YEARNING TO BREATHE FREE

Yearning to Breathe Free

JEWS IN GILDED AGE AMERICA

Essays by Twenty Contributing Scholars

EDITED BY

Adam D. Mendelsohn and Jonathan D. Sarna

WITH A FOREWORD BY SPONSOR

Leonard L. Milberg

Class of 1953

*

PRINCETON, NEW JERSEY

PRINCETON UNIVERSITY LIBRARY

2022

COPYRIGHT © 2022
PRINCETON UNIVERSITY LIBRARY

ISBN 0-87811-065-8 (softcover, regular edition)
0-87811-064-x (hardcover, special edition)

DISTRIBUTED BY
PRINCETON UNIVERSITY PRESS
41 WILLIAM STREET
PRINCETON, NEW JERSEY 08540

*

FRONT COVER IMAGE:

Gerta Ries Wiener, *Emma Lazarus*, 1983, struck in bronze by Johnson Mathey, obverse, 1¾ × 1¾ in. Portrait surrounded by name and quote in Lazarus's handwriting "Emma Lazarus: 'Give me your tired, your poor … yearning to breathe free.'" (Skirball Museum, Cincinnati, Ohio, Jewish-American Hall of Fame Collection. Gift of Mel and Esther Wacks, Debra Wacks, and Shari Wacks).

BACK COVER IMAGE:

Henry Mosler, *Plum Street Temple*, ca. 1866 (Fig. 22.). Oil on canvas, 29½ × 24⅝ in. (Skirball Museum, Cincinnati, Ohio, 41.259. Gift of the Skirball Foundation; Audrey Skirball Kenis, granddaughter of the artist).

TABLE OF CONTENTS

FOREWORD

LEONARD L. MILBERG

YEARNING TO BREATHE FREE is the fifteenth publication I have sponsored in collaboration with the Princeton University Library. The first, *Pride of Place* (1983), focused on my collection of early American prints. It was followed by three more works about graphic art, two on American prints and one on European prints. Then on to modern American poetry. The Spring 1994 issue of the *Princeton University Library Chronicle* contained sixty previously unpublished works by virtually all the living poets in my collection, as well as a number of insightful essays by scholars. Barely catching my breath, I proceeded with six publications on Irish literature—two each on Irish poetry, Irish theater, and Irish prose. Most recently, I have returned to my roots and been responsible now for four publications about Jewish Americans. Most of these volumes have been accompanied by the gift of my collection to Princeton, an exhibition, readings if appropriate, lectures, and a celebratory dinner.

I would not have been able to accomplish any of this without the kind and able assistance of Princeton University's faculty and the staff of the University Library. Sean Wilentz, Harold Shapiro, and Esther Schor are friends who have helped me in my Jewish ventures. Sean, one of America's preeminent historians, wisely suggested that I investigate early American Jewry. When Harold Shapiro was selected president of Princeton, I realized that Jews were, at last, part of the University, and I dedicated my first Jewish collection to him. Starry Schor is a polymath poet who has written books on a variety of subjects, most notably Emma Lazarus.

The last half of the nineteenth century was a period of rapid change and enrichment in America. Mark Twain called that period the "Gilded Age." The Jewish population multiplied fourfold and grew in importance. I have written about four Jewish American institutions and four Jewish lawyers who came to prominence at the end of the nineteenth century and continued to influence Jewish cultural and political issues into the twentieth.

The Jewish Theological Seminary Association, a school for educating rabbis and teachers in traditional Judaism, was established in 1886. Its principal founder and first president, Italian-born Dr. Sabato Morais, took this step to thwart the advance of Reform Judaism in America. By the time of his death in 1897, the institution was near collapse. A new organization called the Jewish Theological Seminary of America was established in 1901 and took over Rabbi Morais's teetering school. The investment banker Jacob Schiff was the moving force behind the seminary, along with Louis Marshall, Cyrus Adler, and Mayer Sulzberger. Schiff was motivated by the need for rabbis who could minister to the growing number of Orthodox Jews from eastern Europe.

Most significantly, Solomon Schechter was immediately recruited to be president of the new seminary. Schechter, born in Romania in 1847, was an extraordinary scholar (Fig. 1). While a student in Berlin, he met Moses Montefiore's nephew Claude, who brought him to England to continue his studies. In 1890, Schechter was chosen as reader in rabbinical studies at Cambridge University. Six years later, he left for Cairo to participate in the excavation of the Genizah, an ancient storeroom of Hebrew prayer books and manuscripts. Schechter brought back to Cambridge tens of thousands of fragments, which he labored to decipher.

Schechter revived the Jewish Theological Seminary, and it continued to thrive after his death in 1915, eventually becoming a center of study and teaching for Conservative Judaism. Through initial donations from some of its founders, its library possesses the world's largest collection of Jewish manuscripts and rare books. (Recently, several books were sold secretly, which has caused some concern in the Jewish community.)

For a number of years in his publication *The Occident*, the Philadelphia rabbi Isaac Leeser advocated the formation of a Jewish publishing organization for the purpose of combating antisemitism and promoting Jewish literature. A group was started in 1845, but membership never exceeded five hundred. In its short six-year existence, the nascent publisher put out fourteen booklets containing tales from the Bible and Midrash, and a few serious books by Isaac Leeser, Moses Samuels, and Grace Aguilar, a pious, short-lived English Marrano lady. The group was forced to close after a fire destroyed the building owned by its publisher and president, Abraham Hart, where all its materials were stored.

In 1871, spurred on by the encouragement of the Reform rabbis Isaac Mayer Wise and Max Lilienthal and others, a national Jewish publication society came to life. Its officers were principally New Yorkers, and it failed for lack of money and leadership. Its most significant achievement was the publication of the fourth volume of Heinrich Graetz's magisterial *History of the Jews* in a translation by Rabbi James Gutheim of New York's Temple Emanu-El.

Fig. 1. Rabbi Solomon Schechter (1847–1915). Founder and president of the United Synagogue of America, president of the Jewish Theological Seminary of America. (Alamy, Inc., Brooklyn, N.Y.).

In the late 1880s there was another call for a Jewish publisher from Polish-born Joseph Krauskopf and American native Dr. Solomon Solis-Cohen. They worked together and summoned a national convention, which took place in Philadelphia in 1888. There was considerable infighting between the clergy and laymen over membership of the board. A compromise agreement was abetted by a donation from the ever-generous Jacob Schiff, and the Jewish Publication Society of America (JPS) came into being. It was principally an elite Philadelphia organization. Members had to be elected. Morris Neuberger, a clothing merchant was the first president. Cyrus Adler and Judge Mayer Sulzberger, head of the publishing committee for twenty-five years, were the guiding lights.

The JPS's initial volume was a reprint of *Outlines of Jewish History*, by an English woman, Lady Katie Magnus, wife of the fascinating Sir Philip, a rabbi, technical educator, and member of Parliament. Henrietta Szold, the brilliant secretary of the society, and Cyrus Adler, who had just completed his studies in Semitics at Johns Hopkins University and would later have active roles in numerous Jewish institutions, co-authored a thirty-three-page summary of Jewish history as an addendum to Lady Magnus's book. The then foremost American Jewish sculptor, Sir Moses Ezekiel, designed a seal for the JPS, which was stamped in gold on the cover of the volume, with the words "Israel's Mission is Peace." The *Outline of Jewish History* was followed by a popular children's book, *Think and Thank*, about the young Sir Moses Montefiore. The first major achievement of the JPS was a six-volume English translation of Graetz's *History of the Jews*, completed in 1898 after seven years of work. A huge success, it was sold as a boxed set until the late 1950s.

When the JPS attempted to capitalize on the late nineteenth-century surge of interest in popular novels, its first two offerings flopped. Fortuitously, in 1890 Mayer Sulzberger had approached the British writer Israel Zangwill about a novel for the JPS. The result was the two-volume *Children of the Ghetto: Being Pictures of a Peculiar People* (1892), which was an instant hit. Zangwill was proclaimed the "Jewish Dickens." Other works written by Zangwill and published by the JPS included *Dreamers of the Ghetto* and *Ghetto Tragedies.*

Henrietta Szold was the first employee of the JPS. Her official title was secretary, but in reality she was the writer, editor, translator, and brains of the society for its first twenty-three years. The eldest of eight daughters, she worked as secretary and translator for her father, the rabbi of a German-speaking congregation in Baltimore. Rabbi Benjamin Szold taught Henrietta religion, literature, and politics, often taking her to the docks of Baltimore to greet Russian and Polish immigrants. Although Szold's formal education ended in high school, she attended lectures at Johns Hopkins and was given permission by Solomon Schechter to take advanced classes at the Jewish Theological Seminary, with the understanding that she would not seek ordination. She was the first woman allowed to attend the seminary. Szold taught at a local girl's finishing school for fourteen years, was a newspaper columnist for the *Jewish Messenger*, and helped to organize a night school for immigrants prior to joining the JPS. Her early achievements included editing Marcus Jastrow's *Talmudic Dictionary* and compiling a widely praised index volume for Graetz's *History*.

After leaving the JPS, Szold devoted her life's work to Zionism. She founded Hadassah, a women's Jewish Zionist organization dedicated to the betterment of health facilities in Palestine. Perhaps influenced by her deeply felt disappointment at the marriage of a younger man, Louis Guinzberg, for whom she had long cherished an unrequited love, she moved to the Holy Land, dying in 1945 in a hospital she had helped to build.

In the last decade of the nineteenth century, the American Jewish Historical Society (AJHS), unlike the teetering Jewish Theological Seminary and the still small JPS, began with a burst of energy. Responding to an invitation from the ubiquitous Cyrus Adler, the voice of Conservative Jewry who had affiliations with both Johns Hopkins and the Smithsonian Institution, a group of forty-one men, including a few prominent Christians, assembled at the Jewish Theological Seminary to discuss the establishment of a society dedicated to the history of Jews in the Americas. German-born Oscar Straus, the wealthy scion of the Macy's department store family and a lawyer active in the administrations of Grover Cleveland and Theodore Roosevelt, was elected chairman of the nascent group, and Cyrus Adler was chosen as secretary treasurer. Other board members included Professor John McMaster; Harvard's Charles Gross; historian of early America Herbert Friedenwald; transportation engineer Mendes Cohen of Baltimore; Lewis Dembitz of Louisville (uncle of Louis Brandeis); Professor Morris Jastrow, holder of the Semitic chair at the University of Pennsylvania; Reform rabbi Bernhard Felsenthal of Chicago; London-born New York rabbi Maurice Harris; and the formidable Henrietta Szold. Many of the same men were board members of all three of these early Jewish organizations and later of the American Jewish Committee.

It was hardly a coincidence that the AJHS came into existence in 1892, the four-hundredth anniversary of Christopher Columbus's departure from the Old World to the New, as well as the same month and year that Spanish Jews were forced to decide between conversion to Catholicism or expulsion. At this time, little was known about the contributions of Jews to the American colonies and the struggle for independence. Charles Gross, the Harvard historian, declared at the founding meeting,

> The object of this Society should be to reveal the past of the Jews of this country.... It will certainly be made evident that the Jews of this Republic have been ready to offer up life and fortune for their country, that they have been patriots in time of war and philanthropists in time of peace.... If we can once make that plain through the researches of the Society ... we shall accomplish a great deal.

In 1893, President Oscar Straus informed the membership that the AJHS had engaged Dr. Meyer Kayserling to research and "bring to light the part taken by Jews" in the voyages of Columbus. The following year, Straus announced that Kayserling's research had culminated in a volume that would be published in an English translation by Charles Gross as *Christopher Columbus and the Participation of the Jews in the Spanish Discoveries* (1894). German by birth, Kayserling was an ordained rabbi who served congregations in Switzerland and Germany and had already written biographies of Manassah Ben Israel and Moses Mendelssohn. Kayserling averred that the "Admiral of the Ocean" was descended from a Spanish Jewish family named Colon and that several Jews accompanied him on his first voyage, including Luis de Torres, his translator and the first person to touch land in the New World.

Today there still is uncertainty about Columbus's background. In 2004, the New York Public Library's Jewish division held an exhibition entitled "Jews in America," showcasing original materials. Citing a book published in Basel in 1493, curator Michael Terry, head of the Jewish division, opined that Columbus recruited only one Jew, Luis de Torres, who knew Hebrew, a little Arabic, and Aramaic, Europe's "oriental languages." Arriving in Cuba—Columbus's China—he was the first crew member to land, and he later returned to live in Cuba.

Other Jews who aided Columbus include Abraham Zacuto, an astronomer and astrologist who produced an astronomical table that correctly predicted a lunar eclipse, thus enabling Columbus to subdue a group of hostile Jamaicans. Terry claimed that Luis de Santangel, a wealthy Converso and adviser to King Ferdinand, financed the first voyage. The second trip was funded by the sale of property abandoned by Jews forced to flee Spain. Columbus's first letter announcing his discovery is known in two copies, written in Spanish, one to Santangel and a duplicate to Gabriel Sanchez, also a New Christian and treasurer of Aragon. It is noteworthy that Jamaica, which was given by the Spanish crown to Columbus's family, was one of the few Spanish colonies not visited by the Inquisition, despite the presence on the island of a number of Conversos.

From its inception, the AJHS's principal mission was to collect, publish, and promote scholarly material bearing upon American Jewish history. The scope included the Caribbean and Central and South America. A library was created to build archives, and research papers were presented at annual public meetings. Other research was printed in annual society publications. In 1893, the first volume contained fifteen essays. One was about the early history of Jews in Canada, and another concerned Americana at an Anglo-Jewish historical exhibition in London. The other thirteen focused upon American Jewish colonial history. One documented how Jews were briefly the majority of the white people in Georgia's first settlement. Sabato Morais, rabbi of the Philadelphia synagogue Mikveh Israel, shed light on the history of his congregation. Morris Jastrow wrote about the early history of Philadelphia Jewry. Dr. Herbert Friedenwald described the Jews who were mentioned in the proceedings of the Continental Congress. Simon Rosendale wrote two articles, one about an act permitting naturalization of Jews in the colonies and another about the early Franks family of New York and Philadelphia. Lewis Dembitz described the early Jewish presence in the state of Kentucky. H. J. Hollander unearthed fascinating facts about Dr. Jacob Lumbrozo, who was born in Lisbon, Portugal, and arrived in Maryland in 1656 via Holland. Arrested in 1658 as a heretic, he was soon released and became a planter. The ubiquitous Cyrus Adler wrote about plantation life and an 1800 political document.

Adler succeeded Oscar Straus when the society's first president returned to political life in 1899. The legendary book dealer Dr. A.S.W. Rosenbach took over in 1922 and presided for some twenty years. The society ran into financial difficulty during his regime. Fortunately, it was rescued and continues to do good work. It now resides on West 16th Street in New York. In 1952, N. Taylor Phillips, one of the AJHS's founders, reminded members of the reasons for its establishment: "You are, of course, aware that the Society found its origin by reason of the severe criticism of and as a protest against the mass [Jewish] immigration of the eighties, which poured in a stream of refugees from religious persecution in Eastern Europe. This produced a reaction against [them]. Even some Jewish predecessors, settled in this country, and some Jewish Press were not entirely free of this attitude."

In 1881, the relatively liberal Tsar Alexander II of Russia was assassinated and succeeded by his reactionary son Alexander III, who soon issued several antisemitic decrees, including one that closed Yiddish theaters. One of the Yiddish troupes, led by its actor-director Jacob Adler, quickly left for Riga, Latvia, and then sailed for London. These nearly destitute players remained there for almost seven years, barely squeaking out a living. In 1889, with funds provided by Adler's great uncle, Hillel Nissim Adler, the chief rabbi of London—

who strongly disapproved of theater—the troupe was able to sail to New York City.

By the turn of the nineteenth century, Adler was a wealthy man. Fondly referred to as Nesher Hagodel, "The Great Eagle," because of his imposing presence, he commanded a guest fee of $1,000 per performance and had his own theater, the Union, on Lower Broadway. In contrast, members of the newly formed Hebrew Actors' Union merely secured a living wage from management. Adler's four-story brownstone on East 72nd Street provided ample room for Jacob, his wife, and their nine actor children. Sara, Jacob's third wife, the mother of eight of the Adler brood, and an accomplished leading lady, furnished her sitting room in the style of Louis Quatorze and traveled annually to Paris to have her gowns made by the House of Worth.

Lulla Rosenfeld, Adler's grandnephew and a historian, ascribes the roots of the Yiddish theater to the nineteenth-century intellectual movement Haskalah, literally, Awakening. Haskalah, in turn, was influenced by the eighteenth-century teachings of Moses Mendelssohn in Germany. Haskalah emphasized secular education, embracing the Christian culture yet remaining faithful to Judaism. It was liberation of the ghetto of the mind. The movement spread eastward, eventually reaching Russia. Maskilim was the name for the proponents of Haskalah.

Abraham Goldfaden, born in Russia in 1840, is acknowledged as the founder of the Yiddish theater. The son of a watchmaker, he attended a rabbinical academy run by a man who embraced Haskalah and arranged dances, masked balls, and visits to the theater for his pupils. Goldfaden traveled to Jassy, Romania, where the local Maskilim welcomed him. While in Jassy, the budding poet and songwriter conceived the idea of a theater combining Yiddish prose and song. His initial effort was *Recruits*, a comic operetta. Goldfaden not only wrote the words and music and directed the performers but also built the stage and painted the scenery. The playwright created a company and returned to Russia, where he was quite popular. He briefly lived in the United States and in 1900 was a delegate to a London Zionist conference. His best-known works were two comedies, *The Two Kuni Lemels* and *Shmendrick*. He also wrote in Hebrew and possessed a wry humor:

> Shakespeare in hatred of the Jews
> Put Shylock on the stage
> The Jews in revenge
> Staged Shylock

Stella Adler was the youngest daughter of Jacob and Sara. After acting on the Yiddish stage, she went on to Broadway, the Group Theatre, and Hollywood, and then became an acclaimed teacher of the Stanislavsky acting method. She later reflected on the state of the American Yiddish theater when her family arrived in 1889: "In America ... Yiddish theater sunk below even its first crude beginnings ... musical productions devoid of merit dominated. The Russian Jewish intelligentsia took no interest ... [then] the overwhelming success of [Jacob] Gordin's the *Yiddish King Lear* ... [the] first realistic play about modern Jewish life ... changed everything overnight ... a mass audience was created of workers, intellectuals, socialists, Zionists, men and women of every class."

Jacob Michailovitch Gordin was born in 1853, the son of a prosperous Ukrainian merchant. He worked as journalist, critic, and shipyard worker in Odessa. He was an atheist, a socialist, and an ardent disciple of Tolstoy who, like his idol, gave Bible readings to peasant farmers. Extremely prolific, Gordin wrote some thirty-five plays and adapted or translated forty others. He arrived in New York at about the same time as Jacob Adler, and these two men were principally responsible for the success of the immensely respected and popular American Yiddish theater in the last decade of the nineteenth century and into the twentieth. Henry James in his book, *The American Scene*, wrote about his viewing a performance of the Yiddish stage during his return visit to the United States in 1904.

There were several other Yiddish playwrights in the mid-1890s, most notably Joseph Latteiner and Moses Horowitz (Moishe Isaac Halevy-Hurvitz). Latteiner, a Maskilim from Jassy, is best known for *The Dybbuk*. Horowitz, a learned former convict, missionary, and socialist, wrote musicals. His play *The Johnstown Flood* blamed Andrew Mellon, Andrew Carnegie, and Henry Clay Frick for the calamity. The works of Gordin sustained the Yiddish theater. In his memoir, Jacob Adler asserted that *The Yiddish King Lear* was "the greatest triumph of all." Other Gordin hits were *Resurrection*, a dramatization of Tolstoy, *The Homeless*, an exploration of an immigrant Jewish domestic tragedy, *Sappho*, a cry for women's sexual freedom, and *The Wild Man*, about a brutalized retarded Jewish child.

There were many fine actors in the Yiddish theater. Sigmund Mogulesko (Siegmund Moguleshka) was a superb song and dance comedian. Sophie Goldstein (Sofia Karp) was praised for her beauty. Bertha Kalich's lovely voice brought her to Broadway. David Kessler and Keni Liptzin had such large followings that each commanded a theater. The legendary Boris Thomashefsky, a friendly rival of Jacob Adler, was born in Kiev and began his career as a singer. He arrived in America in 1881, aged fifteen. Thomashefsky wrote several short plays and had his own company and theater. When he first appeared on stage at the

Thalia Theatre in a performance of *Alexander, Crown Prince of Jerusalem*, it was alleged that women fainted.

Jacob Adler's fame was abetted by the large influx in the late 1800s of eastern European Yiddish-speaking Jews. He also was recognized outside the Yiddish-speaking world. Harold Clurman, a respected American director, critic, co-founder of the Group Theatre, and second husband of Stella Adler, claimed that he decided to enter the American theater after seeing Jacob Adler perform in *Uriel Acosta*, a drama of the Spanish Inquisition: "When [I saw] Uriel Acosta, I was transported.... The man's size—I do not refer to his physique. Grandeur always inspires a sudden shudder at life's immeasurable mystery and might." *Theatre Magazine* compared Adler to Edwin Booth and Sir Henry Irving. The *New York Times* and *Philadelphia Inquirer* wrote glowing reviews of him. In addition to *Uriel Acosta* and *The Jewish King Lear*, Adler's most acclaimed roles were Goldfaden's Shmendrick and Shakespeare's Shylock. Adler played the former for thirty years, referring to it as his *parnosse*, literally, meal ticket. Shylock was Jacob's most meaningful performance, emulating the celebrated English actor Edmund Kean, who is often referred to as a Jew. Adler played the role wearing a rich costume and with dignity (Fig. 2). When Adler performed the part on Broadway, all the cast spoke English except Shylock, who spoke Yiddish.

In 1922 a benefit was held for Adler, who had suffered a stroke and had squandered much of his fortune. In attendance were Jacob J. Schubert, David Belasco, and many other theater celebrities. The entertainers included Will Rogers, Al Jolson, and the opera star Giovanni Martinelli. Adler died four years later at the age of seventy-one. A crowd estimated at between 50,000 and 100,000 walked behind the Great Eagle's bier. Abraham Cahan gave the principal eulogy, and the golden-voiced cantor Josef "Yossele" Rosenblatt chanted the prayer for the dead.

As some of the earliest members of the American Yiddish theater passed on and others, like Paul Muni and Luther Adler, became movie actors, new stars appeared, including Molly Picon, Menasha Skulnick, and Maurice Schwartz. Sholem Aleichem, briefly resident on the Lower East Side, wrote wonderful comedies for the theaters. But by 1920, live theater faced competition from radio, movies, and baseball. All the while, Jews were becoming assimilated. The glory days of the Yiddish theater were over.

In his eulogy of Mayer Sulzberger (1843–1923), Louis Marshall described him as an intellectual leader, a "patron of scholars and literary men" before whom passed a "constant procession of thinkers, philosophers and poets." Though not loved by all, Sulzberger had an impressive career. He arrived in Philadelphia

Fig. 2. A production of *The Merchant of Venice* starring Jacob P. Adler as Shylock. Byron Company, New York, N.Y., photographer. Late nineteenth or early twentieth century. (Folger Shakespeare Library).

from Germany as a child in 1848. A practicing lawyer, he was elected a judge on the Republican ticket. Sulzberger was credited with bringing both the venerable Cambridge scholar Solomon Schechter and the distinguished English novelist Israel Zangwill to the United States. The former resuscitated the moribund Jewish Theological Seminary, and the latter wrote three very popular books for the fledgling Jewish Publication Society. The judge also supported Naphtali Herz Imber, the alcoholic composer of "Hatikvah," the Hebrew national anthem. A voracious bibliophile, Sulzberger generously donated his books to the nascent Jewish Theological Seminary.

Louis Marshall (1856–1929) was born in Syracuse, New York. A lawyer and noted constitutional authority, he enjoyed early success, which brought him recognition and selection several times in the late nineteenth century as a delegate to New York State constitutional conventions. Throughout his life Marshall was active in Republican politics. Cyrus Adler might have been describing himself when he spoke in praise of Marshall: "He has written himself ... in the long and noble annals of the Jewish people." Like Sulzberger and Adler, Marshall was involved in virtually every significant Jewish organization, including the American Jewish Committee, the Educational Alliance, Dropsie College, the Jewish Protectory and Aid Society, Temple Emanu-El, and the Palestine Economic Council. Marshall's charitable work extended to the advancement of African Americans and the preservation of forests and bird sanctuaries. In 1927, he secured an apology from Henry Ford for publishing articles based on the scurrilously antisemitic *Protocols of the Elders of Zion.*

Lawyer Randolph Guggenheimer (1846–1907) was born in Lynchburg, Virginia, and moved to New York City, where he became a partner with two distinguished attorneys, Louis Marshall and Samuel Untermeyer. Beginning in 1887, Guggenheimer held several public offices in the city. As school commissioner, he instituted evening high school classes and a free lecture series. In 1897 he was elected president of the New York City Municipal Council and in that position served several times as acting mayor. Guggenheimer was a visionary early developer of office buildings on Lower Broadway.

Samuel Untermeyer (1858–1940), also from Lynchburg, devoted his early career to representing large corporations. He became one of America's preeminent and wealthiest attorneys. Untermeyer reportedly earned a fee of nearly one million dollars, worth at least twenty-five million in today's dollars, for his work on a merger in the copper industry. He built an estate along the Hudson River with a beautiful garden that has recently been restored. A tireless worker for Jewish causes, Untermeyer is best remembered for his role as lead attorney for the Pujo Committee, a congressional subcommittee that investigated powerful Wall Street financial leaders in 1912. The principal witness was the illustrious J. Pierpont Morgan.

A number of years ago I read, in the *New York Times*, a disclosure of the text of a New York Federal Reserve Board meeting held in the midst of the Great Depression. Morgan's son, J.P. Jr., a member of the advisory council to the board, was able to convince his colleagues to allow the Jewish-owned Bank of United States to fail because Morgan blamed his father's death in 1913 on Untermeyer for his intense and long questioning of him. Eventually, the Bank of United States, the only New York bank allowed to fail, paid its creditors in full.

*

I was tempted to write about three other American Jews whose notable careers began in the late nineteenth century. Lillian Wald, the principal founder of the Visiting Nursing Service of New York and the Henry Street Settlement, who fought for the rights of children and women. Lithuanian-born Bernard Berenson, advisor to Isabella Stewart Gardner and other wealthy patrons, was an esteemed authority on Italian Renaissance art. And finally, Louis Brandeis, the redoubtable "peoples attorney" from Louisville, Kentucky, became the leader of American Zionism, adviser to President Woodrow Wilson, and first true liberal on the U.S. Supreme Court. However, they will have to wait for our next publication.

I express my appreciation to my good friend Adam Mendelsohn and his colleague, the renowned scholar Jonathan Sarna, for their editing skills and contribution of essays. I am also grateful to Esther Schor, Sean Wilentz, and Harold Shapiro for their kindness, wisdom, and encouragement. I would be remiss not to thank Stephen Ferguson of Firestone Library for his advice and patience in preparing the essays for publication.

I wish to acknowledge the assistance I received from Lulla Rosenfeld's annotated memoir of Jacob Adler, Jonathan Sarna's history of the Jewish Publication Society, Melanie Meyers of the AJHS, and my ancient bar mitzvah present, *The Encyclopedia of Jewish Knowledge.*

LEONARD L. MILBERG
Class of 1953

PREFACE

ADAM D. MENDELSOHN & JONATHAN D. SARNA

THE GILDED AGE was a period of paradoxes for America's Jews. Caught up in the currents of a giddy era marked by freedom and disenfranchisement, excess and immiseration, opportunity and exclusion, confidence and anxiety, Jews collectively experienced their own version of these contradictions. Even as their numbers and influence grew, their status became more unsettled. Even as their elite entered the upper reaches of society, Jews encountered new forms of rejection. Even as many achieved prosperity, throngs of newcomers struggled to make ends meet. Because the contradictions of the Gilded Age echo in the present, the period from 1865 to 1900 has received much new scholarly and popular attention. Likewise, the Jewish experience of the Gilded Age has drawn new interest.[1] Yet we still know surprising little of how Jews navigated the currents of this turbulent era.

There are several reasons why. The Gilded Age does not fit neatly into the chronology that long dominated the writing of American Jewish history. That schema divided the past into discrete periods: a "Sephardic period" in the colonial era was thought to be followed by a "German period" initiated when central European Jews first began to flock to the United States after the Napoleonic wars. In turn, an "eastern European period" began when a tidal wave of Jews fled oppression and poverty in Romania and the Russian empire in the 1880s.[2] For many scholars schooled to think of waves of immigration—of a "German period" followed by an "eastern European period"—the Gilded Age sat awkwardly between the two as an interregnum before eastern European Jews came to dominate American Jewish life.

As a transitory moment between epochs, the period was easily imagined to be of little lasting consequence for the trajectory of American Jewish history. This interpretation was compounded by a tendency to look first to Jewish history, rather than to the American context, when framing and writing the American Jewish story. The mass immigration of Jews from Romania and the Russian

1. See, for example, the "Roundtable on Anti-Semitism in the Gilded Age and Progressive Era," *Journal of the Gilded Age and Progressive Era* 19, no. 3 (2020): 473–505.

2. Hasia R. Diner was among the first to challenge this periodization. See *A Time for Gathering: The Second Migration, 1820–1880* (Baltimore: Johns Hopkins University Press, 1992).

empire, for example, was more often explained as a consequence of pogroms and antisemitic legislation rather than presented as part of a broader phenomenon—facilitated by political and economic developments after the Civil War—that attracted millions of other immigrants to the United States. Foregrounding the Jewish dimensions of the story caused the Gilded Age to recede into the background. Scholars who wrote about American Jewish life during the period focused, for the most part, on themes relating to the immigration and acculturation of eastern European Jews, not on the subjects—Reconstruction, citizenship, inequality—that occupied historians of the Gilded Age. Of course, there have been many exceptions to this pattern, not least John Higham and Eric Goldstein, whose interpretations of antisemitism and racial status embed Jews in the social and political currents of the period.[3]

In decoupling the "German period" from the "eastern European period," historians tended to treat each as discrete subjects, obscuring continuities and legacies and drawing boundaries where none existed. A consequence was that the existing Jewish community slipped from the story. Nathan Glazer was not alone in almost entirely writing "German" Jews out of the "eastern European period." When the established community did feature, it was more often as the progenitors of an increasingly deracinated version of Reform Judaism—the status-conscious "uptown Jews" who disapproved of the wretched downtown "greenhorns" and the small coterie of bankers, financiers, and lawyers who formed "our crowd"—rather than as a vital and dynamic population. The virtual "disappearance" of the German American Jewish community was likely part of a broader phenomenon. Christina A. Ziegler-McPherson has described how German Americans "became invisible within a generation" in American life as a consequence of World War I.[4] In addition to treating the Gilded Age as an era worthy of attention in its own right—assessing how the native-born and newcomers engaged with the cultural, political, and religious currents of the day—this volume restores to visibility the experience of Jews of central European origin after 1865.

The thematic essays in *Yearning to Breathe Free* follow a standard format. Each uses a primary source—a book, newspaper, tract, or artwork—as an entry

3. See John Higham, *Send These to Me: Immigrants in Urban America* (Baltimore: Johns Hopkins University Press, 1984), and Eric Goldstein, *The Price of Whiteness: Jews, Race, and American Identity* (Princeton: Princeton University Press, 2008).

4. Christina A. Ziegler-McPherson, *The Great Disappearing Act: Germans in New York City, 1880–1930* (New Brunswick: Rutgers University Press, 2021).

point into the era and as a means to introduce key themes, figures, and developments within the Gilded Age. The essays highlight patterns and trends that in some cases anticipated what came later, and in others demonstrate how developments in the Gilded Age shaped Jewish life in the twentieth century. Collectively, they reveal the variety of ways in which the Gilded Age was a critical period in American Jewish history.

ADAM D. MENDELSOHN
University of Cape Town

JONATHAN D. SARNA
Brandeis University

NOTES ON THE CONTRIBUTORS

SAMANTHA BASKIND is Distinguished Professor of Art History at Cleveland State University. She is the author of five books, most recently *The Warsaw Ghetto in American Art and Culture*, and co-editor of *The Jewish Graphic Novel: Critical Approaches*, the foundational volume in the field. Her publications also include more than 100 articles and reviews, mainly on Jewish art. She served as editor for U.S. art for the 22-volume revised edition of the *Encyclopaedia Judaica* and is currently series editor of "Dimyonot: Jews and the Cultural Imagination," published by the Pennsylvania State University Press.

JUDAH M. COHEN is the Lou and Sybil Mervis Professor of Jewish Culture and Professor of Musicology at Indiana University. He has authored *Through the Sands of Time: A History of the Jewish Community of St. Thomas, US Virgin Islands* (2004); *The Making of a Reform Jewish Cantor: Musical Authority, Cultural Investment* (2009); *Sounding Jewish Tradition: The Music of Central Synagogue* (2011); and *Jewish Religious Music in Nineteenth Century America* (2019). His current projects address Jews and musical expression in the United States, including World War II-era narratives in musical theater, 19th century American synagogue music, and American Jewish singer/songwriter/liturgist Debbie Friedman.

DAVID G. DALIN, a Senior Research Fellow at Brandeis University, is the author, co-author, or editor of twelve books, including *Religion and State in the American Jewish Experience* (co-authored with Jonathan D. Sarna); *Jewish Justices of the Supreme Court, from Brandeis to Kagan*; and *Jews and American Public Life: Essays on American Jewish History and Politics* (forthcoming 2022). His articles and book reviews have appeared in a variety of publications, including *American Jewish History*, the *American Jewish Archives Journal*, *Modern Judaism*, *Commentary*, the *American Jewish Year Book*, and the *Jewish Review of Books*.

NOAH EFRON chairs the Program in Science, Technology & Society at Bar-Ilan University. He was President of the Israeli Society for History & Philosophy of Science and served on the Executive Committee of the International Society for Science and Religion. Efron has been a member of the Institute for Advanced Study in Princeton, Fellow at Harvard University, Columbia Universities, University of Pennsylvania, and MIT. He is author of *A Chosen Calling: Jews in Science in the Twentieth Century* and other books and essays on the complicated intertwine of science, religion, and politics. Efron has also served on the City Council of Tel Aviv-Jaffa.

ZEV ELEFF is president of Gratz College and professor of American Jewish history. He is the author or editor of nine books and more than forty scholarly articles. His *Dyed in Crimson: Football, Faith, and Remaking Harvard's America* will be published by University of Illinois Press in the Fall of 2022.

LORI HARRISON-KAHAN is Full Professor of the Practice of English at Boston College. She is the author of *The White Negress: Literature, Minstrelsy, and the Black-Jewish Imaginary* (Rutgers University Press, 2011). Her edition of *Heirs of Yesterday* by Emma Wolf, co-edited with Barbara Cantalupo, was published by Wayne State University Press in 2020, and her edited collection *The Superwoman and Other Writings by Miriam Michelson* (Wayne State University Press, 2019) received the 2021 Society for the Study of American Women Writers Best Edition Award. She is currently working on a manuscript about Jewish women writers in turn-of-the-twentieth-century San Francisco.

MELISSA R. KLAPPER is Professor of History and Director of Women's & Gender Studies at Rowan University. She is the author of *Jewish Girls Coming of Age in America, 1860–1920* (NYU, 2005); *Small Strangers: The Experiences of Immigrant Children in the United States, 1880–1925* (Ivan R. Dee, 2007); and *Ballots, Babies, and Banners of Peace: American Jewish Women's Activism, 1890–1940* (NYU, 2013), which won the National Jewish Book Award in Women's Studies. She has been awarded numerous fellowships and grants and lectures frequently in academic and community settings. Her most recent book is *Ballet Class: An American History* (Oxford, 2020).

MICHAEL P. KRAMER is Professor Emeritus in the Department of English Literature and Linguistics at Bar-Ilan University. He has authored numerous articles on Jewish and Jewish American Literature and is the editor of *New Essays of "Seize the Day"*; *The Cambridge Companion to Jewish American Literature* (with Hana Wirth-Nesher); *Modern Jewish Literatures: Intersections and Boundaries* (with Sheila Jelen and Scott Lerner); and *The Turn Around Religion in America* (with Nan Goodman). His latest book is an annotated translation of S. Y. Agnon's *And the Crooked Shall be Made Straight.* His current projects include a monograph on the history of Jewish American literary historiography and an edited collection of essays on "The Literature of Jewish American Periodicals" for *Studies in American Jewish Literature.*

ALAN M. KRAUT is Distinguished Professor of History at American University and a nonresident Fellow of the Migration Policy Institute. A past president of the Organization of American Historians and the Immigration and Ethnic

History Society, he specializes in U.S. immigration and ethnic history and the history of medicine and public health in the United States. He currently chairs the Statue of Liberty–Ellis Island History Advisory Committee of the Statue of Liberty–Ellis Island Foundation. Among his many books and articles are *Silent Travelers: Germs, Genes, and the "Immigrant Menace"* (1994) and *Goldberger's War: The Life and Work of a Public Health Crusader* (2003), and he co-authored with his wife, Deborah, *Covenant of Care: Newark Beth Israel and the Jewish Hospital in America* (2007). In 2017 Kraut received the Lifetime Achievement Award of the Immigration and Ethnic History Society for his contributions to scholarship on immigration history. He is an elected fellow of the Society of American Historians.

ELI LEDERHENDLER is the Stephen S. Wise Professor emeritus of American Jewish History and Institutions at the Hebrew University of Jerusalem. His major publications include *The Road to Modern Jewish Politics* (1989); *New York Jews and the Decline of Urban Ethnicity, 1950–1970* (2001); *Jewish Immigrants and American Capitalism* (2009); and *American Jewry: A New History* (2017). He is a co-editor of the annual journal, *Studies in Contemporary Jewry*, and director of the Leonid Nevzlin Research Center for Russian and East European Jewry at the Hebrew University.

ADAM D. MENDELSOHN is Director of the Kaplan Centre for Jewish Studies and Associate Professor of History at the University of Cape Town. The Centre, the only of its kind in Africa, conducts research focused on Jews in southern Africa, past and present. He is the author of *Jewish Soldiers in the Civil War: The Union Army* (2022) and *The Rag Race: How Jews Sewed Their Way to Success in America and the British Empire* (2014.) He co-curated *By Dawn's Early Light: Jewish Contributions to American Culture from the Nation's Founding to the Civil War* at the Princeton University Art Museum in 2016, and edited the companion catalogue containing thirteen original essays on Jewish life in antebellum America.

LEONARD L. MILBERG, Princeton Class of 1953, is Chairman of Milberg Factors, New York. He has received an Alumni as well as the Hyde Award for book collecting from Princeton University. His philanthropic efforts include donations to Princeton University, the Brooklyn Museum, and host of other charitable and educational institutions. In 2018, he was awarded the Mexican Order of the Aztec Eagle—the highest honor given by the Mexican government to foreigners in recognition of outstanding services to Mexico or to humanity—for his key role in returning to Mexico the sixteenth-century manuscript of Luis de Carvajal, the oldest Jewish manuscript in the Americas.

PAMELA NADELL holds the Patrick Clendenen Chair in Women's and Gender History at American University and is a past president of the Association for Jewish Studies. Her books include *Women Who Would Be Rabbis: A History of Women's Ordination, 1889–1985*. Her most recent book, *America's Jewish Women: A History from Colonial Times to Today* (W. W. Norton), won the 2019 National Jewish Book Award's Jewish Book of the Year.

HEATHER S. NATHANS is a professor in the Tufts University Department of Theatre, Dance, and Performance Studies and is the Nathan and Alice Gantcher Professor in Judaic Studies. Her publications include: *Early American Theatre from the Revolution to Thomas Jefferson* (2003); *Slavery and Sentiment on the American Stage, 1787–1861* (2009); and *Hideous Characters and Beautiful Pagans: Performing Jewish Identity on the Antebellum American Stage* (2017). She has received numerous fellowships, including ones from the Guggenheim Foundation, the Mellon Foundation, the National Endowment for the Humanities, and, most recently, the Katz Center for Advanced Judaic Studies at the University of Pennsylvania.

SHARI RABIN is the author of *Jews on the Frontier: Religion and Mobility in Nineteenth-century America* (NYU, 2017), which won the National Jewish Book Award in American Jewish Studies and was a finalist for the Sami Rohr Prize for Jewish Literature. Her second book project is a history of Jews, religion, and race in the U.S. South from the seventeenth century to the present day. She is Associate Professor of Jewish Studies and Religion at Oberlin College.

JONATHAN D. SARNA is University Professor and Joseph H. & Belle R. Braun Professor of American Jewish History at Brandeis University, where he directs the Schusterman Center for Israel Studies. He also chairs the Academic Advisory and Editorial Board of the Jacob Rader Marcus Center of the American Jewish Archives in Cincinnati, and serves as Chief Historian of the Weitzman National Museum of American Jewish History in Philadelphia. His more than thirty books on American Jewish history and life include *American Judaism: A History*; *Coming to Terms with America*; *Lincoln and the Jews: A History* (with Benjamin Shapell); and *When General Grant Expelled the Jews.*

M. M. SILVER is a professor of Jewish History at the Max Stern Yezreel Valley College. His Ph.D. in Jewish History is from the Hebrew University of Jerusalem; and his books, in Hebrew and English, include *Louis Marshall and the Rise of*

Jewish Ethnicity in America, and *Our Exodus: Leon Uris and the Americanization of Israel's Founding Story*. He has been a visiting fellow and professor at Oxford University, and a number of universities in North America. He has recently completed a two-volume history of the Galilee region in Israel, where he works and lives, and is the father of four.

DANIEL SOYER is Professor of History at Fordham University in New York. His books include *Left in the Center: The Liberal Party of New York and the Rise and Fall of American Social Democracy* (Cornell, 2021); *The Jewish Metropolis: New York from the 17th to the 21st Century* (Academic Studies Press, 2021); and (with Annie Polland) *The Emerging Metropolis: New York Jews in the Age of Immigration, 1840–1920* (NYU, 2012). He is a former editor of the journal *American Jewish History*.

BENJAMIN STEINER is a Visiting Assistant Professor of Religious Studies at Trinity College. He is a scholar of American Judaism, and completed his Ph.D. in Near Eastern and Judaic Studies at Brandeis University in 2020. Steiner is currently working on a book about English translations of Jewish marriage contracts (*ketubot*) that illuminate how Jews ensured the economic security of married Jewish women under secular law, how Judaism was received by curious non-Jewish audiences, and how Jewish marriage contracts enshrined gender role expectations of the day. He has also published peer-reviewed articles on Judaism in postwar America.

BETH S. WENGER is Moritz and Josephine Berg Professor of History and Associate Dean for Graduate Studies in the School of Arts & Sciences at the University of Pennsylvania. She is the author of *History Lessons: The Creation of American Jewish Heritage*; *The Jewish Americans: Three Centuries of Jewish Voices in America* (which was named a National Jewish Book Award finalist); and *New York Jews and the Great Depression: Uncertain Promise* (which was awarded the Salo Baron Prize in Jewish History). Wenger co-edited *Encounters With the "Holy Land": Place, Past and Future in American Jewish Culture* (with Jeffrey Shandler); *Remembering the Lower East Side: American Jewish Reflections* (with Hasia Diner and Jeffrey Shandler); and *Gender in Judaism and Islam: Common Lives, Uncommon Heritage* (with Firoozeh Kashani-Sabet).

SHIRA WOLOSKY was Associate Professor of English at Yale University before moving to the Hebrew University, where she is Professor of American Literature, Emerita. Her books include: *Emily Dickinson: A Voice of War*; *Language*

Mysticism; *The Art of Poetry*; *Feminist Theory Across Disciplines*; *Poetry and Public Discourse*; *Defending Identity* (with Natan Sharansky); as well as many essays on poetics, American religious history, and Jewish subjects. Her awards include Guggenheim, ACLS, Fulbright, and Tikvah Fellowships, Fellowships at the Institutes for Advanced Studies at Princeton and Jerusalem, Drue Heinz Visiting Professorship at Oxford, etc.

YEARNING TO BREATHE FREE

AN OVERVIEW OF AMERICAN JEWRY, 1865–1900

BENJAMIN STEINER

Developments in American Judaism

THE GILDED AGE was a formative period in the development of American Judaism. Basic features of contemporary religious practice came together during this era alongside the institutional infrastructure of American Jewish religious life. To study the impact of the Gilded Age on American Judaism, therefore, is not to excavate a distant past but rather to reveal the foundations of the present. In this critical period we find the advent of major Reform institutions, the "awakening" of more traditional religious forms, and the emergence of an embryonic but still amorphous third way forged between the Reform and Orthodox models of Jewish life. We also see the growth of the "post-Jewish" Ethical Culture movement founded by Felix Adler, the scion of one of American Reform's leading lights.

The Reform movement dominated Jewish religious expression during this period. However, its progressive ideology, once heralded by Reform leaders as a means of Jewish rejuvenation, faced headwinds. If the goal was, as some reformers had conceived of it, to cleanse Judaism of elements discordant with their contemporary sensibilities, such ambitions had not inspired synagogue attendance or elevated religious observance among laypersons. A crisis of confidence developed within the Jewish community of the post–Civil War period, and Reform was not spared its implications. In response, the movement labored to redefine itself. Should it choose a moderating posture to attract a wide breadth of Jews, or opt for an ideologically purer but more narrowly appealing religious framework? This question did not originate in the postbellum period, but it grew increasingly pressing as more Jewish institutional infrastructure developed. The Union of American Hebrew Congregations (UAHC), a federation of synagogues formed in 1873 under the leadership of Isaac Mayer Wise (1819–1900), ultimately captured the allegiance of many Jewish congregations. However, no uniform standard of religious practice would emerge, notwithstanding Wise's own efforts and aspirations. While the Cincinnati-based and more moderately minded Wise was Reform's institutional mastermind, the movement's ideological direction trended more radical as the Gilded Age progressed. In 1885, Wise gave that more narrow vision his blessing.

A decade after the advent of the UAHC, Hebrew Union College (HUC) in Cincinnati ordained its first class of rabbis under Wise's leadership, an auspicious affair that augured a homegrown American rabbinate. Yet, more than a source of cohesion, the event ultimately proved a crossroads for American Jewry. Despite the lofty sentiments of unity evoked by the ceremony itself—attended by a diverse group of Jewish rabbinic and lay dignitaries—the infamous trefa banquet that followed on July 11, 1883, destroyed this goodwill. Nine courses of culinary treats greeted the attendees, including all manner of seafoods, non-kosher meats, and a blend of dairy and meat products (Fig. 3). No expense had been spared for the sumptuous occasion—and no dietary restriction, save the prohibition against pork products, was left unbroken. The more traditional Jews at the gathering left enraged. As Jonathan Sarna writes of the affair, "Symbolically, the trefa banquet separated American Jews into two opposing camps that could no longer even break bread together. The incident both anticipated and stimulated further divisions."[1]

For the Reform camp, the trefa banquet presaged an attempt to give systematic direction to an unabashedly liberal vision of Judaism. Gathering in November 1885 just outside Pittsburgh, Reform luminaries under the direction of Kaufmann Kohler hashed out an ideological manifesto. The rabbis sought primarily to regiment the belief system of the Reform movement, enumerating "what it means and aims at," and in that they succeeded. The resulting eight-point Pittsburgh Platform drew on previous liberal Reform thought and spelled out the bedrock tenets of Reform Judaism for another half-century. Among the highlights: the rabbis heralded Judaism as a light unto the nations, "representing the highest conception of the God Idea as taught in our Holy Scriptures." They accepted as binding only the moral provisions in the Bible. They rejected the dietary laws and all ideas "foreign to our present mental and spiritual state." They repudiated Zionism, championing Jewish religion over peoplehood. They embraced what would come to be known as "social justice" as a central pillar of Jewish life. Not every Reform rabbi espoused each and every principle, but the platform became highly influential, so much so that 1885 might be viewed as the year when American Reform definitively broke with Jewish tradition.

What, then, of the Orthodox camp? By the 1870s, almost all Americanized

1. Jonathan D. Sarna, *American Judaism: A History* (New Haven: Yale University Press, 2004), 145.

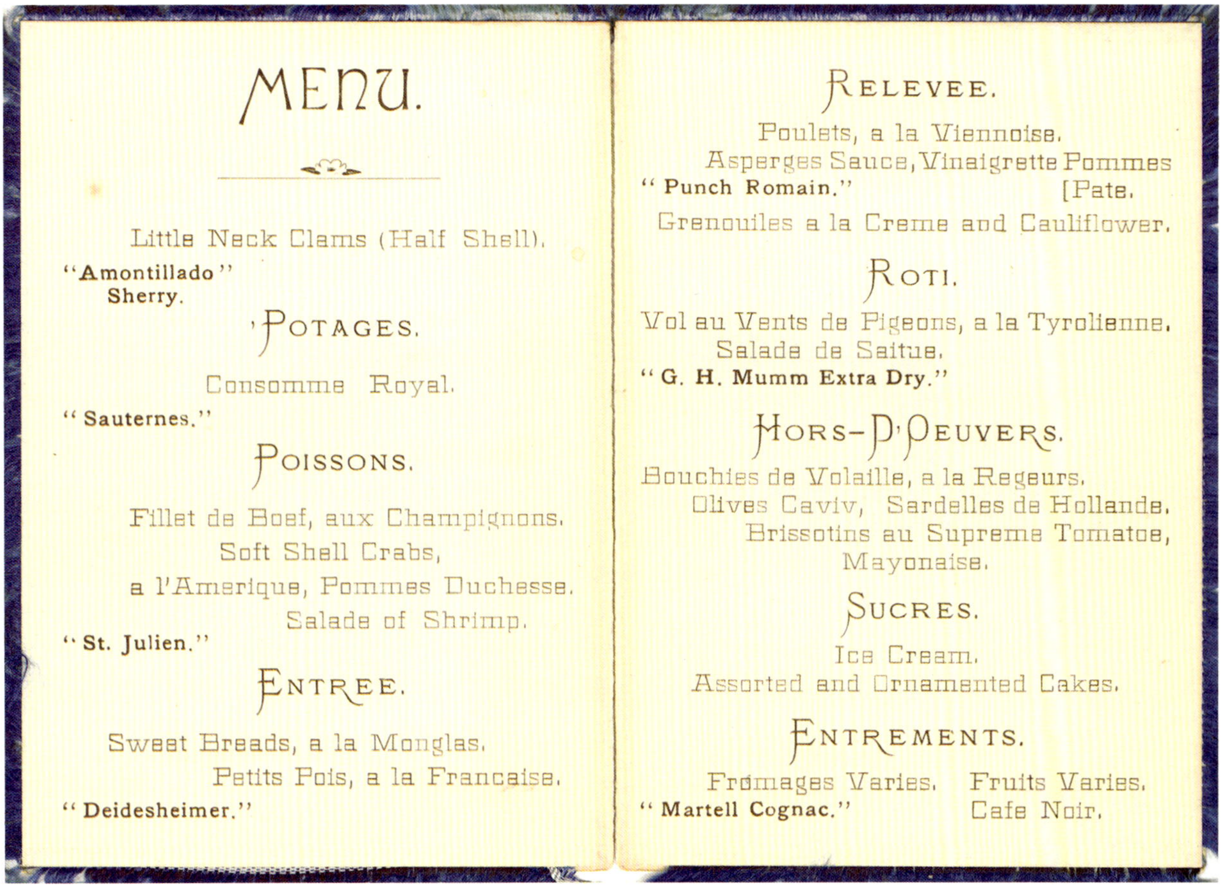

MENU.

Little Neck Clams (Half Shell).
"Amontillado" Sherry.

POTAGES.
Consomme Royal.
"Sauternes."

POISSONS.
Fillet de Boef, aux Champignons.
Soft Shell Crabs,
a l'Amerique, Pommes Duchesse.
Salade of Shrimp.
"St. Julien."

ENTREE.
Sweet Breads, a la Monglas.
Petits Pois, a la Francaise.
"Deidesheimer."

RELEVEE.
Poulets, a la Viennoise.
Asperges Sauce, Vinaigrette Pommes [Pate.
"Punch Romain."
Grenouiles a la Creme and Cauliflower.

ROTI.
Vol au Vents de Pigeons, a la Tyrolienne.
Salade de Saitue.
"G. H. Mumm Extra Dry."

HORS-D'OEUVERS.
Bouchies de Volaille, a la Regeurs.
Olives Caviv, Sardelles de Hollande.
Brissotins au Supreme Tomatoe,
Mayonaise.

SUCRES.
Ice Cream.
Assorted and Ornamented Cakes.

ENTREMENTS.
Fromages Varies. Fruits Varies.
"Martell Cognac." Cafe Noir.

Fig. 3. Dishes served at the trefa banquet, July 11, 1883. (Courtesy of The Jacob Rader Marcus Center of the American Jewish Archives, Cincinnati, Ohio).

synagogues had eschewed Orthodoxy.[2] Still, the postbellum era witnessed a resurgence of traditional Jewish practice, driven initially by laypersons centered largely in New York and Philadelphia. Traditionalists would also soon bring forth their own rabbinic leadership and institutional infrastructure. With synagogue attendance lagging and ritual observance declining, growing numbers of Jews, including young activists, questioned whether the Reform banner served as a helpful rallying point for what they saw as a much-needed religious revival. Following his arrival in America in 1885, the Hungarian rabbi Alexander Kohut (1842–1894) championed a different approach. A celebrated Jewish scholar, Kohut deemed the Judaism shorn of rabbinic law that many Reformers advocated to be a grievous mistake. In seeking a conservative alternative, he aimed

2. Jeffrey S. Gurock, *Orthodox Jews in America* (Bloomington: Indiana University Press, 2009), 83.

to vivify traditional religious observance. In the pulpit and through his writings, Kohut battled with Kaufmann Kohler over the direction of American Jewish life.

As these developments unfolded, Eastern European Jews spilled into the United States in ever growing numbers—two million of them between 1881 and 1914—as part of a global reshuffling of their population. Especially in New York, where most of the immigrants alighted, this massive migration did much to shape the Orthodox Jewish institutions of the day, which worked to keep the immigrants and their children within the religious fold as they acclimated to American ways. Notwithstanding their contemporary reputation for piety and heightened religiosity, the majority of these Jews were not meticulous in their day-to-day observance of Jewish law. They focused instead on the most important lifecycle events (such as birth and death rituals), dietary laws, and calendrical practices (especially the High Holidays) as they navigated an environment of opportunity and hard choices. A decent wage often demanded work on the Sabbath and festival days. Free public education undermined the traditional *cheder*. And of course, the entire edifice of Jewish life in America was wholly voluntary, resulting in the same sort of upheaval that had characterized American Jewish life almost from its inception.

Orthodox laypersons drove the initial charge to bring religious order to the tumult of Eastern European immigrant life. They did so, first, by fashioning synagogues attuned not only to tradition but also to the decorum and aesthetics expected of respectable congregations in America, Jewish and non-Jewish alike. In so doing, they did not hesitate to borrow selectively from the Reform playbook. Grand showplace synagogues, often constructed in the Moorish style, cropped up in immigrant areas. In these edifices, melodious song, often regimented by cantors, and vernacular preaching swept away the more chaotic, foreign feel of the humble *shtiblech* where public ritual observance had largely unfolded. These large synagogues also catered to immigrants hailing from geographically diverse homelands—united now more by their traditionalism than by their place of origin. All told, the goal was to fashion worship spaces that accorded with middle-class American values and about which the rapidly acculturating immigrants could be proud. Advocates of these developments insisted that for Orthodoxy to survive in America, it needed to look different from its mirror in Eastern Europe.

In their efforts to achieve a sustainable Orthodoxy, lay leaders also sought to secure effective rabbinic leadership. Some of these individuals hatched a quixotic plan for a chief rabbi in New York to helm a new body titled the Association of American Orthodox Hebrew Congregations. However, the appointment of Rabbi

Jacob Joseph of Vilna, who took his post in 1888, proved a spectacular failure, as did the association of synagogues intended to pay his salary. Himself a newcomer to America's shores, Joseph could not model the desired Americanized Orthodoxy. His sermons flopped. His cultural vantage point was unrelatable. He did nothing to elevate the position of Orthodoxy and struggled even to make an adequate living, dying impoverished in 1902. And yet, the lesson of Rabbi Jacob Joseph is not simply one of a prominent Old World rabbi unprepared for the cultural circumstances of the New World. Structural forces undermined his position from the start. The unified Orthodoxy so desired by Joseph's early backers had no place in an environment where a title like "chief rabbi" was not backed by a higher governmental authority.

Moreover, the common desire among religious Jews to sustain tradition did not imply a consensus as to who was fit to enter the Orthodox tent. Two philosophies evolved in the fight against Reform, one broad and inclusive and the other narrow and exclusive. In New York, each school of thought became associated with a different physical rabbinical school, although the gap between the philosophies would not spawn two separate movements (Conservative and Orthodox Judaism) until well after the Gilded Age.

The more inclusive vision of Orthodoxy was nurtured at the Jewish Theological Seminary (JTS), incorporated in 1886. Alexander Kohut taught Talmud. The Reverend Henry Pereira Mendes (1852–1937), of the Sephardic Shearith Israel congregation in New York, was another prominent backer. JTS's faculty was ideologically diverse, but united in the quest to save Eastern European immigrants from radical Reform influence. This institution would later gain considerable renown, but suffered in the earliest years from weak internal governance and limited financial support. Were it not for a reorganization in 1902 under the direction of the famous scholar Solomon Schechter (1847–1915), and for considerable financial backing (from prominent Reform Jews seeking to Americanize Orthodoxy), it would likely have failed. In the earliest years, however, JTS did help spawn other enduring Orthodox organizations, including a coalition of synagogues similarly intended to combat Reform, known as the Orthodox Union. Only in the twentieth century would a new generation of mostly JTS-ordained rabbis further the creation of a Conservative movement institutionally and ideologically distinct from Orthodoxy.[3] Even into the post–World War II era, Conservative and modern Orthodox congregations could be difficult to distinguish.

3. See Michael R. Cohen, *The Birth of Conservative Judaism: Solomon Schechter's Disciples and the Creation of an American Religious Movement* (New York: Columbia University Press, 2012).

An exclusive brand of Orthodoxy, more resistant to Americanization but widely overlooked at the time by those outside its reach, coalesced in 1902 under the banner of the Agudat ha-Rabbanim (Union of Orthodox Rabbis). This Yiddish-speaking group shared the concerns of its JTS counterparts with regard to the laxity of Jewish religious observance in America and the dangers of Reform. However, the members viewed the strategy of accommodation to modern conditions—including vernacular preaching and more decorous synagogue worship—as surrender. Instead, they resolved to strengthen the stature of Eastern European rabbinic authority on American soil. Where Jacob Joseph had failed on the American scene, these rabbis saw strength in numbers. They also sought to forge a homegrown rabbinate, and for this purpose supported the recently organized Rabbi Isaac Elchanan Theological Seminary (RIETS). With a curriculum modeled after that of Eastern European *yeshivot*, RIETS in these years made no effort to shape its students in the Americanized manner expected by most Orthodox laypersons. RIETS would struggle until its reorganization in 1915 along more inclusive lines.

While Reform and Orthodox groups stood at odds in this era, both were engulfed in analogous philosophical debates. Each had to decide the extent to which diversity of ideology and practice would be tolerated. As we have seen, these developments were not orchestrated exclusively by the rabbinic class, and the divides were never total. In the Reform movement, however, the tenets of the Pittsburgh Platform heralded a transition from the big tent model of Reform Judaism initially championed by Isaac Mayer Wise. As two visions of traditional religious life coexisted within the Orthodox camp, each enlivened by a different rabbinical school, the Reform movement consolidated. It increasingly embraced an *exclusive* model of Reform Judaism, inaugurating the era of "Classical Reform."

Classical Reform implied a rigorous embrace of modernity and the American way of life, as evidenced by the content of Reform sermons and writings. Changes in synagogue worship also increased, often in tandem with grand new synagogue construction: ritual garb disappeared, vernacular liturgy proliferated, dietary laws were honored in the breech, and organ music complemented the sounds of prayer. A minority of synagogues even moved Sabbath worship services to Sunday to accommodate the working lives of congregants. Yet, Classical Reform was not motivated simply by the desire for inward refinement and modern convenience. Outward social justice activities inspired by Prophetic Judaism and the Protestant Social Gospel movement—which also drove women's growing involvement in synagogue life—proved some of the most enduring and transformative initiatives. Critically, in New York, wealthy German Reform "uptown

Jews" came into contact with their more impoverished Eastern European downtown Jewish coreligionists. This comingling had more than just philanthropic implications. Gradually, a growing number of these Jews were brought into the Reform fold, and some even attended HUC, Reform's Cincinnati citadel.

Universalism also grew more popular in Reform during this period, which furthered its ideological agenda. This principle, coupled with a desire to appear more loyally American, drove many Reform Jews to eschew Zionism. Yet, these same proclivities also pushed some Jews to reject Judaism altogether. Spearheaded by Felix Adler (1851–1933), the son of the rabbi of New York's Reform flagship Temple Emanu-El, the rise of the Ethical Culture movement in the postbellum period rattled the Reform world. Adler's faith coalition renounced theism and rejected all Jewish particularism: the Bible did not contain the highest instantiation of the God Idea, as the Pittsburg Platform would preach; rather, ethics and the universal precepts of world religions should govern the faithful. To Adler, Judaism was not a triumph—it was a dying anachronism. Coming from a man born of Reform royalty, such a diagnosis helped inspire the crisis of confidence that gripped American Jewish life as the Gilded Age began. As it closed, however, a different question emerged. Given the enormous diversity and burgeoning size of the Jewish community, which group, Reform or Orthodox, German or Eastern European, would govern the future? Equally significant to consider is the extent to which each of these groups had elevated American Jewish cultural prestige during this period despite the religious and ethnic divisions among them.

Jewish Print Culture

Critics dismissed America as a Jewish cultural backwater in the postbellum era. As late as 1894, Cyrus Adler, later president of the Jewish Theological Seminary in New York, would lament that American Jewry had "no libraries, no publications and no independent scholars."[4] Judging by these metrics, nineteenth-century European rabbis labeled the United States a *treifene medina*, an "unkosher land." In actuality, as the American Jewish population grew dramatically in the Gilded Age, its cultural output rapidly increased and diversified. By the dawn of the twentieth century, a rising number of publishers, books, newspapers, magazines, and journals operated in as many as four languages—English, Hebrew, German, and Yiddish—solidifying the United States as a center of Jewish culture.

4. Cyrus Adler, *Selected Letters*, ed. Ira Robinson, 2 vols. (Philadelphia: Jewish Publication Society of America, 1985), 1:70.

In the immediate aftermath of the Civil War, American Jews' most significant cultural productions in English were newspapers published by prominent religious leaders such as Isaac Leeser (1806–1868) of Philadelphia and Isaac Mayer Wise of Cincinnati. These two men espoused disparate visions for American Judaism—the former advocated Americanized Orthodoxy and the latter Americanized Reform—but both leveraged their publications to convey Jewish knowledge and promote Jewish unity. Indeed, Leeser's *Occident and American Jewish Advocate* (1843–1869) and Wise's *Israelite* (founded in 1854 and renamed the *American Israelite* in 1874) helped to further these objectives. The newspapers transmitted "a broad range of national, international, and local news, as well as polemics, homiletics and apologetics, serious scholarship, popular fiction, and helpful advice."[5] In so doing, they served as a principal source of in-group information and a forum for religious education and debate. And they connected Jews in far-flung locations, further elevating the concept of a national Jewish culture and community in America. As Jonathan Sarna observes, by the 1860s Jewish newspapers published in urban centers such as New York, Philadelphia, Cincinnati, and San Francisco reached hundreds of smaller communities, including some with only a single Jewish resident.[6]

Another Jewish newspaper in English, the *American Hebrew*, emerged in 1879 (Fig. 4). By then, some young native-born American Jews, many of them descended from central European immigrants but raised reading American newspapers, aspired to a loftier journalistic standard than publications like the *Israelite* practiced. The *American Hebrew* realized this objective in several ways: "its English prose was livelier and less Germanic, its interests broader, its journalism (like that of the *New York Times*) less personal and more highbrow."[7] The paper also espoused a different ideological agenda. Whereas the *Israelite* served as an unofficial organ of the Reform movement, the *American Hebrew* advocated Jewish tradition to boost Jewish renewal while remaining open to different shades of opinion. Its editors sought in this manner to edify the religious and spiritual lives of American Jews and to further their religious knowledge and pride in being Jewish. The *American Hebrew* reached a wide audience and remained the

5. Jonathan D. Sarna, "Two Ambitious Goals: American Jewish Publishing in the United States," in *A History of the Book in America*, vol. 4, *Print in Motion: The Expansion of Publishing and Reading in the United States, 1880–1940*, ed. Carl F. Kaestle and Janice A. Radway (Chapel Hill: University of North Carolina Press, 2009), 380.

6. *Ibid.*

7. Jonathan D. Sarna, "The American Jewish Press," in *The Oxford Handbook of Religion and the American News Media*, ed. Diane Winston (Oxford: Oxford University Press, 2012), 541.

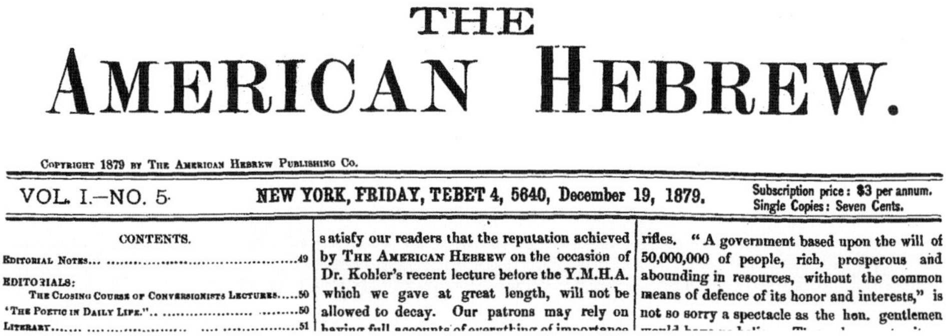
THE AMERICAN HEBREW.

COPYRIGHT 1879 BY THE AMERICAN HEBREW PUBLISHING CO.

VOL. I.—NO. 5. NEW YORK, FRIDAY, TEBET 4, 5640, December 19, 1879. Subscription price: $3 per annum. Single Copies: Seven Cents.

CONTENTS.

EDITORIAL NOTES... 49
EDITORIALS:
THE CLOSING COURSE OF CONVERSIONISTS LECTURES.....50
"THE POETIC IN DAILY LIFE."... 50
LITERARY... 51

satisfy our readers that the reputation achieved by THE AMERICAN HEBREW on the occasion of Dr. Kohler's recent lecture before the Y.M.H.A. which we gave at great length, will not be allowed to decay. Our patrons may rely on

rifles. "A government based upon the will of 50,000,000 of people, rich, prosperous and abounding in resources, without the common means of defence of its honor and interests," is not so sorry a spectacle as the hon. gentlemen

Fig. 4. Masthead of the *American Hebrew*. December 19, 1879. (ProQuest Historical Newspapers).

leading Jewish newspaper in the United States well after its editorial stewardship passed into new hands. However, its national scope was increasingly anomalous for the times. While Jewish newspapers grew in number in the postbellum era, most were locally oriented publications.

Foreign-language periodicals also circulated in the Gilded Age, in German, Hebrew, and Yiddish. The development of Yiddish-language newspapers advanced especially in the last decade of the nineteenth century. A limited number of such ventures had appeared in the 1870s and 1880s, but those periodicals quickly failed. By contrast, numerous successful Yiddish dailies emerged in the 1890s—including several Socialist organs—that played an increasingly important role in immigrant Jewish life.[8] The Yiddish daily *Forward* became the most famous of these, but more than a hundred periodicals of different kinds had emerged before 1905. Some of the publications were geared toward intellectuals, while others catered to more popular audiences. Whoever their readers, these newspapers contained a wider range of content than English-language Jewish newspapers did, including both secular and Jewish news. The Yiddish newspapers also placed greater emphasis upon issues of importance to the immigrant community—matters of immigration, Americanization, and events back in Europe. And they proved more willing to criticize America and American Jewish life than newspapers printed in English.

Jews, most notably Joseph Pulitzer (1847–1911), a Hungarian immigrant initially recruited to the Union Army during the Civil War, and Adolph Ochs

8. Tony Michels, "'Speaking to Moyshe': The Early Socialist Yiddish Press and Its Readers," *Jewish History* 14, no. 1 (2000): 51.

(1858–1935), a son-in-law of Isaac Mayer Wise, also published general newspapers during this period, although the two men championed disparate approaches to the journalistic craft. As owner of the St. Louis *Dispatch* and later the New York *World*, Pulitzer promoted yellow journalism, a style that blended "vigorous promotion, sensationalism, sympathy with labor and the underdog, and innovations in illustration and typography."[9] And his newspapers were wildly successful, so much so that by the time Pulitzer died he was one of the most famous men in America. His bequest endowed the prestigious journalistic prizes that bear his name. Meanwhile, the Cincinnati-born Adolph Ochs got his start as a printer's apprentice and at the age of twenty purchased a controlling interest in the *Chattanooga Times*, which he transformed into a leading Southern newspaper. He is best remembered, however, for his ownership and editorial stewardship of the *New York Times*, which he purchased in 1896. Ochs transformed the once-struggling publication into a preeminent newspaper renowned for its independence. Where Pulitzer advocated sensationalism, Ochs demanded objective, responsible journalism that distinguished news reporting from editorializing.

Jewish book publishing also blossomed in the Gilded Age, reflecting the burgeoning size and growing diversity of the American Jewish population. Some 565 Jewish works were published in the 1860s, a number that nearly quadrupled in the 1890s. Beyond books edited, translated, or written by Isaac Mayer Wise and Isaac Leeser, who together were responsible for almost 150 different works during their lifetimes, American Jewish publishing more broadly came of age in the postbellum era. William Hackenberg's *Statistics of the Jews of the United States* (1880) was an early example. Significant titles of scholarship also included Moses Mielziner's *The Jewish Law of Marriage and Divorce in Ancient and Modern Times and Its Relation to the Laws of the State* (1881) and Marcus Jastrow's groundbreaking *Dictionary of the Targumim, the Talmud Babli and Yerushalmi, and the Midrashic Literature* (1886–1903). Literary works included Emma Lazarus's *Songs of a Semite* (1882), a celebration of her Jewish roots.

The advent of the Jewish Publication Society (JPS) in Philadelphia in 1888 marked a further watershed in American Jewish cultural life. The founders of JPS sought, in part, to unite American Jews across the country through a common culture of print. The Jewish community had doubled in size in the 1880s due to immigration and would do so again in the decade after. This unprece-

9. Irving Rosenthal, "Pulitzer, Joseph," in *Encyclopaedia Judaica*, 2d ed., ed. Michael Berenbaum and Fred Skolnik, vol. 16 (Detroit: Macmillan Reference USA, 2007), 731–32.

dented influx, coupled with growing divisions within the Jewish community itself, highlighted the need for institutions to encourage cultural unity—between natives and newcomers, Germans and east Europeans, Orthodox and Reform Jews, and Jews of different socioeconomic standings. JPS was intended to serve as a resource for all Jews and to stand above such partisan divides.

JPS's founders also aimed to invigorate American Judaism culturally. Believing that rising antisemitism in Germany presaged the cultural decline of the Jewish community there, they championed America as a new center of Jewish culture. "It befits us as free citizens of the noblest of countries," the founders proclaimed, "to take it up in their stead."[10] Patriotism and cultural production thus went hand in hand. JPS would publish books to groom American Jewry for the crucial task of cultural leadership, while proclaiming to the world that the Jews of the United States had matured culturally. Although JPS's most significant early publications were adaptations of European works, with publishing came prestige. As Jonathan Sarna explains, "[a] traditional symbol of unity among Jews, books also historically brought status both to the individuals who wrote them, and to the communities that produced and owned them."[11]

Not surprisingly, significant Jewish libraries were also established in America during the Gilded Age. Founded by B'nai B'rith in New York in 1852, the Maimonides Library was the first major institution of this kind. It was also one of the largest, with a circulating collection of 25,000 volumes by 1885 and 85,000 volumes twenty years later. However, like other significant American Jewish libraries of the nineteenth century, the collection suffered from lack of use, reflecting a broader disconnect between the Jewish high culture promoted by library boosters and the reading preferences of the larger Jewish population. Even Jewish libraries with heavy patronage overwhelmingly circulated books of popular literature. In 1892, New York's Temple Emanu-El transferred its significant collection of European Hebraica—comprising some 2,500 books and 43 manuscripts purchased in 1879—to Columbia University, where it was hoped the works would find greater use.[12] Still, private and institutional Judaica libraries were growing in size and number. Wealthy and learned Jews like Philadelphia's Judge Mayer Sulzberger (1843–1923) and San Francisco's Adolph Sutro (1830–1898) owned significant collections, as did some religious leaders,

10. Quoted in Sarna, "Two Ambitious Goals," 376.

11. *Ibid.*, 382.

12. Robert Singerman, "Books Weeping for Someone to Visit and Admire Them: Jewish Library Culture in the United States, 1850–1910," *Studies in Bibliography and Booklore* 20 (1998): 114.

both Reform and Orthodox. By 1900, the libraries of Cincinnati's Hebrew Union College and New York's Jewish Theological Seminary held 14,000 and 5,000 volumes, respectively.

American Jewish scholarship was also coming of age at the dawn of the twentieth century. First came the publication of volume one of the *Jewish Encyclopedia* in 1901. That effort, spearheaded by Isidore Singer (1859–1939), aimed to bring together Jewish knowledge both traditional and modern, including a century of German Jewish scholarly output. Hundreds of Jewish scholars from around the globe took part in this venture, but the work was centered in New York under the stewardship of mostly American scholars. In this way, Shuly Rubin Schwarz writes, the twelve-volume work signified "the passing of the mantle of scholarly hegemony to the United States ... [and became] the symbol par excellence of the emerging cultural and intellectual independence of American Jewry."[13] And just as the *Jewish Encyclopedia* went to press, Solomon Schechter, one of the world's preeminent Jewish scholars, arrived in the United States to lead the reorganized Jewish Theological Seminary. His coming would further boost the cause of American Jewish scholarship. Schechter worked to turn JTS into an eminent Jewish research institution, and scholarly publications would be a barometer of his success in doing so. Taken together, the *Jewish Encyclopedia* and Schechter's arrival also testified to the growing scholarly confidence and competence of American Jewry, a trend that would continue in the ensuing decades. A new Jewish cultural center was emerging in the very place once decried as a *treifene medinah.* Meanwhile, fueled largely by immigration, American Jewry had grown and fanned out across America's vast geographic landscape.

Jewish Immigration and Demographics

Published as a joint venture of the Board of Delegates of American Israelites and the Union of American Hebrew Congregations, *The Statistics of the Jews of the United States* (1880) provides the most complete demographic portrait we have of American Jewish life after the Civil War and on the eve of mass immigration. From it, we learn that American Jews in the 1870s were still heavily concentrated in urban communities, a sharp contrast to the national population more broadly. Nationwide, 160 towns and cities housed 84 percent of all of America's Jews, and half of them lived in just six cities. New York (Manhattan) had the largest community (approximately 60,000), followed by San Francisco (16,000),

13. Shuly Rubin Schwartz, *The Emergence of Jewish Scholarship in America: The Publication of the Jewish Encyclopedia* (Cincinnati: Hebrew Union College Press, 1991), 16.

Brooklyn (13,000), and Philadelphia (12,000). Chicago and Baltimore were tied with 10,000 Jews each.[14] In addition, America's ten largest Jewish communities took root in its ten largest cities, with only limited differences in rank order.[15]

Notwithstanding this demographic concentration, a significant number of Jews had settled in smaller cities and towns, often to pursue a business venture. Whether they peddled goods or opened shop in these more isolated places, hundreds of Jewish pioneers in the nineteenth century spent part or the entirety of their lives away from other Jews and unaffiliated with Jewish communal life. *Statistics of the Jews* paints a demographic portrait of many of these places: 329 had 10 or fewer Jewish residents, and 190 had between 11 and 20. In total, 868 places of settlement had fewer than 100 Jewish residents. To be sure, a population of fewer than 100 Jews did not preclude the possibility of Jewish communal life. The data demonstrate that 66 towns with fewer than 100 Jewish residents had established a Jewish institution of some kind.[16] Often, these institutions relied upon the involvement of Jews from surrounding areas.

In all, there were more than 200,000 Jews in the United States by 1870. Most were of central European origin. The Jewish population of the United States had increased at least fifty-fold in the four decades before the Civil War, a ripple within the wave of German speakers who crossed the Atlantic in pursuit of religious and political freedom and, above all, economic opportunity. However, already in the 1870s the American Jewish population was changing as immigration from central Europe slowed. Rapid German industrialization opened opportunities for Jews that galvanized significant internal movement from small communities to cities and made migration across the Atlantic less attractive.[17] At the same time, broader Jewish immigration picked up steam. Tens of thousands of Jews from Eastern Europe came, well exceeding the little more than 7,000 east European Jews who arrived during the whole previous half-century. Even though official statistics are not available until the twentieth century, we have considerable information about the 1870s immigration, including rough estimates of its numbers.

14. *Statistics of the Jews of the United States* (Philadelphia: Union of American Hebrew Congregations, 1880); Lee Shai Weissbach, "The Jewish Communities of the United States on the Eve of Mass Migration: Some Comments on Geography and Bibliography," *American Jewish History* 78, no. 1 (1988): 84.

15. Steven G. Mostov, "A 'Jerusalem' on the Ohio: The Social and Economic History of Cincinnati's Jewish Community, 1840–1875" (Ph.D. diss., Brandeis University, 1981), 6.

16. Weissbach, "Jewish Communities of the United States on the Eve of Mass Migration," 91.

17. Rudolf Glanz, "The German Jewish Mass Emigration: 1830–1880," *American Jewish Archives Journal* 22, no. 1 (1970): 49.

Spurred on by misfortune, the Lithuanian Jews who rushed to America in the 1870s made up the largest percentage of Jewish immigrants in that period. In 1868, a cholera epidemic afflicted a large swath of northwestern Russia, followed by severe famine, especially in the provinces of Kovno and Suvalki. Huge numbers of people sought escape, and the early growth of the railroad connecting the Russian empire to central Europe speeded their departure. Survivors crowded into Prussian cities such as Memel, Koenigsberg, and Stettin, from which many were directed on to the United States. In the earliest years, because the established American Jewish community worried about the impact of unchecked migration, Jewish immigrants were mostly young men carefully selected for the journey by relief organizations. Yet, a much larger and more demographically diverse influx soon commenced, especially as earlier arrivals began to bring over their relatives. Mark Wischnitzer "cautiously" estimated the total number of Russian Jews immigrating to the United States from 1869 to 1880 at 30,000, although economist Simon Kuznets later argued that it was likely less than 20,000.[18]

Jews also came from the Austro-Hungarian empire, often to escape economic troubles. Again, no official statistics are available, but it has been estimated that a quarter of the some 63,000 immigrants from the empire to the United States between 1869 and 1880 were Jewish. All told, then, approximately 15,000 Jews came to America from Austria-Hungary in this decade; adding this number to that of Russian Jews gives the considerable figure of some 45,000 immigrants.[19]

After 1880, Jewish immigration from Eastern Europe to America famously accelerated, and the large Jewish communities located in the Northeast absorbed most of the newcomers. In just three decades after the data for *Statistics of the Jews* were gathered, the Jewish population of Brooklyn jumped nearly twenty-fold, New York's ten-fold, Philadelphia's eight-fold, and Baltimore's four-fold. The assassination of Tsar Alexander II in 1881 and the anti-Jewish persecutions and legislation that followed helped to spur the dramatic outflows of Jews to these American urban centers. In the Russian empire, Jews were forced to abandon their prior way of life and journey to approved cities, where they

18. Mark Wischnitzer, *To Dwell in Safety: The Story of Jewish Migration Since 1800* (Philadelphia: Jewish Publication Society of America, 1949), 35; Simon Kuznets, "Immigration of Russian Jews to the United States: Background and Structure," *Perspectives in American History* 9 (1975): 41–42.

19. Salo W. Baron, "United States 1880–1914," in Baron, *Steeled by Adversity: Essays and Addresses on American Jewish Life*, ed. Jeannette Meisel Baron (Philadelphia: Jewish Publication Society of America, 1971), 277.

swelled the ranks of the industrial labor force. There, discriminatory practices and strict quotas prevented numerous Jews from obtaining higher education or well-paying jobs. For both skilled and unskilled young Jews, the "golden land" of America seemed to offer abundant opportunities. Mass migration followed, aided by steamship companies that slashed steerage fares to attract passengers for their trans-Atlantic voyages.[20] Between 1881 and 1900, some 675,000 Jews immigrated to the United States, and the number would accelerate thereafter, so that by 1914 a full one-third of Eastern Europe's Jews, some 2,000,000, had immigrated to the United States.

These historical events account for the surge of migrants in a general sense. What, then, of their more detailed demographic profile? For the most part, they came in families, as evidenced by the significant number of women among the Jewish immigrants entering the port of New York: 41.5 percent between 1886 and 1889, and 47.2 percent between 1895 and 1898. A much higher proportion of Jewish children also made the journey as compared with other immigrant groups. And Jews immigrated at an ever-growing pace during this period: the upwards of 50,000 who arrived annually between 1899 and 1902 more than doubled the annual rate of the previous two decades (and the number would double again in the coming decade, cresting in 1906).

This more than two-fold increase is consistent with the Jewish immigration numbers as a percentage of total immigration to America in these years. Between 1871 and 1901, 11.7 million people immigrated to the United States, with Jews making up 4.3 percent of the total from 1881 to 1889. From 1899 to 1902, that percentage jumped to 11.3, where it plateaued. These are unofficial statistics gathered by Jewish immigrant aid societies. (Immigration officials did not begin to distinguish Jews until 1899, and then based largely on linguistic factors.) Nevertheless, their data reveal important patterns. Yes, the east European Jews had particularly compelling economic and social reasons to make the journey, coming at a much higher rate than other Russian ethnic minority groups. However, it is also true that they formed part of a much larger, predominately east and south European migration of peoples to the United States at this time.

Pull factors also help to explain the accelerating pace of Jewish immigration to America. Once settled there, the first immigrants encouraged and often facilitated the journey for others, fostering a snowball effect. As Simon Kuznets explains:

20. Deborah Dwork, "Immigrant Jews on the Lower East Side of New York: 1880–1914," in *The American Jewish Experience*, ed. Jonathan D. Sarna (New York: Holmes & Meier, 1986), 102.

> Once the mass migration gets under way, other cost-reduction factors are created. The early migration streams establish channels that facilitate the movement of later migrants, such as means of transport, emigrant-aid organizations, institutional patterns of movement, and the like. Also, the additions to the body of immigrants in the receiving country provide further information to their relatives, neighbors, and friends still in the sending country and, after a while, resources and facilities of great help and protection to would-be new emigrants.... [F]requently the immigrants to the United States had their passage paid for by relatives in the country, who also provided initial hospitality to the newcomers. In short, the costs of travel, information, and adjustment are all reduced sharply as the early immigration streams become settled in the country of destination. This reduction of costs undoubtedly was an added incentive for additional groups to emigrate—even with less intensive pressures than those that impelled earlier emigration despite the greater cost of movement.[21]

More often than other immigrant groups, east European Jews stayed permanently in the United States, and often in the port city where they disembarked—overwhelmingly New York City. Social connections with more established friends and family were pivotal for those fresh off the boat. Especially prior to the 1903 Kishinev pogrom and the 1904–1905 Russo-Japanese War, some Jewish immigrants returned to their old hometowns for reasons that included homesickness, economic failure, cultural barriers, difficulty living a traditional Jewish lifestyle, and optimism that life might yet improve for Jews in the Russian empire.[22] Those who stayed—the overwhelming majority—concentrated in New York's industrial workforce. The needle trades provided the largest magnet for Jewish immigrant laborers, and they often found work in factories owned by Jews. The immigrants also dwelt among those of their own kind, concentrating in crowded tenements in lower Manhattan; in some wards they composed upward of 80 percent of the population.

More than the Jews who came to the United States in prior migration waves, east European Jews maintained a noticeable presence in the urban places that offered them the most opportunity. Their omnipresence worried the more established, "uptown" central European Jews who had arrived in America before them, had pursued opportunities across the country, and ultimately had benefited from more rapid upward mobility. Central European Jews cared much about the respect of their Gentile neighbors and had expended much effort to earn

21. For more on these numbers, see Kuznets, "Immigration of Russian Jews to the United States," 35–114.

22. Jonathan D. Sarna, "The Myth of No Return: Jewish Return Migration to Eastern Europe, 1881–1914," *American Jewish History* 71, no. 2 (1981): 256–68.

it. They refined their religious lives along the lines of modern respectability, championed their German cultural heritage as a marker of their commitment to reason and universal human progress, and built opulent "temples" that evoked a general sense of awe and cultural grandeur. They were therefore vexed by the sorry picture presented by their impoverished east European coreligionists, with their unsanitary living conditions, foreign culture, and chaotic worship spaces. These new immigrant masses threatened to disrupt the process of rapid acculturation so earnestly cultivated by earlier arrivals. Worse, the newcomers could fan the flames of racialized antisemitism of the sort ascending back in Germany, which would spare no Jew. In America, consequently, central European Jews showed more concern about the cultural development of east European Jews than non-Jews did.

Although many wealthy uptown Jews privately ridiculed the language, dress, religious rituals, and ideological beliefs of the east Europeans, they publicly defended the downtown Jews and privately donated funds to aid them. The arrival of the east Europeans increased the scope of Jewish philanthropy in all areas of human need. Major Jewish religious and cultural groups, including B'nai B'rith and the Union of American Hebrew Congregations, mobilized for this purpose as well. Their goal, more often than not, was to remake their east European coreligionists in their own cultural image, and education provided the primary means of adjustment. Charities funded an array of educational opportunities, including technical classes and English classes to supplement public school instruction and boost acculturation. Their Americanization agenda was epitomized in the 1889 founding of the Hebrew Institute (later renamed the Educational Alliance), a Jewish-sponsored community house envisioned as a "center of sweetness and light, an oasis in the desert of degradation and despair."[23] The Hebrew Institute became a clearinghouse for impressing the trappings of American culture on immigrant children.

East European Jews, however, also relied on a model of self-help, turning in times of need to their fellow townsmen for assistance. Often, they did so through the infrastructure of *landsmannschaftn*, organizations that bound "the immigrant to his shtetl and birthplace."[24] Founded variously as mutual aid societies, religious groups, and fraternal orders, these bodies afforded members material benefits as well as an arena for social engagement. Their functions were equally diverse, covering everything from burial services and free loan programs to

23. Moses Rischin, "Germans versus Russians," in *American Jewish Experience*, ed. Sarna, 124.
24. *Ibid.*, 127.

insurance and sickness benefits. In New York City, hundreds of these groups sprang up, encompassing the vast majority of the immigrants. By the late 1880s, though, east European Jews had created communal charities as well, providing benefits to a wider range of individuals than the *landsmannschaftn.* The Hebrew Sheltering Home (1889), Hebrew Free Loan Society (1892), and Hebrew Immigrant Aid Society (1902) were a few of the most prominent initiatives. East European Jews also established their own hospitals and built infrastructure for religious education (usually for boys). In the Gilded Age, therefore, Jews divided into two primary subethnic groups—central European and east European—each with its own separate institutions. The gap took generations to close.

The American Jewish community amounted to approximately 150,000 in 1860, 250,000 in 1880, and 1,000,000 by 1900.[25] Along with the masses of Jewish immigrants responsible for the demographic explosion there came a cultural shift. In the early years, most Jews already in America knew that east European immigrants had arrived, but they failed to pay them much heed. Decades later, they realized that the east European Jews had come to greatly outnumber them and that the tenor of the whole Jewish community was changing. Still, the economic fortunes of the new arrivals were intimately tied to the success of the central European Jews who preceded them.

Jewish Economic Profile

In the beginning, there was peddling. For many central European Jews newly off the boat in antebellum America, it afforded the potential for a fresh start. Carrying goods supplied on credit by more established Jewish merchants, penniless immigrants could journey to the hinterlands to hawk their wares with little or no invested capital of their own. They served as foot soldiers of the market revolution on America's rapidly expanding frontier, supplying the wants of settlers who pined for luxuries available only in denser population centers. Peddling was not new to many of these Jews. In the United States, though, the occupation became a point of economic departure and a springboard to more lucrative business ventures; it was rarely the toil of a lifetime.[26] Many of the wealthiest American Jews in the Gilded Age began with humble packs on their backs. Immigrants with names like Lehman, Straus, and Seligman—remem-

25. Jacob Rader Marcus, *To Count a People: American Jewish Population Data, 1585–1984* (Lanham, Md.: University Press of America, 1990), 239–40.

26. Hasia R. Diner, *Roads Taken: The Great Jewish Migrations to the New World and the Peddlers Who Forged the Way* (New Haven: Yale University Press, 2015), 7–8.

bered as titans of finance and manufacturing—started as peddlers. Of course, not every peddler became economically successful, and far fewer marvelously rich; but a good number, particularly those who later wrote about their experiences, certainly did. As the nation boomed, they bounded up the economic ladder in one generation.

Impermanent though it was, peddling impacted the geographic distribution of America's Jews. Often, peddlers were the first Jews to reach small towns that later supported larger Jewish populations. And they settled down and opened their own businesses as soon as they accumulated sufficient capital to do so. For this reason, small-town Jewry in America was more uniformly middle class than urban Jewry. In many small towns, nearly all the Jewish heads of household owned a business that catered to diverse consumer needs. Some worked in retail, others in wholesale, and still others as skilled artisans. Whichever type of business they ran, Jewish shopkeepers often succeeded. Some brought entrepreneurial instincts with them to the places where they settled. Equally important, America's population expanded significantly in the late nineteenth century, and small towns became centers of trade and commerce. Jewish businesses catered not only to local inhabitants but also to those of the surrounding rural areas.

Department stores were the most visible Jewish-owned businesses. Often, they began as small retail establishments run by a single family or a small number of partners, and later expanded into significant institutions that drew in customers from beyond the local community. Their proliferation largely followed the geographic distribution of America's Jews. Almost every town with a triple-digit Jewish community had one, as did numerous towns with smaller Jewish communities (Fig. 5). Frequently, department stores bore the Jewish names of their owners—such as Gimbel, Neiman-Marcus, and Bloomingdale—helping to raise the profile of Jews in towns and cities across America.[27] Such business ventures could also be a springboard to civic leadership or politics, bespeaking the opportunities open to successful Jews, especially in the more newly admitted states: Moses Alexander (1853–1932), a clothing store owner, ultimately became the eleventh governor of Idaho; Julius Meier (1874–1937), scion of the founders of Meier & Frank, Oregon's largest department store, served as the twentieth governor of that state; and entrepreneur Simon Bamberger (1845–1926) was elected the fourth governor of Utah.

In prospering as they did, central European Jews benefited significantly from

27. See Lee Shai Weissbach, *Jewish Life in Small-Town America: A History* (New Haven: Yale University Press, 2005).

Fig. 5. Gimbel's department store, Milwaukee, 1890s. (Milwaukee Public Library).

historical forces beyond their control. Historian Adam Mendelsohn has shown how the Civil War tilted economic fortune in their favor. One-time peddlers and small-town clothing manufacturers received massive contracts to outfit the Union Army, positioning them to dominate the burgeoning ready-made men's clothing industry after the war. All of these developments held significant implications for the economic trajectory of American Jewish life. Not only did central European Jews come to play a disproportionate role in the manufacture and sale of clothing and dry goods, but they also paved the way for east European Jewish immigrants who arrived in America in subsequent decades, went to work for their coreligionists, and in some cases supplanted them. In Mendelsohn's words, without the impetus of the Civil War, "the economic history of American Jews may have been very different."[28]

28. Adam Mendelsohn, "Beyond the Battlefield: Reevaluating the Legacy of the Civil War for American Jews," *American Jewish Archives Journal* 64, no. 1–2 (2012): 84.

Clothing was not the only industry in which central European Jewish immigrants positioned themselves to thrive after the Civil War. For example, historian Michael Cohen has investigated the involvement of Southern Jewish merchants in the cotton industry, which both greatly increased Jewish wealth and contributed to the broader economic restructuring of the postbellum South. He shows that Jews relied on kinship and ethnic networks of trust to secure their economic transactions, including relations with Jewish-owned firms in New York and global Jewish investors. Jews also depended on these connections to bring Northern credit and goods to the South, helping one another to overcome the antisemitic prejudices of lenders and weather the turbulence of economic downturns and agricultural crises. Prominent Jewish-run investment banks such as Kuhn Loeb & Co., J. & W. Seligman & Co., and Lehman Brothers also helped finance railroad expansion. And men such as Meyer Guggenheim and Leonard and Adolph Lewisohn made their fortunes in mining and smelting. Structural economic forces proved pivotal. Jews found themselves in the right place at the right time to clamber up the economic ladder to success.[29]

By the time east European Jews flooded into America in significant numbers in the final decades of the nineteenth century, a shifting economic environment lessened the need for peddling. Railroads vastly reduced travel times between urban and rural areas, and consumers could purchase desired manufactured goods in stores or through mail order catalogues. Still, structural economic forces were equally instrumental to east European Jewish advancement in America after 1880. Some scholars have focused on the skillsets that these Jews brought to the New World, but the rote and repetitive tasks that sweatshop labor demanded of them required only minimal training. More compellingly, Jews took jobs in the garment business because they were plentiful, and Jewish contractors and wholesalers welcomed their cheap labor. And once the first east European Jewish arrivals entered the sweatshops, those who came after them followed their path. The manufacture and sale of clothing developed into a niche economy for American Jews. Employers and employees who shared much in common culturally and linguistically worked side-by-side, sometimes under dangerous and uncomfortable conditions. Together they democratized the clothing industry in America, allowing the poor to emulate the styles of the rich and reducing the price of clothing everywhere.

Thanks to burgeoning demand propelled by America's rapidly expanding

29. Michael R. Cohen, *Cotton Capitalists: American Jewish Entrepreneurship in the Reconstruction Era* (New York: New York University Press, 2017).

population, the clothing trade opened for Jews the potential for upward mobility. Because most clothing at the turn of the century was still made in small workshops rather than large factories, an aspiring entrepreneur needed less than a hundred dollars to get started. Sewing machines and a presser's table could be leased. Immediate family members could forgo wages in hopes of future success. A tenement apartment might double as workspace during the day. And free loan societies helped front the start-up costs. Few immigrants worried about competing with former employers. Their goal was to create a better life for themselves and, especially, for their children.

Self-employment thus became the principal driver of upward mobility for most Jewish immigrants—be they manufacturers, merchants, or small-time professionals. But the road to riches rarely proved linear in America's competitive capitalist economy. In the menswear trade, as many as a third of all contractors folded every year. In addition, most immigrants saw their fortunes undulate with the merciless boom-bust cycles of the national economy as a whole, resulting in movements "back and forth between being employed by someone else and employing others."[30] Slowly, east European immigrants trod the path to material prosperity, although it generally took them two generations to achieve what central European Jews, operating in a more robust economic environment, had achieved in one.

As the geographical production of men's clothing moved away from New York City to cities like Chicago, the production of women's wear opened up vast new opportunities for New York's immigrant Jews. In the early years of the Gilded Age, many women continued to sew clothing for themselves. Mass production did not easily jibe with women's preference for a wide variety of styles and for form-fitting clothes. However, with new technologies and favorable prices, the mass production of women's clothes accelerated after 1880. Turn-of-the-century fashion trends, including such popular items as blouses and skirts, advanced the process, as did the advent of new fabrics. In 1899, New York produced two-thirds of all ready-made women's clothing sold in the United States, and east European Jews dominated the business.

Though the garment industry employed more east European Jewish immigrants than any other, these workers were heavily represented in occupations ranging from the laundry business to cigar- and cigarette-making as well. Others made money in street commerce or entered the scrap business or liquor pro-

30. Adam D. Mendelsohn, *The Rag Race: How Jews Sewed Their Way to Success in America and the British Empire* (New York: New York University Press, 2015), 212.

duction. And those immigrants who succeeded in business sometimes pursued banking as a side enterprise. In New York City, for example, bankers sold ship tickets, offered installment plans to facilitate large purchases, attended to their patrons' savings, and extended business loans and credit. In turn, bankers—most famously among them Sender Jarmulowsky, dubbed "The East Side J. P. Morgan"—invested in real estate, helping to spur development in areas of Jewish settlement, including the Lower East Side, Harlem, and the Bronx. Most Jewish immigrants also trusted their funds to immigrant bankers, so that banks on the Lower East Side became "reservoirs for local investment capital."[31]

The growing presence and burgeoning success of Jews in the decades following the Civil War fueled antisemitism, which "scientific" racism and anti-Jewish hatred born in Europe did much to aggravate. This trend was famously illustrated in 1877, when the Grand Union Hotel in Saratoga Springs, New York, denied banker Joseph Seligman accommodations, its manager proclaiming that "no Israelites shall be permitted in [the] future to stop at this hotel."[32] Within just a few years, social discrimination against Jews spread widely. Jews faced difficulty, for instance, in obtaining credit and loans. They were denied employment in some trades, industries, and professions, and residence in certain neighborhoods. Many elite private schools denied admission to Jewish children, and in the twentieth century colleges and universities established restrictive quotas. Clubs and resorts widely rejected Jews, as did fraternities and sororities. Increasingly, the institutions of elite society closed their doors to Jews, who were depicted as socially backward even as many of them swelled the ranks of the newly wealthy.[33] In response, Jews formed their own separate institutions in cities across the country. Though seemingly "at home in America," they lived in something of an "anxious subculture."[34]

Eric Goldstein has pointed to the economic roots of Gilded Age antisemitism. "Because of social and historical factors that identified them in the popular mind with trade, commerce, and urban life," he explains, "[Jews] served more than any other group as a receptacle for the fears and anxieties that white, middle class Americans harbored regarding the rise of industrial capitalism."[35] By 1915,

31. Deborah Dash Moore et al., *Jewish New York: The Remarkable Story of a City and a People* (New York: New York University Press, 2017), 91–92.

32. Quoted in David S. Koffman et al., "Roundtable on Anti-Semitism in the Gilded Age and Progressive Era," *Journal of the Gilded Age and Progressive Era* 19, no. 3 (2020): 480.

33. *Ibid.*, 477; John Higham, "Social Discrimination Against Jews in America, 1830–1930," *Publications of the American Jewish Historical Society* 47, no. 1 (1957): 7–13.

34. Sarna, *American Judaism*, 222.

35. Eric Goldstein in Koffman et al., "Roundtable," 477.

Jews constituted just 3 percent of the U.S. population but made up a quarter of the population of New York City. Still, antisemitism never became as potent in America during these decades as it did in Europe. For all the discrimination and violations of their civil rights that Jews faced, they also won praise as a group that sustained the bonds of family and community despite the upheavals of modern life.[36] Hard work, traditions of mutual aid, respect for education, centuries of diaspora experience, structural economic forces tied to capitalism, and the fact that most Jews had white skins in a society where Blacks were the principal out-group—all enabled Jews by the middle of the twentieth century to become one of America's most successful minority groups.

36. *Ibid.*, 496.

THE LEGACIES OF THE CIVIL WAR FOR AMERICAN JEWS

ADAM D. MENDELSOHN

IN 1895, Simon Wolf (Fig. 6), who represented the B'nai B'rith fraternal order in Washington, D.C., published a book whose title revealed its purpose. *The American Jew as Patriot, Soldier and Citizen* was an omnibus of articles, running to over 550 pages, that extolled the heroism of Jews and their fidelity to the United States.[1] At its heart was a list of more than eight thousand Jews who had fought in Union blue and Confederate gray in the Civil War, with names, ranks, and regiments, as well as pen portraits of some of the more distinguished among them. The book reflected an ascendant interpretation of the war that emphasized reunion and reconciliation.[2] By 1895, there was no sense of irony in presenting as evidence of Jewish patriotism the names of those who had fought to secede from the Union as well as those who had sought to preserve it. According to Wolf, the brave men he listed were distinctly Jewish, their "keen and responsive sense of duty" rooted in "Torah and Talmud." Yet, whenever possible, he drew proof of their gallantry from officers "entirely non-Jewish in their origin."[3] Wolf provided his readers with battalions of stiff-backed Jewish heroes intended to replace the ghetto-bent eastern European Jewish immigrant—then flocking to America's shores—in the popular imagination. Magnificent in scale and ambition, *The American Jew as Patriot, Soldier and Citizen* has ever since shaped how American Jews recall the Civil War.

Wolf painted on a largely blank canvas. Despite the epochal significance of the Civil War, the conflict was seldom spoken of in Jewish public life between 1865 and the early 1890s in much of the United States. The exception was in the states of the former Confederacy, where Jews embraced the conspicuous modes of remembering favored by their white neighbors. By contrast, in the North—the region that was home to most of America's Jews—the war went almost wholly unmarked by monuments and other forms of public memorialization initiated by

1. Simon Wolf, *The American Jew as Patriot, Soldier and Citizen*, ed. Louis Edward Levy (Philadelphia: Levytype, 1895).
2. On this theme, see David W. Blight, *Race and Reunion: The Civil War in American Memory* (Cambridge, Mass.: Harvard University Press, 2001).
3. Wolf, *American Jew as Patriot, Soldier and Citizen*, 12.

Fig. 6. Simon Wolf. Bain News Service, ca. 1915–1920. (Library of Congress).

Jews, and all but unmentioned in the Jewish press. Undoubtedly, Jewish veterans continued to grapple with the repercussions and traumas of the war as individuals, and perhaps even collectively; but open discussion of the war was muted in Jewish public life, and few veterans published accounts of their experiences between 1861 and 1865. Even if some old soldiers may have been eager to talk about the war, key Jewish communal institutions were not eager to hear them.

Other groups—African Americans, Irish Americans, and German Americans—wielded wartime sacrifice as a potent weapon in their battle for equal treatment after Appomattox. Not so Jews. Only in the 1890s and the decades afterward did this reticence give way. In large part inspired by Simon Wolf, Jews celebrated the contributions of their brethren to the war as never before: in memorial services, in monuments, in a Jewish veteran's organization, and in print. Jews were not the only ones to rediscover the war during this period.[4] But the extent of their suppressing of the war, and the suddenness of their remembering set them apart.

This essay will not focus on why the Civil War was so little spoken of in Jewish public life after 1865. Nor will I recount the experiences of Jewish veterans who returned home after Appomattox. Instead, I will look elsewhere for evidence of how the conflict shaped the lives of Jews in the Gilded Age. My focus will be on how the Civil War shaped popular attitudes toward Jews during this period, as well as on how it encouraged the coalescence of particular forms of Jewish identity in the United States.[5] Past scholarship on both of these subjects bears the imprint of Simon Wolf's 1895 opus. As we will see, the mode of remembering that he promoted obscured more than it has revealed about the legacies of

4. On the new interest in preserving battlefields and adding monuments and markers, see Timothy B. Smith, *The Golden Age of Battlefield Preservation: The Decade of the 1890s and the Establishment of America's First Five Military Parks* (Knoxville: University of Tennessee Press, 2008). On memoirs and reminiscences, see Earl J. Hess, *The Union Soldier in Battle: Enduring the Ordeal of Combat* (Lawrence: University Press of Kansas, 1997), 160; on visits to the battlefields, see 185–90. On the growth of veterans' organizations in the 1880s and their increasing assertiveness in the 1890s, see Stuart McConnell, *Glorious Contentment: The Grand Army of the Republic, 1865–1900* (Chapel Hill: University of North Carolina Press, 1992). On memory in the 1890s, see Nina Silber, *The Romance of Reunion: Northerners and the South, 1865–1900* (Chapel Hill: University of North Carolina Press, 1993); Blight, *Race and Reunion*, chap. 6. On the appeal of Civil War gallantry in "an age increasingly characterized by cynical politics, amoral machines, and the impersonal leviathan of industrialization," see Blight, *Race and Reunion*, 89, 95, 129, 208–11.

5. I have explored these other legacies of the war elsewhere. See Adam Mendelsohn, *Jewish Soldiers in the Civil War: The Union Army* (New York: New York University Press, 2022), and "Beyond the Battlefield: Reevaluating the Legacy of the Civil War for American Jews," *American Jewish Archives Journal* 64, no. 1–2 (2012): 82–111.

the war for American Jews. Wolf's way of interpreting the conflict remained durable and dominant well into the twentieth century and still influences our thinking about Jews and the Civil War.

Simon Wolf and Jewish Memory of the Civil War

The impact of the war on popular attitudes toward Jews prompted Simon Wolf to compile *The American Jew as Patriot, Soldier and Citizen.* His introduction begins by describing how "[i]n December, 1891, there was printed in the *North American Review* a letter in reply to certain statements of a contributor to a previous number of the same magazine regarding the services of American Jewish citizens as soldiers in the Civil War." The contributor was Goldwin Smith—past holder of the Regius Chair of Modern History at Oxford, and more recently a professor at Cornell and a celebrated journalist—who had a history of provocation, particularly when it came to Jews. His claims are easily summarized: Jews brought persecution upon themselves because of a persistent pattern of disloyalty toward and disinterest in the commonweal.

Though Goldwin Smith glanced only in passing at the Civil War in his article, it was this subject in particular that elicited impassioned responses in subsequent issues of the *Review.* Simon Wolf was enraged by a letter from J. M. Rogers, a veteran who claimed that he could not "recall meeting one Jew in uniform or hearing of any Jewish soldier":

> After the war, for twenty-five years I was constantly engaged in travelling, always among old soldiers, but never found any who remembered serving with Jews.... I learned of no place where they stood "shoulder to shoulder," except in General Sherman's department, and he promptly ordered them out of it for speculating in cotton and conveying information to the Confederates. If so many Jews fought so bravely for their adopted country, surely their champion ought to be able to give the names of the regiments they condescended to accept service in.[6]

Under "ordinary conditions," Wolf averred, such claims could have "been left unnoticed." But the situation was far from ordinary. In Germany and France, "anti-Semitism was at floodtide" as politicians and agitators seized upon the Jew as a threat to the nation (and upon Jew-hatred as a means of mobilizing disaffected voters). In the United States, "public attention was being centered on the Jewish refugees from Russia" who were fleeing "Muscovite tyranny."[7] In

6. J. M. Rogers, "Jewish Soldiers in the Union Army," *North American Review* 153, no. 421 (1891): 761–62.

7. Wolf, *American Jew as Patriot, Soldier and Citizen,* 1–2.

such circumstances, the august *North American Review* was difficult to ignore, particularly since Goldwin Smith's article was preceded by an essay in January 1891 penned by Congressman Henry Cabot Lodge calling for "The Restriction of Immigration."[8]

The American Jew as Patriot, Soldier and Citizen was a rebuttal to those who claimed that Jews could be none of these things: patriots, soldiers, and citizens. Wolf sought to prove that Jews, far from being a parasitical people activated only by self-interest, had a storied history of "personal sacrifice and heroism" on behalf of the collective. In insisting that Jews had more than done their part in the Civil War, Wolf was defending Jews against the charge that their values were incompatible with Americanism. Wolf's listing of the sacrifices and contributions of Jews during the Civil War was thus more than merely an effort to restore Jewish honor besmirched by the likes of Goldwin Smith; it also served as the core of his case for why present and future Jewish immigrants made excellent (and deserving) Americans. When he claimed that the "proportion of Jewish soldiers is ... [not] only large, but is perhaps larger than that of any other faith in the United States," he had his eyes fixed as firmly on the future as on the past.[9]

8. Goldwin Smith, "New Light on the Jewish Question," *North American Review* 153, no. 417 (1891): 129–43; Isaac Bendavid, "Goldwin Smith and the Jews," *North American Review* 153, no. 418 (1891): 257–71. This exchange is discussed at length in Sylvan Morris Dubow, "Identifying the Jewish Servicemen in the Civil War: A Re-appraisal of Simon Wolf's *The American Jew as Patriot, Soldier and Citizen*," *American Jewish Historical Quarterly* 59 (March 1970): 357–69. See also Esther Panitz, *Simon Wolf: Private Conscience and Public Image* (Cranbury, N.J.: Associated University Presses, 1987), 178–79; Nils Roemer, "Outside and Inside the Nations: Changing Borders in the Study of the Jewish Past in the Nineteenth Century," in *Modern Judaism and Historical Consciousness: Identities, Encounters, Perspectives*, ed. Andreas Gotzmann and Christian Wiese (Boston: Brill, 2007), 44–45; Jeffrey S. Gurock, "Cautious Defenders," *American Jewish History* 81, no. 2 (1993/94): 168–69. On Goldwin Smith, see Gerald Tulchinsky, "Goldwin Smith: Victorian Canadian Antisemite," in *The Canadian Jewish Studies Reader*, ed. Richard Menkis and Norman Ravvin (Markham, Ontario: Red Deer Press, 2004); Colin Holmes, "Goldwin Smith (1823–1910): A 'Liberal' Antisemite," *Patterns of Prejudice* 6, no. 5 (1972): 25–30. On the *North American Review*, see Pamela Nadell, "Defender of Her Sex and Her People: Nina Morais Cohen," in this volume.

9. Wolf, *American Jew as Patriot, Soldier and Citizen*, 6. Wolf's undertaking echoed that of contemporaneous African American historians who, according to historian Andre M. Fleche, "sought to solidify Black claims to citizenship and equal rights by celebrating the role African-American soldiers played in the Union and ending slavery," as well as other ethnic historians with similar motives. Wolf also had analogues in Europe. Ludwig Phillipson initiated a similar enterprise during the Franco–Prussian War, and later surveys performed a similar function during and after World War I. See Andre M. Fleche, "African-American Soldiering," in *A Companion to the Civil War*, ed. Aaron Sheehan-Dean (Malden, Mass.: Wiley Blackwell, 2014), 298–99; Carole

And yet what is absent from this book is as revealing as what is present. While lavishing attention on Jewish soldiers, Wolf was more circumspect when it came to the experience of Jews on the home front. In particular, he chose not to write about the best-known episodes of discrimination against Jews during the Civil War. Ulysses S. Grant is mentioned several times, but his notorious order expelling Jews from the entire military department under his command is discussed only in passing: "Having enjoyed the friendship of President Grant and of General Sherman ... I can state that I had repeated conversations with them regarding 'Order No. 11,' which was issued over the signature of General Grant, but of which he, at the time, had absolutely no knowledge" (Fig. 7).[10] Entirely unmentioned is the chaplaincy controversy that agitated Jews in 1861 and received national attention: a prospective regimental chaplain was disqualified because, as a Jew, he was debarred by a congressional act that stipulated that only "regularly ordained ministers of some Christian denomination" could be commissioned.

In this partial process of remembering, the war was transformed from a source of hurt into the subject of pride. For Wolf and many of those who followed, the war became unambiguously good for the Jews. The names and deeds of Jewish soldiers assembled by Wolf were paraded so as to inspire a collective espirit de corps among American Jews and to refute anyone who questioned whether Jews could be good Americans. When the chaplaincy controversy and Grant's order were (rarely) recalled, they were remembered as moments when America, shepherded by a sagacious Abraham Lincoln, ultimately lived up to its ideals. Lost were less uplifting interpretations of these same episodes, as well as reflections on the war's more complicated consequences.

This mode of remembering the war, focused on the exploits of individual soldiers, offered little encouragement to university-trained scholars who, in the second half of the twentieth century, began to regard the history of Jews in America as a field worthy of serious attention. The celebratory paeans to patriotism that drew upon Wolf's example and dominated popular Jewish writing about the war were inimical to their scholarly goal of establishing American Jewish history as a credible endeavor. Tales of bravery yielded little beyond

---

Emberton, "'Only Murder Makes Men': Reconsidering the Black Military Experience," *Journal of the Civil War Era* 2, no. 3 (2012): 370; David T. Gleeson, "Ethnicity," in *A Companion to the Civil War*, ed. Sheehan-Dean, 765; Derek J. Penslar, *Jews and the Military: A History* (Princeton: Princeton University Press, 2013), 71, 132, 178.

10. Wolf, *American Jew as Patriot, Soldier and Citizen*, 6.

Fig. 7. Former president Ulysses S. Grant sheds crocodile tears over the "persecuted Jews in Russia," which spill over the "Jewish vote 1884." Cartoon by Bernhard Gillam, *Puck*, Feb. 15, 1882, 376. (Library of Congress).

confirmation that Jews fought too, and certainly not enough evidence to suggest that the war had a durable impact on the development of American Jewry. The war, moreover, did not fit neatly into their chronological framework for understanding American Jewish history. For those schooled to think in terms of waves of immigration—a "German period" and an "eastern European period"—the war seemed sandwiched between the two and of marginal consequence to either.

Tellingly, Bertram Korn, who published *American Jewry and the Civil War* in 1951, was the first professionally trained historian to produce a monograph on the impact of the Civil War on American Jewish life, but also the last scholar to do so for decades. His landmark book focused almost entirely on the home front, paying particular attention to the chaplaincy controversy and to Grant's order, as well as to the relationship of Jews to the heated political questions of the day. Though his work did little to deter the army of chroniclers who continued to trumpet the exploits of Jewish soldiers, Korn demonstrated convincingly that there was a creditable Jewish story to be told about the Civil War. Yet Korn's book left another, less discernible legacy. Despite arguing that the war had "far-reaching effects" on American Jewry beyond 1865, the closing chapter of *American Jewry and the Civil War* encouraged a more limited view of the impact of the war that was picked up by later historians.

Korn's imprint was particularly pronounced on the interpretation of wartime antisemitism. On the one hand, Korn recognized that wartime prejudice was "far greater in articulation, repetition, frequency, and in action too than had ever before been directed against Jews in America." On the other, he downplayed its long-term significance: "these attacks were not typical of America," and "America as a whole, had, perhaps, learned something from the excesses of the Civil War."[11] The war was presented as a moment when American Jewry "learned much about the problems that it would have to solve" and the solutions it should seek, such as a "heightened consciousness of the need for national organizations and institutions" and readiness to resort to "using the right of petition."[12] This framing encouraged many historians who followed to interpret wartime antisemitism as a contained and aberrant phenomenon. Citing Korn, David Gerber, for example, argued that "the brief Civil War experience of Jew-baiting by public officials failed to survive the war" and therefore was of little relevance to

11. Bertram Wallace Korn, *American Jewry and the Civil War* (Philadelphia: Jewish Publication Society of America, 1951), xx.

12. *Ibid.*, 260–61.

understanding later manifestations of antisemitism.[13] Similarly, John Higham, also citing Korn, discounted the import of the Civil War. He instead argued that the rise of modern antisemitism in America should be dated to the 1870s and seen as a consequence of the social and economic competition of that period.[14]

These interpretations are not the only way that Korn shaped later thinking. Korn contended that during wartime "it was almost impossible for the alien to remain aloof.... The national defeats and triumphs were part of his daily life; the high excitements of victory and the depressions of tragedy drove deeply into his nature."[15] Because of the momentum created by the war, Jews "had practically completed the process of acculturation" by the late 1870s. Korn found evidence for this in the "amazing antipathy" between "Americanized Reform Jews" and the eastern European arrivals, as well in as the proliferation of "national organizations and institutions" after the war.[16] Korn was not alone in this interpretation; other historians similarly suggested that the war accelerated the Americanization of Irish and German Americans.[17]

These twin interpretations relating to Americanization and antisemitism emphasized continuity between the prewar and postwar periods: the war accelerated the integration of Jews into American society, and wartime prejudice caused little durable damage. Unintentionally, this framing also made it easier for other scholars to ignore the war. Korn, after all, claimed only a limited and narrow legacy for the Civil War and suggested that it had done little to alter the fundamental dynamics of American Jewish life. Given the modesty of these claims and the proximity of the war to the mass arrival of eastern European immigrants, it was easy to regard it as a minor distraction with limited significance for an American Jewish story that was soon to switch its register from German to Yiddish.

It took more than sixty years—until the sesquicentennial of the Civil War—for scholars to revisit the war in a systematic and sustained way. And yet Korn's

13. David A. Gerber, "Anti-Semitism and Jewish Gentile Relations in American Historiography and the American Past," in *Anti-Semitism in American History*, ed. David A. Gerber (Urbana: University of Illinois Press, 1986), 29.

14. John Higham, *Send These to Me: Immigrants in Urban America* (Baltimore: Johns Hopkins University Press, 1984), 123; John Higham, *Strangers in the Land: Patterns of American Nativism* (New Brunswick: Rutgers University Press, 1955), 13–14.

15. Korn, *American Jewry and the Civil War*, 259.

16. *Ibid.*, 161.

17. For a discussion of the origins of the argument that the war spurred Americanization, see Christian B. Keller, "Flying Dutchmen and Drunken Irishmen: The Myths and Realities of Ethnic Civil War Soldiers," *Journal of Military History* 73, no. 1 (2009): 140; Gleeson, "Ethnicity," 769.

interpretative frame largely remains in place. Although recently historians have added much light and shade to our appreciation of how Jews experienced the conflict—particularly the interactions between Jews and Lincoln and the context and consequences of General Orders No. 11—the Civil War is still rarely thought of as a transformative moment in American Jewish history.[18] The war is discussed only briefly in two of the three recent synthetic histories of American Jews and barely features in new monographs on American Jewry in the nineteenth century.[19] The exception is in new work on the economic history of Jews in the United States that identifies the war as a turning point for Jewish involvement in the clothing and cotton trades.[20]

Contrary to Korn's claims, we will see that wartime antisemitism played a foundational role in shaping and directing hostility toward Jews in the 1870s and after. Likewise, we will see that the war was pivotal in the formation of American Jewish identity, but in a manner and direction different from that traced by Korn. In order to recognize the continuities between wartime antisemitism and what followed, I will first examine the nature of anti-Jewish prejudice before, during, and after the war. As we will see, ideas expressed about Jews between 1861 and 1865 had antecedents, but were molded into new configurations amid

18. For revisionist work that focuses on the period of the war, see Gary Phillip Zola, *We Called Him Rabbi Abraham: Lincoln and American Jewry, a Documentary History* (Carbondale: Southern Illinois University Press, 2014), and Jonathan D. Sarna and Benjamin Shapell, *Lincoln and the Jews: A History* (New York: St. Martin's Press, 2015). Sarna's *When General Grant Expelled the Jews* (New York: Nextbook/Schocken, 2012) devotes as much attention to the long postwar afterlife of General Orders No. 11—and Grant's efforts to make amends for his wartime actions—as to the infamous order itself.

19. Jonathan D. Sarna gives much more attention to the war in *American Judaism: A History* (New Haven: Yale University Press, 2004) than do Eli Lederhendler in *American Jewry: A New History* (New York: Cambridge University Press, 2017) and Hasia R. Diner in *The Jews of the United States, 1654–2000* (Berkeley: University of California Press, 2004). Neither Shari Rabin's book on Jewish mobility nor Hasia Diner's on peddling treats the war as more than a sidebar. See Shari Rabin, *Jews on the Frontier: Religion and Mobility in Nineteenth-Century America* (New York: New York University Press, 2017), 26–32, and Hasia R. Diner, *Roads Taken: The Great Jewish Migrations to the New World and the Peddlers Who Forged the Way* (New Haven: Yale University Press, 2015). The exception is Zev Eleff, who argues that the war had a lasting impact on rabbinic leadership in America; see *Who Rules the Synagogue? Religious Authority and the Formation of American Judaism* (New York: Oxford University Press, 2016), 131, 142.

20. I argue that the war had a decisive impact on the economic standing of the Jewish community in *The Rag Race: How Jews Sewed their Way to Success in America and the British Empire* (New York: New York University Press, 2015). Michael R. Cohen proposes that the Civil War provided the opening that Jews needed to advance within the cotton trade; see *Cotton Capitalists: American Jewish Entrepreneurship in the Reconstruction Era* (New York: New York University Press, 2017).

the overheated anxieties of wartime. Following this survey, I will explore how wartime and postwar antisemitism prompted changes within the American Jewish community.

Wartime Antisemitism and Its Afterlife

When it came to Jews, antebellum Americans drew on a cultural larder well stocked with stereotypes. Among the hostile perceptions of Jews, two interrelated themes dominated. The first imagined the contemporary Jew as the inheritor of the sins of those who betrayed, tormented, and condemned Jesus—every bit as blind, stiff-necked, and stubborn as their forebears who rejected his teaching. The second conceived of the Jew as dishonest and greedy, crafty and crooked in pursuit of lucre, the slippery Judas of the modern-day marketplace. These stereotypes, in a multitude of variations, were reinforced in sermons, folklore, chapbooks, popular literature, and on stage and in the press.[21] "Jew" was used as a slur, and economically exploitative behavior was "portrayed as metaphorically Jewish."[22] But not all the traits associated with Jews were regarded as irredeemable. The imagined Jewish facility with money was admired as well as despised, as was Jewish solidarity and the very survival of Judaism itself.[23] Inconsistency and dissonance abounded. And not all Jews were thought of solely as representatives of their race. As Jonathan D. Sarna has described, Americans differentiated between the "mythical Jew" who embodied an imagined archetype and the "Jew next door," the neighbor or acquaintance whose everyday presence belied the cartoonish stereotype.[24]

War gave new life and purpose to these stereotypes, transfiguring the metaphorically Jewish exploiter into the despised wartime speculator, contractor, and smuggler.[25] Ulysses S. Grant's infamous General Orders No. 11, issued in

21. See Leonard Dinnerstein, *Antisemitism in America* (New York: Oxford University Press, 1994), 17–18; Frederic Cople Jaher, *A Scapegoat in the New Wilderness: The Origins and Rise of Anti-Semitism in America* (Cambridge, Mass.: Harvard University Press, 1996), 170–241. For the varied representations of Jews on stage, see Heather S. Nathans, *Hideous Characters and Beautiful Pagans: Performing Jewish Identity on the Antebellum American Stage* (Ann Arbor: University of Michigan Press, 2017).

22. Quote from Jonathan Judaken, "Jewish Capitalists, Jewish Bolsheviks: Conspiracy Thinking and Modern Judeophobia," *Modern Intellectual History* (April 2020): 4.

23. For the dualistic nature of stereotypes toward Jews, see Higham, *Send These to Me*, 99–101.

24. Jonathan D. Sarna, "The 'Mythical Jew' and the 'Jew Next Door' in Nineteenth-Century America," in *Anti-Semitism in American History*, ed. Gerber, 57–78.

25. On the protean nature of antisemitism, see Francesca Trivellato, *The Promise and Peril of Credit: What a Forgotten Legend about Jews and Finance Tells Us about the Making of European*

Mississippi on December 17, 1862, was an example of word made flesh. As Jonathan D. Sarna has evocatively described, Grant, who had grown frustrated by cotton speculators who proliferated as his army moved into plantation territory along the Mississippi and whose trade he suspected abetted the enemy, pinned his frustrations on "Jews as a class" and ordered all expelled from the Department of the Tennessee within twenty-four hours. To Grant's mind, "Jew" was not only synonymous with speculator and smuggler—shorthand for those who violated "every regulation of trade established by the Treasury Department"—but also described the worst among the speculators and smugglers. In several communications issued prior to General Orders No. 11, Grant called upon his lieutenants to pay particular heed to Jews. Though the order was stifled after President Lincoln was hastily petitioned, the episode received significant attention in the press and reinforced the association in the public mind of Jews with dubious dealings. General Grant, moreover, was far from the last senior military officer to give voice to similar ideas about Jews during the war.[26]

In early 1864, General Benjamin Butler provided a more elaborate exposition of wartime thinking about Jews. As commander of the grandiosely titled Department of Virginia and North Carolina (in reality, a coastal foothold in each state) and the recently designated "special agent" for orchestrating prisoner swaps, Butler issued a short telegraphic dispatch describing the successful return of a raiding party that had ventured up the James River. Listed among the spoils—"22 of the enemy," "99 negroes," "240 boxes of tobacco"—were "five Jews preparing to run the blockade," who were discovered, along with a cache of valuables, concealed in the hold of a captured schooner.[27] Myer Isaacs, son of a prominent New York rabbi, sometime co-editor of the *Jewish Messenger* (his father's newspaper), and secretary of the Board of Delegates of American Israelites, rebuked Butler for identifying the presumptive blockade runners as

---

Commercial Society (Princeton: Princeton University Press, 2019). For an overview of antisemitism on the home front, see Korn, *American Jewry and the Civil War*, 188–209, and Jaher, *Scapegoat in the New Wilderness*, 190–98.

26. For hostile sentiment expressed by other military officials, see Korn, *American Jewry and the Civil War*, 148–49, 122, 153–54, and Jaher, *Scapegoat in the New Wilderness*, 198–200. On Grant's order, see Sarna, *When General Grant Expelled the Jews*, 7, 31–32, 44–45; for the campaign to rescind the order, see 12–23. On Grant's nativism, see Tyler Anbinder, "Ulysses S. Grant, Nativist," *Civil War History* 43, no. 2 (1997): 119–41; see 124n11 for the suggestion that Grant viewed Jewish traders as a persistent "nuisance" before the expulsion order.

27. Butler's dispatch was printed in full in the *Daily Milwaukee News*, January 27, 1864, 1. On the blockade runners, see Sarna, *When General Grant Expelled the Jews*, 43n; Julius Louis Correspondence (SC-7475), Jacob Rader Marcus Center of the American Jewish Archives, Cincinnati.

Jews. His private exchange of letters with Butler became a public contretemps when the correspondence was widely reprinted in both the Union and the Confederacy in March and April 1864.[28] Newspapers from Muscatine, Iowa, to New Orleans and New York picked up the story.

The combative and controversial general, more effective when crossing pens than when crossing swords, refused to apologize for his choice of words. "It was meant, when used," he argued,

> to designate nationality, and not religion, as one would say, five Irishmen, five Germans, or five Italians. I have always considered the Jews a nationality, although possessing no country. The closeness with which they cling together, the aid which they afford each other, on all proper, and sometimes improper occasions; the fact that nearly all of them pursue substantially the same employment, so far as I have known them—that of traders, merchants, and bankers—the very general obedience to the prohibition against marriage with Gentiles, their faith, which looks forward to a time when they are to be gathered together in the former land of their nation—all serve to show a closer tie of kindred and nation among the Hebrews, and a greater homogeneity than belongs to any other nation, although its people live in closer proximity.[29]

Though Butler used the language of nationality rather than race, he was articulating what he regarded as a commonplace: groups exhibit defining characteristics.[30] Careful to disclaim any ill-feeling toward Judaism, he implied that deceit and disloyalty were among the characteristics that defined Jews. Patriotism was a heritable national trait, and so was its obverse. Drawing on an older motif, he imagined Jews as a people adrift. Marshaling the example of the blockade runners (and Judas), he reminded Isaacs that two Jews (and later a third) served in the Confederate cabinet.[31] Butler also understood ethnicity—and not nativity

28. Much of the original exchange was reprinted in *Publications of the American Jewish Historical Society* 29 (1925): 117–28, but it continued for several months longer. For additional letters, see *Board of Delegates of American Israelites Records* (I-2), series 2, box 2, folder 2, Center for Jewish History, American Jewish Historical Society, New York.

29. "General Butler and the Jews," *New York Times*, Feb. 28, 1864, 3.

30. For a fuller description of his thinking about Jews and blood, see Benjamin F. Butler, *Autobiographical and Personal Reminiscences of Major-General Benjamin F. Butler* (Boston: A. M. Thayer, 1892), 33–34. See also Korn, *American Jewry and the Civil War*, 194–97; Jaher, *Scapegoat in the New Wilderness*, 192, 198.

31. Others made similar assertions about prominent Confederates; in reality, only Judah P. Benjamin served in Jefferson Davis's cabinet. See, for example, the claim that Thomas C. Reynolds, the South Carolina–born Confederate lieutenant governor of Missouri and "chief conspirator" for secession in that state was really Thomas C. Reinhold, a German-born Jew. James Peckham, *Gen. Nathaniel Lyon, and Missouri in 1861* (New York: American News Company,

or citizenship—as the defining feature of Americanness. According to this logic, Jews would forever be outsiders.

That this argument was promoted by Benjamin Butler made it that much more noteworthy. When Grant issued his infamous order, he was the coming man, the hero of Forts Henry and Donelson now in pursuit of Vicksburg, the Fortress of the West. By contrast, Butler's words were freighted because of his past. His actions earlier in the war at Fort Monroe—granting haven to runaway slaves and designating them as the legally confiscated "contraband" of war—forever associated him with emancipation. When the Emancipation Proclamation was issued, Jews and other white ethnics fretted that the granting of freedom to African Americans would come at their economic and political expense. Here, seemingly, was confirmation.

Although Grant's and Butler's words and actions created an acute sense of crisis for Jews in the Union, no less corrosive was a steady drip of acrimony that began in the early months of the war and betrayed broader wartime anxieties. Jews felt the sting of prejudice as the "shoddy" scandals captured the public imagination. Military contractors were publicly accused of fleecing the army by supplying substandard uniforms and gear, even as soldiers shivered in the field for want of decent clothing and had large sums docked from their pay for the garments they were required to wear. Several Northern newspapers hostile to the Republican Party led the charge. Army suppliers were lambasted in cartoons and satirical verse as "shoddy contractors" and "shoddy vampires." Contractors whose profits and ostentation were deemed dishonest and immoral were derided as a crass and ill-mannered nouveau riche, a "shoddy aristocracy." In seeking to explain the profiteering and corruption that attended the rush to war, the press summoned the specter of the venal and disloyal Jew.

Although Jews were not exclusively blamed for "shoddy" manufacturing, the term not infrequently took on antisemitic coloration. Wartime scandal accentuated existing fears of the corrupting influence of the market on the nation's morals, and these anxieties were easily projected onto Jews. Here, the hostility drew on older associations of Jews with commerce and the clothing trade, and particularly on the motif of the disreputable Chatham Street "old clo' dealer." Cartoonists delighted in identifying Jews as the archetypal cunning contractors, who not only refused to enlist but also actively undermined the war effort

1866), 27; Frank Moore, ed., *Rebellion Record: A Diary of American Events*, vol. 3 (New York: G. P. Putnam, 1862), 18.

in order to turn a quick profit. In the first year of the conflict several Northern newspapers used the terms "Jew" and "contractor" interchangeably.[32]

Jews were also imagined as the speculators who profited at the expense of the common good and as the smugglers who traded with the enemy.[33] Because they were believed to gorge on the business of war, Jews were spared the canard hurled at Germans and Irish that they were merely wage soldiers, mercenaries whose dedication to the Union cause extended no further than the promise of pay. The assumption that Jews preferred profit to patriotism and therefore evaded enlistment would haunt them after the war. The contractor, smuggler, speculator, and shirker, however, were more than mere figures of scorn. As Brian Luskey has argued, the undermining of the "value of bank paper, products, and people" during the war also "destabilized the power dynamics" in the wider society.[34] Jews and other "shoddy aristocrats" were seen as the creators and beneficiaries of the new economic and social order produced by the war, and as the personification of the injustices of this world made topsy-turvy.[35] This "shoddy aristocracy"—whose morals and manners marked them as undesirable, whose profits were ill gained, and whose power derived from money alone—was imagined to lord it over a new social heap summoned into being by

32. Surveying cartoons that appeared in the illustrated press, Gary L. Bunker and John Appel argue that antisemitic depictions peaked in 1861 and 1864. See Bunker and Appel, "'Shoddy' Anti-Semitism and the Civil War: The Visual Image," *American Jewish History* 82 (1994): 45. On Jews and contracting scandals, see Mendelsohn, *Rag Race*, 164–72.

33. In addition to these ideas, August Belmont, the prominent Democratic grandee, was described by hostile observers as "this Israelite Belmont" in the same breath as Clement Vallandingham, the Copperhead congressman from Ohio who was banished from the Union. See, for example, Moore, ed., *Rebellion Record*, 3:114, and Korn, *American Jewry and the Civil War*, 190. For accusations of a conspiracy of Jews involved in smuggling across enemy lines, see, for example, *Nashville Daily Union*, October 8, 1864, 1. For Jews as spies, see John Fitch, *Annals of the Army of the Cumberland* (Philadelphia: J. B. Lippincott, 1864), 457–66. For representations of the Jew as reluctant recruit, see Bunker and Appel, "'Shoddy' Anti-Semitism and the Civil War," 48, 62. On the idea of "corruption" in the Union, see Michael Thomas Smith, *The Enemy Within: Fears of Corruption in the Civil War North* (Charlottesville: University of Virginia Press, 2011).

34. Brian P. Luskey, "Economic and Social Values in the Civil War," in *The Cambridge History of the American Civil War*, ed. Aaron Sheehan-Dean, vol. 3 (New York: Cambridge University Press, 2019), 92, 97.

35. See Mendelsohn, *Rag Race*, 169–72; Bunker and Appel, "'Shoddy' Antisemitism and the Civil War," 43–71. Isaac Mayer Wise and others did not dispute that the social order had been inverted. But in a twist, Wise argued that the real fault lay with the "lower stratum" that brought along all of its "vices," including antisemitism, when it rose to the top of society. See Naomi W. Cohen, "Antisemitism in the Gilded Age: The Jewish View," *Jewish Social Studies* 41 (Summer/Autumn 1979): 189, 200.

the chaos and disruption of war. Even as the invective of the war years receded after 1865, these ideas remained primed for action. They were returned to service in the Gilded Age.[36]

The toxic residue of wartime antisemitism leached into the landscape. Characteristic was the notion, reinforced during wartime, of "Jews as a class" whose interests, behaviors, and loyalties were distinct. In 1867, for example, five insurance companies in New York and Connecticut (including Aetna Insurance of Hartford) imposed a blanket ban on insuring Jews, claiming "recent numerous heavy losses ... very many of which were on the properties of Jews."[37] A year later, the nomination of Ulysses Grant as the Republican candidate for president thrust General Orders No. 11 into the tumult of a bitter political campaign. Though Grant disowned the order, Jews were again the subject of national attention and discussion.[38]

It was no coincidence that the episode traditionally identified as inaugurating a new wave of antisemitism—the exclusion of Joseph Seligman from the Grand Union Hotel in Saratoga Springs, New York (Figs. 8–11), on May 31, 1877—had at its center a man who had made a fortune as a contractor and banker during the Civil War. His family firm had sold bonds in Europe on behalf of the U.S. government during those years, and now he was a member of the syndicate (alongside August Belmont) that continued to do the same. Seligman was known as to be a friend of President Grant and was viewed as an exemplar of the new capitalism that was remaking America.[39]

By his account, Seligman arrived at the hotel with his wife and two children

36. For a telling example of the hold that these ideas maintained, see the poem "No More Pensions" published in the *Ellsworth Reporter* (Kansas), January 19, 1882, 1. That poem, protesting the mistreatment of veterans, reminded readers of a litany of indignities they had endured when in the army: "They were paid, but not with gold, | In the muster, march and line— | Paid with suffering, curse, and blow, | Borne with fortitude divine. | Paid with loathsome, tainted food; | Paid with shoddy coat and shoe; | In the tent, the camp, the field, | Robbed by sutler, fleeced by Jew." The postscript was telling. "Jew in this connection," the poet noted, "has no reference to the Israelite, but to swindling camp-followers." The idea of the Jew, in other words, had taken on a symbolic life of its own.

37. Protests followed in Richmond, Charleston, Cincinnati, Chicago, Cleveland, and McGregor, Iowa. See *Brooklyn Daily Eagle*, March 14, 1867, 2; *National Republican*, April 2, 1867, 2; *Charleston Daily News*, April 10, 1867, 4; *Israelite*, May 3, 1867, 6, and May 10, 1867, 4; *North Iowa Times*, April 17, 1867, 2.

38. Sarna, *When General Grant Expelled the Jews*, 54–79.

39. For Seligman extolling his relationship with Grant, see *Buffalo Weekly Courier*, June 27, 1877, 3. For discussion of the affair, see Lee Livney, "Let Us Now Praise Self-Made Men: A Reexamination of the Hilton-Seligman Affair," *New York History* 75, no. 1 (1994): 66–98.

Fig. 8. Stereoview card of the Grand Union Hotel parlor, Saratoga Springs, N.Y. Baker & Record, photographers, 1870–1880. (Library of Congress).

late at night after a mechanical failure delayed their journey from New York City. They were met by a clerk who had been instructed to deny accommodation to all Jews, and to Seligman in particular. (The hotel's managers disputed this version, but not the existence of a policy to exclude Jews.) Outraged, Seligman penned an excoriating letter to the proprietor, Judge Henry Hilton, that was also intended for publication. Seligman and Hilton had tangled before. Hilton's reputation, moreover, was already tarnished by his association with the Tweed Ring and the questionable circumstances by which he had acquired the vast interests of "merchant prince" A. T. Steward—including ownership of the Grand Union Hotel—from Stewart's widow.[40] Seligman alluded to Hilton's dubious record in his letter.

Far from backing down, Hilton responded by besmirching Seligman's reputation, characterizing him as a man of "Shylockean meanness," untrustworthy in business, overextended in credit, and successful because of "political influence"

40. On Hilton's reputation, see Livney, "Let Us Now Praise Self-Made Men," 70–71; on the rancorous relationship between Hilton and Seligman, see 75.

Seligman
"JEW"
"Vhere, oh, vhere is my summer home?"
GRAND
A sure device to keep them out..

Fig. 9. Caricature of the antisemitic policies of the Grand Union Hotel in Saratoga Springs, N.Y. Lithograph by Joseph Keppler, *Puck*, June 27, 1877, pp. 8–9. (Library of Congress).

SELIGMAN.

Mr. Seligman does a big banking business and has aided many a great stock enterprise by floating its securities on the street. He made most of his money, however, during the war. He is now a benevolent looking old gentleman on the shady side of sixty. He wears dark bushy side whiskers. He has an abundance of dark hair slightly inclined to curl. His eyes are blue and his nose is aquiline. Mr. Seligman is a great friend of Gen. Grant, who at the close of the war stopped at his house for a long time. Mr. Seligman contributed largely to the Grant fund, of which he is one of the trustees. Mr. Seligman has lately been interested in the West Shore enterprise. He has a large family.

Fig. 10. Joseph Seligman. Clipping from the *St. Louis Post-Dispatch*, Feb. 9, 1884, p. 9. (New York Public Library).

Fig. 11. Cartoon with caption: "CLERK: 'I am very sorry, but my orders are—' TOURIST: 'Yesh, yesh, I know all about your orders; but how voz it dot you knowed I vozn't a Ghristian?'" Cartoon from *Harper's Weekly*, July 28, 1877, p. 592. (Library of Congress).

rather than business acumen. Joseph Seligman was the prime exemplar of what Hilton described as the "Seligman Jew":

> He is of low origin, and his instincts are of the gutter—his principles smell of decayed goods or of decayed principle. But he has extracted cash out of his gutter, his rags, his principles, and he shoves his person upon respectability. He is too obtuse or too mean to see his vulgarity, or go where it may not be on public exhibition. He is shoddy—false—squeezing—unmanly; but financially he is successful, and that is the only token he has to push himself upon the polite.[41]

Embedded within his litany of objections were elements familiar from wartime antisemitism: the Jew as speculator who trafficked in credit and debt; the Jew as obsequious ingratiator who attached himself to the powerful;

41. "Judge Hilton's Position," *New York Times*, June 20, 1877, 1.

the Jew as profiteer who advanced by improper means; the Jew as distasteful and vulgar nouveau riche who flaunted his (and her) obscene wealth and did not know his (or her) place; and the Jew as overlord whose money allowed him (or her) to displace others. In short, the "Seligman Jew" was the "shoddy aristocrat" by another name, a handy template of the Gilded Age parvenu.

Not all hoteliers in Saratoga felt this way. "The question of circumcision has nothing to do with our business," insisted the owners of the Congress Hall Hotel. "If Gen. Sherman, or Phil Sheridan, who are Catholics, should come, we wouldn't deny them entertainment because of their religion, and we have some highly respectable Hebrews in our hotel."[42] The affair attracted national attention. Yet even as Hilton was pilloried in verse by Brett Harte and from the pulpit by the Reverend Henry Ward Beecher, the letter columns of newspapers reflected a less favorable view of the Jew. Typical was a letter in the *New York Times* that defended Hilton's actions as a rational response to "the presence of a class of people so noted for meanness, uncleanliness, and obtrusive vulgarity." Others followed Hilton's lead, including the railroad magnate and developer Austin Corbin, who sought to bar Jews from his Manhattan Beach resort.[43] These were but the most prominent examples of a pattern of social exclusion that was already pronounced during the Civil War. In 1864, the *Jewish Messenger* complained that Jews were more and more often made unwelcome in the "favoured circles of society." This pattern, as Naomi Cohen has shown, troubled Jews well before the Hilton-Seligman affair.[44]

And yet, there was nothing inevitable in the rise of antisemitism in the 1870s and 1880s, nor in the exclusion of Joseph Seligman from the Grand Hotel. Amid the disruptive changes wrought by industrial capitalism and mass immigration, the "shoddy aristocrat" resonated anew. Seligman had the misfortune of serving as an early symbol of Gilded Age excess, much as Jews came to serve as the ideal foil for the particular social anxieties of an era when money was visibly remak-

42. "The Excitement in Saratoga," *ibid.*

43. See Brett Harte, "That Ebrew Jew," *American Jewish Archives* 6, no. 2 (1954): 148–50; Livney, "Let Us Now Praise Self-Made Men," 78–79.

44. *Jewish Messenger*, September 16, 1864. On manifestations of prejudice in the postwar period, see Cohen, "Antisemitism in the Gilded Age," 187–210. Cohen argues for the significance of wartime antisemitism, proposing that postwar discrimination against Jews was rooted in deep-seated religious prejudices that bubbled to the surface during the Civil War. I instead contend that the Civil War was a transition point: after the war, American antisemitism increasingly focused on the economic and social ills imagined to be wrought by Jews. Still, the war was the progenitor of many of these ideas.

ing American society.[45] The motifs of the war years—the Jew as self-seeking, self-promoting, and self-aggrandizing scoundrel—made possible the image of the Jew as the engineer and profiteer of a new economic and social order in which wheeler-dealers, loyal only to lucre and of dubious origin, rigged the system to their advantage. Instead of representing a fresh departure, Seligman's humiliation was but the Lazarus-like return of ideas that had awaited their second coming since the Civil War. In targeting Seligman, a member of the mannered elite, his antagonists made clear that not even the most celebrated of Jews was worthy of social acceptance and inclusion. More than a decade after the war, during an age of mass immigration, Goldwin Smith carried this idea several steps further: no Jew, no matter whether native-born or newcomer, could ever truly be trusted as a citizen of the United States.

Jewish Identity after the War

The indirect effects of wartime antisemitism on postwar Jewish collective identity were no less consequential. Bertram Korn understood this legacy to be largely positive, applauding an "increase in Jewish self-respect which grew out of the victories for Jewish equality won during the war."[46] To his mind, the Civil War, far from alienating Jews from American society, enabled the opposite. Jews on the home front were "drawn into the fray"; the "average immigrant became a partisan" emotionally committed to the progress of arms on the battlefield. "[T]hese and a thousand other aspects of life in a nation at war with itself," he concluded, "Americanized the large immigrant population at a much more rapid rate than that of more peaceful times."[47] Battle-hardened Jewish soldiers attained an "indefinable maturity as Americans" and "emerged from the crucible of the battlefield as Americans in an experiential sense."[48] To borrow Christian Samito's phrase, Jews—on the home front and on the front lines—

45. On Jews as convenient foils for the social ills of the age, see "Roundtable on Anti-Semitism in the Gilded Age and Progressive Era," *Journal of the Gilded Age and Progressive Era* 19 (July 2020): 5, 11, 23.

46. Bertram W. Korn, introduction to "The Jews of the Union," *American Jewish Archives* 13, no. 2 (1961): 135. He made an even stronger case for Americanization in *American Jewry and the Civil War*, 258–59. Howard B. Rock makes a similar argument in *Haven of Liberty: New York Jews in the New World, 1654–1865* (New York: New York University Press, 2012), 252. Their positions mirror those of John Higham and several other influential historians who wrote about the effects of the war.

47. Korn, *American Jewry and the Civil War*, 259.

48. Korn, introduction to "The Jews of the Union," 135.

became American under fire.[49] They identified more closely than before with the United States, loosened ties with their places of origin, and won acceptance into American society.

Such an interpretation, once commonplace for understanding how the war shaped the experience of other ethnic groups, has fallen out of fashion. Instead, scholars of German and Irish America now prefer to argue that the war slowed and muddled rather than hastened the Americanization of immigrants. As Nira Yuval-Davis has noted, belonging "becomes articulated, formally structured, and politicized only when it is threatened in some way."[50] Wartime appears to have provided this impulse for immigrant communities as acute prejudice strengthened ethnic consciousness. Paradoxically, invective against "flying dutchmen"—a favored insult for the supposed failings of soldiers of central European origin—and against Irishmen, often represented as drunken and disorderly, pushed immigrants of diverse backgrounds to embrace a collective identity as Germans and Irish. There was nothing inevitable about this process, given the strength of regional and local identities among immigrants. For central European immigrants, the concept of *Deutschtum* (Germanness) was less familiar than a sense of belonging rooted in origins in Bavaria, Baden, Prussia, and a multitude of other states and principalities. Wartime hostility and postwar nativism forged a sense of common cause among immigrants and demonstrated the benefits of collective and concerted action. When nativists tarred all Germans as cowards and mercenaries, leaders within the immigrant community decried these slurs on behalf of *all* immigrants from the German lands.[51] As Stephen D. Engle has

49. Christian G. Samito, *Becoming American under Fire: Irish Americans, African Americans, and the Politics of Citizenship during the Civil War Era* (Ithaca: Cornell University Press, 2009).

50. Nira Yuval-Davis, *The Politics of Belonging: Intersectional Contestations* (Los Angeles: Sage, 2011), 10.

51. See Christian B. Keller, *Chancellorsville and the Germans: Nativism, Ethnicity, and Civil War Memory* (New York: Fordham University Press, 2007), 10, 77, 93, 105, 113, 123; Keller, "Flying Dutchmen and Drunken Irishmen," 133–40; Keller, "New Perspectives in Civil War Ethnic History and Their Implications for Twenty-First-Century Scholarship," in *This Distracted and Anarchical People: New Answers for Old Questions About the Civil War–Era North*, ed. Andrew L. Slap and Michael Thomas Smith (New York: Fordham University Press, 2013), 131–33, 138–39; Walter D. Kamphoefner and Wolfgang Helbich, eds., *Germans in the Civil War: The Letters They Wrote Home*, trans. Susan Carter Vogel (Chapel Hill: University of North Carolina Press, 2006), xiii; Wolfgang Helbich, "German-Born Union Soldiers: Motivation, Ethnicity, and 'Americanization,'" in *German-American Immigration and Ethnicity in Comparative Perspective*, ed. Wolfgang Helbich and Walter Kamphoefner (Madison, Wisc.: Max Kade Institute for German-American Studies, 2004), 320–21; William B. Kurtz, "'Let Us Hear No More "Nativism"': The Catholic Press in the Mexican and Civil Wars," *Civil War History* 60, no. 1 (2014): 9. For local studies

suggested, collective action of this kind demonstrates that immigrants were "moving in both directions (towards assimilation and towards constructing an ethnic identity) simultaneously—creating firmer ethnic solidarity, on the one hand, and acting effectively in the public sphere, on the other hand."[52] This dynamic continued after the war as nativism nagged at these same communities.

Similar processes were evident among Jews. The public expression of antisemitic sentiment and discriminatory action obliged Jews to present a united front to counteract their detractors. The chaplaincy controversy and Grant's order required collective action on the home front, persuading a diverse population of immigrants to quell internal differences in order to express their grievances as a singular ethnic group.[53] Much as it did for other immigrant communities, this response strengthened a sense of ethnic consciousness, common cause, and collective identity. To be sure, this effort was only an early stage in the consolidation and coalescence of a national community. Isaac Leeser and Isaac Mayer Wise, preeminent religious leaders of very different stripe, began working toward this goal well before the war. And the Board of Delegates of American Israelites, which sought to speak on behalf of all American Jews, was founded in 1859, a year prior to South Carolina's secession from the Union. Though now best remembered for its efforts "to keep a watchful eye on occurrences at home and abroad" that threatened the "civil and religious rights of Israelites," the Board's ambitions were broader, including a desire to play a role in the religious affairs of the Jewish community.[54] Yet for this and other reasons, the Board was challenged by prominent detractors who questioned its authority and legitimacy. Though such fractures, divisions, and rivalries did not disappear after the war, wartime prejudice amply demonstrated the advantages of concerted and collective action, as well as of the establishment of organizational structures necessary to coordinate a geographically dispersed Jewish population.

Wartime prejudice was disillusioning for Jews, much as it was for other

---

that demonstrate this ethnicization in action, see Joseph R. Reinhart, "Louisville's Germans in the Civil War Era," *Register of the Kentucky Historical Society* 117 (Autumn 2019): 478; Andrew P. Yox, "Bonds of Community: Buffalo's German Element, 1853–1871," *New York History* 66, no. 2 (1985): 152–53.

52. Stephen D. Engle, "A Raised Consciousness: Franz Sigel and German Ethnic Identity in the Civil War," *Yearbook of German-American Studies* 34 (1999): 10 (quote on 1).

53. See, for example, the collective action stimulated by Grant's order; Sarna, *When General Grant Expelled the Jews*, 13–18.

54. See clauses 1–3 of the *Constitution and By-Laws of the Board of Delegates of American Israelites* (New York: Jewish Messenger Office, 1860).

immigrant communities. Earnest patriotism and conspicuous sacrifice were repaid with public scorn that questioned motives and loyalties. Instead of fulfilling initial hopes that the war might, as the *Jewish Messenger* anticipated, "purify the nation of its social as well as political relations," abundant evidence showed the opposite.[55] Disillusionment propelled a turn inward, encouraging some Jews to assert their identity as Jews during and after the war. That decision was driven less by a new confidence and prosperity than by chastening memories of a war that had demonstrated how uncertain the position of Jews was in American society. It also reflected another practical effect of wartime prejudice. Alternative forms of identification—as German American, for example—became that much harder for Jews to claim because of the solidification of the boundaries of other ethnic groups and heightened prejudice from these groups against Jews. German associational life in America, for instance, became less welcoming of Jews following the unification of Germany in 1871.[56]

This inward turn among Jews was reflected in the cascade of local and national Jewish organizations, institutions, and initiatives—cultural, literary, welfare, and religious—launched in the decades after the war.[57] Whereas before the war efforts to create, consolidate, and centralize were often frustrated or resisted, particularly at the national level, the Gilded Age was an era of building. Jonathan Sarna has described this period as a "late nineteenth-century American Jewish awakening" and as a "renaissance."[58] During these same decades German Americans likewise "constructed a national German American ethnic identity based on language, culture, and values," buttressed by social clubs, beer gar-

55. See *Jewish Messenger*, January 17, 1862, 15; *Allgemeine Zeitung des Judenthums* 26 (1862): 660.

56. Tobias Brinkmann writes about this process of ethnicization in Chicago. See Brinkmann, "Charity on Parade: Chicago's Jews and the Construction of Ethnic and Civic 'Gemeinschaft' in the 1860s," in *Celebrating Ethnicity and Nation: American Festive Culture from the Revolution to the Early 20th Century*, ed. Geneviève Fabre, Jürgen Heideking, and Kai Dreisbach (New York: Berghahn, 2001), 156–74; Brinkmann, "Jews, Germans, or Americans? German-Jewish Immigrants in the Nineteenth-Century United States," in *The Heimat Abroad: The Boundaries of Germanness*, ed. Krista O'Donnell, Renate Bridenthal, and Nancy Reagin (Ann Arbor: University of Michigan Press, 2005), 131–32; and Brinkmann, "'We Are Brothers! Let Us Separate!': Jewish Immigrants in Chicago between Gemeinde and Network Community before 1880," in *German-Jewish Identities in America*, ed. Christof Mauch and Joseph Salmons (Madison, Wisc.: Max Kade Institute for German American Studies, 2003), 54–58.

57. On the building of new synagogues, see Sarna, *American Judaism*, 124–25.

58. *Ibid.*, 138. See also Jonathan D. Sarna, "Introduction," in *Jewish Renaissance and Revival in America: Essays in Memory of Leah Levitz Fishbane*, ed. Eitan P. Fishbane and Jonathan D. Sarna (Waltham, Mass.: Brandeis University Press, 2011), 5–10.

dens, theaters, churches, and German-language newspapers.[59] This exercise in identity formation was reinforced by events abroad. The Franco-Prussian War and the unification of Germany caused an explosion of "Teutonic patriotism" in America.[60] German Americans trumpeted their "German-ness wherever possible," much as Irish Americans celebrated their shared Celtic roots.[61]

Paradoxically, this embrace of ethnic pride and particularism also involved the assertion of national belonging as citizens of the United States. Immigrant communities publicly extolled their virtues and touted their contributions to American society "as special gifts that only immigrants could provide their new country, and the young United States was portrayed as badly in need of them."[62] Simon Wolf's book was a typical expression of this claim to citizenship. By invoking the sacrifices of Jews for the United States from the American Revolution to the Civil War, he was demonstrating the rootedness of Jews in American society. He and others, including the newly formed American Jewish Historical Society, were seeking what Jonathan D. Sarna has described as "legitimation in history."[63] Their quest aimed to prove to others that Jews were not undesirable newcomers and to create a self-conscious attachment to being American Jews.

As such, *The American Jew as Patriot, Soldier and Citizen* encapsulated two of the key legacies of the war for Jews. On the one hand, Wolf's book was a response to antisemites who drew upon a set of ideas about Jews that crystallized during the Civil War and sharpened thereafter. Their feverish imaginings would be familiar to Benjamin Butler: Jews were vigorous in pursuit of money but not in defense of patria, self-seeking and clannish, and incapable and unworthy of citizenship. Wolf's book also reflected the inward turn of Jews after the Civil War. Wolf served in Washington, D.C., as representative of the B'nai B'rith, one of the national Jewish organizations that thrived during the Gilded Age. In his public role and in his magnum opus he sought to speak on behalf of Jews to

59. Reinhart, "Louisville's Germans," 478.

60. Helbich, "German-Born Union Soldiers," 321.

61. Keller, "New Perspectives in Civil War Ethnic History," 139, 141.

62. *Ibid.*, 133.

63. Sarna, "The 'Mythical Jew' and the 'Jew Next Door,'" 73. See, for example, the contents of the *Publications of the American Jewish Historical Society*, which first appeared in 1893. Many of the articles related to the earliest period of Jewish settlement in the United States, reminding readers that Jews were not recent interlopers. In 1892, Jews participated enthusiastically in the celebrations to mark the 400th anniversary of Columbus's landing in the New World. Some even claimed Columbus as a Jew. See Jonathan D. Sarna, "Columbus and the Jews," *Commentary* 94, no. 5 (1992): 38–41.

America, but also to his fellow Jews. He offered the latter much to celebrate. In place of the calumnies advanced by antisemites, Wolf presented an alternative vision: the Jew as the beau idéal of American citizenship. In doing so, Wolf also erased any sense that the Civil War was less than glorious for Jews. Discrimination and prejudice had little place in an account that looked to the Civil War as America's finest hour and the proving ground of patriotism. Ironically, then, *The American Jew as Patriot, Soldier and Citizen* was both a product of these two legacies of the war and an agent of their erasure from memory. As we have seen, the book drew scholarly attention away from the effects of the Civil War and its aftermath on antisemitism. Both are now overdue for reappraisal. Much as we cannot understand the Gilded Age without understanding what came before, we cannot adequately understand Jews in the Gilded Age without appreciating the legacies of the Civil War.

POLITICS AND PUBLIC LIFE, 1865–1900

DAVID G. DALIN

AS THE presidential election of 1868 approached, American Jews were in a quandary. This first national election since the end of the Civil War would be a referendum on Reconstruction, Black suffrage, and civil rights—and the Jewish vote would be a factor.[1] Jews who supported the Democratic Party's presidential candidate, former New York governor Horatio Seymour, accused the Republican candidate and Civil War hero, General Ulysses S. Grant, of antisemitism. On the other side, leading Jewish Republicans with close ties to the organized Jewish community, including Simon Wolf, Joseph Seligman, and Lewis Dembitz, staunchly defended Grant, reminding Jewish voters that their community owed much to the party of Abraham Lincoln and that Seymour, while a gubernatorial candidate in 1862, had described emancipation as "a proposal for the butchery of women and children, for scenes of lust and rapine, and of arson and murder."[2]

The presidential election of 1868 was not, as Jonathan D. Sarna has documented,[3] the first in which both political parties actively sought the Jewish vote. In 1864, when Lincoln was running for re-election and his popularity had plummeted, members of the Jewish Union Republican Associations from New York, Pennsylvania, and Indiana actively campaigned on his behalf. In a letter calling upon their fellow Jews to pledge their support, they declared that "the votes of the immense number of Jewish citizens will go far to determine the re-election of Abraham Lincoln to the presidency."[4] Thus, Jews *as Jews* were

1. John Hope Franklin discusses the background and significance of the election in "Election of 1868," in *History of American Presidential Elections, 1789–1968*, ed. Arthur M. Schlesinger Jr. and Fred L. Israel, vol. 2 (New York: Chelsea House, 1971), 1247–66.

2. For the 1862 New York State Democratic Party platform, see James McPherson, *Battle Cry of Freedom: The Civil War Era* (New York: Oxford University Press, 1988), 560. Seymour is quoted in Jonathan D. Sarna, *When General Grant Expelled the Jews* (New York: Nextbook/Schocken, 2012), 66.

3. Jonathan D. Sarna, "Jews, Lincoln, and the American Election of 1864: A Newly-Discovered Document and Its Larger Significance" (paper presented at the conference "The Practice of Jewish Politics, 1492–1880," held at the University of Maryland, October 22–23, 2017), 1–9.

4. Quoted in Naomi W. Cohen, *Encounter with Emancipation: The German Jews in the United States, 1830–1914* (Philadelphia: Jewish Publication Society, 1984), 134.

for the first time actively engaged in partisan public politics, setting a precedent for the election of 1868 and beyond.

The issue that caused the greatest controversy between Jewish Democrats and Jewish Republicans in the 1868 election was General Grant's decision early in the Civil War to order the expulsion of all Jews "as a class" from the territory under his military command, the Department of the Tennessee, which included northern Mississippi and parts of Kentucky. Issued on December 17, 1862, only weeks before the Emancipation Proclamation, General Orders No. 11 gave Jews twenty-four hours to leave the area and further stipulated that any Jew who returned would be summarily arrested.[5] Although President Lincoln rescinded the order two weeks later, it remains the most notorious anti-Jewish edict by a government official in American history.

As Grant's most recent biographer, Ron Chernow, has noted, Republicans and Democrats alike "knew the Jewish issue would surface" because of General Orders No. 11.[6] Indeed, in 1867, Schuyler Colfax, the Republican Speaker of the House of Representatives who would be Grant's first vice-presidential running mate, had argued against Grant's nomination because of "the danger of losing at one blow the whole Jew vote, by his having banished the whole of them publicly."[7] The Republican Party feared that the large number of Jewish voters in Cincinnati, Chicago, and St. Louis "might defect to the Democrats" and take the overall Jewish vote in Ohio, Illinois, and Missouri with them.[8] The Democrats seemed to confirm the Republicans' worst fears by making General Orders No. 11 a major campaign issue and by vilifying Grant as an antisemite. Thus, in 1868, "for the first time since the founding of the United States, the question of a presidential candidate's alleged anti-Semitism became a central political issue."[9]

Grant's nomination posed an "unprecedented and deeply vexing dilemma" for America's Jews, who began increasingly to evaluate political candidates and engage in partisan politics *as Jews* and would continue to do so throughout the late nineteenth century. Could they vote for a candidate—even a national war hero such as Grant—who once had expelled "Jews as a class" from the territory

5. *The Papers of Ulysses S. Grant*, ed. John Y. Simon et al., 32 vols. (Carbondale: Southern Illinois University Press, 1967–2012), 7:50 (hereafter *Grant Papers*).

6. Ron Chernow, *Grant* (New York: Penguin Books, 2017), 620.

7. Letter from Schuyler Colfax to John Russell Young, August 12, 1867, quoted in *ibid.*

8. *Ibid.*

9. Joakim Isaacs, "Ulysses S. Grant and the Jews," in *The American Jewish Experience*, ed. Jonathan D. Sarna (New York: Holmes & Meier, 1986), 64.

under his command?[10] How were Jewish voters, especially Jewish Republicans, to view Grant's candidacy? Many Jewish Democrats, still outraged over Grant's edict of six years earlier, called for Jewish voters to seek revenge through the ballot box, by casting their votes *as Jews* against the Republican Party's nominee. A viciously anti-Grant pamphlet entitled *General Grant and the Jews*, published in June 1868, shortly after Grant's nomination, made the most polemical case for revenge (Fig. 12). Its author, writing under the pseudonym Ph. von Bort and claiming to speak "in the name of all American Jews," denounced Grant "as unfit for the first office of this Government" and as "unworthy of the dignity" of the position. "As a CLASS, you have stigmatized and expelled us!" he declared. "As a CLASS, we rise up and vote against you, like one man!" The sixteen-page pamphlet concluded with the unqualified assertion that American Jews had the political and financial power to defeat Grant. "We are numerous," the author warned, "we are influential, we are wealthy, we are diffused over the whole continent, we are as one family; wherever our influence reaches, every Jew—no matter what political party—every Jew, with the votes he can command, will endeavor to defeat, and with God's blessing, *will* defeat you!"[11]

Other Jewish Democrats shared the pamphleteer's sentiments and would not forgive what they viewed as Grant's hatred of the American Jewish community. Prominent among them was the outspoken Cincinnati rabbi Isaac Mayer Wise, the preeminent leader of Reform Judaism in America. He founded and served as editor of the *Israelite*, one of the country's leading Jewish newspapers, and would later organize the Union of American Hebrew Congregations and establish the Reform movement's seminary, Hebrew Union College. A longtime and staunch Democrat with pro-Southern leanings, Wise was an uncompromising critic of the abolitionists.[12] Writing in the *Israelite* several months before the May 1868 Republican National Convention, he argued that "no one in the nineteenth century, in civilized countries, has abused and outraged the Jew" more than Grant. "In case of his nomination to the presidency, which we hope will not take place, we will consider it our duty to oppose him and the party nominating him."[13]

10. Sarna, *When General Grant Expelled the Jews*, 53.

11. Ph. Von Bort, *General Grant and the Jews* (New York: National News Company, 1868), 16. This pamphlet, signed simply "A Jew," is an early and important example of late nineteenth-century Jewish political campaign literature.

12. David G. Dalin and Alfred J. Kolatch, *The Presidents of the United States and the Jews* (Middle Village, N.Y.: Jonathan David Publishers, 2000), 78–79.

13. *Israelite*, February 28, 1868, 4, quoted in Sarna, *When General Grant Expelled the Jews*, 55.

Throughout the presidential campaign, in city after city, Jewish Democrats vilified Grant, comparing him to the historic enemies of the Jewish people, including the pharaohs of ancient Egypt and "the wicked Haman, vizier of Persia and villain of the biblical book of Esther, whose order to exterminate the Jews of his day was overturned by Persia's King Ahasuerus—with disastrous consequences for Haman and his family." Jews "will defeat Grant as they defeated Haman," Jewish Democrats in Atlanta proclaimed. In unprecedented political rallies in Memphis, Nashville, Atlanta, St. Louis, and Los Angeles, Jewish voters gathered to oppose Grant's nomination and election.[14]

Several prominent Jewish Republicans came to Grant's defense. One of the most notable was the legal scholar Lewis N. Dembitz, a cofounder of the Republican Party in Kentucky and the uncle of the future Supreme Court justice Louis Dembitz Brandeis. An Orthodox Jew and a fervent abolitionist, Dembitz named one of his sons after Henry Clay and the other after Abraham Lincoln.[15] By the age of twenty-seven, Dembitz had already become an important Republican leader in Kentucky, and "tradition holds" that he gave one of the nominating speeches for Lincoln at the Republican National Convention of 1860.[16] Eight years later, Dembitz responded immediately when Grant came under attack, sending a letter of inquiry about General Orders No. 11 to Grant's campaign headquarters. He received a "long courteous reply" from John A. Rawlins, Grant's assistant adjutant general back in 1862 and one of his main presidential campaign advisers and spokesmen in 1868. Rawlins told Dembitz what he and other Jewish Republicans very much wanted to hear: allegations that General Orders No. 11 "was issued on account of the religion of the Jews cannot be seriously entertained by any one who knows the General's steadfast adherence to the principles of American liberty and religious toleration."[17] Rawlins's letter, as intended, was widely distributed among Jewish Republicans, who were reassured that they could vote for Grant *as Jews.*

However, some Jewish leaders, such as Liebman Adler, rabbi of Chicago's oldest synagogue, contended that Jews should not vote *as Jews* on the basis of specifically Jewish interests, but should cast their ballots in support of what he called general American interests. Although proud to be a Jew, he maintained

14. Sarna, *When General Grant Expelled the Jews*, 49, 68–69.

15. David G. Dalin, *Jewish Justices of the Supreme Court, from Brandeis to Kagan: Their Lives and Legacies* (Waltham, Mass.: Brandeis University Press, 2017), 25.

16. Jonathan D. Sarna and Benjamin Shapell, *Lincoln and the Jews: A History* (New York: St. Martin's Press, 2015), 55; and Dalin, *Jewish Justices of the Supreme Court.*

17. John A. Rawlins to Lewis N. Dembitz, May 6, 1868, *Grant Papers*, 19:38–39n.

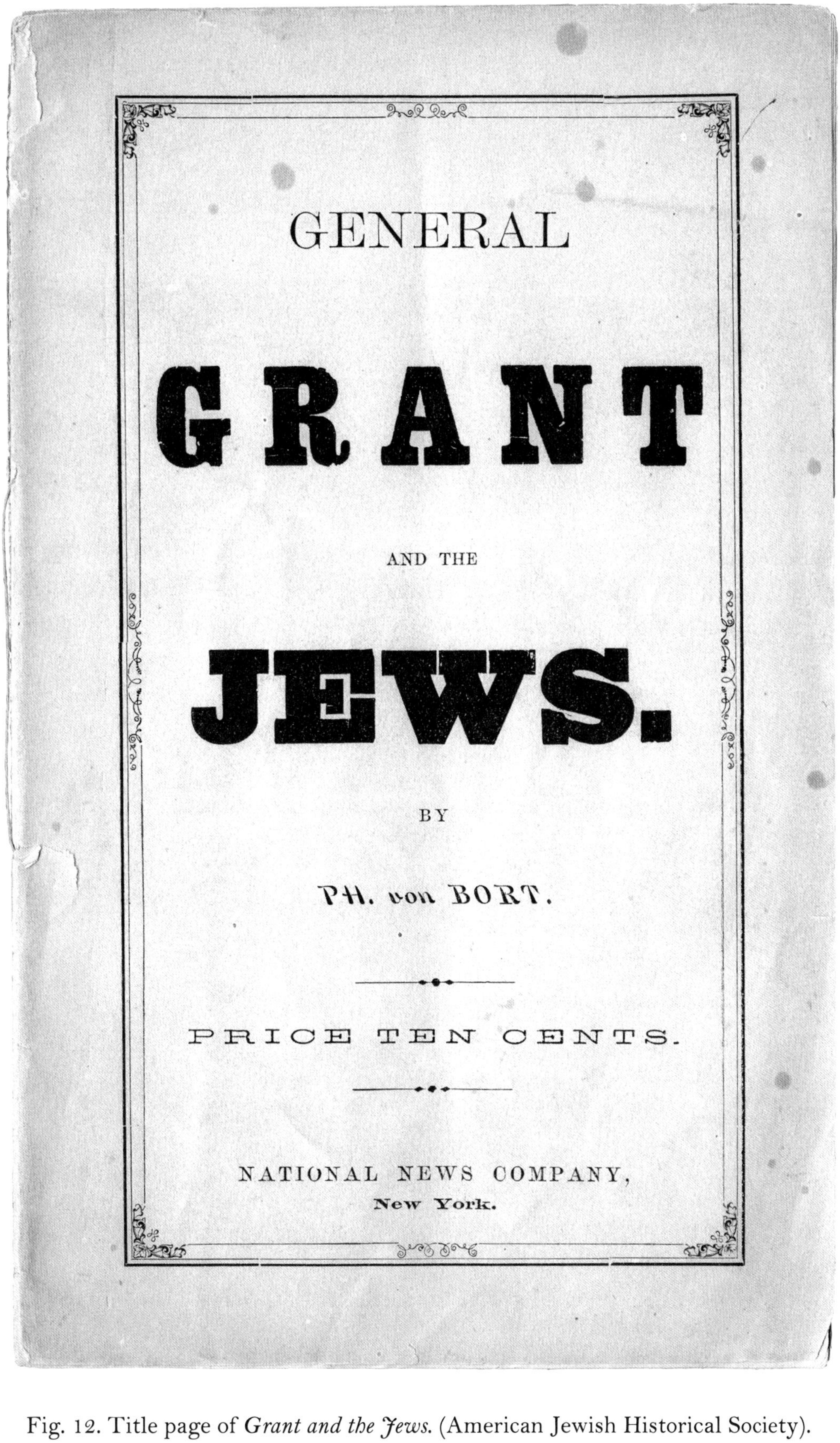

GENERAL

GRANT

AND THE

JEWS.

BY

PH. von BORT.

PRICE TEN CENTS.

NATIONAL NEWS COMPANY,

New York.

Fig. 12. Title page of *Grant and the Jews.* (American Jewish Historical Society).

that "it is different when I take a ballot in order to exercise my rights as a citizen. Then I am not a Jew, but I feel and act as a citizen of the republic." On election day, "I do not ask what pleases the Israelites. I consult the welfare of the country." Adler publicly supported Grant, believing that the principles of the Republican Party, especially its promise that "all men of all races should be equal," was the most important consideration. In the end, if Grant is the best man for the American people and the welfare of the country, "he is the best man for the Israelites, despite General Orders No. 11."[18]

Throughout the presidential campaign of 1868, Washington, D.C., attorney and lobbyist Simon Wolf (Fig. 13), then the most influential Jewish Republican leader in the country, mobilized support for Grant among Jewish voters throughout the United States. After the election, he was recognized by President Grant as the spokesman for the American Jewish community on all issues pertaining to their political interests and their relations with the administration.[19] Wolf, who had emigrated from his native Germany with his grandparents at the age of twelve in 1848 and who grew up in the small rural town of Ulrichsville, Ohio, moved to Washington in 1862, where he practiced law and became involved in politics. Having begun his political life as a Democrat, Wolf acted upon his fervent antislavery beliefs and his admiration of Abraham Lincoln by becoming a Republican in 1860.[20] He personally congratulated Lincoln on the Emancipation Proclamation in 1862,[21] and he would go on to campaign for and advise every Republican president from Grant to William Howard Taft. In 1868 he emerged as the most vocal and public defender of Grant against allegations of antisemitism.

Many campaign observers expected that a majority of American Jews would vote for Horatio Seymour. It is not known how many Jews voted for Grant, nor can the extent of Simon Wolf's influence be estimated precisely. There was, however, a general perception that Wolf helped Grant carry more of the Jewish vote than initially anticipated, which impressed Republican Party leaders.[22] Wolf himself hoped and expected to receive a political appointment from the new president and wrote a formal request to Grant three days after the inauguration. The prominent St. Louis Jewish communal leader Isidor Bush added

18. Quoted in Sarna, *When Grant Expelled the Jews*, 73–74.

19. *Ibid.*

20. Simon Wolf's early life and career are discussed in Esther L. Panitz, *Simon Wolf: Private Conscience and Public Image* (Cranbury, N.J.: Associated University Presses, 1987), 17–26.

21. Sarna and Shapell, *Lincoln and the Jews*, 124.

22. Panitz, *Simon Wolf*, 32.

Fig. 13. Simon Wolf. Plate facing page 31 in Simon Abram, *A History of the Washington Hebrew Congregation* (Washington, D.C., 1905). (Library of Congress).

his support: "if Presidt Grant wants to prove his impartiality towards Israelites and to disprove any unfriendliness attributed to him on account of Order No. 11—there is probably no better opportunity than by appointing Mr. Simon Wolf."[23] In gratitude for Wolf's early and tireless support, his "ardent" services to the Republican Party during the election campaign, and his successful efforts "to overcome the reluctance of the Israelites" to vote for him, Grant appointed Wolf the federal Recorder of Deeds for the District of Columbia, a post created specifically for him.[24]

During his eight-year tenure as recorder, Wolf would develop a close relationship with Grant and would later claim in his (decidedly self-serving) autobiography that, with the exception of his own family and cabinet members, Grant saw Wolf more frequently than any other individual.[25] To be sure, President Grant manifested his warm friendship for Wolf and his appreciation for Wolf's political support in various ways. In January 1869, for example, Grant accepted Wolf's invitation to serve as godfather to his newborn son and sent his White House aide to represent him at the circumcision ceremony at Wolf's home. Wolf, in turn, showed his appreciation by naming the child Adolf Grant Wolf.[26]

The controversy over General Orders No. 11 and the unprecedented division among Jewish voters that it precipitated finally ended in late November 1868, when Grant, as president-elect, allowed a private letter he had written two months earlier to be published in the press and widely distributed. In it, he unequivocally repudiated General Orders No. 11 and apologized for the anti-Jewish prejudice it contained: "I do not pretend to sustain the order.... The order was made and sent out, without any reflection, and without thinking of the Jews as a sect or race to themselves...." American Jews were especially pleased with Grant's forthright concluding statement: "I have no prejudice against sect or race but want each individual to be judged by his own merit. Order No. 11 does not sustain this statement, I admit, but then I do not sustain that order. It never would have been issued if it had not been telegraphed the moment penned, without one moments reflection."[27] After months of internecine political bat-

23. Isidor Bush to Senator Carl Schurz of Missouri, March 12, 1869, *Grant Papers*, 19:19n.

24. Panitz, *Simon Wolf*, 32–33; Sarna, *When General Grant Expelled the Jews*, 84–85.

25. Panitz, *Simon Wolf*, 34; Simon Wolf, *The Presidents I Have Known from 1860–1918* (Washington, D.C.: B. S. Adams, 1918), 71.

26. Panitz, *Simon Wolf*, 34; Wolf, *Presidents I Have Known*, 97.

27. Grant to Isaac N. Morris, September 14, 1868, *Grant Papers*, 19:37; Sarna, *When General Grant Expelled the Jews*, 76.

tling, American Jews, Republicans and Democrats alike, were delighted with Grant's apology, in which he conveyed unequivocally the liberal idea that prejudice against Jews would never be acceptable in his post–Civil War America.

Jews in late nineteenth-century America did not view the state as an enemy, as European Jews frequently did.[28] Beginning in the early republic and throughout the nineteenth century, American Jews looked to the state for political recognition in the form of presidential appointments to public office. Presidents James Madison and James Monroe, for example, appointed Jews to several consular posts.[29] Likewise, between 1865 and 1900, most Jews who received presidential appointments were nominated for diplomatic posts. Often their religion was important in the decision regarding particular assignments. In 1870, for example, President Grant, with the support and lobbying of Simon Wolf, appointed Benjamin Franklin Peixotto, a prominent San Francisco attorney, Jewish communal leader, and former national president of B'nai B'rith, as U.S. consul to Bucharest, Romania, which was then a hotbed of virulent antisemitism. Grant endorsed the new consul's intention to use the American consulate to promote Jewish rights and political emancipation in Romania.[30] Peixotto would remain as U.S. consul in Bucharest throughout the Grant presidency.

In 1868, Wolf had been assisted in his campaign for Grant's election by other prominent Jewish Republicans. Especially notable was the financial and political support from the Seligmans, America's preeminent Jewish banking family. During his first term in office, Grant offered to appoint his longtime friend Joseph Seligman as secretary of the Treasury. Seligman had come to America from his native Bavaria in 1837, and during the 1840s he was joined by his ten brothers and sisters. Seligman's first contact with Grant dated back to the late 1840s, when two of his brothers opened a general store in Sackett's Harbor, New York, where young Lieutenant Grant was stationed.[31] Grant became a regular

28. Howard B. Rock, "The Jews and the State, 1776–1865," in *By Dawn's Early Light: Jewish Contributions to American Culture from the Nation's Founding to the Civil War*, ed. Adam Mendelsohn (Princeton: Princeton University Library, 2016), 42.

29. David G. Dalin, "Presidents, Presidential Appointments, and Jews," in *Jews in American Politics*, ed. L. Sandy Maisel and Ira N. Forman (Lanham, Md.: Rowman and Littlefield Publishers, 2001), 31.

30. *Ibid.*, 31. Max Kohler and Simon Wolf cite a letter that Peixotto carried with him from President Grant to Prince Charles of Romania; see Max J. Kohler and Simon Wolf, "Benjamin F. Peixotto's Mission to Romania," in *The Jewish Experience in America*, vol. 2, *In the Early Republic*, ed. Abraham J. Karp (Waltham, Mass.: American Jewish Historical Society, 1969), 382.

31. George S. Hellman, "Joseph Seligman, American Jew," *Publications of the American Jewish Historical Society* 41 no. 1 (1951): 31.

customer, and a friendship developed with the entire Seligman family, particularly Joseph. Together, Joseph and his brothers prospered in business and later, as influential international bankers headquartered in New York, established branches in San Francisco, New Orleans, London, Paris, Berlin, Frankfurt, and Amsterdam. During the Civil War, the Seligman brothers strongly supported the Union cause and the Republican Party. They "helped to outfit New York's Seventh Regiment" and traveled to Europe to sell $200 million of U.S. government Treasury bonds (while winning government contracts to supply uniforms and accessories to the Union Army).[32]

In the presidential elections of 1868 and 1872, Joseph, Jesse, and James Seligman were among Grant's most important financial and political supporters. Much to Grant's disappointment, Joseph Seligman declined the office of secretary of the Treasury, an appointment that would have made him the first Jewish cabinet member in U.S. history, choosing instead to continue managing his family's banking interests. Seligman would later also turn down the Republican nomination for mayor of New York City, explaining that "the bank needs me, and my brothers beg me to leave politics and public office to others."[33] He would remain, with Simon Wolf, one of the most influential Jewish Republican leaders in the country until his death in 1880.

Perhaps the most notable of Grant's Jewish appointees was his longtime friend Edward S. Salomon, who in 1870 was named governor of Washington Territory. Salomon, who had assumed command of the Eighty-second Illinois Infantry during the Battle of Gettysburg, became the first professing American Jew to serve as governor of a state or territory. Isaac Mayer Wise, who had earlier called General Orders No. 11 an "outrage," now applauded Grant's decision: "The appointment shows that *President* Grant has revoked *General* Grant's notorious Order No. 11."[34]

On Simon Wolf's recommendation, President Grant appointed Jews to other government posts, including consuls, district attorneys, deputy postmasters, and a superintendent of Indian affairs for Arizona Territory. Grant, according to Wolf, appointed "more Israelites to office than any other President since the

32. Howard B. Rock, *Haven of Liberty: New York Jews in the New World, 1654–1865* (New York: New York University Press, 2012), 244; Sarna, *When General Grant Expelled the Jews*, 62.

33. Quoted in Stephen Birmingham, *"Our Crowd": The Great Jewish Families of New York* (New York: Harper and Row, 1967), 142.

34. Quoted in Ronald C. White, *American Ulysses: A Life of Ulysses S. Grant* (New York: Random House, 2016), 495; in Sarna, *When General Grant Expelled the Jews*, 90; and in Lee M. Friedman, *Jewish Pioneers and Patriots* (Philadelphia: Jewish Publication Society of America, 1942), 353–64.

founding of the Government."[35] Years later, Wolf estimated that, at his personal request, "more than fifty appointments were made by Grant."[36] No American Jew until then had been so influential in the White House, and Wolf holds the distinction of having been the preeminent Jewish presidential advisor in late nineteenth-century America. As Jonathan D. Sarna has noted, "no previous American president ever appointed a Jew to so high a position of trust, and none before Grant ever sought to have a Jew in his administration to represent his 'co-religionists' before the government."[37]

Notwithstanding Wolf's "propensity to self-aggrandize and exaggerate," the historical record confirms that he "found numerous opportunities to intervene with Grant" on behalf of Jewish office seekers and "causes important to the Jewish community." If the author of the pamphlet *General Grant and the Jews* had opposed Grant's presidential nomination "in the name of all American Jews," Wolf, as the recognized spokesman for the American Jewish community, supported and advised (and was widely viewed as advising) President Grant "in the name of all American Jews." Wolf would be viewed as representing all his coreligionists before the government during the Republican administrations of Presidents Rutherford B. Hayes, James Garfield, Chester A. Arthur, and Benjamin Harrison.

The presidential campaign of 1884 and Grover Cleveland's victory over Republican James G. Blaine, the first by a Democrat since 1856, brought new Jewish voters into the Democratic Party. The most prominent Jewish Democrat of the Cleveland years was Oscar Straus (Fig. 14), a former Republican who would leave the Democratic Party in 1896 to support and advise Republican presidents William McKinley and Theodore Roosevelt. Born in Otterberg, Bavaria, in 1850, Straus immigrated to the United States with his parents and two older brothers a few years later. After graduating from Columbia University Law School, Straus practiced law before joining L. Straus and Sons, his family's china and glassware business. With financial help from his brothers Isidor and Nathan (who later owned and developed R. H. Macy's into the world's largest department store), Straus was able to devote his life to public service. In 1882, having become a member of the Young Men's Republican Club in Manhattan, where he first met and befriended Theodore Roosevelt (then beginning his political career as a young assemblyman in Albany), Straus entered politics as a

35. Chernow, *Grant*, 642; and Sarna, *When General Grant Expelled the Jews*, 88–89.

36. *American Israelite*, October 20, 1916, 841. Cited in Panitz, *Simon Wolf*, 35; Sarna, *When General Grant Expelled the Jews*, 88.

37. Wolf, *Presidents I Have Known*, 71–73; Sarna, *When General Grant Expelled the Jews*, 86.

Fig. 14. Oscar Straus at a World War I Liberty Bond rally in front of Federal Hall, Wall Street. Bain News Service, 1918. (Library of Congress).

leader of a citizens' movement dedicated to municipal and civil service reform.[38] But in the 1884 presidential campaign, as secretary of the executive committee of the New York City Merchants' and Business Men's Association and as a Mugwump (a Republican who detested the corruption associated with Blaine), Straus actively campaigned for Cleveland.

In 1887, President Cleveland named Straus to be the U.S. minister to Turkey.

38. Naomi W. Cohen, *A Dual Heritage: The Public Career of Oscar S. Straus* (Philadelphia: Jewish Publication Society of America, 1969), 18–19.

When the appointment was announced, detractors pointed out that the U.S. minister in Constantinople was responsible for protecting Christian missionaries and colleges. However, several Protestant clergymen supported Straus, including the enormously popular Brooklyn preacher Henry Ward Beecher, who wrote to Cleveland: "The bitter prejudice against Jews, which obtains in many parts of Europe, ought not to receive any countenance in America. It is because he is a Jew that I would urge his appointment as a fit recognition of this remarkable people who ... deserve and should receive from our government such recognition."[39] Straus was an immensely successful and popular minister to Turkey.

Cleveland established a precedent followed by Republican and Democratic presidents alike over the next thirty years. The ambassadorship to Turkey came to be considered a quasi-Jewish domain, comparable to the later "Jewish seat" on the U.S. Supreme Court.[40] American presidents recognized the symbolic importance of the Turkish embassy for American Jews, and especially for the growing number of Zionists within the American Jewish electorate, since the Jewish homeland in Palestine remained under the direct control of the Turkish government. Thus, when Oscar Straus resigned in 1889, President Benjamin Harrison invited Simon Wolf to the White House and expressed his desire "to appoint a representative American citizen of the Jewish faith to Turkey."[41] Acting on Wolf's recommendation, Harrison named Solomon Hirsch, a Republican merchant, Jewish communal leader, and state legislator from Portland, Oregon. Hirsch held the position until 1892.[42]

By inviting Wolf to the White House to advise him on Straus's successor, President Harrison recognized Wolf as the spokesman for the American Jewish community on all political issues and presidential appointments of interest to American Jews. Wolf first met and campaigned for Harrison when the Republican ran for governor of Indiana in 1876. They maintained a cordial friendship over the next decade, and, following Harrison's successful run for president, Wolf was appointed a member of the select committee that planned and organized the inauguration in March 1889. Harrison subsequently offered Wolf the diplomatic post of U.S. consul general to Egypt, which Wolf declined so as to resume his private law practice.

39. Quoted in Dalin, "Presidents, Presidential Appointments, and Jews," 32.

40. *Ibid.*

41. Wolf, *Presidents I Have Known*, 111.

42. Biographical information on Hirsch can be found in Robert E. Levinson, "Solomon Hirsch," *Encyclopedia Judaica*, vol. 8 (Jerusalem: Keter Publishing House, 1971), 516–517, and Donald Altschiller, "Solomon Hirsch," in *Jews in American Politics*, ed. Maisel and Forman, 354.

As president, Harrison expressed public concern and sympathy for the worsening predicament of the Jews in tsarist Russia. As the pogroms and antisemitic persecution of Jews worsened in 1890 and 1891, a delegation of Jewish leaders that included Simon Wolf, Oscar Straus, Jacob Schiff, Jesse Seligman, and Louis Marshall took it upon themselves to speak on behalf of the entire Jewish community and met with Harrison in the White House in April 1891 to discuss what the U.S. government could do. At the group's suggestion, Harrison appointed a special commission, headed by John B. Weber, the U.S. commissioner of immigration at Ellis Island, to travel to Russia and report on the situation firsthand.

Several months later Weber issued a damning assessment of Russian anti-Jewish edicts and persecutions. In his annual message to Congress on December 9, 1891, Harrison expressed his sympathy for the Jews of Russia in the most unequivocal terms. Based on the findings contained in the Weber report, Harrison informed Congress that his administration had expressed its concern to the Russian government over "the harsh measures now being enforced against the Hebrews in Russia."[43] Harrison noted that the Weber report "estimated that over one million [Jews] will be forced from Russia within a few years. . . ."[44]

In November 1892, Benjamin Harrison was defeated in his bid for re-election, despite the efforts of American Jewish Republican leaders like Wolf, Schiff, Marshall, Jesse Seligman, and Hirsch. In this election, following the precedent set in 1868, Jewish leaders *as Jews* actively engaged in campaign politics, taking it upon themselves to speak for the entire Jewish community. In so doing, they were adhering to the belief that Jewish community spokesmen could legitimately support or oppose a political candidate "in the name of all American Jews," echoing the sentiments of *General Grant and the Jews*, which had done so much to influence and shape Jewish politics since 1868.

With the exception of Isaac Mayer Wise, all the German Jewish leaders in the late nineteenth century—among them, Wolf, Schiff, Mayer Sulzberger, Jesse Seligman, Straus, Marshall, Hirsch, and Julius Rosenwald—were staunch Republicans who remained so throughout their public careers. By the 1880s and 1890s, however, not all Jewish Republicans came from that wealthy, upper-class circle. A growing number of Yiddish- or Hebrew-speaking working-class east

43. Gary Dean Best, *To Free A People: American Jewish Leaders and the Jewish Problem in Eastern Europe, 1890–1914* (Westport, Conn.: Greenwood Press, 1982), 32; Dalin and Kolatch, *Presidents of the United States and the Jews*, 113.

44. Oscar S. Straus, *Under Four Administrations: From Cleveland to Taft* (Boston and New York: Houghton Mifflin Company, 1922), 107.

European Jewish immigrants, living in the tenements of New York City's Lower East Side, were affiliating with the local Republican Party. As early as the 1870s, as Moses Rischin has noted, east European Jewish immigrants who idolized Lincoln "followed the lead of their German coreligionists and supported the party of the Great Emancipator."[45] During the 1890s, many Jewish voters in New York City's Eighth Assembly District, on the Lower East Side, consistently voted Republican. There, "Stitch" McCarthy, born Sam Rothberg, a Yiddish-speaking saloonkeeper and Republican politician, mobilized immigrant Jewish voters on behalf of Republican candidates.[46] These east European Jewish Republican voters, like their wealthy German Jewish coreligionists, were grateful to Presidents Grant and Harrison for their administrations' vigorous protests against antisemitic outrages and pogroms in Russia and Romania.

But not all Yiddish-speaking east European Jewish immigrants in the Eighth Assembly District voted Republican. Many were instead committed socialists who, during the late 1880s and the 1890s, voted for the Socialist Labor Party (SLP). They were poor, working-class Jews, primarily garment workers who toiled for negligible wages in the city's factories and sweat shops and had little in common with the "uptown" German Jewish elite. Many east European Jewish immigrants first became involved in left-wing politics in 1886, when the United Labor Party chose the radical single-tax theorist Henry George as its candidate for New York City mayor. As literary and social critic Irving Howe noted, George "won the hearts of immigrant Jews, and for the first time a sizable number of them became active in local politics."[47] Henry George clubs sprang up on the Lower East Side, where Jewish immigrants enthusiastically joined the Henry George Tailors League and the Henry George Tobacco Workers League, and street meetings were held in Yiddish. According to Howe, "a few days before the election, a large rally was organized at which George made an impassioned speech comparing the liberation of the Jews from the Pharaohs ... with the campaign to ease the lot of New York wage earners."[48] George ran especially well in the East Side's Second, Fourth, and Eighth Assembly Districts, all heavily Jewish; in the city as a whole, his total Jewish vote was estimated to

45. Moses Rischin, *The Promised City: New York's Jews, 1870–1914* (Cambridge, Mass.: Harvard University Press, 1962), 221.

46. *Ibid.*, 223.

47. Irving Howe, *World of Our Fathers: The Journey of the East European Jews to America and the Life They Found and Made*, 30th Anniversary Edition (New York: New York University Press, 2006), 366.

48. *Ibid.*

be anywhere between 5,000 and 15,000.[49] Thousands of Jewish workers made their entry into American politics through their active participation in the George campaign.

When the United Labor Party disbanded after Henry George's defeat in 1886, most of the east European immigrant working-class Jews who had been radicalized by his campaign joined the SLP, which enjoyed its greatest success under the leadership of its Jewish leader, Daniel DeLeon, during the 1890s. In the aftermath of the Panic of 1893 and in the midst of the most severe economic depression in the nation's history to date, the SLP began to challenge the hegemony of Republican and Democratic politicians throughout Manhattan. When DeLeon twice ran for Congress from the city's hardest-hit area, the Jewish Lower East Side, he received 10 percent of the vote in 1894 and 18 percent in 1896, "the most impressive total by far of any SLP candidate in the city."[50] In the late 1890s, DeLeon "consistently received 30% of the ballots cast" when he ran for assemblyman in his own Lower East Side Eighth Assembly District.[51]

Throughout the 1890s, leading Jewish radical polemicists Benjamin Feigenbaum and Louis Miller wrote passionate articles in the Yiddish socialist press about the virtues of socialism and in support of SLP candidates for public office. Dismayed by the results of the 1896 presidential election, when William McKinley became the first Republican in many years to carry New York City, Louis Miller raged in *Zukunft*, the most distinguished of all Yiddish socialist periodicals, "Socialism seems so clear, simple and logical to us that only a dunce or a scoundrel could fail to understand it."[52] In 1901, the Jewish attorney and socialist theoretician (and future socialist candidate for Congress) Morris Hillquit would become a founding father of the Socialist Party of America, and east European immigrant Jews "would support the candidates of that party in increasing and disproportionate numbers."[53]

Although a growing number of American Jews were elected to public office between 1865 and 1900, none of them won on the SLP ticket. Eighteen Jews were elected to the U.S. Congress, nine in the decade of the 1890s alone. They represented districts throughout the country, from New York, California, Louisiana, Pennsylvania, Massachusetts, Michigan, Maryland, Missouri, and

49. *Ibid.*

50. Rischin, *Promised City*, 226.

51. *Ibid.*

52. Quoted in *ibid.*, 227.

53. Gerald Sorin, *The Prophetic Minority: American Jewish Immigrant Radicals, 1880–1920* (Bloomington: Indiana University Press, 1985), 79.

Illinois.[54] Seven were elected from New York, where the largest Jewish population was concentrated.

Among the most notable of these Jewish congressmen were Julius Kahn of San Francisco and Lucius Littauer of New York. Kahn, a German-born actor turned lawyer and Republican politician, was elected to the California state assembly in 1892. Six years later, he won a seat in Congress, where he would spend twenty-four years, serving for several terms as the powerful Republican chairman of the House Military Affairs Committee. Kahn would be the only Jew ever seriously considered for the speakership of the House of Representatives.[55] Littauer, a wealthy glove manufacturer and Republican congressman, first elected to the House of Representatives in 1896, had been Theodore Roosevelt's college roommate at Harvard in the 1870s and his close friend and supporter in the years afterward. Littauer's re-election to Congress in 1898 coincided with Roosevelt's election as governor of New York. At a Harvard Club dinner at the Waldorf Astoria Hotel in February 1900, Governor Roosevelt declared that "it is a Harvard Man and Congressman, Lucius Littauer, who is my most intimate friend and close political advisor."[56] After Roosevelt succeeded to the presidency in 1901, Littauer was a frequent guest at the White House. A prominent philanthropist, Littauer endowed the Nathan Littauer Professorship of Hebrew Literature and Philosophy at Harvard, the first chair in Jewish studies in the United States.

During the period 1865–1900, twelve Jews were elected mayors of large cities: Denver, Colorado; Boise, Idaho; Grand Rapids, Michigan; Jersey City and Patterson, New Jersey; Portland, Oregon; Savannah, Georgia; Toledo, Ohio; Tampa, Florida; and San Francisco, California.[57] There would be no Jewish mayor of New York City until the election of Abe Beame in 1973.

The presidential election of 1896 is widely acknowledged as one of the most important in American history, one of the few that brought about a fundamental realignment in American politics.[58] As Lewis L. Gould has noted, the Republican

54. Kurt F. Stone, *The Jews of Capitol Hill: A Compendium of Jewish Congressional Members* (Lanham, Md.: Scarecrow Press, 2011), 31–61, 66–72.

55. *Ibid.*, 66–68; Burton Alan Boxerman, "Kahn of California," *California Historical Quarterly* 55, no. 4 (1976): 340–51.

56. Quoted in Stone, *Jews of Capitol Hill*, 59.

57. Appendix J in *Jews in American Politics*, ed. Maisel and Forman, 469–70.

58. R. Hal Williams, *Realigning America: McKinley, Bryan, and the Remarkable Election of 1896* (Lawrence: University Press of Kansas, 2010), xi.

Party's nomination and election of William McKinley "signaled a transformation in American politics" that would mark the beginning of a new "era of Republican dominance."[59] Republicans became the new majority party and would remain so, governing the country—with the exception of Woodrow Wilson's years in the White House—until the election of Franklin D. Roosevelt in 1932.

William Jennings Bryan's advocacy of the silver standard in U.S. monetary policy, and the antisemitism on the part of many of Bryan's Populist Party supporters, convinced the German Jewish elite to campaign actively for, and contribute financially to, the Republicans. Beginning in the 1870s, the economic plight of Midwestern and Southern farmers, who by the early 1890s made up the Populist Party's rank and file, continually worsened. When the Panic of 1893 swept the United States, those farmers "increasingly began to identify Jews as the sources of their woes,"[60] as did Populist writers, orators, and politicians. For the agrarian Populists, who often referred to Jews as Shylocks and Rothschilds and who crusaded passionately against the gold standard, "the Jews stood not only for plutocracy in general, but also for the financial power of gold in particular."[61] The historian Richard Hofstadter concluded that by the time of the presidential campaign of 1896, "anti-Semitism had become, if not all pervasive, at least common" among the Populist supporters of Bryan.[62] Populists used religious metaphors to link the hated gold standard to a conspiracy of Jewish Republican bankers and plutocrats. Thus, Bryan, a mesmerizing orator, could conclude his speech accepting the presidential nomination at the Democratic National Convention by interspersing Christian biblical imagery with his advocacy of the silver standard. Defenders of the gold standard, he thundered, "shall not press down upon the brow of labor this crown of thorns. You shall not crucify mankind upon a cross of gold." The antisemitism conveyed by the powerful metaphor of the crucifixion appealed to rural Protestant fundamentalists in the Midwest and South, farmers and small businessmen alike.[63] During the presidential campaign and thereafter, Bryan's Populist supporters reiterated crucifixion metaphors in their crusade against the gold standard. For them, it

59. Lewis L. Gould, *The Republicans: A History of the Grand Old Party* (New York: Oxford University Press, 2014), 88.

60. Leonard Dinnerstein, *Antisemitism in America* (New York: Oxford University Press, 1994), 48–49.

61. John Higham, *Send These to Me: Jews and Other Immigrants in Urban America* (New York: Atheneum, 1975), 123.

62. Richard Hofstadter, *The Age of Reform, from Bryan to FDR* (New York: Knopf, 1955), 80.

63. Dinnerstein, *Antisemitism in America*, 49–50.

was a symbol of the oppression of the big-city Republican Jewish bankers and businessmen they detested.

The presidential election of 1896 was the first since that of 1868 in which the Jewish vote and the alleged antisemitism of a presidential candidate became a central issue for American Jews. McKinley's victory was applauded by longtime German Jewish Republican leaders like Schiff, Wolf, Sulzberger, Hirsch, and Marshall, who had actively supported him. It also brought Oscar Straus back into the Republican Party after serving as a member of Cleveland's "Kitchen Cabinet."[64] These and other Jewish Republicans received increasing political recognition throughout McKinley's presidency. Straus again had easy access to the White House and advised McKinley on monetary policy and a variety of issues relating to international diplomacy and foreign affairs. In 1898, McKinley asked Straus to resume his former post as U.S. minister to Turkey. Although at first reluctant, Straus concluded that his "destiny" was to return to Constantinople. As he wrote to McKinley, "I deem it my patriotic duty to you and to the country to accept."[65] Straus served in Turkey until December 1900.

President McKinley recognized other Jewish Republican supporters as well. Simon Wolf was appointed a member of the committee that planned the inauguration ceremonies that took place on March 4, 1897. A frequent guest at the McKinley White House, he was offered presidential appointments as Postmaster in Washington, D.C., and as commissioner of the District of Columbia, both of which he declined. Together with Straus, Wolf was recognized by McKinley as a Jewish spokesman and White House advisor who spoke "in the name of all American Jews" on issues of Jewish politics and Jewish presidential appointments. In 1897, on Wolf's recommendation, McKinley offered Solomon Hirsch the post of ambassador to Belgium, which Hirsch declined.

Throughout the 1890s and the first decade of the twentieth century, the Jewish role in American government and public life was shaped and influenced by a small group of German Jewish communal leaders and philanthropists who "by virtue of their economic standing, official post or access to power brokers and opinion molders were able to command attention for their fellow Jews from the government."[66] Jacob Schiff, Oscar Straus, Simon Wolf, Jesse Seligman, Solomon Hirsch, Judge Mayer Sulzberger, Congressman Lucius Littauer, and Louis

64. Dalin, "Presidents, Presidential Appointments, and Jews," 32.
65. Cohen, *Dual Heritage*, 77.
66. Cohen, *Encounter with Emancipation*, 232.

Fig. 15. Jacob Schiff before the Industrial Commission. Bain News Service, 1915. (Library of Congress).

Marshall, who had achieved great financial success and a considerable measure of political influence in late nineteenth-century America, were the most prominent of this group. "Bound to each other by ties of friendship, business, marriage," and affiliation with and support for the Republican Party, "they formed an intimate circle" and enjoyed a close relationship with Republican presidents.[67]

In the presidential elections of 1896 and 1900, this group of Republican Jewish notables worked together to mobilize financial and political support for William McKinley. Chief among them was Jacob Schiff (Fig. 15), head of Kuhn, Loeb and Company and the wealthiest and most influential German Jewish banker and railroad financier in the last decade of the nineteenth century. During the

67. *Ibid.*

1890s, Schiff, whose stature as a banker was second only to that of J. P. Morgan,[68] contributed generously to McKinley's campaign and rejoiced in his victory. "Would the grass look as green, the sky as blue, the people as pleasant" if the Republicans had lost, Schiff asked a business ally and friend in 1896.[69] Schiff, who occasionally advised the administration on tariff issues and monetary policy, publicly supported McKinley's re-election campaign in 1900.

Jews voted in even greater numbers for McKinley in 1900. His selection of Theodore Roosevelt as his vice-presidential running mate consolidated and increased Jewish Republican enthusiasm for the ticket. Roosevelt had enjoyed widespread support among Jews since his appointment as New York City's police commissioner in 1895. When the notorious German antisemite Hermann Ahlwardt arrived in the city that year to preach a crusade against Jews, Roosevelt assigned only Jewish policemen to guard him. As Roosevelt would later recall, Ahlwardt "made his harangue against the Jews under the active protection of some forty policemen, every one of them a Jew."[70] The Jewish community of New York loved this kind of grand political gesture and voted for the charismatic Roosevelt in great numbers when he ran for governor of New York in 1898 and then as McKinley's running mate in 1900. The fact that Ahlwardt had been a vocal supporter of William Jennings Bryan's presidential aspirations was one further reason many Jewish voters abandoned the Democratic Party to support McKinley in 1896 and 1900.

German Jewish Republicans were not alone in their enthusiastic support for Roosevelt. Yiddish-speaking east European Jewish immigrants who read the two Yiddish Republican newspapers, the *Tageblat* and the *Morning Journal*, voted for Roosevelt for governor in 1898 and for the McKinley–Roosevelt ticket in 1900. Indeed, when Roosevelt ran for governor of New York in 1898, Yiddish handbills distributed throughout the city's Lower East Side echoed the admonition of the author of *General Grant and the Jews* thirty years earlier: "every true Jew must and will vote for Theodore Roosevelt."[71]

Schiff, Straus, Wolf, Littauer, and Marshall had an especially close relationship with Roosevelt, who succeeded to the presidency after McKinley's assassination in 1901. Schiff, one of Roosevelt's foremost financial supporters, was an increasingly familiar figure in the White House, "often invited to discuss issues

68. Naomi W. Cohen, *Jacob Schiff: A Study in American Jewish Leadership* (Hanover, N.H.: University Press of New England for Brandeis University Press, 1999), 130–31.

69. *Ibid.*, 12–13, and Jacob Schiff to James J. Hill, November 9, 1896, quoted in *ibid.*, 29.

70. *Theodore Roosevelt, An Autobiography* (New York: Macmillan, 1913), 205–6.

71. Quoted in Dalin and Kolatch, *Presidents of the United States and the Jews*, 116.

of banking, railroads and regulation of corporations," as well as issues of Jewish concern, with the president and members of his cabinet. Schiff "made ready use of his entrée into government circles" to promote Jewish political interests.[72] During one White House conference in 1902, for example, Schiff told Roosevelt about a new wave of antisemitism in Romania, after which Straus, Wolf, and Congressman Littauer each contacted Roosevelt on behalf of the Jews there. At their urging, Roosevelt instructed Secretary of State John Hay to send a note of protest to the Romanian government, officially objecting to the antisemitic treatment "to which the Jews of Romania are subjected."[73]

Oscar Straus was also a close friend and an especially close political confidant of Roosevelt, whom Straus had first met and befriended in the early 1880s. In 1902, Roosevelt appointed Straus to a six-year term on the recently established Permanent Court of International Justice in The Hague. Later, in 1906, Straus accepted Roosevelt's offer to be secretary of the Department of Commerce and Labor, the first Jewish appointee to a cabinet position in American history.

Beginning with the presidential election of 1880, Louis Marshall's support for the Republican Party was especially unwavering. William Jennings Bryan's runs for president in 1896 and 1900 "decisively alienated" Marshall from the Democratic Party, which he would never again consider supporting.[74] Two weeks after the election of 1900, during which Marshall had actively campaigned for the McKinley-Roosevelt ticket, he wrote to Felix Adler, the founder of the Ethical Culture movement, "I am and have always been a Republican."[75]

Marshall (Fig. 16) was the best-known proponent of the Jewish ideal of political neutrality, a view notably similar to that of Rabbi Liebman Adler during the presidential election of 1868. As Naomi W. Cohen has cogently analyzed, Schiff, Wolf, Sulzberger, Littauer, and Straus also adhered to this conception of individual political engagement. While ready "to accept eagerly the political responsibility of voting and office-holding that citizenship entailed," these members of the German Jewish elite "laid down strict guidelines circumscribing the political activity of Jews as a group."[76] This prescription for Jewish po-

72. Cohen, *Jacob Schiff*, 130–31.

73. *Ibid.*, 131; Cohen, *Dual Heritage*, 123–26; Dalin and Kolatch, *Presidents of the United States and the Jews*, 123, 125.

74. David G. Dalin, "Louis Marshall, the Jewish Vote, and the Republican Party," *Jewish Political Studies Review* 4, no. 1 (1992): 56.

75. Louis Marshall to Felix Adler, November 19, 1900, *Louis Marshall Papers* (MS-359), series A, box 1571, Jacob Rader Marcus Center of the American Jewish Archives, Cincinnati.

76. Cohen, *Encounter with Emancipation*, 129.

Fig. 16. Louis Marshall. Photograph dating between 1910 and 1930. (Courtesy of the Adirondack Experience).

litical neutrality was predicated on the assumption that Jewish lay leaders and rabbis had no right to advise the Jewish community on how to vote. Politics "concerned the individual Jews but not the community. Jewish group interests, if indeed there were any, had no place under that name in any political forum."[77] Committed in public to this ideal, Marshall continuously called upon his fellow Jews to vote not *as Jews*, but as American citizens. Time and again, in apparent rejection of the view of Jewish politics espoused by the author of *General Grant and the Jews*, Marshall warned that in the polling booth Jews had to decide who would do the best job for the country.[78] At the same time, however, Marshall was

77. *Ibid.* 78. Dalin, "Louis Marshall," 58.

always ready to use his high standing in the Republican Party to seek support for Republican candidates "in the name of all American Jews" and to leverage the Jewish vote to urge or pressure Republican presidents and secretaries of state on issues of Jewish concern.[79]

In theory, Marshall, Schiff, Wolf, Straus, and Littauer publicly deplored the concept of a Jewish vote. In practice, however, they knew there were Jewish voters, especially among the newly enfranchised east European Jewish immigrants, who might be instructed and advised on political candidates and issues, and they not infrequently sought to undertake this task.[80] Thus, while in private they adopted the political view and tactics advocated by the author of *General Grant and the Jews*, they publicly claimed to do just the opposite.

In retrospect, the presidential election of 1868 ushered in a new era of Jewish politics and marked a coming of political age for American Jews. By engaging Jews *as Jews* on behalf of explicitly Jewish interests in the political arena, it set a precedent for Jewish participation in national politics throughout the second half of the nineteenth century. The idea that a recognized Jewish community spokesman such as Simon Wolf (or a delegation of such spokesmen) might legitimately support or oppose a political candidate or issue "in the name of all American Jews," echoing the author of *General Grant and the Jews*, shaped and influenced Jewish politics in the presidential elections of 1896, 1900, and 1904.

Between 1868 and 1900, every president with the exception of Grover Cleveland was a Republican. During this period, Jewish Republican leaders such as Simon Wolf and Jacob Schiff (and beginning in 1896, Oscar Straus) emerged as influential Jewish community spokesmen and presidential advisers, who were viewed as speaking "in the name of all American Jews." When in 1891 Wolf, Schiff, Straus, Seligman, and Marshall met, as a formal delegation of Jewish communal leaders, with President Benjamin Harrison to protest antisemitism in tsarist Russia, they were, echoing the sentiments of *General Grant and the Jews*, responding "as a class." So, too, in 1896, when the antisemitism of the Populist supporters of William Jennings Bryan was directed at Jews "as a class," Jewish Republican leaders such as Wolf, Schiff, Straus, and Marshall responded on behalf of the entire Jewish community, "in the name of all American Jews."

In the presidential campaign of 1904, thirty-six years after the author of *General Grant and the Jews* set the tone for Jewish engagement *as Jews* in politics by opposing Grant's presidential nomination, Jacob Schiff sought to speak "in

79. *Ibid.*, 56–57.

80. *Ibid.*, 61.

the name of all American Jews" by urging every "eligible Jewish voter" to support the presidential candidacy of Theodore Roosevelt. Indeed, he famously said that he could not imagine any Jewish voter not doing so.[81] Schiff, together with Oscar Straus, Simon Wolf, Lucius Littauer, and Louis Marshall, believed that Jews should (and would) engage in presidential politics *as Jews*.

81. Nathan Weyl, *The Jew in American Politics* (New Rochelle, N.Y.: Arlington House, 1968), 94.

Fig. 17. Grand Duke Aleksei. *Frank Leslie's Illustrated Newspaper*, Dec. 9, 1871, p. 208. (Library of Congress).

AMERICAN JEWS AND THE INTERNATIONAL ARENA

ELI LEDERHENDLER

DURING November and December 1871 a small Russian naval flotilla visited New York as part of a high-profile goodwill tour, following a visit by a squadron of the U.S. Navy, commanded by Admiral David G. Farragut, at the Russian capital of St. Petersburg. Arriving with the Russian expedition was the twenty-one-year-old naval lieutenant Grand Duke Alexei Alexandrovich Romanov, the fourth son of the reigning tsar, Alexander II (Fig. 17).[1] Alexei journeyed from New York for an abbreviated and rather understated visit to the White House, where he met President Ulysses S. Grant, his family, and members of Grant's cabinet. Traveling with his entourage in a private, three-carriage train, Alexei visited the U.S. Naval Academy at Annapolis, then returned to New York City, where he resumed a crowded schedule of events. The itinerary took him to West Point, Boston, Niagara Falls, Chicago, and several stops in Canada and points west, including a rousing buffalo hunt in the company of William "Buffalo Bill" Cody and General George Armstrong Custer.

Grand Duke Alexei became something of a celebrity during the tour, despite the brusqueness of his Washington reception. Apart from the carping of some skeptics, who complained about the inordinate fuss and extravagant expense squandered by a supposedly self-respecting democratic republic on a crowned European personage, the affable young man was afforded the finest royal tour that American money and hoopla could provide. He was fêted, entertained, fawned over, and shielded from possible ill-wishers.[2]

1. Aleksei and Aleksandr, respectively, are the correct transliterations from Russian, but I opt for the standard English usage, which also appears in contemporary reports. The choice in favor of Western usage applies as well to my reference below to Nicholas (Nikolai).

2. Lee Farrow, *Alexis in America: A Russian Grand Duke's Tour, 1871–1872* (Baton Rouge: Louisiana State University Press, 2014); NYU Jordan Center for the Advanced Study of Russia, web post, dated January 8, 2016: jordanrussiacenter.org/news/alexis-america-grand-tour-russian-grand-duke-1871-1872/#.XIU82GgzaUk (accessed Feb. 2, 2020); *New York Times*, November 22, 1871, 1; November 23, 1; November 24, 5; November 29, 5; December 2, 1, 5; Norman E. Saul, *Historical Dictionary of United States–Russian/Soviet Relations* (Lanham, Md.: Scarecrow Press, 2009), xxii, 13. On the reign of Alexander II in general, see Edvard Radzinsky, *Alexander II: The Last Great Tsar*, trans. Antonina W. Bouis (New York: Free Press: 2005); Geoffrey

Unbeknownst to his dazzled American hosts, the grand duke's grand tour was not just a goodwill gesture at the highest level of state diplomacy. Back home in Russia, Alexei's lover was just then giving birth to their illegitimate son. Alexei was distraught over the entire affair, for the imperial household had concocted the trip in the hope of severing the errant grand duke from a "dishonorable" match with a commoner.[3]

There were several other behind-the-scenes issues around which complications might have arisen. For one, Russian-American diplomacy was just then under a cloud in Washington, owing to persistent friction with the Russian ambassador, whose recall the Americans were demanding; hence the somewhat subdued tenor of Alexei's White House reception. Also, there were indeed ill-wishers. Specifically, some Polish patriots in the United States reportedly sought an occasion for causing bodily harm, or worse, to the son of the Russian emperor. These events took place, after all, a scant eight years after the Russian regime's repression of the latest Polish insurrection in 1863. With this categorical assertion of imperial power, Russia doomed Polish nationalists' aspirations for (at the very least) a greater measure of home rule under the Romanov crown—aspirations that remained unrealized until Poland's independence was restored in 1919 upon the demise of the Russian empire.[4]

In that somewhat uncertain, not to say sensitive, context Alexei became the object of attention of the worthy members of the Board of Delegates of Ameri-

---

Hosking, *Russia: People and Empire, 1552–1917* (Cambridge, Mass.: Harvard University Press, 1998).

3. Farrow, *Alexis in America.*

4. Norman Davies, *God's Playground: A History of Poland,* rev. ed., vol. 2, *1795 to the Present* (Oxford and New York: Oxford University Press, 2005), 256–71; Stephen R. Burant, "The January Uprising of 1863 in Poland: Sources of Disaffection and the Arenas of Revolt," *European Historical Quarterly* 15, no. 2 (1985): 131–56. On American-related aspects, see John Kutolowski, "The Effect of the Polish Insurrection of 1863 on American Civil War Diplomacy," *The Historian* 27, no. 4 (1965): 560–77; Joseph Wieczerzak, "American Reactions to the Polish Insurrection of 1863," *Polish-American Studies* 22, no. 2 (1965): 90–98; George L. Lerski, "Jewish-Polish Amity in Lincoln's America," *Polish Review* 18, no. 4 (1973): 34–51. The post-1863 russification campaign against the free expression of Polish culture incidentally reinforced Jewish literary and journalistic activities in the Russian language. Another spinoff of the Polish defeat was the development of a Jewish "positivist" school of secular thought that paralleled similar trends among the Polish intellectual elite. See Timothy Snyder, *The Reconstruction of Nations: Poland, Ukraine, Lithuania, Belarus, 1569–1999* (New Haven and London: Yale University Press, 2003), 30–32; Theodore R. Weeks, "Russification: Word and Practice, 1863–1914," *Proceedings of the American Philosophical Society* 148, no. 4 (2004): 471–89; Eliyahu Stern, *Jewish Materialism: The Intellectual Revolution of the 1870s* (New Haven and London: Yale University Press, 2018).

can Israelites, led by its secretary, Myer Samuel Isaacs (1841–1904). The Board, initially organized in 1859 amid the public uproar over the infamous Mortara case in Italy, represented a coalition of Jewish congregations and claimed to speak in the name of collective Jewish interests, particularly regarding issues that troubled Jews living in other lands.[5] After the Civil War, the group was active in mounting vocal protests against anti-Jewish actions and policies in the Turkish empire and Romania (then still under the titular suzerainty of the Turks), in Russia, and in North Africa. In 1869 the Board, along with B'nai B'rith, petitioned the Grant administration to object through official channels to the Russian authorities' intent to oust Jews from territory along the newly renegotiated Russian-Romanian border. The expulsion order applied to Jewish residents who had recently settled along the western edge of the province of Bessarabia (modern Moldova), including the city of Kishinev.[6]

Figuring just as prominently in the news of that time and highlighted in Jewish protests was the matter of Romania's Jews, who still suffered under second-class status and were the target of violent attacks (to be discussed later). By 1871, with the adoption in January of that year of the new German empire's constitution, the only countries of Europe in which significant numbers of

5. Bertram Wallace Korn, *The American Reaction to the Mortara Case, 1858–1859* (Cincinnati: American Jewish Archives, 1957). Myer S. Isaacs was the son of the prominent New York Jewish spiritual leader Samuel Myer Isaacs. Dutch-born, the elder Isaacs had lived in London before immigrating to America in 1839. Although not an ordained rabbi, he served as the religious leader (preacher and *hazan* [cantor]) of the Orthodox Ashkenazi ("German") B'nai Jeshurun congregation in New York, and afterward of the breakaway Anglo-Dutch Orthodox congregation Temple Shaaray Tefila. A cofounder of the Board of Delegates, he was also remembered as an officiant at the funeral of Abraham Lincoln and as the founder and editor of the New York *Jewish Messenger* (1867–1878). See the "Historical Note" to the *Records of the Board of Delegates of American Israelites* (I-2), Center for Jewish History, American Jewish Historical Society (AJHS), New York, https://archives.cjh.org/repositories/3/resources/13256 (accessed March 11, 2021). See also the Myer Isaacs Collection (P-2), Center for Jewish History, AJHS; Robert P. Swierenga, "Samuel Myer Isaacs: The Dutch Rabbi of New York City," *American Jewish Archives Journal* 44, no. 2 (1992): 607–21.

6. Robert Jensen, "The Politics of Discrimination: America, Russia, and the Jewish Question 1869–1872," *American Jewish History* 75, no. 3 (1986): 280–95; Evelyin Levow Greenberg, "An 1869 Petition on Behalf of Russian Jews," *American Jewish Historical Quarterly* 54, no. 3 (1965): 278–95; Eliyahu Feldman, "Hanisayon harishon shel pe'ulah amerikayit lema'an yehudei rusiyah (1869–70) [The First Attempt at American Action on Behalf of Russia's Jews, 1869–70]," *Ziyyon* 30 (1965): 206–23. On the Board of Delegates in general, see Jonathan D. Sarna, *American Judaism* (New Haven and London: Yale University Press, 2004), 110–11; Allan Tarshish, "The Board of Delegates of American Israelites (1859–1878)," *Publications of the American Jewish Historical Society* 49, no. 1 (1959): 16–32. For the Board's activities at the time, see the Records of the Board of Delegates of American Israelites, series V, boxes 4, OS1, OS2.

Jews were living, but where they as a group were not recognized as equal in civil status along with Christians of similar social rank, were Russia and Romania.[7] Moreover, these Jews were saddled with broadly discriminatory disadvantages. These incipient signs of a major "Jewish Question" in eastern Europe furnished the occasion for American Jewish leaders to try their hand at public diplomacy.

For the historian, there are at least two issues at stake in closely examining this turn of events. First, as I have maintained elsewhere, American Jewish history does not stop at the American border. Indeed, a distinctive characteristic of the Jews in America, more apparent when compared with other American ethnic groups, is that they conceived and preserved a persistent concern for Jews abroad that spanned several generations; and this "European nexus" prompted them to speak and act on the world stage, even when neither they nor their forebears had originated from the countries or communities that elicited their concern.[8] This pattern was in the process of being established during the events to be discussed below, which may, therefore, be regarded as precedent setting.

The second metahistorical issue at stake here is what R. Laurence Moore referred to in his classic essay, "Insiders and Outsiders in American Historical Narrative and American History."[9] The initiative, mobilized resources,

7. There were some exceptions, hence my qualification regarding "significant numbers of Jews." For example, the tiny Jewish population of Switzerland, numbering about 7,000, waited until 1866 to be granted the right to settle at will anywhere in the country, and their citizenship and religious freedom would not be constitutionally recognized until 1874. Starting in the early 1850s, the lower status of Jews under Swiss law had become an issue in American, American Jewish, and British circles. Jews in America protested against the 1854 U.S.-Swiss Treaty of Friendship, which extended privileges only to Christian U.S. citizens visiting Switzerland. See Lance J. Sussman, *Isaac Leeser and the Making of American Judaism* (Detroit: Wayne State University Press, 1995), 212–13; Natalie Isser, "Diplomatic Intervention and Human Rights: The Swiss Question, 1852–1864," *Journal of Church and State* 35, no. 3 (1993): 577–91; Cyrus Adler and Aaron M. Margalith, *With Firmness in the Right: American Diplomatic Action Affecting Jews, 1840–1946* (New York: American Jewish Committee, 1946), 299–322; Lucien Wolf, *Notes on the Diplomatic History of the Jewish Question* (London: Jewish Historical Society of England, 1919), 65–68; Sol M. Stroock, "Switzerland and American Jews," *Publications of the American Jewish Historical Society*, no. 11 (1903): 7–52; Marcus Lipton, "The Jewish Question in Anglo-Swiss Diplomacy," *Transactions* (Jewish Historical Society of England) 10 (1921–1923): 207–20.

8. Eli Lederhendler, *American Jewry: A New History* (Cambridge and New York: Cambridge University Press, 2018), xiii, xiv, xix, 190–247. Cf. Naomi W. Cohen, "American Jewish Reactions to Anti-Semitism in Western Europe, 1875–1900," *Proceedings of the American Academy for Jewish Research* 45 (1978): 29–65.

9. R. Laurence Moore, "Insiders and Outsiders in American Historical Narrative and American History," *American Historical Review* 87, no. 2 (1982): 390–412.

and sense of entitlement required on the part of Jews in the United States, members of a small religious minority, in order to project their parochial concerns onto the American public stage present a question of narrative ambiguity. Were they "insiders" working within the "mainstream" of American society? Or were they using their "outsider" status to effect change, raising grievances in the name of Jewish "victimhood" in order to shake up the established order?

Moore contended that narratives of American history in which the issues hinge on demonstrating the marginalization of "others" by a hegemonic, white, Christian, male, and affluent upper caste run the risk of missing what is "mainstream" in the behavior and rhetoric of "outsiders." The opposite approach, however—"mainstreaming" the history of small groups who vocally challenge hegemonic institutions and who demand change (from within? from without?)—not only misses seeing the "others" as a category that must be treated as such, but may also overlook the significance of how, when, and why those "others" choose to assert the agenda of victimhood as a part of their self-construction. As Moore noted, "An outsider identification pursued by a group over time can provide the group with well-recognized social status within the structure of existing social arrangements."[10]

Further to Moore's argument, in the final years of the twentieth century and at the beginning of the new millennium, the oxymoronic doubling of the Jews' status inside/outside the general social and political realm has become an often-featured trope, and several historians have placed the insider-outsider ambiguity at the very core of the American Jewish case.[11] Marc Dollinger and Michael Alexander, respectively, phrased the issue in terms of the Jews' pursuit of "inclusion," on the one hand and, on the other, as a "downward identification" with victimhood, enacted within an experience of greater social acceptance.[12] The present essay is part of this long, continuing discussion.

10. *Ibid.*, 391–95, 399–403, quotation at 404.

11. *Insider/Outsider: American Jews and Multiculturalism*, ed. David Biale, Michael Galchinsky, and Susannah Heschel (Berkeley: University of California Press, 1998); Hasia R. Diner, *A Time for Gathering: The Second Migration, 1820–1880*, vol. 2 of *The Jewish People in America*, ed. Henry L. Feingold (Baltimore and London: Johns Hopkins University Press, 1992), chap. 8 ("Inside/Outside"). Note also *Insiders and Outsiders: Dilemmas of East European Jewry*, ed. Richard I. Cohen, Jonathan Frankel, and Stefani Hoffman (Portland, Ore.: Littman Library of Jewish Civilization, 2010).

12. Marc Dollinger, *Quest for Inclusion: Jews and Liberalism in Modern America* (Princeton: Princeton University Press, 2000); Michael Alexander, *Jazz Age Jews* (Princeton: Princeton University Press, 2001).

Emancipation Now! American Jews and Public Diplomacy

The records of the Board of Delegates contain a ceremonial testament of welcome addressed to the visiting grand duke (who was commonly known abroad as Alexis). The message in full reads as follows (Fig. 18):

> *To His Imperial Highness the Grand Duke Alexis*
>
> In common with other bodies of citizens of the United States, the BOARD OF DELEGATES OF AMERICAN ISRAELITES proffer your Imperial Highness a cordial welcome to these shores.
>
> RECOGNIZING in the Emperor of Russia, your august father, a sovereign who has devoted himself to the WELFARE OF HIS PEOPLE and under whose reign the BLESSINGS OF LIBERTY have been extended to millions and the condition of our brethren in faith has perceptibly improved, we pay our respects to you as the representative of the Czar as endowed by Heaven with great opportunities for the good of mankind.
>
> THE PROGRESS made in the imperial dominions since the accession of the good Czar, your father, encourages us to hope that every vestige of discrimination against the Jews of Russia will soon be swept away and that relieved from the prejudice against them which yet lingers in the minds of the populace in some of the provinces, our brethren will occupy a position commensurate with their morality and intellectual ability.
>
> WE PRAY that you will preserve with other recollections of your sojourn in this country, the impressions conveyed of the capacity of Israelites to become useful citizens, and that on your return to your home, your generous influence will be exerted to second the Imperial measures *for the complete emancipation of the Jews of Russia* [emphasis added].
>
> New York, December 1, 1871 — for the Executive Committee,
> Board of Delegates of American Israelites
>
> Myer S. Isaacs, Secretary[13]

The salutation, bearing the seal of the Board of Delegates and clearly intended for formal presentation at a public meeting with the imperial Russian entourage, is safely stored in the archives of the American Jewish Historical Society, which raises the question of whether in fact it was ever actually delivered to the grand duke. Although I have found no evidence to confirm such an event, it is conceivable that the document in New York is a copy, the original of which was tendered to Alexei. Whatever the case may be, the text holds a great deal of interest as a reflection of Jewish political sensibility. Its phrasing lends color,

13. Records of the Board of Delegates of American Israelites, box OS2.

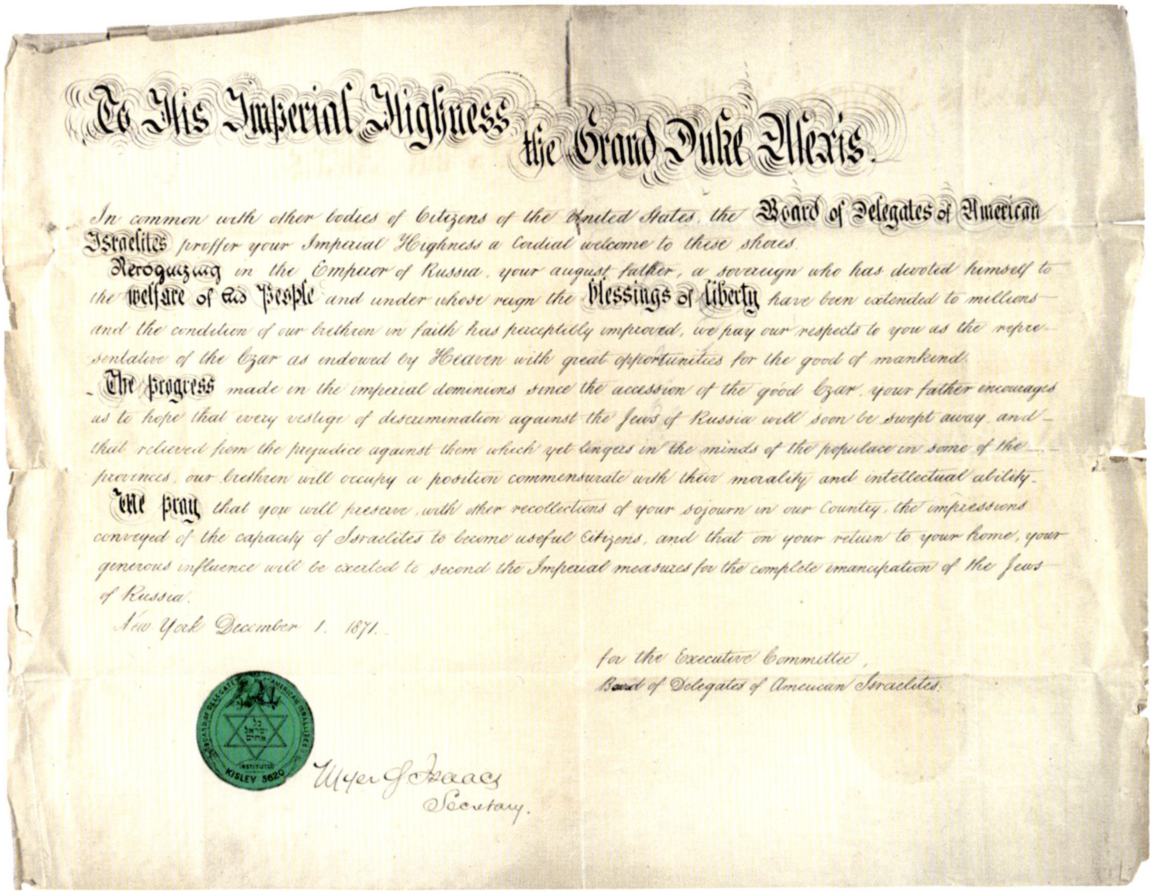

To His Imperial Highness the Grand Duke Alexis.

In common with other bodies of Citizens of the United States, the Board of Delegates of American Israelites proffer your Imperial Highness a cordial welcome to these shores.

Recognizing in the Emperor of Russia, your august father, a sovereign who has devoted himself to the welfare of his People and under whose reign the blessings of Liberty have been extended to millions and the condition of our brethren in faith has perceptibly improved, we pay our respects to you as the representative of the Czar as endowed by Heaven with great opportunities for the good of mankind.

The progress made in the imperial dominions since the accession of the good Czar, your father encourages us to hope that every vestige of discrimination against the Jews of Russia will soon be swept away, and that relieved from the prejudice against them which yet lingers in the minds of the populace in some of the provinces, our brethren will occupy a position commensurate with their morality and intellectual ability.

We pray that you will preserve, with other recollections of your sojourn in our Country, the impressions conveyed of the capacity of Israelites to become useful Citizens, and that on your return to your home, your generous influence will be exerted to second the Imperial measures for the complete emancipation of the Jews of Russia.

New York December 1. 1871.

for the Executive Committee,
Board of Delegates of American Israelites.

Board of Delegates of American Israelites — Instituted Kislev 5620

Myer S. Isaacs
Secretary.

Fig. 18. Ceremonial testament of welcome, addressed to Grand Duke Alexei, from the Board of Delegates of American Israelites. Records of the Board of Delegates of American Israelites, series V, box OS2, American Jewish Historical Society. (Photo courtesy of the American Jewish Historical Society).

character, and detail to an array of other actions (to be sketched in as we go along) that were carried out in the public arena during those years.

The timing of the imperial visit is pointedly relevant. Russia was still attempting to recover politically, economically, and militarily from its stinging defeat in the Crimean War (1853–1856) and was eager to reinforce its ties with various Western countries, including the United States. In that context, Russia had supported the Union during the Civil War. Memorably also, Russia had sold Alaska to the United States, and the transfer took effect in October 1867.

Alexander II, who had succeeded his father, Nicholas I, in 1855 under the cloud of the unsuccessful military campaign, opened his reign with an ambitious agenda of domestic reform, symbolized most famously by the abolition of serfdom in February 1861—two years before Abraham Lincoln's Emancipation Proclamation. It was to this act of manumission that the Board's memorial chiefly alluded when it cited "the progress made in the imperial dominions since the accession of the good Czar, your father," and rejoiced in "the blessings of liberty [that] have been extended to millions." Pertinent as well, Alexander considerably eased some of Nicholas's draconian policies in areas such as censorship of the press, education, and the judiciary. Under the relaxed press laws, for example, a new and vibrant Jewish periodical literature emerged in Russia, with publications in Hebrew, Russian, Yiddish, and eventually Polish.[14]

Among the beneficiaries of these Great Reforms were the Jews living in the Pale of Settlement, and the Board's message subsumed the idealization of Alexander's reforms when it gratefully acknowledged that "the condition of our brethren in faith has perceptibly improved." Jews also reaped the boon of the "tsar-liberator's" overhaul of the onerous, sometimes punitive forms of military conscription, which were common abuses in the first half of the nineteenth century. Announced on the occasion of Alexander's coronation, the measures ended the dreaded impressment of child-recruits (sometimes younger than twelve

14. For a brief summary of the period, see Olga Litvak, "Russian and Soviet Jewry," in *The Cambridge History of Judaism*, vol. 8, *The Modern World, 1815–2000*, ed. Mitchell B. Hart and Tony Michels (Cambridge and New York: Cambridge University Press, 2017), 51–55. Cf. Werner E. Mosse, *Alexander II and the Modernization of Russia*, rev. ed. (New York: Collier Books, 1967); John Doyle Klier, *Imperial Russia's Jewish Question, 1855–1881* (Cambridge and New York: Cambridge University Press, 1995); Eli Lederhendler, *The Road to Modern Jewish Politics: Political Tradition and Political Reconstruction in the Jewish Community of Tsarist Russia* (Oxford and New York: Oxford University Press, 1989), 111–53; Benjamin Nathans, *Beyond the Pale: The Jewish Encounter with Late Imperial Russia* (Berkeley: University of California Press, 2002), 31, 45–72; Benjamin Pinkus, *The Jews of the Soviet Union: The History of a National Minority* (Cambridge and New York: Cambridge University Press, 1988), 20–22; Hans Rogger, *Jewish Policies and Right-Wing Politics in Imperial Russia* (Berkeley: University of California Press, 1986), 12–13, 16; Brian Horowitz, *Jewish Philanthropy and Enlightenment in Late-Tsarist Russia* (Seattle: University of Washington Press, 2009), esp. 20–21, 29–31, 55–56, 61–63. On Jews in the imperial army, see Yohanan Petrovsky-Shtern, *Jews in the Russian Army, 1827–1917: Drafted into Modernity* (Cambridge and New York: Cambridge University Press, 2009), 1–8, 29–73, 90–130; Olga Litvak, *Conscription and the Search for Modern Russian Jewry* (Bloomington: Indiana University Press, 2006); Michael Stanislawski, *Tsar Nicholas I and the Jews: The Transformation of Jewish Society in Russia, 1825–1855* (Philadelphia: Jewish Publication Society of America, 1983), 25–34, 184; Nathans, *Beyond the Pale*, 27–29, 37–38, 45–47; Lederhendler, *Road to Modern Jewish Politics*, 64–67. For a perception of Alexander II's reforms from the point of view of a Jewish woman in White Russia (Belarus), see Pauline Wengeroff, *Memoirs of a Grandmother: Scenes from the Cultural History of the Jews of Russia in the Nineteenth Century*, vol. 2, trans. Shulamit S. Magnus (Stanford: Stanford University Press, 2014), esp. 107–8.

years of age) for twenty-five years of service, haunted by the specter of forced baptisms, in the infamous "cantonist" cadet schools and army units.[15] Emma Lazarus, who will figure later on in this discussion, eulogized Alexander II, following his assassination in March 1881, perpetuating his image as an emancipator-tsar. In her poem "Sic Semper Liberatoribus!" ("It is always the liberators"), she wrote: "What alien current urged on to smite him dead | Whose word had loosed a million Russian chains?"[16]

The Board of Delegates' address in 1871 to the tsar-liberator (via the youthful grand duke) was complimentary and deferential—quite as one would expect, given the mannered courtliness demanded of such an occasion. In contrast to some contemporary declarations, resolutions, and diplomatic protests against discriminatory policies and actions aimed against Jews, this salutation reduced the hint of protest to a fleeting, almost apologetic reference to "vestige[s] of discrimination against the Jews of Russia." The effusiveness of this letter should be compared with the tone of the note addressed by Myer Isaacs two years earlier to the U.S. State Department, which was no less polite but rather more candid in recounting the reported Bessarabian expulsions. Responsibility was laid squarely at the feet of the Russian sovereign: "An ancient ukase of Russia has been enforced so as to exile two thousand Bessarabian Jews into the interior of the Empire.... [R]ecognizing the great moral influence our government may exercise in advising the Emperor of Russia, through our Minister near St. Petersburgh [*sic*], that such a ukase is contrary to the spirit of justice and civilization, I am directed to ask of your Department its characteristic kindly interest in behalf of the distressed."[17]

The next day, on November 30, 1869, President Grant received Isaacs and other members of a Jewish delegation, who presented him with a petition that forwarded the notion that Alexander II, as an enlightened reformer, should be expected to live up to more liberal standards than those prevailing among the uneducated masses. It explicitly acknowledged that "we well know, that it is against the policy of this Government to interfere with the internal affairs of any other people," but went on to an uncompromising condemna-

15. American Jewish historians should bear in mind this chronology in light of popular myths in Jewish immigrant memoirs, which erroneously project the cantonist episode forward into the 1880s as an explanation for the desire to emigrate.

16. Quoted in Bette Roth Young, "Emma Lazarus and Her Jewish Problem," *American Jewish History* 84, no. 4 (1996): 298.

17. M. S. Isaacs to Secretary of State Hamilton Fish, November 29, 1869, reproduced in Greenberg, "An 1860 Petition," 284.

tion: "yet there are crimes committed in the name of municipal jurisdiction, that by their nature and magnitude become offences against humanity, and thus are violations and infractions of the law of nations."[18] Blunt speech was also evident in a resolution adopted in the House of Representatives in May 1872 to condemn anti-Jewish abuses occurring in Romania. Proposed by Congressman Samuel S. Cox (D, New York) and unanimously consented to by the House, it minced no words: "Be it resolved. That the President of the United States be respectfully requested to join with the Italian Government in its protest against the intolerant and cruel treatment of the Jews of Roumania [*sic*]."[19]

Despite the softened tone of the 1871 welcoming note, its subtext was subtly astute and, I would argue, unexpectedly daring. Consider, for instance, the way it brandished compliments to Alexander II, imputing to the tsar-liberator a commitment to enlightened humanistic values ("the blessings of liberty ... the good of mankind")—deployed here as a reciprocal, common denominator linking America (and America's Jews) and the Russian emperor. The text follows up on the compliment by implying that the tsar is obliged to honor his own principles with "complete emancipation" for his Jewish subjects. The message then segues smoothly, but with unmistakable condescension, to characterizing the anti-Jewish attitudes prevalent in Russia as a "prejudice ... which yet lingers in the minds of the populace in some of the provinces"—"prejudice," "populace," and "some of the provinces" being coded terms to acknowledge that such benighted opinions could be attributed only to the common riffraff far removed from the centers of enlightened policy and generally accepted notions of civilization. Hence, such attitudes must be reckoned as inconsistent with the magnanimous spirit of the tsar's other policies (the Polish issue, naturally, being absent here!). Correspondingly, and in deliberate counterpoint, the letter proffers the opinion that "our brethren" stand on a higher plane in terms of "their morality and intellectual ability" and, hence, ought to be viewed not only as meriting civil liberties as a matter of principle but also as deserving of better treatment by reason of their virtuous and refined character. Gingerly, but rather creatively, the document aimed to burnish the reputation of the Jews at the tacit expense of simple Russians of the "provinces."

18. Petition to President Grant, November 1869, Miscellaneous Correspondence of the State Department, Part 11, National Archives, Record Group 59, reproduced in Greenberg, "An 1869 Petition," 280. Cf. Jonathan D. Sarna, *When General Grant Expelled the Jews* (New York: Nextbook/Schocken, 2012), 99–102.

19. *The Congressional Globe*, 42d Congress, 2d sess., May 20, 1872, vol. 45, p. 3655.

Salient, too, is the specific use of the term *emancipation*, so resonant in the American milieu of that time, as well as fully attuned to the epithet with which Alexander II was extolled as the ruler who freed Russia's peasants from servitude. Although it is clear, in historical retrospect, that there are substantive conceptual difficulties in any attempt to apply the term *emancipation* to the Russian Jewish case,[20] it is also clear that the American and generally Western Jewish rhetoric of the day did not appreciate these analytical distinctions and, rather, conceived and spoke of the Russian Jewish issue in the terms most familiar to them.

Finally, we ought also to consider the self-flattery and the sense of privilege that are implied in the last sentence: "that you will preserve with other recollections of your sojourn in this country, the impressions conveyed of the capacity of Israelites to become useful citizens."

As a deliberately crafted piece of Jewish apologetics, calibrated to woo the Russian emperor (via his globe-trotting son), the Board of Delegates salutation displays many characteristics of its day and age. It is, nonetheless, an early example of what would come to be called "public diplomacy." I use the term here as a way to allude to the open contest for political interests, a contest in which interested parties within civil society ("public opinion" or, in our case, Jewish spokespersons) become engaged in the "project" of international relations, an effort that could no longer be limited to the exclusive purview of government officials.[21] In that sense, "public diplomacy" is not merely the notion that international exchanges must be "open to public scrutiny," which was the more restricted meaning of the phrase in its first-ever recorded American usage, coincidentally enunciated in the year 1871 by Congressman Samuel S. Cox.[22]

20. Nathans, *Beyond the Pale*, 6, 10, 23–24, 49, 67, 75–79.

21. "Public diplomacy," though it has a venerable history as a phenomenon, is of fairly recent vintage as a term used in international relations, and therefore I use it consciously as an anachronism. *The Oxford Handbook of Modern Diplomacy* defines "public diplomacy" as "an instrument used by states, associations of states, and some sub-state and non-state actors to understand cultures, attitudes, and behaviour; build and manage relationships; and influence thoughts and mobilize actions to advance their interests and values. It is therefore ... a metaphor for the democratization of diplomacy, with multiple actors playing a role in what was once an area restricted to a few." Jan Melissen, "Public Diplomacy," in *Oxford Handbook of Modern Diplomacy*, ed. Andrew F. Cooper, Jorge Heine, and Ramesh Thakur (Oxford: Oxford University Press, 2013).

22. Nicholas J. Cull, "Public Diplomacy Before Gullion," in *Routledge Handbook of Public Diplomacy*, ed. Nancy Snow and Philip M. Taylor (New York and London: Routledge/Taylor and Francis, 2009), 19. The quote by Representative Cox is from the *New York Times*, January 20, 1871, 2. As Nicholas Cull puts it, Cox "spoke in high dudgeon against secret intrigue to annex the Republic of Dominica, noting he believed in 'open, public diplomacy.'"

Rather, my intent is to include the active role of members of the public in the open pursuit of political change around the world.[23]

American Jewry's Emergence in the World Jewish Context

During the years of Reconstruction and on into the Gilded Age, the American Jewish community absorbed an ever-increasing flow of new immigrants. Their greater numbers augmented American Jews' role in world Jewish affairs. It is estimated that by 1881, just before the annual influx surged forward significantly, there were about a quarter million Jews in the United States, roughly half the estimated number of Jews in Germany or, to cite another comparison, about one-third the number of Jews living in the Austrian-ruled provinces of Galicia (a territory divided today between Poland and Ukraine).[24] Like other sizeable Jewish communities at that time, particularly in countries where a developed civil society and parliamentary regimes existed and where an affluent group of citizens contended for leadership within the community, U.S. Jewry was emerging as a politically aware and civically active group. As in France, England, Germany, Austria-Hungary, and Russia, where Jewish initiatives led to the creation of, for example, the Anglo-Jewish Association and the Israelitisch Allianz zu Wien, American Jewish figures, committees, and journals aimed to project an audible Jewish voice in public affairs.[25]

23. I rely on one of the early academic definitions of "public diplomacy" in a brochure issued in 1965 by Edmund Gullion, dean of the Fletcher School of Law and Diplomacy at Tufts University and founder of the Edward R. Murrow Center of Public Diplomacy: "Public diplomacy ... encompasses dimensions of international relations beyond traditional diplomacy; the cultivation by governments of public opinion in other countries; the interaction of private groups and interests in one country with another ... and the process of intercultural communication." Quoted in Cull, "Public Diplomacy Before Gullion," 19.

24. On Jewish population figures of the nineteenth century, see: Gustav Adolf Schimmer, *Statistik des Judenthums in den im Reichsrathe Vertretenen Königreichen und Ländern* (Vienna: K. K. Statistischen Central-Commission, 1873), 4; Jits van Straten and Harmen Snel, "The Jewish 'Demographic Miracle' in Nineteenth-Century Europe: Fact or Fiction?" *Historical Methods, A Journal of Quantitative and Interdisciplinary History* 39, no. 3 (2006): 123–31. Cf. Sergio DellaPergola, "Changing Patterns of Jewish Demography in the Modern World," *Studia Rosenthaliana* 23 (1989): 154–74.

25. Lisa Moses Leff, *Sacred Bonds of Solidarity: The Rise of Jewish Internationalism in Nineteenth-Century France* (Stanford: Stanford University Press, 2006); Abigail Green, "Old Networks, New Connections: The Emergence of the Jewish International," in *Religious Internationals in the Modern World: Globalization and Faith Communities since 1750*, ed. Abigail Green and Vincent Viaene (New York: Palgrave Macmillan, 2012), 53–81; Horowitz, *Jewish Philanthropy and Enlightenment*; Rachel Manekin, *Yehudei galitsiya vehaḥukah haostrit: Reishitah shel politikah yehudit modernit* [Gali-

The documents discussed above, related to the Board of Delegates of American Israelites, were not isolated American forays into public diplomacy. Rather, they attest to a wider mobilization of Jewish notables and public opinion. The Board was, in fact, formally affiliated with the French Alliance Israélite Universelle (AIU), established in Paris in 1860, which sought broad amelioration of Jewish civil and social status in lands where masses of Jews were subject to discriminatory political and socioeconomic conditions.[26] Thus, the emergent voices of American Jewish international activism fit quite naturally within the patterns set by other emancipated Jewries and, in retrospect, may be considered as an early prefiguring of the larger role that American Jewish groups and individual leaders would come to play in world Jewish affairs in the following century. Still, during the second half of the nineteenth century and right up to World War I, the European groups usually proved to be far more effective. They worked more steadily and intensively, partly for reasons growing out of their countries' deep involvement, as imperial powers, across the far reaches of Europe, Asia, and North Africa. They were also far better able to sustain their own existence as organizations, situated at the top of a pyramid-like communal structure dominated by a central elite.

As in America, the leaders of Europe's Jews were also rather new on the scene. They tended to represent the less traditional, more secularized, and more civically integrated ranks of the upper bourgeoisie, allied with a new meritocracy of journalists, lawyers, writers, and physicians. The era's new Jewish leaders were devoted to an ideal of personal activism within the predominant public culture of their countries and their social and professional milieux. Their approach to Jewish affairs drew inspiration from modern ideologies of legal parity and democratic rights. Along with many other, less well-remembered Jewish

---

cian Jews and the Austrian Constitution: The Beginning of Modern Jewish Politics] (Jerusalem: Zalman Shazar Center for Research in Jewish History, 2015); Jonathan Frankel, "Jewish Politics and the Press: The 'Reception' of the Alliance Israélite Universelle (1860)," *Jewish History* 14, no. 1 (2000): 29–50; Jonathan Frankel, *The Damascus Affair: "Ritual Murder," Politics, and the Jews in 1840* (Cambridge and New York: Cambridge University Press, 1997); Shulamit Volkov, "Mif'al hamoderniyut shel yehudei eiropah: Piẓul ve`aḥidut" [The European Jewish Project of Modernity: Fragmentation and Solidarity], in *Haẓiyonut ve-haḥazarah lahistoriyah: Ha'arakhah meḥadash* [Zionism and the Return to History: A Reevaluation], ed. S. N. Eisenstadt and Moshe Lissak (Jerusalem: Yad Ben-Zvi, 1999), 292–93.

26. The AJHS "Historical Note" to the records of the Board of Delegates states, "As a dues[-paying] and alms constituent of the Alliance Universelle, the goals and aims of the Board of Delegates converged greatly with those of the Alliance, [as well as parallel Jewish defense and welfare organizations in other lands:] the Anglo-Jewish Association, the Roumanian Committee, the Israelitisch Allianz zu Wien, and the Board of Deputies [of British Jews]."

advocates, Adolphe Crémieux (1796–1880)—an attorney, public activist, founder of the AIU, and briefly a minister in the French government—best personified the new European Jewish leadership of that era.[27] Yet these "new" leaders were still unmistakably European, embedded within a Jewish legacy that included a tradition of patronage politics. They were able to co-opt, if not entirely to displace, the legitimate heads of an official, state-recognized "Jewry," an entity acknowledged in various forms under public law in countries where, unlike the United States, organized and established religion retained a recognized place in the governmental system. That structure included, among other things, registration (births, marriages), tithing of citizens according to religious affiliation, a tax-supported clergy, and institutionalized sectarianism in such areas of life as education.

American Jewish leaders operated in a very different environment and in a markedly more improvised manner. Even with the leadership of prominent figures in the Jewish community, such organizations as the Board of Delegates of American Israelites were far less able to direct a domestic Jewish infrastructure that was embraced and accepted by the larger community. By the same token, they were not demonized in the antisemitic press, as were the Rothschilds and the AIU, as representing a "powerful" clique with designs on manipulating the politics of the nation.[28]

Nonetheless, the foreign interventions of American Jews and Jewish organizations played a crucial role in American Jewish life for the very reason that overseas activism was one of the only available platforms for the expression of Jewish solidarity across congregational and denominational lines. American Jewry was very decentralized compared with most of Europe's Jewish communities. There, Jewish communal solidarity was reinforced by the collective answerability of all Jews to the heads of their communities, who, in turn, were answerable to state authorities. In America, by contrast, Jews were never collectively congregated under a state-supervised, super-communal apparatus. They had no consolidated rabbinical establishment; nor did they possess a European-style coterie of (en)titled nobility that could adopt a patronage model for Jewish public life.[29]

American Jews' leadership patterns were individualistic rather than dynastic,

27. Michael Graetz, *The Jews in Nineteenth-Century France: From the French Revolution to the Alliance israélite universelle*, trans. Jane Marie Todd (Stanford: Stanford University Press, 1996).

28. Leff, *Sacred Bonds of Solidarity*, chap. 6.

29. For these and further comments on the changing structure of Jewish political activism, see Eli Lederhendler, "Shtadlanut and Stewardship: Paternal Diplomacy and Leadership in American Jewry, 1860s to 1920s," *Jewish Culture and History* 19, no. 1 (2018): 97–110.

and their organizational structures were diffused rather than centralized. The advantages of status that came with enhanced financial means, compounded by an ethos of co-responsibility—reinforced by social distinctions defining Jews' relations with non-Jews—enabled American Jews to develop leaders and consultative bodies in a non-hierarchical fashion. When those leaders' and those organizations' activities crystallized around foreign Jews' problems, this arrangement conferred upon them a sense of corporate identity that otherwise nearly always eluded them. Averse to acknowledging that this mission represented a form of politics and favoring instead a stance of moral advocacy, they invoked the urgency of helping their brethren abroad without, at the same time, defining themselves as a political interest group.[30]

It is significant in this regard that one of the key cofounders of the Board of Delegates of American Israelites, Samuel M. Isaacs, consciously and vocally separated the project of international intervention from any notion of partisan "politicking" and similarly declined to invoke communal discipline to rally a hypothetical constituency of Jewish voters. During the 1868 presidential campaign, when the question of Ulysses S. Grant's attitude toward Jews was brought into play by Democratic Party supporters and given public resonance by Isaac Mayer Wise, Samuel M. Isaacs (a firm opponent of Wise's Reform Judaism) rejected out of hand the notion that Jews should take a "Jewish" position or coalesce around a "Jewish issue": "Israelites are too intelligent and too self-asserting to be driven, or led by their ministers, especially in matters that have no connection with religion."[31]

As other historians have pointed out, there were at least two good reasons why American Jewish leaders of that day might have opposed "mixing politics with religion" in the domestic sphere. One entailed their anxiety over a backlash if Jews as a group were to close ranks for a political purpose. Although not as virulent as in Europe, anti-Jewish sentiment had surfaced in the United States during the Civil War.[32] The second source of resistance arose from a theologically

30. Lederhendler, *American Jewry*, 191–92; Lederhendler, "Shtadlanut and Stewardship," 99–100.

31. Quoted in Joakim Isaacs, "Candidate Grant and the Jews," *American Jewish Archives* 17, no. 1 (1965): 12; Sarna, *When General Grant Expelled the Jews*, 50–79; Joseph Lebowich, "General Ulysses S. Grant and the Jews," *Publications of the American Jewish Historical Society*, no. 17 (1909): 73–76.

32. One of the classic discussions of this issue is John Higham, "Anti-Semitism in the Gilded Age: A Reinterpretation," *Mississippi Valley Historical Review* 43, no. 4 (1957): esp. 564–66. Cf. Leonard Dinnerstein, *Antisemitism in America* (New York and Oxford: Oxford University Press, 1994), 40; Jonathan D. Sarna, "The 'Mythical Jew' and the 'Jew Next Door' in Nineteenth-

divided Jewish clergy, keen to oppose any encroachment upon their individual opinions or their denominational autonomy if any one Jewish body, self-nominated to speak in the name of "American Judaism," should presume to issue statements on its own authority. The Board of Delegates had faced just that sort of searing opposition from within rabbinical ranks when it sponsored a domestic campaign during the Civil War to allow Jews to serve as chaplains in the Union army.[33]

To some extent at least, the campaign for benign policies toward Jews in other countries was immune from these caveats. It could be insulated from domestic partisan manipulation, especially when framed within the broadest terms of American democratic values, and it could attract support from a diverse Jewish public across denominational lines. In due course, this naturalization in American terms of Jewish interventions on behalf of Jews abroad or in defense of the rights of émigré Jews who, as American citizens, returned as visitors to their homelands would be honed as an operational strategy and as an ideology. It was easily married to the emergent discourse on humanitarian causes, and despite the non-interventionist bias of governments invoking the sanctity of state sovereignty, it could be wielded under the aegis of state-to-state intercession. By 1905, this approach had gathered enough support among prominent Jewish figures to inspire efforts not only to defend the Jewish propriety of international interventionism, but also to propose it as a precedent-based manual of American policy.[34]

A concise rationale that rendered the notion into legal-political terms, after having been conceived, refined, and reiterated in practice over several decades, may be found in remarks prepared in 1912 by Oscar Straus (1850–1926), who was appointed several times as U.S. envoy (later ambassador) to Turkey (1887–1889, 1898–1899, 1909–1910) and served as the first Jewish cabinet secretary under

---

Century America," in *Anti-Semitism in American History*, ed. David A. Gerber (Urbana and Chicago: University of Illinois Press, 1986), 57–78; Diner, *A Time for Gathering*, chap. 7.

33. Avraham Barkai, *Branching Out: German-Jewish Immigration to the United States, 1820–1914* (New York and London: Holmes & Meier, 1994), 109–10, 119–24; Naomi W. Cohen, *Encounter with Emancipation: The German Jews in the United States, 1830–1914* (Philadelphia: Jewish Publication Society, 1984), 129–30; Bertram W. Korn, *American Jewry and the Civil War* (1951; repr. Marietta, Ga.: R. Bemis Publishing, 1995), 56–97; Albert Isaac Slomovitz, *The Fighting Rabbis: Jewish Military Chaplains and American History* (New York and London: New York University Press, 1999), 10–22.

34. Cyrus Adler, "Jews in the Diplomatic Correspondence of the United States," *Publications of the American Jewish Historical Society*, no. 15 (1906): 1–117, 119–22. Cf. Adler and Margalith, *With Firmness in the Right*, iv.

President Theodore Roosevelt. Straus was speaking shortly after the American Jewish Committee had spearheaded a successful campaign to abrogate the 1832 Russian-American commercial treaty, a political victory that seemed to vindicate the strategy of interventionism:

> There is another class of causes where intervention is not recognized as strictly as [an] international right, but where it is justified "by a high act of policy above and beyond the domain of law," especially if such intervention ... is not used as a cloak for national ambition, but undertaken solely and singly in the interest of humanity for the purpose of ending revolting barbarities, inhuman oppressions or religious persecutions.... The diplomacy of humanity ... has made a stronger appeal to our sympathies and had a wider application in our relations than in the foreign relations of other countries.[35]

Just six years earlier, however, Straus's patron had reflected on the potential risks of exerting diplomatic or presidential pressure on behalf of the oppressed in foreign lands. In May 1905 Theodore Roosevelt asked the veteran British civil servant and government minister Sir George Trevelyan (1838–1928) whether he agreed that the England of the 1860s,

> like the United States of today, is too apt to indulge in representations on behalf of weak peoples which do them no good and irritate the strong and tyrannical peoples to whom the protest is made. It seems to me that the [British] protest on behalf of the Poles to Russia in '63, and the protest on behalf of the Danes to Germany about the same time, were harmful rather than beneficial.... I am always being asked to say something on behalf of the Jews in Russia, of the Armenians in Turkey, of the people in the Congo Free State, etc., etc. It does not always do to refuse. England rendered a real and great service to Italy by her sympathy and championship, for instance. But it certainly does harm to be always harping on the sympathy which finds expression only in words.[36]

It would be well, therefore, to appreciate the persisting structural and political challenges that would-be Jewish spokespersons would continue to face in their attempts to convince those in power to project humanitarian concerns as a principle of statecraft.

35. Oscar S. Straus, "Humanitarian Diplomacy of the United States," *Proceedings of the American Society of International Law* 6 (April 25–27, 1912): 45–59, quotations from pp. 46–47, 48. Straus did not himself deliver the remarks at the scheduled session of the society because his brother Isidor and his sister-in-law Rosalie Ida had lost their lives in the Titanic disaster some ten days earlier.

36. Roosevelt to Sir George Trevelyan, May 13, 1905, *The Letters of Theodore Roosevelt*, ed. Elting E. Morison et al., 8 vols. (Cambridge, Mass.: Harvard University Press, 1951–1954), 4: 1173.

The Romanian Crisis and the Peixotto Mission, 1870–1876

An example of the peculiar strengths and weaknesses of Jewish Americans' communal solidarity and their overseas interventions "in the Jewish cause" may be shown in the case of the mission of Benjamin Franklin Peixotto to Romania in 1870. The frequent abuses against Jews in the Balkan principality (later, kingdom) were an ongoing concern among Jewish groups around the world, and reactions to such events seeped into the practice of international statecraft at several critical points, most famously at the Congress of Berlin in 1878, when German Chancellor Otto von Bismarck (1815–1898) intervened to place the issue of Jewish civil rights on the table.[37] The American episode (1870–1876) was thus a link in a longer chain of events, and it has been overshadowed by the more dramatic events of 1878 and subsequent developments. In the context of our discussion, Peixotto's mission may be viewed as another example of the impromptu nature of American Jewish activities regarding Jewries in distress overseas.[38]

Peixotto was a Cleveland merchant and lawyer with some standing in Jewish circles. He led the B'nai B'rith fraternal order at the national level (1863–1864) and later oversaw the organization of the Midwestern Jewish orphan asylum

37. Fritz Stern, *Gold and Iron: Bismarck, Bleichröder, and the Building of the German Empire* (New York: Knopf, 1977), xvii, 351–52, 355–57, 369–92. Cf. Wolf, *Diplomatic History of the Jewish Question*, 23–54; Carole Fink, *Defending the Rights of Others: The Great Powers, the Jews, and International Minority Protection, 1878–1938* (Cambridge and New York: Cambridge University Press, 2004), 3–38.

38. The events are summarized in Sarna, *When General Grant Expelled the Jews*, 103–16. Cf. Max J. Kohler and Simon Wolf, *Jewish Disabilities in the Balkan States: American Contributions Toward Their Removal, with Particular Reference to the Congress of Berlin* (New York: American Jewish Committee, 1916), 2–24; Max J. Kohler, "Simon Wolf," *American Jewish Year Book* 26 (1924–1925): 409; I. Lifshitz, "'Al shliḥuto shel binyamin franklin peishoto beromaniah," *Ziyyon* 26 (1961): 85–102; Lloyd P. Gartner, "Roumania, America, and World Jewry: Consul Peixotto in Bucharest, 1870–1876," *American Jewish Historical Quarterly* 58, no. 1 (1968): 34, 44–107; Lloyd P. Gartner, "Documents on Roumanian Jewry: Consul Peixotto and Jewish Diplomacy, 1870–1875," in *Salo Wittmayer Baron Jubilee Volume on the Occasion of His Eightieth Birthday*, ed. Saul Lieberman and Arthur Hyman, 3 vols. (New York and Jerusalem: American Academy for Jewish Research, 1974), 1:467–90; Deborah Dash Moore, *B'nai B'rith and the Challenge of Ethnic Leadership* (Albany: State University of New York Press, 1981), 30–32; Gary Dean Best, *To Free a People: American Jewish Leaders and the Jewish Problem in Eastern Europe, 1890–1914* (Westport, Conn., and London: Greenwood Press, 1982), 14–15; Peter Adams, *Politics, Faith, and the Making of American Judaism* (Ann Arbor: University of Michigan Press, 2014), 128–30; Fink, *Defending the Rights of Others*, 16–17; Lederhendler, "Shtadlanut and Stewardship," 101–3; Norbert B. Stern and William M. Kramer, "A Pre-Israeli Diplomat on an American Mission, 1869–1870," *Western States Jewish Historical Quarterly* 8 (1976): 232–34.

in Cleveland, Ohio, a major Jewish philanthropic enterprise.[39] Peixotto set off to Bucharest without much of a specific plan, apart from an intention to bring relief to Romanian Jewry, and without any governmental backing other than President Grant's goodwill. Hoping to receive financial support from his fellow members of B'nai B'rith, he found himself chronically short of cash, spurned by the Romanian regime, and sometimes at loggerheads with leading Bucharest Jews. He lasted about five years before moving on to a more official (but not Jewishly connected) diplomatic appointment as U.S. consul at Lyons.

Yet, Peixotto's effort received attention in the press, at the State Department and in both houses of Congress. In the early months of 1872, Peixotto relayed numerous messages expressing urgent concern for Jewish safety. On February 6 and 8, for example, he sent dispatches reporting news of "deplorable scenes" in several towns:

> Ismail contains a population of 20,000, of whom 2,000 are of the Hebrew faith. The assault upon the Israelites was commenced on the evening of the 24th of December, and lasted three days; another account says seven.
>
> During this time the houses of the Israelites were broken into, the inmates beaten and driven forth, valuables robbed, the furniture destroyed, and the premises gutted. One hundred families took refuge in Tultscba, on the opposite Turkish shore. Some fewfound an asylum on board the Austrian national ship Pest; others fled to the fields. The Austrian subjects were protected at their consulate, except the rabbin, who was arbitrarily carried off and imprisoned. The consul-general of Austria, resident here, has made a demand for his liberation.
>
> Dispatches received here this evening confirm accounts of similar outrages at Vilcovu and Cabool. Thirty families of the former place are reported as plundered, driven from their homes, and exposed to the rigors of the season.
>
> At Cabool the Israelites defended themselves, taking refuge finally in the barracks; two are reported killed, ten to twelve wounded. The excesses appear to be spreading, and are said to be instigated by enemies of the government.[40]

In answer to a resolution of the House on May 20 "requesting me to join the Italian Government in protest against the intolerable and cruel treatment of the Jews of Roumania," President Grant transmitted a report from his secretary of state. Hamilton Fish noted that Peixotto had added his name to a collective

39. Sarna, *When General Grant Expelled the Jews*, 103–11.

40. Peixotto to [Second Assistant Secretary of State William] Hunter [Jr.], February 6 and 8, 1872, *Papers Relating to the Foreign Relations of the United States, Transmitted to Congress with the Annual Message of the President, December 2, 1872*, pt. 1 (Washington, D.C.: GPO, 1873), docs. 474 and 476 (https://history.state.gov/historicaldocuments/frus1872p1/, accessed Feb. 24, 2020). For a selection of Peixotto's memoranda sent from Romania, see Adler and Margalith, *With Firmness in the Right*, 99–110.

"note of remonstrance" to the Romanian government sent by "Representatives of other Powers," and that the State Department had instructed him "not to be backward in joining any similar protest or other measure ... with a view to avert or mitigate further harshness toward the Israelites residents in or subjects of the Principalities"[41]

Peixotto's decision to champion the cause of Jewish emigration to America as a comprehensive solution to the Romanian Jewish crisis—arguably the most practical and, in retrospect, the most far-sighted vision for Romanian Jewish relief—angered European Jewish leaders, including some in Romania, who were pressing for sweeping acts of Jewish emancipation.[42] These considerations, his subsequent retreat to Lyons in 1877, and the great powers' intervention at the Congress of Berlin in 1878 have largely obscured Peixotto's mission in the larger historical narrative.

Knowledge Is Power: Steering the Transnational Discourse

The pan-Jewish bonds of common concern that I have called the "European nexus," which helped to shape American Jewish activity and self-image, were evident far beyond the actions of a few leading figures who ventured into the rarified sphere of diplomacy, congressional resolutions, and White House interventions. Proclamations, delegations, and official protests may claim greater visibility on the international scene, and they tend to dominate in historians' reviews of the past. However, the "Jewish Question" became not only politicized at the state level by the end of the nineteenth century, but also enmeshed in a globalized system of transmission of ideas, information, and disinformation. What was said about Jews and their living conditions abroad—in eastern Europe, for example—bore ever-wider potential consequences for the status of Jews in emancipated societies, such as in the United States. In light of the efforts of local Jews to maintain and enhance their own positions in U.S. society, and in view of the anticipated reception and heightened public awareness of Jewish refugees and migrants, it became ever more critical to intervene in popular media, such as newspapers, magazines, and pamphlets. American Jews who were involved in rebutting antisemitic propaganda were well aware of the transnational impact of anti-Jewish opinion and of pro-Jewish advocacy, and their interventions produced an arsenal of words in the cause of Jewish self-

41. *The Papers of Ulysses S. Grant*, ed. John Y. Simon et al., vol. 23 (Carbondale: Southern Illinois University Press, 2000), 116n.

42. Fink, *Defending the Rights of Others*, 16–17; Gartner, "Consul Peixotto in Bucharest," 93–94.

defense. Their presence on the stage of public discourse was a necessary adjunct to efforts being made at the diplomatic level.

A myriad of examples might be adduced as expressions of Jewish solidarity in the arena of public opinion that carried transnational implications. Here I will examine two cases that, to my mind, offer something a little extra in terms of their authorship, content, and context: *The Semitic Nations* (1872), by the Russian academic Daniil Avraamovich Khvol'son (Daniel Chwolson, 1819–1911),[43] and Emma Lazarus's pungent retort to a defamatory magazine article in 1882 on the gross faults and blameworthy actions of Russian Jews.

The Semitic Nations may be considered a transnational exemplar of philo-Jewish polemical literature. It was rendered into English in the United States by Ephraim M. Epstein, M.D. (1829–1913), who published it in 1874.[44] Both Chwolson and Epstein were "post-Jewish" converts to Christianity. Epstein, for part of his mercurial career, was a Baptist minister who had been trained at Andover Seminary, the birthplace of the eschatological missionary movement known as the American Board of Commissioners for Foreign Missions (ABCFM).[45]

To contextualize this early defense of the "Semites," we need first to grasp the significance of Chwolson's authorship in the decade that would see the first enunciation of the term *antisemitism* by Wilhelm Marr.[46] Chwolson retains a reputation in Russian intellectual history as the founder of the field of Semitics

43. Between the choice of transliterating the name from Russian or using the German spelling that he used himself, I opt for the German one. Readers should refer, however, to the Khvol'son spelling when consulting the biographical entry by Christoph Gassenschmidt, "Daniil Khvol'son," in the *YIVO Encyclopedia of Jews in Eastern Europe*, ed. David Gershon Hundert et al., 2 vols. (New Haven: Yale University Press, 2008), https://yivoencyclopedia.org/article.aspx/Khvolson_Daniil_Avraamovich.

44. D. Chwolson, *The Semitic Nations*, trans. Eph. M. Epstein, M.D. (Cincinnati: Bloch, 1874). The original tract was published in both Russian and German in 1872 following its delivery as a lecture at the University of St. Petersburg in February 1871. The Russian version, "Kharaktaristika semitskikh narodov," appeared in the Moscow literary and political journal *Russkii vestnik* (a high-profile publication featuring, among others, works of Russia's leading writers of the day). The German title was *Die semitischen Völker: Versuch einer Charakteristik* (Berlin: Franz Duncker, 1872).

45. I thank my friend and colleague Yaakov Ariel of the University of North Carolina for insights on Epstein and the ABCFM. See the guide to the Epstein collection at the University of South Dakota, https://libguides.usd.edu/ephraim, where Ephraim Menahem Epstein was the founding president (briefly, in 1882). Epstein's life inspired a historical novel, *The Extraordinary Dr. Epstein*, written by his great-granddaughter, Susan Lee Kerr (© Susan Lee Kerr, CreateSpace Independent Publishing Platform, 2015).

46. Wilhelm Marr (1819–1904), author of *Der Weg zum Siege des Germanenthums über das Judenthum* (1880) and founder, in 1879, of the Antisemiten-Liga (League of Antisemites).

in St. Petersburg. Born in Vil'na (today, Vil'nius, Lithuania) in a traditional Jewish environment, he pursued academic studies after his typically religious Jewish training. He moved first to Riga, Latvia, and then, at the urging of Rabbi Max Lilienthal,[47] to Breslau, Germany (today, Wrocław, Poland), where, with the blessing of Abraham Geiger, he completed his university training. In 1855, Chwolson converted to Russian Orthodoxy to meet the requirements for holding the chair in Hebrew and Syrian Studies at the University of St. Petersburg. Like some other renowned converts of convenience of the nineteenth century, Chwolson retained a benevolent, almost custodial concern and affinity for his Jewish heritage. He was a member of the leading circle of Russified Jewish public activists, the Society for the Promotion of Enlightenment among the Jews of Russia (OPE), and he penned notable pro-Jewish works, among them, a defense of the Jews against the "blood libel," published in 1861, which he later put to good use in a Russian criminal investigation into an alleged Jewish "ritual murder" case.[48]

Chwolson's decision to write and publish *The Semitic Nations* was almost inevitable, because of the wide reception afforded to *Histoire générale et système comparé des langues sémitiques* (1855), by French Semiticist Ernest Renan (1823–1892). Renan's foray into a quasi-racial anthropology of the ancient Hebrews in fact presented only a "historical" introduction to the topic, rather than the declared linguistic program. Renan cast the inner history of languages as an emanation from the history of their speakers and as defining the conceptual borders of their mentalities.[49] More to the point at hand, Renan fostered an essentialist typology that compared the "Semitic peoples" unfavorably ("race inférieur"), in terms of their cultural attributes, to the Indo-European (Aryan) peoples.[50]

47. Lilienthal moved shortly thereafter to New York and, from there, to a rabbinical post at the Reform Congregation Bene Israel in Cincinnati.

48. Gassenschmidt, "Daniil Khvol'son." Cf. Dimitri Bratkin, "Manuscripts, Images, and Biographies of Daniel Chwolson: New Details from the Archives of St. Petersburg," *PaRDES: Zeitschrift der Vereinigung für jüdische Studien*, no. 24 (2018): 171–89; Lederhendler, *Road to Modern Jewish Politics*, 97, 105, 113; Andrew C. Reed, "For One's Brothers: Daniil Avramovich Khvol'son and the 'Jewish Question' in Russia, 1819–1911" (Ph.D. diss., Arizona State University, 2014); Andrew C. Reed, *Contested Identity: D. A. Khvol'son, Ritual Murder, and the Battle for Tolerance in Late Imperial Russia* (forthcoming).

49. "Les langues sémitiques doivent être envisagées comme correspondent à une division du genre humain; en effet; le caractère des peuples qui les ont parlées est marqué dans l'histoire par les traits aussi originaux que les langues qui ont servi de formule et de limite à leur pensée." Ernest Renan, *Histoire générale et système comparé des langues sémitiques*, pt. 1, 2d ed. rev. (Paris: L'Imprimerie Impériale, 1858), 2–3.

50. Paul Lawrence Rose, "Renan versus Gobineau: Semitism and Antisemitism, Ancient Races

Chwolson, as both a (post-)Jew and as a Semitics scholar, defended the reputation of the "Semites," albeit with terminology no less essentialist, no less Orientalist, and no less immersed in the Aryan-Semitic typology than Renan's: "the character of a nation is as immutable as is that of an individual.... The real and main representatives of the *Cultur* races are the Aryans and the Semites."[51] Chwolson sniffed that Renan's book was "still excellent ... in spite of its defects," but went on to eviscerate it, point by point, as well to bemoan the near-universal acceptance of Renan's inflammatory claims: "the words of Renan are met with in a rechewed condition *ad nauseum*," particularly in Germany.[52]

Among other standard Jewish apologetic tropes, Chwolson used one that resonated strongly at the time throughout Western Jewish cultures (including in America), namely, the glories of the Spanish "Golden Age": "Mohammedans and Jews distinguished themselves by loftiness and clearness of spirit, and even kindled many a spark in Christian Spaniards.... With the expulsion of the Jews from Spain, there vanished industry, commerce, and enterprise ... there were entire districts without any physician...."[53] In another note that would acquire added resonance when transmitted in English in "Protestant America" (a construct already facing egregious challenges in the post–Civil War decades), Chwolson claimed: "The Semites could never subject themselves to an infallible Pope.... But about one hundred millions [*sic*] of Aryans do this. In the Vatican reside those who possess a vast knowledge of human nature, who know very well what they are doing."[54]

If Chwolson was the "inevitable" rebuttal witness against Renan, then Ephraim Epstein, a Russian-born Jew and older brother of the now-celebrated memoirist Pauline (Epstein) Wengeroff, was Chwolson's "inevitable" English translator.

---

and Modern Liberal Nations," *History of European Ideas* 39, no. 4 (2013): 528–40. Cf. Geoffrey Nash, "Aryan and Semite in Ernest Renan's and Matthew Arnold's Quest for the Religion of Modernity," *Religion and Literature* 46, no. 1 (2014): 25–50; Joan Leopold, "Ernest Renan (1823–1892): From Linguistics and Psychology to Racial Ideology (1840s to 1860s)," *Historiographia Linguistica* 37, no. 1–2 (2010): 75–104.

51. Chwolson, *Semitic Nations*, 12, 15. Quotations are from the English translation by Epstein.

52. *Ibid.*, 17. Renan's reception aside, he has been the subject of a longstanding argument over the ways in which he mixed elements of anti- and philo-semitism, and over his attempts to dissociate himself from racial antisemitic politics. One pro-Jewish bibliography on the "Jewish Question" proudly featured an epigraph from Renan in the Jews' defense: "Les ennemis du judaïsme, regardez-y de près, vous verrez que ce sont en général des ennemis de l'esprit moderne." Joseph Jacobs, *The Jewish Question, 1875–1884: Bibliographical Hand-List* (London: Trübner and Co., 1885).

53. Chwolson, *Semitic Nations*, 9.

54. *Ibid.*, 37.

Epstein had immigrated to America twice, once before the Civil War and then again in 1867 after serving as a naval surgeon in the Imperial Austrian Navy. A convert, a missionary, a man of science, and a popularizer, Epstein had crossed paths with Chwolson in several ways. Both had in their youth encountered Max Lilienthal in Russia (Epstein later turned to him in Cincinnati as well), and Chwolson is alluded to in Wengeroff's work (though not by name and not appreciatively, considering his conversion).[55]

We associate the need to counter the rhetoric of antisemitism in America more with the later 1870s; the Seligman affair of 1877 is frequently cited as a critical juncture.[56] Therefore, we might ask what circumstance or urgent cause in 1874 prompted Epstein to enter the public arena with a counternarrative? In fact, however, we must look at other contexts to account for the timing of Epstein's translation and publication of *The Semitic Nations.* The first such factor would be Epstein's familiarity with the contemporary European scene, where the "Jewish Question" was already reaching a critical point—the Romanian case continued to smolder throughout the decade—as well as his firsthand knowledge of Chwolson's role as a (post-)Jewish advocate. The original German- and Russian-language editions of *The Semitic Nations* had been published in 1872; thus, the idea for translating it for English readers would have been fresh in Epstein's

55. For biographical notes, see Wengeroff, *Memoirs of a Grandmother*, 34, 38–41, 176–77n24; Shulamit S. Magnus, *A Woman's Life: Pauline Wengeroff and Memoirs of a Grandmother* (Oxford and Portland: Littman Library of Jewish Civilization, 2016), 114 (re: Chwolson), 116–18, 166–207. Epstein translated his younger sister's memoirs into English and tried unsuccessfully to have them published by the Jewish Publication Society of America. On this and other details, see Magnus, *A Woman's Life*, 117–18, 174–87; Shulamit S. Magnus, "Wengeroff in America: On the Resonance of Conversion and Fear of Dissolution in Early Twentieth-Century America," *Jewish Social Studies*, n.s. 21, no. 2 (2016): 142–87. Among the publications authored by Epstein, the following are preserved among his records, held at the library of the University of South Dakota and elsewhere: *Nathaniel, or The Israelite Indeed: A Periodical Devoted to the Illustration and Defence of the Hebrew Christianity*, ed. Gideon R. Lederer and Ephraim M. Epstein (New York: Association of Hebrew Christians in the United States of America, July 1857–April 1871); *Why Do I Live So Long?* (Chicago: Clinic Publishing Co., 1908; repr. from *American Journal of Clinical Medicine*, April/May 1908); *The Mosaic Names of God and What They Denote* (Chicago: Open Court, 1907; repr. from *The Monist*, July 1907); *The Construction of the Tabernacle* (Chicago: Open Court, 1911; repr. from *The Monist*, October 1911).

56. Naomi W. Cohen used 1875 as her boundary between an era described by American Jewish spokespersons, rabbis in particular, as one of prolonged progress and the following decades, in which antisemitism at home and abroad fed a trend of doubt and anxiety. Cohen, "American Jewish Reactions," 30. The earliest selection in a textbook collection of American antisemitic writings is a document from the later 1870s; see *Anti-Semitism in America, 1878–1939* (New York: Arno Press, 1977).

mind. A second factor may have been the subjective effect of Epstein's passing reversion to Judaism while in Europe with his family in the first half of the 1860s.

The third, and perhaps most important factor influencing Epstein's reception of Chwolson's polemic against Renan would have been Epstein's immersion in Hebrew-Christian missionary discourse, which operated independently of other catalysts. It was, in this latter context, entirely in character for Epstein to enter the propaganda wars with a retort to Renan, whose ideas fit into a European (especially Protestant) trend that sought to detach the figure of Jesus from the Jewish historical context. The de-Jewing of the historical Jesus was a feature of this Christian Aryanism, and it required derogation of the "Semitic" heritage as something that Jesus had transcended.[57] This insult was something that Epstein, the devoted Hebrew-Christian, could not abide. Thus, it was only to be expected that he would try to control the narrative by publishing a tract that concluded with the affirmation that "our culture consists of a union of the products of both the Semitic and the Aryan culture" and that in Christianity "Semite" and "Aryan" are ineluctably and "happily" (re)connected.[58]

Turning now to my second example of Jewish solidarity in the arena of public opinion that carried transnational implications, I will examine Emma Lazarus's scathing response to the assertion by Russian émigré writer Zinaida A. Ragozin, published in a prominent New York magazine, that Russian Jews "merited" the wrath meted out to them by "simple Russians" in the pogroms of 1881–1882.[59] New York was home to a cosmopolitan public, including individuals who were

57. Susannah Heschel, *Abraham Geiger and the Jewish Jesus* (Chicago: University of Chicago Press, 1998), esp. 157–61, 276–77n120.

58. Chwolson, *The Semitic Nations*, 54.

59. Zinaida Alexeyevna Ragozin, "Russian Jews and Gentiles: From a Russian Point of View," *Century* 23 (April 1882): 905–20. Of Ragozin we are told the following by a sympathetic historian: "Zenaide [*sic*] Ragozin, a prolific author, historian, artist, musician—and eccentric—of the Russian nineteenth-century diaspora.... This remarkable woman represents an unusual duality: a Russian exile in America for twenty-five years, from around 1875 to 1900, and then an American exile in Russia for the next quarter century until her death in 1924. She excelled as a tutor of foreign language, music, art, and history to a generation of New York debutantes, which included the Pulitzer, Tiffany, and Putnam families." She authored four volumes for G. P. Putnam's "Story of the Nations" series in the 1880s and 1890s and won a special grant from Tsar Nicholas II for her work in children's literature (1910). After the 1917 Revolution, she translated for the Comintern, commenting to a friend, "Beggars can't be choosers." Saul, *Historical Dictionary of United States–Russian/Soviet Relations*, 290–91; Norman E. Saul, "American Collections on Immigrants and Émigrés from the Russian Empire," *Russian and East European Books and Manuscripts in the United States: Proceedings of a Conference in Honor of the Fiftieth Anniversary of the Bakhmeteff Archive of Russia*, ed. Tanya Chebotarev and Jared S. Ingersoll (London and New York: Routledge, 2014), 57.

literate in the languages and cultures of many countries, with a resultant mix of sometimes agitated opinions. Lazarus, already emerging as a formidable Jewish polemicist in both prose and poetry, was scandalized by Christians' Jew-hatred.[60] Her pugnacious, withering, and sarcastic article appeared in the very next issue of the same high-profile New York magazine, *The Century*, edited by her very close friend and supporter Richard Gilder. This unplanned exchange took place between April and May 1882, on the heels of the first arrivals of Russian pogrom refugees in New York, some of whom Lazarus had visited at the shelter on Wards Island in the East River.[61]

Lazarus's piece is filled with fairly standard "defenses" of the Talmud, of Judaism, and of the Jews of Russia, pointing out flaws in the slurs against them.[62] These are set alongside high-flown, acerbic thrusts of ridicule against Ragozin's thesis that Jews are, regrettably, not only weak, filthy, and miserable creatures, but also (simultaneously) the stronger contestant in the head-to-head confrontation between Jews and Russians: "But is it not as puerile as it is monstrous to assert that the Christians, who outnumber the Jews by millions, who have the whole power of the law and the throne to back them, not to speak of the prejudice of the whole civilized world in their favor, can find no other weapons

60. Young, "Emma Lazarus and Her Jewish Problem," 291–313. Cf. Bette Roth Young, *Emma Lazarus in Her World: Life and Letters* (Philadelphia and Jerusalem: Jewish Publication Society, 1995), esp. chap. 8; Esther Schor, *Emma Lazarus* (New York: Nextbook/Schocken, 2006), 79–90, 107, 119–33, 142–74; Ranen Omer-Sherman, "Emma Lazarus, Jewish American Poetics, and the Challenge of Modernity," *Legacy* 19, no. 2 (2002): 172–73; Ranen Omer-Sherman, "'Thy People Are My People': Emma Lazarus, Daniel Deronda, and the Ambivalence of Jewish Modernity," *Journal of Modern Jewish Studies* 1, no. 1 (2002): 51–53.

61. Emma Lazarus, "Russian Christianity versus Modern Judaism," *Century* 24 (May 1882): 48–56. On the visit to Wards Island, see *Proceedings of the Conference of Hebrew Emigrant Aid Societies and Auxiliary Committees, New York, 4th June 1882, American Hebrew* 12, no. 10 (October 20, 1882), 114–15, 119–20; Yaakov Kellner, "Mered hamityashvim berishon leẓiyyon be-1887 umered hamehagrim hayehudim benyu-york be-1882" [The Settlers' Revolt in Rishon Leziyyon in 1887 and the Immigrants' Revolt in New York in 1882], *Kathedra* 5 (1978): 3–29. Cf. Lederhendler, *American Jewry*, 76. On the relationship between Lazarus and Richard and Helena deKay Gilder, see Young, *Emma Lazarus in Her World*; Schor, *Emma Lazarus*, 128, 130–32, 148–50.

62. Lazarus dwelled at length on refuting charges that Jews were secretly conniving against Christian society, an accusation that was in the judeophobic spotlight, especially in the wake of writings by the Russian Jewish convert Yakov Brafman. His *Book of the Kahal* (Kniga kagala) was a supposed exposé based on Jewish communal records. Brafman, upon whom Ragozin relied as a reputable source, targeted the prominent Jewish leadership groups both within and beyond the level of the local kahal (community), including such new leadership organizations as the OPE in St. Petersburg and the AIU in Paris. See Horowitz, *Jewish Philanthropy and Enlightenment*, 56, 58–59; Lederhendler, *Road to Modern Jewish Politics*, 116–17, 142–43.

than tyranny, violence, and murder to preserve them against the Jew, who has nothing but his wits?"[63]

The point of these remarks in the context of transnational discourse may be brought home by one of the many objections raised by Ragozin: "The readiness with which they [the Jews] appeal to foreign sympathy and interference," something that ought rightly to be labeled "treason of the worst kind," was characteristic of "their oriental nature."[64] On this point Lazarus, working within the vein of Jewish solidarity, begged to differ. The issue, she sought to convince her readers, was not one of loyalty, but of humanity. A different reading would have us view Lazarus's polemic in terms of the insider/outsider conundrum to which I alluded to earlier. In Dianne Lichtenstein's assessment, Lazarus "provides us with an alternative model of women's lives because she used her words, rather than her assigned female roles, to affirm her American and Jewish citizenships [*sic*]; and she provides us with a vivid example of how women, Jews, and other 'outsiders' have had to struggle to belong to the American nation...."[65] It would be appropriate to note, however, that Emma Lazarus, the fourth-generation descendent of an established New York family, was arguably more the "insider" than was the relative newcomer Zinaida Ragozin, despite her upper-crust connections. Ragozin would return to Russia, whereas Lazarus would eventually leave a particularly celebrated stamp (albeit posthumous) on American public culture. The question for us, therefore, is not only whether Lazarus was an outsider seeking inclusion, but also how she framed her "outsider" writings to stake

63. Lazarus, "Russian Christianity," 55. That same issue of *The Century* included a kind of postscript, in the form of an unsigned comment running to half a dozen long paragraphs. It bears many of the earmarks of Lazarus's arguments. Perhaps these were "outtakes" from previous drafts that the editor (or Lazarus herself) excised from her main article; or perhaps the notes simply restate opinions that Lazarus expressed in discussions with her intimate friends, the Gilders. Published in a group of similar unsigned comments, and thus ostensibly representing the editor's opinions, headlined as "Topics of the Time," the note is entitled "Jews and Jew-baiters." It ends with the observation: "Oppression no doubt degrades the oppressed, as it certainly does the oppressor, but it will not do to take the word of the tyrant for the character of the slave under his heel." "Jews and Jew-baiters" (unsigned), *Century* 24 (May 1882): 149. The extra note of spoken outrage may have been a gesture by Richard Gilder, who "owed" his friend Emma Lazarus some added compensation since *The Century* had seen fit to publish the scurrilous Ragozin article in the first place.

64. Ragozin, "Russian Jews and Gentiles," 919–20. The quotation is also noted by Ann E. Healy, "Tsarist Anti-Semitism and Russian-American Relations," *Slavic Review* 42, no. 3 (1983): 408–25; see 408n1.

65. Diane Lichtenstein, "Words and Worlds: Emma Lazarus's Conflicting Citizenships," *Tulsa Studies in Women's Literature* 6, no. 2 (1987): 247.

a claim as a native daughter before the American public. And, by extension, is this paradigm appropriate as a lens for viewing the entire range of American Jewish "interventions" in the transnational arena?

Reviewing the cases presented in this essay, I suggest that the international arena provided American Jews with a forum for flexing their communal awareness and their pan-Jewish sense of solidarity, and also to carry their claims to American citizenship into the heart of the public square.

JEWISH ARTISTS BEGIN TO MAKE THEIR MARK

SAMANTHA BASKIND

AT THE second national convention of the Jewish fraternal organization Independent Order of B'nai B'rith (Sons of the Covenant), held in Chicago in January 1874, the group passed a resolution to commission a statue in recognition of religious liberty. The monument was to be presented to the United States at the upcoming Centennial International Exhibition, the world's fair in Philadelphia celebrating the one-hundredth anniversary of the signing of the Declaration of Independence. Publicity indicates that following the exhibition B'nai B'rith planned to gift the work to the U.S. government, "to remain as a lasting monument to the great truths it is designed to illustrate," as later touted by newspapers across the country.[1] B'nai B'rith brothers were asked to raise funds to pay for the monument. Soon after, Moses Jacob Ezekiel (1844–1917), an untried sculptor, an expatriate living in Rome, and a member of B'nai B'rith, was named the artist of choice.[2] Unfortunately, delayed by both Ezekiel's perfectionism and the failure of B'nai B'rith to provide timely payment, *Religious Liberty* did not touch U.S. soil until the centennial had ended its six-month run in November 1876.

The highly classical, twenty-four-foot tall, thirteen-ton allegorical marble presents Liberty as a woman clothed in a coat of mail and partly covered by a toga (Fig. 19).[3] She wears a Phrygian cap, the Roman *pilleus libertatis* bestowed

1. "Israelites Centennial Monument, To the Officers and Members of the Union of American Hebrew Congregations," misdated "Cleveland, July 14–16, 1873," B'nai B'rith International Archives, 1843–2015 (MS-900; hereafter BBIA), box D4-18/8, folder 8 (Statue of Religious Liberty, 1873–1989), Jacob Rader Marcus Center of the American Jewish Archives (hereafter AJA), Cincinnati. The resolution should be dated 1874. The *American Israelite* urged representatives from congregations to attend that year's meeting of the Council of the Union of American Hebrew Congregations in Cleveland (as well as to join, if not yet a member). Undoubtedly, this date is accurate, considering that the resolution for the sculpture was not passed until January 1874. See *American Israelite*, July 17, 1874, 1.

2. Simon Wolf, "The B'nai B'rith and the Philadelphia Statue of Religious Liberty" (1921), in *Selected Addresses and Papers of Simon Wolf: A Memorial Volume* (Cincinnati: Union of American Hebrew Congregations, 1926), 277–80.

3. Measurements for the sculpture vary in newspaper accounts. This measurement was taken

upon freed slaves, with a border of thirteen gilded stars to represent the original colonies. The laurel wreath of victory in her left hand rests on fasces, a bundle of birch rods bound with a ribbon, which symbolizes power and strength in unity. Also atop the fasces is an open book, meant to represent the U.S. Constitution. Liberty extends her right arm protectively over an idealized nude boy, a personification of Faith, who balances a flaming lamp in one hand as he raises the other up to heaven. At Liberty's feet an eagle, a central emblem denoting America, attacks a serpent, signifying Intolerance. The group stands on a pedestal bearing the inscription "Religious Liberty, Dedicated to the People of the United States by the Order B'nai B'rith and Israelites of America."

On a cold Thanksgiving Day, Jews and non-Jews stood together—along with Ezekiel, members of his family, and representatives from B'nai B'rith—as *Religious Liberty* was finally and triumphantly unveiled in Philadelphia's Fairmount Park. About 250 dignitaries processed to a platform impressively decorated in red, white, and blue bunting, accompanied by patriotic songs—"The Star-Spangled Banner," "Home Sweet Home," and "Yankee Doodle Dandy"—played by McClurg's Cornet Band. When the initial pomp ended, Rabbi George Jacobs addressed approximately 1,500 spectators. Jacobs carefully mentioned God but avoided Hebrew language and Hebrew prayers. Rather, he spoke in large part about the good fortune of American Jews, thus implying their misfortune elsewhere: "Almighty God, Sovereign of the Universe, who art enthroned high above all mortals and rulest the destinies of all nations, we approach Thee this day with thankful spirits for having preserved us alive and sustained us to behold the advent of this joyous occasion to which every Hebrew heart, as well as the heart of every lover of religious liberty, has looked forward to with anxious and blissful expectation ... to unveil a precious monument—one that belongs not to any creed or sect, but which interests the good and the true of all denominations."[4]

Considering some of the major goals of B'nai B'rith, the rabbi's inclusive word choice made sense. Later in the ceremony, A. L. Sanger, chairman of the B'nai B'rith Centennial Committee, recited verbatim a portion of the preamble to the

---

during an assessment of the sculpture in 2009. Institutional files of the National Museum of American Jewish History (hereafter NMAJH), Philadelphia.

4. Quoted in "Religious Liberty," *Philadelphia Inquirer*, December 1, 1876. The unveiling was covered by a number of newspapers, including the Philadelphia *Jewish Record*, the *Philadelphia Public Ledger and Daily Transcript*, and the *New York Herald*. Clippings in a scrapbook kept by State Senator Horatio Gates Jones (hereafter Jones Scrapbook), archives of the NMAJH (1998.33.1), gift of Garry G. Greenstein. See also *Richmond Daily Dispatch*, December 2, 1876, 1.

Fig. 19. Moses Jacob Ezekiel, *Religious Liberty*, 1876. Height: 24 ft. Stands in front of the National Museum of American Jewish History, Philadelphia.

order's most recent constitution, stating its guiding principles: "to develop and elevate the mental and moral character of our race, by a liberal support of science and art, and the inculcation of the holiest and purest principles of philanthropy, honor and patriotism."[5] This broad mandate focused on philanthropy and personal growth rather than on promoting religious Judaism; and, to be sure, the organization has primarily been secular and unifying, committed, as the first sentence of its constitution expansively proclaimed, to "the highest interests of humanity."[6] The order's mission explicitly encouraged patriotism—in other words, becoming one with the nation in which Jews reside—in line with the sculpture's strongly American conception.

B'nai B'rith and the American Jewish community have publicly acclaimed *Religious Liberty* for more than a century. Its wide popularity after the unveiling led to its reproduction in other formats. For example, the monument was featured in the masthead of the *Jewish Exponent*, first published in April 1887, which reported news about Jewish life in Philadelphia and beyond. The masthead was designed by Louis Levy, better known for developing the halftone printing process with his brother Max. *Religious Liberty* rises high at the center, demonstrating how the monument had become a symbol of pride for Jews in late nineteenth-century America, especially in Philadelphia.

Religious Liberty also appeared as the cover image, repeated inside as the frontispiece, for *The American Jew as Patriot, Soldier and Citizen* (1895), written by Simon Wolf and published by Louis Levy.[7] A lawyer and activist who had the ear of presidents, Wolf was a vigorous promoter of "patriotic citizenship," which for him centered on military service. Wolf, who served as lodge president of the Washington, D.C., chapter of B'nai B'rith and eventually led the national organization, wrote the book to dispel antisemitic claims that Jews had reneged on their military obligations in American wars, especially the Civil War. Like Ezekiel's sculpture, Wolf's book aimed to prove that Jews were very much American, participating in American life and deserving of religious freedom.

The monument's intriguing history includes two relocations and four ded-

5. Quoted in "Statue to Religious Liberty: The Gift of the Israelites of America to the Nation," *Jewish Record*, December 1, 1876. Clipping in Jones Scrapbook.

6. "Constitution of the Independent Order B'nai B'rith," 1868, unpaged, BBIA, box B1a-37, folder 2. An earlier, less expansive version from 1843 referred to "the highest interests of Judaism." See also Edward E. Grusd, *B'nai B'rith: The Story of a Covenant* (New York: Appleton-Century, 1966), 47–49.

7. Simon Wolf, *The American Jew as Patriot, Soldier and Citizen*, ed. Louis Edward Levy (Philadelphia: Levytype Company, 1895).

ications. In August 1985, after more than a century in Fairmount Park, with financial assistance from B'nai B'rith International and individual benefactors, a carefully wrapped *Religious Liberty* journeyed seven miles to the grounds of the National Museum of American Jewish History, from its former location in front of a synagogue just east of Independence Mall. Three considerations shaped the decision to relocate the statue: its theme is well suited for Independence Mall; more people could see *Religious Liberty* in such a conspicuous location; and its message of freedom coincides with that of the museum. Ezekiel's tribute to religious tolerance was relocated again, in 2010, to the front of the museum's new, enlarged building at the corner of Market and Fifth Streets, a major upgrade from the former space. Having been transported only some 500 feet, *Religious Liberty* fittingly remains on Independence Mall, mere steps from the Liberty Bell, a block south of the National Constitution Center, and a block north of Independence Hall, where American liberty was born. Well over a century since *Religious Liberty* was unveiled, the monument continues to serve as a proud reminder of the liberties that have allowed Jews to thrive, finally in freedom, in America.

Religious Liberty is the first and still the most prominent work of art commissioned by the Jewish American community, fittingly executed by the first Jewish American artist of international prominence. The commission, however, did not usher in a grand era of Jewish patronage, or even signal a growing stature of Jews on the art scene. The lack of Jewish artists cannot be attributed to widespread acceptance of the Second Commandment, the misunderstood prohibition against graven images, which has been a talking point in the modern era. Nor did that paucity stem from antisemitism in the art world, for which there is scant evidence.[8]

Nineteenth-century American Jews simply did not readily enter the profession. Ezekiel provides a case in point. One of his early efforts as a sculptor, *Moses Receiving the Law on Mount Sinai* (ca. 1860, lost), dismayed his grandmother. When the plaster model collapsed because Ezekiel had failed to provide proper supports, his grandmother interpreted that event as an omen that he should abandon sculpting as a career. In this case, her reaction can be attributed both to belief in the Second Commandment and to concern that her grandson would choose a profession that might not allow him to make a proper living, both

8. On the misconception that Jews are aniconic, see Kalman P. Bland, *The Artless Jew: Medieval and Modern Affirmations and Denials of the Visual* (Princeton: Princeton University Press, 2000); Margaret Olin, *The Nation without Art: Examining Modern Discourses on Jewish Art* (Lincoln: University of Nebraska Press, 2001).

subjects that Ezekiel addressed in his memoir.[9] As a young man, Ezekiel spent a year at the Medical College of Virginia only because he felt that a career in art was unrealistic and that medicine would provide financial security.[10] The father of painter Tobias "Toby" Rosenthal (1848–1917) also did not support his son's choice of profession, at least at first. As the artist recalled in his memoir: "At the beginning my father called it a waste of time, because he regarded painting as did others of his environment as an unprofitable activity. Since everyone was trying to get rich, and because there seemed to be no possible way to give me a chance to study art, his disapproval was understandable."[11]

Few coherent patterns fit the careers of Jewish artists working in postbellum America up to the turn of the twentieth century. In many cases, the attempt to excavate the lives and work of these artists, now mostly obscure, proves to be challenging. Scattered and often elusive extant materials allow only patchy reconstructions.[12] Nonetheless, because of the equality afforded to American Jews, and celebrated by *Religious Liberty*, Jewish American artists could—and some did—contribute to their country's artistic life and culture. Those contributions were rarely of an explicitly Jewish nature, and Jewish identity was largely inconsequential to the artists described here. Thus, the Jewish-themed works mentioned in this essay should not offer a false impression. Ezekiel himself, the

9. Moses Jacob Ezekiel, *Memoirs from the Baths of Diocletian*, ed. Joseph Gutmann and Stanley F. Chyet (Detroit: Wayne State University Press, 1975), 102.

10. *Ibid.*, 124, 127, 130.

11. William M. Kramer and Norton B. Stern, *San Francisco's Artist Toby E. Rosenthal, with Rosenthal's Memoir of a Painter*, trans. Marlene Rainman (Northridge, Calif.: Santa Susana Press, 1978), 144–45.

12. For the pioneering work on this period, see Joseph Gutmann's survey, "Jewish Participation in the Visual Arts of Eighteenth- and Nineteenth-Century America," *American Jewish Archives Journal* 15, no. 1 (1963): 21–57. There are only nine paragraphs about nineteenth-century Jewish American artists in the first major survey of Jewish art (327 pages); see Cecil Roth, ed., *Jewish Art: An Illustrated History*, rev. ed. by Bezalel Narkiss (Greenwich, Conn.: New York Graphic Society, 1971), 203–5, 315–16. There is nothing on the topic in its successor: Gabrielle Sed-Rajna et al., *Jewish Art*, trans. Sara Friedman and Mira Reich (New York: Abrams, 1997). Matthew Baigell devoted three pages to nineteenth-century artists in his slim volume on the subject: *Jewish Art in America: An Introduction* (Lanham, Md.: Rowman and Littlefeld, 2007). On the two leading Jewish American artists from the years before the Civil War, see Dale Rosengarten, "Portrait of Two Painters: The Work of Theodore Moïse and Solomon Nunes Carvalho," in *By Dawn's Early Light: Jewish Contributions to American Culture From the Nation's Founding to the Civil War*, ed. Adam Mendelsohn, exh. cat. (Princeton: Princeton University Library, 2016), 138–87. One point of note: Gutmann identified Robert Frederick Blum as a Jewish sculptor. To set the record straight, Blum was not of Jewish descent. See Bruce Weber, "Robert Frederick Blum (1857–1903) and His Mileu," vol. 1 (Ph.D. diss., City University of New York, 1985), 33n1.

most connected to his religio-cultural heritage—and the favored artist when it came to Jewish patrons' needs in postbellum America (as well as the most distinguished of the era)—was adamant about avoiding categorization:

> I must acknowledge that the tendency of the Israelites to stamp everything they undertake with such an emphasis [as Jewish art] is not sympathetic with my taste. *Artists* belong to no country and to no sect—their individual religious opinions are matters of conscience and belong to their households and not to the public. In reference to myself, this is my standpoint. Everybody who knows me knows that I am a Jew—I never wanted it otherwise. But I would prefer as an artist to gain first a name and reputation upon an equal footing with all others in art circles. It is a matter of absolute indifference to the world whether a *good artist* is a Jew or a Gentile and in my career I do not want to be stated with the title of "Jewish sculptor." [13]

Yet, even as a lifelong bachelor living in Rome for forty years, Ezekiel remained strongly connected to his Jewish identity, religious and otherwise. In a letter to his brother he affirmed: "My relief *Israel*, my *Judith*, *David*, and *Christ in the Tomb* show that my ideals have always been deeply connected with Jewish traditions and ideals." [14]

During Ezekiel's lifetime, he primarily made monumental sculptures, works with religious themes, and portraits.[15] Notably, he crafted three likenesses of Thomas Jefferson, a fellow Virginian and author of the Virginia Statute for Religious Freedom, which guaranteed the separation of church and state and became a model for the First Amendment of the U.S. Constitution. A commission from Isaac and Bernard Bernheim, two Jewish philanthropist brothers who prospered in the whiskey business, resulted in a statue of Jefferson by Ezekiel, placed in front of the Jefferson County Courthouse in Louisville, Kentucky (1900; Fig. 20). At 5½-feet tall, Jefferson stands atop a replica of the Liberty Bell, seven-feet tall with a diameter of 6¼ feet. He appears as drafter of the Declaration of Independence, holding the document outward. Ezekiel depicted Jefferson in his early thirties, an inventive approach, indicating the future president's age at the time when he wrote the new nation's charter. Four winged, allegorical female

13. Quoted in David Philipson, "Moses Jacob Ezekiel," *Publications of the American Jewish Historical Society* 28 (1922): 9–10.

14. Moses Jacob Ezekiel to Henry Ezekiel, July 11, 1903, reprinted in *ibid.*, 27.

15. On Ezekiel, see Stan Cohen and Keith Gibson, *Moses Ezekiel: Civil War Soldier, Renowned Sculptor* (Missoula, Mont.: Pictorial Histories Publishing Company, 2007); Alice M. Greenwald, ed., *Ezekiel's Vision: Moses Jacob Ezekiel and the Classical Tradition*, exh. cat. (Philadelphia: National Museum of American Jewish History, 1985); Philipson, "Moses Jacob Ezekiel," 1–62; and most valuably, Ezekiel's extensive *Memoirs from the Baths of Diocletian.*

figures surround the bronze bell at evenly spaced intervals to represent Jeffersonian ideals: Liberty, Equality, Justice, and the Brotherhood of Man, the last a term Ezekiel coined to denote religious freedom. Remarkably and progressively, the Brotherhood of Man holds a tablet bearing the inscription, "The Statute of Religious Freedom," along with the names of deities: Jehova (Hebrew God), Brahma (creator God in Hinduism), Atma (individual's essence in Hinduism), Ra (Ancient Egyptian sun god), and Alla (Muslim name for God).[16] In the upper left corner Ezekiel placed the Om of Hinduism in Sanskrit, and in the right corner he singled out his own God in Hebrew, Adonai Echad, meaning one God.

Isaac Bernheim wrote retrospectively in his memoir that he commissioned the statue because of the opportunities allowed him in America, as an immigrant who finally lived in freedom because of Jefferson's words and actions: "After deliberation, it occurred to me, that as my brother and I were foreign born, had been naturalized in and protected by this government, and under its benign rule had enjoyed so many blessings, that it would be a fitting thing to present the statue of him who had done more than any other man to make this country free, and who had made our success and happiness possible by inspiring Americans with the truth and justice of that immortal declaration, All men are created equal."[17] A second version of Ezekiel's *Jefferson*, in front of the iconic Rotunda at the University of Virginia, was dedicated nine years later. Ezekiel's marble bust of Jefferson for the U.S. Senate's Vice Presidential Bust Collection (1888) sits conspicuously above the rostrum in the Senate Chamber on the gallery level, visible to visitors and viewers of televised Senate hearings.

Ezekiel's contributions to American sculpture are important but complicated. Born in a home with enslaved people and partly raised by mammies, Ezekiel

16. All spellings conform with Ezekiel's, as written on the tablet.

17. Isaac Wolfe Bernheim, *The Story of the Bernheim Family* (Louisville: John P. Morton and Company, 1910), 118–19. Uriah Phillips Levy, the first Jewish commodore in the U.S. Navy, also greatly admired Jefferson for his support of the separation of church and state. He commissioned and donated the first full-length portrait statue for the Capitol Building, a seven-and-a-half-foot-tall bronze of Jefferson (1834) by French sculptor Pierre-Jean David D'Angers. So appreciative was he of Jefferson, Levy purchased a run-down Monticello in 1836 and was pivotal in restoring the mansion and its grounds. See Marc Leepson, *Saving Monticello: The Levy Family's Epic Quest to Rescue the House That Jefferson Built* (Charlottesville: University of Virginia Press, 2003), and Melvin I. Urofsky, *The Levy Family and Monticello, 1834–1923: Saving Thomas Jefferson's House* (Charlottesville: Thomas Jefferson Foundation, 2001).

Fig. 20 (*facing*). Moses Jacob Ezekiel, *Thomas Jefferson*, 1900. Height: 12½ ft. Stands in front of the Louisville Metro Hall, Louisville, Kentucky. (Library of Congress).

OF THE REPUBLIC

always remained a Southerner at heart. The first Jew to attend the Virginia Military Institute (VMI), he fought for the Confederacy as a teenaged cadet in the brutal Battle of New Market (1864). Later, on commissions from the United Daughters of the Confederacy, Ezekiel proudly sculpted VMI professor and Confederate general Thomas J. "Stonewall" Jackson for the grounds of the West Virginia State Capitol in Charleston (1909) and the thirty-two-foot-tall Confederate Memorial in Arlington National Cemetery (1914).[18]

Well respected and feted, Ezekiel consorted with celebrities, royalty, and political dignitaries in America and Europe. He portrayed his friends General Robert E. Lee and Lee's wife, Mary Custis Lee, as well as composer Franz Liszt, in sculptures or drawings. The guest of presidents at the White House, Ezekiel also welcomed American leaders to his famed studio in the ancient Baths of Diocletian, notably Ulysses S. Grant, Theodore Roosevelt, and William Taft. Regard for Ezekiel was so high that he was asked to broker the deal to sell the Villa d'Este by Cardinal von Hohenlohe-Schillingsfürst, one of his dearest companions and the subject of a portrait bust (1886). Gabriele D'Annunzio wrote a poem about Ezekiel, and novelists Carel Vosmaer and Mary Agnes Tincker modeled characters on him.[19] Ezekiel received numerous honors. In 1887, George II, Grand Duke of Saxe-Meiningen, bestowed on him the cavalier's Cross of Merit for Art and Science. Six years later, Kaiser Wilhelm II of Germany presented him with the Golden Cross of the House of Hohenzollern, and in 1906, King Victor-Emanuel III conferred on him the honorary title of Cavaliere, officer of the crown of Italy. Ezekiel was buried with full military honors beneath his own Confederate Memorial in Arlington National Cemetery. A eulogy by President Warren Harding, read at his funeral, lauded Ezekiel as "a great Virginian, a great artist, a great American, and a great citizen of world fame."[20]

Ezekiel's contemporary Henry Mosler (1841–1920) was born in Silesia, the son of lithographer Gustavus Mosler, and arrived in the United States at age eight.[21] After a stint in New York City, the Mosler family settled in Cincin-

18. Ezekiel donated a replica of the Jackson monument to his alma mater in 1912. See Samantha Baskind, "The Jewish Sculptor of the Confederacy," *Tablet*, January 21, 2021, https://www.tabletmag.com/sections/arts-letters/articles/stonewall-jackson-moses-jacob-ezekiel-vmi (accessed January 28, 2021).

19. Carl Vosmaer, *The Amazon* (1880), trans. E. J. Irving (New York: William S. Gottsberger, 1884); Mary Agnes Tincker, *The Jewel in the Lotos* (London: W. H. Allen and Company, 1884).

20. "Lesson of Americanism Drawn By Harding From Monument Marking Ezekiel's Grave," *Cincinnati Enquirer*, March 31, 1921, 16.

21. A 1995 retrospective exhibition mounted by the Skirball Cultural Center resurrected Mosler's œuvre and life from near obscurity. See Barbara C. Gilbert, ed., *Henry Mosler Rediscovered: A*

nati, which boasted a large German Jewish population.[22] For an aspiring artist, Cincinnati held great promise; among others, sculptors Henry Kirke Brown and Hiram Powers were once based there, as were painters John Twachtman and James H. Beard (with whom Mosler studied). Mosler, too, was involved in the Civil War, though not as a soldier; as an artist-correspondent for *Harper's Weekly*, he joined ranks with the likes of Winslow Homer. In the mid-1860s, Mosler studied at the Düsseldorf Academy before returning to the Queen City in 1866. There he became acquainted with Ezekiel, whose family had moved to Cincinnati from ravaged Richmond after the war. The two artists' fates could very well have been intertwined if Ezekiel had taken up Mosler's offer to go with him to Paris in 1874. An expatriate for two decades, Mosler ran a studio there, where students took private lessons and artists visited him, including Ezekiel and Toby Rosenthal. The *American Israelite* praised Ezekiel and Mosler in a single headline: "Two Israelites in Cincinnati have recently attained high distinction in fine arts."[23]

Mosler achieved significantly more success in France than he did in the United States. He frequently pictured peasant costume and life in Brittany, although he painted in a much more conventional, literal manner than the Dutch Jewish artist Jacob Meijer de Haan. Non-Jews, such as Emile Bernard and Paul Gauguin, were also attracted to the region but followed their avant-garde aspirations.[24] Mosler meticulously recorded Breton dress, customs, and domestic interiors, and he painted Breton wedding traditions on several occasions, such as *The Wedding Feast* (ca. 1892, collection unknown), which was exhibited at the Paris Salon.

Nineteenth-Century Jewish-American Artist, exh. cat. (Los Angeles: Skirball Museum, 1995). Since then, his work has attracted more interest. The Archives of American Art, the largest repository of archival materials about American artists in the world, produced an online exhibition about Mosler's Civil War years based on a diary he kept in October 1862 ("Henry Mosler's Civil War Diary," https://www.aaa.si.edu/collection-features/civil-war-diary).

22. In 1860, between 7,500 and 10,000 Jews lived in Cincinnati; by 1870, their estimated population was 8,000–12,000. Jonathan D. Sarna and Nancy H. Klein, *The Jews of Cincinnati* (Cincinnati: Center for the Study of the American Jewish Experience, 1989), 181.

23. *American Israelite*, August 1, 1879, 6. Years later, they were again coupled: "Ezekiel-Mosler: Two Famous Cincinnatians," *American Israelite*, March 31, 1898, 8.

24. The first substantial number of Jews to become professional fine artists in Europe was well surveyed in a Jewish Museum exhibition on nineteenth-century Jewish artists, with an accompanying catalog: Susan Tumarkin Goodman, ed., *The Emergence of Jewish Artists in Nineteenth-Century Europe*, exh. cat. (New York: Jewish Museum, 2001), which includes artists from Germany, France, England, Italy, the Netherlands, Austria, and the Pale of Settlement (modern Poland, Ukraine, and Russia).

Interested in accurate representations and fascinated by the rural exotic, Mosler collected Breton costumes and objects to ensure his paintings' authenticity. In a revealing essay, an exemplar for the type of critical discussion needed to expand the field of nineteenth-century Jewish American art, Albert Boime argues that Mosler was attracted to traditional Breton spirituality because of the region's ability to retain traditional customs in a rapidly modernizing world. He claims that by painting Breton life, Mosler reconciled his attachment to tradition without producing parochial imagery of Jewish subjects.[25] Boime's unearthing of Jewish influence in work without overt Jewish subjects offers an important recuperative approach.

Mosler's 1879 entry in the prestigious French Salon, *Le Retour* (Fig. 21), received an honorable mention from the jury and was purchased for the Musée du Luxembourg, the first canvas by an American to be bought by the French government and the highest-priced purchase up to that date.[26] Tightly rendered in a dark palette, *Le Retour* recounts the oft-told redemption story of the Prodigal Son, a traditional New Testament subject embraced by artists such as Rembrandt and Murillo, but relocated to a Breton setting. Here, the errant son returns home to find his mother on her deathbed, arriving too late to ask for her forgiveness. He kneels in despair at the base of an authentic, intricately carved oak Breton bed. Mosler contrasts the anguished son, wearing threadbare clothes and kneeling in dirt, with his mother, who rests peacefully in white as two candles cast a golden glow around her head. On the basis of this foundational work and others, Mosler won major awards: a gold medal at both the 1883 Paris Salon and the 1884 International Exposition in Nice; a third-class medal at the 1888 Paris Salon; and a silver medal at the Universal Exhibition in Paris (1889). Mosler was named Chevalier of the Legion of Honor and an Officer of the French Academy. After returning permanently to the United States in 1894, Mosler spent the remainder of his days in New York and painted scenes from American history and genre works.

During his career, Mosler executed a few works that indicate a relationship with the Jewish community. Without a commission, he elected to paint *Plum Street Temple* (ca. 1866; Fig. 22), a canvas detailing the exterior of the newly constructed house of worship for B'nai Yeshurun in Cincinnati, led by the pioneering rabbi Isaac Mayer Wise. He precisely delineated the Moorish-style

25. Albert Boime, "Henry Mosler's 'Jewish' Breton and the Quest for Collective Identity," in *Henry Mosler*, ed. Gilbert, 91–127.

26. W. A. Cooper, "Artists in Their Studios, IV: Mr. Henry Mosler," *Godey's Magazine* 130 (June 1895): 569, with three photographs of Mosler's studio.

Fig. 21. Henry Mosler, *Le Retour*, 1879. Oil on canvas, 47¼ × 39½ in. (Musée Departemental Breton-Quimper, France).

architecture, which dominates the canvas, dwarfing the well-dressed congregants who mingle before the structure. A color-tinted lithograph based on Mosler's painting graced the cover of a musical score, "Progress March," written for the synagogue's dedication. Portraits commissioned from Mosler by the Jewish community include a likeness of Wise's first wife, Therese Bloch Wise (ca. 1867, Skirball Museum, Cincinnati). Despite these explicit religious associations, Mosler characterized art as his spiritual connection: "I am an eternal worshipper of the Creator. When I transfer a beautiful model to the canvas, I am engaged in an act of divine worship."[27] This belief in art as religion would be repeated among a number of later Jewish American artists.

Moses Jacob Ezekiel, too, had affiliations with Isaac Mayer Wise and Plum Street Temple. On one of several occasions when he provided service to the Jewish community, he created a bronze portrait bust of Rabbi Wise (1899; Fig. 23), most likely the first sculpture modeled from life of any rabbi by a Jewish artist.[28] Commissioned by the rabbi's congregation to honor his eightieth birthday, the bust shows Wise as a fully acculturated American, attired in line with current fashion and the norm for members of his Reform congregation. In contrast to most Orthodox Jews, Wise wears a high-buttoned vest with one button undone beneath a wide V-notched lapel outercoat that accentuates his shoulders. The rabbi has a jaunty ascot around his neck, the left corner partially tucked into his vest and the right crossing over onto his coat. A bushy mustache spreads across his cheeks to his thick sideburns, with hair, long in the back, tucked behind his ears and reaching a little past the bottom of his neck. The rabbi's dress reveals how most assimilated Jews wanted to be perceived by the larger American population. Ezekiel's Sephardic family dressed in this fashion, as did the artist himself. Three months after her husband's death in March 1900, Selma Bondi Wise donated the bronze to Hebrew Union College (now held by the Skirball Cultural Center, Los Angeles).[29]

27. Quoted in "New York Jews in Art: No. 11—Henry Mosler," *Federation Review* 4 (March 1910): 77.

28. Four decades earlier, Rabbi Wise had opposed a monument to philanthropist Judah Touro. Wise's later acceptance of a bust made in his honor demonstrates that his thinking about the Second Commandment had evolved. On the Touro monument, see Jonathan D. Sarna, "The Touro Monument Controversy: Aniconism vs. Anti-Idolatry in a Mid-Nineteenth-Century American Jewish Religious Dispute," in *Between Jewish Tradition and Modernity: Rethinking an Old Opposition: Essays in Honor of David Ellenson*, ed. Michael A. Meyer and David N. Myers (Detroit: Wayne State University Press, 2014), 80–95.

29. Letter from Selma Wise to the president and members of the board of governors of Hebrew Union College, June 26, 1899, bust of I. M. Wise file, curatorial files, Skirball Museum,

Fig. 22. Henry Mosler, *Plum Street Temple*, ca. 1866. Oil on canvas, 29½ × 24⅝ in. (Skirball Museum, Cincinnati, Ohio, 41.259. Gift of the Skirball Foundation; Audrey Skirball Kenis, granddaughter of the artist).

Fig. 23. Moses Jacob Ezekiel working on bust of Isaac M. Wise, 1899. (Courtesy of The Jacob Rader Marcus Center of the American Jewish Archives, Cincinnati, Ohio).

Four years later, at the request of Wise's son-in-law Adolph Ochs, publisher of the *New York Times*, Ezekiel translated the likeness into marble for his patron's home, a work eventually donated to Hebrew Union College in Cincinnati by the rabbi's heirs. In 1906, Ochs asked Ezekiel for a third copy of the bust, intended for display at the National Jewish Hospital for Consumptives in Denver (now National Jewish Health), an organization that Wise supported. Since 1956, that bronze has resided in the lobby of the Hebrew Union College branch in New York City. Another notable commission of a Jewish nature was Ezekiel's design for a stained glass memorial window in honor of Isaac Mayer Wise (1909) at Philadelphia's Temple Keneseth Israel, since destroyed by fire. Ezekiel also designed the first seal, in use from 1890 to 1906, for the Jewish Publication Society (JPS), the foremost nonprofit, nondenominational Amer-

Cincinnati. In June 1956, Wise's son Rabbi Jonah Wise donated the second bronze to the Union of American Hebrew Congregations, at the time representing 530 Reform congregations. "Isaac Mayer Wise is Honored By Son," *New York Times*, June 17, 1956, 49.

ican press to focus on Jewish subjects, founded in 1888 and still producing books.

The career trajectory of Ephraim Keyser (1850–1937) resembles that of Ezekiel, but with less success, to the extent that he is now erased from the annals of art history.[30] Born in Baltimore, Keyser traveled to Germany for art instruction, studying at the Royal Academy of Art in Munich and also with Ezekiel's mentor Albert Wolff in Berlin. Keyser's fifty-seven-inch idealized marble statue of *Psyche* (1877) was the first piece of original sculpture given to the Cincinnati Museum of Art. As did Ezekiel, Keyser earned his reputation as a maker of portrait busts and commemorative sculptures, including a memorial at President Chester Arthur's tomb in the Albany Rural Cemetery (1889; Fig. 24). A classically inspired bronze angel gently places a large palm frond atop a polished black sarcophagus. Her draping wings hug her flowing robes as she mourns the late president. Fellow sculptor Lorado Taft, author of the first survey of American sculpture, praised the Chester memorial as "a graceful and expressive work." He also singled out as demonstrative of the artist's "poetic imagination" Keyser's bronze relief *Hope* (1903) in the Baltimore Hebrew Cemetery, which portrays a seated boy holding a branch and looking at a Star of David.[31]

Keyser's most public commission is a bronze statue of Baron Johann de Kalb (1886; Fig. 25). A German who served as an officer in the French army, de Kalb was offered a command with the Continental Army during the Revolutionary War and died in South Carolina at the Battle of Camden (1780). Because de Kalb had led Maryland troops, the Maryland House of Delegates commissioned a statue in his honor. Like Ezekiel, who sculpted fellow Virginians, Keyser received the commission because of his connections to Maryland. The heroic de Kalb statue, rendered from a photograph of a painted portrait, shows the major general in a Continental uniform striding forward with his sword raised.[32] Completed in Rome and shipped to Annapolis, the statue stands on the grounds of

30. "Ephraim Keyser, Sculptor," *New Era Illustrated Magazine* 6 (March/April 1905): 397–99; *Ephraim Keyser: Memorial Exhibition* (Baltimore: Maryland Institute, 1937), a small pamphlet with a list of works; Dianne W. Feldman, "Ephraim Keyser: Catalogue Raisonné" (M.A. thesis, University of Maryland, 2008). Feldman's recuperative effort to locate Keyser's work is admirable. This kind of investigation needs to be done for many of the artists described here.

31. Lorado Taft, *The History of American Sculpture* (New York and London: Macmillan, 1903), 521. Keyser also sculpted a nine-foot-tall statue of President Arthur (1892), originally slated for Plaza Circle in New York City but rejected by park commissioners as substandard. After a period in a private collection, the statue currently stands at Union College in Schenectady, Arthur's alma mater. Feldman, "Ephraim Keyser," 51.

32. "The De Kalb Statue," *Harper's Weekly*, August 28, 1886, 549.

Fig. 24 (*above*). Ephraim Keyser, *Chester A. Arthur Memorial*, 1889. Bronze. Albany Rural Cemetery, New York.

Fig. 25 (*facing*). Ephraim Keyser, *Baron Johann de Kalb*, 1886. Bronze. Height: 21 ft. Stands in front of the Maryland State House, Annapolis. (Collection of the Maryland State Archives; MSA SC 1545-0761).

the Maryland State House. Keyser returned to his hometown in 1893, where he became one of the most influential instructors at the Maryland Institute College of Art.

The creative Keyser family also lays claim to Ephraim's nephew Ernest Wise Keyser (1876–1959), a minor artist who became a sculptor as well, frequently making portrait busts and small figures.[33] Ephraim's sister Fannie married

33. "Biographical Sketches: Ernest Wise Keyser," *American Jewish Year Book* 6 (Philadelphia: Jewish Publication Society of America, 1904–1905), 128. Also following in his family's footsteps was Herman N. Hyneman (1849–1907), a cousin of Moses Ezekiel. In his twenties, the Philadelphia-born Hyneman traveled to France for study and became a portraitist, sometimes painting works with literary themes. Gutmann, "Jewish Participation in the Visual Arts," 51–52.

DeKALB

photographer David Bachrach (1845–1921), discussed below; when Ephraim moved back to the United States, he lived with the Bachrachs and maintained a studio at the back of their property (their home, since 1985, is on the National Register of Historic Places). Amelia Keyser, the sister of Ephraim and Fannie, was the mother of Leo and Gertrude Stein, extremely important art patrons in Paris. They never specifically sought out art by Jews; rather, in the early years of the twentieth century the Stein siblings lent their support to progressive artists like Pablo Picasso and Henri Matisse. While living with the Bachrachs in Baltimore in 1892 after the deaths of her parents, Gertrude met Claribel and Etta Cone, who bequeathed their prestigious collection of works by Matisse and other avant-garde artists to the Baltimore Museum of Art.[34] That museum's first director, Florence Nightingale Levy (1870–1947), was a Jewess who had studied art history abroad, wrote a number of books, and founded the directory *American Art Annual* in 1898, which she edited for more than two decades. America had few nineteenth-century Jewish art patrons, but Jews such as the Steins and the Cones, and later Edith Halpert and Peggy Guggenheim, acquired crucial collections in the early twentieth century.

Another prominent portraitist in his day was George Da Maduro Peixotto (1859–1937), but he did not exhibit widely.[35] Peixotto was born into a notable Sephardic family; his father, Benjamin Franklin Peixotto, was U.S. consul to Bucharest, and the younger Peixotto received his art education in Europe during his father's overseas service. He painted portraits of notables, such as President McKinley (ca. 1898, lost), Sir Moses Montefiore (1886, Jewish Museum, New York), and printmaker Julius Bien (1886, National Portrait Gallery, Washington, D.C.), discussed below.[36] Peixotto's canvas *Family Group* (1893, lost) was exhibited at the French Salon, and he was elected an officer of the French Academy.

Born in Prussia, Toby Rosenthal (1848–1907) made an impression on San

34. Janet Bishop, Cécile Debray, and Rebecca Rabinow, eds., *The Steins Collect: Matisse, Picasso, and the Parisian Avant-Garde*, exh. cat. (New Haven: Yale University Press, 2011); *Four Americans in Paris: The Collections of Gertrude Stein and Her Family*, exh. cat. (New York: Museum of Modern Art, 1970); Karen Levitov, *Collecting Matisse and Modern Masters: The Cone Sisters of Baltimore*, exh. cat. (New Haven: Yale University Press, 2011); Brenda Richardson, *Dr. Claribel and Miss Etta: The Cone Collection of the Baltimore Museum of Art*, exh. cat. (Baltimore: Baltimore Museum of Art, 1985).

35. "George Peixotto, Portrait Painter," *New York Times*, October 13, 1937, 23.

36. The Corcoran Gallery of Art in Washington, D.C., purchased the portrait of Moses Montefiore in 1886. Files indicate that the canvas was deaccessioned in 1959, at which time it entered the collection of the Jewish Museum. "Peixotto, George DaM.—Sir Moses Montefiore, Aged 100," Cor.5.1.rg: Corcoran Registrar Series 16.1, box 96, folder 94, Corcoran Archives, George Washington University.

Francisco, the city of his youth.[37] *Overland Monthly* featured Rosenthal when a young man in his late twenties; the author points out the artist's Jewish origins at the outset and enthuses that at his birth, "none could have suspected what new honor the God of Israel was about to put upon that chosen race...."[38] Such accolades were often showered on Rosenthal, minus the Jewish hyperbole. Like Moses Ezekiel, Rosenthal was widely admired, and he received most of his commissions from Americans, especially the California Jewish community, even though he lived across the Atlantic. Rosenthal was honored in Europe as well, accepting the Cross of the Bavarian Order of St. Michael. Unlike Ezekiel's work, however, Rosenthal's is mostly hidden today in museum basements, his career largely forgotten.

As a teen, Rosenthal studied at the Royal Academy in Munich and aspired to be a history painter, then viewed by the academic art establishment as the pinnacle of success. He favored dramatic subject matter with a romantic bent, painted in a Germanic style. A genre painting, *Sebastian Bach and his Family at their Morning Devotions* (1870; Fig. 26), was exhibited in Vienna and purchased by the Leipzig Museum not long after Rosenthal arrived in Germany. Henry Mosler, too, had painted historical genre scenes; his canvas *Pilgrim's Grace* also depicts a moment of piety, in this case that of a solemn Puritan family celebrating their first Thanksgiving (1897; Fig. 27). *Sebastian Bach and his Family at*

37. In his autobiography, Rosenthal claimed that he was born in New Haven, Connecticut, where his family did live at one point; this misinformation was reprinted for decades in newspaper accounts. On Rosenthal, see *Toby Rosenthal: Exhibition, San Francisco*, exh. cat. (San Francisco: Bosqui Engraving and Printing Co., 1884), unillustrated but with some of the artist's letters reprinted and a biography. In J. Nilsen Laurvik, *Catalogue of a Museum Loan Exhibition of Work by the California Group of Contemporary American Artists and Toby E. Rosenthal Memorial Exhibition*, exh. cat. (San Francisco: Palace of the Fine Arts, 1919), Rosenthal's exhibition begins on page 45 with a catalogue listing of works. Rosenthal's brief autobiography, appended at the end of Kramer and Stern, *San Francisco's Artist*, is the only full translation from German; written late in life and published posthumously, the memoir covers Rosenthal's early years, training in Munich, and first successes.

38. Walt M. Fisher, "Toby Rosenthal: How He Became a Painter," *Overland Monthly* 14, no. 3 (1875): 284. Later that year, a brief note on Rosenthal was included in Charles W. Stoddard, "A Note from Abroad," *Overland Monthly* 15, no. 6 (1875): 589. Twenty years later, he was mentioned in an article about prominent Jewish San Franciscans in Gustav Adolf Danzinger, "The Jew in San Francisco: The Last Half of the Century," *Overland Monthly* 25, no. 148 (1895): 401–2.

Fig. 26 (*overleaf*). Toby Edward Rosenthal, *Sebastian Bach and His Family at Their Morning Devotions*, 1870. Oil on canvas. Location unknown. (Photo: akg-images).

Toby E. Rosenthal.
Munich

their Morning Devotions and other paintings by Rosenthal garnered such acclaim that they were lithographed and widely distributed in Europe.

The 1875 *Overland Monthly* article pointed to *Elaine* (1874; Fig. 28) as being "*the* great picture of this year," and indeed, for that canvas Rosenthal attained fame.[39] Painted on commission, *Elaine* melodramatically portrays a moment from Alfred Lord Tennyson's "Lancelot and Elaine," one of twelve poems in *Idylls of the King*: "In her right hand the lily, in her left | The letter—all her bright hair streaming down." Rosenthal's richly colored canvas dramatically pictures the tragic young maiden after her affections were rebuffed by Lancelot and she died from a broken heart. Her corpse floats resplendently on a small boat bedecked with flowers, to be reunited in serene death at Camelot with the object of her unrequited love.

This somber painting captured the imagination of Americans, sparking an Elaine craze of sorts and leading to the composition of "The Elaine Waltz," the organization of Elaine clubs, and reprintings of *Idylls of the King* for admirers of the painting. Exhibited soon after its completion in Berlin, the canvas was shown in Boston, New York, and Philadelphia, where it was awarded a gold medal at the Centennial Exhibition. Most famously, in San Francisco the sizeable painting was stolen from the gallery where it was on display.[40] The theft, and the painting's quick recovery, were covered by newspapers nationwide, even reaching the front page of the *New York Times*.[41]

Two Jewish artists were at the forefront of chromolithography: Julius Bien (1826–1909), from Germany, and Max Rosenthal (1833–1918), born in Poland. Chromolithography, a printing process that gained immense popularity in the years around the Civil War, allowed Americans to decorate their homes with inexpensive color images, so millions of brightly hued, eye-catching prints soon hung in homes across the country. Chromolithograph techniques were employed widely for advertisements, posters, postcards, and reproductions of fine art.[42] Not only did Bien and Rosenthal follow their artistic muse, but they also demonstrated entrepreneurial skills, homing in on a new and profitable process that broadened the market for art beyond the elite.

39. Fisher, "Toby Rosenthal," 286. Italics in original.

40. William M. Kramer and Norton B. Stern, "The Great 'Elaine' Robbery: The Crime Against Civilization," *Journal of the West* 10, no. 4 (1971): 585–95. This article is an earlier version of the most useful chapter of the authors' *San Francisco's Artist.*

41. "A Valuable Painting Stolen From an Art Gallery," *New York Times*, April 3, 1875, 1; "Recovery of a Stolen Picture," *New York Times*, April 5, 1875, 1.

42. Peter C. Marzio, *The Democratic Art: Pictures for a 19th-Century America, Chromolithography 1840–1900* (Boston: David R. Godine, 1979).

Bien received valuable training in color lithography in his native land, acquiring techniques still unknown in America. After fighting in the 1848 Revolution, he fled to New York, where he lived a life in service to the Jewish people and art. Bien led B'nai B'rith as the organization's president for more than three decades, just as comfortably as he did in his ten-year presidency of the National Lithographers' Association.[43] His technical proficiency and attention to detail as a printer of maps included service to the Union cause during the Civil War, to Pacific Railroad surveys, and to U.S. census reports for forty years. Aided by more than two hundred artists in his large workshop, Bien was recognized as the most prolific and respected practitioner in the field. To cite one of many encomiums, Charles P. Daly, the president of the American Geographical Society (and chief justice of the New York Court of Common Pleas), declared one Bien map to be "the finest geographical work that has yet appeared in this country, and will compare with any I know of in any other country."[44] Bien's work was also acclaimed by the larger public, winning medals at world expositions in Paris, Philadelphia, and Chicago.[45]

Bien's magnum opus was an illustrated edition of artist-naturalist John James Audubon's *Birds of America* (1858–1860). That edition, which relied on direct examination of the original color drawings rather than the copper plates used as models for other editions, has been lauded as a landmark in the chromolithographic process in the United States and widely admired for its soft, more accurate color varieties (Fig. 29). Unfortunately, the financial troubles of his Audubon collaborators, the advent of the Civil War, and newer scientific approaches in ornithology halted the project. Images of only 150 of the original 435 species were produced and eventually bound in one volume.[46]

Following study in Berlin and Paris, seventeen-year-old Max Rosenthal reunited with four of his brothers in Philadelphia and enrolled in classes at the

43. Benjamin F. Peixotto, "Julius Bien," *Menorah: A Monthly Magazine for the Jewish Home* 8 (June 1890): 284–95.

44. Quoted in *ibid.*, 288.

45. "Biographical Sketches: Julius Bien," *American Jewish Year Book* 6 (Philadelphia: Jewish Publication Society of America, 1904), 63.

46. Ann Lee Morgan, "The American Audubons: Julius Bien's Lithographed Edition," *Print Quarterly* 4, no. 4 (1987): 362–79. For a facsimile, see Joel Oppenheimer, *The Birds of America: The Bien Chromolithographic Edition* (New York: W. W. Norton, 2013).

Fig. 27 (*overleaf*). Henry Mosler, *Pilgrim's Grace*, 1897. Oil on canvas, 38¾ × 51¾ in. (Allentown Art Museum, Allentown, Pennsylvania. Gift of Mr. and Mrs. Norman Hirschl, 1977; 1977.04).

Henry Mosler.
Copyright 1897.

Fig. 28. Toby Edward Rosenthal, *Elaine*, 1874. Oil on canvas, 38 9/16 × 62 1/2 in. (Art Institute of Chicago. Gift of Maurice Rosenfeld).

N° 6

Drawn from Nature by J.J. Audubon F.R.S. F.L.S.

Great White Hero

Fig. 29. Julius Bien, *Great White Heron*, 1860. Chromolithograph on paper, 24¾ × 36¾ in. (Smithsonian American Art Museum).

Pennsylvania Academy of Fine Arts.[47] The Rosenthal brothers—Lewis, Maurice, Solomon, Simon, and Max—established a profitable family lithography business, with Max as the primary artist.[48] The firm printed a variety of images, from city views to sheet music covers to advertisements. Max's interior view of the grand lodge room of Philadelphia's New Masonic Hall (1855; see Fig. 31) measures 22 by 25 inches and was the largest American chromolithograph to date. This commemorative print exemplifies the vibrancy of chromolithographs, especially in the turquoise hues featured throughout the ornate Gothic architecture, patterned carpet, and cushioned benches. Like Ezekiel and Mosler, Rosenthal's career was touched by the Civil War; he served as official illustrator for the U.S. Military Commission, making sketches of army camps that he then translated into lithographs. Later he found appreciation for his technically rich mezzotint portrait engravings of distinguished Americans, mostly made after original paintings by other artists (Fig. 30).

Rosenthal attained some notoriety for daring to show Jesus as a Jew—with Semitic features and wearing a tallis, phylacteries, and prayer shawl—in a painting titled *Jesus at Prayer* (1904, lost). At the bottom right corner of the canvas a thorny bush presages Jesus's fate. Each corner of the specially designed ornate frame featured plentiful grapes, a symbol of the Eucharist or, as mistakenly reported in the Jewish press, a symbol of Judah.[49] More easily identified is the lion carved at bottom center, surely symbolizing the Tribe of Judah, with Judah's name printed in Hebrew. Created on commission for a Protestant church in Baltimore, the painting was promptly rejected by its Christian patrons. In defense of the conception, one writer countered that in art, over the ages,

> Jesus has been everything, except what he was—a Jew.... His [Rosenthal's] readings in the New Testament have given him no reason to believe that all the

47. Albert Rosenthal, "Max Rosenthal: Lithographer, Painter, Designer, Etcher, and Engraver in Mezzotint," *Print Connoisseur: A Quarterly Magazine for the Print Collector* 2, no. 1 (1921): 3–25. This article includes a brief biography, a catalogue raisonné of Rosenthal's forty-seven mezzotints, and twenty-one reproductions. For a more complete listing of works by Max Rosenthal and his son Albert, alphabetized and numbering over 700, see *List of Portraits: Lithographs, Etchings, Mezzotints* (Philadelphia: privately printed, 1923).

48. On the Rosenthal family, see Harry T. Peters, *America on Stone: The Other Printmakers to the American People* (1931; repr. New York: Arno Press, 1976), 343–46.

49. "A Jewish Painter's Idea of Jesus," *New Era Illustrated Magazine* 5, no. 1 (1904): 76.

Fig. 31 (*overleaf*). Max Rosenthal, *Grand Lodge Room of the New Masonic Hall, Chestnut Street Philadelphia*, 1855. Chromolithograph on paper, 22 × 25 in. (Library of Congress).

Fig. 30. Max Rosenthal, *George Washington*, 1904. Mezzotint on paper. (Cleveland Museum of Art. Gift of Albert Rosenthal).

On Stone by Max Rosenthal.

Entered, according to Act of Congress, in the year 18[illegible]

Grand Lodge Room of the NEW M

To the R. W. Grand Master, Grand Officers, and Members of the Grand

PUBLISHED

Sloan & Stewart Architects.

IC HALL, Chesnut Street Philadelphia.

...en.^c and the Order in general, this print is respectfully dedicated by L. N. Rosenthal. of No 9

ROSENTHAL, PHILADA PA

MICROFILMED

> Jewish customs in regard to prayer were not observed by Jesus. ... Mr. Rosenthal has, therefore, painted Jesus standing erect and open-eyed, instead of kneeling with bowed head, as Christian painters have been accustomed to represent him, an attitude unknown among Jews, and therefore unlikely to have been assumed by Jesus.[50]

Rosenthal himself understood the canvas, which he said was the dream of his life to paint, not "as a religious, but distinctly as an historic picture, aiming at conscientious accuracy."[51]

At the same time in Europe, Jewish artists—Polish painter Maurycy Gottlieb; Russian sculptor Mark Antokolsky; German painter Max Liebermann; and German Zionist graphic artist Ephraim Moses Lilien—were producing imagery that portrayed Jesus very much as a Jew.[52] Moses Ezekiel stressed Jesus' Jewish origins as well, including a powerful *Ecce Homo* (1899, Cincinnati Art Museum) as a bronze torso with a heavy beard and pronounced crown of thorns. Highly admired in its time, but now hidden in an obscure church in Paris, is Ezekiel's *Christ in the Tomb* (1896; Fig. 32) in the Chapelle de Notre Dame de Consolation. The marble sculpture presents a life-sized recumbent Jesus encased in a winding sheet of drapery. Ezekiel conceived this Jesus as possessing Semitic features and, surprisingly, giving the ancient priestly blessing with four fingers separated into two groups, as decreed in Numbers 6:24–26. This sculpture resembles Ezekiel's recumbent funerary monuments for Mary Outwater White (1889), wife of President Andrew D. White of Cornell University, and Jennie McGraw Fiske (1908), who bequeathed generously to the university. Both monuments remain in Cornell's Sage Chapel.

Max Rosenthal's son and protégé, Albert Rosenthal (1863–1939), was likewise a printmaker of colonial and historical portraits and a portrait painter, trained at the École des Beaux-Arts in Paris. The Independence Hall Committee of

50. *Ibid.*, 75, 76. Rosenthal's painting gained such notice that *Literary Digest*, a general interest weekly, partly reprinted the article with the same title: "A Jewish Painter's Idea of Jesus," *Literary Digest* 29, no. 2 (1904): 51–52. For *New Era*'s follow-up, see "Of Interest to Jewish Readers," *New Era Illustrated Magazine* 5, no. 6 (1904): 652. This small snippet reported the reaction of Baltimore's Cardinal Gibbons to the canvas: "I was a little surprised at Mr. Rosenthal's use of the phylacteries, because our Lord condemned the wearing of them and said that the truth should be found in our hearts, not worn on the outside. But I am very glad to have seen the painting. It is a very striking picture."

51. Quoted in "A Jewish Painter's Idea of Jesus," *New Era Illustrated Magazine*, 76.

52. Ziva Amishai-Maisels, "Origins of the Jewish Jesus," in *Complex Identities: Jewish Consciousness and Modern Art*, ed. Matthew Baigell and Milly Heyd (New Brunswick: Rutgers University Press, 2001), 55–62.

Philadelphia commissioned him to copy the original portraits of the members of the Federal Convention, and he painted some original portraits of the Supreme Court associate justices, twelve from life. Rosenthal medaled at the St. Louis Exposition (1904) and the Panama-Pacific Exposition in San Francisco (1915). A respected collector and art expert for museums and private collections, the younger Rosenthal was heavily involved in promoting his father's art, publishing several small catalogues reproducing Max's prints.[53] Together, father and son created portraits of the Supreme Court justices for a limited edition history of the Court.[54]

Just as Jews were pioneers in lithography, they were innovators in photography, though histories of the medium have slighted them. Before discussing Jewish photographers during the years covered in this essay, it is worth looking briefly at the important accomplishments of three predecessors from the antebellum period: Jules Lion (ca. 1806–1866), Philip Haas (ca. 1808–ca. 1864), and Solomon Nunes Carvalho (1815–1897).

Questions surround the heritage of lithographer and photographer Jules Lion (sometimes spelled Lyon), born Jacob Isaac in Paris. Lion has alternately been identified as "a free man of color," based on six annual editions of the New Orleans city directory that list him with the designation "f.m.c.," and as a Jew, the religion of his parents as given in French census records, among many other sources.[55] Already recognized for his lithography in Paris and in New Orleans, where he arrived at age thirty, Lion returned to France to learn the new daguerreotype process. With a series of city views (all lost), Lion was the first artist to exhibit daguerreotypes in New Orleans and introduce the invention to his adopted city. He soon opened his own daguerreotype studio, but over time he became less interested in photography and returned to lithography. Lion made lithographic portraits of patriots and influential Louisianans, including John James Audubon (1860).[56]

53. See Albert Rosenthal, "Albert Rosenthal: Painter, Etcher, Lithographer," *Print Connoisseur* 9, no. 2 (1929): 97–103, for a short autobiographical statement followed by a "List of Plates Executed by Albert Rosenthal" (106–30), counting over 200 works, with six reproductions.

54. Hampton L. Carson, *The History of the Supreme Court of the United States: With Biographies of All the Chief and Associate Justices*, 2 vols. (Philadelphia: P. W. Ziegler and Co., 1902–1904). The Rosenthals provided fifty-eight engravings.

55. Charles East, "Jules Lion's New Orleans," *Georgia Review* 40, no. 4 (1986): 913–20; Sara M. Picard, "Racing Jules Lion," *Louisiana History* 58, no. 1 (2017): 5–37. Picard's lengthy article, based on extensive, meticulous research, offers a more compelling case for Lion's Jewish ancestry than for his identification as a Black man.

56. Sara Picard, "Facing Jules Lion: Portraits of Louisiana's Distinguished Men," *Imprint:*

Fig. 32. Moses Jacob Ezekiel, *Christ in the Tomb*, 1896. Marble. Mémorial du Bazar de la Charité, Paris. (Photos © Mémorial du Bazar de la Charité, Marie-Béatrice Vallet).

Before immigrating to America in his twenties, Philip Haas trained as a lithographer in Germany and later gained skills as a daguerreian artist, perhaps in Paris.[57] Expert in both fields, Haas was able to reproduce his own daguerreotypes as published lithographs, an entrepreneurial move that garnered financial reward beyond that of peers who worked only in one medium. Because few of his one-of-a-kind daguerreotypes are extant, the surviving lithographs provide the best means to get a sense of Haas's style and legacy. In addition, Haas created lithographs after other artists' paintings and daguerreotypes, notably of Presidents Martin Van Buren (1837) and William Henry Harrison (1841), and prints in other genres. To cite just one example, he printed a map and atlas of the Bridgeport, Connecticut, harbor for the U.S. Navy (1836). Over the years

---

Journal of the American Historical Print Collectors Society 41, no. 2 (2016): 17–33; Patricia Brady, "Jules Lion, F.M.C.: Lithographer Extraordinaire," in *Printmaking in New Orleans*, ed. Jessie J. Poesch (Jackson: University Press of Mississippi, 2006), 160–75.

57. For the only comprehensive discussion of Haas, a valuable work of research, see William and Estelle Marder with Sally Pierce, "Philip Haas: Lithographer, Print Publisher, Daguerreotypist," *Daguerreian Annual* (1995): 20–39.

he maintained studios in Washington, D.C., and New York City. Well respected in his field, Haas exhibited his work to acclaim and was elected a member of the American Daguerre Association as well as vice president of the New York Daguerreian Association. During the Civil War, Haas lied about his advanced age to enlist in the Union army. Together with Washington Peale, from the distinguished Peale family of artists, Haas took photographs of combat in Charleston Harbor in the summer of 1863, along with camp scenes; twenty-five original negatives signed by the pair are in the collection of the Library of Congress.[58]

Haas made news in 2017, when the National Portrait Gallery paid more than $300,000 to acquire his daguerreotype portrait of John Quincy Adams (1843; Fig. 33), the earliest surviving photograph of an American president.[59] In his diary, Adams mentions two sittings, specifying Haas's name. Congressman Adams's visit to the photographer's studio in Washington also marked the first time that a current or former president sat for a photographic portrait. Haas's likeness of Adams, one of three, offers yet another first. The artist's subsequent lithograph, dated the same year as its prototype, is acknowledged as the first directly from a daguerreotype.

Born in Charleston, South Carolina, to a Sephardic family, Solomon Nunes Carvalho primarily painted portraits and landscapes. He saw new possibilities for portraiture after the introduction of the daguerreotype and established his photographic practice in several cities. Carvalho was well respected for a technical innovation that provided protective coating for daguerreotypes. His fame,

58. Milton Kaplan, "The Case of the Disappearing Photographers," *Quarterly Journal of the Library of Congress* 24, no. 1 (1967): 40–45; Bob Zeller, *The Blue and Gray in Black and White: A History of Civil War Photography* (Westport, Conn.: Praeger, 2005), 119, 131–33.

59. Jennifer Schuessler, "Found: The Oldest U.S. Presidential Photo," *New York Times*, August 17, 2017, C2; https://www.antiquesandthearts.com/360500-for-earliest-known-photograph-of-an-american-president-at-sothebys/ (accessed January 4, 2021). For early musings about Haas's identity and the whereabouts of the original daguerreotype of Adams before its discovery, see Beaumont Newhall, "A Daguerreotype of John Quincy Adams by Philip Haas," *Metropolitan Museum Journal* 12 (1977): 151–54.

Fig. 33 (*facing*). Philip Haas, *John Quincy Adams*, 1843. Daguerreotype, 5⅜ × 4 in. (National Portrait Gallery, Smithsonian Institution. Acquired through the generosity of the Secretary of the Smithsonian and the Smithsonian National Board; The Burnett Family Fund; Carl and Marilynn Thoma; Connie and Dennis Keller; Tim Lindholm and Lucy Gaylord Lindholm; Mr. and Mrs. John W. McCarter, Jr.; Mr. and Mrs. Ronald J. Gidwitz; Ellen G. Miles and Neil R. Greene; Ronnyjane Goldsmith; David D. Hiller; Richard and Janet Horwood; and Mary Martell).

though, chiefly rests on his work as a daguerreotypist for John C. Frémont's 1853 expedition through Kansas, Utah, and Colorado, an exploration undertaken to map a transcontinental railway route from the Mississippi River to the Pacific Coast. Unfortunately, Carvalho's photographs and sketches of the trip are presumed lost in an 1881 fire, although a single badly damaged picture survived (Library of Congress, Washington).[60] Carvalho's account of the expedition, the only record of the trip, was widely reprinted, four times before 1860.[61] The volume discusses both the rigors and the discoveries of the journey while also providing Carvalho's personal reflections. After the Civil War, his artistic production mostly ceased because of failing eyesight. Instead, he dedicated his efforts to the betterment of the Jewish community and to his business ventures, including a patented heating invention.

Commercial photographer Theodore Lilienthal (1829–1894) straddles the ante- and postbellum periods. Arriving in the United States from Prussia in his twenties, he opened a daguerreian gallery in New Orleans before the Civil War, specializing in commercial portraits and urban photography, and later in the popular stereoview format.[62] When Ulysses S. Grant was in the area during the Vicksburg campaign, he stopped at the well-regarded studio to have a vignetted portrait taken (1863). Lilienthal's portrait photographs, which he wisely copyrighted, were translated into wood engravings in publications such as *Harper's Weekly* and *Frank Leslie's Illustrated Newspaper*. He also had the foresight to patent usage of the Lambertype, a printing process, in Louisiana.

When Lilienthal received the commission to produce a portfolio of 150 views of

60. Robert Shlaer, "An Expeditionary Daguerreotype by Solomon Carvalho," *Daguerreian Annual* (1999): 151–59; Robert Shlaer, *Sights Once Seen: Daguerreotyping Frémont's Last Expedition Through the Rockies* (Santa Fe: Museum of New Mexico Press, 2000). On Carvalho more broadly, see Joan Sturhahn, *Carvalho, Artist-Photographer-Adventurer-Patriot: Portrait of a Forgotten American* (Merrick, N.Y.: Richwood Publishing Company, 1976); Elizabeth Kessin Berman, "Transcendentalism and Tradition: The Art of Solomon Nunes Carvalho," *Jewish Art* 16/17 (1990/1991): 64–81. Rosengarten, "Portrait of Two Painters," 161–86, also discusses the Carvalho family's history.

61. Solomon Nunes Carvalho, *Incidents of Travel and Adventure in the Far West with Colonel Frémont's Last Expedition* (1856; repr. Lincoln: University of Nebraska Press, 2004).

62. Peter E. Palmquist and Thomas R. Kailbourn, *Pioneer Photographers from the Mississippi to the Continental Divide: A Biographical Dictionary, 1839–1865* (Stanford: Stanford University Press, 2005), 398–99; Margaret Denton Smith and Mary Louise Tucker, *Photography in New Orleans: The Early Years, 1840–1865* (Baton Rouge: Louisiana State University Press, 1982), 136–38. Of interest, Lilienthal's brother married the Civil War diarist Clara Solomon; see *The Civil War Diary of Clara Solomon: Growing Up in New Orleans, 1861–1862*, ed. Elliott Ashkenazi (Baton Rouge: Louisiana State University Press, 1995).

New Orleans for the 1867 Paris Universal Exposition, he set himself to the task with alacrity.[63] Documents from the era indicate that a major goal of the project was to attract new residents and investors to the city during the challenging postbellum period. Lilienthal won a bronze medal for this ambitious effort (and other prestigious accolades during his career), the first large-scale municipal commission of topographic scenes of an American city. Measuring a sizeable 12 by 15 inches, Lilienthal's albumen prints portray monuments, bodies of water, festivals, and a range of hospitals, churches, hotels, residences, commercial establishments, and more. Photographs of a Jewish nature include views of the newly constructed Gates of Prayer synagogue (Fig. 34) and the Jewish Widows' and Orphans' Asylum, established in the wake of the yellow fever epidemic of 1853. Lilienthal's consistency and clarity in capturing the qualities of light in varied contexts, and his sensitive eye for detail and framing, render this large endeavor a technical and aesthetic tour-de-force. At the exposition's close, *La Nouvelle Orléans et ses environs* was presented to Napoleon III in an effort to shore up commercial bonds between the city and the country of its original founders.

Lilienthal's New Orleans contemporary, Bavarian-born Gustave Moses (1836–1915), who had arrived in the United States as a child, also thrived as a photographer.[64] He and his three brothers learned how to make daguerreotypes from their father, Samuel Wolfgang Moses (1798–1885). At different times, Gustave partnered with his brother Bernard (1832–1899), with whom he opened galleries before and after the Civil War. The brothers specialized in portraits, with Bernard making oil paintings as well as photographs.[65] The Moses brothers closed their gallery to join the Confederate army (their father and other brothers also fought for the Confederacy). In 1864, following his discharge, Gustave was commissioned to take albumen photographs of the aftermath of battle at Fort Morgan in Alabama.[66] Later, Gustave opened Gustave Moses and Son, a studio that operated until the 1930s.

Originally from Germany, David Bachrach (1845–1921) took his first photograph of a president on assignment for *Harper's Weekly*. As a young apprentice, Bachrach made one of only three confirmed photographs of Abraham

63. Gary A. Van Zante's admirable study, *New Orleans 1867: Photographs by Theodore Lilienthal* (London: Merrell, 2008), contextualizes and reproduces all 126 surviving photographs and discusses Lilienthal's career and techniques.

64. Palmquist and Kailbourn, *Pioneer Photographers*, 453–54.

65. *Ibid.*, 452–53; Smith and Tucker, *Photography in New Orleans*, 142–44.

66. Frances Osborn Robb, *Shot in Alabama: A History of Photography, 1839–1941, and a List of Photographers* (Tuscaloosa: University of Alabama Press, 2016), 55–56.

Fig. 34. Theodore Lilienthal. *Jackson St. Synagogue, New Orleans.* 1867. (Tulane University Archives).

Lincoln at Gettysburg (housed in the National Archives), which shows him seated in a large crowd after delivering his powerful address. During the Civil War, Bachrach was dispatched by the army to take photographs of Union prisoners. After the war, he founded Bachrach Photography Studio in 1868, which has been operated for over a century by four generations: patriarch David; sons, Louis Fabian and Walter; grandsons, Louis Fabian Jr. (known as Fabian) and

Bradford; and great-grandsons, Louis Fabian III and Robert Bachrach.[67] Initially based in Baltimore, the family business specializes in portrait photography and, at its height and until the Great Depression, maintained forty-eight studios in twelve states with up to 600 employees. The eldest Bachrach lived through the rapid-fire evolution of photography and contributed to it as well: He patented several photographic and printing processes, including a widely used method of making photo-relief plates for printing illustrations, and published important articles about photography in journals such as *Wilson's Photographic Magazine.* Among the fascinating figures who sat for the Bachrachs are Grover Cleveland, Ulysses S. Grant, and Thomas Edison. Bachrachs have taken formal photographs of every president from Andrew Johnson until George H. W. Bush, in addition to such notables as Amelia Earhart and Muhammad Ali. The family business is the country's longest-running photography studio, having made photographs for more than 150 years, from wet plates to the digital age.

A word needs to be said here about the absence of female artists. In her foundational essay, Linda Nochlin points to the institutional barriers facing women in the art world, such as difficulty gaining admission to art schools and prohibitions against attending life drawing class.[68] The only female Jewish artist about whom we have more than an inkling is Philadelphian Katherine M. Cohen (1859–1914). Her impressive artistic pedigree includes study at the Pennsylvania Academy of Fine Arts with Thomas Eakins and then at the Art Students League in New York City with the eminent sculptor Augustus Saint-Gaudens. She maintained her own studio in Philadelphia before embarking to Paris in 1887 to work for several years in the studios of two sculptors.

Little evidence remains about Cohen's subjects or the locations of her works beyond her execution of formal portrait busts. Among those are: Judge Mayer Sulzberger (date unknown, lost), a congregant at her synagogue; a plaster bust of Harry Souther (1890, lost), displayed at the 1893 Columbian Exposition in Chicago; and *General James A. Beaver* (ca. 1900; Fig. 35), for the *Smith Memorial Arch* in Philadelphia's Fairmount Park, a multi-figure monument honoring supporters of the Union in the Civil War.[69] Cohen also made works with Jewish

67. Douglas Collins, *Photographed by Bachrach: 125 Years of American Portraiture* (New York: Rizzoli, 1992). Samantha Baskind, "Personal Best: The Photography Dynasty That Made Everyone Look Great," *Smithsonian Magazine* (June 2021): 7–9.

68. Linda Nochlin, "Why Have There Been No Great Women Artists?" in Nochlin, *Women, Art, and Power and Other Essays* (New York: Harper and Row, 1988), 145–78.

69. Moses Ezekiel's bust of Pennsylvania Governor Andrew Gregg Curtin (1903) occupies a niche in the memorial as well. On Beaver, see Penny Balkin Bach, *Public Art in Philadelphia*

themes. In 1896, her sculpture *The Israelite* (ca. 1895–1896, lost) was exhibited at the French Salon. She modeled a group sculpture, titled *Vision of Rabbi Ben Ezra* (date unknown, lost), and also designed the seal for Gratz College in Philadelphia.[70] A book for kindergartners that Cohen illustrated with twelve full-page pictures depicting ceremonies at home and in synagogue is said to be one of the earliest printed in color for Jewish children.[71] According to the *American Jewish Year Book*, which featured her with a short biographical sketch, Cohen sometimes painted portraits and landscapes in oil and watercolor.[72] At the Women's Pavilion of the Chicago World's Fair, Cohen gave a speech encouraging greater support of artists and made special mention of female artists. Cohen's sister, Mary M. Cohen, was an accomplished journalist, author, and poet, often writing on Jewish themes.[73]

Jewish American artists would stand at the forefront of major visual arts movements in the twentieth century. Social Realists, a cadre of artists who addressed political, social, and economic issues, especially during the Great Depression, were overwhelmingly Jewish. They included William Gropper, Raphael Soyer, and Jack Levine, among many others. A number of leading Abstract Expressionists were Jewish. Barnett Newman, Mark Rothko (born Rothkowitz), Adolph Gottlieb, and Lee Krasner eschewed representation in the fifties and sixties. Pop art boasts Roy Lichtenstein, Jim Dine, and Larry Rivers (born Yizroch Loiza Grossberg). Two Jewish artists, Judy Chicago and Miriam Schapiro, initiated the Feminist Art Movement. The only female Photorealist, Audrey Flack, painted meticulous canvases commenting on stereotypes of femininity, and she was the first living female to be included in H. W. Janson's landmark survey of Western art. At the beginning of the twentieth century, the field of photography was

(Philadelphia: Temple University Press, 1992), 208. On Souther, see Carolyn Kinder Carr et al., *Revisiting the White City: American Art at the 1893 World's Fair*, exh. cat. (Hanover, N.H.: University Press of New England, 1993), 362.

70. Michele Siegel, "Katherine M. Cohen," Jewish Women's Archive, Encyclopedia of Jewish Women, https://jwa.org/encyclopedia/article/cohen-katherine-m.

71. Katherine Myrtilla Cohen, *A Jewish Child's Book* (Philadelphia: Jewish Publication Society of America, 1913).

72. "Biographical Sketches: Katherine M. Cohen," *American Jewish Year Book, 1904–1905* 6 (Philadelphia: Jewish Publication Society of America, 1904), 76.

73. Dianne Ashton, "Crossing Boundaries: The Career of Mary M. Cohen," *American Jewish History* 83, no. 2 (1995): 153–76.

Fig. 35 (*facing*). Katherine H. Cohen, *General James A. Beaver*, ca. 1900. Bronze. Smith Memorial Arch, Philadelphia. (Courtesy of the Association for Public Art, Philadelphia).

brought to artistic legitimacy by Alfred Stieglitz, followed over the decades by such crucial figures such Weegee, Diane Arbus, and Lee Friedlander. This partial listing barely begins to probe the vital contributions by American Jews in the arts during the last century and does not touch on the myriad ways that Jewish identity would overtly and covertly shape their visual output.[74]

Early Jewish American artists mostly worked independently and were not readily known to each other beyond the families who worked together in the lithography and photography businesses. They created works in divergent styles and genres, usually along the trends of the artistic mainstream. Not until the twentieth century did Jewish American artists begin to interact regularly and take art classes together—most notably at the Educational Alliance, a settlement house on the Lower East Side—and when they did, their prominence belies their small numbers.[75] If one were to try to find even a few commonalities among the distinct group of postbellum artists described here, we could point to a cosmopolitan group who often traveled to Europe for artistic training and sometimes remained for long periods, although this trajectory is not unique to Jewish artists of that generation. They also tended to congregate in cities populated by Jews. Of greater salience is that artists did not face obstacles because of their religion and were afforded the same opportunities as their non-Jewish peers. Neither were they confined by their Jewish roots: they did not feel personally compelled by their religio-cultural identity to make works of an overtly Jewish nature or forced to focus on Jewish subjects to please Jewish patrons, even if they benefited from that support. In these ways, Jewish Americans strongly differed from their European Jewish contemporaries, who were navigating political, religious, and social upheavals that inspired a more personal artistic response or a nostalgic turn to a Jewish life rapidly disappearing. Reexamination of some of these artists is long overdue, not because they were "Jewish artists" per se—and most of them would not want to be categorized as such—but because they are neglected artists who made intriguing, unfairly forgotten works that enriched the American cultural landscape and merit deeper exploration.

74. Samantha Baskind, *Encyclopedia of Jewish American Artists* (Westport, Conn.: Greenwood Press, 2007).

75. Norman L. Kleeblatt and Susan Chevlowe, eds., *Painting a Place in America: Jewish Artists in New York 1900–1945* (New York: Jewish Museum, 1991).

JEWS AND MUSIC: INTO THE SYNAGOGUE

JUDAH M. COHEN

JUDGING from Sidney Luska's 1885 novel *As It was Written: A Jewish Musician's Story*, music played a powerful role in late nineteenth-century human expression, affecting Jewish and non-Jewish Americans alike.[1] Luska, the Jewish-sounding pen name of non-Jewish writer Henry Harland, told the sordid story of Jewish violinist Ernest Neuman, who finds his fiancée, Hungarian Jewish contralto Veronika Pathzuol, mysteriously murdered. Luska portrays musicality in the novel as a power transcending religious identity: Ernest is as enraptured listening to Veronika in a New York City synagogue on Saturday as he is at a Hoboken church on Sunday. The musician's craft and career similarly defy social boundaries. Veronika's fluency in all kinds of music—the lovers meet when Ernest distantly hears Veronika sing Charles Gounod's 1859 setting of "Ave Maria"—highlights her talent as part of "a freemasonry, so far as we were concerned."[2] And his readers were expected to follow along: at one point, in a moment of foreshadowing, the book freely transitions from written narrative to musical score and back as if both registers connected naturally (Fig. 36).

Music's central role in the plot goes deeper than just the characters' occupations: it also opens channels between the conscious mind and a subconscious history of inherited family grievances. In final two chapters, music comes to its full psychological power. Neuman, after learning of past tensions between his family and Veronika's family, spontaneously improvises a rapturous violin solo. In a dreamlike state he transcribes it; but when he wakes the next day, he sees his musical notation transforming into a written murder confession. To his horror, he reads that he killed Veronika in a subconscious stupor, avenging a buried injustice between the two families.[3]

Jewish newspaper reviews gave the book a mixed reception, largely based on

1. Sidney Luska/Henry Harland, *As It Was Written: A Jewish Musician's Story* (New York: Cassell & Co., 1885).

2. *As It Was Written*, chaps. 1 and 2. Gounod created this piece in 1853 by adding an improvised melody over J. S. Bach's C-major prelude from *The Well-Tempered Clavier, Book I* (BWV 846).

3. *As It Was Written*, chaps. 13 and 14.

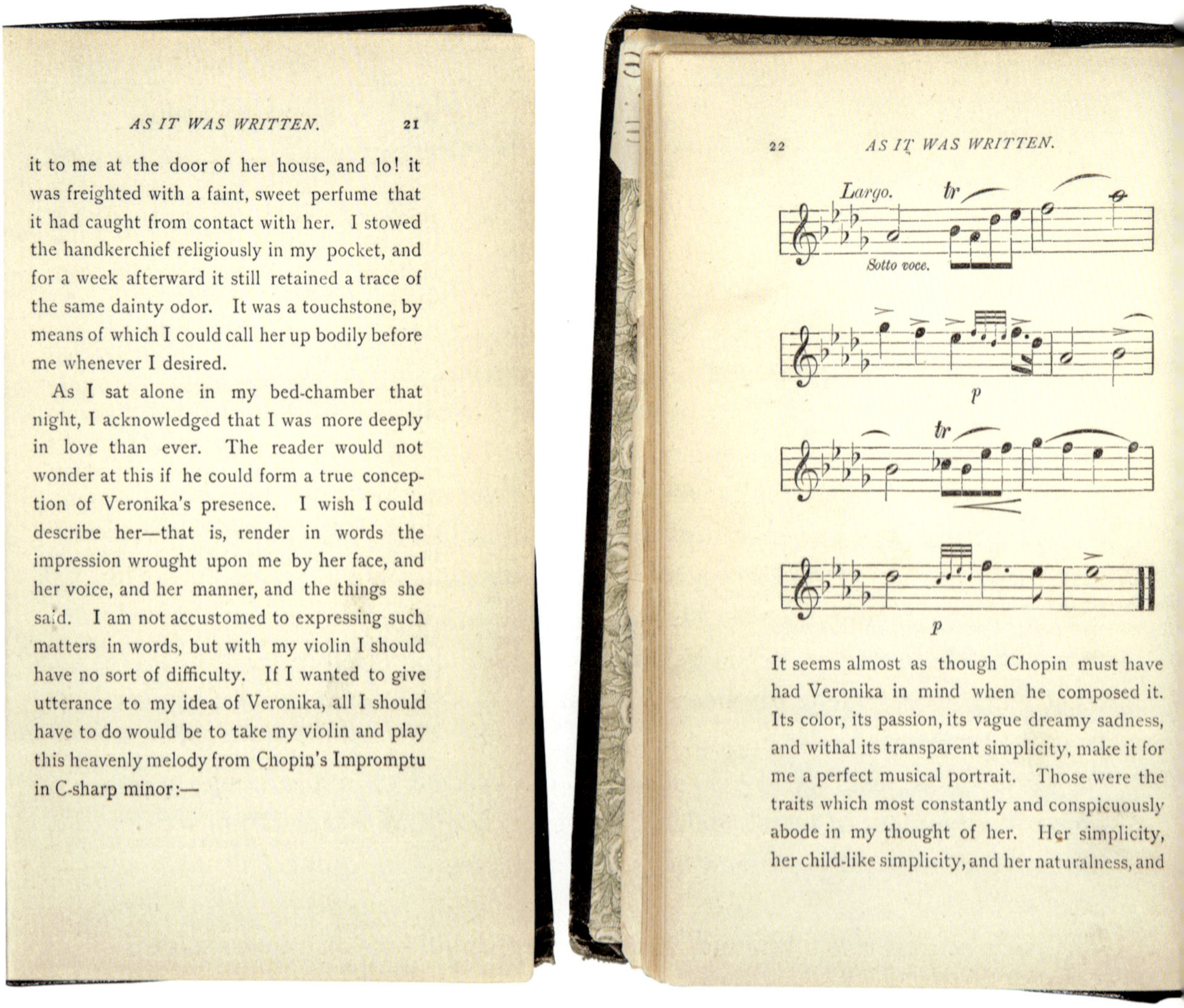

AS IT WAS WRITTEN. 21

it to me at the door of her house, and lo! it was freighted with a faint, sweet perfume that it had caught from contact with her. I stowed the handkerchief religiously in my pocket, and for a week afterward it still retained a trace of the same dainty odor. It was a touchstone, by means of which I could call her up bodily before me whenever I desired.

As I sat alone in my bed-chamber that night, I acknowledged that I was more deeply in love than ever. The reader would not wonder at this if he could form a true conception of Veronika's presence. I wish I could describe her—that is, render in words the impression wrought upon me by her face, and her voice, and her manner, and the things she said. I am not accustomed to expressing such matters in words, but with my violin I should have no sort of difficulty. If I wanted to give utterance to my idea of Veronika, all I should have to do would be to take my violin and play this heavenly melody from Chopin's Impromptu in C-sharp minor:—

22 AS IT WAS WRITTEN.

It seems almost as though Chopin must have had Veronika in mind when he composed it. Its color, its passion, its vague dreamy sadness, and withal its transparent simplicity, make it for me a perfect musical portrait. Those were the traits which most constantly and conspicuously abode in my thought of her. Her simplicity, her child-like simplicity, and her naturalness, and

Fig. 36. Sidney Luska, *As it Was Written* (New York, 1885). Pages 21 and 22 showing transitions into music and back again. (Princeton University Library).

Luska/Harland's Jewish characterizations, and offered little commentary on the music itself.[4] Yet the book's seemingly incidental pairing of Jewish characters with musical careers also allowed readers to peer into hidden depths of human experience and connection. Music's potential to captivate the collective imagination, in other words, had more to do with its "universal" affect than with any specific ethnic or religious identity. Discussions of the characters' talent certainly magnified musical narratives, but largely to dramatize the dark psychological underpinnings of a common middle-class experience.

4. *Jewish Messenger*, September 25, 1885; *American Israelite*, October 2, 1885, 3.

This conception of music as a social discourse tended to supersede ideas about "Jewish music" throughout much of the late nineteenth century. In a slowly healing postbellum America, where a lack of state support for the arts complemented a lively commercial infrastructure, one musical style after the next filtered through the American landscape, affecting the public square, the home, the theater, and the house of worship at the same time. Americans participated in musical activities analogous to those in Europe, including festivals, music lessons, and concerts; but they also fostered a series of experimental and creative conventions that reflected specifically American cultural practices, such as political rallies, balls, civic observances, and social clubs.

These musical activities, which spanned both "popular" and "classical" genres, ultimately became the basis from which a distinct category of "Jewish music" could gain increasing interest and refinement.[5] Community-wide music making, deeply woven into American life, coincided with the rise of Jewish movements and institutions, such as the Union of American Hebrew Congregations (founded in 1873) and the Jewish Theological Seminary (1886). These institutions, in turn, sought to circumscribe specific Jewish domains of activity, including music and art, and emphasized the synagogue sanctuary as a central site for defining Jewish identity. Music, through such efforts, became identified with Jewish ritual, thus generating a need to preserve it and keep it away from corrupting outside influences (such as the music of beer halls and the opera). By the end of the century, such Jewish institutional efforts to define and regulate music became important strategies for reinforcing communal identity, determined in part through ideologically connected claims to "tradition" that both reflected and superseded the surrounding musical practices.

An examination of Jews' broad engagement across the musical spectrum provides an alternate path through the musical developments of the second half of the nineteenth century. Following a broad survey of the ways that Jews participated in the popular and classical musical activities of the time, I will briefly chronicle events that brought a more focused "Jewish music" category into the synagogue sanctuary. I then turn to one of the era's musical capstones: Alois Kaiser and William Sparger's 1893 collection *Songs of Zion*, distributed by the National Council of Jewish Women as a souvenir for Chicago's Columbian Exposition. Building on the developments of these decades, Kaiser and Sparger presented "Jewish music" as a unique sonic form born of Jewish history, while

5. For a parallel account of Jews and music in late tsarist Russia, see James Loeffler, *The Most Musical Nation: Jews and Culture in the Late Russian Empire* (New Haven: Yale University Press, 2010).

modeling practical techniques for propagating that form across the Jewish calendar. That approach, as I will show, set a standard for describing and evaluating Jewish music ever since.

Jews and Music in the Late Nineteenth Century

To explore how Jews engaged with sound in the late nineteenth century requires a consideration of how a heterogeneous collection of musical practices can give rise to a musical tradition. Scholarship has shown how, despite a rhetorical aura of permanence, musical "traditions" can change rapidly as nations, religious groups, and political parties (among others) rethink their core values—often relying on music's ambiguously immaterial status to pivot from one ideology to another.[6] In other words, in order to understand how Jewish music came to be, we must also consider how Jews participated in widespread middle-class practices, such as parlor music, social dance, pop songs, sacred music concerts, community ensembles, balls, and other creative gatherings—genres that involved porous boundaries, overlapped with the music of other communities, and often borrowed from each other. For the sake of illustration, we can separate Jews' non-synagogue musical activities during this era into three primary realms: commercial and professional performance, amateur networks, and institutions devoted to Jewish community and identity.

COMMERCIAL AND PROFESSIONAL MUSIC PERFORMANCE

In both large cities and smaller towns, postbellum American Jews had access to a wide range of musical options across social, business, and entertainment networks. Most areas, regardless of size, had a theater or concert hall that hosted traveling entertainment troupes and local events, allowing residents to experience the latest musical dramas, vaudeville acts (including ethnic impersonators), operas, burlesques, minstrel shows, and concerts of all types. Cities with Jewish newspapers, including New York, Chicago, Cincinnati, Milwaukee, St. Louis, and San Francisco, regularly included performance listings in their pages, as well as advertisements by local sheet music retailers, instrument importers, and music teachers (especially of voice and piano). Readers saw the entertainment on offer as a potential source of pleasure, cultivation, and, occasionally, moral

6. Karen Ahlquist, for example, has pointed out that, despite the assumptions of "high" and "low" culture emerging in the late nineteenth century, a closer look at the music scene shows a far more complicated situation. See Karen Ahlquist, "Balance of Power: Music as Art and Social Class in the Late Nineteenth Century," in *Rethinking American Music*, ed. Thomas Riis and Tara Browner (Urbana: University of Illinois Press, 2019), 7–33.

concern. Just as significantly, newspaper editors developed their own voices as arts critics, vetting the appropriateness of performances for Jewish audiences, promoting Jewish performers, and offering aesthetic critiques of the musical styles they encountered.

This kind of coverage presented musicians and music making as a regular part of Jewish life, with a specialized pedagogy and canon that emphasized talent as a key criterion for acceptance. In an era before commercial recordings, musical artists with proficient training and good reputations enjoyed significant demand, providing entertainment for all manner of gatherings. Some Jewish instrumentalists held steady jobs in local professional ensembles, while vocalists and keyboardist/organists addressed the need for high-quality worship music in synagogues and churches alike. Supplemented by private lessons and occasional solo engagements, these jobs allowed some musicians to lead a middle-class lifestyle.

For American musicians who made their careers playing in commercial ensembles, such as Amsterdam-born violinist Jacques Oliveira, Jewish identity was largely incidental. Oliveira, for example, worked in New York and New Orleans, partly in the employ of troupes managed by P. T. Barnum.[7] When career musicians settled into a single location, however, their Jewish identities became a significant factor, as Jewish populations hired them regularly to play at their community functions and celebrations. St. Louis's Jewish musicians, for example, included: William Weil, whose orchestra regularly performed at the functions of Jewish social clubs; Aaron Pareira, a violinist admitted to the local musicians' union at age seventeen and hired by the city's Standard Theatre orchestra; violinist Isaac Schoen; and local-boy-made-good Herman Epstein, whose travel to Berlin for piano training received note in the local paper.[8] In most of these cases, as Brian Thompson notes in his essay on Oliveira, Jews integrated with other musicians as a community embracing its own artistic class. Yet, while Jewish identity resonated less in their public personae, their accomplishments were recognized by other Jews wishing to include music as a symbol of progress and a paradigm of communal achievement.

European Jewish musicians, meanwhile, received coverage in Jewish newspapers as paragons of public and cultural accomplishment, including opera composers Giacomo Meyerbeer (1791–1864) and Jacques Fromenthal Halévy

7. Brian C. Thompson, "Journeys of an Immigrant Violinist: Jacques Oliveira in Civil War–Era New York and New Orleans," *Journal of the Society for American Music* 6, no. 1 (2012): 51–82.

8. *Jewish Voice*, June 2, 1881, 3; November 8, 1887, 2; June 22, 1888, 5; August 3, 1888, 5; January 5, 1894, 7.

(1799–1862), and pianist Sigismond Thalberg (1812–1871). On a national level, American musicians such as New York conductor Max Maretzek (1821–1897), alto Henrietta Sulzer (1832–1907, daughter of Vienna cantor Salomon Sulzer), pianist Fannie Bloomfield-Zeisler (1863–1927), and the husband and wife musicians Julie Rosewald (soprano, 1847–1906) and Jacob Rosewald (conductor, violinist, 1841–1895) offered well-publicized models for Jewish musical success.[9] American virtuoso pianist Louis Moreau Gottschalk (1829–1869), meanwhile, represented a more variable figure. His father was of Jewish heritage, but he made little personal claim to Judaism. Isaac Mayer Wise referred to Gottschalk's Jewish identity in the past tense while the pianist was still alive, and Christian preachers sometimes included Gottschalk's name when seeking to point out Jews of note. In the latter years of the nineteenth century he began to appear occasionally in similar lists by Jewish authors.[10]

Jews also supported the growing American music infrastructure. Especially in urban areas, a few wealthy Jewish families appeared to incorporate music into a salon model similar to the one that had helped to acculturate Jews into European society. Jewish women of means in Berlin and Vienna hosted gatherings of writers and artists across the creative spectrum, supporting intellectual culture while raising the reputations and connections of the hosts.[11] American Jews had the literary salon of poet Penina Moïse (1797–1880) in Charleston, South Carolina, where music likely had a presence (though it is not clearly documented). Music factored more openly in the 48th Street parlor of clothier, financier, and philanthropist Elkan Naumburg (1835–1924) in New York City, where famous musicians stopped in to play and socialize, young artists were nurtured, and the Oratorio Society of New York was founded by conductor Leopold Damrosch (1832–1885) in 1873. The Naumburgs also helped to establish the New York Philharmonic and a longstanding series of free concerts in the city's parks,

9. Beth Abelson Macleod, *Fannie Bloomfield-Zeisler: The Life and Times of a Piano Virtuoso* (Urbana: University of Illinois Press, 2015), 102–14; Judith S. Pinnolis, "'Cantor Soprano' Julie Rosewald: The Musical Career of a Jewish American 'New Woman,'" *American Jewish Archives Journal* 62, no. 2 (2010): 1–53. Julie Rosewald in particular became a "lady cantor" for San Francisco's Temple Emanu-El for nearly a decade at the end of the nineteenth century.

10. S. Frederick Starr, *Bamboula! The Life and Times of Louis Moreau Gottschalk* (New York: Oxford University Press, 1995), 15–24; "Another Voice of a Christian: Money and Music," *Israelite*, November 21, 1856, 157; [Isaac Mayer Wise,] "Modern Jews," *Israelite*, December 18, 1863, 196; "Lafayette, Ind.," *American Israelite*, June 17, 1887, 6; "The Jewish Race: Its Greatness, Its Tribulations, Its Destiny," *American Israelite*, February 19, 1886, 7.

11. Marjanne E. Goozé, "What Was the Berlin Jewish Salon around 1800?" in *Sara Levy's World: Gender, Judaism, and the Bach Tradition in Enlightenment Berlin*, ed. Rebecca Cypess and Nancy Sinkoff (Rochester: University of Rochester Press, 2018), 21–38.

created the Naumburg Fellowship Fund at Harvard University to support young musicians' study in Europe, and underwrote the university library's acquisition of music books and scores.[12] Although the Naumburgs represented a high level of investment, numerous Jewish families across the country offered smaller contributions by sponsoring "musicales" or "literary evenings" that supported local musicians. Taken together, such families helped to foster an active musical scene through both direct and indirect support of musical organizations and venues.

On the other side of musical support lay the task of music education, which increasingly became its own professional activity after the Civil War.[13] Both Jewish and non-Jewish music teachers taught middle-class students of all backgrounds. In just one 1888 issue of Cincinnati's *American Israelite*, for example, readers could find advertisements for voice lessons by Charles J. Coleman and Fanny Levy, and a "piano-forte school" directed by Henry G. Andres.[14] Jewish music pedagogues sometimes bolstered their teaching incomes with other specifically Jewish musical activities. Gustavus S. Ensel of Paducah, Kentucky, taught music independently throughout the 1880s and 1890s and gave a presentation on Jewish music at a national conference of music educators in 1887; he also served the town's synagogue as rabbi and choir director between 1880 and 1886. During the summers between 1861 and 1863, composer and synagogue musician Sigmund Schlesinger taught at the female seminary of Noxubee County, Mississippi, a few hours away from his home base of Mobile, Alabama. Jewish religious leader Gustav M. Cohen similarly alternated between musical and teaching positions in New York, Cincinnati, Chicago, and Cleveland. Music teachers thus became beloved fixtures in many communities, helping to prepare young people of all backgrounds for the meaningful engagements of adulthood.

Alongside the emphasis on Western music literacy after the Civil War, the rapidly expanding sheet music industry provided another medium for Jews to participate in a broader cultural landscape. By the 1860s, music sellers, who doubled as publishers, had established both regional and national distribution networks, supplying inexpensive sheet music to both amateurs and professionals.

12. "Elkan Naumburg Dies in 90th Year," *New York Times*, August 1, 1924, 11. Notably, a memorial concert held the following month in the Naumburg Bandstand at Central Park had an audience of 15,000 and featured cantor Josef Rosenblatt singing two selections.

13. In 1876, music publisher Theodore Presser helped to create the Music Teachers National Association (MTNA), which gave the profession broad recognition. Music also became a staple of female colleges in the South, as a part of young society women's secondary education, and at dedicated music academies in the North, such as the Peabody Institute (Baltimore, 1866), Cincinnati Conservatory/College of Music (1867/1878), and the New England Conservatory (Boston, 1867).

14. *American Israelite*, September 7, 1888, 7.

Mass publication in the late nineteenth century played a role similar to social media in the twenty-first, and Jews, like others, treated popular dances, songs, and solo works as public declarations of social, personal, and professional relationships. Several publications reproduced the sounds of celebrated Jewish communal events: as early as 1857, consumers could purchase Philadelphia bandleader Mark Hassler's "Society Schottische ... composed and dedicated to the Hebrew Literary Association" (Fig. 37). In 1863, Henry Mayer dedicated his "Souvenir de Purim"—a continuous, multi-movement set of dances that may have reflected the music actually played at a recent Purim ball—to Miss Rachel Wolff (Fig. 38).[15] Pianist, composer, and future financier Isaac L. Rice dedicated his 1871 "Hildise March" to the Hildise Bund (from "Hilf dir Selbst," or "help yourself"), a German American mutual aid society founded the previous year. The notice on the title page that it had been "Arranged for the piano from the original score" suggests that the march premiered during the group's August 14 "festival" in New York's Hamilton Park.[16] Max Frankel dedicated his 1880 "Zion Glide Schottische" to the Zion Literary Association, a discussion circle organized by young people at Chicago's Zion Temple (Fig. 39); and William Jonas's 1885 "Montefiore March" carried a dedication to the Hebrew Charity Ball Association of Philadelphia (Fig. 40).[17] Even Isaac Mayer Wise's first wife, Theresa, received a dedication on the cover of P. Martens's 1867 "Progress March," which featured a lithograph image of Cincinnati's Bene Jeshurun synagogue (Plum Street Temple), possibly from its recent rededication (Fig. 41).[18] These publications today offer a sonic historical record of popular music as a part of Jewish social life, affirming the complex commercial relationships that existed among musicians and Jewish families or groups. When preserved in piano arrangements, moreover, they joined a larger culture of sheet music collection and performance, especially for domestic production by and for young women.[19]

15. Henry Mayer, "Souvenir de Purim: Caprice pour le Piano" (New York: William A. Pond, 1863), advertised in *Musical Review and World* 14, no. 9 (1863), 107; Mark Hassler, "Society Schottische" (Philadelphia: Edward L. Walker, 1857).

16. I. L. Rice, "Hildise March" (New York: J. Amuel, 1871); "The Hildise Bund," New York Times, October 10, 1870, 8; "The Hildise Bund Festival," New York Times, August 15, 1871, 8.

17. Max Frankel, "Zion Glide Schottische," arr. E. G. Klein (Chicago: Theodore Root & Sons, 1880); William Jonas, "Montefiore March" (Philadelphia: J. W. Jost & Son, 1885). Frankel, likely the son of Philadelphia rabbi Jacob Frankel, was also the composer of the 1888 comic opera *Ujiji*, with Charles Hartley's libretto (*Jewish Exponent*, March 2, 1888, 7). See also Sigmund Schlesinger, "Fidelia Schottische" (Mobile: Bromberg Bros., 1871).

18. P. Martens, "Progress March" (Cincinnati: J. J. Dobmeyer, 1867).

19. Recent scholarship has highlighted the role of women in collecting sheet music, often

Fig. 37. Mark Hassler, "Society Schottish" (Philadelphia, 1857). (Library of Congress).

Fig. 38. Henry Mayer, "Souvenir de Purim" (New York, 1863). (University of Michigan).

Fig. 39. Max Frankel, "Zion Glide Schottische" (Chicago, 1880). (Library of Congress).

Fig. 40. William Jonas, "Montefiore March" (Philadelphia, 1885). (Levy Sheet Music Collection, Sheridan Libraries, Johns Hopkins University).

Fig. 41. P. Martens, "Progress March" (New York et al., [1867]). (Levy Sheet Music Collection, Sheridan Libraries, Johns Hopkins University).

AMATEUR MUSIC

Music making outside of the processional sphere also contributed to local community building. Middle-class Americans banded together in ensembles that transformed liberal democratic ideals into acts of aesthetic beauty, with people of different backgrounds and identities engaging in group musical activities through religious institutions, fraternal organizations, political organizations, and even family/parlor units. The most visible of the civic ensembles in the postbellum period—the men's choirs (*Männerchöre*) and singing societies (*Gesangvereine*) imported from German models—became the basis of a flourishing amateur choral movement, with substantial local support, well-defined regional networks, and annual conventions (known in English as Sängerfests) that attracted tens of thousands of people.[20] Groups soon expanded beyond the core male members to enlist women in more complex works, such as operas and oratorios (including the 1879 American premiere of Giuseppe Verdi's *Requiem*), and festivals included events for all genders and ages.[21]

Major Jewish religious figures such as Isaac Mayer Wise and Max Lilienthal took leadership roles in regional Sängerfests. Jewish groups across the nation also sponsored their own amateur choral unions and societies, cultivating the popular art of part-singing—sometimes led by local *Gesangverein* conductors—as a way to keep young people in Jewish institutional life. Temple Beth Or in Montgomery, Alabama, for example, established a choral union in 1878 "for the purpose of promoting vocal culture and establishing a healthy taste for music and singing." "There is also another purpose in originating such a union," the local correspondent to the *American Israelite* admitted, "namely, to have a source from which to get good voices for our choir in the Temple."[22] Public choral singing thus fostered a musical language across a variety of religious and civic experiences; and accounts of people singing at each other's social functions and houses of worship reinforced music's role as a "universal" language that transcended social differences.

---

brought together in "binder's volumes" as a major domestic activity. See, for example, Petra Meyer-Frasier, *Bound Music, Unbound Women: The Search for an Identity in the Nineteenth-Century* (Missoula, Mont.: College Music Society, 2015), and Mark Slobin, James Kimball, Katherine K. Preston, and Deane Root, eds., *Emily's Songbook: Music in 1850s Albany* (Middleton, Wisc.: A-R Editions, 2011). Although "thousands" of such volumes are purported to exist, there has as yet been no study of albums specifically compiled by Jewish women.

20. Cincinnati's May Festival offers a contemporary version of one of these singing festivals.

21. Karen Ahlquist, "Musical Assimilation and 'the German Element' at the Cincinnati Sängerfest, 1879," *Musical Quarterly* 94, no. 3 (2011): 381–416.

22. *American Israelite*, July 12, 1878, 2.

For young women, musical proficiency held particular relevance in preparing for middle-class adult life, complementing their projected expectations as mothers, educators, and homemakers. Contemporary accounts describe women using these skills as both participants in and organizers of arts-based gatherings, public galas, and fundraisers to benefit local organizations. Their voices anchored volunteer choirs in synagogues and churches across the country (with men far less constant). Many also served as organists and conductors for these groups, as Laura Z. Wineman did in Charleston, South Carolina, in the 1870s.[23] Amateur musical knowledge thus played an active role in women's cultural, religious, economic, and social contributions to late nineteenth-century American society.

MUSIC IN JEWISH INSTITUTIONS

When Jews organized musical experiences for themselves and the public, they worked mainly through three local institutions: the synagogue, the B'nai B'rith lodge (from the 1840s), and the Young Men's Hebrew Association (YMHA; from the 1850s). As Jewish analogs to churches, masonic lodges, and YMCAs, these institutions offered variations on familiar configurations of spiritual, cultural, and social service, and provided accessible spaces for numerous forms of expression. The groups that originated in these settings spilled over into to the home, school, sanctuary, theater, literary salon, professional club, and political rally, allowing Jews to profess a robust compatibility with the local culture.

In synagogues, for example, Jewish congregational religious schools encouraged musical competence as an important part of the Jewish life cycle. Music instructors taught young Jews to sing hymns, a skill that would accompany them into both Jewish and civic adulthood. But music also marked students' progress from year to year. Schools typically held public opening and closing exercises in September and May, which brought in local residents of all backgrounds in addition to parents and congregants, and involved the recitation of prepared speeches and musical numbers. Students also sang together during synagogue-sponsored family picnics in late spring and summer, and participated in plays with music during Chanukah and Purim. As finances became tight during the relatively lean 1870s, moreover, congregations increasingly looked to children to anchor their choirs, replacing paid choristers and keeping parents connected to congregational life. What seemed a natural social skill outside of the synagogue thus became a symbol of communal health inside of it.

23. Uriah Zevi Engelman, "Jewish Education in Charleston, South Carolina, During the Eighteenth and Nineteenth Centuries," *Publications of the American Jewish Historical Society* 42, no. 1 (1952): 43–70, esp. 68–70.

Other forms of musical activity developed through formal and informal clubs. One significant example was the "literary club," where young men and women could meet under the pretense of cultural self-improvement. Often named after aspirational concepts (such as Baltimore's Eureka Club, Louisville's Progress Club, or Rochester's Beacon Light Association) or famed historical names (including Schenectady's Montefiore Society and New York's Henry Clay Society), literary clubs convened on weekday evenings or weekend afternoons at a synagogue, YMHA, B'nai B'rith hall, or local auditorium. Their hours-long meetings would include formal presentations, discussions of literature and current events, rhetorical dialogues, and amateur musical performances. Men tended to participate in the debates, recitations, and readings, while women offered more of the musical performances. Often overseen by a prominent older member of the community (such as a rabbi), these meetings ensured that young people had an opportunity to mingle while modeling the sophistication associated with their aspirations to "cultural uplift." Chicago had at least three such societies during the late 1870s, covering different regions of the city: the Sinai Literary Association connected with Sinai Congregation (south side); the Zion Literary Association affiliated with Bernard Felsenthal's Zion Congregation (west side); and a third association downtown sponsored by the YMHA. The announcement for a March 1878 "entertainment" of the Sinai Literary Association provides a sample of the proceedings, which included a pair of musical sister acts interwoven with other intellectual activities:

PROGRAMME:

Declamation, "Der Erl-Koenig" [Goethe poem, recited by] M. M. Schultze

Reading, "Searching for the Slain" [a common elocution selection, recited by] A. F. Leopold

Instrumental Duet [by] Misses Rose and Grace Meyer

Essay, "Die Mode" [by] Julius Kuh

Paper [by] Miss Leah Felsenthal

Instrumental Duet [by] Misses Minnie and Sophie Price

DEBATE:

"Resolved that a limited monarchy, like England's[,] is the best form of government."

Affirm—Julius Rosenberg, I. Mass // Deny—S. J. Kline, Alfred Depres.[24]

24. *American Israelite*, March 15, 1878, 6.

Established adults and families looking for more highbrow entertainment could also attend events sponsored by local Jewish social clubs. Supported by wealthier Jewish families, these associations often allowed only male membership, occupied their own buildings, held their own events (both all-male and all-community), and offered places of social gathering without the religious expectations of the synagogue. Some, including the Harmony Club of New Orleans (founded 1862), even built their own well-appointed music halls.[25] Women's social clubs existed as well, including Ladies Hebrew Benevolent Societies in New Orleans and Quincy, Illinois, among other places; they focused on community welfare and organized their own charity dances and performances, though they rarely kept their own buildings.[26] Both men's and women's clubs took pride in transforming halls into places for public enjoyment, employing Jewish performers as local talent, and translating Jewish-interest causes into civic causes. Many of their events received notice in both local and Jewish newspapers as community events to be recognized and celebrated.

Perhaps most prominently, Jewish social clubs annually planned elaborate and musically significant Purim balls from the 1860s onward. As events where well-heeled society could gather in costume and with gaiety during the general carnival season, the balls allowed attendees to mingle, try the social dances of the day, and hobnob to strains of high-class music. Purim balls became increasingly significant musical symbols around the country in the final decades of the nineteenth century, presenting opportunities for local Jewish populations to show their neighbors a good time while employing the area's most prominent musicians. In smaller communities, organizational responsibilities frequently fell to the local Jewish social club. A single column in an April 1886 issue of the *American Israelite*, for example, printed reports of Purim balls held by the Standard Club (Chicago), Concordia Society (Toledo), Harmony Club (Shreveport, Louisiana), Liederkranz Society (Toronto), and Unique Club (San Antonio)—all Jewish groups devoted to social progress both inside and outside of the Jewish community.[27]

In New York City, perhaps the epicenter of this practice, the city-wide Purim Association (founded in 1862) had made its annual ball a highlight of the social calendar by the late 1860s, attracting thousands of attendees, Jewish and

25. John H. Baron, *Concert Life in Nineteenth-Century New Orleans: A Comprehensive Reference* (Baton Rouge: Louisiana State University Press, 2013), 22. The YMHA building in New Orleans housed another music hall (the Athenaeum) from 1896 (*ibid.*, 24).

26. See *American Israelite*, August 16, 1894, 5 (Quincy, Ill.).

27. *American Israelite*, April 2, 1886, 10.

otherwise, to such august sites as Irving Hall, the New York Academy of Music, and Pike's Opera House (in the latter case, interrupting the opera season for an evening).[28] Music held a crucial role in shaping each evening's activities and highlighting its elaborately themed decorations. For example, the association's fifth ball, held at the Academy of Music on March 1, 1866, employed two large musical ensembles to entertain the three thousand attendees. One ensemble, the city's National Guard Seventh Regiment Band, accompanied a series of Jewish-themed processions, one of which was described in advance in the *New York Sun*:

> The first procession will represent the centuries during which the Hebrews were oppressed, each century marching past until the nineteenth is reached, when the Goddess of Liberty will appear in a chariot, with a temple within which rises a structure, bearing the names of Hebrew celebrities of the time in which they lived. As the cortege reaches the stage, the clouds will open, and Prince Carnival and his Court will appear and pay homage to the Queen, after which a grand ballet by harlequins and amazons, will bring the ceremonies to a close.[29]

Between the processions, a second ensemble/orchestra led by celebrated conductor Theodore Thomas played a series of fashionable social dances—quadrilles, galops, polkas, redowas, and lanciers—some composed specifically for the occasion and all listed in order on a large sign and (likely) a hand-out card.[30] Although the format of the ball, the number of attendees, and the extent of Jewish-themed programming varied greatly over the remainder of the century (including a gap during the economic downturn of the 1870s), the event itself endured as a prominent site for social and sonic crossover, connecting the festivities of the season, the sounds of high society, and the charity-based theme through a Jewish framework that emphasized social compatibility and full participation.

On the same night as the Purim Association's 1886 ball, however, other groups of amateur entertainers ("vorshtellers" by one paper's account) roamed the streets. One of these was "a Minstrel Band [of blackface entertainers], which

28. Philip Goodman, "The Purim Association of the City of New York (1862–1902)," *Publications of the American Jewish Historical Society* 40, no. 2 (1950): 135–72.

29. *New York Sun*, February 26, 1866, 1; cited on the website "Music in Gotham: The New York Scene, 1862–75," https://www.musicingotham.org/event/70498. See also Goodman, "Purim Association," 149–50. In 1867, some of the selections played by the Seventh Regiment Band included "Prof. Woolf's Purim March," and the dances included Woolf's "Purim Mazourka" and the "Hebrew Melodies Quadrille." *Jewish Messenger*, March 29, 1867, 2.

30. See, for example, the image of the 1877 Purim Association charity ball from *Frank Leslie's Popular Monthly*, 4 (August 1877): 141 (reprinted in Goodman, "Purim Association," 134).

was quite numerous and powerful and went through a selected programme of negro melodies, not to mention the jokes."[31] "Low culture" variety performance, including popular songs, parody, and minstrelsy, appeared largely the domain of young people in this era—derided as crude by community leaders, but still presented in limited settings. Complementing mainstream stage troupes, for example, community groups used the racially offensive form of the minstrel show to present gags, skits, and popular songs with transgressive and physical humor likely disallowed elsewhere.[32] Jewish newspapers of the era provide accounts of one-off performances by St. Louis's "High-Toned Korkers" (1879), troupes of "YMHA Minstrels" in Cincinnati (1884) and Savannah, Georgia (1891), and Chicago's "Standard Club Minstrel Co." (1887).[33] Even synagogues appeared to schedule occasional minstrel performances as part of youth programs. A show by "Our Young People" (eight women and four men) for Sunday school students in Youngstown, Ohio, for example, followed the genre's standard three-act format and included Stephen Foster's popular song "Swanee River."[34] Notably, while many professional minstrel performances of the time added spirituals to project greater "authenticity" to audiences, Jewish-sponsored performances appeared to emphasize the comic elements, thus avoiding Christological subjects.[35] In an era of proliferating ethnic impersonation acts on the vaudeville stage, including

31. *Jewish Messenger*, March 9, 1866, 4; see also March 17, 1865, 4.

32. Contemporary research on this controversial form suggests that in addition to its ubiquity and overt offensiveness, minstrel performance in the late nineteenth century also generated its own body of songs now described as classically American (including "Blue-Tail Fly," "O Susannah," and "Camp-Town Races") and provided opportunities for African American entertainers through mixed-race troupes. Thomas Riis, "Defying Boundaries and Escaping Stereotypes: African American Entertainers in the Late Nineteenth Century," in *Rethinking American Music*, ed. Riis and Browner, 200–220.

33. *Jewish Tribune*, September 19, 1879, 3 (High-Toned Korkers); *American Israelite*, December 5, 1884, 6 (Cincinnati YMHA minstrels); *American Israelite*, May 27, 1887, 2 (Chicago Standard Club Minstrel Co.); *Jewish Voice*, October 2, 1891, 6 (Savannah, Georgia). Mentions of several other minstrel performances appear in Jewish newspapers through the 1880s and 1890s, including a performance by the Entertainment Committee of the (Cincinnati) Excelsior Club on February 23, 1885 (*American Israelite*, March 6, 1885, 6), suggesting that the form was widespread.

34. *American Israelite*, March 9, 1888, 7. After an introduction of the troupe, part 1 of the program involved a series of minstrel songs and recitations; part 2 proceeded with a set of comic recitations and dialogues, ending with the (apparent) song "The Little German Band," which received four encores; and part 3 (the "Finale") involved a short comic play called "I'll Do Well Here," presumably with some music. Another recorded synagogue-based minstrel show took place in Detroit around Chanukah 1881, where the officers and members of Congregation Beth El performed for the children. *American Israelite*, December 23, 1881, 203.

35. See Sandra J. Graham, *Spirituals and the Birth of a Black Entertainment Industry* (Urbana: University of Illinois Press, 2018), chap. 8.

a number that exploited Jewish stereotypes, this problematic form of entertainment contributed to a complex historical landscape.[36]

Taken as a whole, the range of musical opportunities facilitated by local Jewish institutions reveals an active and creative populace deeply connected as both citizens and Jews with the musical infrastructure around them.

The 1880s: Nationalism, Mass Production, and the Emergence of Jewish Music

In the last third of the nineteenth century, national entities began to use music as a powerful tool for reinforcing common history and heritage, while affirming specific styles and sounds as essential components of communal culture and purity. Musicologist Heike Bungert describes how, for example, American *Männerchor* repertoire made a decided shift in the late 1880s from progressive poetry and art music to German folk tunes.[37] The transnational expansion of music history as a scientific pursuit (under the term "musicology"), moreover, built music into the cultural fabric of the West by establishing a succession of stylistic eras, iconic figures, and celebrated compositions, all grounded in the systematic study of texts and scores.

Jews on both sides of the Atlantic followed suit, pursuing the idea of a distinctly Jewish sound through simultaneous efforts at professionalization, scholarship, and new composition. Yet they were also motivated, in part, by longstanding discussions of Jews as "unmusical" or noisy and as lacking music of their own. Most notably, composer and German nationalist Richard Wagner published the second part of his influential anti-Jewish screed *Judaism in Music* in 1868.[38] While Jews continued to engage with popular and classical musical activities, the concept of "Jewish music" thus increasingly emerged as its own circumscribed category.

36. Harley Erdman, *Staging the Jew: The Performance of an American Ethnicity, 1860–1920* (New Brunswick: Rutgers University Press, 1997).

37. Heike Bungert, "The Singing Festivals of German Americans, 1849–1914," *American Music* 34, no. 2 (2016): 155. Religious groups made similar efforts. As Katherine Bergeron has noted, Catholics revised/"purified" their chant traditions in the 1870s through a gathering at the Solesmes monastery in France that eventually produced the chant reference called the *Liber Usualis.* See Katherine Bergeron, *Decadent Enchantments: The Revival of Gregorian Chant at Solesmes* (Berkeley: University of California Press, 1998).

38. Richard Wagner, "Judaism in Music," in *Judaism in Music and Other Essays*, trans. William Ashton Ellis (Lincoln: University of Nebraska Press, 1995), 75–122. For a far more involved discussion of these stereotypes against Jewish musicality over time, see Ruth HaCohen, *The Music Libel Against the Jews* (New Haven: Yale University Press, 2011).

The perceived longevity and durability of the synagogue ritual, seen as a cornerstone of synagogue reform, became one basis for Jews' "folk" music, complementing the rural populations that other nationalities identified as their musical stewards. To a newly organized class of synagogue music professionals who consolidated under the title of "cantor," the evocation of the millennia-old chain of tradition in the synagogue sanctuary brought claims of a longstanding, conservative musical practice and a connected wellspring of Jewish musical content. Cantors engaged in a number of strategies to reinforce this perspective, borrowing from the playbooks of other emerging musical traditions: they created a sophisticated music theory based on a combination of distinctive intervals and melodic motives ("modes"), distilled a "purified" repertoire of traditional tunes, and embarked on a public effort to identify and weed out "secular" influences in Jewish prayer music, all while arguing for music as an age-old entity that could inspire a viscerally familiar response in Jews.

The push toward a category of "Jewish music" comprised part of a larger movement to place Jewish sonic knowledge into the hands of religious specialists. In 1879/80 European synagogue music leaders around the urban centers of Vienna and Berlin banded into a pair of professional cantorial organizations. Through conferences, pamphlets, and a regular journal, cantors in each group began to disseminate new liturgical creations, write scholarly histories of Jewish music, assemble elaborate narratives of the cantorate, and offer extended musical analyses of core synagogue works. One of the most influential developments was Vienna cantor Josef Singer's 1886 treatise on synagogue modes, which synthesized synagogue music into a set of scales that could parallel Christian church modes and be used to evaluate the authenticity of synagogue music old and new.[39] This approach captured the cantorial imagination, coming over to the United States in the following years through the students of Vienna Obercantor Salomon Sulzer.

And none too soon. A congregational singing movement had arisen in the United States in the 1880s, born partly from the economic downturn of the 1870s, partly from desires to empower congregants as the Union of American Hebrew Congregations began to take shape, and partly from a national Christian revivalist movement of congregational song spearheaded by Dwight L. Moody and Ira K. Sankey. Isaac Mayer Wise at first derided Moody and Sankey's efforts as simplistic, appealing to the lowest common denominator and requiring little direct knowledge; but over time Wise came to respect the pair's sincerity and

39. Josef Singer, *Die Tonarten des traditionellen Synagogalegesangs: Ihr Verhältnis zu den Kirchentonarten und den Tonarten der vorchristlichen Musikperiode* (Vienna: E. M. Wetzler, 1886).

success. And while American Jewish music figures like Gustavus Ensel looked to Sankey as the model for their own hymnal efforts, the nation's few cantors faced the dilemma of maintaining professional standards while satisfying the desire for congregational participation.[40] By turning to the modes and the distillation of traditional melodies, the rising cantorial organizations in the United States found a medium for establishing their musical authority while preserving a collaborative spirit with their congregations.

These considerations, among others, remained in play by the early 1890s. A growing number of cantors, seeking to improve their standing with the Central Conference of American Rabbis, made efforts to present themselves as indispensable pulpit officiants and public clergy. And in the lead-up to the world's fair of 1892/93, a new opportunity to assert musical primacy arose through a collaboration between two of the era's most prominent émigré cantors, Baltimore's Alois Kaiser and New York City's William Sparger.

CHICAGO'S COLUMBIAN EXPOSITION

Like its predecessors in Paris (1855/1867/1878/1889) and Philadelphia (1876), the Chicago World's Columbian Exposition offered a mélange of exhibits that played with concepts of high and low culture, all in the service of a heterogenous yet geographically bounded vision of global human progress. As Barbara Kirshenblatt-Gimblett describes, different Jewish groups looked to these expositions as opportunities for self-definition, presented through a range of Jewish historical and cultural displays.[41] In Chicago, as Kiri Miller notes, the organizers sought to prove to the world "that America was capable of artistic enlightenment as well as massive industry and unrefined ostentation." To fulfill this mission musically, a "self-styled American musical elite" planned an elaborate program of musical activities highlighting American musical innovation and creativity.[42]

Kaiser and Sparger, looking for a stronger Jewish platform, turned to the emerging and increasingly powerful network of Jewish women's organizations.[43]

40. G. S. Ensel, review of M. Landsberg and Sol Wile, *Hymn Book for Jewish Worship*, *Die Deborah*, May 14, 1880, 3.

41. Barbara Kirshenblatt-Gimblett, "Exhibiting Jews," in *Destination Culture: Tourism, Museums, and Heritage* (Berkeley: University of California Press, 1998), 79–128.

42. Kiri Miller, "Americanism Musically: Nation, Evolution, and Public Education at the Columbian Exposition, 1893," *19th-Century Music* 27, no. 2 (2003): 137–55; Marie McCarthy, "American Music Education as Reflected in the World's Columbian Exposition, 1892–93," *Bulletin of Historical Research in Music Education* 15, no. 2 (1994): 111–42.

43. This and the next several paragraphs are based on Cohen, *Jewish Religious Music*, 233–36.

Synagogue-based women's groups had provided significant support for orderly worship and congregational singing as facilitators of education and home life, suppliers of choir members, recipients of "proper" musical education, and self-appointed keepers of congregational order. More significantly, as part of the call to prepare for the Columbian Exposition, a newly organized National Council of Jewish Women looked to music to symbolize their contributions to Jewish communal life. As member Emma Frank later recounted:

> That it is peculiarly [in the] women's sphere to introduce divine and sacred music into the household is self-evident; why should not we, then, deem it a duty to become familiar with the beautiful echoes of the past and the histories that surround them? ... In our new and easy methods of teaching in the Sabbath School, it has been found unwise and unnecessary to bother the children with the study of Hebrew, but music, the language understood by young and old the world over, must not be buried....[44]

In March 1893, the committee of the Jewish Women's Branch of the World's Fair Religious Congress commissioned Kaiser and Sparger to "compile and arrange the hymns" for a "Memorial Hymnal, to be at once a bibliography and a collection of traditional Jewish music."[45] Julia K. Simpson, "Jewess delegate to the world's congress of religions," followed up by noting that the committee is "also endeavoring to make a collection of traditional Jewish synagogical music, beginning as far back as possible and containing notes relating to the authors of the hymns. We hope to make this a very interesting volume and think of publishing about 1,000 copies."[46] Their comments hint at an approach that transcended denominationalism and used longevity to craft a pluralistic vision associated neither with the reform-leaning Union of American Hebrew Congregations nor with the more conservative supporters of the Jewish Theological Seminary (nor with more independent orthodox congregations). By June, Kaiser and Sparger had compiled a series of musical pieces prefaced by an extensive historical and analytical introduction: *Songs of Zion: A Collection of the Principal Melodies of the Synagogue from the Earliest Times to the Present.*[47]

44. Emma Frank, "Presentation of the Hymn Book," *Papers of the Jewish Women's Congress, Held at Chicago, September 4, 5, 6 and 7, 1893* (Philadelphia: Jewish Publication Society of America, 1894), 168–69.

45. "A Memorial Hymn-Book," *Jewish Exponent*, March 17, 1893, 7. See also Faith Rogow, *Gone to Another Meeting: The National Council of Jewish Women 1893–1993* (Tuscaloosa: University of Alabama Press, 1998), 13.

46. Fannie Fitzgerald, "Congress of Religions," *Atchison Daily Globe* (Kansas), June 7, 1893.

47. Alois Kaiser and William Sparger, *Songs of Zion: A Collection of the Principal Melodies of the Synagogue from the Earliest Times to the Present* (Chicago: T. Rubovits, 1893).

INSIDE 'SONGS OF ZION'

Kaiser and Sparger attempted to realize more fully the status of Jewish music as a hallmark of Jewish identity, especially as presented through the National Council of Jewish Women. Their collection used an assortment of formats to highlight "traditional" melodies while making them accessible to a wide variety of users and practical for presentation in Jewish communities. More significantly, Kaiser and Sparger's introduction fenced off Jewish music as a distinct musical tradition that they promoted as a source of pride, with its own inherent value, countering previous scholarly studies that had sought to include Jewish musical expression as part of a broad continuum of human progress. Jewish music could contribute to such genres as classical and popular music, but it needed to do so on its own clearly defined terms first—and only in ways consistent with underlying values of Jewish tradition.

This conservative shift to Jewish music as its own *sui generis* form relied heavily on recent cantorial research. Rather than seeing Jewish musical modes as an outcropping of Christian modes, the two cantors instead cited Vienna cantor Josef Singer to claim that Jewish musical modes came *first* and had been preserved since the Temple period through oral tradition. But this was only one step in an extensive revision of musical history. Kaiser and Sparger drew a crucial distinction between "traditional melodies" and "ritual chant" in the service.[48] The former, mainly German-based hymn tunes from the previous century, were "characterized by a childlike simplicity" and "mostly composed in the modern major key."[49] In contrast, they claimed, "ritual chant" demonstrated a much older provenance and comprised a richer trove of source material.

The twisty logic behind this assertion is instructive for understanding how changing views of ethnic history and identity shifted the course of Jewish music. Kaiser and Sparger, through Singer, identified three modal scales that they advanced "as the foundations of the liturgical songs of the Synagogue."[50] Two of these modes, roughly associated with the minor/Aeolian and Mixolydian Greek modes, could be found in contemporary pre-Christian musical treatises. But the third, which featured a more exotic augmented second interval, "does not find its parallel in any of the ancient or modern systems of tonality." They interpreted this discrepancy as proof of Jewish modes' primacy, continuing: "And it

48. William Sparger, "Literature on the Music of the Jews: An Attempt at a Bibliography," *American Hebrew*, December 9, 1892, 197–99; December 16, 229; December 23, 265–66.

49. Kaiser and Sparger, *Songs of Zion*, ix.

50. *Ibid.*, xii. Kaiser and Sparger described the scales as "1st C, D, E♭, F, G, A♭, B♭, C. // 2d. C, D, E, F, G, A, B♭, C; and // 3d. C, D♭, E, F, G, A♭, Bb, C."

is this fact which marks it as peculiarly important for the development of music of the synagogue. It is exclusively Jewish."[51] "What, then, are the relations of the Church modes to the ritual chant of the Jews?" they asked rhetorically. "None. In constructing his system, Ambrosius [who codified an early version of Gregorian chant] adopted among others those modes which the Jews had in common with other nations, and were of the least importance in the Temple service, while he rejected the *one* (exclusively Jewish) that had grown upon Jewish soil."[52] Such sweeping statements, made in the absence of granular data, reflect the methods of music scholarship at the time; to Kaiser and Sparger, they reclaimed Jewish music from historical obscurity.

Kaiser and Sparger also crafted their introduction to set boundaries between "Jewish" music and "popular" music, criticizing the relatively common practice of adapting popular melodies in Jewish contexts. Once again taking a historical angle, the authors criticized practices of melodic borrowing that had worked their way from secular songs into sacred poetry, and thence into Jewish liturgical music (a process also seen, in their view, in the contemporary practices of the Salvation Army). After presenting a series of carefully chosen examples that emphasized the moral gulf between secular music and sacred text, they applied their mode-based filter to repertoires they deemed questionable, thus pointedly rejecting "the antiquity and Jewish origin of the Sephardic melodies." They then cast the same moral alarm over the broader communal repertoire that German Jewish populations had used for hymn singing, which dated to at least the 1810s.[53] Through such arguments, Kaiser and Sparger sought to sideline "popular music" as a short-term corrupting influence on a centuries-old tradition, while prioritizing recent cantorial scholarship as the basis of restoration efforts.

Introducing this new, elite approach to Jewish music presented challenges in a volume aimed at a general readership. To avoid too dense a thicket of technical language, Kaiser and Sparger turned to melody as a top-level organizing factor that could superimpose "tradition" on common musical practices. The seventy-four selections that the compilers included in their collection followed a broad range of performance formats, from four-part table songs, to parlor songs for solo and duet, to instrumental keyboard solos, organ-based sacred songs, and refined choral works. Each, however, either identified or reused a melody that the authors deemed to have an appropriate provenance. Like their contemporary British counterpart Francis L. Cohen, Kaiser and Sparger accompanied their

51. *Ibid.*, xiii. 52. *Ibid.*, xiv.

53. *Ibid.*, xiv. For a history of German Jewish hymn singing, see Cohen, *Jewish Religious Music*, 58–61.

musical selections with English-language texts, presumably to ensure a wide appeal while adhering to the conventions of popular psalmody and hymnody. But their mission, succinctly stated in the introduction, came through: "Simplify the traditional chant, but preserve carefully its inherent characteristics and originality, and plant it again in the Synagogue and homes of our people in the only form in which this can be achieved now, namely, in the form of hymns."[54]

The music itself came in two parts. A first part, "Traditional Melodies," featured a series of consumer-level scores, interspersed with select monochrome illustrations of Jewish ceremonial objects, domestic and religious scenes, and ancient artwork. The five dozen authorless tunes with English words, organized by holiday according to the Gregorian year and arranged for a variety of basic vocal and instrumental formats, illustrated what Kaiser and Sparger viewed as the oldest and, therefore, "the most important melodies and chants of the Synagogue."[55] Almost every holiday's section began with an arrangement of an "ancient melody" for solo organ or keyboard, followed by a combination of hymn-style choral arrangements (usually for four voices) and solo songs. The high holidays sections, meanwhile, included somewhat more elaborate music involving keyboard, choir, and solo voice (male or female). Taken together, the pieces in this section offered a guide to Jewish (synagogue) musical literacy, instilling a basic core knowledge for amateurs to integrate each tune idiomatically into home and synagogue use.[56]

The second part of the book consisted of seventeen "Modern Compositions" that showcased prominent European, British, and American synagogue music composers, similarly adapted to English texts and arranged as a kind of spiritual trans-Atlantic journey to the United States. The first seven of these selections, mostly by aged or recently deceased European composers, featured mainly unnamed "Traditional Themes."[57] Ten elaborate and technically involved "Original" pieces followed, seven written by cantors or music directors active at major American synagogues.[58] By organizing the second half of the book this

54. Kaiser and Sparger, *Songs of Zion*, xvi (original in italics).

55. *Ibid.*, vii, xvii. The holiday sections carried the following titles, in order: Sabbath, Passover, Feast of Weeks, the Ninth of Ab, New Year, Atonement, Feast of Booths, and Feast of Lights.

56. Kaiser and Sparger arranged these works in three frequently used formats—keyboard alone, keyboard and single voice (cantor/solo), and four-voice choral (probably with keyboard colla parte)—thus providing versatility for potential users.

57. The composers were Moritz Deutsch (Breslau, 1818–1892), Salomon Sulzer (Vienna, 1804–1890), Louis Lewandowski (Berlin, 1821–1894; two compositions), and Samuel Naumbourg (Paris, 1815–1880), in addition to active Baltimore synagogue cantor/composers Jacob D. Marmor (Madison Street Congregation) and Alois Kaiser (Eutaw Place Synagogue).

way, Kaiser and Sparger portrayed America as a site of Jewish creative rebirth, where ancient musical modes could find new life through a return to tradition.

Through *Songs of Zion*, Kaiser and Sparger attempted a public transformation of Jewish music that carefully filtered existing music practices into the synagogue. Their efforts did not represent the first reproductions of popular styles for Jewish usage: previous works such as G. M. Cohen's *Sacred Harp of Judah* (1864) and *The Orpheus* (1878), in addition to several Jewish hymnals, accomplished similar feats. Yet Kaiser and Sparger built onto these practices a layer of musical discernment, presenting a Judaism with its own distinctive sound born of collective experience. Rather than looking to the broad civic singing movements of the previous decades, the two cantors argued for a musical outflow *from* the traditions of the synagogue sanctuary *into* the activities of the public square.

Kaiser and Sparger's combination of scholarly writing and accessible music accomplished its task. As a professionally formatted and illustrated music collection with a limited printing (advertised as 1,000 copies), the book drew praise for the National Council of Jewish Women, and gained a status as a desired domestic object. A paragraph-long review in the Chicago *Daily Inter-Ocean* twice described the book as "handsome."[59] George Alexander Kohut, in his review for the B'nai B'rith journal *The Menorah*, expressly identified women as its core audience, briefly noting, "The selections are happily made and cannot but appeal to the heart of every sentimental Jewess, who 'hath music in her soul.'"[60] And Chicago Jewish historian Morris Gutstein recalled the volume's value as a commemorative object, oddly advertised as "[a] book for every Jewish household, most appropriate as a confirmation, wedding or birthday gift, and in use by many Church choirs."[61]

On a practical level, however, the book's music appears to have had a limited reach. Although the English translations provided guidance to the uninitiated and helped "the volume, like all the work of these congresses, [show] how the world is moving, and ushering in and proclaiming the brotherhood of mankind

58. In addition to Kaiser, Sulzer, and Lewandowski, this section had works from Munich cantor M. G. Lowenstamm (1814–1881) and New York synagogue personnel A. J. Davis (organist, Temple Emanu-El, 1820–1902), Herman Goldstein (cantor, Shaar Hashomayim, 1847–1906), Theodore Guinsburg (cantor, Ahawath Chesed, 1847–1923), and S. Kantrowitz (music director, Zichron Ephraim).

59. "Current Literature," *Daily Inter-Ocean* (Chicago), August 19, 1893.

60. George Alexander Kohut, review of *A Collection of the Principal Melodies of the Synagogue*, *Menorah: A Monthly Magazine for the Jewish Home* 16 (February 1894): 159.

61. Morris A. Gutstein, *A Priceless Heritage: The Epic Growth of Nineteenth Century Chicago Jewry* (New York: Bloch Publishing, 1953), 308.

the wide world over," they appeared less useful as an actual accessory to Jewish ritual.[62] Far more influential was the book's introduction, which became a source for later musicologists hoping to tie "Jewish music" to the church music that served as the center of Western music histories. Scholars and pedagogues such as Oberlin's Edward Dickinson (1870–1946) quickly added it to the scant scholarly materials he found on synagogue music.[63] In 1898, music critic and scholar Sam L. Jacobson quoted Kaiser and Sparger's introduction extensively in a short article arguing for the existence of Jewish music.[64] Francis L. Cohen included it as a source in his "Music" entry in the *Jewish Encyclopedia*, and Joseph Rieder mentioned it in his 1914 review of the first volume of Abraham Z. Idelsohn's *Hebräisch-Orientalischer Melodienschatz* (later called the *Thesaurus of Hebrew-Oriental Melodies*).[65] More than twenty years later, the book's distributor still saw it as a viable volume and advertised copies for sale in the *American Jewish Chronicle*.[66] *Songs of Zion* thus became both a memory piece and a link in a chain of scholarly discussions that bound "Jewish music" ever more tightly to the synagogue.

"JEWISH MUSIC" AND THE BOUNDARIES OF SYNAGOGUE SOUND

Since the Gilded Age, scholars exploring the relationship between Jews and music have drawn on the developments of this era. On one hand, authors ascribed to Jews a sonic or philosophical essence, born in a long collective history or memory, that created a definable music of their own: unique and deeply imprinted scales, modes, and melodic formulae that reached back centuries or even millennia. Some made reference to the Temple period as a source of authenticity, and nearly all credited the continuity and conservatism of Jewish prayer as a vehicle for musical longevity.[67]

Such literature became a prescriptive road map for refining Jewish music. But it countered the real practices of American Jewish populations, who maintained multiple engagements with civic society, negotiated identity within a variety of

62. Cyrus Adler, in his preface, reinforced the outward-looking task of the book, describing the compilers as "embarrassed by the necessity, in many cases, of preparing an English text to set the music." Kaiser and Sparger, *Songs of Zion*, v.

63. Edward Dickinson, *Guide to the Study of Musical History and Criticism* (Oberlin, Ohio: Pearce and Randolph, 1895), 5, 84, 90; Edward Dickinson, *The History of Church Music: Syllabus with Bibliographic References*, published as vol. 1, no. 3 of the *Oberlin College Library Bulletin*, 4–5.

64. Sam L. Jacobson, "The Music of the Jews," *Music* (Chicago) 14 (August 1898): 412–16.

65. Francis L. Cohen, "Music," *The Jewish Encyclopedia*, vol. 9 (New York: Funk and Wagnalls, 1905), 135; Joseph Rieder, "Jewish and Arabic Music," *Jewish Quarterly Review* 7, no. 4 (1917): 636.

66. Advertisement, Bloch Publishing Co., *American Jewish Chronicle*, April 6, 1917, 729.

67. The most elaborate studies, such as those of Abraham Z. Idelsohn in the first third of the

different spaces, and in many cases actively promoted porous boundaries with other ethnic and religious populations. They engaged openly in messy discourses of cultural identity and social progress that, as Shari Rabin has noted, defied institutional attempts at simple classification.[68] Just as authorities such as Isaac Leeser and Isaac Mayer Wise sought to tame communal instability by compiling statistics, promoting religious hierarchy, and reinforcing definitions of Jewish identity, so scholars such as Kaiser and Sparger sought to promote Jewish sound as part of an effort to define what we know today as "Jewish music."[69]

Jews' sonic connection to the synagogue service deepened further as the twentieth century began, due to efforts by an organized, empowered, and professionalizing group of American cantors. Cultivating a culture of expertise, these cantors gave Jewish music a history and a moral imperative while continuing to reinforce melody as the central criterion for Jewish music. This approach, as in the late nineteenth century, effectively reversed the flow of cultural knowledge: Jewish music became the exclusive domain of the sanctuary in this arrangement, but its newly defined origins in synagogue chant also opened up options for composers and songwriters to draw on those melodies to indicate Jewishness in all manner of musical works, from songs to symphonies. For a while, cantorial music became its own popular music, as cantors developed their own star system, made well-received audio and film recordings, and concertized in ways that highlighted the line between sacred and secular performance. The appearance of famed cantor Josef Rosenblatt in the 1927 classic talking film *The Jazz Singer* presents one such example of the ways that Jewish music *became* a distinct commercial genre.[70] Such success, in turn, reinforced careful monitoring of the sanctuary as the ancient, originating source of Jewish music, spurring on scholars and cantors alike to highlight the moral dangers of bringing in "outside" melodies.

While these standards have shifted over time, they have largely remained in

---

twentieth century, traced the pathways of Jewish music over millennia, casting a suspicious eye on anything outside of the synagogue sanctuary. Others credited Jewish music as an inspiration for well-known compositions and tunes, while conversely condemning "popular" music imported from outside the synagogue.

68. Shari Rabin, *Jews on the Frontier: Religion and Mobility in Nineteenth-Century America* (New York: New York University Press, 2017).

69. Shari Rabin, "'Let Us Endeavor to Count Them Up': The Nineteenth-Century Origins of American Jewish Demography," *American Jewish History* 101, no. 4 (2017): 419–40; Zev Eleff, *Who Rules the Synagogue? Religious Authority and the Formation of American Judaism* (New York: Oxford University Press, 2016); Judah M. Cohen, *Jewish Religious Music in Nineteenth-Century America: Restoring the Synagogue Soundtrack* (Bloomington: Indiana University Press, 2019).

70. Jeffrey Shandler, "Cantors on Trial," in *Jews, God, and Videotape: Religion and Media in America* (New York: New York University Press, 2009), 13–55.

place into the twenty-first century, manifesting in a number of different ways. Art music composers from Mario Castelnuovo-Tedesco to Ernest Bloch, A. W. Binder, A. Z. Idelsohn, and Michael Isaacson, have created "Services"—large-scale, single-author compositions covering the core liturgical parts of Jewish religious rituals—most of which adhere in concept if not always in practice to ideas of musical Jewishness and modes. The augmented second interval highlighted as distinctive by Kaiser and Sparger would continue to code Jewishness in popular culture, perhaps most ubiquitously in Idelsohn's 1918 composition "Hava Nagila" (from a Hasidic source).[71] Even more significantly, subsequent discussions around the concept of Jewish music gave it a nearly genetic quality fabled to pass involuntarily from one generation to the next. Scholars, critics, and laypeople alike would scrutinize the compositions of musicians with Jewish ancestry, including George Gershwin, Aaron Copland, and Leonard Bernstein, for evidence of a Jewish musical inheritance. And when melodic proof seemed unclear, sensibility and method became factors as well—especially for wholesale claims about the relationship between Jews and the music of Tin Pan Alley.[72] Similar expectations affected the reception of Jews in popular music, including Al Jolson, Bob Dylan, Neil Diamond, the Beastie Boys, and Matisyahu.[73] New forms of music for Jewish worship, moreover, continue to face scrutiny and criticism on the basis of Jewish melodic content, with cantors interpreting popular interest in "folk-rock" services and the music of Debbie Friedman (for example) as troubling signs of disinterest in Jewish modes—and by association Jewish "tradition."[74]

These and many other instances highlight the late nineteenth century as a crucial era that fundamentally transformed Jews' relationships with popular and art music, ostensibly distilling their "own" music as a freestanding category gathered from a wide array of common practices. Such activities were hardly unique: during times of nation building, many groups sought to distinguish their sounds by creating circumscribed sets of modes, tones, and heritage-based mel-

71. James Loeffler and Edwin Seroussi, "The Secret History of 'Hava Nagila.'" *Tablet*, December 19, 2019, https://www.tabletmag.com/jewish-arts-and-culture/music/291493/secret-history-hava-nagila.

72. See, among others, Jack Gottlieb, *Funny, It Doesn't Sound Jewish: How Yiddish Songs and Synagogue Melodies Influenced Tin Pan Alley, Broadway, and Hollywood* (Albany: State University of New York Press, 2004).

73. See, among others, Ben Sidran, *There Was a Fire: Jews, Music, and the American Dream*, rev. ed. (Madison, WI: Nardis Books, 2021).

74. Judah M. Cohen, *The Making of a Reform Jewish Cantor: Musical Authority, Cultural Investment* (Bloomington: Indiana University Press, 2009), 219–22.

odies that reinforced national narratives. For Jews, however, these shifts also created space in the sanctuary for the cantor to become a Jewish music professional, subsequently offering a new sonic guardian of Jewish identity. Jewish musicians continued to participate in all kinds of musical expressions, from the parlor to the concert stage, the theater to the large-scale arena. In those settings, the boundaries between what was "Jewish" and what was not remained messy and complex. The synagogue, by contrast, increasingly offered a site of sonic clarity, where those who wished could explore a heritage of "Jewish music" with ever growing confidence and erudition.

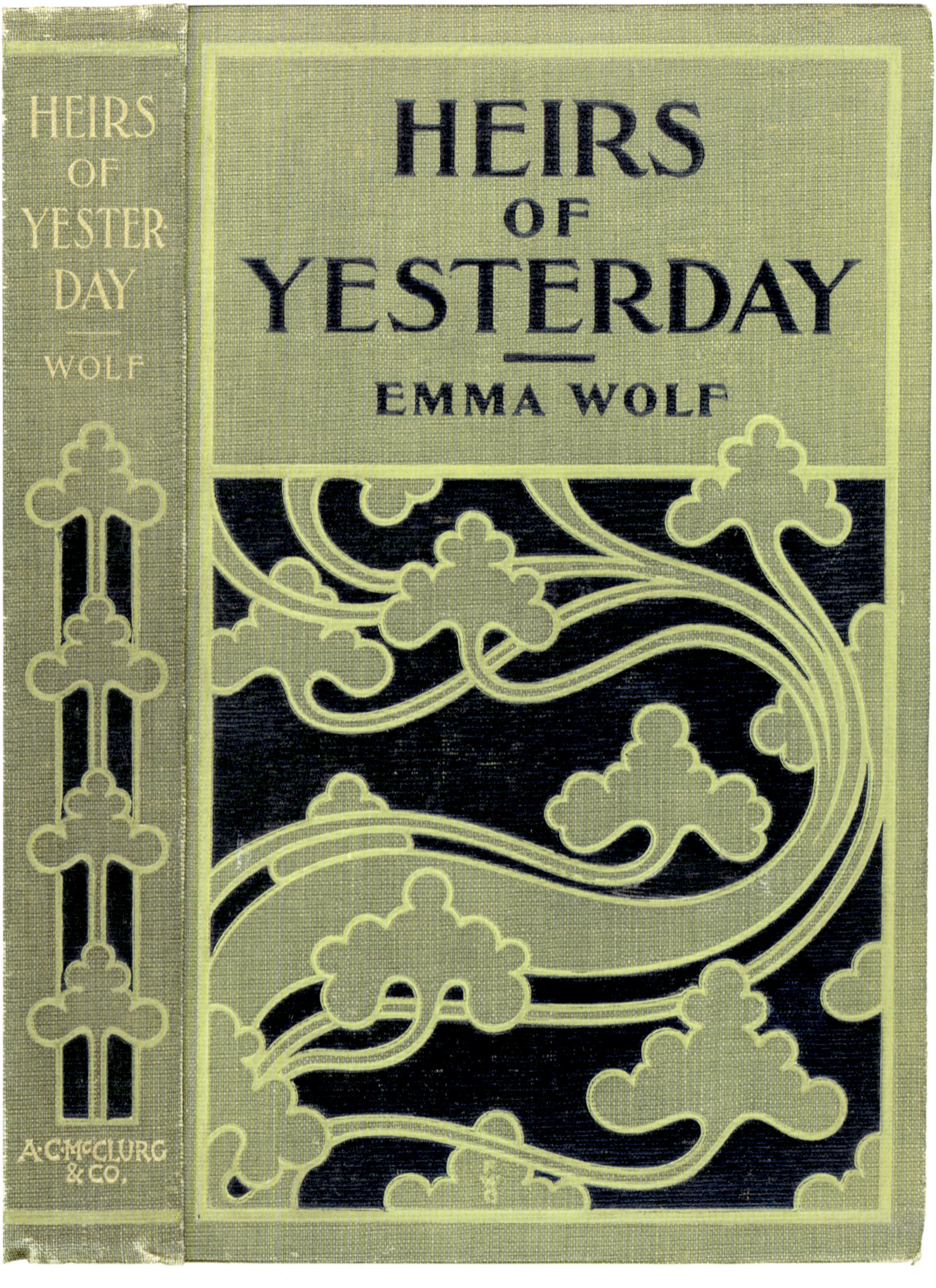

Fig. 42. Front cover and spine of Emma Wolf, *Heirs of Yesterday* (Chicago: A. C. McClurg, 1901). (Princeton University Library).

"TRUTH-TELLING SHOULD BE AN AUTHOR'S RELIGION": JEWISH FICTION AND AMERICAN LITERARY REALISM

LORI HARRISON-KAHAN

PUBLISHED in 1900, Emma Wolf's fourth novel, *Heirs of Yesterday*, centers on a love story between two middle-class, American-born, Jewish characters: physician Philip May and musician Jean Willard (Fig. 42). Supplying the familial and communal conflicts at the heart of the novel, Philip's and Jean's dissenting views about Jewish identity present an obstacle to their romance. To Philip, Judaism is "a dead letter, a monument to the past." Eager to free himself from the "unfit shackle" of his Jewish background, Philip goes so far as to pass for non-Jewish in order to "override" barriers to his professional and social success.[1] Jean, in contrast, embraces her religious difference and disagrees with Philip's decision to cut himself off from his heritage. Set in Gilded Age San Francisco, *Heirs of Yesterday* explores topics such as ethno-religious assimilation, genteel antisemitism, and the rise of Reform Judaism. Despite the continued salience of such topics in the twentieth and twenty-first centuries, Wolf's novel has only recently begun to receive attention from literary scholars and historians. In her time, however, Wolf was a widely known Jewish American novelist, and the press took notice when she published *Heirs of Yesterday*. A front-page review in the *Jewish Messenger*, for example, praised the novel and its author. "She is expressly omitted from the category of Jewish novelists who exploit their religion and special class of people and call the result literature," the reviewer stated, declaring Wolf to be "one of the rare exceptions to the general rule" in the recent explosion of Jewish fiction.[2]

The 1890s proved to be a watershed moment for the Jewish American novel. For the first time, the work of Jewish American fiction writers could be grouped into an identifiable "category" of its own—as evidenced by the *Jewish Messenger*'s

1. Emma Wolf, *Heirs of Yesterday*, ed. Barbara Cantalupo and Lori Harrison-Kahan (Detroit: Wayne State University Press, 2020), 101–2, 100, 99. Parts of this essay are drawn from the introduction to this edition of *Heirs of Yesterday*. As such, I would like to acknowledge Barbara Cantalupo's significant contributions to this essay and her groundbreaking research on Wolf.

2. "Miss Wolf's New Story," *Jewish Messenger*, Dec. 14, 1900, 1.

observation that Wolf's novel broke with conventions employed by other authors of her religious background. Even though a Jewish American poetic tradition had emerged in the decades immediately following the Civil War, with the publication of works by Emma Lazarus, Penina Moïse, Minna Cohen Kleeberg, and Adah Isaacs Menken, Jewish fiction writers were few and far between. The most significant Jewish American novelist of the postbellum period was Nathan Mayer, whose serialized historical novels appeared in the *Israelite* in the 1850s. In 1867, Mayer published *Differences*, which, according to Karen Keely, is considered "one of the first works of fiction to depict the contemporary lives of American Jews." Like the protagonists of *Heirs of Yesterday*, most of the Jewish characters in *Differences* are genteel and acculturated. Set during the Civil War, the novel features a prosperous Jewish family that lives on a Southern plantation and enslaves Black people for labor. As Keely points out, Mayer's novel fits the genre of the Civil War reconciliation romance, but it "ultimately cares far more about Jewish continuity than national unity," as indicated by "the fact that all of the major characters finish the novel preparing to settle in the North and not holding onto any Lost Cause ideology."[3] *Differences* explores how to maintain Jewish continuity in the face of assimilation through intersecting sentimental plotlines that depend on courtship and marriage, including Jewish-Christian intermarriage—a topic that Wolf, too, would take up in her first novel, *Other Things Being Equal*, published in 1892.

Few works of Jewish fiction appeared in the period between Mayer's *Differences* and Wolf's *Other Things Being Equal.* During the 1870s, Emma Lazarus tried her hand at fiction, publishing *Alide* (1874), a novel based on the life of Johann Wolfgang von Goethe, and a short story, "The Eleventh Hour," in *Scribner's* in 1878. Neither dealt directly with Jewish themes or met with the success that she achieved with her poetry.[4] By the 1890s, however, the publication of short stories and novels by Jewish American fiction writers became a regular occurrence, prompting essayist and book critic Josephine Lazarus to observe, "To-day, we have almost a new Jewish literature of our own, springing up in our midst, dealing not with foreign conditions and circumstance, but with the facts as they are here and now among us."[5] Her prescient essay, "Judaism, Old

3. Karen A. Keely, "Reform Judaism, Reconciliation Romance, and the Civil War: Nathan Mayer's *Differences* and Nineteenth-Century Reform Jewish American Life," *American Jewish History* 104, no. 2/3 (2020): 265, 278.

4. On Emma Lazarus's attempts at fiction writing, see Esther Schor, *Emma Lazarus* (New York: Nextbook/Schocken, 2006), 44–46, 63–65.

5. Josephine Lazarus, "Judaism, Old and New," in Lazarus, *The Spirit of Judaism* (New York: Dodd, Mead, 1895), 70–71.

and New," originally published in 1894, illuminates the confluence of historical and literary factors that fertilized Jewish American fiction at the end of the nineteenth century. The coming of age of the American-born children of mid-nineteenth-century immigrants from central Europe, such as Wolf, coincided with a major influx of eastern European immigrants to the United States. Settling largely in New York, the new immigrants forged a socialist Yiddish literary culture; at its helm was journalist, editor, and fiction writer Abraham Cahan (1860–1951), a Lithuanian émigré who helped found the *Jewish Daily Forward* in 1897. Concurrent with these shifting patterns of Jewish immigration, American literature took a significant turn away from romance and sentimentalism and toward realism and naturalism. Writers were increasingly invested in using fiction to represent "the facts as they are here and now among us," in Josephine Lazarus's words.

Closely associated with Cahan's journalistic work and his first novel, *Yekl: A Tale of the New York Ghetto* (1896), the ghetto tale became Jewish American writers' best-known contribution to the broader movement of American literary realism. In contrast to the genteel Jewish characters who appear in fiction by Mayer and Wolf, the ghetto tale centers on working-class, eastern European immigrants striving to adapt to American culture while living in ethnic enclaves on the East Side of New York. The setting consists of tenements, sweatshops, and streets teeming with people and pushcarts. The Yiddish-inflected dialect of the "greenhorn" characters brings additional color to the gritty, but lively atmosphere.

The ghetto tale continued to enjoy a wide readership well into the twentieth century. While Cahan and Anzia Yezierska remain the best-known of the early ghetto storytellers, a broader catalogue of writers and works affiliated with this genre evinces the ghetto tale's tremendous popularity, as well as its often unacknowledged diversity. The list includes Isaac Kahn Friedman's *The Lucky Number* (1896); Nathaniel Isaiah Gillman's *Circumstantial Affection: A Realistic Romance of the New York Ghetto* (1901); the comic stories of Bruno Lessing, whose work was collected in *Children of Men* (1903) and *With the Best Intention* (1914); Herman Bernstein's *In the Gates of Israel: Stories of the Jews* (1902) and *Contrite Hearts* (1905); the novels of Lithuanian American writer Ezra Brudno, notably his fictionalized autobiography, *The Fugitive: Being Memoirs of a Wanderer in Search of a Home* (1904); another autobiographically inspired fiction, *The Mediator: A Tale of the Old World and the New* (1907), by the Christian convert Edward A. Steiner; Rabbi Henry S. Stollnitz's self-published *Glimpses of a Strange World* (1908); James Oppenheim's *Dr. Rast* (1909); Montague Glass's

"Potash and Perlmutter" series (ca. 1908–1927), a comic sensation responsible for widely disseminating stereotypes of the Jew as parvenu industrialist, especially when the "Ventures and Adventures" of business partners Abe Potash and "Mawruss" (Morris) Perlmutter were adapted for stage and screen; and Fannie Hurst's *Just Around the Corner* (1914), the debut collection by an author who would go on to become a sensation in her own right as a best-selling novelist and the highest-paid magazine contributor of her time.[6]

In addition to novels and story collections with ghetto settings, tales and sketches of ghetto life appeared regularly in magazines such as *Cosmopolitan, Everybody's, McClure's*, and the *Saturday Evening Post* beginning in the 1890s. The ghetto in its various manifestations captured the imaginations of American readers and appealed to the reform-minded social conscience of the Progressive Era. Ghetto literature was also critically acclaimed, famously championed by "the Dean of American letters," William Dean Howells, who praised writers of the "Hebraic school" for displaying "an instinct for reality."[7]

However, as suggested by the *Jewish Messenger*'s singling out of *Heirs of Yesterday* as a "rare exception to the general rule," the popular genre of the ghetto tale had its detractors. In both the mainstream and the Jewish press, critics accused Jewish writers of sacrificing truth for caricature and exoticism in their depictions of ghetto life, betraying their own people as well as the very principles of realism that Howells extolled. Surveying the debate over ghetto fiction, as well as Wolf's deviation from the prevailing generic conventions, this essay explores Jewish writers' varied contributions to fin-de-siècle American literary culture and illuminates how fiction became a contested site for defining Jewish American identity at the end of the nineteenth century.

6. While the majority of works by Jewish American writers focused on ghettos in the United States, some looked back to the ghettos of the Old World; Martha Wolfenstein's *Idylls of the Gass* (1901) and *The Renegade and Other Stories* (1905) are cases in point. A rich tradition of ghetto fiction written in Yiddish by writers such as Sholem Asch also developed in the twentieth century. To the list of Jewish writers we can add many other works by non-Jewish writers who found source material in the Jewish ghetto: Edward King's *Joseph Zalmonah* (1893); the sociological tales of Hutchins Hapgood and Jacob Riis; Irish American writer Myra Kelly's stories of Jewish schoolchildren; E. R. Lipsett's "Denny the Jew" series about an Irish boy who becomes a Jew; and the writings of Henry Harland, who took on a Jewish persona, publishing under the pseudonym Sidney Luska. The tradition of Jewish ghetto writing extended far beyond World War I, evident, for example, in works by Samuel Ornitz, Mike Gold, Henry Roth, and Daniel Fuchs. Contemporary Jewish American literature, too, contains many nostalgic narratives of ghetto life.

7. William Dean Howells, "Editor's Easy Chair," *Harper's Monthly Magazine* 130 (May 1915): 959.

Abraham Cahan's "Yekl" and Ghetto Fiction

Abraham Cahan's short novel *Yekl* addresses the Americanization of Jewish immigrants through the character of Jake, formerly Yekl, a garment worker eager to shed his identity as a Yiddish-speaking greenhorn and become a modern, English-speaking Yankee (Fig. 43). Jake is forced to confront his past when his wife, Gitl, and young son, Yoselé, arrive in New York. Unable to reconcile his self-perception as "an *American feller*" with his wife's Old World appearance and manners, Jake gravitates toward Americanized Mamie, whom he meets at a dance hall. The novella resolves with Jake and Gitl's divorce. Jake ends up with Mamie, and Gitl pairs off with Bernstein, a learned grocer who holds on to his Jewish identity, continuing to study the Talmud on the side. As its subtitle, *A Tale of the New York Ghetto*, suggests, *Yekl* is very much a story about place, rife with evocative depictions of urban squalor. Jake's walk through the ghetto in the book's second chapter takes him past "dense swarms of bedraggled half-naked humanity," garbage "lining the streets in malicious suggestion of rows of trees," and "tiers and tiers of fire escapes," all of which create a "pent-in sultry atmosphere ... laden with nausea."[8]

Yekl's status in American literature owes much to the influence of William Dean Howells. In the 1890s, Cahan was working as a journalist for papers ranging from Socialist Yiddish weeklies to the New York *Sun*. One of his short stories, "A Providential Match," came to Howells's attention when it was published in a literary magazine in 1895. Howells subsequently took the Jewish writer under his wing, helped him secure D. Appleton and Company as a publisher, and advised him to change his book's title from *Yankel the Yankee* to *Yekl*. In an 1896 article titled "New York Low Life in Fiction," which appeared in the *New York World*, Howells promoted Cahan as a "new star of realism," pairing *Yekl* with the slum writing of Stephen Crane. While acknowledging that "there is much that is painful in [Cahan's] story, as there is much that is dreadful in Mr. Crane's work," Howells argued that both writers succeed because they "persuade us that they have told the truth." Part of this truth, for Howells, lies in the use of dialect. Although Howells praised Cahan's facility with English ("In its simplicity and its purity, as the English of a man born to write Russian, it is simply marvelous"), he also singled out the characters' speech as a distinctive

8. Abraham Cahan, *Yekl and the Imported Bridegroom and Other Stories of Yiddish New York* (1896; New York: Dover, 1970), 70, 13. Cahan used italics in the text to indicate English words within a Yiddish sentence.

"New York jargon" that incorporated Yiddish and American slang, reproducing the sound of the ghetto.[9]

The multilingualism of Cahan's narrative has continued to garner significant attention from contemporary critics. In an early article arguing for the inclusion of *Yekl* in the realist canon, Sanford Marovitz notes that the "polyglot" quality of Cahan's prose reinforces the novel's realism. "This is language not of caricature but of living people," he explains.[10] In a more recent analysis, Hana Wirth-Nesher attends to the linguistic complexity of Cahan's novel, exploring how the text reproduces processes of translation and language acquisition to transcend the "plain speaking realism" of Howells with local color dialect conventions. For Wirth-Nesher, *Yekl*'s linguistic complexities exemplify a poetics of ethnicity in Jewish American literature.[11]

Cahan's synthesis of Jewish and American culture has secured *Yekl*'s standing as a celebrated, formative work of Jewish American fiction. However, Howells's reputation has obscured the fact that most initial responses to Cahan's debut novel were not so laudatory. Critics at the time were attuned to what Susan K. Harris identifies as the "problems of representation in turn-of-the-century immigrant fiction."[12] Alluding to Howells without naming him, reviewer Nancy Huston Banks took issue with "eminent American critics" who lavished only praise on *Yekl*. Banks commended the story's novelty and "curiously lifelike" characters, "conceding" that the book represents "realism in the narrowest sense of the term," but she questioned "the work's realism in a wider sense":

> Does Mr. Cahan wish us to believe that the types and phases of the life of the Ghetto thus presented by him are truly representative of his race? That it is as sordid, selfish, as mean, as cruel, as degraded as he has here shown it to be? ... It

9. William Dean Howells, "New York Low Life in Fiction," *New York World*, July 26, 1896, 18. The scholarship on *Yekl* is extensive. See, for example: Sanford Marovitz, "Yekl: The Ghetto Realism of Abraham Cahan," *American Literary Realism* 2, no. 3 (1969): 271–82; Dalia Kandiyoti, *Migrant Sites: America, Place, and Diaspora Literatures* (Hanover, N.H.: Dartmouth College Press, 2009), 49–80; Aviva Taubenfeld, "'Only an 'L': Linguistic Borders and the Immigrant Author in Abraham Cahan's *Yekl* and *Yankel der Yankee*," in *Multilingual America: Transnationalism, Ethnicity, and the Languages of American Literature*, ed. Werner Sollors (New York: New York University Press, 1998), 144–65; Hana Wirth-Nesher, *Call It English: The Languages of Jewish American Literature* (Princeton: Princeton University Press, 2008), 32–51; and Joan Zlotnick, "Abraham Cahan, A Neglected Realist," *American Jewish Archives* 23, no. 1 (1971): 33–46.

10. Marovitz, "Yekl," 273.

11. Wirth-Nesher, *Call It English*, 51.

12. Susan K. Harris, "Problems of Representation in Turn-of-the-Century Immigrant Fiction," in *American Realism and the Canon*, ed. Tom Quirk and Gary Scharnhorst (Newark: University of Delaware Press, 2004), 127–42.

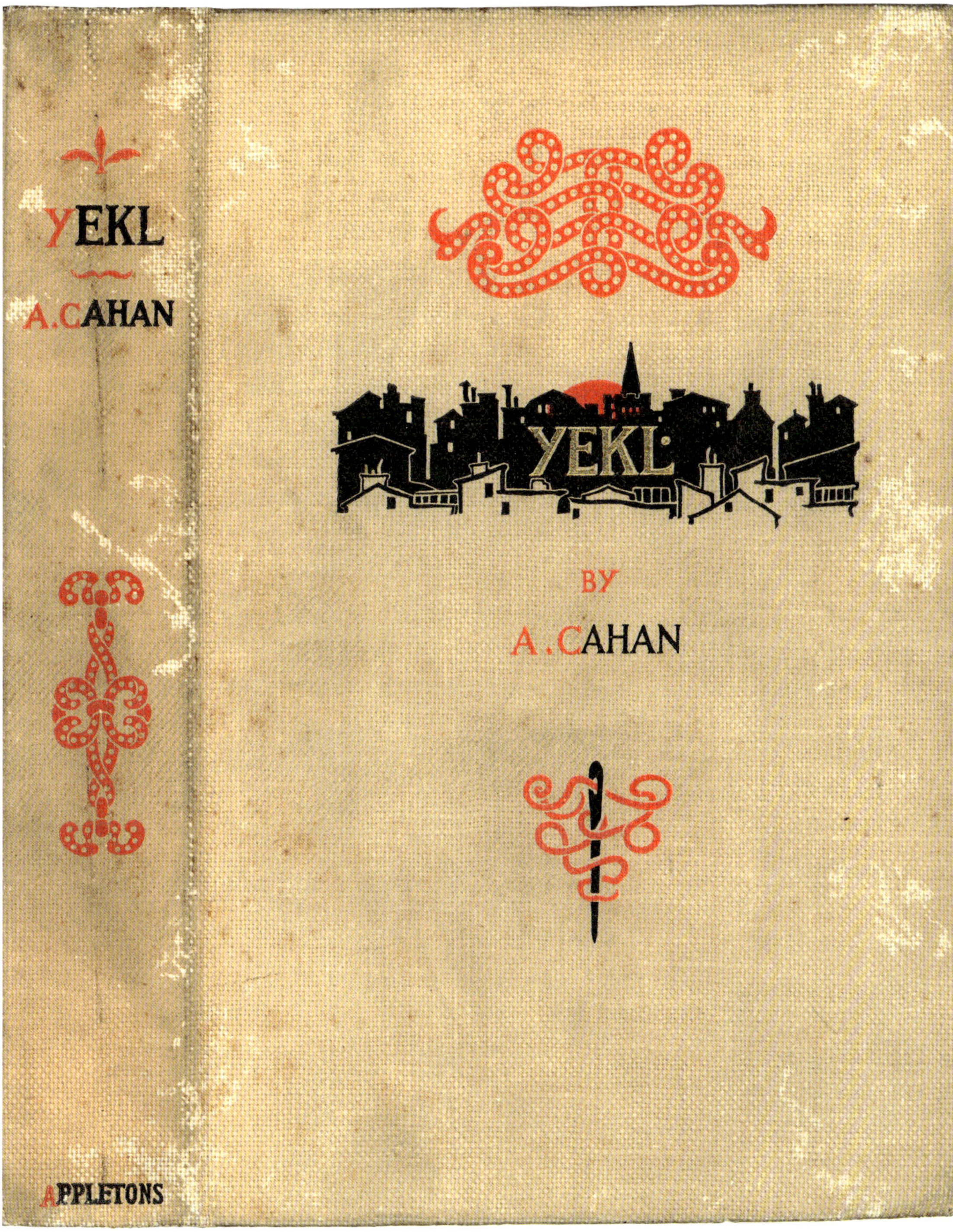

Fig. 43. Front cover and spine of Abraham Cahan, *Yekl* (New York: Appleton, 1896). (Princeton University Library).

> is a hideous showing, and repels the reader, who misses ... that dignity of faith which compels respect from Christians; that helpfulness of each other which shames the selfishness of the Gentile.... If, then, these likenesses and these views are reproduced from life, was it wise to develop the pictures? Can it be true that we care much in fiction for what has so little interest in life? that we are attracted in literature by characters and scenes that we would shrink from in the flesh? Are such books ever worth while? Do they serve any purpose, even to amuse? Do they add anything to literature? above all, *are* they literature?[13]

Banks's litany of questions addresses two key aspects of the text: the ethics of representation and its literary value. Her review further suggests that these aspects are connected. By rendering Jewish life in an aesthetically unappealing way, Cahan does a disservice to his people, Banks suggests. He misses an opportunity to depict Judaism as a dignified religion and thus win the sympathy of his book's Gentile readers by stressing commonalities with Jews.

That Cahan's novel might stoke fears of Jewish difference is clear from a review in *The Critic* that similarly focuses on the text's "revolting details": "Without wearing the white carnation of the anti-Semitic crusade, one may differentiate Jews so far as to admit that the manners and customs of Suffolk street are ... 'neither pleasing nor delightful.'" Reading *Yekl* as a realist text, *The Critic*'s reviewer took it to be a sociological document and found in it a justification for antisemitism: the novel does not offer a critique of the urban conditions that circumscribe immigrants' lives and opportunities but instead provides evidence of inherent differences between Jews and Gentiles. The reviewer's attack on Cahan's use of dialect as "giving grotesque and repulsive shapes to familiar words" expresses anxiety about how attempts to integrate Jewish immigrants led to the corruption of the English language and, by extension, Anglo-Saxon ideals.[14]

Reviews in the Jewish press echoed Banks's concerns. Comparing the author of *Yekl* unfavorably to the British Jewish writer Israel Zangwill, author of *Children of the Ghetto* (1892), they expressed outrage, compounded by personal betrayal. Jewish reviewers went further than Banks in their critique of the novel's realism, challenging both the ethics and the veracity of Cahan's representations. Several reviews pointed out that Cahan had captured but a sliver of Jewish life, narrow even within the confines of the ghetto. Filled with "disgust" at Cahan's unfaithful (in both senses of the word) characterizations, a reviewer in *The Menorah*, for instance, stated that the book was "not representative" of ghetto life because the characters do not "retain any of the principles of the Russian Jew,

13. Nancy Huston Banks, "New York Ghetto," *Bookman* 4 (October 1896): 157–58.

14. Review of *Yekl*, *The Critic*, July 25, 1895, 53.

who comes here saturated thoroughly with the moral fortitude of the Jewish religion."[15] A review in the *American Hebrew* warned that readers of Cahan's novel will be "grievously disappointed" with the "dark, sordid picture of Ghetto life." The reviewer took aim at the novel's aesthetic qualities, stating that the story "does not contain a single specimen of word-picture" nor a "pleasing literary style" and suggesting that Cahan should have chosen material "that would give the Gentile reader a better opinion of the Russian Jew, and at the same time, make a more readable novel." Cahan "may be a successful leader of the socialist workman," the reviewer concluded, "but ... cannot be accounted a successful novelist."[16] The *American Jewess* was more conciliatory toward Cahan's skill as a realist novelist, but its review similarly ended with the hope that "the author of 'Yekl' will soon, with equal veracity, pen-picture the nobler types of Jews dwelling" in the ghetto.[17]

In the years after the publication of *Yekl*, the debate over whether the grittiness of the ghetto was a fit subject for literary art came to a head in 1899 with the American premiere of the dramatic adaptation of Zangwill's *Children of the Ghetto.* As a writer in *Bookman* observed of the debate playing out in the Jewish press, "frankly realistic" depictions of ghetto life were viewed by some Jews as "an offence only slightly less heinous than treason." Dissenters were largely middle-class, American-born Jews who feared that they would be grouped with such lowly literary representations of the ghetto Jew and sought to distance themselves from their newly arrived eastern European coreligionists. The *American Israelite* was harshest in its criticism. In its pages, Julius Wise, a prominent Chicago physician and the son of Rabbi Isaac Mayer Wise, one of the innovators of American Reform Judaism, issued a scathing attack on Cahan. Writing under the pseudonym "Nickerdown," Wise accused Cahan of "intentionally exaggerat[ing] what is worst among his own class of people," labeling him "a scoundrel [who lies] for the sake of a few dollars" and calling for a boycott of magazines that publish his "vile lucubration."[18]

A similar but more measured critique came from the pen of Sephardic Jewish writer Annie Nathan Meyer. Participating in a debate about ghetto literature that

15. Review of *Yekl*, *The Menorah: A Monthly Magazine for the Jewish Home* 21, no. 2 (1896): 127–28.

16. "Judaica: Rev. of *Yekl*," *American Hebrew*, July 17, 1896, 274–75.

17. Review of *Yekl*, *American Jewess* 2 (August 1896): 609.

18. Quoted in "Chronicle and Comment," *Bookman* 10 (January 1900): 428–29. For another example of a negative review of *Yekl* in the *American Israelite*, see "Notes and Comments," *American Israelite*, July 30, 1896, 1.

appeared in the *Bookman* in 1900, Meyer acknowledged the "genius" of Zangwill and Cahan while summarizing the concerns of her affluent, professional class:

> The Americanised Hebrew is growing a little tired of this reiteration of the Ghetto type which the Gentile world find so interesting within the covers of a book. After all, when the good American used to be piqued because the cowboy filled the horizon of literary London, it was given him to point to some novels dealing with the average American banker who prefers to take his promenades without his six-shooter. But to the Americanised Hebrew is denied *in toto* the luxury of pointing to any literature that pretends to describe him seriously. ... [T]here is implanted in the breast of the Jew, quite as well as in the breast of his Gentile brother, the ... desire to hold up his resemblances rather than his differences. The Jew is doing his best to show off his fine Oxford cloth coat of latest cut, while the public persists in looking for the gabardine.[19]

While Meyer occasionally gave voice to what she called "the unwritten-up Jew" in stories such as "Henry Brooke, Jr.," which appeared in the *American Jewess* in 1895, California novelist Emma Wolf offered the most sustained articulation of Jewishness through the lens of genteel, rather than ghetto, realism.[20] Yet, even as Wolf steered clear of sordidness and exoticism, depicting cultured, well-off characters who could not be differentiated from their Gentile neighbors except in their religious practices and affiliations, her work, too, provoked controversies that illuminate the challenges of seamlessly synthesizing Jewishness and Americanness in fin-de-siècle culture.

Genteel Realism and the Marriage Plot in "Other Things Being Equal"

In 1892, four years before Cahan's *Yekl*, Emma Wolf published her first novel, *Other Things Being Equal.* Like *Heirs of Yesterday*, the novel is set in the Jewish community of Gilded Age San Francisco, a community the novelist knew firsthand. Born in 1865 in California to French-Alsatian immigrants turned pioneers, Wolf grew up in middle-class Pacific Heights, where her family attended Temple Emanu-El, a Reform congregation founded by traders and merchants during the Gold Rush of 1849. Educated at San Francisco Girls' High School, where a reform-minded principal advocated a strong foundation in literacy as well as religious tolerance among the students, Wolf was part of a Bay Area cohort of Jewish women with artistic and professional aspirations. Her classmates

19. Annie Nathan Meyer, "Concerning Sensitive Epiderms," *Bookman* 10 (February 1900): 533.

20. See Annie Nathan Meyer, "Henry Brooke, Jr. (A Sketch)," *American Jewess* 2 (December 1895): 123–27. It is worth noting that neither of Meyer's two novels features explicitly Jewish characters.

included fellow writer Harriet Lane Levy, who became part of the expatriate circle surrounding Gertrude Stein; Rebekah Bettelheim, who would go on to marry Rabbi Alexander Kohut and become a prominent Jewish communal leader in her own right; and Florence Prag, who in 1925 became the first Jewish woman to serve in the House of Representatives, succeeding her husband, Congressman Julius Kahn, after his death.[21] Following graduation, Wolf and several of her classmates continued to study and learn together as members of the Philomath Club, a literary society for elite Jewish women founded by another California novelist, Bettie Lowenberg. While the intellectual environment of Gilded Age San Francisco provided fertile ground for Wolf's art, the fact that she had a congenital physical disability removed her from the marriage market, making it possible for her to prioritize literary pursuits over childbearing and other domestic obligations that occupied most women of her class.[22] Over the course of a twenty-five-year career, she published five novels, as well as short stories and poems in magazines ranging from the *American Jewess* to *Century* and the *Smart Set* (Fig. 44).

An auspicious beginning for Wolf's literary career, *Other Things Being Equal* was a popular success, in part because of its controversial depiction of interfaith romance between its Jewish heroine and her Unitarian lover. When Ruth Levice, the only child of prosperous French immigrants, falls in love with her Gentile neighbor, physician Herbert Kemp, the couple is forced to confront the cultural taboo against intermarriage. Ruth's father voices his opposition to their union, objecting on the grounds of the "great difference between the Jewish race and traditions, and the Christian" and fearing that his daughter, and her future children, would face a lifetime of social ostracism from both religious communities. Ultimately, however, *Other Things Being Equal* presents intermarriage as a viable option for the couple, given that they are members of the same social class. By the end of the novel, Mr. Levice is persuaded by the force of Ruth and Kemp's love to overturn his objections. Stricken ill while doing business on the East Coast, he returns home to San Francisco, where his daughter and Kemp grant him his deathbed wish, marrying that very day so that he can bless their

21. Both Harriet Lane Levy and Rebekah Bettelheim Kohut published autobiographical writings about growing up Jewish in Gilded Age San Francisco. See Harriet Lane Levy, *920 O'Farrell Street: A Jewish Girlhood in Old San Francisco* (1947; repr. Berkeley, Calif.: Heyday Books, 1997), and Rebekah Kohut, *My Portion* (New York: Thomas Seltzer, 1925).

22. For more on Wolf's disability, see Lori Harrison-Kahan, "We Shouldn't Ignore This Groundbreaking Jewish Novelist's Disability," *Alma*, June 21, 2021, https://www.heyalma.com/we-shouldnt-ignore-this-groundbreaking-jewish-novelists-disability/.

new life together and publicly sanction their union as "a grave experiment" in social equality.[23]

In Wolf's novel, both genteel realism and the intermarriage plot function, in Meyer's words, to "hold up ... resemblances rather than ... differences" between Jews and Gentiles.[24] Through the accumulation of class signifiers in her characterizations of the Levices, Wolf indicates that religion is the sole factor differentiating Ruth and her family from Kemp and their other Christian neighbors. In contrast to the chaotic scene in the "overcrowded stuffy" sweatshop that opens *Yekl*, for instance, the opening of *Other Things Being Equal* places Ruth in a peaceful and elegant domestic setting, where she is "lazily rocking" by a window as "the long, drowsy call of a crowing cock came from afar off" and the "hazy splendor" of San Francisco "lifted its jocund hills." Ruth's reverie is interrupted by the arrival of her cousin, who is "glistening in jewels and silk."[25] In addition to material objects such as clothes, speech reinforces the gentility of Ruth and her family. Even her father's acquired English, spoken in "a full, musical voice with a marked French accent," adds to the cultured elegance of their lifestyle.[26] Because the characters' French accents are noted but not rendered in dialect, dialogue functions as a cultural marker of sameness in the novel. Mr. Levice's French accent serves another purpose as well, reminding readers that his American-born daughter speaks in unaccented English. Unlike Yekl, whose polyvocality shows him to be in the process of becoming the American Jake, Ruth is depicted as already assimilated, free of the gauche Americanisms that define ghetto girls like Mamie. One step removed from her parents' immigrant past, Ruth can express her Jewish identity without significantly compromising her standing as an American.

Urbane and well-mannered, products of the same affluent, cosmopolitan social milieu, Ruth and Kemp are drawn to each other more by their similarities than by their differences. Nor does Ruth's attraction to a Christian man reflect a desire to eradicate her ethno-religious difference in order to achieve acceptance by mainstream society, as is often the case in Jewish American narratives of intermarriage.[27] Instead, as the novel's title suggests, intermarriage functions as a

23. Emma Wolf, *Other Things Being Equal*, ed. Barbara Cantalupo (Detroit: Wayne State University Press, 2002), 184, 254. This volume is a reissue of the 1916 revised edition.

24. Meyer, "Concerning Sensitive Epiderms," 533.

25. Cahan, *Yekl*, 2; Wolf, *Other Things Being Equal*, 63.

26. Wolf, *Other Things Being Equal*, 69.

27. See Leslie Fiedler, "Genesis: The American-Jewish Novel Through the Twenties," *Midstream* (Summer 1959): 21–33; Adam Sol, "Longings and Renunciations: Attitudes Towards

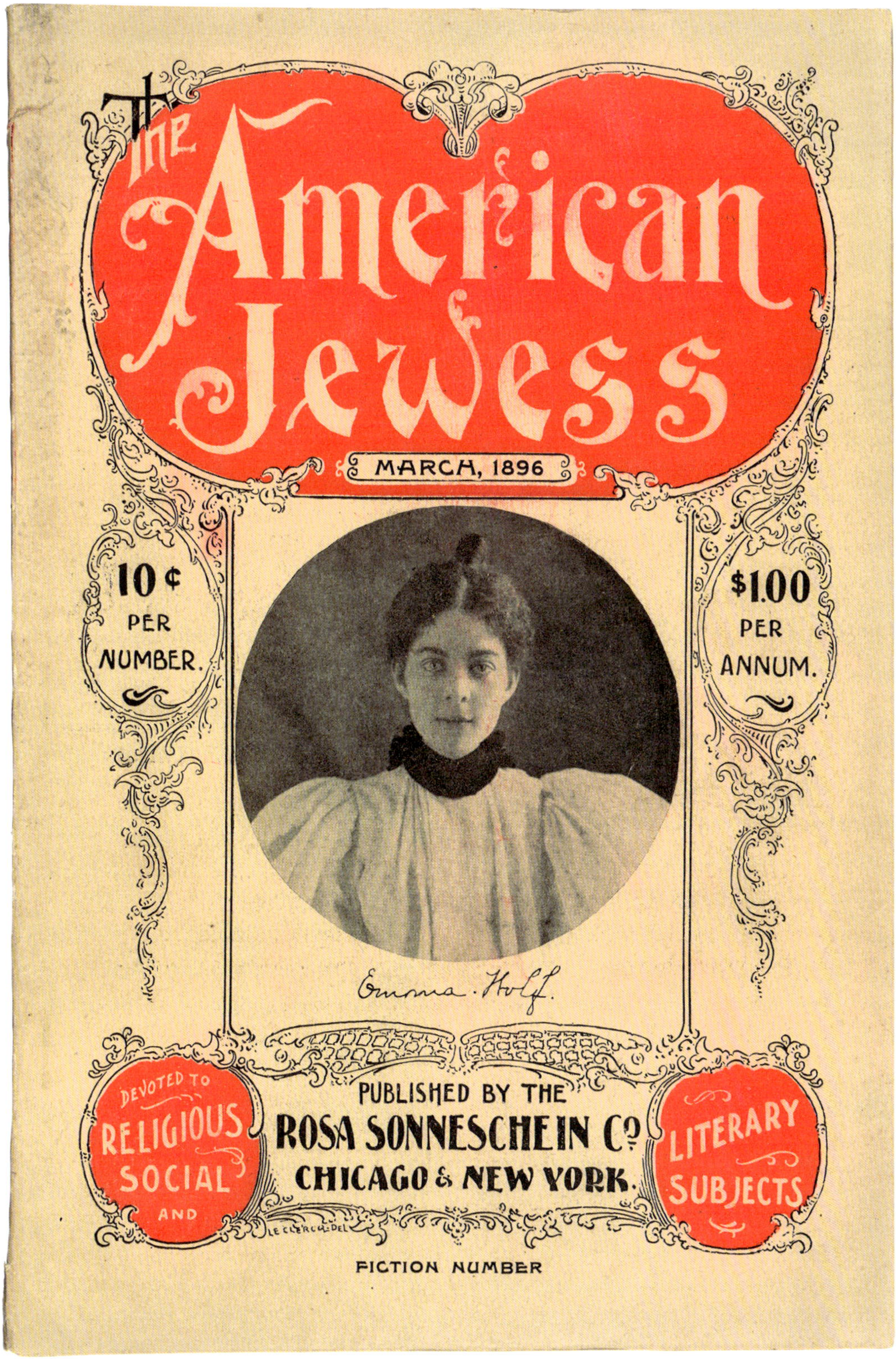

Fig. 44. Emma Wolf on the front cover of the *American Jewess* 2, no. 6 (March 1896). (Princeton University Library. Gift of Leonard Milberg).

public affirmation of a social equality that has mostly been achieved. It is telling that the primary objection to their marriage comes not from Gentile society but from within the Jewish community, via Ruth's father.

Rather than presenting an argument about the value of accepting difference, Mr. Levice's explanation of how he overcame his opposition to the couple's marriage relies on the rhetoric of equivalence:

> I grasped your two images before me and drew parallels: Socially—in my opinion society is a mutual drawing together of resemblances—socially each was as fair as the other. Mentally, the woman of the same stratum as the man. Physically, both were perfect types of pure, healthy blood. Morally, both were irreproachable. Religiously, both held a broad, abiding love for man and God. I stood convicted. I was in the position of a blind reactionary who, with a beautiful picture before him, fastens his critical, condemning gaze upon a rusting nail in the wall behind—a nail even now loosened, and which, some day, please God, shall fall.[28]

Ruth's father reverses his initial judgment, replacing it with a "beautiful picture" of equality.

This visual image suggests an outward similarity of appearance that derives foremost from commonalities in social environment. When set in the ghetto, narratives of interethnic romance necessitate spatial crossings. Inhabiting distinct social environs, the lovers of Anzia Yezierska's *Salome of the Tenements* (1923), for instance, must transcend the walls of the ghetto, moving between uptown and downtown; thus, ethno-religious difference becomes inextricable from class difference. In *Other Things Being Equal*, in contrast, socioeconomic class brings the lovers together; they reside in the same middle-class neighborhood, fortuitously discovering that they live only "a few blocks" apart from one another.[29] Class sameness once again overrides the possibility of ethno-racial difference, as suggested by Mr. Levice's reference to his daughter and future son-in-law

---

Intermarriage in Early Twentieth Century Jewish American Novels," *American Jewish History* 89, no. 2 (2001): 215–30; Ann Shapiro, "The Ultimate Shaygets and the Fiction of Anzia Yezierska," *MELUS* 21, no. 2 (1996): 79–88; and Josh Lambert, *Unclean Lips: Obscenity, Jews, and American Culture* (New York: New York University Press, 2014), 118–30. For considerations of intermarriage in *Other Things Being Equal* specifically, see my "'A Grave Experiment': Emma Wolf's Marriage Plots and the Deghettoization of American Jewish Fiction," *American Jewish History*, 101, no. 1 (2017): 5–34, and Jessica Kirzane, "Women, Love, and the Reform Jewish Mission: Jewish-Christian Marriage in Emma Wolf's *Other Things Being Equal* and Its Literary Successors," *American Jewish History* 104, no. 2/3 (2020): 289–322.

28. Wolf, *Other Things Being Equal*, 253–54.

29. *Ibid.*, 70.

as "perfect types of pure, healthy blood." This assertion bolsters the claim that Ruth and Kemp are "each ... as fair as the other," thus affirming his daughter's white racial identity.[30] The sequence of Mr. Levice's "parallels" indicates that outward signs of social and physical sameness lead to assumptions about interior similarities and compatibility, extending beyond blood to morality and religious belief.

As a realist writer, Wolf did not shy away from confronting antisemitism in *Other Things Being Equal.* More pragmatic than Kemp, Ruth remains aware that she could be subjected to prejudice based on imagined notions of racial difference and inferiority. "Involuntarily, the Christian mind always rears its ghettoes," she tells Kemp in response to his insistence that there is no distinction between Christian and Jew. "And in that mental ghetto, I want you to know, I belong—and proudly." This statement echoes Ruth's earlier declaration, "I am a Jewess, and will die one."[31] In response to her father's suggestion that her marriage would be perceived by others as a renunciation of Judaism, Ruth maintains that intermarriage need not require conversion. The "mental ghetto" may be a means of articulating elusive differences, but for Ruth, these differences become a source of pride rather than anxiety. Her class status ensures that she can embrace her Jewishness without threat to her social standing. Wolf's use of genteel realism allows her to create believable upper-middle-class Jewish characters who counter antisemitic caricatures. In the process, she persuades her readers that an interfaith union based on the principle of sameness—"other things" besides religion "being equal"—is realistic as well.

Not surprisingly, Wolf's treatment of intermarriage generated significant debate among her Jewish readers, and the novel continued to be a source of controversy more than a decade after its initial publication. In an 1896 speech before the New York Section of the National Council of Jewish Women, for instance, Annie Josephine Levi warned that Wolf's story, though "charmingly told," might "sow dangerous seeds in the minds of youth," who would disregard "religious sympathy" and view intermarriage as a real possibility.[32] Levi's concern that life might imitate fiction was not unfounded. An article on Wolf in the *San Francisco Chronicle* reported that although the author "has no idea how many marriages her story is responsible for," she has received wedding announcements from interfaith couples accompanied by notes thanking her for

30. On Jews and whiteness in late nineteenth-century America, see Eric Goldstein, *The Price of Whiteness: Jews, Race, and American Identity* (Princeton: Princeton University Press, 2006).

31. Wolf, *Other Things Being Equal*, 238, 194.

32. Annie Josephine Levi, "Intermarriage," *American Hebrew*, May 22, 1896, 73.

"untangl[ing] a knotty problem" in her novel.[33] In a 1904 sermon about intermarriage as apostasy, Los Angeles rabbi Sigmund Hecht, like Levi, expressed his disapproval of Wolf's imaginative resolution to the American quandary of difference and equality. "There were those among the readers of her book who roundly denounced the spirit in which it was conceived and written and declared that the author had broken with her ancestral religion and was trying to undermine the faith of her co-religionists," he stated, while acknowledging that "others ... hailed the sentiments expressed in that book as the powerful manifestation of the progressive spirit of Judaism."[34]

Wolf was unapologetic about her religious beliefs and her positive representation of intermarriage. When *Other Things Being Equal* was republished in 1916, the slightly revised edition contained a new foreword in which the novelist doubled down on the importance of her theme: "In presenting this revised edition to a new generation, the author feels that the element of change has touched very lightly the romantic potentialities obtaining at the time of the original writing.... Christian youth still chances upon Jewish youth, and with the same difference of historic background, the same social barriers and prejudices—the same possibilities of mutual attraction. The humanest love knows no sect.... It is the story of that beauty, which the author, in this revised edition, for a new generation, has not cared to revise."[35]

Wolf was far from the only writer to perceive the narrative and symbolic potential of romances between Christians and Jews. Intermarriage would become one of the most prevalent themes in works of Jewish American literature in the twentieth century, as Leslie Fiedler observed in his landmark 1958 essay, "Genesis: The Jewish-American Novel Through the Twenties." Although Wolf herself did not return to the specific topic of interfaith romance in her other published works, she continued to employ genteel realism and the narrative structure of the marriage plot as means of exploring questions of gender and class. Like other nineteenth-century women writers, she also viewed fiction as a means to participate in the public discourse on religion. Her adherence to "the progressive spirit of Judaism" is best exemplified by her fourth novel, *Heirs of Yesterday*, which engages explicitly with the development of Reform Judaism, as articulated in the Pittsburgh Platform of 1885 and implemented

33. "Writes About Home: Emma Wolf and Her Two Books," *San Francisco Chronicle*, July 15, 1894, 2.

34. "Spoke on 'Apostasy': Rabbi Hecht Discusses Intermarriage of Jews and Christians," *Los Angeles Herald*, March 6, 1904, 6.

35. Emma Wolf, foreword to *Other Things Being Equal*, 61.

by the leadership of her San Francisco synagogue, Temple Emanu-El. Wolf's novelistic treatment of religion continued to stoke controversy in the Jewish community, as evidenced by the Jewish Publication Society's reluctance to publish *Heirs of Yesterday*, among other works of fiction that she submitted for consideration.

Realism and Reform Judaism in "Heirs of Yesterday"

First published in 1892, *Other Things Being Equal* is among the earliest Jewish American novels.[36] In its realistic representation of middle-class Jewish life in San Francisco, it anticipated many of the debates surrounding the ghetto genre, including Meyer's call for literature that highlights resemblances rather than differences between Jews and Gentiles. By 1900, when Wolf published *Heirs of Yesterday*, not only had ghetto fiction firmly secured its niche in Anglo-Jewish letters with the emergence of figures such as Cahan and Zangwill, but antisemitic representations were also increasingly pervasive in American print culture and in fiction by non-Jewish writers. Popular periodicals, for instance, regularly published dialect stories in which Jews appeared as one-dimensional caricatures, as well as cartoons and jokes whose punchlines depended on the audience's knowledge of Jewish stereotypes. While some Gentile American writers voiced respect and sympathy for Jews, leading at times to complex literary portrayals, scholars such as Donald Pizer have exposed the extent of antisemitic representation in the work of canonical writers of the era—including Wolf's fellow San Franciscan, novelist Frank Norris.[37]

In his 1899 novel *McTeague: A Story of San Francisco*, Norris describes the character of Zerkow, a Polish Jewish junk dealer, in demonic and animalistic terms: "a dry, shriveled old man" with satanically red hair; "eager, catlike lips of the covetous; eyes that had grown keen as those of a lynx from long searching

36. See, for example, Josephine Lazarus's 1894 essay, "Judaism, Old and New," which includes a discussion of *Other Things Being Equal*, and D. J. Myers, "Emma Wolf's Stories," http://dgmyers.blogspot.com/2010/05/emma-wolfs-stories.html. Myers argues that Wolf is "the mother of American Jewish fiction" because *Other Things Being Equal*, published by the "Christian-owned house of A. C. McClurg," was "the first American novel written by a Jew, on a Jewish subject, but aimed at a general audience." This designation has since been challenged by Jonathan Sarna's recovery of Cora Wilburn's work, especially her novel *Cosella Wayne*, which was serialized in the Spiritualist journal *Banner of Light* in 1860. See Sarna, "The Forgetting of Cora Wilburn: Historical Amnesia and *The Cambridge History of Jewish American Literature*," *Studies in American Jewish Literature* 37, no. 1 (Spring 2018): 73–87.

37. See Donald Pizer, *American Naturalism and the Jews: Garland, Norris, Dreiser, Wharton, and Cather* (Urbana and Chicago: University of Illinois Press, 2008).

amid muck and debris; and clawlike, prehensile fingers—the fingers of a man who accumulates, but never disburses." Zerkow's "inordinate, insatiable greed" leads him to marry a poor Mexican charwoman, Maria, in order to get his hands on a set of gold dishes that her family once purportedly owned.[38] By the end of the novel, Zerkow's lust for gold turns murderous, and he kills his wife in pursuit of the illusory dishes. As Elisa New writes, "Norris' depiction of the greedy Jew reflects a particularly American anti-Semitism that was very much of the 1890s and was shared by other naturalist writers."[39]

Throughout *Heirs of Yesterday*, Wolf refers to antisemitic tropes and stereotypes in an effort to counter them, and she fully develops her Jewish characters as individuals in response to depictions that appeared in the work of her contemporaries. Whereas antisemitic discourse relayed Jewishness through a character's outward appearance, Philip May is visually indistinguishable from his Gentile counterparts. As Philip himself explains, his father "endowed [him] with a name which tells no tales," while "thanks to [his] mother [his] features are equally silent." When the novel states that Jean Willard's "religion had always lain lightly upon her," it refers at once to spirituality and to the fact that her appearance is not readily identifiable as Jewish. Wolf's attention to the visual signifiers of Jewishness is especially evident in the plotline involving Jean's refusal to model for the antisemitic painter Stephen Forrest, who is enamored of the heroine's "shadowy dark" beauty. Although Forrest attempts to reassure Jean that her "sex unsects" her when she reminds him of her Jewish background, his view remains circumscribed by the archetype of *la belle juive* (the beautiful Jewess), an image of erotic fascination for Christian men.[40] Orientalized femininity rendered Jewish women as exotic, while bringing into relief the repulsive physical features that marked Jewish male difference in antisemitic representations. As Wolf makes clear, such representations run the gamut from fine art to low comedy. At a gallery exhibition, Jean is distressed to find that Forrest has created her portrait from memory and without her consent, titling it "The Jewess." In another scene, a group of Jean's friends debates how best to respond to cartoons in popular humor magazines such as *Puck*, in which corporeal excess served as a visual marker of Jewish men's greed and undesirability.[41]

38. Frank Norris, *McTeague: A Story of San Francisco* (1899; New York: Signet, 1981), 37–38.

39. Elisa New, "My Favorite Anti-Semite: Frank Norris and the Most Horrifying Jew in American Literature," *Tablet*, October 24, 2013, https://www.tabletmag.com/jewish-arts-and-culture/books/149884/mcteague-frank-norris.

40. Wolf, *Heirs of Yesterday*, 99, 117, 90, 114.

41. On antisemitic representations in late nineteenth-century cartoons, see Matthew Baigell,

The novel's references to antisemitic stereotyping help to explain why Philip decides to suppress his Jewish background. In making a case for resemblances between Jews and Gentiles, the novel combines its marriage plot with a narrative of passing. "I was an American—with a difference. I hated the difference," confesses Philip, explaining to his father how he came to pass for Gentile while in medical school at Harvard. By omitting any mention of his Jewish background and attending a Unitarian church, Philip became part of "a crowd of young Bostonians" who "took [him] for one of their own persuasion."[42] Like many African American authors who wrote novels of passing, Wolf uses the trope to expose discriminatory practices and challenge notions of racial difference while ultimately rejecting passing as a means of attaining social equality. Through his relationship with Jean, Philip comes to see his decision to pass as misguided and moves toward an increasing acceptance of his heritage.

Conveying admirable aspects of Jewishness that Jewish and non-Jewish critics alike felt were missing from ghetto tales such as *Yekl*, Wolf portrays characters such as Jean with "that dignity of faith which compels respect from Christians" and "that helpfulness of … other[s] which shames the selfishness of the Gentile."[43] Like *Other Things Being Equal*, *Heirs of Yesterday* deploys genteel realism to characterize its middle-class characters and to portray life in the hills of Pacific Heights. Once again, we are far from the cramped atmosphere of the New York ghetto. Instead, the novel opens with Jean walking "westward … swiftly, lightly, the joyous wind of motion in her going," and taking off her jacket in the warm February sun "to enjoy the freedom." A talented pianist and sought-after companion in her circle of young intellectuals and artists, Jean is defined by freedom of movement and thought. During Philip's sojourn in the East, Jean, who was born in Los Angeles, came to live next door to his father, Joseph May, with her uncle, Daniel Willard, who lovingly raised her after the deaths of her parents. As an orphan, Jean is seemingly released from filial obligations and afforded an opportunity to reinvent herself, in keeping with her passionate belief in "the development of individuality at any cost."[44] But Jean takes the possibility of reinvention in a different direction from Philip's when he makes his decision to cut off ties to the past. Instead, she devotes herself to her father's brother, Daniel, and his neighbor and closest friend, Joseph. Calling

---

The Implacable Urge to Defame: Cartoon Jews in the American Press, 1877–1935 (Syracuse, N.Y.: Syracuse University Press, 2017).

42. Wolf, *Heirs of Yesterday*, 99–100.

43. Banks, "New York Ghetto," 158.

44. Wolf, *Heirs of Yesterday*, 87, 138.

both of them "Uncle," she defines kinship by bonds of love and affection above blood. She views Judaism, too, as an inheritance that can be redefined to better suit her modern lifestyle.

Whereas the cultural taboo against interfaith unions proved an obstacle in the marriage plot of *Other Things Being Equal*, in *Heirs of Yesterday* the would-be lovers, both Jewish by birth, find that their conflicting attitudes toward ethno-religious identity interfere in what would otherwise be a providential match. Initially viewing Philip as a "coldly ambitious man," Jean cannot tolerate his renunciation of his Jewishness for the purpose of "climbing up the social ladder." When Joseph dies, heartbroken at the idea that his son, in rejecting Judaism in order to become a self-made man, had also rejected his father, Jean holds Philip responsible for the death, accusing him of violating the Fifth Commandment. Orphaned, like Jean, and disinherited by his father, who had revised his will upon hearing of his son's intent to pass as Gentile in order to promote his career and gain membership in the city's best social club, Philip seems free of the "unfit shackle" that threatened to confine him. But both his attraction to Jean and the death of his father propel Philip into a reencounter with Judaism and an opportunity to find new meaning in the religion that he once viewed as no more than a "social handicap."[45]

If religious practice is a fairly minor consideration in *Other Things Being Equal*, it is central to *Heirs of Yesterday*, which depicts everyday life and ritual in Jewish homes, as well as the dynamics of the broader religious community, with San Francisco's Temple Emanu-El at its center. The novel's historically informed engagement with the rise of the Reform movement allows Wolf to represent Judaism as a modern religion well suited to New World values, rather than as a sentimental vestige of Old World traditions. Wolf's realistic treatment of religion was shaped by her personal experience with the Reform movement, specifically her family's involvement in Temple Emanu-El. By the late nineteenth century, Emanu-El, under the leadership of Rabbis Elkan Cohn and Jacob Voorsanger, had become one of the nation's leading Reform synagogues, initiating looser interpretations of religious law in order "to remake the Jewish liturgy, ritual, and credo to suit the values of the New World."[46] Emanu-El was one of the first synagogues in the country to prioritize Friday evening services above Saturday morning, thus leaving Saturday open for business or leisure. As Marc Lee

45. *Ibid.*, 112, 111, 100, 101.

46. Fred Rosenbaum, *Visions of Reform: Congregation Emanu-el and the Jews of San Francisco, 1849–1999* (Berkeley: Judah L. Magnes Museum, 2000), 16.

Raphael has demonstrated, Voorsanger, who was appointed rabbi of Emanu-El in 1886, one year after the Pittsburgh conference, strongly emphasized the progressive potential of Reform Judaism by drawing links to the American belief in "manifest destiny" and its implied assumption of white superiority. A proponent of assimilation in all matters but religion, Voorsanger was concerned that the influx of newly arrived Eastern European coreligionists, with their "meaningless, Oriental rites," would "chain Jews to the ghetto." He went so far as to support immigration restrictions to ensure that Jews who were already settled in the United States would not be deemed backward and racially inferior by association. According to Raphael, Voorsanger's convictions resulted in a "general rejection of all which stood between Judaism and the non-Jewish world" for many Emanu-El members.[47] Thus, in accordance with the Pittsburgh Platform, practices that would have interfered with Jews' ability to socialize and conduct business with their Gentile counterparts, such as kosher dietary laws or strict Sabbath observance, were largely abandoned. Members of Emanu-El formed an elite society of Jews who had emigrated from central Europe in the mid-nineteenth century and who lived in close proximity to one another in Pacific Heights. Although the Jews of Emanu-El modeled their community and social lives on those of their Gentile neighbors, they continued to identify publicly as Jews, believing that the practice of liberal Judaism created "alternatives to assimilation," in the words of Alan Silverstein, a historian of the American Reform movement.[48]

As opposed to Philip, who associates his abandoned religion with the cramped confinement of the ghetto, Jean embraces the tenets of the Reform movement, viewing Judaism as "singularly free, unhampered, broad, open to the light of day." When Philip finds himself a reluctant guest at the Willards' Passover Seder, Jean introduces him to the versatile doctrine of the nineteenth-century reformers and shares with him her religious philosophy: Judaism is not an ancient practice but an evolving one. Jean's lessons are reinforced by her uncle, who accompanies Philip to Temple for Friday night services during his father's

47. Marc Lee Raphael, "Rabbi Jacob Voorsanger of San Francisco on Jews and Judaism: The Implications of the Pittsburgh Platform," *American Jewish Historical Quarterly* 63, no. 2 (1973): 191, 192, 203.

48. Alan Silverstein, *Alternatives to Assimilation: The Response of Reform Judaism to American Culture* (Waltham, Mass.: Brandeis University Press, 1994). On the Reform movement, see also Dana Evan Kaplan, *American Reform Judaism: An Introduction* (New Brunswick: Rutgers University Press, 2003), and Jonathan D. Sarna, *American Judaism* (New Haven: Yale University Press, 2004), 82–88, 144–51.

shivah. There Philip experiences Judaism "robbed of provincialisms and anachronisms." As Daniel explains to the man who aspires to become his nephew-in-law, "the Talmudic idea—was that the Law was never to be a sealed matter—that it was always to remain open to the interpretation of the search-light of progress."[49] Like intermarriage in *Other Things Being Equal*, Reform Judaism is depicted as an open "experiment," with the potential to forge reconciliation between religious belief and modernity. This expansive vision of Judaism is made possible in part by Wolf's Western setting, which removes her characters from the confines of the ghetto. The Jewishness of Wolf's characters is thus shown to be compatible with the freedoms of American identity, and this compatibility is emphasized via the temporal context of the novel's ending, which coincides with the start of the Spanish-American War.

Although Philip maintains some of his skepticism, by the end of the novel he comes to accept, if not Judaism, then love as his religion. "You have become my religion," he tells Jean in an effort to win her over. "If you are Jewish, must I not too be Jew?"[50] But *Heirs of Yesterday* does not end with the neat resolution of the marriage plot. Instead, the novel zooms outward to the national and world stage, as the historical backdrop of the Spanish-American War overtakes the lives of Wolf's fictional characters. As Jeanne Abrams's analysis of the war's coverage in the *American Israelite* demonstrates, the Reform community in particular saw its interests as Jews aligned with its interests as Americans and supported the nation's efforts to expand its borders and spread democracy.[51] Indeed, Wolf's Jewish characters are subsumed into the national narrative. In a show of patriotism, Philip enlists as an army surgeon—a historical reference to Colonel Joseph M. Heller, a surgeon who roused Jewish pride when he left a thriving medical practice to become the first man to volunteer following the United States's declaration of war.[52] Jean, meanwhile, devotes herself to the San Francisco Red Cross, preparing packages for soldiers and entertaining them with "patriotic airs." The historical event of the Spanish-American War offers

49. Wolf, *Heirs of Yesterday*, 212. The reference to Friday night services is significant, given that Wolf's congregation, Temple Emanu-El, was among the first synagogues in America to hold services on the evening of the Sabbath. See Rosenbaum, *Visions of Reform*, 46.

50. Wolf, *Heirs of Yesterday*, 240.

51. Jeanne Abrams, "Remembering the Maine: The Jewish Attitude Toward the Spanish-American War as Reflected in *The American Israelite*," *American Jewish History* 76, no. 4 (1987): 440, 444.

52. See Seymour "Sy" Brody, *Jewish Heroes & Heroines of America* (Hollywood, Fla.: Frederick Fell, 2004), 104, and "Col. Joseph M. Heller Dies; Doctor in Two U.S. Wars," *Washington Post*, October 12, 1943, 8.

yet another way for Wolf to portray the nobility of her Jewish characters, who find "an absorbing interest beyond self" through their service to the nation.[53]

In the novel's final pages, an image of Philip and Jean walking together over the hills and into the future is followed by a coda depicting the Manila expedition departing for the Philippines from San Francisco Bay, with Philip on board and Jean standing with the crowds from Pacific Heights in a farewell salute. Through their participation in American expansionism, Wolf's characters have become part of the nation; they have done so, however, while reclaiming and redefining, rather than creating greater distance from, their Jewish identities. Instead of resolving with the union of its two main characters, *Heirs* concludes with a narrative ambiguity that furthers its author's commitment to realist aesthetics. In raising the specter of Philip losing his life at war or at sea, the ending leaves readers with uncertainty about the future, thus reflecting the sociopolitical and global changes taking hold at the turn of the new century as America's path through modernity became intertwined with its status as an imperial power. For many of Wolf's readers, the uncertainties about daily American life at the end of the nineteenth century extended to the future of Judaism—as suggested by the backstory of how *Heirs of Yesterday* made its way into print.

The Jewish Publication Society and the Politics of Print

The controversial nature of *Heirs of Yesterday* is illuminated by its publication history. The novel was published by A. C. McClurg, the Chicago-based firm that had previously taken a chance on *Other Things Being Equal* and subsequently published Wolf's third novel, *The Joy of Life*, in 1896. Neither *The Joy of Life* nor Wolf's sophomore novel, *A Prodigal in Love* (1894), contains explicitly Jewish content, suggesting, at first glance, that Wolf turned away from the religious themes that sparked contention with the publication of her debut novel. However, recent archival research has shown that Wolf was actively writing Jewish fiction throughout the 1890s. *Heirs of Yesterday* was one of three manuscripts she submitted to the Jewish Publication Society of America (JPS) between 1894 and 1900, only to have her work repeatedly rejected by the society's publication committee. The other two manuscripts—a Jewish-themed novel titled *A Dreamer of Dreams*, which she sent to the JPS in 1893, and a children's story, "Little Jaffa," which she submitted for a literary contest—are now lost. Knowledge of them, along with the subsequent publication of *Heirs of Yesterday* by McClurg, elucidates the politics of print in the Gilded Age and the gatekeeping

53. Wolf, *Heirs of Yesterday*, 229, 227.

role played by the Jewish publishing industry in shaping mainstream representations of Jewishness.

Founded in the mid-nineteenth century with the purpose of promoting Jewish literature, the JPS was in its heyday in the 1890s, with the publication of acclaimed works like Zangwill's *Children of the Ghetto*.[54] Following the success of *Other Things Being Equal*, the JPS reached out to Wolf in the hope of nurturing American talent. She was then at work on *A Dreamer of Dreams*. The little we know about this novel comes from Wolf's correspondence with the JPS and the minutes from publication committee meetings. The cover letter that Wolf sent with the manuscript states, "Should you find any objections upon points which you think I could remedy, I trust you will not hesitate to mention them."[55] This sentence might suggest that Wolf anticipated pushback. The JPS toed the line between Orthodoxy and Reform in order to maximize its audience, with the goal of unifying American Jews through culture. Based on the response to *Other Things Being Equal*, Wolf knew that her progressive religious principles were likely to meet with opposition. The publication committee's deliberations on *A Dreamer of Dreams* confirm the JPS's interest in her work, as well as its members' desire to steer clear of overly controversial material. The "objections" mentioned in the minutes focused on content rather than style. One member, for example, acknowledged that the novel was "good from a story-teller's point of view," but "considered some of the characters immoral, and the Rabbi hero impossible": "the fact that whenever a traditional Jewish custom is discussed …, the Rabbi declares himself conscientiously unable to observe it, ought to suffice to prevent the publishing of the book." Other members wanted to prioritize aesthetics and popularity, resulting in a tie vote. Ultimately, the committee decided that it was "not expedient" for the JPS to publish the novel.[56]

These minutes offer a tantalizing glimpse of Wolf's lost work. Like *Heirs of Yesterday*, *Dreamer* appears to deal with the modernization of American Juda-

54. On the Jewish Publication Society, see Jonathan D. Sarna, *JPS: The Americanization of Jewish Culture, 1888–1988* (Philadelphia: Jewish Publication Society, 1989).

55. Letter from Emma Wolf, November 14, 1893, written from 1711 Geary Street, San Francisco, to Mayer Sulzberger, chairman of the publication committee of the JPS. Held by the National Library of Israel's Abraham Schwadron Autograph Collection. In the introduction to the 2020 edition of *Heirs of Yesterday*, Cantalupo and I raise the possibility that Wolf did not completely abandon *A Dreamer of Dreams* and that *The Joy of Life* may be a revision that stripped the novel of its Jewish content.

56. Henrietta Szold, "Minutes of the Publication Committee of the Jewish Publication Society of America, 1888–1905," 37, Jewish Publication Society Archives, series 4, box 130, folder 2, Temple University Libraries Special Collections Research Center, Philadelphia.

ism. But unlike Wolf's other fiction, the narrative may have featured a rabbi as its main character. From the committee's description, it appears that Wolf was again using fiction—one of the few public forums available to women in the nineteenth century—as a means of grappling with theological questions. That her "Rabbi hero" forgoes traditional observance implies that the book, like *Heirs*, was sympathetic to Reform Judaism. If the minutes are too spare to shed substantive light on Wolf's manuscript, they do capture the competing demands on the JPS and the factors that went into the production of late nineteenth-century Jewish fiction. Prioritizing the ideological function of art over its literary value, the JPS made a pragmatic decision: Wolf's work would highlight ruptures within the Jewish community rather than create continuity.

Despite the rejection, Wolf was not dissuaded from trying to publish with the JPS. Several years later, in an effort to reach the younger generation, the JPS promised a prize of $1,000 for the best children's story. The prize committee's debate was contentious, and some of the dispute was sparked by Wolf's submission. Among the twenty-seven manuscripts, Wolf's "Little Jaffa" was favored by one vote over the other top-rated story. Unable to arrive at consensus, the JPS decided not to award a prize. Like all of the contestants, Wolf was informed that no winner was selected because "no story of Jewish interest suited to young readers and satisfactory to the Judges" was offered.[57] The content of "Little Jaffa" remains a mystery, although it likely had a female protagonist ("Jaffa," which means beauty in Hebrew, was probably used as a girl's name). Events that transpired afterward heighten the mystery and offer potential clues about Wolf's lost work. The JPS decided to publish two of the stories submitted for the contest: Sara Miller's *Under the Eagle's Wing* and Louis Pendleton's *Lost Prince Almon*. The latter was the submission that tied with Wolf's. What makes the decision to publish Pendleton's and not Wolf's story curious is its author's background. Despite the JPS's mission to promote Jewish writers, Pendleton was a Christian Southerner. Miller's and Pendleton's tales were adventure stories featuring young male protagonists. Combining religious and historical content with the exotic veneer of Orientalism, both share the didacticism common to nineteenth-century children's literature. Based on the JPS's decision not to publish "Little Jaffa," we can assume that Wolf's text defied expectations for religious children's literature of the time.

A few years later, Wolf's friendship with the JPS's star author, Israel Zangwill, reignited her interest in publishing with the house. Although the two writers

57. *Ibid.*, 100.

never met in person, they engaged in a trans-Atlantic correspondence about their craft for at least four years, beginning in 1896, when Wolf sent the British author an admiring letter accompanied by a copy of *The Joy of Life.* Taking place at a pivotal moment in the careers of both writers, the correspondence would significantly shape the work that they went on to produce.[58] In a letter to Wolf, Zangwill encouraged her to write "the Jewish story which is stirring in your subconscious" and submit it to the JPS for consideration. Interestingly, Zangwill's endorsement of the JPS was not unequivocal. He had his own hesitations about its agenda and urged Wolf not to compromise her beliefs.[59] Wolf took Zangwill's advice and submitted the manuscript for *Heirs of Yesterday* to the JPS. Although the publication committee called the novel "an admirable piece ... from a literary point of view," it ended up rejecting Wolf's work for a third time. The minutes reveal that several members "thought it inadvisable ... to publish ... on account of the treatment of its subject" and that, "in view of the division existing in the Committee, the publication of Miss Wolf's novel was impracticable."[60] Once again, the committee praised Wolf's artistry while questioning whether the content fulfilled the JPS's mission. In rejecting Wolf's work, the publisher may have missed an opportunity to expand the regional parameters of Jewish fiction and contribute to a pluralistic Jewish culture that extended beyond the ghetto, in this case to the West Coast.

Fortunately, Wolf persevered, placing *Heirs of Yesterday* with A. C. McClurg, which would later become known for publishing other groundbreaking works of ethnic American literature, such as W. E. B. Du Bois's *The Souls of Black Folk* (1903) and Sui Sin Far's *Mrs. Spring Fragrance* (1912), the first collection of fiction by an Asian American writer. According to Lucas Dietrich, McClurg developed a reputation for its ability "to mediate between an ethnic author and a mainstream, predominantly white literary readership," positioning these works so that they simultaneously "bridge[d] cultural divisions" and "reinscribe[d] existing social hierarchies."[61] The first edition of *Heirs of Yesterday* bears

58. For more on the relationship with Zangwill and especially Wolf's influence on his 1908 play *The Melting Pot,* see Harrison-Kahan, "'A Grave Experiment.'" On the correspondence between Zangwill and Wolf, see Barbara Cantalupo, "The Letters of Israel Zangwill to Emma Wolf: Transatlantic Mentoring in the 1890s," *Resources for American Literary Study* 28 (2002): 121–38. Only Zangwill's side of the correspondence has survived, preserved and bound by Wolf's family.

59. Israel Zangwill to Emma Wolf, February 5, 1897. Zangwill's letters to Wolf can be found in Cantalupo, "The Letters of Israel Zangwill to Emma Wolf."

60. Szold, "Minutes," 136.

61. Lucas Dietrich, "'At the Dawning of the Twentieth Century': W. E. B. Du Bois, A. C. McClurg & Co., and the Early Circulation of *The Souls of Black Folk,*" *Book History* 20 (2017): 315.

evidence of such mediation. The book's cover design (see Fig. 42) is divided horizontally, with the plainly rendered title above the author's name in the top section. The lower section is filled with a floral design, bordered in black. One of the vine-like flowers bleeds over the border into the top section, coming in close proximity to the name "Wolf." With that flower creating a bridge between the staid upper half and the lusher imagery below, the design at once signals containment and crossover.

The book's epigraph is a quotation from Zangwill's *Dreamers of the Ghetto*, a book published by the JPS in partnership with Harper & Brothers: "For something larger had come into his life, a sense of a vaster universe without, and its spaciousness and strangeness filled his soul with a nameless trouble and a vague unrest. He was no longer a child of the Ghetto."[62] The epigraph page is followed by a one-page foreword, which contains the novel's first explicit reference to Jewishness. The text sets the scene as middle-class San Francisco, where "the tide of Jewish social culture runs its mimic parallel alongside" Gentile culture. It introduces Philip with his cry of denial: "Bah! … what have I to do with Ghettoes!"[63] Through these paratexts, *Heirs of Yesterday* is placed in dialogue with Zangwill and ghetto literature (and, by extension, with the kind of literature published by the JPS). In this introductory moment, Philip may even be said to represent Wolf herself. If Wolf's character rejects the idea that anyone born a Jew must be defined by the ghetto, Wolf rejects the idea that Jewish fiction must be circumscribed by the ghetto genre. Thus, the text mediates between Wolf as a Jewish author and non-Jewish readers via references to more familiar representations of Jewish identity. The narrative, however, overturns those familiar representations through its depiction of Jewish characters who are well-off, cultured Americans and, in most ways, indistinguishable from their Gentile counterparts.

In an interview with the *San Francisco Examiner* that appeared after the publication of *Heirs of Yesterday*, Wolf addressed the controversies surrounding her work, especially among her coreligionists. "My purpose in writing … is to give genuine pleasure to my readers," she stated,

> But one must not place heart before art. I try to paint the subject as truthfully as possible in the colors in which I see it myself mentally. Truth-telling should be an author's religion. It is mine, and because of it I have caused considerable

62. Israel Zangwill, *Dreamers of the Ghetto* (Philadelphia: Jewish Publication Society, 1898), 20.

63. Wolf, *Heirs of Yesterday*, [85].

> discussion among my own people. But all that I have written has been said in the spirit of love—the love that has the courage to point out a fault in its object.[64]

Undeterred by those who viewed her treatment of themes such as intermarriage and Reform theology as a threat to the future of Judaism, Wolf held fast to the principles of realism above idealization and professed an allegiance to "truth-telling" above her faith. The debates about both ghetto fiction and Wolf's novels of manners speak not only to the challenges of ethno-religious representation in art but also to the slipperiness of realism as a literary mode.

Today, Cahan's *Yekl* continues to enjoy its privileged status as an ur-text of Jewish American fiction. Yet, Wolf, too, is beginning to get her due. With the heirs of so many generations of eastern European Jews now flourishing throughout the United States, her themes have become relevant once again. As Josh Lambert writes in an essay about the 2020 reissue of *Heirs of Yesterday*, "Because many American Jews today resemble the ones in Wolf 's San Francisco more than their ancestors could have imagined … *Heirs of Yesterday* resonate[s] … with a surprising contemporaneity."[65] Reconsidering the mixed reception of Cahan's work and making space in the canon for writers like Wolf allows for a fuller and more textured evaluation of the relationship between Jewish fiction and American literary realism. This account attests to the diversity of Jewish American experiences, within and beyond the ghetto, while recognizing the wide-ranging contributions of Jewish novelists to American culture by the end of the nineteenth century and their impact on the production of Jewish American literature to come.

64. Lillian Ferguson, "Leading Epigrammist in Recent Fiction is a California Girl: Great English Critics Have Given High Praise to Miss. Emma Wolf's Novels," *San Francisco Examiner*, Dec. 1, 1901, 25.

65. Josh Lambert, "The Jewish Jane Austen Whose Novels Were Almost Forgotten," *Lilith* 46 (Spring 2021): 25.

OVERLAPPING COMMUNITIES: EMMA LAZARUS AND AMERICAN JEWISH POETICS

SHIRA WOLOSKY

Pluralist Communities

AMERICA was never solely an English Protestant land. There were Germans of various sects in Pennsylvania, Spanish Catholics in Florida and the Southwest, French Catholics in Louisiana and Canada, and English Catholics in Maryland. Nevertheless, English Protestantism established the model of the American. The "New Americans" described by J. Hector St. John de Crèvecœur in his *Letters from an American Farmer*, in whom "individuals of all nations are melted into a new race of men," closely resembled the English Protestant ones, as also did the melting pot American at the turn of the twentieth century.[1] Up through perhaps the second half of the twentieth century, two main options were available to newcomers: inclusion as American by conforming to the English Protestant model; or exclusion by being forbidden to do so. Nativism flourished with the Know-Nothings in reaction against the Irish Catholic immigration of the 1820s and culminated in the anti-immigration legislation of the 1920s. The Civil War to an extent marks a moment of shifting identifications and more pluralist expression. Black freedmen, women, and a new sense of regionalism all emerged as literary voices. The failure of Reconstruction and the growth of nativism presented countertrends against this postbellum pluralist expression.[2] Yet a notion of "cultural pluralism," a term first introduced by Horace Kallen in 1906,[3] also emerged, elaborated in turn by William James and John Dewey.

1. Crèvecœur, "What Is an American," Letter 3 in *Letters from an American Farmer* (London: T. Davies, 1782). According to John Higham, white English Protestants "were the Americans and all others were outsiders." Higham, *Hanging Together: Unity and Diversity in American Culture*, ed. Carl Guarneri (New Haven: Yale University Press, 2001), 91. Milton Gordon posits that the melting pot concept "embraces a view of acculturation which is hardly distinguishable from that of Anglo-conformity." Gordon, *Assimilation in American Life: The Role of Race, Religion, and National Origins* (New York: Oxford University Press, 1964), 116, 125.

2. John Higham, *Send These to Me: Jews and Other Immigrants in Urban America* (New York: Atheneum, 1975), 102–15.

3. He did not use it in print until 1915. See Sidney Ratner, "Horace M. Kallen and Cultural Pluralism," *Modern Judaism* 4, no. 2 (1984): 185–200.

American Jewish communities by their very definition mark a pluralist configuration. Pluralism and memberships are mostly studied through statistics, answering questions regarding rituals, synagogue attendance, and other institutional involvements. But literature, including poetry, can offer a window into how American Jews experienced pluralism and also constituted themselves as members of both Jewish and American communities in ongoing and shifting interrelationships. Such reflection on plural memberships occurs even before its more dramatic expression in the migration literature that flourished at the end of the nineteenth century.

The Jewish postbellum period was of course radically bifurcated by the onset of immigration from the pogroms of eastern Europe. On the whole, in the period before and after the Civil War American Jews, numbering between 250,000 and 300,000 until the 1880s, mainly participated in what I would call overlapping pluralist communities. Individuals could consider themselves both Jewish and American, where each identity was seen to express and support the other. American values and goals were largely shared alongside distinctive Jewish practices, organizations, and learning.

Isaac Leeser's *Occident and American Jewish Advocate* was a forum for such overlapping, yet distinct and even contending communities. The first general Jewish periodical in the United States, the *Occident* published poetry, essays, letters, sermons, editorials, and news from Europe as well as America. The leader of the traditional (Orthodox) stream in Philadelphia, Leeser was also a social activist, tracking and protesting against the exclusion of Jews in American legal and social contexts and countering threats to their particular existence, notably the proselytizing efforts of missionary societies. Jews were perhaps the only non-Christian citizens in America that missions could target, because Blacks and Native Americans had no rights at all. Leeser appealed not to religious principles but to a republican equality based on the Enlightenment ideals of the Declaration of Independence. This conception countered long-held notions of America as a Christian nation, which was in complex relation and also tension with republican definitions of nationhood. In his 1840 pamphlet, *The Claims of the Jews for Equality of Rights*, Leeser demanded equality for Jews, not as mere toleration nor as "a special act of grace" nor as based in religious arguments. His grounds are Enlightenment principles in defense of Jewish American rights.[4] Leeser

4. Jonathan D. Sarna, *American Jews and Church-State Relations: The Quest for "Equal Footing"* (New York: American Jewish Committee, 1989), 1-43, available at https://www.brandeis.edu/hornstein/sarna/christianjewishrelations/Archive/AmericanJewsandChurchStateRelationsEqualFooting.pdf. Naomi W. Cohen, *Jews in Christian America: The Pursuit of Religious Equality*

attacked oaths and other exclusions from public offices, still a very live topic due to the ongoing controversy over the 1826 Maryland "Jew Bill," which would allow Jews to hold public office. He joined with Seventh Day Adventists in opposing Sunday laws (unsuccessfully);[5] drafted the letter from the Jewish Board of Delegates protesting the 1864 proposed amendment to introduce Christian language into the Constitution;[6] published articles by Warder Cresson and covered the 1849 trial that eventually exonerated him, on the grounds of religious freedom, of charges of insanity brought by his ex-wife after his conversion to Judaism and move to Palestine.[7] Cresson's legal battle is a striking case of how American Jews not only benefited from the rise of American pluralism but were core figures in shaping it.[8]

Emma Lazarus

Emma Lazarus's career exemplifies this pluralist unfolding. She was among the first intellectuals to consciously propose and perform what came to be called a hyphenated identity as American-Jewish. Her writings register and pursue the course of American Jewish identities in the second half of the nineteenth century, including the radical turn at 1881 with Jewish mass immigration from

---

(New York: Oxford University Press 1992), discusses the embrace of Enlightenment ideas "as a bulwark against Christian nationhood" (48). Cf. Naomi W. Cohen, "An Overview of American Jewish Defense," in *Religion and State in the American Jewish Experience*, ed. Jonathan D. Sarna and David G. Dalin (Notre Dame: Notre Dame University Press, 1997), 13–45. On Leeser, see also Kyle G. Volk, *Moral Minorities and the Making of American Democracy* (New York: Oxford University Press, 2014), 49–52.

5. Maxine S. Seller, "Isaac Leeser: A Jewish-Christian Dialogue in Antebellum Philadelphia," *Pennsylvania History: A Journal of Mid-Atlantic Studies* 35, no. 3 (1968): 231–42.

6. The first sentence of the Constitution would have been amended to say, "Almighty God, Lord Jesus Christ." Sarna and Dalin, eds., *Religion and State in the American Jewish Experience*, 134; Robert T. Handy, *A Christian America: Protestant Hopes and Historical Realities* (New York: Oxford University Press, 1971), 51–52.

7. Isaac Leeser, "The Lunacy Trial of Warder Cresson," *Occident and American Jewish Advocate* 21 (August 1863): 203–13; Gershon Greenberg, *The Holy Land in American Religious Thought, 1620–1948: The Symbiosis of American Religious Approaches to Scripture's Sacred Territory* (Lanham, Md.: University Press of America, 1994), 144. Abraham Karp describes the trial as a "[s]ignificant landmark in America's growth in religious equality." Karp, "The Zionism of Warder Cresson," in *Early History of Zionism in America: Papers Presented at the Conference on the Early History of Zionism in America, ed. Isidore S. Meyer* (New York: American Jewish Historical Society and Theodor Herzl Foundation, 1958), 8.

8. See Higham, *Send These to Me*, on how immigrants helped in the "forging of urban mass culture to replace the traditions they could not transplant intact," notably as pioneers of "mass media," where they "found the substance of common life" (25–26).

eastern Europe. Born in 1849, she produced early work within the main currents of American women's verse. Yet, even then she displayed specifically Jewish characteristics, beginning with her multilingualism. In America, then as now, Lazarus's command of languages was unusual. It was not grounded in an ethnic Jewish language, such as Yiddish or Hebrew (which she began to learn later), but instead centered on Italian, French, and German. Her own ancestry was mixed German and Portuguese Jewish, that is, the characteristic background of Jewish Americans before 1880 (Fig. 45). Though native born, she was nonetheless tied in transnational ways to German Jewish learning and literature as well as to Hebrew verse through German translations. Her outlook was shaped through her readings of the Jewish German *Wissenschaft* writers such as Abraham Geiger and Heinrich Graetz, who were historicizing Judaism in ways also current in Christian and biblical studies. In literary terms, besides contemporary American verse, she was drawn early to the German Jewish poet Heinrich Heine, publishing translations as well as her own verse in *Poems and Translations* in 1866 and *Poems and Ballads of Heinrich Heine* in 1881. She likewise pursued study of Yehuda Halevi, Ibn Gabirol, and Ibn Ezra when asked in 1876 to translate these medieval *piyuttim* at the request of Rabbi Gustav Gottheil, to be included in his new prayer book, *Hymns and Anthems Adapted for Jewish Worship* (1886), for his New York Reform synagogue, Temple Emanu-El.

Gottheil's prayer book project is itself markedly overlapping and pluralist, intertwining Jewish and American religious forms. Hymns are fundamental in American Protestant worship, going back to Isaac Watts and then flowering with Charles Wesley. Gottheil's collection is in fact made up preponderantly of Protestant hymns, including ones by Watts, Wesley, Harriet Beecher Stowe, John Greenleaf Whittier, Walter Scott, Oliver Wendell Holmes Sr., William Cullen Bryant, James Russell Lowell, Robert Burns, and Thomas Moore, to cite only the more familiar names.[9] Lazarus, Gottheil, and Penina Moïse are among the few Jewish authors. Earlier in the century Moïse herself had written pluralist hymns intertwining Jewish trends and terms with evangelical, republican, and liberal Protestant ones.[10]

9. Gustav Gottheil, comp., *Hymns and Anthems Adapted for Jewish Worship* (New York: G. P. Putnam's Sons, 1886).

10. Gottheil included Moïse's "One God! one Lord! one mighty King!" (2), "Pray when the morn unveileth" (3), "Praise ye the Lord, for it is good" (69), "Between the past and future year" (90), "Great Arbiter of human fate" (102), "In God, the holy, wise, and just" (15), and "Into the tomb of ages past" (89). Lazarus contributed translations of Ben Ezra's "Infatuate I trifled faith away" (145) and "Unto the house of peace my spirit yearns" (144) and of Halevi's "Long in the lap of childhood didst thou sleep" (46), along with her rather grim rendering of

Fig. 45. Emma Lazarus. Engraving by T. Johnson after a photograph by William Kurtz. Published in *Century* 36, no. 5 (September 1888), p. 802. (Library of Congress).

Lazarus thus showed interest in Jewish culture even prior to 1881. Yet Judaism was uncertainly placed in her work and engagement. In response to Gottheil's invitation she wrote, "[T]he more I see of these religious poems, the more I feel that the fervor and enthusiasm requisite to their production are altogether lacking in me."[11] She had responded to Longfellow's 1858 portrait of dead Jewish voices "In the Jewish Cemetery at Newport" ("No Psalms of David now the silence break | No Rabbi reads the ancient Decalogue | In the grand dialect the Prophets spake") by moving the reflection from "In the Jewish Cemetery" to "In the Jewish Synagogue at Newport," written in 1867. The site, however, remains more crypt than living place or language: "No signs of life here: the very prayers | Inscribed around are in a language dead." At the end, somewhat weakly, she mitigates the emptiness: "Nathless the sacred shrine is holy yet."[12]

Most of Lazarus's early writings remained devoted to meditative verse on inner states, beauty, dreams, and nature in an interiorized and reflective aesthetic. She presents herself almost entirely as an American writer, associating with an elite group that included the Ward family of Julia Ward Howe, Thomas Wentworth Higginson, Nathaniel Hawthorne's daughter Rose, Ralph Waldo Emerson's daughter Ellen (who marveled at meeting a "real unconverted Jew"), and, above all, Emerson himself, whom she regarded as her mentor.[13] As the epigraph to her sixteen-part poem "Epochs," published in 1871, she took a statement by Emerson of emphatic interiority: "The epochs of our life are not in the facts, but in the silent thought by the wayside as we walk."[14]

Thus, when Rabbi Gottheil invited Lazarus to accompany him to the immigrant station at Wards Island in 1881, the encounter with Russian refugees marked a dramatic turn in her writing—in subject, in address, in aesthetics.[15]

Ecclesiastes 13, "Remember Him, the only One" (46). Lazarus was asked to review the English of Gottheil's hymns and to contribute five translations of her own. See Richard Gottheil, *Life of Gustav Gottheil: Memoir of a Priest in Israel* (Williamsport, Pa.: Bayard Press, 1936), 17; Esther Schor, *Emma Lazarus* (New York: Nextbook/Schocken, 2006), 76–79. See also Shira Wolosky, "The First Reform Liturgy: Penina Moïse's Hymns and the Discourses of American Identity," *Studies in American Jewish Literature* 33, no. 1 (2014): 130–46.

11. Letter of February 6, 1877, quoted in Gottheil, *Life of Gustav Gottheil*, 62.

12. Emma Lazarus, *Admetus and Other Poems* (New York: Hurd and Houghton, 1871), 160–62.

13. Schor, *Lazarus*, 53.

14. Lazarus, *Admetus and Other Poems*, 137.

15. The continuities and discontinuities of Lazarus's Judaic interest are variously argued. See Louis Harap, *The Image of the Jew in American Literature: From Early Republic to Mass Immigration* (Philadelphia: Jewish Publication Society, 1974), 283–88. Morris Schappes notes that Lazarus

Her awakening was not to Jewish religion but rather to Jewish history and Jewish peoplehood, in further transnational investment from Russia to America to Palestine. Her voice was transformed from genteel reflection to urgency, in prose as well as in verse, as she confronted immediate questions of nationality, policy, and the place of the Jew in her contemporary world. Hers is a powerful public intervention. As John Higham writes, Emma Lazarus emerges as "the first modern American laureate of Jewish history and culture."[16]

Lazarus's response led her to both political and prophetic writing, to appeals to ancient Israel as a heritage to be reclaimed, alongside reflections on modern nationhood in balance and counterbalance with particularist belonging. She endorsed Zionism as a concrete historical project while investing in American cultural Judaism at home. Her range of writing is reflected both in the topics and forms of her verse and in the venues in which she published. The varied Jewish journals and periodicals in which Lazarus's writings appeared were flourishing in the later nineteenth century. They took part not only in the current debates, including over Americanization, nationality, reform, and religion, but also in the formation of the American Jewish community itself. Ethnic journals and newspapers played a central role in giving voice to Jewish communities as well as in shaping them.[17] Readership was a form of belonging, both as receivers of news, views, politics, and religious invitation and competition, and as responders to the print media in letters and opinion pieces. The periodicals provided a powerful platform in which community members could express themselves and

---

had a "residual Jewish consciousness," as glimpsed in her earlier poetry, but that it was transformed from "a passive mainly cultural expression of Jewish identity" into an "active sharply focused combative sense of solidarity." Emma Lazarus, *An Epistle to the Hebrews*, ed. Morris U. Schappes (New York: Jewish Historical Society, 1987), ix–x; quotations from this work will be cited in the text as E with page number. Cf. Max Cavitch, "Emma Lazarus and the Golem of Liberty," *American Literary History* 18, no. 1 (2006): 13–15. Bette Roth Young offers a quite skeptical reading of Lazarus as "an improbable champion of a people she scarcely knew," someone attempting to assimilate into a New York high society not prepared to forgive her "Jewish blood." Young sees Lazarus recirculating anti-Jewish stereotypes, in the context of her father's sugar business, as implicating him in slavery, which she did not protest. Jewish nationalism gave her a safe evasion. Young, *Emma Lazarus in Her World: Life and Letters* (Philadelphia: Jewish Publication Society, 1995), 42–45, 49–51.

16. Higham, *Send These to Me*, 80.

17. Robert E. Park, *The Immigrant Press and Its Control* (New York: Harper and Brothers, 1922), 89–93. According to Sally Miller, "Newspapers appeared where the nucleus of a particular community existed toward which publication might help give form." Miller, "Introduction," in *The Ethnic Press in the United States: A Historical Analysis and Handbook*, ed. Sally Miller (Westport, Conn.: Greenwood Press, 1987), xi.

address each other, actively binding them together. Editors set out to "stand for" and "to interest all sections" of the Jewish community."[18]

One striking characteristic of the Jewish periodicals, compared to other ethnic newspapers, newsletters, weeklies, and monthlies, is the prominence and endurance of the English-language publications. Immigrant groups tended to read and publish in the languages they brought to America, as was also the case for Yiddish speakers after the mass migration began. In most cases, immigrant publications ceased to be printed once a second generation had moved to English and turned to mainstream sources of information. On the contrary, Jewish-focused periodicals continued to be published in English even after journals in Yiddish and Hebrew had declined, a mark of continued plural and overlapping identities. Periodicals flourished on the national, regional, and local levels, first with active journalism on religious affairs as defense against missionary activity, then presenting claims and counterclaims as the different streams of Judaism emerged, mirroring the denominationalism of Protestant America. Periodicals also reported commercial or community ventures without specific religious connection. Jewish/English publications both shaped and mirrored the senses of belonging to more than one community in sustained and inter-relational ways. They stood between the Jewish and other American communities, sharing textual space, issues, and arguments between them and thus acting as an interface between communities in mutual address and contention. And it was in periodicals that poetry largely appeared and participated in the public discourse that newspapers conducted.

Other venues of publication for Lazarus were single volumes of poetry and verse anthologies, including Gottheil's liturgical collection. Gottheil's project was one of several revisions of Jewish prayer books undertaken to reach American Jews who did not have Hebrew language skills.[19] Like periodicals, these volumes were intended to build an American Jewish community in response to new conditions, interests, and values. Other outstanding examples are Isaac Mayer Wise's *Hymns, Psalms and Prayers* in English and German and Penina Moïse's hymn book, the first original American liturgy.[20] These compilations

18. Arthur Goren, "The Jewish Press," in *Ethnic Press in the United States*, ed. Miller, 203–28; Jonathan D. Sarna, "Two Ambitious Goals: American Jewish Publishing in the United States," in *A History of the Book in America*, vol. 4, ed. Carl F. Kaestle and Janice A. Radway (Chapel Hill: University of North Carolina Press, 2009).

19. Gottheil, *Life of Gustav Gottheil*, 38. The revised prayer book was to include more English selections as well as a shorter service for American congregations (162).

20. *Hymns, Psalms and Prayers* (Cincinnati: Bloch, 1868) was part of Isaac Mayer Wise's project

were undertaken within the emerging American Reform movement and were countered by traditionalist Jews through their own collections and publications. Isaac Leeser translated the Torah, edited *The Form of Prayers: The Custom of the Spanish and Portuguese Jews*, and wrote instructional books, all self-published due to reluctance by established publishers to take on his materials. Tensions between Reform and traditional Judaism characterized his *Occident and Jewish Advocate* and other journals. George Alexander Kohut, an early literary historian of Jewish writing, was a strong voice against Reform. He helped to found and served as librarian at the new Jewish Theological Seminary in 1886, which set out to counter the Reform movement, later becoming a center of Conservative Judaism. The *American Hebrew*, where Lazarus often published, declared its allegiance to this movement "identified with historical traditional Judaism" and urged balance: Jews should not preserve their practices only "because it is traditional but also not ... discard it because it is traditional."[21]

Lazarus wrote for both Jewish and non-Jewish audiences, representing each to the other with significant impact on how Jewish communities were perceived and perceived themselves. She was in the forefront of urgent emerging issues of Jewish identity and community, ignited for her by the mass immigration. These questions include the beginnings of a political Zionism committed to the establishment of a Jewish homeland in Palestine; Jewish nationality in relation to and distinct from religion, within the context of emerging Reform and rationalist arguments; and the enduring examination of particularism as a valid and valuable commitment in relation to universal claims. Each of these issues posed questions of belongingness to both American and Jewish communities.

Promised Lands

Zionism, as Lazarus encountered it, was not exclusive to Jewish discourses. In nineteenth-century America, Jewish imaginings of a return to Zion were profoundly shaped by British and American Christian ones. In these movements, the heritage of Puritan identification as a New Israel in Exodus from Europe, crossing the Atlantic/Red Sea to the American Promised Land, became incorporated into both a religious American national self-definition and a notion of republican exceptionalism as democratic exemplar to the world. Enlightenment,

---

of *Minhag Amerika*. Jonathan D. Sarna, *American Judaism: A History* (New Haven: Yale University Press, 2004), 98. Penina Moïse, *Hymns Written for the Service of the Hebrew Congregation, Beth Elohim* (Charleston, S.C.: Levin and Tavel, 1842).

21. Yehezkel Wyszkowski, "*The American Hebrew*: An Exercise in Ambivalence," *American Jewish History* 76, no. 3 (1987): 348.

republican, and religious discourses intertwined. Enacted westward through Manifest Destiny, an American sense of mission also extended eastward through new access to the Holy Land in Palestine. Technological advances in transportation and political developments—the weakening of Ottoman power and European incursions into the Middle East—made travel to the Near East newly possible and enticing. The eastern Holy Land provided a kind of mirror for America's own sense of Manifest Destiny, and a Holy Land mania ensued. Travel accounts, geographic and geological mappings, murals and dioramas, tourism and diplomatic efforts proliferated. Christian missions attempted to penetrate into Ottoman Palestine, even as revivals, the remnants of the Second Great Awakening, intensified across the United States.

Lazarus's own awakening to Zionism originated in non-Jewish sources: George Eliot's and Laurence Oliphant's calls for a Jewish homeland. Zion offered solutions to several distinct problems. First, it would provide territory for the mass of Jews fleeing eastern European pogroms and persecutions. An added benefit would be to deflect an influx of these alien Jews into America, feared as overwhelming the established American Jewish community and its carefully crafted affiliations. Further, Zion offered a refuge from the Christian missions that, in both America and the Holy Land, targeted Jews, because the Muslim regime in Palestine had taken draconian measures to prevent conversions from Islam.[22]

Christian discourses of repatriation or restoration of the Holy Land thus inspired Jewish ones, both defensively and assertively. Age-old prayers were redirected toward concrete action. Mordecai Noah's "Ararat" colony for interim resettlement of Jews near Niagara Falls is one early, if rather eccentric, venture. Rebekah Hyneman, writing in the 1840s and 1850s is another precursor voice. Raised in a Jewish household and converted to Judaism by Leeser, she published poems in Leeser's *Occident.* Their central scene is the Holy Land, with settings reflecting new geographic reports and populated by distinctive Jewish characters. Leeser himself explored the question of restoration extensively in the *Occident* and made his own translation of a *Descriptive Geography of Palestine* in 1850 as a Jewish response to the many Christian travel narratives that leave "the Jewish people to receive an account of its possessions ... from the mouths of others." He instead relied on Hebrew and the Talmud, to which others did not have access. His essays move from a general, traditional longing for Zion to concrete projects of fundraising and organizing agricultural and industrial

22. Jonathan D. Sarna, "The American Jewish Response to Nineteenth-Century Christian Missions," *Journal of American History* 68, no. 1 (1981): 49.

settlements and training for the Jews of Palestine, taking Sir Moses Montefiore as his particular model.[23]

Lazarus's near-prophetic poems look at once back to ancient Jewish history in the Israelite homeland and forward to a reconstituted Jewish land. But they can sound like Protestant Zionist hymns, sharing terms and even modes of address. For example, Thomas Hastings's "Dawn of the Millennium" opens:

Hail to the brightness of Zion's glad morning!
  Joy to the lands that in darkness have lain;
Hush'd be the accents of sorrow and mourning;
  Zion in triumph begins her mild reign.[24]

This hymn, better known as "The Latter Day," was collected alongside many others in the 1917 *Standard Book of Jewish Verse*, a retrospective anthology reflecting and also constructing Jewish community through a body of poetry.[25] Lazarus's "The Banner of the Jew" is included, along with other national, ritual, historical, and liturgical poems (as well as a series of tributes to her), and takes its place among many other awakenings of Zion verses, Jewish and Christian. First published in *Songs of a Semite* in 1882, the poem is a kind of declaration of Lazarus's Jewish poetic independence. It opens in ways similar to numerous Christian hymns also collected in the *Standard Book*, such as Thomas Moore's "But Who Shall See?": "But who shall see the glorious day | When, throned on Zion's brow, | The Lord shall rend that veil away | Which hides the nations now?" (SB 482). Likewise, the second stanza of "The Restoration of Israel," by James Montgomery, rings out: "Awake, awake, put on thy strength, ... The day of freedom dawns at length | The Lord's appointed day" (SB 485).

"The Banner of the Jew" similarly opens with a prophetic call: "Wake, Israel, wake!" Lazarus, however, stands out from Christian Zionist poets as more historical, asserting a past she sees as concrete and temporal, rather than mythically biblical, and linked to an attainable historical future. Like her poem "Bar

23. See, for example, *Occident* 2:347–49, 407–8 449–52 552–56; 4: 616; 5: 156–158; 210–12. See also Maxine S. Seller, "Isaac Leeser's Views on the Restoration of a Jewish Palestine," *American Jewish Historical Quarterly* 58, no. 1 (1968): 118–35; Lance J. Sussman, *Isaac Leeser and the Making of American Judaism* (Detroit: Wayne State University Press, 1995); Lance J. Sussman, "Isaac Leeser and the Protestantization of American Judaism," *American Jewish Archives* 38, no. 1 (1986): 1–21.

24. Thomas Hastings, *Spiritual Songs for Social Worship* (Boston: Carter, Hendee and Co., 1834), 164.

25. Joseph Friedlander and George Alexander Kohut, comp., *The Standard Book of Jewish Verse* (New York: Dodd, Mead and Company, 1917), 483; further quotations will be cited in the text as SB followed by page number.

Kochba," which describes an actual historical figure acting in the name of political sovereignty beyond a spiritual state, "The Banner of the Jew" invokes the Maccabees. Her call is immediately political:

> Oh, for Jerusalem's trumpet now,
> To blow a blast of shattering power,
> To wake the sleepers high and low,
> And rouse them to the urgent hour!
> No band for vengeance—but to save,
> A million naked swords should wave.
>
> Oh, deem not dead that martial fire,
> Say not the mystic flame is spent!
> With Moses' law and David's lyre,
> Your ancient strength remains unbent.
> Let but an Ezra rise anew,
> To lift the banner of the Jew! (SB 309)

"Moses' law and David's lyre" signal the reconstitution of a Judaic polity reaching from governmental rule to poetic culture, from the ancient world to the present as a historical continuity.

The overlapping of discourses shared across poets with varied community membership can be seen in the verse of Cora Wilburn. Wilburn's writings have been recently recovered by Jonathan Sarna, including probably the first Jewish novel in America. She resides at a far edge of American/Jewish identity, raising questions about what that is and the boundaries of community membership. In the course of her life, Wilburn converted to Catholicism and returned to Judaism ("I had repented before I began," she wrote in her diary). As Sarna traces, she then joined the Spiritualist movement, without "denying her Jewish heritage," but also, as Sarna puts it, "eschewing the Bible or any specific creed." Still later, she was attracted to the Reform movement as embracing "liberalism and progressive causes."[26]

Interestingly, Wilburn's poetry is included in the *Standard Book of Jewish Verse*, admitting her into this community. The selections include a liturgical verse, "After Yom Kippur," an homage to "My Heritage," and "A Call to Israel." These were culled from increasingly Jewish-affiliated poems published in the later decades of her life in a variety of largely Jewish periodicals.[27] Wil-

26. Jonathan D. Sarna, "Jewish Women without Money: The Case of Cora Wilburn (1824–1906)," *Nashim: A Journal of Jewish Women's Studies & Gender Issues*, no. 32 (Spring 2018): 23–37.

27. Jonathan D. Sarna "The Forgetting of Cora Wilburn: Historical Amnesia and The Cam-

burn's work reflects the overlaps, syncretism, and transmutations of American/Jewish communities, combining trends from a range of religious contexts. "After Yom Kippur," for example, spiritualizes, interiorizes, and universalizes. What Wilburn calls the "Great white fast" is cast in Protestant Spiritualist terms as a "gracious summons of the Voice Divine | That bade the soul before truth's inner shrine." Truth is inward reflection. Judgment is an interior event where "conscience struggles with its deadly fear" and "introspection's force [is] by memory driven." Such experiences are far from exclusive or particular to Jewish worship; indeed, they erase particularist ritual, although set on the Jewish holiest day. Her questions, "has justice entered in | the Awakened conscience?" and whether "the worldly din | Died into silence 'neath the voice of God," confirm an inward spirituality above and, indeed, apparently contrary to the outward world. They are at once solitary and yet general. She ends with an American appeal to freedom:

> Cleansed from the idol worship of our pride,
> White robed humility be teaching guide;
> And Israel's heart of kinship link the hands,
> Of the compassionate throughout all lands.
> The righteousness of freedom, understood
> Bind all of life in one vast brotherhood. (SB 294–95)

"Kinship" links hands not within the bounds of "Israel's heart" but among "the compassionate throughout all lands." Yom Kippur's general virtue of "humility" converges into an American "righteousness of freedom" to "bind all of life in one vast brotherhood." Distinctions seem overwhelmed, including those between particular communities.

"My Heritage," or, as Wilburn opens the text, "A Glorious heritage is mine," seems to declare her self-definition through attachment to tradition. From the poem's outset, the terms remain general, if not Christianized: "Enhaloed of Light Divine, | My mission's truth appears." This opening is followed by liberal American creed: "Great Freedom's light aglow!" What emerges as specifically Jewish is "Persecution" in "the Ghetto's drear abode," out of which emerges a generalized "Hope's world-wide message." And the ultimate mark of this "Glorious heritage ... Refulgent with the Light Divine" is "To conquer Prejudice and Wrong" (SB 547–48). The movement of the poem is therefore from a bounded heritage to one that overcomes just such boundedness.

---

bridge History of Jewish American Literature," *Studies in American Jewish Literature* 37, no. 1 (2018): 73.

The title of Wilburn's "Call to Israel" resembles other verse summonses, Jewish and Christian, to awakened national resurgence, as does its opening demand for a "modern Judah Maccabee." But the call is then pursued in distinctly American terms, "To lead anew the world's hope of the free." The "New Deliverer" is set "to summon all the hosts of Liberty." American and Jewish terms enforce yet also elide each other. The poem then strikingly adds another strand of identity, that of gender:

In Israel's glorious past transcendent shone
 The reverent daring of the Woman-soul;
Fair Esther proved her birthright to a throne ...

May not the wise, omnipotent decree ...
Find 'mid the multitude of brave and free,
 Some modern Judith? in ascendance won
For Freedom's holiest cause.... (SB 709–10)

The poem's dedication to "Freedom's holiest cause" sounds rather like Julia Ward Howe's "Battle Hymn of the Republic" ("as you died to make men holy let us die to make men free").[28] But Wilburn is more daringly gendered in her recasting of both Israel and America than anyone else.[29] The modern Judah Maccabee becomes "some modern Judith"; "Israel's glorious past" is feminized, its genealogy of leadership traced back to "Fair Esther." Republican freedom, religious election, America as a sacred cause,[30] Jewish imagery, and gendered radicalism intertwine in a cacophonic harmony of multiple communities and discourses:

Rise valiant daughters of the prophetic line
Rise, Jewish warriors with the rage divine
That scorns subjections! ...
Arise! Arm! Strike! do Freedom's holy will! (SB 711)

A woman's poetic voice invokes, constructs, and joins "valiant daughters of the prophetic line," likened to "Jewish warriors" in the name of a republican religious "Freedom's holy will." Does this poem answer or pose questions of community, of national, religious, and cultural belonging, and which is which?

28. Ernst Lee Tuveson, *Redeemer Nation: The Idea of America's Millennial Role* (Chicago: University of Chicago Press, 1968), 191–202.

29. The only exception may be Adah Isaac Menken's "Judith." See Wolosky, *Poetry and Public Discourse*, 106–7.

30. Nathan O. Hatch, *The Sacred Cause of Liberty: Republican Thought and the Millennium in Revolutionary New England* (New Haven: Yale University Press, 1977).

Liberal Nationhood

In "The Banner of the Jew," Lazarus's call to "Let but an Ezra rise anew" echoes her urgent prose writings. She stands out for the polemical essays she published alongside her poetry in mainstream as well as Jewish journals. "The Jewish Problem," her single fullest treatment of Judaism as a historical phenomenon, and her agitation toward immediate urgent action, appeared in *Century* magazine, where major figures such as Henry James regularly published.[31]

The essay is striking for presenting Jewish history from a Jewish point of view rather than through the Christian frameworks that prevailed in mainstream American culture. As Lazarus wryly reminds her audience, she is setting out to "review history since the Scriptural age where ordinary readers are content to close it."[32] The very notion of an independent Jewish history, one that is not a prelude to Christ and his betrayal, is a momentous step. Based on the recent work of Graetz and Leopold Zunz, which she read in German even before the transformative visit to Wards Island, hers is an insistently historical approach. Yet, it is not free from apologetics. Writing in a rhetoric of polemic, Lazarus parries, defends, claims, and advocates. Incensed by a defense of the Russian pogroms by one Madame Ragozin in the April 1882 issue of *Century*, Lazarus admits to the decisive influence on her of George Eliot's *Daniel Deronda* and Laurence Oliphant's *Land of Gilead*, but declares that Jews need a "new Ezra for their own people" (JP 611). There must be immediate leadership of concrete programs. Her image in "The Banner of the Jew" of "Jerusalem's trumpet" in this sense differs from much missionary verse. It is not apocalyptic, but rather a reminder of a historical event of uprising and the possibility of its recurrence in the present.

One force pushing toward Jewish consolidation, as registered in Lazarus's verse, is antisemitism. Besides protesting Madame Ragozin's defense of pogroms, Lazarus's poems counter a long list of attacks against Jews, from her short lyrics, such as "The Crowing of the Red Cock" (where, paradoxically, in attacking Jews, Christians betray Christ: "The folk of Christ is sore bestead; | The Son of Man is bruised and banned"), to long historical poems, such as "The Death of

31. Another contributor to *Century*, the critic, essayist, and poet Edmund Clarence Stedman, once encouraged Lazarus: "there is a wealth of tradition you are heir to." She replied at the time that she was "proud of my blood and heritage but Hebrew ideals do not appeal to me." Quoted in Harap, *Image of the Jew in American Literature*, 289.

32. "The Jewish Problem," *Century* 25 (February 1883): 602–11; reprinted in *Emma Lazarus: Selected Poems and Other Writings*, ed. Gregory Eiselein (Orchard Park, N.Y.: Broadview Press, 2002), 264–81. Further references will be cited as JP with the *Century* page number.

Raschi" and the drama *The Dance to Death.* Two of Lazarus's poems collected in the *Standard Book*, "Lines on Carmen Sylva" and "To Carmen Sylva (Queen of Roumania)," address Queen Elizabeth, wife of King Carol I of Romania. Under the pen name "Carmen Sylva," Queen Elizabeth wrote more than fifty books promoting art and artists (notably women) in a country that was at the same time increasingly and severely antisemitic, as Lazarus notes in her prose writings (JP 608).[33] Jews were forbidden to lease land, settle in villages, establish factories, or attain citizenship, and they were subject to expulsion, plundering, and pogroms.[34] As Lazarus exposes, the Jew in Queen Elizabeth's Romania remains "An alien in his land of birth | An outcast from his brethren's earth." While "Some little Jew is falling | Clubbed in his narrow pale— | The Queen is singing sweetly | Songs of the Nightingale" (SB 684).

The problem of illiberal nationalism, where all too often the assertion of national identity takes the form of suppressing or violating another nationality, is one of the tensions that permeate Lazarus's prose and poetry. Antinomies include religion and race, the rational and the prophetic, the particular ("tribal") and the universal or humanitarian, the public and the private, the past and the future. These are the terms available to her; but in using them, she is also caught within the very oppositions she is trying to transform. Thus, she herself, in Epistle I of *Epistle to the Hebrews*, dismisses "the hackneyed question whether Judaism be a race or a religion," saying "it is both" (E 9).[35] But she is far from solving the challenge of defining identities that are necessarily inter-relational and evolving. On one hand, she warns against "entrenching ourselves behind a Chinese wall of petrified religious forms," lest "the great modern stream of scientific philosophy ... sweep past" us (E 14). She clearly leans toward a rationalizing of religion, claiming there is a "reconciliation of science and religion in Judaic principles re pure monotheism, reign of law and historic development" (E 55). She even cites as support the Talmud's dictum that "law speaks in the language of the sons of man" to argue that tradition itself allows a "skilled readjustment and simplification of code" (E 25). There is an "elasticity in the unchangeable word that could never permit of any contradiction between Faith and Science" (E 55). Letting go the "antiquated body of ceremonials" that scorns "Reform, i.e. Progress, Advancement, Improvement" (E 14) would still preserve "the

33. Doina Pasca Harsanyi, "Blue Blood and Ink: Romanian Aristocratic Women before and after World War I," *Women's History Review* 5, no. 4 (1996): 497–511.

34. Stanford J. Shaw, *The Jews of the Ottoman Empire and the Turkish Republic* (New York: New York University Press, 1991), 189–95.

35. Schappes, "Introduction" to Lazarus, *An Epistle to the Hebrews*, ix–xvii.

spiritualized form of our belief—the Unity of the Creative force, the necessity of the moral law" (E 25).

Lazarus thus enlists religion as rationally reformed yet historically continuous. But her plea for national awakening is far from one of abstract reason. It is instead prophetic and inspired.[36] Lazarus's very language changes, becoming imagistic and soaring when she appeals to "sacred fires of historic memory" (E 15) as a "seed of fire" (E 31). She likewise invokes traditionally religious language. Epistle VIII is something of a commentary on the Talmudic saying "Let the fruit pray for the welfare of the leaf," which serves as her epigraph (E 42, 45). And she adds another core saying, "it is not incumbent for thee to complete the work; thou must not therefore cease from pursuing it" (Avot 2:16). These are invitations to participate in a community of textual tradition and orientation—a call to community participation as such—that rests on more than reason, even if not pious or orthodox. One thinks of Abraham Lincoln's "mystic cords of memory."

In May 1883, three months after "The Jewish Problem" appeared in *Century*, Rabbi Abram Isaacs, editor of the *Jewish Messenger*, criticized the essay in the same magazine.[37] Isaacs objected to an opinion Lazarus attributed to a "Russian Jew," that "the religious mission of the Jews belongs to the past." He retorted, "If it be true that 'the racial tie binds Jews together even though they discard all religion,' why form a separate nationality, unless to establish a free religious and atheistic *commune* under the Jewish name?" What Isaacs pinpointed is the conundrum of how both, in Lazarus's later words, to "emancipate and fortify our reason to keep pace with the intellectual advance of our age" while "at the same time nourishing the sacred fires of historic memory" (E 15). How does Lazarus propose to build a new and different Jewish future without abandoning or betraying the past?

Isaacs's main objection, however, is to Lazarus's "advocacy of a separate Jewish nationality" through "the restoration of Palestine to the Jews." His dismissal of this scheme as "utopian" is weakened when he proposes an even wilder fantasy to solve the "Jewish problem" in Russia: "the Russian Israelites ... must remain where they are" and work "to secure political emancipation and social and educational reform," while the Church "should strive to awaken a Christianity more in accord with the gentle teachings of its Founder."[38] The extreme

36. At this time, the Reform movement largely rejected Zionism, although Gottheil himself supported it. Sarna, *American Judaism*, 202.

37. Abram S. Isaacs, "Will the Jews Return to Palestine," *Century* 26 (May 1883): 156–57.

38. Isaacs, "Will the Jews Return to Palestine," 157.

unlikelihood of achieving a better life for Jews in Russia is one reason Lazarus argues for "Repatriation and Auto-emancipation in Palestine" (E 74). As she acknowledges, given the "insuperable objections existing against all other propositions" and the "tremendous difficulties which it presents," repatriation nevertheless remains "the only possible issue from a desperate situation" (E 77).

Lazarus's arguments are less theological or theoretical than urgently historical as a response to immediate crisis: "a crisis has arrived in Jewish history presenting for millions of Jews the sharp alternative of extinction or separation" (E 66). Her strongest argument is community. She herself was skeptical of a Judaism of pure reason, mocking as "shallow and frivolous" those who absorb "skepticism and materialism and call themselves agnostics or freethinkers" (E 15). Yet religious ritual is not fundamental to her and in fact is divisive among the warring streams of Reform, Orthodox, and a "historical" conservative Judaism. The American Jewish "community" was further divided in terms of wealth, background as German, Sephardic, or Russian/eastern European, and length of time in the country, raising the perhaps most daunting question: Can a Jewish community be sustained in overlapping yet distinct modes as both Jewish and American?

One target of Lazarus's indictment, materialism, applies to both of her communities. On one hand, her apologetics defends Jews against accusations of materialist reduction and greed, and is tied to another of her projects, the need to train Jews in agriculture and other practical and technical skills. Expanding the range of Jewish productivity is a necessity for repatriation because "we need second only to closer union and warmer patriotism, the building of our national physical force," the "practical pioneer work of founding a new nation," which the "new Ezra [must] recruit" (E 30). Lazarus repeatedly argues that Jewish separation from practical labor, with the accompanying association of Jews with commerce and moneylending, is not essential or natural to them, but the result of centuries of restriction and persecution.[39] On the other hand, wealth is an American value that Jews share. Wealth becomes problematic, however, when it cuts off the privileged from the rest of the community, threatening solidarity. Lazarus rails against private interests that ignore public responsibility, a trend in American culture that solidarity of the Jewish community must offset. Is it the American or the stereotypical Jew that Lazarus chides: "are we to look

39. Lazarus writes: "Accusations of materialism and tribalism are all due to the history of persecution, which has also lost that homogeneity and united national sentiment which it is our first duty to revive in order to concentrate our efforts towards their regeneration and rehabilitation" (E 30).

for the new Ezra, the living Mordecai, among the stockjobbers, the merchants and tradesmen, absorbed in the accumulation of wealth," who would "sneer" at the "great moral principle, of fulfilment of a national mission" as against "the pursuit of gain?" (E 14). Jews have benefited from America's "new and marvelous facilities for acquiring wealth," "the defiant self-confidence and inordinate ambition engendered by the material success of Democracy" (E 17). Lazarus's address, then, seems to be to the Jewish community against American privatization. Raising George Eliot's figural "torch of visible community," Lazarus sets out to rally "faithful hearts of Israel" who "for the good of their people and their kind [shall] gather scattered workers from an insignificant minority to a resolute and homogeneous nation" (E 15).

But which nation is intended here? Community as a positive image has a darker shadow that worries Lazarus: tribalism. Lazarus challenges this notion along with other antisemitic tropes and yet also attempts to claim and transform it. "Tribal" is a "perpetual taunt" (E 30), a "prevalent theory" that "Jews always form a close corporation, financially, socially, and politically." Such a "comparative compact and homogeneous body," she counters, occurs only when a group is "subjected to external pressure." In free circumstances, Jews "develop opinions in exact proportion to the number of individuals" (E 80). Here the individual is defended against group collectivism. Far from being "tribal," Jews, whenever treated freely, "have adapted ourselves to the varying customs and climates of every nation in the world" (E 30). Yet she also claims that "we are not 'tribal' enough," that "we have not sufficient solidarity to perceive that when the life and property of a Jew in Caucasus are attacked the dignity of a Jew in free America is humiliated" (E 30).

After she confronts individual and group, rights and nationality, private interest and public belonging, American and Jewish, the final rhetorical gap into which Lazarus falls is perhaps the most seductive: universal and particular. Western moral language posits universalism as the highest norm, leaving the particular as at best a mere part, at worst in conflict with and undermining truths that by definition must transcend difference. Like tribalism, Jewish particularism is an antisemitic trope implying that loyalty to a particular betrays the universal. Lazarus attempts to circumvent this trap first by claiming that universalism originated with the Jewish people, who are its exemplar. She agrees that ethical theory sees "Humanity as a grand whole towards whose common weal every individual must strive" (E 12). But that theory has grown through a "gradual and orderly evolution," advancing through a "deepening and broadening charity of Deuteronomy and the Prophets to the Rabbis of the Talmud including the immortal Hillel," then intercrossing with Greek philosophy to be formulated by Philo of Alexandria, "in whom the new doctrine of Universalism finds complete expression" (E 12–13). As exemplars, Jews have not stood apart and against other cultures, but rather have "imbibed and assimilated the broad notion of a common humanity" and interpreted "into new significance the teachings of the older prophets" (E 13). Nevertheless, even while proving "swift and prompt to assimilate all that was desirable in the surrounding civilization," Jews have done so "without abandoning their own intellectual stronghold" (E 12). Lazarus's task is to awaken Jewish solidarity and community without seeming to betray universalism.

Poetic Crossings

Lazarus's projection of her verse as public voice redefined poetry for her. No longer meditative and interior, no longer in a genteel language remote from immediate address, hers becomes a language charged with biblical force and prophetic vision. Poetry may also offer other ways of configuring the antinomies she exposes. Is there a way to interrelate particulars, each with its own commitments, while also extending responsibility and participation to each other? A way not to erase differences but to inter-confirm them so that they respect or even support each other? This project would suggest ethical particularism as an alternative to traditional universalism. Lazarus writes: "To combine the conservation of one's own individuality with a due respect for the rights of every other individuality, is the ideal condition of society but it is a foolish perversion of this truth to deduce therefrom the obligation to renounce all individuality and this remark is no less applicable to nations than to persons" (E 13).

Lazarus imagines such interrelated particularisms as combining the "practical requirements of American life without losing the fire of Oriental blood to hope to find united the special aptitudes of both races" (E 20). In civic terms, commitments to more than one community would strengthen each. "Tribalism" is a "separate nepotism." Nevertheless, "he who would faithfully serve the larger interests of humanity must learn in due order to become the valiant protector of his own hearth, his own kin, his own people, his own kind" (E 13). There is a mirroring confirmation when Lazarus writes, "we possess the double cosmopolitanism of the American and the Jew" (E 67), bringing the two together in their very separation.

As a poetics, Lazarus's texts inter- and counter-weave terms, words, strands from her various affiliations, intercrossing idioms. This strategy sometimes takes strange turns. "In Exile" was written upon Lazarus's learning that a group of

Russian Jewish refugees had resettled in Texas. There, they claimed, they found a life of "unbroken paradise," a promised land—or rather lands.

> Freedom to love the law that Moses brought
> To sing the songs of David, and to think
> The thoughts Gabirol to Spinoza taught,
> Freedom to dig the common earth, to drink
> The universal air—for this they sought
> Refuge o'er wave and continent, to link
> Egypt with Texas in their mystic chain,
> And truth's perpetual lamp forbid to wane.[40]

Lazarus characteristically insists on Jewish national culture as including all spheres of social life: civic and legal, here as Moses's law; poetic and prophetic, as are the songs of David and Gabirol; philosophical, as in Spinoza; and not least, "Freedom to dig the common earth," which is a vital part of her proto-Zionist vision for Palestine, except here the earth is in Texas. Like the Puritan pilgrims, who thought of themselves as the heirs to the ancient Hebrews, these Russian Jews have "sought refuge o'er wave and continent" now to link "Egypt with Texas in their mystic chain." Europe, as for the Puritans, is a typological Egypt. Texas is Canaan. Yet at the same time, or in this very promise, all breathe together "the universal air."

This poem brings to the surface an anxiety about Zionism as competitive rather than concurrent with Jewish American membership. Abram Isaacs expressed this worry in "Will the Jews Return to Palestine," and it was not uncommon. In the *Epistle* Lazarus felt called upon to correct what she is "mistakenly supposed to encourage," that is, the "idea of restoring the Kingdom of Israel in Palestine by means of a general ingathering from Europe and America" (E 73). She clarifies: "My plea for the establishment of a free Jewish State therefore has not the remotest bearing upon the position of American Jews." The possibility of concurrent, even overlapping memberships comes under pressure: "A man can no more acknowledge two 'nationalities' than he can profess two religions" (E 42). "We are ready and glad to pay the full price ... for the privileges of American citizenship, viz: the forfeiture of all claim to an alien nationality." In America, "all differences of race and faith were fused in a refined cosmopolitanism" (E 73), rather a different formulation than distinctive Jewish identity. "There is not the slightest necessity for an American Jew, the free citizen of a republic, to rest his

40. *The Poems of Emma Lazarus*, 2 vols. (Boston and New York: Houghton, Mifflin, 1889), 2:6; further citations to these volumes will appear in the text as P1 and P2 with page numbers.

hopes upon the foundation of any other nationality soever." In sum, "wherever we are free we are at home" (E 73).

Lazarus's Statue of Liberty poem, "The New Colossus" (P 1: 138), addresses the conundrum of plural memberships with a complexity that opens avenues other than those posited in her prose (Fig. 46). The poem in one swerve radically altered the significance, indeed the whole profile, of the Statue. As James Russell Lowell wrote to Lazarus, "I liked the poem more than I liked the Statue."[41] Donated by France as a monument to French-American friendship, the Statue still required a pedestal. Lazarus's poem, written to help raise funds, in effect redefined the Statue into an image of America as feminized Mother of Exiles, extending "world-wide welcome" to all who are "homeless, tempest-tossed."

The restrictions placed on immigration in the years after the poem's composition make it obvious that Lazarus's pluralist interpretation of America was not the only one. Indeed, the poem was not mounted at the entrance of the Statue until 1945 when its message for rescue was too late.[42] George Eliot's phrase spoken by Mordecai in *Daniel Deronda*—"torch of visible community"—is twice quoted in the *Epistle* (E 15, 32). But the Statue's torch also registers "liberty's contradictory meanings."[43] The perplexities of legitimate particular community solidarity, at once open and bounded, emerges in tensions and negotiations between Jewish nationalism, Jewish diaspora, American nationalism, American nativism and antisemitism, individual liberties, and ideals of universalism. These questions remained for Lazarus, as for us, an urgent challenge.

The "New Colossus" is extraordinarily intricate in its interweaving of cultural strands in ways that multiply, intercross, and realign their different and overlapping senses. These include Jewish and American, biblical and mythological,

41. James Russell Lowell to Emma Lazarus, December 17, 1883, in *Letters to Emma Lazarus in the Columbia University Library*, ed. Ralph L. Rusk (New York: Columbia University Press, 1939), 74.

42. Higham, *Send These to Me*, 82–85, recounts the history of the poem's circulation as a nexus between visions of America as welcoming or warding off immigration. In 1903 Georgina Schuyler had the poem placed on an interior wall of the statue's pedestal. It was moved to the main entrance of the Statue in 1945.

43. Cavitch, "Emma Lazarus and the Golem of Liberty," 5, 1. Cavitch places Lazarus within transnational as well as national discourses, and describes the complexity of "her poetic exploration, re-creation, and refutation of shared identities" as a "plural voice" (8, 13). Ranen Omer-Sherman approaches Lazarus through methods of culture studies, yielding a hermeneutic of suspicion, but one that reifies inconsistencies as well as categories such as universalism that he is trying to critique. Omer-Sherman, "'Thy People Are My People': Emma Lazarus, Daniel Deronda, and the Ambivalence of Jewish Modernity," *Journal of Modern Jewish Studies* 1, no. 1 (2002): 49–72.

Fig. 46. The grave of Emma Lazarus at Beth Olam Cemetery, Cypress Hills, Brooklyn, New York.

male and female tropes.[44] Mythological, male, and European, the "Brazen Giant of Greek fame" contrasts with the "mighty woman" of a feminized America. Here Lazarus brings to powerful image women's benevolent activism and community building that characterized nineteenth-century America.[45] But woven through this American figuration is a Hebrew one encoded as double or hidden meanings.

> A mighty woman with a torch, whose flame
> Is the imprisoned lightning, and her name
> Mother of Exiles.

"Lightning" evokes Deborah as *eshet lapidoth* (woman of lightning); "Mother of Exile" evokes Rachel. The poem's final line, in which she lifts her "lamp beside the golden door" as a sign of welcome to an America made up of diverse particular communities, joins with a chain of images of beacons in Lazarus's writings, such as the "perpetual lamp" at the conclusion of "In Exile." The image is linked by Lazarus to the Chanukah Menorah of Maccabean national rebirth against the Greeks, as in "The Feast of Lights":

> Kindle the taper like the steadfast star
>   Ablaze on evening's forehead o'er the earth,
> And add each night a lustre till afar
>   An eightfold splendor shine above thy hearth. (P2: 18)

In the "New Colossus," the lamp flares out at once as American liberty and Jewish awakening.

Such encoding is intrinsic to poetry; meanings multiply through different figurative levels. Lazarus's figures are strongly historical, but extend through analogical metaphors, metonymic contiguities, parallelisms, antitheses, and paradoxical oxymora between the two peoples to which she belongs. When "Bar Kochba" is conjured from the past—the first-century rebel against Roman rule and Jewish persecution in Palestine—he is framed in terms close to those of the American/Jewish "New Colossus": "the last Warrior Jew," he led "[t]he weak, the wronged, the miserable" (P2: 22). Ancient Jews, who in the aftermath of Bar Kochba's revolt were sent into their millennia of exile, are uncannily like the Jewish and other refugees that the Statue has been recast to welcome.

44. Shira Wolosky, "An American-Jewish Typology: Emma Lazarus and the Figure of Christ," *Prooftexts* 16, no. 2 (1996): 113–25.

45. Wolosky, *Poetry and Public Discourse*; Shira Wolosky, *Feminist Theory across Disciplines: Feminist Community and American Women's Poetry* (New York: Routledge, 2013).

Such multiple encodings across overlapping cultural memberships resonate through the Lazarus hymn "New Year: Rosh-Hashanah, 5643" (P2: 1–2):

> Not while the snow-shroud round dead earth is rolled,
> And naked branches point to frozen skies, —
> When orchards burn their lamps of fiery gold,
> The grape glows like a jewel, and the corn
> A sea of beauty and abundance lies,
> Then the new year is born.

The opening "Not" distinguishes the Jewish New Year from the American one in January in its "snow-shroud," but situates it in America, where "orchards burn their lamps of fiery gold" in the northeastern autumn. Yet "lamps," here American leaves, feature largely as a Jewish emblem. And the New Year celebrated is Rosh Hashanah, in *Tishre*, the "mother of the months," as the next stanza declares, whose "ivory horn of plenty" evokes the harvest season of Palestine. The "sacred cornet" is the ram's horn shofar, which is sounded on the New Year. Lazarus makes it into a prophetic "Call back" at once awakening the past "ancestral blood" but also pointing forward toward an "undreamed-of morn." The dawn, rising at once in east and west, reaffirms the poem's double locations:

> Even as the Prophet promised, so your tent
> Hath been enlarged unto earth's farthest rim.
> To snow-capped Sierras from vast steppes ye went
> Through fire and blood and tempest-tossing wave,
> For freedom to proclaim and worship Him
> Mighty to slay and save.
> . . .
> In two divided streams the exiles part,
> One rolling homeward to its ancient source,
> One rushing sunward with fresh will, new heart.
> By each the truth is spread, the law unfurled,
> Each separate soul contains the nation's force,
> And both embrace the world.

The geography here is westward: from the "vast steppes" of eastern Europe to the "snow-capped Sierras" of the western United States as emblems of "freedom." Yet the Prophet's promise seems to extend in all directions: "enlarged unto earth's farthest rim." Is this image self-contradictory, or plural? Here the "two divided streams," America and Palestine, are both valid, individual choices for "each separate soul" that nonetheless confirm a "nation's" communal connection, at once particular and general to "embrace the world" exactly in this mutual confirmation of particularity. "Truth" is not betrayed nor "law" dissolved by this pluralism, but "spread" in "each" distinct particularization of it. This juxtaposition is not pitting universal against particular, but imagining a meaningful order as relations among particulars.

Lazarus wrote in "The Jewish Problem": "I would not have all Jews congregate in a single community. Their fate and their purpose is to be separated. They are to serve as the connecting link between hostile people and advance the glorious cause of our common humanity" (JP 611). She seems to me to be attempting to formulate an ethical particularism where actions are taken only as individuals, and as individual nations, but in commitment to each other. How challenging, how recalcitrant it can be to do so is demonstrated in a companion sonnet to "The New Colossus," "1492," and written at the same time. It offers a layered enigma of the several cultures and communities in complex interchange and distinction:

> Thou two-faced year, Mother of Change and Fate,
> Didst weep when Spain cast forth with flaming sword,
> The children of the prophets of the Lord,
> Prince, priest, and people, spurned by zealot hate.
> Hounded from sea to sea, from state to state,
> The West refused them, and the East abhorred.
> No anchorage the known world could afford,
> Close-locked was every port, barred every gate.
> Then smiling, thou unveil'dst, O two-faced year,
> A virgin world where doors of sunset part,
> Saying, "Ho, all who weary, enter here!
> There falls each ancient barrier that the art
> Of race or creed or rank devised, to rear
> Grim bulwarked hatred between heart and heart!" (P 1: 22–23)

The image of "Mother" recurs here, but less as consoling than as herself caught in the mystery of the "two-faced year." Is this doubling a veil over hidden truths, or duplicity? The year 1492 is immediately recognizable in American history as the date of Columbus's discovery and in Jewish history as the year of the expulsion from Spain. Rumors that some of Columbus's crew, if not Columbus himself, were Jews escaping Europe link the two events. Lazarus extends the dimensions of both, as separate issues and in relation to each other. To be "cast forth with flaming sword" recalls the expulsion from Eden, which Spain in its Golden Age seemed to echo. Israel, too, is constituted here in the terms Lazarus claims for nationhood: "Prince, priest, and people." Jews here are despised precisely as a people, reified into a spurned collective. Their hounding "from sea to sea and state to state" re-creates, or pre-creates, the condition of the refugees Lazarus was agitating for in her very public prose and poetry as well as in her social activism.

In its first eight lines, the sonnet faces toward the Jew-hatred and Jewish statelessness of 1492 as also of 1882. But it then turns from East to a new West—the hidden face the year now "unveil'dst." Mother becomes virgin, and the New World itself beckons, like the Statue in New York Harbor four hundred years later, in promise of its now unveiled true "Fate." But what is that fate?

> There falls each ancient barrier that the art
> Of race or creed or rank devised, to rear
> Grim bulwarked hatred between heart and heart!

Is the fall of "each ancient barrier" a transcending of difference as erasure? The elimination of "race or creed or rank" an overcoming of "hatred between heart and heart" or of distinctions as such, including distinct, particular communities? The poem poses a continuing challenge: how to honor differences in ways neither of hatred nor of rank, allowing for concurrent and overlapping commitments that at once distinguish and bind together in shared as well as distinct communities.

"THE VEIL OF FICTION": JEWISH AMERICAN CULTURE AND THE REPERTOIRE

HEATHER S. NATHANS

Prologue to Change

TEXTS are tenacious. Even events as cataclysmic as civil wars seldom wholly eradicate an entire body of work or set of performance traditions. However, while melodrama remained a staple of the post–Civil War theatrical repertoire, the explosion of burlesque and vaudeville, the eruption of working-class entertainments in industrial centers, the arrival of Yiddish theatre troupes, and the development of the Theatrical Syndicate and the Little Theatre Movement disrupted traditional programming of Eurocentric drama on American stages. And so, while many familiar *texts* remained in the U.S. repertoire, they collided with new performance genres and created fresh meanings in the process.

Performance studies scholar Diana Taylor defines the repertoire as the enactment of "embodied memory: performances, gestures, orality, movement, dance, singing." She argues that while the archive (texts) and the repertoire work in tandem, "the repertoire requires presence: people participate in the production and reproduction of knowledge by 'being there,' being part of the transmission." Taylor contrasts the (assumed) stability and authority of the archive of material documents with the way that the repertoire "both keeps and transforms choreographies of meaning."[1] Following familiar literary and theatrical texts such as *The Merchant of Venice*, *Ivanhoe*, *La Juive*, and *Leah, the Forsaken* over a half-century of "production and reproduction," I use Taylor's concept of repertoire to trace oscillations in the performance of Jewish identities on the U.S. stage in the second half of the nineteenth century. Theatre scholar Tracy Davis has described the nineteenth-century repertoire in particular as "multiple circulating recombinative discourses of intelligibility that create a means by which audiences are habituated to understand one or more kinds or combinations of performative tropes and then recognise and interpret others that are unfamiliar,

1. Diana Taylor, *The Archive and the Repertoire: Performing Cultural Memory in the Americas* (Durham: Duke University Press, 2007), 21.

so that the new may be incorporated into repertoire."[2] Following Davis's argument, I also explore the ways in which Jewish Americans constructed culture and identity through performance.

Popular Phantoms

"Hath not a Jew eyes?" The familiar cry uttered by Shakespeare's money-lender Shylock haunted eighteenth- and nineteenth-century Jewish American audiences. While the speech pleaded for recognition of Jews' humanity, even the most seemingly sympathetic stage representations of Shylock perpetuated Jewish stereotypes, and the character's name persisted as an antisemitic epithet beyond the playhouse. *The Merchant of Venice* debuted in colonial theatres in 1752 and remained a staple of the colonial and early national repertoires. In 1804, Jewish audiences petitioned Charleston theatre managers to withdraw the play from the repertoire, and antebellum Jewish American playwrights, including Isaac Harby, Jonas B. Phillips, and Mordecai Manuel Noah, did their best to repudiate Shakespeare's Shylock or create Jewish stage avatars in the guise of Roman senators or Native Americans that might push back against this pernicious stereotype of the grasping Jewish father.[3] Although they never succeeded in fully eradicating the character, his meaning fluctuated over the years as philo- and antisemitic sentiments waxed and waned in the United States. In 1880, New York's *Jewish Messenger* declared Shylock to be the "Jew of the popular imagination, not the Jew of history," and the paper observed with satisfaction that a host of essays published recently in England and Germany, as well as a collection of sermons in the United States, had (supposedly) demonstrated that the "real" Shylock was not a Jew but in fact a *Christian* merchant of Rome named Paolo Maria Secchi. The *Messenger* claimed that a Jew named Simson Ceneda had been trapped by Secchi's treachery into sacrificing a pound of flesh. Despite this supposed correction to the historical and literary record, the paper acknowledged that "Shylock will still be quoted by many Judeophobists for many a decade.... Superstitions die hard; but as the veil of fiction is torn aside, and history is allowed to testify on its own behalf, the Shylock myth will pass into the region of other popular phantoms, born of a specious theology."[4] Interestingly, the *Messenger*'s prophecy implies that a "true" Jewish character and history existed to be revealed.

2. Tracy C. Davis, "Nineteenth-Century Repertoire," *Nineteenth-Century Theatre and Film* 36, no. 2 (2009): 7–8.

3. Heather S. Nathans, *Hideous Characters and Beautiful Pagans: Performing Jewish Identity on the Antebellum American Stage* (Ann Arbor: University of Michigan Press, 2017), 36.

4. *Jewish Messenger*, January 9, 1880, 4.

However, in dismissing a "popular imagination" reliant upon repetition and adaptation of histories, the author subtly prioritized the positive power of the archive over the potentially destructive power of the repertoire. By contrast, I argue that attention to the always fluid relationship *between* the archive and the repertoire invites contemporary scholars to tear away the "veil of fiction" that settled over Jewish stereotypes enshrined in long-familiar texts. I invoke Jonathan Freedman's term "imaginative formations" to describe the processes by which Jewish culture was translated into American vernaculars throughout the second half of the nineteenth century.[5]

How to establish a clear focal point in the dizzying whirl of changes like the ones I have described above? Throughout this essay, I return to the father-daughter dyad that remained at the heart of many of the stories about Jewish characters presented in the post–Civil War American theatre. While Jewish American sons might bear the burden of becoming future leaders and patriarchs, in the context of nineteenth-century domestic culture, daughters traditionally carried the responsibility of raising a new generation of Jewish American citizens and sustaining the daily practice of faith in the home. Fraught father-daughter dynamics had long been a staple of Jewish representation on the U.S. stage, including Shylock and Jessica in *The Merchant of Venice*, Isaac and Rebecca in numerous adaptations of *Ivanhoe* (1819), Eleazar and Rachel in *La Juive* (1835; adapted in English that same year as a melodrama called *The Jewess, or The Council of Constance*), and *Leah, the Forsaken* (1862). In the next section, I explore how artists reimagined these canonical texts to comment on Jewish American identity in the post–Civil War period.

The Special Grace of Melodrama

Post–Civil War audiences enjoyed a wide range of entertainments and experienced them in an increasingly diverse array of performance spaces. Major middle- and upper-class urban theatres held thousands of spectators and enveloped them in luxuriously appointed surroundings of gilt and velvet. New York City newsboys carved tiny theatres into tenement basements. Western saloon theatres were often exactly what their names implied: spaces in which the bar served as the main attraction and the entertainers vied for the attention of drunken patrons. Small towns unable to afford dedicated theatre buildings frequently created multipurpose spaces that combined town halls, lecture halls,

5. Jonathan Freedman, "Jews on Film," in *The Cambridge History of Jewish American Literature*, ed. Hana Wirth-Nesher (New York: Cambridge University Press, 2016), 276.

concert halls, and improvised performance venues. The Little Theatre Movement of the late nineteenth century stepped away from ornate architecture toward experimental sites that often held fewer than one hundred patrons. The increasingly popular genre of pageant performances hosted at open-air fairs sometimes involved hundreds of performers and thousands of spectators. The impact of *space* on audiences and performers—who "owned" the space, who felt welcome in the space, and who saw themselves reflected on the stage—played a significant role in shaping repertoires in the post–Civil War era.

Performance culture after the Civil War also juggled many seemingly conflicting questions. Could the theatre portray reconciliations between the North and the South while at the same time dealing with race relations and burgeoning immigrant populations that challenged long-held notions of white supremacy? Could it promote the glory of westward expansion while documenting the eradication of indigenous communities and the catastrophic toll of rapid industrialization on the urban poor? The proliferation of postwar genres reflects these often conflicting needs. Racist minstrel shows played in the same theatres that showcased the plight of immigrant factory girls. Melodramas promoting religious tolerance toured small towns that also hosted antisemitic burlesques. *All* of these theatrical transformations would provide opportunities for Jewish American artists and audiences to challenge stereotypes, rewrite familiar texts, and craft new narratives in the post–Civil War United States. Within less than half a century, topics that would have been taboo on the stage before the war made their way into the repertoire, and characters that might once have fit certain preconceptions received renewed consideration. And, as I have suggested, even canonical works upended through parody or satire can shed new light on particular cultural moments.

For many modern readers, melodrama seems tailor-made for parody. Images of maidens tied to railroad tracks and mustache-twisting villains may inspire giggles rather than terror.[6] Modern readers may mock reports that audiences wept at the death of Little Eva or gasped in fright as a hero writhed with *delirium tremens*. That failure to grasp the power of melodrama reveals a shift in the theatre's emotional lexicon from the end of the Civil War into the turn of the twentieth century. To be sure, nineteenth-century melodramas frequently conclude with lessons that affirm white, Christian, middle-class, heteronormative values. Therein lay much of their power and also much of their vulnerability

6. Amy E. Hughes, *Spectacles of Reform: Theater and Activism in Nineteenth-Century America* (Ann Arbor: University of Michigan Press, 2012).

to parody. Yet the plays also had an *aspirational* universality that accounted for much of their appeal. In 1911, drama critic Clayton Hamilton argued that to label a piece as melodramatic might be regarded as insulting. But in fact, "It is the special grace of melodrama to represent not what a particular person would do in a given situation, but what *anybody* would do under such a stress of circumstance."[7]

The "leveling" potential of melodrama appears in a cluster of actors' interpretations of the Jewish father from the mid-nineteenth century. James William Wallack (1795–1864) was a prolific performer and a member of one of the best-known Jewish-descended acting families in the United States. Originally from England, the Wallacks established themselves as talented managers and star-makers, nurturing the careers of Jewish American performers such as Rose Eytinge. When impresario Lester Wallack retired from the management of Wallack's Theatre in 1888, stars from across the United States and Europe gathered to pay tribute in one of the most spectacular productions of *Hamlet* ever staged. The Wallack name was one to be reckoned with, as was James William Wallack's interpretation of Shylock. His performance appeared unusual to critics accustomed to actors such as Edmund Kean and Junius Brutus Booth because Wallack focused on Shylock's *rage*, to the point that in 1856 the *Charleston Courier* commented that Shylock's "vindictiveness" was apparent from his very first interaction with Antonio.[8] Although the critic might have preferred a subtler build-up, Wallack's Shylock suggested a man who had *already* been pushed past his limits by the daily antisemitic acts he encountered. To interpret Shylock as a Jewish man filled with rage from the outset pushed back against the prevailing depictions of the character at that point, which tended to emphasize his more sympathetic qualities until the moment of his eruption in the trial scene. Wallack's apparent fury challenged the notion that Jews would meekly accept abuse, and it obviously startled the predominantly Gentile audience members out of their complacency and their intention to find Shylock pathetic rather than powerful.

Black tragedian Ira Aldridge (1807–1867) highlighted another humanizing, and perhaps distinctively American, interpretation of Shylock in the melodrama era. When he began playing Shylock—his most frequently performed role—during his European tours in the early 1830s, some critics assumed that Aldridge was merely imitating the white British performer Edmund Kean. Yet by the 1860s, critics lauded his ability to transform Shylock into a "hero," with one writer

7. Clayton Hamilton, "Melodrama, Old and New," *The Bookman* 33 (May 1911): 311.

8. "The Theatre—Mr. Wallack's Engagement," *Charleston Courier,* December 4, 1856, [2].

proclaiming that he "reads Shakespeare between the lines." Perhaps it is not surprising that a Black man born in New York in 1807, when many Black New Yorkers still lived in slavery, would understand Shylock's sense of bitterness and oppression, particularly at the loss of his beloved Jessica. Aldridge, who would have heard tales of so many enslaved families torn asunder, played Shylock's bond with Jessica as the "type of love that increases because of this fear of losing it."[9] As another critic wrote, "Ira Aldridge is a mulatto born in America and feels deeply the insults levelled at people of another colour by people of a white colour in the New World. In Shylock he does not seem particularly a Jew, but a human being in general, oppressed by the age-old hatred shown towards people like him, and expressing this feeling with wonderful power and truth."[10] Aldridge's interpretation was not the only one to link Shylock and Jessica's father-daughter dynamic with Black Americans. As Kimberly Manganelli argues, the plight of the beautiful Jewish woman, prey to the machinations of Gentile men, invited many comparisons with the dangers faced by enslaved Black women at the hands of white slaveholders.[11]

The opera *La Juive* (1835), by Eugène Scribe and Jacques-François-Fromental-Élie Halévy, performed another kind of aspirational universality in the post–Civil War repertoire. It was quickly translated into English, with some publishers printing versions with the original French libretto and the English translation on facing pages, which would enable English-speaking audiences to follow along during a French-language performance. The opera was also adapted by W. T. Moncrieff as the English-language melodrama *The Jewess, or The Council of Constance* ([1835]).[12] The story at the heart of these multiple adaptations exemplifies another powerful Jewish father-daughter dynamic circulating in the American repertoire, as well as the burden both figures carried in the popular imagination. Both Halévy's *La Juive* and Moncrieff's *The Jewess* became perennial favorites on the American stage. Like the many iterations of *The Merchant of Venice* and *Ivanhoe*, both the opera *La Juive* and the drama *The Jewess* invite scholars to explore how the "veil of fiction" alternately concealed or revealed themes of Jewish rights, father-daughter dynamics, and gender roles for postbellum American audiences. Because the work may be less familiar to some

9. Quoted in Bernth Lindfors, "'Mislike Me Not for My Complexion . . .': Ira Aldridge in Whiteface," *African American Review* 33, no. 2 (1999): 352.

10. Quoted in *ibid.*, 354.

11. Kimberly Snyder Manganelli, *Transatlantic Spectacles of Race: The Tragic Mulatta and the Tragic Muse* (New Brunswick: Rutgers University Press, 2012).

12. It can sometimes be difficult to determine which version of *The Jewess* is being performed at any one venue, since the characters retained the same first names.

scholars of U.S. theatre (particularly the opera's multiple musical and nonmusical adaptations), I will delve into the plot details and link them to issues that might have been particularly relevant for postwar Jewish American audiences.

Eleazar Mendizabel is the long-suffering Jewish father figure in *La Juive / The Jewess.* His daughter, Rachel, has fallen in love with a Gentile prince named Leopold, who has disguised himself as a Jew to be near her and who has also neglected to mention that he already has a fiancée. From the outset, Eleazar proclaims his refusal to assimilate into Gentile culture or to acknowledge its power over him. In *La Juive,* Eleazar demands, "Ne suis-je pas fils d'Israël | Et le Dieu des Chrétiens m'ordonne-t-il à moi?" (Am I not a son of Israel | And can the God of the Christians command me?).[13] In Moncrieff's *The Jewess,* Eleazar declares, "Can'st tell me what we have in common save the broad earth, and the wide air, our flesh and blood, feeling and sense, our frailties and mortality!"[14] Instead of touting Jews' *similarities* to Gentiles as a means of establishing a common ground, as Shylock does ("If you prick us, do we not bleed?"), Eleazar dismisses the authority of the Gentile deity as well as considerations of "flesh and blood" as irrelevant, pointing to the fundamental differences in faith and practice that continued to distinguish the two religions. Moreover, he steadfastly refuses to bridge those divides.

As the action begins, Eleazar has fallen afoul of local authorities by opening his goldsmith business on Sunday. When Catholic officials threaten him for violating the "Sabbath," he retorts that Gentiles refuse to respect *his* Sabbath; therefore, he should not be obliged to honor theirs. In Moncrieff's version, Eleazar declares, "I am not of thy faith. The God of Jacob whom I serve does not deny that on this day I should both toil and prosper, though chance an unbeliever [Gentile] may do so."[15] Eleazar offers ups the history of his persecution at the hands of the Church, which forced him to watch his two sons burned at the stake. He had to "look on their dying agonies ... while they perished for their father's faith."[16] Disdaining the "butcheries" of the Church officials, he refuses to bow to those "wily hypocrites," declaring, "Our people seek naught from yours."[17]

13. *La Juive* (New York: F. Rullman, Inc., 1919), [4] (translation by the author). For a bilingual text, see https://archive.org/stream/lajuivethejewess00halv/.

14. W. T. Moncrieff, *The Jewess; or, The Council of Constance* (New York: Samuel French, [1853]), 11. The full text is available through https://catalog.hathitrust.org/Record/012393133.

15. *The Jewess,* 10. In the original French version, Eleazar asks, "Et pourquoi l'aimerais-je?" ("And why should I love [the Sabbath]?").

16. *The Jewess,* 10. In the original French version, Eleazar says, "J'ai vu périr mes fils" ("I watched my sons perish.")

17. *The Jewess,* 10.

Eleazar's declarations might have evoked a number of important issues for post–Civil War Jewish American audiences.[18] His protest about laws prohibiting work on the Christian Sabbath would have resonated with individuals who had long resisted the compulsory closures, fines, and loss of business on Sundays; Jewish merchants and other businesses were often forced to stay open on Saturdays (the Jewish Sabbath) to avoid financial loss. But perhaps more than the financial cost of the Sabbath debates, Jewish Americans weighed the damage in sustaining Judaism among local communities. For example, a letter published in the *Jewish Messenger* in 1867 called upon "every true Israelite" to join the newly created "Hebrew Sabbath Association" to promote "the general observance of the Sabbath among the Israelites of New York."[19] One year later, the *Jewish Messenger* described how B'nai B'rith lodges were considering the "Sabbath closing" proposed by more than twenty congregations in New York.[20] Yet, the question over which Sabbath might prevail persisted, touching on widespread concerns about religious freedom as well as anxieties about labor unrest. When an 1880 *New York Times* essay decried the Jewish Sabbath Movement as "an act of bigotry," it drew protest from the *Jewish Messenger*, which defended the movement as "aiming to create a sentiment of reverence and respect for Sabbath rest and sanctity."[21] In 1889, an essay in the New Orleans *Times-Picayune* noted with dismay the ongoing attempts to enforce a national "Sunday Rest" law that would close businesses and halt transportation, mail delivery, and all other nonreligious activities on Sundays. As the author observed, a mandated day of rest was advantageous for the health of the laboring classes, but any requirement that the day be *Sunday*, given its implicit religious connotation, might "oppress the religious preference of some or promote the religious preference of others, or to force religious observances on any against their will." The author added, "Any attempts to connect church and state must inevitably work great injury to the cause of religion."[22]

This debate over Sabbath labor proves to be the inciting incident for *La Juive*/

18. They would also certainly have resonated with the strong anti-Catholic sentiment that pervaded the United States during much of the mid-nineteenth century. Isaac Mayer Wise's *Israelite* occasionally reminded Jewish Americans that nativist politicians were not allies of the Jews simply because of their anti-Catholic policies.

19. "Local Intelligence. New York City," *Jewish Messenger*, June 7, 1867, [5].

20. "The Sabbath Movement. Action Of Benai Berith Lodges," *Jewish Messenger*, September 25, 1868, [2].

21. *Jewish Messenger*, January 9, 1880, 4. For more on this topic, see Jonathan D. Sarna, *American Judaism: A History* (New Haven: Yale University Press, 2004).

22. "Sunday Rest," *Times-Picayune*, May 19, 1889, 6.

The Jewess. As Eleazar remains defiant, the crowd turns violent. Cardinal di Brogni enters and recognizes Eleazar as a man he banished from Rome many years ago. Once again, the cardinal banishes Eleazar, telling him that he has three days to leave Constance; if he remains, he will be killed. Fearing for his daughter's safety, Eleazar confides a great secret to her: after the murder of his two sons and the death of his wife, he adopted Rachel, who was actually born a Christian. He gives her a sealed packet of information that will safeguard her against Christian persecution should the need arise. Mid-century American audiences had seen this device used in numerous dramas, comedies, and novels. It often unlocked the vital piece of information that, usually, allowed an apparently Jewish heroine to marry a Gentile suitor.

La Juive also features a clandestine Passover celebration. Lyrics in the French version describe the traditional setting of the table: "Partagez vous ce pain | par mes mains consacré | Et qu'un levain impur n'a jamais altéré" (Share this bread, consecrated by my hands and untouched by any leaven). Eleazar implores God to "cache nos mystères | A l'œil des méchants" (Hide our rites from evil eyes).[23] Similarly, the stage directions in Moncrieff's melodrama have the Jews and Jewesses "enter in stealth and secrecy." Under the cloak of darkness, Eleazar welcomes his guests to a table decked with "Paschal lamb, Unleavened Bread, Bitter Herbs, &c.," bidding them, "Children of Moses, eat and rejoice. Welcome the season of your deliverance from the fierce furnace of affliction, the house of bondage."[24]

The secrecy of the rites depicted in *La Juive / The Jewess* contrasts strongly with the more open celebration of religious rituals many Jewish Americans enjoyed after the Civil War. For example, in 1880, the *Jewish Messenger* featured an announcement from D. Canter's bakery to the "Jewish community" of New York that he was "ready to receive orders as usual for his best class of Matzoh and choice Confectionary for the ensuing Passover." The advertisement also reminded customers that the shop would be "positively closed on Saturdays and Holidays."[25] Though the notice is small, its text is telling. Canter obviously had both Jewish and Gentile clients, otherwise he would not need to address the advertisement specifically to the Jewish community. Additionally, the phrase "as usual" establishes Canter as a fixture of the neighborhood *and* suggests that he does not anticipate any reprisals for openly celebrating Passover. Jonathan Sarna has explored how producing matzoh became a significant venture for Jewish Americans during the Passover season—to the point that Jewish American

23. *La Juive*, 12. 24. *The Jewess*, 20–21.

25. "Advertisement," *Jewish Messenger*, February 6, 1880, 6.

communities sometimes commissioned Gentile bakeries to produce the volume of matzoh needed. Recognizing a ready market, newspapers—sometimes those specific to the Jewish community and sometimes those aimed at broader audiences—began to include ads for matzoh during the Passover season.[26] One year after Canter's ad, the *Jewish Messenger* gently teased middle-class Jewish housewives about the challenges of keeping a cook during Passover, "when so much of a culinary character has to be arranged in the cleanly fashion in which our mothers delighted since the days of Pharaoh."[27] Jonathan Sarna observes that Passover's "ritual demands," ultimately, "demanded more time, effort, and forethought, than any other Jewish holiday." He adds that the observance also "generated more artifacts than any other holiday."[28]

Despite this apparent progress in openly celebrating Jewish religious holidays, an 1882 issue of the Macon, Georgia, *Telegraph* reported that negative superstitions about Passover still persisted, including the longstanding rumor that Jews used the blood of murdered Christians in Passover food.[29] In 1899, an issue of the San Diego *Evening Tribune* suggested at least slightly more tolerance, reminding readers that "Passover began Saturday.... Among Jews this is one of the most important church occasions of the year and is strictly observed by all orthodox Jews."[30] That same year the *Jewish Messenger* hailed the "authenticity" of *La Juive*, observing that Halévy had been president of the committee of synagogue music in Marseilles and that the opera included "a portion of the Seder service on the evening of Passover."[31]

The Passover scene in *La Juive / The Jewess* proves another turning point in the drama. Leopold's treachery is exposed, and in her anger Rachel steps forward to proclaim that he "hath dared to hold unlawful commerce with one your faith prescribes, accurses—an Israelite, a Jewess!"[32] The cardinal pronounces a death sentence on Leopold, Rachel, and Eleazar. Aghast that she has betrayed her former love, Rachel nobly declares that she brought a *false* charge against

26. Jonathan D. Sarna, "Marking Time: Notes from the Arnold and Deanne Kaplan Collection of Early American Judaica on How Nineteenth-Century American Jews Lived Their Religion," in *Constellations of Atlantic Jewish History*, 1555–1890, ed. Arthur Kiron, exh. cat. (Philadelphia: University of Pennsylvania Libraries, 2014).

27. "Our Gossip," *Jewish Messenger*, March 25, 1881, [1].

28. Sarna, "Marking Time," 54.

29. "The Jews Are Vindicated," *Macon Telegraph*, March 13, 1891, 3.

30. *Evening Tribune*, March 27, 1899, 1.

31. "Foreign," *Jewish Messenger*, July 7, 1899, 3.

32. *The Jewess*, 34. The French version reads: "Chretien, il eut commerce | Avec une maudite, | Une Juive, une Israélite."

Leopold, thus sacrificing herself to save his life. Yet she fails to realize that in acquitting Leopold, she also implicates her father, who is accused of plotting with her to injure the prince. For the alleged crime of conspiring against Leopold, Rachel and Eleazar are condemned to be plunged into boiling oil. The cardinal offers them one chance to save themselves if they will convert and declare that they have found salvation in Christ. Flinging his defiance at the cardinal, Eleazar taunts him with one final jibe. He reveals that when the cardinal's palace in Rome was sacked and his wife and daughter attacked, Jews secretly smuggled the baby away and that only he, Eleazar, knows the fate of the child. The cardinal falls on his knees to beg Eleazar to reveal her whereabouts. Eleazar refuses, and the cardinal declares that he and Rachel shall be put to death instantly. Realizing he has just doomed Rachel—who is the cardinal's long-lost daughter—Eleazer debates whether saving her life or giving her a martyr's crown is the more worthy choice. Rachel refuses to embrace Christianity to save her own life. In the end, she chooses to die with Eleazar—the only father she has ever known.

In the operatic version, as the cardinal begs Eleazar to reveal his daughter's whereabouts, Eleazar refuses until the moment Rachel is flung into the cauldron:

BROGNI: Réponds: ma fille existe-t-elle encore? (Answer me: Does my daughter still live?)
ÉLÉAZAR: Oui! (Yes!)
BROGNI: Dieu! Où donc est elle? (O God! Where is she?)
ÉLÉAZAR: La voilà! (There she is!)
On précipite Rachel dans le bûcher. (*Rachel is thrown into the cauldron.*)[33]

As Rachel is thrown into the boiling oil, the Chorus closes the tale in a moment of horrible irony: "'Tis done at last, | And we have been avenged, | Upon the Jews!"[34]

Although refutation of antisemitism lies at the heart of *La Juive*, its melodramatic tone initially invited critics to interpret a more universal message of religious tolerance. As an 1846 review in the New Orleans *Jeffersonian Republican* described it, "the tender bonds of family and life are ruthlessly broken by fanaticism and burned on the scaffold in the name of Charity and religion."[35] Some

33. *La Juive*, 36 (translations by the author).

34. *Ibid.*, 37 (English libretto). Note that Moncrieff's version allows Rachel to be saved at the last minute.

35. "les plus tendres liens de la famille et de l'existence sont impitoyablement brises par le fanatisme et immolé sur l'echafaud de la superstition au nom de la Charité et de la religion." "Theatre D'Orleans," *Jeffersonian Republican*, December 23, 1846, [3] (translation by the author).

two decades later, audiences still sought a universal message in the melodrama. In 1867 the *New-Orleans Times* proclaimed it one of those operas that "stirred ... nobler thoughts" in the audience.[36] Yet, as the *Jewish Messenger* made clear in an 1889 review, Jewish American audiences still appreciated the pro-Jewish message at the core of the work. The paper approved the actors' fine performances as Eleazar and Rachel (the "notable Jewish pair"), and hailed Rachel's "strong love" for her "aged companion in persecution" and her "heroic devotion to her creed," which "raises the old tragedy above the commonplace."[37]

As with every show that underwent multiple revivals, critical responses differed based on the quality of the company, the performers' level of preparation, and so on. Thus, assessments in the decades following the Civil War varied widely. By 1888, the *New York Herald* described *La Juive*'s ongoing presence in the repertoire as "somewhat wearing."[38] But even if some New York audiences had lost their enthusiasm for the text, the New Orleans *Times-Picayune* claimed in 1892 that "Halevy's *La Juive* has become the traditional opera for the debut of opera troupes in New Orleans." The author added that "*La Juive*, which was first presented about sixty years ago, should be too familiar to opera-goers and music lovers to require any retrospective history."[39] Interestingly, by 1900, the *Times-Picayune* observed that the work no longer matched "modern ideas of the music drama."[40] The range of opinions reflected here suggests that while the *text* remained largely stable, audiences' understanding of the work's meaning, impact, and relevance continued to shift.

A Fine Bit of Caricature

Like melodrama, minstrelsy evolved long before the Civil War, but in the postwar years it shifted from what Eric Lott has characterized as a primarily Northern phenomenon, exploiting white working-class discontent via blackface, to a nationwide genre vaunting an ersatz nostalgia for the vanished land of Dixie alongside lampoons of "high" culture (including Shakespeare).[41] Burlesque—a form that grew out of the minstrel show—also parodied familiar works, even as it rapidly transformed into a sexualized spectacle that exploited the female

36. "Amusements," *New Orleans Times*, December 14, 1867, 2.

37. "Music and Drama," *Jewish Messenger*, January 25, 1889, 6.

38. "Curtain Raisers," *New York Herald*, November 25, 1888, 7.

39. *Times-Picayune*, October 12, 1892.

40. "Amusements 'La Juive' at the French Opera House," *Times-Picayune*, December 23, 1900, 7.

41. See Eric Lott, *Love and Theft: Blackface Minstrelsy and the American Working Class*, 20th anniversary ed. (Oxford: Oxford University Press, 2013).

body.[42] Canonical texts such as Shakespeare's *The Merchant of Venice* and Sir Walter Scott's *Ivanhoe* became fodder for both minstrel and burlesque performances by both Gentile and Jewish performers. Interestingly, the only parody I have found of *La Juive* was produced in France in the years just after its première in 1835 and does not seem to have traveled to the United States.[43] However, the *role* of Rachel Mendizabel sometimes became conflated with Jewish American actresses targeted by antisemitism, particularly the controversial star Adah Isaacs Menken. All of these parodies, attacks, and appropriations offer insight into postwar performances of Jewish American identities, and especially into the all-important father-daughter relationships that lie at the heart of each story.

Even as Jewish moneylenders remained a constant on the postwar stage, many of the post–Civil War adaptations of *The Merchant of Venice* also took aim at the ubiquity of Jewish peddlers across the American landscape.[44] Those parodies included George Melville Baker's *The Peddler of Very Nice* (published 1867), which parodied the infamous trial scene between Shylock and Antonio, and G. W. H. Griffin's *Shylock, a Burlesque* (published ca. 1874), played by Griffin & Christy's Minstrels. Both scripts describe Shylock's costume in some detail. The directions in *The Peddler of Very Nice* call for "A long dressing gown, high colored; long white hose; sandals; a coarse wig, made from horse-hair, that can easily be detached in 'handfuls;' three hats, one on top of the other, in imitation of the old Jew peddlers."[45] While that description might not convey much

42. It should be noted that some women embraced burlesque as a route to liberation from traditional female roles. See M. Alison Kibler, *Rank Ladies: Gender and Cultural Hierarchy in American Vaudeville* (Chapel Hill: University of North Carolina Press, 1999), and Robert C. Allen, *Horrible Prettiness: Burlesque and American Culture* (Chapel Hill: University of North Carolina Press, 1991).

43. Diana R. Hallman's study, *Opera, Liberalism, and Antisemitism in Nineteenth-Century France: The Politics of Halévy's "La Juive"* (New York: Cambridge University Press, 2002), reveals that *La Juive* spawned French parodies soon after its Parisian debut. The title of the 1836 publication *La Juive de Pantin; ou, La Friture manquée* puns on the action of the play: *friture* means to fry in oil and *manquée* means "missed" or "failed." Pantin is both a suburb of Paris *and* slang for a doll or puppet. So, the title might be translated as "The Jewish Puppet, or The Failed Fry." The parody depicts Eleazar as a miser, much like Shylock.

44. For more on this topic, see Shari Rabin, *Jews on the Frontier: Jews and Mobility in Nineteenth-Century America* (New York: New York University Press, 2017), and Michael R. Cohen, *Cotton Capitalists: American Jewish Entrepreneurship in the Reconstruction Era* (New York: New York University Press, 2017). Other burlesques targeting moneylenders include *Much Ado About a Merchant of Venice* (1869) and *The Water Cure* (1883). For more on these burlesques and post–Civil War Jewish stage types, see Harley Erdman, *Staging the Jew: The Performance of an American Ethnicity, 1860–1920* (New Brunswick: Rutgers University Press, 1997).

45. George Melville Baker, *The Peddler of Very Nice, a Burlesque, in Baker, Amateur Dramas for Parlour Theatricals, Evening Entertainments and School Exhibitions* (Boston: Lee and Shepard, 1867), 201. The full text is available at https://catalog.hathitrust.org/Record/011630892.

to a modern-day reader, in fact it played on the familiar Shylock persona then popular on the melodrama stage, which often featured "Oriental" robes and a flowing beard. Slight variations on that costume can be seen in images of the famous Shylocks portrayed by James William Wallack, Ira Aldridge, and, later, Henry Irving. The addition of the *three* hats echoes cartoons of Jewish peddler characters sometimes circulated in the mid-nineteenth century and undercuts the seriousness of Shylock's character. *The Peddler of Very Nice* even entered the realm of parlor theatricals. In just one example of its wide reach, the *Goodhue County Republican* of Red Wing, Minnesota, proudly listed the comedy among an evening's amateur entertainments at a local literary society gathering in 1871.[46] In Griffin's *Shylock, A Burlesque*, the role of Jessica was played by a male performer in the troupe. (This kind of drag performance grew out of the "burlesque" section of the minstrel show.) The character sings saucy songs, including "Naughty, Naughty Men."[47] Thus, Shylock's fear that losing his daughter means losing his future degenerates into a drag piece that reduces the characters to objects of ridicule. The male impersonation of Jessica subverted the desirability and vulnerability that had long marked the role of the Jewess on the American stage. But a male performer in drag could also parody the supposed aggressive sexuality of Jewish women.

Not all burlesques of *Merchant* satirized Jewish identity from the "outside." In 1867, the *Jewish Messenger* drew readers' attention to *Shylock, the Jew* at Garland's Theatre, in which Miron (or Myron) Leffingwell played Shylock. Leffingwell had begun in more serious roles, playing Antonio to Edwin Booth's Shylock, for example. But as his career progressed, he became known for his burlesque interpretations of well-known parts. Thus, it seems likely that *his* Shylock would have parodied Booth's interpretation. It also seems probable that the newspaper identified Leffingwell as Jewish, particularly because his performance is listed among a roster of other Jewish American artists, including Rose Eytinge. Putting these clues together, a reader of the *Jewish Messenger* might conclude that Leffingwell's Shylock would play as an inside joke for Jewish American audiences (Fig. 47).[48]

Ivanhoe also made a shift from melodrama to parody by the second half of the nineteenth century. Sir Walter Scott's novel tells the story of the young Saxon

46. *Goodhue County Republican*, December 28, 1871, 4.

47. G. W. H. Griffin, *Shylock, A Burlesque* (New York: Happy Hours Company, 1874).

48. "Music and the Drama," *Jewish Messenger*, November 1, 1867, [5]. Leffingwell also played Shylock in another *Merchant* parody, *The Merchant of Venice Preserved*, which puns on the title of a well-known eighteenth-century drama, *Venice Preserved*. Leffingwell's obituary outlines his career: "M. W. Leffingwell," *New York Times*, June 11, 1879.

Fig. 47. Miron Leffingwell (ca. 1880s), a Jewish performer who played in some of the burlesques of *The Merchant of Venice.* (Laurence Senelick Collection).

knight Ivanhoe, betrothed to the Christian aristocrat Rowena, but secretly in love with the wise and lovely Rebecca, a Jewess. Throughout the story, Rebecca and her father, Isaac, face constant persecution and ultimately leave England to escape intolerance. Multiple dramatic adaptations of *Ivanhoe* had enthralled American audiences from the novel's debut in 1819. Many dramatists even reconfigured the action around the Jewish father and daughter, focusing on their devoted relationship and reducing Ivanhoe to a secondary character. Unfortunately, these versions still portrayed Isaac as powerless to protect Rebecca from attack by the Gentile knight Sir Brian de Bois Guilbert.

Within fifty years of its debut, however, the stage tale of a weak Jewish father and a beleaguered Jewish woman had become a cliché to many U.S. audiences. In 1860, burlesque actress Mrs. John Wood and comic star Joseph Jefferson III (best known for playing Rip Van Winkle) spoofed the famous showdown between Ivanhoe and Sir Brian after Sir Brian's attack on Rebecca.[49] In Scott's original novel and in its more faithful stage adaptations, Sir Brian corners Rebecca in his castle and threatens to assault her if she will not convert to Christianity and marry him. She vows to throw herself from the tower if he comes one step closer.

MR. JEFFERSON AND MRS. WOOD IN "IVANHOE."

Fig. 48. Mrs. Wood and Mr. Jefferson boxing in *Ivanhoe.* From Laurence Hutton, *Curiosities of the American Stage* (New York: Harper & Brothers, 1891), 196. (Princeton University Library).

Wood and Jefferson reconceived this epic confrontation as a boxing match, thus perhaps collapsing the roles of the beautiful Rebecca and her defender, Ivanhoe, with Wood as the male/female combatant in the ring (Fig. 48). A sketch of this "grand fistic encounter," with a forceful Wood clad in chain mail (which also scandalously reveals the outline of her legs) and an over-the-top Jefferson sporting

49. "Advertisement," *New York Herald,* March 6, 1860, 7.

an exaggerated moustache and giant crusader cross on his tunic, seemingly displaces the father-daughter relationship at the heart of the drama.[50] In a nod to current political events in 1860, the Wood/Jefferson production of *Ivanhoe* concluded with a "Brilliant Tableau emblematic of the Union between the North and the South."[51] Thus a tale of the conflict between Norman and Saxon, Gentile and Jew, became subsumed in a political spectacle about the coming war. The Wood/Jefferson parody was so popular that it persisted into the 1870s.

Subsequent parodies continued to undermine the importance of the Isaac-Rebecca relationship, as well as the "popular phantom" of Jewish women's irresistible allure. In 1869, comic actor James Lewis played Rebecca at New York's Waverley Theatre, dressing in drag to satirize the supposed helplessness and sexual allure of the Jewish female character. As the *New-York Tribune* reported, "Mr. Lewis indulges his humorous propensities in a fine bit of caricature."[52] That comment raises a compelling question about the "veil of fiction": if Lewis's Rebecca was seen as a "caricature" of the beautiful Jewess Rebecca, did a Gentile audience assume that the original melodrama character represented the *real* Jewess?

The question of what defined an "authentic" Jewess persisted throughout the second half of the nineteenth century and was embodied in the person and the repertoire of actress, activist, and author Adah Isaacs Menken (Fig. 49). Menken played Rachel Mendizabel, the female lead in *The Jewess*, beginning in 1858. The role offered her a platform to perform her Jewish identity—a bold choice in an era in which the French star Rachel Félix had met with a vicious outpouring of antisemitism during her 1855 American tour. While some American audiences lauded Félix's passionate style of performance, others mocked her as "the veriest Shylock of her race" and a "Jewish sorceress" of low "moral repute."[53] This cluster of epithets from just one review encapsulates all of the stereotypes that still encircled Jewish female stage characters and Jewish actresses well into the second half of the nineteenth century. Menken fought this bigotry throughout her career.

Born in 1835, Menken was a complex figure, given to spinning fanciful and often contradictory tales of her origins—including whether she had been born

50. "Advertisement," *New York Herald*, March 11, 1860, 7.

51. *Ibid.*

52. "The Drama," *New-York Tribune*, April 3, 1869, 4.

53. The *Republican Quarterly Review*, quoted in David Anthony, "Fantasies of Conversion: The Sensational Jewess in Poe and Hawthorne's America," *American Literary History* 26, no. 3 (2014): 431–61.

Fig. 49. Adah Isaacs Menken at her writing desk. Photograph by McLean & Haes, London, ca. 1864. (Laurence Senelick Collection).

to a Jewish family or had converted upon her marriage. As Renée Sentilles has chronicled, Menken courted controversy throughout her life in the roles she played, the causes she championed, and the choices she made for her personal life.[54] Some audiences hailed her as an inspired talent and moving spirit. When she played Rachel in *The Jewess*, the *Cincinnati Daily Commercial* chronicled the "favourable impression" and warm applause she earned in the role.[55] She even performed *The Jewess* for a benefit performance, which suggests the popularity of the piece as well as Menken's delight in playing the pious and courageous heroine who willingly goes to her death in defense of her faith.[56]

Throughout her career Menken persistently proclaimed her devotion to Judaism, penning articles for *The Israelite* and asserting that Jewish women could prove just as militant in the defense of religion as Jewish men. In "Hear, O Israel," from her posthumously published collection of poems, *Infelicia* (1868), she exhorts Jews everywhere to "Come forth with the signs and wonders, and thy strong hands, and stretched-out arms, even as thou didst from Egypt! Courage, courage! trampled hearts!"[57] In her poem "Judith," Menken imagines herself as the biblical character facing Holofernes:

> Stand back!
> I am no Magdalene waiting to kiss the hem of your garment.
> It is mid-day.
> See ye not what is written on my forehead?
> I am Judith!
> I wait for the head of my Holofernes!
> Ere the last tremble of the conscious death-agony shall have shuddered, I will show it to ye with the long black hair clinging to the glazed eyes, and the great mouth opened in search of voice, and the strong throat all hot and reeking with blood, that will thrill me with wild unspeakable joy as it courses down my bare body and dabbles my cold feet!
> My sensuous soul will quake with the burden of so much bliss.[58]

But, as many scholars of Menken's life have documented, neither her artistic talents nor her faith could defend her from scurrilous antisemitic attacks like the ones so often faced by the heroines she played (or her role model, Rachel

54. Renée M. Sentilles, *Performing Menken: Adah Isaacs Menken and the Birth of American Celebrity* (Cambridge and New York: Cambridge University Press, 2003).

55. *Cincinnati Daily Commercial*, December 27, 1858.

56. "Advertisement," *Daily Ohio Statesman* (Columbus), February 4, 1859, [2].

57. Adah Isaacs Menken, *Infelicia* (Philadelphia: J. B. Lippincott, 1868), 85; accessed at https://quod.lib.umich.edu/a/amverse/BAD8997.0001.001/1:26?rgn=div1;view=toc.

58. *Ibid.*, 23.

Félix). Her poem "Where the Flocks Shall Be Led" hints at her frequent sense of persecution and her determination not to yield: "But I shall not plead for mercy | Weak and fainting as I am, I fear you not!"[59] Despite her resistance, critics persisted in aligning her with the often hyper-sexualized images of Jewish women. In 1862 a reviewer in the *Sacramento Daily Union* characterized her as a "handsome, dark-eyed brunette, a Jewess," praised her "beautiful underpinnings [legs]," and described her as a "voluptuous person" who presented a "delicious arrangement of flesh and blood."[60] One year later, an article in the same paper called her a "pretty, shapely Jewess" who was "coining money" on her tours, suggesting that she was little better than a prostitute (and once again linking a Jew with love of gold).[61] Menken's independence (artistically and personally) invited some critics to make *her* into the parody of Jewish female identity.

Ironically, the same passion and militancy that critics mocked in Menken's life initially won plaudits for stage characters in the theatrical repertoire, particularly in Augustin Daly's 1862 *Leah, the Forsaken*, an adaptation of German Jewish author Salomon Hermann Mosenthal's play *Deborah.* Leah falls in love with a Gentile named Rudolph but is unable to marry him. He marries his Gentile sweetheart, Madelena, and Leah departs, cursing the community that rejected her. When she returns as a beggar some years later, she discovers that her former love has named his daughter after her. She ultimately forgives those who wronged her.

The play proves an exception to the familiar father-daughter dynamic I have emphasized here. Instead, the ghost of the father looms over Leah's identity and fate. Daly's melodrama frames Leah as the "daughter of an accursed race" rather than of one man. And Leah acknowledges her responsibility to "carry the little lamp" of faith left to her by her father into the future, thus claiming the roles of both son and daughter simultaneously.[62] She honors her father's memory by sustaining her faith but can also fight in her own defense. Her resolve appears most clearly in the final moments of the play, when she denounces the character of Nathan the Schoolmaster as an apostate and murderer. She draws her knife on him, declaring, "As Judith to Holofernes, so I to you!"[63]

59. *Ibid.*, 88–89.

60. *Sacramento Daily Union*, February 6, 1862. The author even suggested that she was a "honey pot" in which men (aside from her husband) had reveled.

61. *Sacramento Daily Union*, December 7, 1863. This attack also echoes those leveled against Félix.

62. Augustin Daly, *Leah, the Forsaken* (New York: Samuel French, [1862]); the full text is available at https://catalog.hathitrust.org/Record/008611697.

63. *Ibid.*, 44.

Leah's advent on the American stage suggests that as the nation entered the second half of the nineteenth century, *some* authors, actors, and audiences had begun to challenge stereotypes in the repertoire, struggling to banish the "popular phantoms" of the troubled Jewish father-daughter representations. When *Leah* debuted, it featured actress Kate Bateman, a performer apparently noteworthy for her distinct *lack* of any recognizable Jewish identity.[64] Yet, as with some of the earlier melodramas discussed above, Bateman presented a kind of aspirational universality in her heroine that drew sympathy to her plight as the "daughter of an accursed race" and made the figure of the betrayed Jewess the quintessential melodrama heroine. As Jonathan Sarna has noted, some spectators imagined the play would combat antisemitism, while others read in it a message of healing for a nation fractured by the Civil War.[65]

Within a year of *Leah*'s debut, playwright, journalist, and theatre critic Frank Wood penned the parody *Leah the Forsook* (1863), which included a male performer as Leah and mocked the tearjerker aspects of the original.[66] *Leah, the Forsaken* also inspired the minstrel song "Leah the Shook or Was She Forsook," which featured a male performer in drag *and* blackface playing Leah. As Jonathan Hess argues, the female impersonation combined with the blackface might suggest one of two possibilities to an audience. First, Leah's character was already so exaggerated in Daly's version that these excesses simply made those qualities manifest. Or, viewers might recall the pejorative descriptions often used about Jewish women, including "black, but comely," a reference to the *Song of Solomon*, but often invoked in problematic ways.[67]

The stage parodies of famous Jewish fathers and daughters described above represent only a handful of the performance pieces that circulated in the post–Civil War repertoire. As Harley Erdman has argued, such representations continued to portray Jewish fathers "as oriental grotesques."[68] The beautiful Jewess also became a stock figure, hovering somewhere between a shrew, a harlot, and a character whose marginal racial identity was often conflated with that of Black Americans.

In contrast to the often grotesque aspects of burlesque, vaudeville emerged

64. Nathans, *Hideous Characters*, 170–71.

65. Jonathan D. Sarna and Benjamin Shapell, *Lincoln and the Jews: A History* (New York: St. Martin's Press, 2015), 190.

66. Jonathan M. Hess has argued that some portions of Daly's *Leah* verge on parody themselves. Hess, *Deborah and Her Sisters: How One Nineteenth-Century Melodrama and a Host of Celebrated Actresses Put Judaism on the World Stage* (Philadelphia: University of Pennsylvania Press, 2017), 103.

67. *Ibid.*

68. Erdman, *Staging the Jew*, 31.

as a more family-friendly genre of entertainment and was frequently stocked with sketch acts featuring comic tales of immigrant life (such as the Jewish immigrant "Dutch" duo Weber and Fields or the Irish duo Harrigan and Hart). Some vaudeville acts built loyal followings among the very communities they gently satirized, since the artists themselves came from those same immigrant or working-class backgrounds.[69] Harley Erdman suggests that "never before or since in the American theatre had Jewish characters enjoyed such a highly visible presence" as they did in the 1870s and 1880s. Moreover, many Jewish vaudeville stars, including Miron Leffingwell, used the vaudeville stage to "translate" Jews from villains to figures of comedy. Erdman argues that many Jewish actors walked a "performance tightrope" in the 1880s and 1890s "in their transition from the margins to the mainstream of commercial popular entertainment."[70] Leffingwell, like other Jewish vaudeville comics, helped to revolutionize the repertoire of dour Jewish fathers, particularly Shylock. Finding the humor—especially the *insider* humor of a figure like Shylock—"invites the repudiation of this tradition."[71]

The Idol of the Ghetto

On May 9, 1903, the *Salt Lake Telegram* informed its readers that Jacob Adler, the "idol of the New York ghetto," would play *The Merchant of Venice* "in Hebrew" during the coming theatrical season.[72] The paper's characterization of Adler, one of the greatest stars of the Yiddish theatre, raises intriguing questions about the meaning of "ghetto" by that point in U.S. history. Playwright Israel Zangwill had proudly claimed it in his dramas. Yet, it had also begun to signify slum areas: Jack London would use the term "working-class ghetto" in 1908 to describe a neighborhood hard hit by the San Francisco earthquake. An article in an 1892 issue of the *New-York Tribune* noted the increasing conflation among some "provincial New Yorkers" of the words "slum" and "ghetto." The writer rebuts this misconception, arguing that too many audience members have swallowed the stage caricature of the "thick-witted and outlandish-looking fellow speaking a barbarous jargon." He invites them to explore the Lower East

69. For more on the development of signature vaudeville characters, see Rick DesRochers, *The New Humor in the Progressive Era: Americanization and the Vaudeville Comedian* (New York: Palgrave Macmillan, 2014).

70. Erdman, *Staging the Jew*, 64.

71. *Ibid.*, 65.

72. "Plays and Players Here and Elsewhere," *Salt Lake Telegram*, May 9, 1903, 5. Adler was playing in Yiddish, not Hebrew.

Side, where they will see "Hebrew papers … Hebrew shops with Hebrew signs … Hebrew restaurants … [and] a Hebrew playhouse." As the author reminds his readers, foreign does not equal "slum," signifying impoverishment or illiteracy, and he rebukes those who lack the imagination to appreciate Jewish culture.[73] However the Salt Lake newspaper understood Adler's identity as a hero of the "ghetto," the notice of his upcoming tour confirms that his appearance as Shylock was a significant theatrical event.[74]

The Russian-born Adler had emigrated to the United States in 1887 and within a few years founded the Independent Yiddish Art Company and the Yiddish-language Union Theatre. Yiddish theatre had debuted in America in 1881–1882 and found ready audiences in urban centers with high concentrations of recent Jewish immigrants, such as New York and Chicago. For many recent immigrants, Yiddish theatre troupes reinforced cultural ties to the "old country." Nahma Sandrow has described the escapist quality of many late nineteenth-century Yiddish theatre productions, particularly the ones that featured "glorious periods of Jewish history."[75] Sandrow describes American Jews' eager anticipation to enjoy Yiddish theatre, noting that the popularity of songs that had traveled with and circulated among new immigrants created a ready market for its arrival.

Avrom Goldfadn (Abraham Goldfaden, 1840–1908), often described as the "Father of Yiddish Theatre," blended traditional European forms with Jewish cultural ones to produce what Seth Wolitz describes as a "successful aestheticization of Jewish life and custom."[76] Goldfadn's works, including *The Sorceress* (1877) and *The Fanatic, or, The Two Kuni-Lemls* (1887), became hits with many Jewish American audiences, and, as Sandrow notes, many of their themes or songs persist in Jewish "folk culture" to this day.[77] And although Goldfadn remains among the best-known late-nineteenth century Jewish playwrights, authors such as Jacob Gordin (1853–1909) also revolutionized Jewish theatre,

73. "New-York. A City Unknown To New-Yorkers," *New-York Tribune*, January 31, 1892, 21.

74. For more on the ways in which Jewish Americans were represented in late nineteenth- and early twentieth-century American culture, see M. Alison Kibler, *Censoring Racial Ridicule: Irish, Jewish, and African American Struggles over Race and Representation, 1890–1930* (Chapel Hill: University of North Carolina Press, 2015).

75. Nahma Sandrow, "Yiddish Theatre in America," in *The Cambridge History of Jewish American Literature*, ed. Wirth-Nesher, 225.

76. Seth Wolitz, "Avrom Goldfadn," in *The YIVO Encyclopedia of Jews in Eastern Europe*, ed. Gershon David Hundert, 2 vols. (New Haven: Yale University Press, 2008), https://yivoencyclopedia.org/article.aspx/Goldfadn_Avrom.

77. Sandrow, "Yiddish Theatre in America," 224–25.

infusing it with some of the more modern themes seen in the works of Henrik Ibsen. As Sandrow argues, Gordin aspired to create a "pure" and politicized form of Yiddish theatre, rather than a "folksy" one that catered to the whims and tastes of uneducated audiences.[78] Though they had different aims, Goldfadn and Gordin inspired new waves of theatrical activity, training, and performance culture in the final decades of the nineteenth century. Their work launched the careers of numerous stars, spurred the development of subsequent generations of Yiddish playwrights, and enshrined Jewish culture in the U.S. theatrical lexicon.

Given the popularity of Yiddish theatre, it seems unsurprising that by the time he undertook the role of Shylock in 1903, Jacob Adler had established himself as a star in several well-known roles, including his much-lauded turn as Lear in the Yiddish-language version of *King Lear.* However, as Boston's *Sunday Herald* commented, because Adler generally appeared with a Yiddish-speaking company, "his clientele … has heretofore been almost exclusively confined to the Jewish part of the population."[79] The paper anticipated that Adler's choice to play Shylock in Yiddish with the company around him playing in English would increase the accessibility of the work to non-Jewish patrons, or what the paper described as "theatregoers of all classes." I suggest that the phrase "all classes" may evoke the *assumed* economic and social disparity between Yiddish and non-Yiddish speakers.

The use of the term "ghetto" to describe Adler's Jewish American audience persisted, with all its potential complexities. In June 1903, the *Kansas City Star* reprinted a story from a New York newspaper that recounted the supposed resentment of Adler's "Ghetto population" at his defection from the Lower East Side to Broadway. Some New Yorkers claimed that Adler owed allegiance to the Jewish Americans who had been loyal audience members since his arrival in the city and for whom he was "the embodiment of an ideal." Others claimed that a move to Broadway would prove that "art is universal," even when performed in Yiddish.[80]

Adler had other barriers to overcome. Memories of previous Shylocks still lingered in audiences' imaginations, and he found himself haunted by the persistence of the theatrical repertoire.[81] A review in the *Philadelphia Inquirer*

78. *Ibid.*, 227–29.

79. *Boston Herald,* May 10, 1903, 38.

80. "A Ghetto View of Shylock," *Kansas City Star,* June 4, 1903, 7.

81. For more on this phenomenon, see Marvin Carlson, *The Haunted Stage: The Theatre as Memory Machine* (Ann Arbor: University of Michigan Press, 2001).

observed that spectators could not respond to Adler's Shylock without recalling the performances of Edwin Booth or Henry Irving in the role. However, as the reviewer noted with pleasure, the actor introduced "an entirely new conception of the part." Adler repudiated the tradition of presenting Shylock as a man broken by the machinations of the Gentile characters and shamed by his forced conversion to Christianity. Instead of a "broken, pitiful old man," Adler's Shylock was "bold, haughty, and proud, walking from the scene arrogant and defiant." The reviewer added with admiration, "*Never is he a caricature*, never is he anything but the foremost figure in the tragic-comedy."[82] Although the Philadelphia critic found Adler's performance inspiring, some New York critics attacked it as "the narrow presentment of one individual Jew" rather than "the poet's universal conception."[83] These divergent opinions reveal the ongoing challenges Jewish artists faced in embodying Jewish characters on the American stage. Were they supposed to transcend their religious and ethnic identities, "translating" Jewishness into a performance that would be intelligible to non-Jewish audiences? Or could they play "one individual Jew," unburdened by the need to somehow represent all Jews everywhere?

Coda: What Is and Is Not Art

As I have suggested, throughout the second half of the nineteenth century, minstrelsy, burlesque, and vaudeville proved highly adaptable forms, often twisting canonical texts to address contemporary social and political issues. Similarly, Yiddish theatre reinvented familiar stories and characters for new immigrant communities. It remains important to note that these forms never eliminated melodrama from the nineteenth-century repertoire. For example, Jewish American impresario David Belasco took the form to new heights at the end of the century. He "captivated audiences by the atmosphere of the entire production," which might include real stoves cooking real food onstage, sound effects to mimic the squeak of an elevator or the rumble of carriages, or what he described as the "poetry of light" conjuring a sunset on the desert or a night of stars.[84] Mark Hodin has described Belasco's approach to production as the "theatricalization

82. "Adler as Shylock," *Philadelphia Inquirer*, May 10, 1903, 5. The reviewer also added that the Yiddish-speaking members of the audience found the evening "doubly enjoyable," an acknowledgment that those spectators were clearly privy to another layer of the performance.

83. "A Ghetto View of Shylock," *Kansas City Star*, June 4, 1903, 7.

84. "Green Room Gossip," *Times-Picayune* (New Orleans), February 1, 1903, 34.

of psychological affect."[85] As Hodin argues, melodrama *always* acknowledged its manipulation of the audience. The same artificiality that opened it to parody was what made the genre so compelling.

New theatrical venues and rising communities of Jewish artists and producers supported the transformation of American theatrical culture as well. Although it is beyond the scope of this essay to examine the breadth of their accomplishments, their artistic interventions fundamentally reshaped both the archive *and* the repertoire of American theatre. The Theatrical Syndicate offers just one example. Beyond the big urban centers, the expansion of railroad networks brought touring companies and great stars to small towns, allowing far-flung audiences to savor cosmopolitan delights (like the opportunity to see Sarah Bernhardt starring in *Leah, the Forsaken*). The rapid mushrooming of theatrical venues across the United States spurred the creation of a series of theatrical monopolies, including what became known as the Theatrical Syndicate.[86] Created by six Jewish businessmen (Abe Hayman, Charles Frohman, Marc Klaw, Abe Erlanger, Sam Nixon, and J. F. Zimmerman), this group "nearly monopolized theatrical production nationwide, wielding control over all levels of management and production and forging the twentieth-century concept of a centralized 'show business' industry."[87] As Harley Erdman argues, the power of the Syndicate raised anxieties among Gentile producers and critics who imagined a Jewish conspiracy to subsume "American" art in a Jewish American agenda. Not surprisingly, this antisemitism emerged in editorials, theatrical reviews, and ongoing efforts to undermine Jewish managers. For example, a *New-York Tribune* article in 1898 accused the Syndicate management team of "going into politics" in support of a particular candidate. The article listed all the leaders of the Syndicate by name; it also added a group of other Jewish managers and producers as well, including Theodore Moss (Wallack's former theatre manager, who had faced numerous antisemitic attacks in the past), Alfred E. Aarons, and Al Hyman.[88]

85. Mark Hodin, "Late Melodrama," in *The Oxford Handbook of American Drama*, ed. Jeffrey H. Richards and Heather S. Nathans (Oxford: Oxford University Press, 2014), 168–69.

86. The Shubert brothers (Sam, Lee, and J.J.) would give the Syndicate a run for its money beginning in the early twentieth century. For more on this rivalry, see Annie Polland and Daniel Soyer, *Emerging Metropolis: New York Jews in the Age of Immigration, 1840–1920* (New York: New York University Press, 2012), 236–37.

87. Erdman, *Staging the Jew*, 93.

88. "Tammany Theatrical Managers," *New-York Tribune*, November 4, 1898, 2.

The Syndicate tended to regulate its repertoires closely, focusing on works that would please mainstream audiences rather than more avant-garde productions. Perhaps not surprisingly, artists who wanted to experiment with form, genre, and subject matter began to push back against the Syndicate, including a handful of Jewish American artists. Companies such as New York's Neighborhood Playhouse, founded in 1915 by Alice and Irene Lewisohn near the Henry Street Settlement, would become key laboratories for nurturing new generations of professional theatre artists and amateur players as well. Indeed, by 1925, the *Jewish Chronicle* of Newark, New Jersey, credited the Little Theatre Movement and Samuel S. Grossman of the Jewish Art Theatre in New York with inspiring the creation of Newark's own Community Theatre Guild, through the Y.W.H.A. and Y.M.H.A.[89] Little more than a year later, the community produced *The Dybbuk*, the Vilna Troupe work that had created such a sensation in Europe and New York City.[90]

Born partly from frustration with the Syndicate, the Little Theatre Movement emerged to showcase plays that grappled with controversial subject matter in ways that sidestepped familiar melodrama endings, which generally dictated that the bad characters be punished and the good rewarded. Sholom Asch's controversial Yiddish drama *God of Vengeance* (*Got fun nekome*) debuted in the United States in 1907 before being translated into English and produced on Broadway in 1923 (where it was promptly shut down on obscenity charges). *God of Vengeance* returns to the familiar father-daughter dynamic, but with a wildly different twist. The play tells the story of a Jewish brothel owner planning to marry his daughter to a respectable member of the Jewish community, not realizing that she has fallen in love with one of the prostitutes. The work ignited a storm of controversy over *how* Jewish characters should appear onstage. Just as Adler had faced criticism for portraying Shylock's downfall as the story of "one" Jew rather than all Jews, Jewish Americans questioned the potential damage an outspoken work like Asch's might do to their efforts to combat persistent stereotypes.[91]

Jonathan Freedman suggests that the "imaginative formations" shaping Jewish American culture represent a long process of collaboration between artists and audiences as they have created and critiqued each other.[92] Some of the plays discussed above have dropped out of the repertoire, but their residue can be

89. "Society Community Theatre Guild," *Jewish Chronicle*, May 8, 1925, 6.

90. "Local Players To Present 'Dybbuk,'" *Jewish Chronicle*, November 12, 1926, 9.

91. Kibler, *Censoring Racial Ridicule*, 110–11.

92. Freedman, "Jews on Film."

seen in contemporary television series such as "The Marvelous Mrs. Maisel," with its exaggerated Jewish father figures and ingénue daughters. Others, such as *The Merchant of Venice* and *La Juive*, remain in the repertoire, but the ways in which artists produce them and audiences view them has been fundamentally altered, particularly in a world so alive to the danger of antisemitism. If, as Diana Taylor argues, repertoires create "choreographies of meaning," then any investigation of Jewish American culture in the postbellum period reveals that the dance is still in motion.[93]

93. Taylor, *The Archive and the Repertoire.*

THE ISRAELITE.

A weekly Periodical, devoted to the Religion, History and Literature of the Israelites.

PUBLISHED BY
CHAS. F. SCHMIDT & CO.
OFFICE:
NO. 21, EAST THIRD STREET.

יהי אור
"LET THERE BE LIGHT"

EDITED BY
ISAAC MAYER WISE.
RESIDENCE:
NO. 141, EAST THIRD STREET.

Vol. I. Cincinnati, O., July 28, 5614 A. M., 1854 A. C. No. 3.

ISRAELITE

יהי אור

DEVOTED TO LITERATURE RELIGION HISTORY AND NEWS

BLOCH & CO., PRINTERS, 150 W. FOURTH ST. LET THERE BE LIGHT ISAAC M. WISE, EDITOR AND PROPRIETOR.

VOL. XXII. CINCINNATI, JUNE 26, 1874, 5634 A. M. NO. 26

58439

THE AMERICAN ISRAELITE.

Let there יהי אור be Light.

VOL. XXIII. WHOLE NO. 1041. CINCINNATI, O., JULY 3, 1874. NEW SERIES, VOL. I. NO. 1.

Fig. 50. Masthead of the inaugural issue of *The Israelite*, July 28, 1854 (*top*). Masthead of the June 26, 1874, issue (*middle*). Masthead of *The American Israelite*, July 3, 1874 (*bottom*). (Balch Institute, Philadelphia; YIVO, New York).

THE AMERICAN ISRAELITE AND AMERICAN ISRAELITES IN THE ERA OF CITIZENSHIP

SHARI RABIN

ON JULY 3, 1874, *The Israelite*, Isaac Mayer Wise's twenty-year-old newspaper, appeared under a new masthead: *The American Israelite.* The motto—"Let there be light"—remained the same, although the original Hebrew was more subtly displayed, and the year on the Jewish calendar was no longer included (Fig. 50). Ironically, perhaps, the first two pages were dedicated to a novel about Protestant townsfolk set during the reign of Oliver Cromwell, the Lord Protector who had informally readmitted the Jews to England in the mid-1650s.[1] Entitled "King, 'By the Grace of God.' An Historical Romance," it was originally written in German by Julius Rodenberg, a Jewish writer who would soon become prominent in German letters as the founding editor of the influential *Deutsche Rundschau.*[2] To the left of Rodenberg's story on the front page was a poem about nature written by Max Meyerhardt, a Prussian-born teenager living in Rome, Georgia.[3] These choices, idiosyncratic though they may seem, reflected Wise's middle-brow literary aspirations and his extensive ties, both across the Atlantic and across the recently reunited sectional divide.

Isaac Mayer Wise had immigrated to the United States from Bohemia in 1846. According to his memoir, "I landed in New York with wife and child and two dollars in my pocket."[4] After a tumultuous tenure in Albany, New York, he made his way in 1854 to Cincinnati, a bustling city on the Ohio River, where he served as the rabbi at Bene Yeshurun congregation.[5] Wise was part of a mass migration of German-speaking Jews, many of them young single men who worked as peddlers in the South and West. In places across the country, these Jews had gradually settled down and banded together for mutual support and worship.

1. *The American Israelite*, July 3, 1874, 1 (hereafter, this issue is referred to as *AI*).

2. Paul H. Emden, "Baron Paul Julius de Reuter," *Transactions* (*Jewish Historical Society of England*) 17 (1951–52): 216n3.

3. 1860 U.S. Federal Census, ancestry.com.

4. Isaac Mayer Wise, *Reminiscences*, trans. David Philipson (Cincinnati: Leo Wise and Company, 1901), 13.

5. Sefton D. Temkin, *Isaac Mayer Wise: Shaping American Judaism* (New York: Oxford University Press, 1992).

Whereas in 1820 there were six congregations in the United States serving a few thousand Jews in Eastern port cities, by 1850 there were seventy-five congregations, a national Jewish fraternal order, countless local Hebrew benevolent and other societies, and a Jewish population approaching 150,000, which was scattered throughout an expanding continental empire.[6]

From the beginning, Wise's aspirations went beyond those of the typical congregational rabbi. By the early 1850s, there were two American Jewish periodicals, Philadelphia's *The Occident and American Jewish Advocate*, founded in 1843, and New York's *The Asmonean*, founded in 1849, where Wise cut his editorial teeth.[7] Within three months of arriving in Cincinnati, he founded *The Israelite*, which, he promised, would "declare war against error, superstition, prejudice, ignorance, arrogance, hypocrisy and bigotry, in whatever shape or form they may fall under our notice."[8] It was soon followed by *Die Deborah*, a German-language supplement.[9] With no denominational infrastructure to link American Jews, *The Israelite*, *Die Deborah*, and their competitors became important sites of communal discourse and development. For many, a subscription was their only Jewish affiliation. As one Jew wrote to Wise from Dakota Territory in 1869, "In my solitude the Jewish papers (I read all of them) keep me in connection with the Hebrew community. I read and imagine to be a member of society."[10] This anonymous Jew anticipated and confirmed Benedict Anderson's famous argument that newspapers help to create an "imagined community."[11] Wise's publication was arguably the most important in this regard because it had the farthest reach and lasted the longest. By 1860, it had had more than 5,100 subscribers in 860 locations.[12] Both *The Asmonean* and *The Occident* had ceased publication by 1874, along with a few other short-lived publications, although *The Jewish Messenger* (1857) and *The Jewish Times* (1869) had entered onto the scene.[13]

6. Shari Rabin, *Jews on the Frontier: Religion and Mobility in Nineteenth-Century America* (New York: New York University Press, 2017).

7. Temkin, *Isaac Mayer Wise*, 86.

8. Isaac Mayer Wise, "To the Reader," *Israelite*, July 15, 1854, 4.

9. Temkin, *Isaac Mayer Wise*, 124; Wise, *Reminiscences*, 292.

10. "A Radical Voice," *Israelite*, August 13, 1869.

11. Benedict Anderson, *Imagined Communities: Reflections on the Origin and Spread of Nationalism* (New York: Verso, 1983).

12. Rudolf Glanz, "Where the Jewish Press was Distributed in Pre-Civil War America," *Western States Jewish Historical Quarterly* 5 (October 1972): 1–14.

13. Shari Rabin, "People of the Press: Religious Periodicals and the Creation of American Judaism," in *Religious Periodicals and Publishing in Transnational Contexts: The Press and the Pulpit*, ed. Oliver Scheiding and Anja-Maria Bassimir (Newcastle upon Tyne: Cambridge Scholars Publishing, 2017), 73–90.

By 1900, a list of Jewish periodicals in the *American Jewish Yearbook* would run to twelve pages; those listed were printed in cities across the country, almost half of them in Yiddish, although they varied widely in regularity, longevity, popularity, and quality.[14]

For Wise, *The Israelite* was part of a broader project of coordination among American Jewish communities. His ultimate goal was an institutional "union" that would bring together all American Jews in order to standardize and regularize Judaism across the continent. Toward this end, in the 1850s he organized gatherings of American Jewish leaders, founded a short-lived rabbinical college, and published a prayer book, *Minhag America* (1857). He also encouraged congregations to adopt modernizing religious reforms like choirs, organs, and confirmation ceremonies.[15] In an 1863 editorial, he insisted that "the conceptions of the Ghetto can not stand the benign rays of freedom and the sentiments of a persecuted and oppressed race can not well be harbored by the free and happy citizen ... we want reforms in order to endear and preserve our religion."[16] There was heated conflict over these initiatives within congregations and among rabbis. Wise regularly castigated those who clung to traditionalism as well as more radical reformers like Rabbi David Einhorn of Baltimore, who privileged the immediate implementation of Reform principles above the goal of achieving unity.[17]

After decades in this struggle, the year 1873 proved a momentous one for Wise (Fig. 51). His lay allies succeeded in creating the Union of American Hebrew Congregations (UAHC), the national body that he had long advocated. Professionally, he contemplated leaving Cincinnati for a position in New York, and personally, his wife, Theresa, fell into what would become her final illness.[18] In a May prospectus for the newspaper, he requested that readers solicit new subscribers, pay their postage in advance, and submit payments on time. "We work the whole blessed year, day and night sometimes," he noted, adding that the paper's publishing costs ranged "from $15,000 to $18,000 a year."[19]

14. A. S. Freidus, comp., "A List of Jewish Periodicals Published in the United States," *American Jewish Year Book* 1 (1899–1900): 271–82. See also Jonathan D. Sarna, "The American Jewish Press," in *The Oxford Handbook of Religion and the American News Media*, ed. Diane Winston (New York: Oxford University Press, 2012).

15. Temkin, *Isaac Mayer Wise*; Rabin, *Jews on the Frontier*.

16. Isaac Mayer Wise, "To the Israelites of the West," *Israelite*, August 14, 1863.

17. Temkin, *Isaac Mayer Wise*, 142.

18. *Ibid.*, 251–58, 213–15.

19. "Prospectus of the Twenty-first Volume of Israelite and Deborah," *Israelite*, May 30, 1873, 7. These figures are the equivalent of an estimated $300,000–400,000 in 2020 dollars. "Historical Currency Conversions," https://futureboy.us/fsp/dollar.fsp (accessed March 27, 2020).

Fig. 51. Isaac Mayer Wise, ca. 1870. (Courtesy of The Jacob Rader Marcus Center of the American Jewish Archives, Cincinnati, Ohio).

Concerns about funding the paper surely intensified after September 18, when railroad bonds failed, leading to the bankruptcy of Jay Cooke & Company and the stock market crash known as the Panic of 1873.[20] Wise's biographer, Sefton Temkin, argues that Wise made the decision to change his publication's name "impetuously," given that "the appearance of the first issue in the new guise was delayed and it did not mark a regular break, such as the beginning of a new volume." Yet, he also notes that Wise was turning reflective in the summer of 1874; indeed, the first part of Wise's *Reminiscences* was published in his German-language publication *Die Deborah* on July 3, 1874, the very same day that *The American Israelite* first appeared.[21]

Then in his mid-fifties, Wise may have been going through something like a mid-life crisis. The pulpit offered to him in New York had been given to his rival, the radical reformer David Einhorn, the UAHC had finally been brought into being by others, and his wife's condition continued to deteriorate.[22] His *Reminiscences* were peppered with expressions of disappointment, regret, and defiance. Describing a moment after the Panic of 1857, but plausibly relaying his own feelings in the aftermath of the Panic of 1873, he wrote,

> Life is bitter indeed, if one has to think, read, and write day and night; is scolded and criticized on all sides; is poor as a church-mouse, and has to put up with all possible objectionable conditions, in order to have the pleasure of being permitted to unload one's ideas upon a highly-honored public. And yet I owed it to my friends not to retire from the public arena, nor would I give my enemies the satisfaction. Somehow or other I imagined that Judaism needed my work and my aid; and therefore I could not give up.[23]

In traditional Judaism, those who are sick are given a new name in order to trick the angel of death.[24] Perhaps Wise thought a new name would change his fortune, or at least remind people of his importance and that of the city where he labored. It might have been a gesture to the postwar project of national reunion or a marketing decision intended to recognize a landmark anniversary and lure subscribers in a time of economic hardship. Whatever the immediate cause of the new name, it was an admission that after twenty years of publication, much

20. Richard Schneirov, "Thoughts on Periodizing the Gilded Age: Capital Accumulation, Society, and Politics, 1873–1898," *Journal of the Gilded Age and Progressive Era* 5, no. 3 (2006): 189–224

21. Temkin, *Isaac Mayer Wise*, 266. 22. *Ibid.*, 258.

23. Wise, *Reminiscences*, 347.

24. Dov Noy, "Angel of Death," *Encyclopaedia Judaica*, 2d ed., ed. Michael Berenbaum and Fred Skolnik, vol. 2 (New York: Macmillan Reference USA, 2007), 147–50.

had changed. Wise looked back on *The Israelite*'s two decades of publication as a "brilliant success." His paper had, he argued, "fought the battles of the Lord in this blessed land, for truth, reform, progression, light, and charity."[25] Indeed, *The American Israelite* of 1874 bore signs of the maturation of Wise, his readers, and, almost one hundred years after independence, the United States itself.

This essay takes the inaugural issue of *The American Israelite* as a starting point for an exploration of Isaac Mayer Wise and American Judaism more broadly in the decade after the Civil War. Newspapers have long been used as a source for information about nineteenth-century American Jews. But as communications scholar James W. Carey argues, they not only disseminate information but also facilitate "a symbolic process whereby reality is produced, maintained, repaired and transformed."[26] Newspapers are interactive spaces that reflect and reinforce the shifting and contested contours of communal identity. According to Wise's biographer, "the *Israelite* was much more the auditorium for one man's voice than a forum for the exchange of opinions"; yet it always included the words of others, through corrections, correspondence, and contributions.[27] In any given issue, sermons abut literature abut correspondence abut advertisements, giving us a snapshot view—perhaps not representative, but certainly telling—of American Jewish life and thought in a particular moment. The contents range from scholarly articles to Wise's random musings, like his praise for the Mishnah's prohibition on dogs in Jerusalem because the dog, "except the watch dog in solitary homes, and the shepherd's dog, is the most useless of all quadrupeds."[28] It is impossible to wrest into a single interpretive framework the rich and idiosyncratic content found within a single issue without creating a map that is the same size as the territory. It is possible, however, to identify the central concerns and influences coursing through its pages.

Whatever the nature of his personal motivations, Wise changed the name of his publication at the tail end of what is usually described by American Jewish historians as the "German period," but which is better known to U.S. historians as the "Reconstruction Era," the "Era of Citizenship," and even the "Second

25. Wise, "The American Israelite," *AI*, 4. On Wise's boosterism of Cincinnati, see Jonathan D. Sarna, "'A Sort of Paradise for Hebrews': The Lofty Vision of Cincinnati Jews," in *Ethnic Diversity and Civic Identity: Patterns of Conflict and Cohesion in Cincinnati since 1820*, ed. Henry D. Shapiro and Jonathan D. Sarna (Urbana: University of Illinois Press, 1992), 152–53.

26. James W. Carey, *Communication as Culture: Essays on Media and Society* (1989; repr. New York: Routledge, 1992), 23.

27. Temkin, *Isaac Mayer Wise*, 116.

28. *AI*, 4.

Founding."[29] In the summer of 1874, Wise—along with his contributors, advertisers, and correspondents—continued the long-simmering project of building an American Judaism, albeit under new pressures. As meanings of American citizenship shifted, Jews ascended in class status, and new understandings of the world gained traction, they reconsidered the fundamental building blocks of American Jewish life: identity, organization, and belief. In the pages of *The American Israelite*, leaders and laypeople offered differing visions of what they meant by "American" and by "Jewish," although they united in affirming their compatibility.

Defining American Jewish Citizenship

The challenge for immigrant Jews in the United States was how to maintain Jewish identity once they were surrounded by enthusiastic Protestants and cut off from the communities where they had learned to be Jews. Despite these challenges, and periodic threats to Jewish belonging, American Jews deeply valued the United States, which offered them rights questioned or denied elsewhere in the world. In the years after the Civil War, as historian Heather Cox Richardson has written, "All inhabitants of the nation—men and women; black, white, Indian, and immigrant; North, South, and West—had to reconsider what it meant to be an American."[30] The inaugural *American Israelite* never mentions the Civil War, Reconstruction, or the word "citizenship," and yet these concerns lay just beyond the page. Wise's newspaper helped his readers reconsider what it meant to be American Jews by negotiating between the competing lures of European Jewry and American Christianity.

In the aftermath of the ratification of the Constitution of 1787 and the passing of the Naturalization Act of 1790, European Jews in the United States had been determined without much fanfare to be "free white persons." In their August 1790 address to George Washington, for example, the Jews of Newport, Rhode Island, praised the new nation for "affording to All liberty of conscience, and immunities of citizenship" and the "blessings of civil and religious liberty."[31]

29. Hasia R. Diner has questioned this periodization. See Diner, *Jews of the United States, 1654 to 2000* (Berkeley: University of California Press, 2004); Heather Cox Richardson, "North and West of Reconstruction: Studies in Political Economy," in *Reconstructions: New Perspectives on the Postbellum United States*, ed. Thomas J. Brown (Oxford and New York: Oxford University Press, 2006), 66; Eric Foner, *The Second Founding: How the Civil War and Reconstruction Remade the Constitution* (New York: W. W. Norton, 2019).

30. Richardson, "North and West of Reconstruction," 66.

31. "From the Newport Congregation to the President of the United States, August 17,

In the decades to follow, Jewish immigrants claimed these blessings for themselves, becoming naturalized as U.S. citizens.[32] Many of them came from Germany, which would not grant Jews full citizenship rights until after unification in 1871.[33] Migrants maintained ties to their hometowns through travel, correspondence, and chain migration, and they connected with other Germans in the United States by, for instance, joining German clubs. At the same time, they rapidly learned English, joined American organizations, and became involved in politics.[34]

For his part, Wise argued, "The Jew must be Americanized ... for every German book, every German word reminds him of the old disgrace" of persecution.[35] On an 1850 trip to Washington, D.C., where he met President Zachary Tyler and other notables, "I felt that I was one of the American people, although I had not yet been naturalized, and from that time I said 'we,' 'us' and 'our' quite unconsciously whenever I spoke of American affairs." He remembered thinking that if he had been treated the same way in the Austrian capital, "the newspapers would talk about it for months; all Jewry would be carried away with enthusiasm."[36] And yet there was also a history of limits to Jewish political inclusion in the United States. While the First Amendment protected religious freedom on the federal level, in practice it varied by state and locality, and Christianity exerted a sizeable influence in public life. Throughout the country, the Protestant Bible was taught in public schools, governors offered Christian prayers of thanksgiving, and laws forbade work on Sunday, requiring most Jews to work on the Jewish Sabbath. North Carolina did not eliminate Christian oaths for officeholders until 1868, when a new state constitution was drafted.[37]

During the Civil War, Jews, like their neighbors, had divided largely along

---

1790," in *A Documentary History of the Jews in the United States, 1654–1875*, 3d ed., ed. Morris U. Schappes (New York: Schocken Books, 1971), 79.

32. One archival example from North Carolina in 1857: Seligman Hoffman citizenship document, BANC MSS 2010/558, Magnes Collection of Jewish Art and Life, Bancroft Library, University of California, Berkeley.

33. Werne E. Mosse, "From 'Schutzjuden' to 'Deutsche Staatsbürger Jüdischen Glaubens': The Long and Bumpy Road of Jewish Emancipation in Germany," in *Paths of Emancipation: Jews, States, and Citizenship*, ed. Pierre Birnbaum and Ira Katznelson (Princeton: Princeton University Press, 1995), 59–93.

34. Rabin, *Jews on the Frontier*, 50–52.

35. Wise, *Reminiscences*, 331.

36. *Ibid.*, 139.

37. Morton Borden, *Jews, Turks, and Infidels* (Chapel Hill: University of North Carolina Press, 1984).

sectional lines, enduring injuries and casualties as well as four years of conflict with relatives, friends, and coreligionists.[38] Living in a border city, Wise had been a "Peace Democratic" who advocated for the preservation of the Union, even at the cost of perpetuating Southern slavery.[39] In 1854 he had claimed that *The Israelite* "is a religious paper, but not a sectarian or sectional one," and at the outbreak of the Civil War he declared in an editorial, "Silence [is] Our Policy."[40] He did speak up, however, in the face of wartime antisemitism. In response to General Ulysses S. Grant's General Orders Number 11, which expelled "the Jews, as a class" from the area under his command, Wise protested, "Israelites, citizens of the United States, you have been outraged, your rights as men and citizens trampled into the dust, your honor disgraced, as a class you have officially been degraded!"[41] Even at a moment of peak exclusion, Wise confidently invoked the power of Jewish citizenship.

Following the Civil War, the contours of American citizenship dramatically shifted. A series of landmark constitutional amendments abolished slavery and extended political rights to African Americans, in the process defining as American citizens "all persons born or naturalized in the United States."[42] Yet, even as new pathways to legal U.S. citizenship were established, many asserted narrower, more exclusionary visions of political belonging. Women continued to be excluded from suffrage, despite renewed efforts to obtain it. It was made clear to African Americans as well as to Native Americans, Mormons, and Chinese immigrants in the West that there were prerequisites for full inclusion in the polity, namely, "uplift" or "civilization" through commitment to individualism, capitalism, the monogamous family, and secular rule.[43] The U.S. Army occupied

38. Jonathan D. Sarna and Adam Mendelsohn, *Jews and the Civil War: A Reader* (New York: New York University Press, 2010).

39. Bertram W. Korn, "Isaac Mayer Wise on the Civil War," *Hebrew Union College Annual* 20 (1947): 635–38.

40. Isaac Mayer Wise, "To the Reader," *Israelite*, July 15, 1854, 4; "Silence Our Policy," *Israelite*, April 19, 1861, 334.

41. Isaac Mayer Wise, "The Outrages in Major-General Rosencrans' Army," *Israelite*, January 2, 1863, 202.

42. Martha S. Jones, *Birthright Citizens: A History of Race and Rights in Antebellum America* (New York: Cambridge University Press, 2018).

43. Faye E. Dudden, *Fighting Chance: The Struggle over Woman Suffrage and Black Suffrage in Reconstruction America* (New York: Oxford University Press, 2011); Christopher M. Span, *From Cotton Field to Schoolhouse: African American Education in Mississippi, 1862–1875* (Chapel Hill: University of North Carolina Press, 2012); Jennifer Graber, *The Gods of Indian Country: Religion and the Struggle for the American West* (New York: Oxford University Press, 2017); Sarah

the South in order to guarantee black political rights, but racial egalitarianism increasingly took a backseat to the project of "reunion" between Northern and Southern whites. Some commentators argued that a diverse and fractured nation could best be brought together through the embrace of a common Christian identity.[44] The National Reform Association, for instance, expanded its efforts to add an amendment to the Constitution "recogniz[ing] God as the source of all power, Jesus Christ as the chief ruler, and the Bible as the supreme ruler of all national conduct."[45] In this vision, political belonging would be limited not only by race or gender but also by religion.

Wise and his Jewish readers were part of these conversations, coupling ardent nationalism with a principled resistance to any whiff of Christianization. In the early 1870s, he supported a national petition to Congress to drop the proposed "Christian Nation" amendment, and he was involved in the so-called Cincinnati Bible Wars of 1869–1872, which sought to eliminate vestiges of Protestantism from the public schools.[46] Beyond this kind of political activism, Wise worked in more subtle ways to present Judaism as an American religion. Toward this end, *The American Israelite* regularly demonstrated a kind of genteel ecumenism. A letter describing "Notes and Gossip" from New York mentioned the expansion of the liberal Christian paper *The Golden Age* and the publication of *Tempest Tossed: A Romance*, written by that paper's founder, Theodore Tilton.[47] Tilton was an assistant to Henry Ward Beecher, a celebrity preacher and social reformer

---

Barringer Gordon, *The Mormon Question: Polygamy and Constitutional Conflict in Nineteenth-Century America* (Chapel Hill: University of North Carolina Press, 2002), 111; Joshua Paddison, *American Heathens: Religion, Race, and Reconstruction in California* (Berkeley: University of California Press, 2012), 5; Derek Chang, *Citizens of a Christian Nation: Evangelical Missions and the Problem of Race in the Nineteenth Century* (Philadelphia: University of Pennsylvania Press, 2010); Cathleen D. Cahill, *Federal Fathers and Mothers: A Social History of the United States Indian Service, 1869–1933* (Chapel Hill: University of North Carolina Press, 2011), 2.

44. Edward J. Blum has argued that "religious revivals, benevolence, common suffering, and religious reform provided many of the needed opportunities for northern whites to imagine former Confederates as equal partners in the nation and to treat them as such." Blum, *Reforging the White Republic: Race, Religion, and American Nationalism, 1865–1898* (Baton Rouge: Louisiana State University Press, 2005), 15. See also David Blight, *Race and Reunion: The Civil War in American Memory* (Cambridge, Mass.: Harvard University Press, 2001).

45. Tisa Wenger, "The God-in-the-Constitution Controversy: American Secularisms in Historical Perspective," in *Comparative Secularisms in a Global Age*, ed. Linell E. Cady and Elizabeth Shakman Hurd (New York: Palgrave Macmillan, 2010), 86; Temkin, *Isaac Mayer Wise*, 227.

46. Benny Kraut, "Judaism Triumphant: Isaac Mayer Wise on Unitarianism and Liberal Christianity," *AJS Review* 7/8 (1982/83): 190–91.

47. *AI*, 6.

whom Tilton would soon sue for improper conduct with his wife, Elizabeth.[48] Wise, who had published a number of excerpts from Beecher's sermons in the past, regularly engaged with liberal Christians, especially Unitarians, whom he described as "enlightened men of broad principles who on the greatest religious questions of the day fully coincide with us."[49] He lectured in churches and even served as a vice president of the Free Religious Association, a group founded in 1867 by elite radical Unitarians that advocated religious liberty and universalism.[50]

At the same time, Wise insisted on the need to maintain the integrity of Judaism as a distinct religious community. Wise was a longstanding critic of Christian theology; one historian likens his published editorials and sermons on Judaism to "'pep-talks' to the faithful to keep the faith."[51] In first issue of *The American Israelite*, advertisements appeared for two of Wise's books, *Judaism, Its Doctrines and Duties* and *The Martyrdom of Jesus of Nazareth*, which promised to answer the "questions every Israelite in this country is frequently asked," namely, "Why are you a Jew? What do the Jews believe? Why are you no Christian? What do the Jews think of Jesus? Did the Jew crucify Jesus?" Another ad offered *The Deicides: Analysis of the Life of Jesus, and of the Several Phases of the Christian Church in Their Relation to Judaism*, authored by Joseph Cohen, translated by Anna Maria Goldsmid, and sold by *The Jewish Messenger* of New York.[52] Both Wise and Cohen were taking part in a broader project in the nineteenth century of reinterpreting Jesus as a Jewish figure. They asserted Jewish claims over Christian origins, but also worked to gird Jewish readers against Christian influence.[53]

Wise encouraged his readers to consider not only their Christian neighbors

48. Debby Applegate, *The Most Famous Man in America: The Biography of Henry Ward Beecher* (New York: Doubleday, 2006).

49. For instance, "Henry Ward Beecher's Heaven," *Israelite*, October 14, 1870, 7; "Keokuk Iowa," *Israelite*, August 13, 1869, 6.

50. Kraut, "Judaism Triumphant," 191. By 1874, Wise had become frustrated with the efforts of members of this group, which he saw as still committed to Christianity and the erasure of Judaism. According to Kraut, "he began to acknowledge that the ties liberal Christians had to their Christian past were no less deep than his own to Judaism, and, of necessity, would separate liberal Christians from Jews and Judaism for the immediate and foreseeable future" (206).

51. *Ibid.*, 184.

52. Advertisements, *AI*, 7.

53. Stephen Prothero, *American Jesus: How the Son of God Became a National Icon* (New York: Farrar, Straus and Giroux, 2004), 229–66; Susannah Heschel, *Abraham Geiger and the Jewish Jesus* (Chicago: University of Chicago Press, 1998).

but also their coreligionists across the Atlantic. In the inaugural *American Israelite*, he argued that the new name was appropriate for "the organ of American Israel." Furthermore, it distinguished his newspaper from all the others named *The Israelite* "in Mainz, Lemberg, Australia and elsewhere."[54] He thus indicated that "American Israel" was its own entity even as he placed it within a trans-Atlantic Jewish republic of letters. Wise celebrated the United States as a setting for Judaism, writing that he never cared about "what the European press might say or not say concerning us" and that "American Hebrew congregations stand higher in the scale of reform and progress than the[ir] European sisters."[55] His regular reports on Jews' status in Europe helped draw further distinctions between the Old World and the New. He included reports of a bill in the National Assembly at Versailles that "appears not to be more favorable to the Jews and Protestants than the old law" and of a recent honor granted to a Jewish physician by the Duke of Saxe-Coburg-Gotha.[56]

At the same time, Wise wrote that he "had no intention to separate the American Israel from the whole house of Israel," and in many ways he cultivated transnational Jewish ties, whether to bolster religious commitments or appeal to his immigrant readership. He regularly published articles translated from German, listed contributors from Vienna and Frankfurt, and accepted an advertisement for the consulate of the German empire.[57] Wise wished a pleasant journey to a friend, Tobias Cohn, who was returning to his native Hungary for the first time since emigrating.[58] Readers learned that Chief Rabbi Nathan Adler of England had recently completed a continental tour, and there was a report from the *Levant Herald* of a famine in Lebanon, although "it seems not to have affected the Jews as much as it did their neighbors of other creeds."[59] The renowned philanthropist Sir Moses Montefiore, at age ninety, was allegedly considering journeying to Damascus to help. Adler and Montefiore were both staples of the American Jewish press, celebrated as heroes because of their public acclaim and commitments to Jewish affairs.[60]

In advertisements for functionaries, congregations identified themselves in a number of ways: two described themselves as followers of Wise's *Minhag America*; one called itself "the German congregation"; and at Beth Elohim in Charleston,

54. Isaac Mayer Wise, "The American Israelite," *AI*, 4.

55. *Ibid.*

56. *AI*, 2.

57. *AI*, 1, 4, 6, 8. In his *Reminiscences*, Wise took credit for having brought German Jewish writers to American attention through his newspaper (224).

58. "Local and Domestic," *AI*, 6.

59. *AI*, 2.

60. Adam Mendelsohn, "Tongue Ties: The Emergence of the Anglophone Jewish Diaspora in the Mid-Nineteenth Century," *American Jewish History* 93, no. 2 (2007): 188–90.

"the service is conducted in the Portuguese Minhag."[61] Even with these distinctions on the ground, the project of elaborating an American Judaism took on new importance at a time when understandings of citizenship and political belonging were rapidly shifting. In *The American Israelite*, Wise made the case for the compatibility of Judaism and American citizenship through his engagement—both actual and imaginative—with American Christians and European Jews. He offered tools for refuting Christian theology and maintaining transnational religious community while at the same time arguing that the United States was unique and placing Judaism within its liberal religious firmament. And yet, the assertion that there was an American Judaism did not make clear how best to implement or understand it. These details would be worked out in *The American Israelite* by Wise and his readers as they responded to shifting contexts of Jewish class status and religious knowledge.

Organizing Middle-Class Jews

The pages of *The American Israelite* not only advocate for an American Judaism but also show where and how it was being enacted. Wise continually endorsed the newly founded Union of American Hebrew Congregations, arguing that Judaism would be truly "American" when it was united in a national institution. For most of his correspondents, however, American Judaism was already being constructed in local communities. By the 1870s, there were an estimated 200,000–300,000 Jews in the United States, many of whom had achieved some level of economic security, weathering the war years and their aftermath through the support of Jewish networks of trade and credit.[62] For instance, Jews found profitable niches in the garment and cotton industries, which, Michael R. Cohen argues, created a "golden age" of prosperity in the decades after the Civil War, as increasing numbers of Jews entered the new middle class.[63] These Jews

61. Advertisements, *AI*, 3.

62. Jonathan D. Sarna, *American Judaism: A History* (New Haven: Yale University Press, 2004), 354.

63. Adam D. Mendelsohn, *The Rag Race: How Jews Sewed Their Way to Success in America and the British Empire* (New York: New York University Press, 2014); Michael R. Cohen, *Cotton Capitalists: American Jewish Entrepreneurship in the Reconstruction Era* (New York: New York University Press, 2017); Richard L. Bushman, *The Refinement of America: Persons, Houses, Cities* (New York: Vintage Books, 1993); Linda Young, *Middle-Class Culture in the Nineteenth Century: America, Australia, and Britain* (New York: Palgrave MacMillan, 2003); Burton J. Bledstein and Robert D. Johnston, eds., *The Middling Sorts: Explorations in the History of the American Middle Class* (New York: Routledge, 2001); Stuart M. Blumin, *The Emergence of the Middle Class: Social Experience in the American City, 1760–1900* (New York: Cambridge University Press, 1989).

patronized 250 congregations and countless Jewish societies, charities, and fraternal lodges across the country.[64] Even as *The American Israelite* communicated Wise's national vision, it also showed clearly how middle-class respectability—enacted through consumerism, philanthropy, and the nuclear family—was reshaping Judaism on the ground.

Throughout the antebellum period, Wise and other Jewish leaders had attempted to create a "union" of American Jews. As Wise described it in his *Reminiscences*, "the pet project which was continually in my thoughts was the union of the congregations of America by firm and harmonious cooperation ... to found and direct useful institutions."[65] Wise's colleague and competitor Isaac Leeser had first raised the idea in 1841, two years before he founded *The Occident* and five years before Wise stepped foot on U.S. soil. After a false start in 1848, Wise made his first real attempt at creating a union at a meeting of squabbling rabbinic leaders in Cleveland in 1855. Four years later, the Board of Delegates of American Israelites was founded, with Leeser among its leaders, although its already limited scope was further inhibited by the outbreak of war. Leeser died in 1868, leaving the organizational field to Wise and his allies. In February 1873, Henry Adler informed Wise that he wanted to donate $10,000 for the founding of a rabbinical college, an offer that encouraged a group of Cincinnati laymen to organize the first official conference in Cincinnati in July of that year.[66]

The Civil War, as historians have noted, facilitated the consolidation and centralization of American state power.[67] This development likely added encouragement to longstanding arguments for a Jewish union. Indeed, when Wise reported in *Die Deborah* in June 1871 that the first congregation had committed to joining what would become the UAHC, he concluded his report by echoing the motto of the United States: *E Pluribus Unum*.[68] Wise was so committed to the cause of the new organization that he declared, "Whenever the Union of American Hebrew Congregations shall have become a universal fact and the Hebrew

64. Leon Jick, *Americanization of the Synagogue* (Hanover, N.H.: University Press of New England, 1976), 57.

65. Wise, *Reminiscences*, 307.

66. Steven A. Fox, "On the Road to Unity: The Union of American Hebrew Congregations and American Jewry, 1873–1903," *American Jewish Archives Journal* 32, no. 2 (1980): 145–93; Joseph Buchler, "The Struggle for Unity: Attempts at Union in American Jewish Life, 1654–1868," *American Jewish Archives Journal* 2, no. 1 (1949): 21–46; Rabin, *Jews on the Frontier*, 112–17; Temkin, *Isaac Mayer Wise*, 251.

67. Drew Gilpin Faust, *This Republic of Suffering: Death and the American Civil War* (New York: Random House, 2008).

68. Temkin, *Isaac Mayer Wise*, 246.

College be in full blast, the editor will consider his task performed, and might just as well retire from the periodical press."[69]

The Union and the newspaper went hand in hand. Envisioned as a body for all American Jews, the UAHC's membership had risen to fifty-two congregations by 1874, almost double the twenty-seven that had joined at the first meeting.[70] At the upcoming conference in Cleveland, just ten days off, Wise advised, "Matters will come before the Council of interest not only to every congregation, but to every Israelite who desires that his faith be perpetuated." The crowd there was expected to be "very large," Wise wrote, adding, "It is not too late yet for the others to come in in time to be represented." Congregations from Lafayette and Fort Wayne, Indiana, and St. Louis, Missouri, had recently joined, and representatives were attending from Shreveport, Louisiana, and Pittsburgh, Pennsylvania.[71] He emphasized the Union's ability to bring together Jews from across the country, including from both North and South. In reality, however, the UAHC was overwhelmingly western in its makeup, reflecting longstanding regional tensions among American Jewish leaders, and it never received universal support.[72]

Even within the pages of *The American Israelite*, it was clear that Judaism was being profoundly shaped by local communities enacting new class standards. Most of Wise's readers had arrived in the United States in the antebellum period as young single men with few resources. Many of them took up peddling, which was seen as a suspect occupation because of its transience, and they lived in boardinghouses, which were denigrated because they seemed to threaten the nuclear family and the private home.[73] Some Jewish migrants had faced serious economic hardship. In 1851 Isidor Bush, who was trying to succeed in the Judaica business, wrote of his "struggle [as] a beginner who is fighting for his mere existence, as well as my insufficient speaking and writing knowledge of the

69. Isaac Mayer Wise, "The American Israelite," *AI*, 4.

70. Temkin, *Isaac Mayer Wise*, 262; Fox, "On the Road to Unity," 150.

71. "To the Hebrew Congregations of the United States," *AI*, 4; "Local and Domestic," *AI*, 6.

72. Fox, "On the Road to Unity," 152.

73. Hasia R. Diner, *Roads Taken: The Great Jewish Migrations to the New World and the Peddlers Who Forged the Way* (New Haven: Yale University Press, 2015); Rowena Olegario, "'That Mysterious People': Jewish Merchants, Transparency, and Community in Mid-Nineteenth Century America," *Business History Review* 73, no. 2 (1999): 161–89; Shari Rabin, "You are Where You Live: Jews, Religion, and the New York Boardinghouse," December 22, 2015, The Gotham Center for New York History, http://www.gothamcenter.org/blog/you-are-where-you-live-jews-religion-and-the-new-york-boardinghouse; Wendy Gamber, *The Boardinghouse in Nineteenth-Century America* (Baltimore: Johns Hopkins University Press, 2007).

English language."[74] In most Jewish communities, benevolent societies were among the first Jewish institutions created, in large part because of the need to care for an emergent class of "friendless," impoverished Jews.[75] Congregations varied membership dues by economic and marital status, while acknowledging that some members would be unable to pay at all.[76]

In the postwar years the U.S. economy was transformed by free labor and fossil fuels.[77] This new economy ossified antebellum class distinctions, creating a politicized working class, an elite of fabulously wealthy industrialists, and a new middle class. An article in *Scribner's* described a tripartite division of New Yorkers; the middle encompassed "a broader and more numerous class, ... embracing the well-to-do, from those who may live handsomely with economy, down to those whose income does not exceed twenty-five hundred to three thousand a year."[78] Whether or not they saw themselves as a distinct "class," a growing population of nonmanual laborers was paid in salaries rather than wages and lived in suburban areas. Between 1870 and 1880 the number of clerks and copyists in the United States more than quadrupled, and new home construction in the so-called streetcar suburbs exploded.[79] These patterns resulted in distinct, if inchoate, "life-styles, outlooks, and aspirations."[80] By 1874, many of the Jews who had started out as single peddlers had learned English, settled down, and become merchants or wholesalers.[81] While shaped by the postbellum U.S. context, the rise of the middle class was a transnational development, and American Jews—like their counterparts back in Germany—embraced middle-class domesticity, leisure, and the values of "law, order, and respectability," ideals that fit nicely with German Jewish notions of *bildung*, or self-cultivation.[82]

74. Isidor Bush to Isaac Leeser, Isaac Leeser Papers (MS-197), box 1, folder 1, Jacob Rader Marcus Center of the American Jewish Archives, Cincinnati, Ohio.

75. "Charitable Institutions," *Occident* 5 (December 1847): 1; Rabin, *Jews on the Frontier*, 32.

76. Rabin, *Jews on the Frontier*, 45.

77. Rebecca Edwards, *New Spirits: Americans in the Gilded Age* (New York: Oxford University Press, 2010), 19, 39.

78. James Richardson, "The New Homes of New York: A Study of Flats," *Scribner's Monthly* 8 (May 1874): 70.

79. Blumin, *Emergence of the Middle Class*, 267.

80. *Ibid.*, 3. See also Bushman, *Refinement of America; Young, Middle-Class Culture in the Nineteenth Century*; Bledstein and Johnston, eds., *The Middling Sorts*; Robert Wuthnow, *American Misfits and the Making of Middle-Class Respectability* (Princeton: Princeton University Press, 2017).

81. Mendelsohn, *Rag Race*; Cohen, *Cotton Capitalists*.

82. Eric Foner, *Reconstruction: America's Unfinished Revolution, 1863–1877*, rev. ed. (New York: Harper Collins, 2011), 521; Marion Kaplan, *The Making of the Jewish Middle Class: Women, Family, and Identity in Imperial Germany* (New York: Oxford University Press, 1991).

Two important vehicles of middle-class identity in both Europe and the United States were construction and consumption. American Jews erected beautiful new synagogues across the country, including Plum Street Temple in Cincinnati, built in 1866 in a majestic, Moorish style by Wise's congregation.[83] According to the U.S. census of religious bodies, the value of synagogue buildings increased from $1.1 million in 1860 to more than $5 million in 1870.[84] Jews increasingly became participants in the emergent consumer culture, as is made clear in the advertising section of *The American Israelite*.[85] Whereas there had been one page of advertisements for furniture, modest hotels, a printing company, and Jewish books in the first issue of *The Israelite* in 1854, now there were three pages of advertisements, offering up luxuries ranging from marble works to pianos to cigars.[86] To be sure, middle-class status was not universal. There continued to be listings of "Jewish Boarding-Houses" in urban centers and entry-level job openings; for instance, a proprietor in Wabash, Indiana, was looking for "a Jewish lady, to make herself generally useful in Millinery and Fancy Goods Store." And yet, on the same page, readers read of railroad lines that could transport them for business or leisure, as well as of hotels like The Pleasant Home, run by Mrs. F. Rich in the spa town of Saratoga Springs, that promised readers "first-class board and lodging."[87]

Most advertisements anticipated that readers had expendable income, leisure time, and families. Middle-class culture valorized the private nuclear family, which was understood to be shaped by affection and dedicated to the nurture

83. Sarna, *American Judaism*, 124–25. In the European context, see Saskia Coenen Snyder, *Building a Public Judaism: Synagogues and Jewish Identity in Nineteenth-Century Europe* (Cambridge, Mass.: Harvard University Press, 2013). On U.S. church construction, see Jeanne Kilde, *When Church Became Theatre: The Transformation of Evangelical Architecture and Worship in Nineteenth-Century America* (New York: Oxford University Press, 2002).

84. Jick, *Americanization of the Synagogue*, 179.

85. On consumer culture, see William Leach, *Land of Desire: Merchants, Power, and the Rise of a New American Culture* (New York: Vintage Books, 1994); T. J. Jackson Lears, *Fables of Abundance: A Cultural History of Advertising in America* (New York: Basic Books, 2004); Neil Harris, *Cultural Excursions: Marketing Appetites and Cultural Tastes in Modern America* (Chicago: University of Chicago Press, 1990); Leigh E. Schmidt, *Consumer Rites: The Buying and Selling of American Holidays* (Princeton: Princeton University Press, 1995). On gender and consumption, see Mary Louise Roberts, "Gender, Consumption, and Commodity Culture," *American Historical Review* 103, no. 3 (1998): 817–44; Riv-Ellen Prell, "The Economic Turn in American Jewish History: When Women (Mostly) Disappeared," *American Jewish History* 103, no. 4 (2019): 485–512. On European Jews, see Gideon Reuveni, *Consumer Culture and the Making of Modern Jewish Culture* (New York: Cambridge University Press, 2017).

86. *Israelite*, July 15, 1854, 8.

87. Advertisements, *AI*, 3, 7, 8.

of children.[88] Readers of *The American Israelite* were encouraged to purchase "children's carriages and boys' velocipedes," which reflected what one historian has described as "the growing [middle-class] belief … that recreation was a good way to build ties between parents and children."[89] They were also urged to "secure all of the benefits of a Life policy in case of death." Six different life insurance companies ran advertisements; one firm used an illustration of a Revolutionary soldier, presenting insurance as a patriotic necessity (Fig. 52).[90] The life insurance business had begun in earnest in the United States in the 1840s and, despite concerns about its morality, had expanded considerably by the early 1870s. Its presence in *The American Israelite* is an indication both of the need to manage uncertainty in an increasingly complex economy and of the new middle-class status of many American Jews.[91] Occupations were seldom mentioned outside of the advertisements, but Wise nevertheless gave a sense of his aspirations for the community when he described his friend Tobias Cohn as "a manufacturer and gentleman of many merits."[92] If not all Jews were middle class, *The American Israelite* gave the impression that most were or soon would be.

Another sign of this expectation was a letter from New York that tracked the presence of Jews in recent college commencement ceremonies.[93] At the College of the City of New York, or "the Free College"—later to attain renown for its education of the children of eastern European Jewish immigrants—a "young co-religionist, Mr. Samson Lachman, carried off the largest share of the honors."[94] The correspondent listed six other Jewish students at that institution, four Jewish award winners at Columbia, and Abram S. Isaacs, who earned a master's degree at New York University.[95] Elsewhere in *The American Israelite*,

88. Stephanie Coontz, *The Social Origins of Private Life: A History of American Families, 1600–1900* (New York: Verso, 1988); Steven Mintz, "Foreword," in *Children and Youth During the Civil War*, ed. James Marten (New York: New York University Press, 2012), ix–xii; Blumin, *Emergence of the Middle Class*, 187; James Marten, "Bringing Up Yankees: The Civil War and the Moral Education of Middle-Class Children," in *The Middling Sorts*, ed. Bledstein and Johnston, 86–100.

89. Gary S. Cross, *Kids' Stuff: Toys and the Changing World of American Childhood* (Cambridge, Mass.: Harvard University Press, 1997), 23.

90. Advertisements, *AI*, 7.

91. Viviana A. Rotman Zelizer, *Morals and Markets: The Development of Life Insurance in the United States* (New York: Columbia University Press, 1979).

92. *AI*, 6.

93. Among the "specific strategies for securing the family's foothold in the developing middle class" was extended schooling. Blumin, *Emergence of the Middle Class*, 187–88.

94. Sherry Gorelick, *City College and the Jewish Poor: Education in New York, 1880–1924* (New Brunswick: Rutgers University Press, 1981).

95. "New York Letter," *AI*, 6.

Fig. 52. Advertisement from *The American Israelite*, June 3, 1874, p. 7.

advertisements for "Educational Institutes" in New York invoked middle-class values of the sentimental family and higher education. S. H. Kleinfeld offered "thorough instruction with parental care," and the Reverend Dr. M. Mielziner promised to prepare pupils "for commercial pursuits as for college."[96] Higher education was expanding in this period, and antebellum Jewish immigrants now had native-born children, for whom attending college was a clear path to elevated social standing.[97]

96. Advertisements, *AI*, 8.
97. John R. Thelin, *A History of American Higher Education* (Baltimore: Johns Hopkins University Press, 2004).

One New York correspondent, who signed as "Phil Point," argued that Jewish collegiate success reflected not only on the individuals themselves but also on the American Jewish community. But while he lauded "our young men [for] thus bravely maintaining the reputation of the race," he critiqued Jewish women. "[T]he daughters in Israel do not seem to cherish any desire for the best education," he wrote, noting the lack of Jews among the graduates of Vassar College. There were educational options for Jewish women—Mrs. H. Simons of Chicago advertised a "Day and Boarding School for young ladies of the Hebrew faith"—and increasing numbers of them were attending college, but they still represented under one-quarter of all new college graduates in this period.[98] That there were no Jewish graduates from Vassar was a measure less of Jewish women's own desire for education than of the limits placed on them by family and society, if not by Vassar itself.[99] Indeed, Jonathan Sarna has found that growing numbers of Cincinnati Jewish women were attending college in this period.[100] "Phil Point"'s public chiding can be seen as an indication of—and possibly an impetus for—broadening expectations of American Jewish women.

Overall, however, women's activities appeared to be limited to music and literature, the ballroom, and the family home. The same correspondent from New York wrote about Emma Lazarus, whose new volume of poetry was forthcoming, but described her in patronizing terms as a "talented authoress" of "dainty verse." He also noted "young ladies fond of dance-music," who could be expected to purchase a newly composed waltz.[101] Women appeared as brides in marriage notices and in the titles of advertised novels like Herman M. Moos's *Hannah, or, A Glimpse of Paradise* and its sequel, *Carrie Harrington*, which used female protagonists to "dispel some prejudices … [and] raise the claims of Israel to a partial acknowledgment of its deserts."[102] In a note about the disappearance

98. Edwards, *New Spirits*, 118.

99. Melissa R. Klapper, *Jewish Girls Coming of Age in America, 1860–1920* (New York: New York University Press, 2007), 97–98.

100. Sarna, "'A Sort of Paradise for Hebrews,'" 22–23.

101. "New York Letter," *AI*, 6.

102. "Betrothals," *AI*, 6; advertisement, *AI*, 7. Herman M. Moos, *Hannah, or A Glimpse of Paradise* (Cincinnati: Literary Eclectic Publishing House, 1868), 4. On Jewish female characters in Christian-authored literature of the nineteenth century, see Regine Rosenthal, "Inventing the Other: Ambivalent Constructions of the Wandering Jew/ess in Nineteenth-Century American Literature," in *Representations of Jews Through the Ages*, ed. Leonard Jay Greenspoon and Bryan F. Le Beau (Omaha, Neb.: Creighton University Press, 1996). On middle-class women and literature in the nineteenth century, see Ann Douglas, *The Feminization of American Culture* (New York: Farrar, Straus, and Giroux, 1998).

of Moritz Pfeffer, a "well-to-do" Jewish husband and father in Philadelphia, readers were encouraged to imagine "the anguish of a loving wife seeing her husband departing from home to attend his daily business in the city, and not having returned after three days."[103] Even in its reporting on a potential tragedy, *The American Israelite* cultivated gendered middle-class behavior and affect.

Jewish religion was also represented as an aspect of middle-class consumption. The same advertising pages that promoted cigars and velocipedes featured a growing market of Jewish goods and services tailored for a refined American clientele. One of the men advertising his services as a ritual circumcisor—Simon Gerstmann of Meridian, Mississippi—included an endorsement from four medical doctors, who lauded his "skillful, rapid manner, with apparently no pain to the child."[104] There was also a growing cadre of Jewish musical entrepreneurs seeking "idiomatic improvements of music in the public ritual."[105] Cantor A. Kaiser of Baltimore sold a setting of Psalm 29 for choir and organ, and a group of music professionals offered the second volume of *Zimrath Yah*, an ambitious compendium of liturgical music.[102] This text was designed to be inclusive and flexible, and came with arrangements for choir and organ. Its creators described their goal as "contributing toward maintaining the elevated character of our service ... [and] propagating our peculiar sacred music on the American soil."[107]

This attention to sacred music was in keeping with local congregational trends, as evidenced by the six advertisements for congregational *hazanim*. For instance, the ad for Beth Elohim in Charleston noted that their "mode of reading could be acquired here in a short time" but that candidates must be comfortable "with an organ and choir." There was some variability, to be sure. The congregation in Petersburg, Virginia, wanted someone with the ability to slaughter kosher meat—"a Chasan [and] Schochet"—while Adath Israel in Boston explicitly described its service as "Reform." And yet, almost all of the congregations expressed a desire for leaders with professional skills like teaching, lecturing, and choir leading. Beth Elohim's notice began with its "desire to secure the services

103. *AI*, 6.

104. Advertisements, *AI*, 7. On medical authority in the nineteenth century, see Carroll Smith-Rosenberg, *Disorderly Conduct: Visions of Gender in Victorian America* (New York: Knopf, 1985).

105. Judah M. Cohen, *Jewish Religious Music in Nineteenth-Century America: Restoring the Synagogue Soundtrack* (Bloomington: Indiana University Press, 2019), 188.

106. Advertisements, *AI*, 7, 3.

107. Cohen, *Jewish Religious Music*, 198–200.

of a competent minister, who is also capable of delivering English lectures."[108] Local congregations with diverse religious priorities were all in search of religious leaders who could teach children and present a respectable public face for local Jews.

As the name of the UAHC indicated, Wise was a champion of congregations as vehicles of Jewish life, but *The American Israelite* also attested to flourishing alternatives, often organized along gendered lines and toward charitable ends. Fraternal lodges, gendered benevolent societies, and charitable institutions alike dated to the antebellum period; they offered mutual aid and financial support that promised to keep Jews from falling victim to Christian missionaries or acquiring a bad reputation.[109] In the years after the Civil War, these endeavors expanded. Among the associations whose resolutions were published in *The American Israelite*—for a fee—were two lodges of the Independent Order of B'nai B'rith, the Hebrew Ladies' Benevolent Society of Kansas City, and the orphan asylums in Louisville and Cleveland.[110] All offered forms of gendered Jewish solidarity that also demonstrated middle-class respectability. Jewish men had a site of sociability apart from the feminized synagogue, Jewish women had an acceptable means of public activism, and the community as a whole showed its moral rectitude in providing for impoverished children.[111]

American Jewish charitable endeavors not only expanded but also took new forms, like the newly founded Hebrew Female Orphans' Dowry Society of New York, which was mentioned in the "New York Letter": "It is to be composed of seventy trustees, and every minister acceptable to the Board of Directors, every president of a Jewish congregation in New York and of the Orphan Asylum are honorary trustees. The dowry is to be paid to deserving applicants only after diligent investigation by the committee appointed for that purpose."[112] This benefit was an extension of longstanding Jewish charity to widows and orphans, transformed in a time of increasing economic inequality and concern about young people. The society was also part of a broader transformation that

108. Advertisements, *AI*, 3. See Shari Rabin, "Working Jews: Hazanim and the Labor of Religion in Nineteenth-Century America," *Religion and American Culture: A Journal of Interpretation* 25, no. 2 (2015): 178–217.

109. "Charitable Institutions," *Occident*, 1; Rabin, *Jews on the Frontier*, 32.

110. Resolutions, *AI*, 6.

111. Karla Goldman, *Beyond the Synagogue Gallery: Finding a Place for Women in American Judaism* (Cambridge, Mass.: Harvard University Press, 2001). On American women's charity, see Elizabeth Alice White, "Charitable Calculations: Fancywork, Charity, and the Culture of the Sentimental Market, 1830–1880," in *The Middling Sorts*, ed. Bledstein and Johnston, 73–85.

112. *AI*, 6.

sought to make charity efficient, institutional, and masculine.[113] Even though it was concerned with the fate of young women, the society was run entirely by men, who sought a city-wide alliance of Jewish leaders. That this description came immediately after "Phil Point" commented on the lack of Jewish students at Vassar and dismissed Emma Lazarus's poetry indicates that young Jewish women were a particular cause of communal anxiety, perhaps anticipating the Jewish male-female antagonism that Riv-Ellen Prell has identified in the early twentieth century: "the nightmare of excessive Americanization and desire projected by professionals and middle-class Jews onto young working-class women."[114] Women were crucial to Jewish continuity, yet also worryingly susceptible to insufficient, improper, or excessive Americanization.

These benevolent organizations not only enabled good work but also publicized it, drawing attention to their members and patrons. Local lodges and societies regularly published the results of their elections. The Orphan Asylum School in Louisville announced that it would soon hold a public examination of its "inmates," followed by a picnic for "friends and patrons of the institution." Individual men—and women—who supported the asylum were acknowledged through the publication of a list of donations. These included $21 from "A friend to the Orphans" in Albany, New York, and $25 from the Hebrew Benevolent Association of Chillicothe, Missouri, but also $20 from B. A. Feineman of Kansas City, $50 from Mrs. Elias Friend of Milwaukee, and more than thirty smaller donations.[115] Attention was also paid to a growing cadre of individual Jewish philanthropists. Charles Kahn Jr., "proving especially liberal on account of his filial love," had donated $3,000 to charity upon the recent death of his mother, including "$500 to the Theological institution, and $1000 to the Orphan Asylum."[116]

These notices burnished the reputations of the individuals involved, pointedly distinguishing them from those in need of charity. They also offered a model to readers of *The American Israelite*, advocating for Jewish benevolence as a marker of American Jewish citizenship in addition to—or potentially instead of—

113. Idana Goldberg, "'Sacrifices Upon the Altar of Charity': The Masculinization of Jewish Philanthropy in Mid-Nineteenth Century America," *Nashim: A Journal of Jewish Women's Studies & Gender Issues*, no. 20 (Fall 2010): 34–56.

114. Riv-Ellen Prell, *Fighting to Become Americans: Assimilation and the Trouble between Jewish Women and Jewish Men* (Boston: Beacon Press, 1999), 24. See also Roberts, "Gender, Consumption, and Commodity Culture," 817–19.

115. "Donations to Orphan Asylum," *AI*, 6.

116. *Ibid.*

congregations or the UAHC. That there were multiple visions of how to enact and preserve American Judaism was made plain by the fact that the UAHC conference in Cleveland conflicted with the anniversary celebration of that city's orphan asylum. Wise sent a representative to the asylum celebration while he attended the conference.[117] Even as Wise's editorials touted his vision of a national union, the paid resolutions, advertisements, and other notices in his newspaper showed that American Jews were prioritizing local organizations and forms of consumption and charity that were gendered, often youth-oriented, and above all middle-class. The newspaper allowed Wise to assert his vision of how to perpetuate American Judaism, but it did not go uncontested.

Elaborating a Rational Judaism

Debates about American Judaism were not limited to the medium but extended to the question of message, as Wise and his contributors offered different conceptions of Jewish belief. By the 1870s, Darwinism and historical criticism of the Bible, both of which had previously been dismissed or ignored, were becoming more widely accepted, raising serious questions about the authority of the Bible. In the face of this challenge, Wise and his contributors sought to defend Judaism's reputation as both authoritative and progressive, a project often conducted through engagement with Jewish history. At the same time, ordinary Jews showed little interest in this debate, instead constructing a lay theology rooted in popular postwar conversations about death and the afterlife. These different approaches coexisted but also competed, as was made particularly clear in debates about what to teach the new generation of American Jews.

Most of the Jews who had immigrated to the United States before the Civil War came from traditional religious backgrounds. As Wise's colleague and competitor Isaac Leeser put it in 1866, "Their education at home may have been religious, such as is met with in the villages of the old country; they probably have learned to read Hebrew, some indeed imperfectly; a few may have been instructed in translating some chapters of the Scriptures and a portion of the prayers and have obtained an insufficient knowledge of the theoretic part of Judaism from catechisms and Bible histories."[118] In the new American setting, leaders like Leeser and Wise were deeply concerned that these Jews would abandon Judaism or convert to Christianity. The evidence indicates that most maintained belief in a providential God, although they may have decoupled this belief from a

117. "Local and Domestic," *AI*, 6; *AI*, 4.

118. "The Season," *Occident* 24 (September 1866): 1–18.

requirement for strict observance of Jewish law.[119] This development was part of a broader trans-Atlantic project of modernizing Judaism, which meant making it compatible with the nation-state, science, and privatized, Protestant-inflected conceptions of "religion." Wise described his ideal as "American Judaism free, progressive, enlightened, united, and respected."[120] This vision led him to reject aspects of traditional Jewish belief, most controversially, the idea of a personal messiah and a bodily resurrection, references to which were altered or eliminated in Wise's 1857 *Minhag America* prayer book.[121] It also meant emphasizing the biblical text over later rabbinic interpretations; indeed, this is one possible explanation for Wise's use of the title "Israelite" for his periodical in the first place.

Jewish theological ideas had already been transformed in the antebellum era, but new challenges would emerge in the 1870s. Charles Darwin's ideas had been circulating on both sides of the Atlantic since the 1859 publication of *On the Origin of Species*, to which most religious leaders responded by questioning its scientific basis.[122] Darwin expanded his theory of evolution to humans in *The Descent of Man* (1871), and by the mid-1870s, his work had been accepted by most members of the scientific community and some religious leaders. Wise and other reformers had spent decades arguing that Jews should both embrace modern culture and place the Bible at the center of Judaism. Now that the historicity of the Genesis creation story was in question, these two projects seemed directly at odds.[123] In January 1874, Rabbi Kaufmann Kohler gave a sermon in Chicago supporting both Darwinism and biblical criticism. In March, Wise's collaborator Solomon Sonneschein published an article in *The Israelite* pointing to the fifteenth-century Jewish philosopher Joseph Albo as a precursor of evolutionary thought. Just a few weeks into *The American Israelite*'s run, on July 31, Wise would publish a pro-evolution sermon written by Jacob Mayer of Cleveland along with his own critical response. Indeed, in the words of historian Marc Swetlitz, Wise was "American Jewry's harshest and most persistent critic of evolutionary theory."[124]

119. Rabin, *Jews on the Frontier*, 90–95.

120. Wise, *Reminiscences*, 317.

121. Zev Eleff, *Who Rules the Synagogue? Religious Authority and the Formation of American Judaism* (New York: Oxford University Press, 2016), 117.

122. Jon Roberts, *Darwinism and the Divine in America: Protestant Intellectuals and Organic Evolution, 1859–1900* (South Bend, Ind.: University of Notre Dame Press, 2001), 84.

123. Naomi W. Cohen, "The Challenges of Darwinism and Biblical Criticism to American Judaism," *Modern Judaism* 4, no. 2 (1984): 121–57.

124. Marc Swetlitz, "American Jewish Responses to Darwin and Evolutionary Theory, 1860–

And yet, in an editorial entitled "The Remains," Wise tried to find a broader middle ground between religion and science. He affirmed that men of science represented "the tendency of our age," but argued that they were too quick to ignore "the religious spirit of the age." Citing a range of European thinkers like "Darwin and Agassiz, Haeckel and Wigand, Schoppenhauer and Hartmann, Venitianer and Volkert, Mill and Spenser," he singled out German philosophers in particular as atheist zealots. According to Wise, "it may be justly said" that the German scientist Ernst Haeckel "forced Darwin to write his unscientific 'Descent of Man.'" He argued that the "facts of science are neither theistical nor atheistical," but admitted that they necessitated a reconsideration of religious tradition. Once science, philosophy, and biblical criticism had been taken into consideration, "Is that which remains in harmony with Judaism, or do we stand charged before the spirit of the age with error and superstition?"[125] His response consisted of twenty-two lectures delivered in Cincinnati and published in *The American Israelite* beginning that fall under the title "Soph Dabar: A Last Word on Philosophical Problems in Popular Lectures."[126]

Wise also exposed his readers to higher criticism of the Bible, which had originated in German universities in the late eighteenth century and produced evidence of multiple human authors. Outside of certain Unitarian circles, these scholarly investigations had largely been met with timidity.[127] Wise reprinted a favorable review of French scholar Ernest Renan's work on the Song of Songs from the *Westminster Review*, an elite English political journal. Renan dated the poem to the tenth century BCE, arguing that it was not written by King Solomon and that it originated in the northern kingdom of Israel as a profane work of drama. In the words of the reviewer, it was actually the "bridal drama of a rude Semitic tribe" rather than the "fantastic and mystical allegory" theologians had understood it to be. Although Renan had close Jewish associates and was seen as friendly to Jews, his writings and the review were typical of biblical criticism's tendency to contrast an idealized ancient Israelite past with Judaism's later denigration.[128] The review spoke of "the happiest age," when

---

1890," in *Disseminating Darwinism: The Role of Place, Race, Religion, and Gender*, ed. Ronald L. Numbers and John Stenhouse (New York: Cambridge University Press, 1999), 216.

125. Isaac Mayer Wise, "The Remains," *AI*, 4

126. The first lecture appeared in *The American Israelite*, October 16, 1874, 4; the last appeared on April 16, 1875, 4.

127. William R. Hutchison, *The Modernist Impulse in American Protestantism* (1976; repr. Durham: Duke University Press, 1992), 76.

128. Robert D. Priest, "Ernest Renan's Race Problem," *Historical Journal* 58, no. 1 (2015): 309–30.

"the Hebrew genius was most free and untrammeled," in contrast to a "wave of misfortune and fanaticism [that] had swept over it, and envelops it with the darkness and littleness of religious monomania."[129] According to this interpretation, Judaism had lost its nobility and wisdom around the time of the Babylonian exile in 586 BCE.

Historian Naomi W. Cohen argues that by the 1890s, Wise was a "veteran opponent of higher criticism," but in 1874 he merely criticized Renan for showing "no originality."[130] In particular, he complained that the *Westminster Review* never mentioned Heinrich Graetz, a leading German Jewish scholar "who deserves probably the principal credit" for Renan's ideas. Graetz, whose work had been published in *The Israelite* before, was one of a number of scholars associated with *Wissenschaft des Judentums*, the scientific study of Judaism, which used the tools of biblical criticism to contest Christian interpretations of Jewish history.[131] Two years earlier, *The Israelite* had published Elias Eppstein's three-part review of Graetz's translation and study of the Song of Songs.[132] Directly addressing Renan's work, Graetz had dated the text to the much later, supposedly backward post-exilic period, and argued that it was not a drama but an ethical allegory about chaste love.[133] By invoking Graetz, then, Wise pointed toward a Jewish critique of Renan, but he also argued for the Jewish origins of cutting-edge modern thought, much as Sonneschein had done when he identified a Jewish precursor for Darwin. Wise inserted Jews into modern science, even if he was ambivalent about the religious consequences.

Despite his unease with specific scientific developments, Wise was invested in an understanding of Judaism as "progressive" and "rational." This stance meant that he argued not only against atheistic science but also against irrational superstition. In his *Reminiscences*, Wise recalled a long-past battle against a kabbalah-expounding Christian minister who had published anonymously in *The Occident* with evangelistic aims. Wise claimed that he had responded from "the rationalistic Maimonidean standpoint," invoking the twelfth-century Spanish-born rabbi-philosopher, and "quoted from the Zohar and other cabalistical

129. "The Song of Solomon—Shir Hashirim," *AI*, 4–5.

130. Cohen, "Challenges of Darwinism and Biblical Criticism," 144.

131. Heinrich Graetz, *The Israelite*, November 21, 1873, 1. See Ran HaCohen, *Reclaiming the Hebrew Bible: German-Jewish Reception of Biblical Criticism* (New York: DeGruyter, 2010).

132. Dr. Eppstein, "Review," *The Israelite*, August 16, 1872, 9.

133. He thus "maintain[ed] that post-exilic Judaism remained an era of literary, ethical, religious, and cultural flourishing." Alexandra Zirkle, "Heinrich Graetz and the Exegetical Contours of Modern Jewish History," *Jewish Quarterly Review* 109, no. 3 (2019): 371.

works, in order to fight mysticism with its own weapons."[134] In the inaugural *American Israelite*, he published the first part of a biographical sketch of the notorious self-proclaimed messiah Shabbatei Zevi, which attacked mysticism because it "twists the words of Scriptures into arguments in favor of its whimsical doctrines."[135]

Written by the reform rabbi Nehemiah Bruell, "Shabbatei Zevi" began by describing medieval Jewish culture and the intellectual advancements of Muslim Spain before attacking the Zohar as "a great danger for Judaism" and Zevi as a man of great intellect who had tricked the "ignorant masses."[136] The article, translated from the German, was a product of European Jewish thought and participated in the rational monotheism and celebration of the "Sephardic mystique" that was so widespread in German Jewish culture of the era.[137] Wise affirmed these arguments, but also added his own perspective in a brief introduction to the piece. He critiqued "[t]hat excrescence of Judaism, mysticism and chasidism, which wields such unbounded sway over some Eastern provinces of Europe," arguing that such ideas "will never gain a foothold in the present stage of civilization" because "science and erudition enjoy, now-a-days, that authority which in former times was claimed by religious jugglery and the vain pomp of priestly attire."[138] Wise distinguished between bad and good forms of Judaism, mapping them respectively onto the past and the future and onto eastern Europe and, it was implied, the United States.

Another article in the same issue attacked an American "superstition," Spiritualism, although it never explicitly named the movement.[139] Spiritualism had its roots in the antebellum period and flourished in the 1870s as part of a broader effort among Americans to cope with the massive loss of life suffered during the Civil War. In this context, Americans increasingly rejected the idea that there was an absolute divide between this world and the next. For instance, *The Gates Ajar*, a novel by Elizabeth Stuart Phelps depicting a sentimental vision of a heavenly afterlife, became a bestseller in 1868. Many Americans experimented with or embraced Spiritualism because it promised the opportunity to speak to deceased loved ones.[140] The article in Wise's newspaper, written "For

134. Wise, *Reminiscences*, 80. 135. "Sabbathai Zevi," *AI*, 6. 136. *Ibid.*

137. Michael A. Meyer, *Response to Modernity: A History of the Reform Movement in Judaism* (Detroit: Wayne State University Press, 1995); Ismar Schorsch, "The Myth of Sephardic Supremacy," *Leo Baeck Institute Year Book* 34 (1989): 47–66.

138. "Sabbathai Zevi," *AI*, 6.

139. "A Speech for School," *AI*, 2.

140. Faust, *A Republic of Suffering*, 171–210; Molly McGarry, *Ghosts of Futures Past: Spiritu-*

the Israelite" by "M.R.M.," lamented that "[m]any of the best educated of our country are now firm believers in immediate communication with the spirits of the dead, and they first had to reject the Bible as an infallible rule before they entered on this belief."[141]

Addressing an imaginary classroom of rural Gentiles, the author encourages the audience both to embrace their individual consciences and to abide by the wisdom of Jewish scriptures, which dictates that "[a]ll consultations with the spirits of the dead were contrary to the law." This argument was embedded within a broader vision of education as a vehicle for human progress. It would, the author argued, improve quality of life and "drive superstitious fears from the neighborhood somewhat as a bright lamp puts darkness out of a room." Whereas the review of Renan invoked the glories of a long-lost Jewish past and raised questions about the Bible, this Jewish author pointed to the Bible as a Jewish source of rational wisdom for a Gentile public and to episodes in English and American history, including the Salem witch trials, as examples of "what it is to be ignorant."[142]

Even if Jewish religious leaders rejected Spiritualism, ordinary Jews—who were coping with the aging of the immigrant generation in addition to wartime losses—expressed considerable interest in the nature of the afterlife. In his poem on the front page of *The American Israelite*, Max Meyerhardt offered a pastoral vision of nature before shifting to an imagination of the afterlife that would have been perfectly familiar to readers of *The Gates Ajar*:

> And as I gaze upon that scene,
> Grave thoughts within me rise
> Of that fair land—the good man's goal—
> That lies beyond the skies.
> The brightest flowers forever bloom
> On that celestial shore,
> Where all is love, and peace, and joy,
> And pain comes nevermore.[143]

A lay theology of death also emerges in three sets of resolutions from local organizations that lamented the deaths of beloved friends. These reports from B'nai B'rith lodges in Indianapolis and Hudson, New York, and from a Hebrew Ladies Benevolent Society in Kansas City formulaically but movingly detail their authors' collective grief, the meritorious characteristics of the deceased,

---

alism and the Cultural Politics of Nineteenth-Century America (Berkeley: University of California Press, 2008).

141. "A Speech for School," *AI*, 2. 142. *Ibid.* 143. "Thoughts," *AI*, 1.

their sympathy for the family, and finally their determination to publish the resolutions. They invoke "the will of God, who wounds and heals, and who is abundant in mercy unto all that depend on his protection." God is "all-wise and merciful," a "Heavenly" and "Almighty Father" who "doeth all things well," providing comfort and enacting "His mysterious providence." Two of these resolutions described death euphemistically as the individual being "removed from our midst."[144] Proximity to death occasioned heart-felt entreaties to the wisdom of the divine in a vague, providential mode that was unconcerned with the Bible or its veracity.

The diversity of approaches to understanding and perpetuating Judaism was also made clear in discussions of education. A layman named Max L. Guttman wrote from Rochester to complain about "the poor opinion of Judaism which our youths are left to infer, because they do not receive sufficient instruction in Jewish history." Such an education, he argued, would be much more effective in "attract[ing] and induc[ing] the growing youth to attend divine service" than the current method of implementing religious reforms. Guttman placed the burden of Jewish education on religious functionaries, who, he wagered, had plenty of free time, since sermons took up only a few hours a week. Calculating that they had 254 days per year of vacation, he concluded, "If these gentlemen would take pains and patience to instruct and inspire, we should have filled synagogues of a growing youth, animated with a glowing veneration for God, their ancestors, and their good and brave teachers."[145] Guttman made Jewish history the engine of Jewish commitment, rather than the Bible.

If Guttman pitted teaching history against religious reforms, Wise warned against congregational schools that emphasized history and catechism at the expense of biblical Hebrew. Wise himself had written Jewish historical fiction and a book entitled *History of the Israelitish Nation, from Abraham to the Present Time.* But when reporting on the annual examination at his congregation's Talmud Yelodim Institute, he declared, "A Sabbath-school in which Hebrew grammar is not the main feature is a failure."[146] He insisted that his students still had plenty of time for other subjects: "In history [the pupils] progressed this year to the destruction of the Second Temple by Titus; in catechism 'Judaism,' etc., to the commandments, including the holidays." At the annual examination, prizes had been given out to one girl and one boy who were best able

144. Resolutions, *AI*, 6.

145. *AI*, 6.

146. Isaac Mayer Wise, *History of the Israelitish Nation, from Abraham to the Present Time* (Albany: J. Munsell, 1854); "Talmid Yelodim Institute," *AI*, 4.

to translate and explain the grammar of five Bible verses on the spot.[147] For Wise, the fundamental element of what should be passed to the next generation was the language that would allow them to read the Bible, which he still saw as the core of an American Judaism that eschewed both atheistical science and superstitious mysticism.

At least one private teacher advertising in *The American Israelite* offered "competent and experienced" instruction in "the Hebrew, German, and French languages," placing Hebrew in the context of cultured language acquisition and private schooling.[148] Indeed, education became an increasingly central locus for working out the central questions of American Judaism: where should it happen and what should it consist of? Here again we seen Wise at odds with his own contributors and advertisers. Wise elevated a vision of a rational, biblical Judaism that combatted Darwinism and higher criticism on the one hand and forms of "superstition," both Jewish and American, on the other. Ironically, however, the real threat may have been from his readers, who were more interested in a Judaism that could accommodate a robust afterlife or engender Jewish pride than in one that could hold its own against scientific advances or Old World mysticism.

Conclusion

In some ways, the 1870s are a postbellum era like others in U.S. history—the 1780s, the 1920s, and the 1950s come to mind.[149] Wars cause rupture: demographic changes, new ideas of citizenship and belonging, new technologies and economic paradigms, and new ways of understanding the nature of existence. Their effects reverberate long after the fighting stops and far beyond individual soldiers. Within Jewish communities, postwar years have demanded broader reconfigurations of the structures and ideas that together constitute American Judaism.

In a new and complicated postwar moment in which U.S. citizenship was expanding legally to include African Americans but contracting rhetorically to white Christian men, the United States and its Jewish congregations were moving to centralization, Jewish immigrants were becoming middle-class

147. "Talmid Yelodim Institute," *AI*, 4.

148. "A Card," *AI*, 6.

149. See William Pencak, *Jews and Gentiles in Early America* (Ann Arbor: University of Michigan Press, 2005); Deborah Dash Moore, *At Home in America: Second Generation New York Jews* (New York: Columbia University Press, 1981); Rachel Kranson, *Ambivalent Embrace: Jewish Upward Mobility in Postwar America* (Chapel Hill: University of North Carolina Press, 2017).

parents, and the Bible seemed less reliable but the afterlife surer than ever, Wise renamed his newspaper *The American Israelite.* A search of the ProQuest Historical Newspapers database will find *The Israelite* and *The American Israelite* listed as separate publications. While they were in many ways continuous, it is clear that Wise—as a rabbi but also as an editor and businessman—wanted to start fresh. In 1874, Isaac Mayer Wise did not know that he would have twenty-six more years ahead of him to continue elaborating his vision of American Judaism, one informed by the correspondence and other contributions that were being sent to his office. In 1875, the same year his son Leo began to work with him on *The American Israelite,* Hebrew Union College was finally founded, with Wise as president; he would also serve as president of the Central Conference of American Rabbis, founded in 1889.[150] Nor did he know that *The American Israelite* would exist to the present day, albeit with the much more limited goal of "connecting Jewish Cincinnati."[151] He did know that the times were changing and that it was an important moment to argue yet again that his readers could wholeheartedly be both citizens and Jews, at once part of a multireligious nation-state and a global religious community.

The American Israelite is an indispensable document for understanding the life and thought of Isaac Mayer Wise, but it is also an important source for understanding the ordinary Jews whose words and subscriptions he relied upon. As it turns out, there were multiple and competing visions of American Judaism, enacted in daily life and private belief, that found expression in Wise's publication, implicitly if not explicitly challenging his own prescriptions. If Wise was intent upon creating a national Jewish institution, his readers seemed more concerned with consumption and charity. If Wise was determined to present Judaism as both rational and biblical, his correspondents seemed more interested in contemplating their past history and future afterlife. The overlapping of these possibilities in different genres in *The American Israelite* shows how rabbis and laypeople alike used the press to argue with and to perform to one another what it meant to be American Jews. In the process, they helped American Jews

150. Temkin, *Creating American Judaism,* 280, 281, 297. Leo had previously "absconded with funds entrusted to his father for the forthcoming Hebrew Union College"; after a four-year absence, he returned to Cincinnati during his mother's final illness in November or December 1874. He then repented and became his father's colleague at *The American Israelite.* Janice Rothschild Blumberg, *Prophet in a Time of Priests: Rabbi Alphabet Browne, 1845–1929,* Kindle ed. (Baltimore: Apprentice House Press, 2012), location 998–1015.

151. Home page, *The American Israelite,* http://www.americanisraelite.com (accessed Mar. 27, 2020).

to understand themselves as part of a collective with a diverse, if not totally unbounded, set of organizational and theological options.

While the specifics changed over time, American Jews continued to hold a multiplicity of viewpoints, and the press continued to be an important venue for the ongoing process of American Jewish self-creation. There never has been universal agreement on what it means to be "American" or what constitutes "Judaism," nor are those markers ever free from the political, economic, and intellectual contexts in which they take shape. The period from 1865 to 1900 was one of particularly intense upheaval; the new approaches to Judaism pioneered in the antebellum period were put under pressure by the Civil War, by industrialization, by scientific thought, and, eventually, by the mass migration of a new group of Jews who would think differently about whether and how to become "American Israelites."

THE "AMERICAN JEWESS" IN TRANSITION: PATTERNS AND OPPORTUNITIES

MELISSA R. KLAPPER

ON MAY 18, 1880, a woman small in stature but mighty of pen rose to address an audience of St. Louis women and men who had gathered to celebrate the "annual entertainment" of the Pioneers, the first Jewish women's literary society in the United States. Assigned to trace the august history of the Pioneers, she explained that she had quailed before the task, given that the literary society was only sixteen months old. To prepare her remarks, she purported to have visited the Mercantile Library downtown and perused a book written in 2189 A.D. Therein, she found a history of the world that fully justified the modest yet essential work of the Pioneers three centuries earlier: lady politicians flying on mechanized wings to Russia to assist with the election of a "Presidentress" there; a mind-reading machine that had "saved womankind from the great annoyance of talk and gossip"; and peace among all people in a United States no longer subject to Death's sting, that malign power having been banished in an effort to maintain a stable population in an era of scant immigration. All these edifying transformations stemmed, according to the 2189 tome, from the founding on January 24, 1879, of the Pioneers, an association that proved without doubt that women could band together to debate issues of the day, to celebrate with coffee and cake, and to rationally, respectably, and professionally provide education and entertainment not only to themselves but also to the former members of the lately collapsed Young Men's Hebrew Literary Association, whose demise predicted the 2189 future of women's dominion.[1]

Rosa Sonneschein's (1847–1932) tongue was planted firmly in her cheek when she delivered this address to a group so appreciative of her wit that they arranged for the immediate publication of *The Pioneers: An Historical Essay* (Fig. 53). She was already well known in St. Louis's Jewish community, not just as the wife of Rabbi Solomon Sonneschein (1839–1908), with whom she immigrated to the United States in 1869, but also on her own merits for organizing choral societies

1. Rosa Sonneschein, *The Pioneers: An Historical Essay* (St. Louis: Woodword, Tiernan & Hale, 1880).

Fig. 53. Rosa Sonneschein. Detail from cover of the *American Jewess* 5, no. 2 (May 1897). (Princeton University Library. Gift of Leonard Milberg).

and ladies auxiliaries at the two congregations he served in the city. Born in the Austrian empire, Sonneschein was the daughter of Rabbi Dr. Hirsch Baer Fassel, a renowned figure who gave his intellectual daughter the run of his library and allowed her to attend the literary salons he hosted at their home. A uniquely well-educated woman in both secular and religious realms, she was a public figure in St. Louis's expansive German cultural life and literary circles as well as in the Jewish community. Perhaps heartened by the success of the Pioneers, which had already doubled its membership by the time she spoke at the May 1880 program, she began to publish stories and articles in both American Jewish periodicals and the broader German-language press. She also worked as a correspondent for several Chicago and St. Louis newspapers while attending the Paris Exposition in 1889. These credentials served her well when she became self-supporting after her acrimonious divorce. By the time of the Chicago World's Fair in 1893, she was a prominent member of a panel of women journalists at the World Press Congress held there. During her speech, she suggested the need for a periodical especially for American Jewish women.[2]

Sonneschein stayed in Chicago after the World's Fair. In 1895, inspired in part by the establishment of the National Council of Jewish Women (NCJW) two years earlier, she founded the *American Jewess*, an illustrated monthly magazine. Though persistent financial troubles meant that the *American Jewess* lasted only four years, during its brief run it simultaneously reflected and predicted the "New Jewish Woman," a figure committed to women's interests in education, health, philanthropy, reform, literature, travel, and good taste, as well as to a variety of explicitly Jewish causes, including, controversially, Zionism. The *American Jewess* assumed that a consonance of identities—American, Jewish, female—was not only feasible but also both desirable and inevitable for its readers, a proposition not always taken for granted by American Jewish women during the latter decades of the nineteenth century.[3]

2. For biographical details, see Jack Nusan Porter, "Rosa Sonneschein and The American Jewess: The First Independent English Language Women's Journal in the United States," *American Jewish History* 68, no. 1 (1978): 57–63; Jack Nusan Porter, "Rosa Sonneschein and The American Jewess Revisited: New Information on an Early American Zionist and Jewish Feminist," *American Jewish Archives Journal* 32, no. 2 (1980): 124–31; Carole S. Kessner, "Rosa Sonneschein: The Woman and Her Work," in *Proceedings of the World Congress of Jewish Studies*, 1989, vol. 2 (Jerusalem: World Union of Jewish Studies, 1989), 325–30; and Jane H. Rothstein, "Rosa Sonneschein," in *Jewish Women in America: An Historical Encyclopedia*, ed. Paula E. Hyman and Deborah Dash Moore, vol. 2 (New York: Routledge, 1997), 1289–91.

3. Barbara Straus Reed, "Rosa Sonneschein and 'The American Jewess,'" *Journalism History* 17 (Fall 1990): 54–62.

When a later Pioneers president, Laura D. Jacobson (1868–1953), chronicled the literary society's history in the *American Jewess*, she straightforwardly explained that the group was the brainchild of "a few energetic, intellectual and progressive Jewish women of St. Louis," not least among them Sonneschein herself.[4] But these adjectives so blithely stated in 1895—"intellectual," "progressive"—appeared nowhere in Sonneschein's earlier address on the Pioneers; more significantly, she also did not include the word "Jewish." Only those who knew that "Y.M.H.L.A." referred to the recently defunct Young Men's Hebrew Literary Association would have had any idea that the Pioneers was a Jewish women's group and that Sonneschein's original audience was mostly, if not entirely, Jewish. There were references to the biblical "wisdom of Solomon" in her talk, but also to the "art of Terpsichore." Both would have been intelligible to educated listeners and readers regardless of religious background. The constitution and bylaws of the Pioneers resembled those of any other women's literary society of the day, with no indication of Jewish affiliation.[5]

This reticence is in stark contrast to Jacobson's 1895 history, which proudly claimed the Pioneers as "the first literary society of Jewesses" and described the club's program of the past year, which focused on Jewish history. "No course of study could have stirred the ethical consciousness of the club more deeply than the tragic, yet divinely glorious history of the Jews," Jacobson asserted.[6] Even though her account appeared in a magazine expressly aimed at American Jewish women, the differences in masked versus vocal pride in Jewishness between the 1880 and 1895 narratives of the Pioneers are striking. Both cheerfully predicted the growing, though still hotly debated, political power and public activities of American women; yet in just fifteen years something about the position of American Jewry had shifted enough that American Jewish women like Jacobson felt comfortable establishing their own organizations, reading their own magazine, and expanding their roles in public life.

Their confidence came in part from a late nineteenth-century moment of promise for American women. Secondary and higher educational opportunities expanded greatly; new jobs and professions opened; the legal status of married women improved; new inventions altered domestic duties; technological innovations benefited women in everything from clothing to travel; and a great wave of activism fundamentally shifted women's roles in society and politics. American Jewish women participated in and enjoyed the advantages of all these changes,

4. Laura D. Jacobson, "The Pioneers," *American Jewess* (hereafter *AJ*) 1 (August 1895): 240.

5. Sonneschein, *The Pioneers*, 13, appendix with constitution and bylaws.

6. Jacobson, "The Pioneers," 242.

though their individual experiences were always filtered through class status, family role, and geographic location, among other factors. Yet the question of what role their Jewishness, however defined, would play in their encounters with all the transformations of the modernizing age lingered on, whether they were wealthy Jewish women whose families had lived in America for generations or poor Jewish women who had recently come to the United States as part of the new wave of migration from southern and eastern Europe that began in the 1880s. Many of these women embraced their Jewish identity, while others downplayed, hid, or rejected it; but few could ignore it altogether, especially given the rise of a rarely violent but nonetheless pervasive antisemitism at the end of the nineteenth century. Changes in gender roles and ideas about gender thus intersected with changes in Jewish life during this period. There was pressure from all sides to achieve a balance between tradition and innovation.

The differences between the two accounts of the history of the Pioneers also reflect some of the changes within the American Jewish community during even that brief time frame. In 1880 the American Jewish community was growing steadily but not yet in huge numbers, whereas in 1895 the impact of mass Jewish migration from eastern Europe was already being felt. In 1880 there were Jewish women's benevolent associations with relatively narrow missions and, as the Pioneers demonstrated, the beginnings of a few Jewish women's literary societies; but in 1896 there were already fifty chapters of the new NCJW across the country, and the impulse to organize synagogue sisterhoods oriented toward philanthropy and social work was stirring.[7] In 1880 there were congregational Sabbath schools staffed by Jewish women with good intentions but little education; there were more Jewish schools by 1895, and the slowly rising standard was increasing Jewish educational and professional opportunities for girls and women. In both 1880 and 1895, Jews lived in cities, towns, villages, and farms across America; but by the latter date, the urban Jewish population was becoming ever more dominant, and the spate of new Jewish organizations and institutions like the American Jewish Historical Society and the Jewish Publication Society tended to cluster in cities, as did the new Jewish immigrants. In only a few short years since Sonneschein's circumspect lecture, the contours of the American Jewish community had changed in ways that emboldened Jewish women and contributed to Jacobson's greater willingness to claim Jewish identity explicitly as part of the history of the Pioneers.

During its brief run, the *American Jewess* covered all of the topics that con-

7. Faith Rogow, *Gone to Another Meeting: The National Council of Jewish Women, 1893–1993* (Tuscaloosa: University of Alabama Press, 1993), 26.

cern the balance of this essay: American Jewish women's multifaceted identity, religious education for girls, and women's activism in a new age of opportunity. Also like the *American Jewess*, this essay acknowledges the presence of immigrants and their undeniable impact on the American Jewish community but focuses primarily on the American-born Jewish women of the late nineteenth century, whose histories are sometimes overshadowed by the great dramas attendant on Jewish mass migration. As a cohort, these women participated in a transformation of their private and public lives that played an important role in the creation of modern American Jewry.

Whatever Rosa Sonneschein's and Laura Jacobson's opinions of the organization they headed, they surely would have recognized that, in the grand scheme of the benevolent empire that reform-minded Americans created during the mid-nineteenth century, the Pioneers was not of much significance. But Jewish women had been making their mark since the early days of the creation of civic, religious, and social groups earnestly dedicated to changing the world, and the Pioneers did continue in that tradition.[8] During the antebellum era, Rebecca Gratz (1781–1869) had perhaps been the most visible example of a Jewish woman who was not only involved in the charitable and educational institutions of her beloved city of Philadelphia but also saw the need for creating organizations within her Jewish community (Fig. 54). Gratz belonged to Philadelphia's Female Association for the Relief of Women and Children in Reduced Circumstances and served on the board of the Philadelphia Orphan Asylum. But she also established the Female Hebrew Benevolent Society to assist poor Jewish women without subjecting them to Protestant missionizing and the Hebrew Sunday School Society to provide Jewish children with religious education. Gratz joined, founded, and remained involved in benevolent organizations both inside and outside the Jewish community for the rest of her life, with her name becoming a byword for generations of Jewish women's dedication to reform and ultimately to activism. She herself hoped that it was not "too much to expect from the daughters of a noble race that they will be foremost in the works of Charity." Gratz wore her Jewish identity as a badge of honor and was lovingly cited for decades as a role model.[9]

8. On nineteenth-century American women and reform, see Lori D. Ginzberg, *Women and the Work of Benevolence: Morality, Politics, and Class in the Nineteenth-Century United States* (New Haven: Yale University Press, 1990), and Judith A. Giesberg, *Civil War Sisterhood: The U.S. Sanitary Commission and Women's Politics in Transition* (Boston: Northeastern University Press, 2000).

9. Rebecca Gratz, "Female Hebrew Benevolent Society Annual Report (1835)," in *Four Centuries of Jewish Women's Spirituality: A Sourcebook*, ed. Ellen M. Umansky and Dianne Ashton, rev. ed.

Fig. 54. Rebecca Gratz. (Courtesy of The Jacob Rader Marcus Center of the American Jewish Archives, Cincinnati, Ohio).

Another Jewish woman in antebellum America whose activism led to a certain fame—or perhaps notoriety—was Ernestine Rose (1810–1892). Rose was not actually an American, though she lived in the United States for several decades, nor did she generally identify as Jewish. A rabbi's daughter from Poland, she proclaimed herself an atheist and arrived in the United States in 1836 after a winding path that took her through numerous European countries and a utopian community in England. Rose played an important role in abolition and several other reform causes before and just after the Civil War. Like many other women involved in antislavery activism, she also became committed to women's rights and attended many conventions, gaining acclaim as a skilled platform speaker.[10] She was a particularly fierce advocate of married women's property rights. "What right has the law to entrust the interest and happiness of one being into the hands of another?" she thundered in 1851. "And if the merging of the interest of one being into the other is a necessary consequence on marriage, why should woman always remain on the losing side? Turn the tables. Let the identity and interest of the husband be merged in the wife."[11] Rose and other supporters of married women's property rights saw some success in the decade before the Civil War, with the laws changing in their favor in Massachusetts in 1855 and New York in 1860, though progress was piecemeal and slow.[12]

For much of her American career, Rose dismissed her religious origins as irrelevant and delivered a stump speech that was also published in pamphlet form as *A Defence of Atheism.* But in the wake of antisemitic attacks that began to appear in the *Boston Investigator* in 1863, Rose entered the fray, despite her longstanding relationship with the paper as a correspondent. She defended Jews and Judaism and spoke out fervently in favor of nondiscrimination on the basis of religion. "[I]n spite of the barbarous treatment and deadly persecution [Jews] suffered," she wrote to the *Boston Investigator* in one of a series of letters, "they have lived and spread and outlived much of the poisonous rancor and prejudice

---

(Waltham, Mass.: Brandeis University Press, 2009), 93. On Gratz, see Dianne Ashton, *Rebecca Gratz: Women and Judaism in Antebellum America* (Detroit: Wayne State University Press, 1997).

10. On Rose, see Carol A. Kolmerten, *The American Life of Ernestine Rose* (Syracuse, N.Y.: Syracuse University Press, 1998), and Bonnie S. Anderson, *The Rabbi's Atheist Daughter: Ernestine Rose, International Feminist Pioneer* (New York: Oxford University Press, 2017).

11. Ernestine Rose, "Remove the Legal Shackles from Woman," in *Voices from Women's Liberation*, ed. Leslie B. Tanner (New York: Signet, 1970), 65.

12. On married women's property acts, see Linda E. Speth, "The Married Women's Property Acts, 1839–1865: Reform, Reaction, or Revolution," in *Women and the Law: A Social Historical Perspective*, ed. D. Kelly Weisberg, vol. 2 (Cambridge, Mass.: Schenkman, 1982), 69–85.

against them.... Are the Jews in Boston so much worse, that their spread is to be dreaded ... ? Let us ... not add to the prejudice already existing towards the Jews, or any other sect." She rigorously deployed the sharp tongue and cutting pen that had made her an admired rather than beloved figure, earning her some level of appreciation within the Jewish community she had once renounced, though never anything like the adulation reserved for Gratz. When she departed in 1869 for England, never to return to the United States, her memory faded somewhat; but she, like Gratz and countless others who never achieved such renown, had helped set the stage for later nineteenth-century American Jewish women's intense activism in a number of causes.[13]

Like many of her peers, Rose tirelessly campaigned for women's rights in the belief that empowered women would remedy all manner of social ills. While some activists eventually rejected the argument that women were morally superior beings who would purify politics and cure all the world's ailments, this strain of thinking meshed nicely with emerging nineteenth-century ideas about women in general. Rabbi Samson Raphael Hirsch of Frankfurt, Germany, and other important rabbinic figures of the mid-nineteenth century began to extol Jewish women's innate spirituality and superior moral compass. Such thinking, which reflected the gender norms emerging in an industrializing western world that increasingly separated home from work, operated simultaneously both to restrict women's sphere of activity and to provide motivation for stepping beyond it in the name of social and religious improvement.[14] When Sonneschein founded ladies auxiliaries at the synagogues in St. Louis where her husband served as rabbi, or when Rabbi Emil Hirsch (1851–1923) of Chicago's Sinai Temple encouraged his female congregants to engage in good works—though using modern philanthropic methods instead of older models of charity work—they followed in the footsteps of Gratz and Rose.[15]

Not all Jewish women followed Rose all the way to the women's rights movements, but many adopted new ideas about women and girls. After the Civil

13. Anderson, *The Rabbi's Atheist Daughter*, 119; Ernestine Rose, letter to the Boston Investigator, February 10, 1864, https://www.brandeis.edu/wsrc/ernestine-rose-society/about/speeches/index.html.

14. On this dynamic in both western Europe and the United States, see Paula E. Hyman, *Gender and Assimilation in Modern Jewish History: The Roles and Representation of Women* (Seattle: University of Washington Press, 1995).

15. On Hirsch, see Tobias Brinkmann, *Sundays at Sinai: A Jewish Congregation in Chicago* (Chicago: University of Chicago Press, 2012).

War, it was abundantly clear that women could engage in careers they had not been allowed to enter before, such as nursing and civil service work. They would benefit not only themselves but also all of society through new educational and professional opportunities. While most American women continued to choose traditional domesticity, they faced a practical problem: in the wake of more than 600,000 wartime casualties, not all of them could rely on wifehood and motherhood to structure their lives. Even those in traditional roles found that in an era of so much technological and organizational change, they required new skills just to keep their families secure. Working-class and rural women joined groups like the Knights of Labor and the Grange in an effort to expand their rights and prerogatives, while middle-class women pushed for significant expansion of higher education and professions for women. All of them drew on the rhetoric of gender to justify their public interests and public work. And all of them participated in the cultural conversation around the "New Woman" of the late nineteenth century, a figure of good health, education, and independence who enjoyed more opportunity than women ever had before, whether riding a bicycle, graduating from college, or choosing her own husband based on affection and companionship.[16]

The question of "Our Girls" became one of the most urgent issues of the day. As public education (at least for white students) continuously expanded and high schools appeared all over the country, there were debates over the best way to raise daughters in a rapidly modernizing age. The growing recognition of adolescence as a distinct stage of life between childhood and adulthood contributed to the question of how girls could best develop into women.[17] Renowned women's

16. The literature on women during the late nineteenth century is too vast to cite in full here. For representative works, see Frances B. Cogan, *All-American Girl: The Ideal of Real Womanhood in Mid-Nineteenth-Century America* (Athens: University of Georgia Press, 1989); Lara Vapnek, *Breadwinners: Working Women and Economic Independence, 1865–1920* (Urbana: University of Illinois Press, 2009); Nancy Woloch, *A Class by Herself: Protective Laws for Women Workers, 1890s–1990s* (Princeton: Princeton University Press, 2015); Rebecca Edwards, *Angels in the Machinery: Gender in American Party Politics from the Civil War to the Progressive Era* (New York: Oxford University Press, 1997); Kathryn Kish Sklar, *Florence Kelley and the Nation's Work: The Rise of Women's Political Culture, 1830–1900* (New Haven: Yale University Press, 1995); Jean V. Matthews, *The Rise of the New Woman: The Women's Movement in America, 1875–1930* (Chicago: Ivan R. Dee, 2003); and Martha Patterson, *The American New Woman Revisited: A Reader, 1894–1930* (New Brunswick: Rutgers University Press, 2008).

17. G. Stanley Hall, *Adolescence: Its Psychology and Its Relations to Physiology, Anthropology, Sociology, Sex, Crime, Religion, and Education*, 2 vols. (New York: D. Appleton, 1904), is the classic text. For representative works on American adolescence, see Joe Austin and Michael Nevin Willard, eds., *Generations of Youth: Youth Cultures and History in Twentieth-Century America* (New York:

rights activists Elizabeth Cady Stanton (1815–1902) and Mary Ashton Rice Livermore (1820–1905) both delivered hundreds of lecture circuit talks about the American girl throughout the 1870s and 1880s. In Stanton's most popular lecture, titled variously "The Coming Girl," "The Girl of the Future," and "Our Girls," the doughty reformer drew on her own experience as a mother of seven as well as an activist to critique gender norms that limited girls' freedom of movement, expression, and ambition. Famously opining, "I would have girls regard themselves not as adjectives but nouns," Stanton encouraged girls to pursue aspirations other than—though not necessarily exclusive of—marriage and motherhood and to seek out good health, intellectual development, and honest work for their own sake, not merely as precursors to a preordained domesticity.[18] In "What Shall We Do With Our Daughters," a speech Livermore delivered more than eight hundred times, she similarly expressed the hope that "it is for our young women that the great changes of the time promise the most" and urged parents to attend to their daughters' physical, practical, and academic education so that they would be prepared to face the challenges of their lives and their expanding responsibilities in the wider world with independence, a strong constitution, and a finely calibrated moral compass.[19]

American Jewish women shared in this debate, as is evident in discussions about girls in the American Jewish press. From the 1860s through at least World War I, American Jewish periodicals published lively exchanges on the subject, drawing comments from parents, educators, rabbis, and sometimes girls or young women themselves. In many respects these responses echoed the broader discussion and dealt with issues ranging from dress reform to higher education to economic independence. However, the debate over "Our Girls" in the English-language American Jewish press virtually always included—and often prioritized—the additional component of religious education. As opposed to the

---

New York University Press, 1998); Sarah E. Chinn, *Inventing Modern Adolescence: The Children of Immigrants in Turn-of-the-Century America* (New Brunswick: Rutgers University Press, 2009); Glen Elder, "Adolescence in Historical Perspective," in *Growing Up in America: Historical Experiences*, ed. Harvey J. Graff (Detroit: Wayne State University Press, 1987); Thomas Hine, *The Rise and Fall of the American Teenager* (New York: Avon, 1999); and Grace Palladino, *Teenagers: An American History* (New York: Basic Books, 1996).

18. Lisa Shawn Hogan, "Elizabeth Cady Stanton, 'Our Girls' (Winter 1880)," *Voices of Democracy* 1 (2006): 104–17, https://voicesofdemocracy.umd.edu/wp-content/uploads/2010/08/hogan-stanton.pdf; Elizabeth Cady Stanton, "Our Girls," https://voicesofdemocracy.umd.edu/stanton-our-girls-speech-text/ (quotation in paragraph 11).

19. Mary Ashton Rice Livermore, *What Shall We Do With Our Daughters? Superfluous Women and Other Lectures* (Boston: Lee and Shepard, 1883), 15.

vague moral or spiritual development referenced by Stanton and Livermore, the religious education of Jewish girls in America was to be explicitly Jewish, something that would firmly ground their identities. Though not everyone involved in this debate agreed about the appropriate practice of Judaism in the modern world, virtually all commentators concurred that Jewishness should be part of the conversation about girls. In this way, Jewish girls' religious education came to represent a path forward for a community interested in integrating new opportunities for women with traditional family life and domesticity.[20]

Even before the Civil War, the English-language American Jewish press had launched the discussion. The *Jewish Messenger*, a New York weekly with a traditionalist bent, editorialized in 1860 that "as teachers and as parents, we have been unmindful of our trust, in neglecting to store the minds of Israel's daughters with the tenets of that faith which is to guide them through this life, and to prepare them for the next." The editorial went on to lament the passing of the days when Jewish mothers knew enough to teach their daughters at home. Another *Messenger* article the following year echoed the critique that in America, Jewish girls learned too much in the way of French and dancing but not enough in the way of Hebrew and "the duties which devolve on them as daughters of Israel."[21] In both cases, the authors were most concerned about girls' ability to fulfill their undoubted destiny as mothers and hoped that if more young American Jewish women became religious educators, they could improve both their own level of knowledge and that of their children and students, to the benefit of all. This perspective matched the goals of the Hebrew Sunday School movement started by Rebecca Gratz in Philadelphia in 1838, which employed women as teachers and offered them training in an effort to shore up observance and knowledge in the then diminutive American Jewish community.[22] Both articles, in decrying the greater willingness of American Jewish parents to provide their daughters with an ornamental rather than a religious education, also made very clear the folly of this priority.

An 1867 series on "The Education of Jewish Females" in the *Jewish Messenger* incorporated analogous themes, once again calling especially on mothers to supervise their daughters' religious training and also blaming the increasingly

20. On adolescent Jewish girls during this period, see Melissa R. Klapper, *Jewish Girls Coming of Age in America, 1860–1920* (New York: New York University Press, 2005).

21. "Religious Education for the Daughters of Israel," *Jewish Messenger* (*JM* hereafter), October 19, 1860; J.A.L., "The Education of American Jewesses," *JM*, November 1, 1861.

22. See Ashton, *Rebecca Gratz*, and Lance J. Sussman, *Isaac Leeser and the Making of American Judaism* (Detroit: Wayne State University Press, 1995).

popular Reform movement for the atrophy of women's traditional responsibilities for keeping kosher kitchens and observing Shabbat.[23] The *Occident*, another religiously conservative American Jewish periodical, took a similarly dim view of the impact of religious reform on Jewish girls' education: it was all very well for girls to display their finery while sitting in family pews in Reform synagogues, but they would be better off "if they had been trained in the same unostentatious schools as their pious mother[s]" and "worship[ped] unobtrusively as was done before our times."[24] It was not that Jewish parents neglected religious education altogether. Advertisements for Jewish girls' schools in the *Occident* made sure, as did Rosenbaum's Institute in 1868, to promise that "particular attention will be paid to Hebrew." Mrs. H. Simons's "Select Boarding School for Young Ladies" likewise assured parents that "moral and religious training will be under the superintendence of the Principal, whose endeavours will be to give her pupils a love and veneration for their holy faith." But Rosenbaum's Institute preceded any mention of Hebrew with details of the French and German language instruction available at the school, and Mrs. H. Simons had more to say about music, sewing, and embroidery lessons than anything related to Judaism.[25]

Concerns about Jewish girls' education also became part of larger discussions in the American Jewish press about the role of women. An 1875 article "About Our Girls," perhaps purposely echoing the title of Stanton's well-known lecture, sharply criticized Jewish girls for thinking of nothing but fashion and marriage.[26] Even though it appeared in the *American Israelite*, a Cincinnati weekly founded by the influential Reform rabbi Isaac Mayer Wise (1819–1900), the condemnation of American Jewry for neglecting girls' religious responsibilities and intellectual capacities strongly resembled the criticisms found in more traditionalist periodicals. The *American Israelite* published numerous responses to "About Our Girls" over the following weeks, allowing a glimpse into what ordinary individuals thought about these issues. Indignant girls from around the country defended themselves. Minnie from Charleston insisted that "[we] are perfectly conversant with the works of Shakspeare [*sic*], Scott, Lamb, and above all, that greatest of all novelists, Charles Dickens, his works are proverbial with us"; as a parting blow, she added, "I regret exceedingly that your correspondent should be so unfortunate as to reside among so many ignorant

23. "The Education of Jewish Females," *JM*, June 21, 1867; "The Religious Education of Our Females II," *JM*, June 28, 1867; "The Religious Education of Our Females III," *JM*, July 12, 1867.

24. "Education," *Occident* 25, no. 9 (December 1867): 426.

25. School advertisements, *Occident* 26, no. 1 (April 1868).

26. Hyacintha, "About Our Girls," *American Israelite* (*AI* hereafter), January 8, 1875.

girls." One man attributed the problem to the American Jewish community's insistence on marrying off girls so young that they had to leave school. A young woman from Louisville blamed Jewish men for the fact that "the young lady of high moral culture, possessed of enviable talents, modest and unassuming—the result of intellectual training—receives far less attention at the hands of the majority of young gentlemen" than the beribboned, frivolous girl who remained ignorant of religion and culture.[27] Virtually all the correspondents agreed that expanded schooling for girls was a positive development. During the decades following the Civil War, this value was shared in the United States more generally, as evidenced by the establishment of more high schools and more colleges and universities open to women.[28] Unlike the earlier *Jewish Messenger* articles, however, hardly any of the *American Israelite* correspondents mentioned religious education. Organized Jewish education was at something of a low point in America during this period, even though Sabbath schools continued to serve many communities and congregations. American Jews had nearly unanimously adopted the "Protestant model" whereby religious education was supplemental to secular public or private education and not seen as central to American Jewish life or communal priorities.[29]

It was left to a lengthy symposium conducted by the *Jewish Messenger* in 1890 to bring religious education back into the popular discussion of Jewish girls. The *Messenger* invited renowned Jewish women from all over the country to participate in this symposium, asking them "what should be the training of the American Jewess and her relation to the changed conditions of the times."[30]

27. Minnie, "Our Girls," *AI*, January 22, 1875; L.D., "Our Girls," *AI*, January 22, 1875; C.S., "Something More About 'Our Girls,'" *AI*, February 12, 1875.

28. On high schools, colleges, and expanding education for girls and women, see Elizabeth Seymour Eschbach, *The Higher Education of Women in England and America, 1865–1910* (New York: Garland, 1993); Lynn D. Gordon, *Gender and Higher Education in the Progressive Era* (New Haven: Yale University Press, 1990); Karen Graves, *Girls' Schooling during the Progressive Era: From Female Scholar to Domesticated Citizen* (New York: Garland, 1998); William J. Reese, *The Origins of the American High School* (New Haven: Yale University Press, 1995); Sally Schwager, "Educating Women in America," *Signs* 12, no. 2 (1987): 333–72; Barbara Miller Solomon, *In the Company of Educated Women: A History of Women and Higher Education in America* (New Haven: Yale University Press, 1985); David Tyack and Elisabeth Hansot, *Learning Together: A History of Coeducation in American Schools* (New Haven: Yale University Press; New York: Russell Sage Foundation, 1990); and William G. Wraga, *Democracy's High School: The Comprehensive High School and Educational Reform in the United States* (Lanham, Md.: University Press of America, 1994).

29. Jonathan D. Sarna, "American Jewish Education in Historical Perspective," *Journal of Jewish Education* 64 (Winter/Spring 1998): 8–21.

30. "The American Jewess: A Symposium for Purim," *JM*, March 7, 1890.

The very wording of this question reflected the transformation of women's roles since the end of the Civil War twenty-five years earlier. Girls and women had more educational, professional, legal, and personal opportunities than ever before. Most of the women who contributed to the symposium, with educators, writers, activists, communal workers, and homemakers among their ranks, expressed strong feelings about what Jewish girls should do with these opportunities. While some focused on proper gender roles and others on the meaning of American identity for Jewish girls, a significant number highlighted the essential need for religious education.

Mrs. F. Noot, whose husband was involved with the Hebrew Free Schools in New York, prescribed for the American Jewish girl "a love and veneration for the traditions of her race," along with "regular attendance at synagogue service." She should also "be taught to read the Hebrew, translate the prayers, and comprehend the fundamental principles of Judaism." Ella Jacobs (1862–1917), a school principal in Philadelphia, agreed: "As a Jewess she must necessarily be trained in Judaism, be it orthodoxy or reform, it matters not ... she must be proud of her faith, her race, her religion." Fanny Binswanger (1862–1949), a founder of the Young Women's Union in Philadelphia, specified that the American Jewish girl needed to be "well-versed in the history, literature, and ethics of Judaism so that she may be a living representative and illustration of those truths which have been the guiding star for all humanity." These and other symposium contributors felt strongly that religious education for girls would achieve a number of goals. It would strengthen the community; as Helen K. Weil of Kansas City explained, "[our daughters] are the future mothers of its Hebrew citizens, and upon them depends what the coming Jew will be." It would serve as a bulwark against the troubling growth of antisemitism, since religiously educated young people would be better able to respond to prejudice with their heads held high, proclaiming, in playwright Martha Morton's (1865–1925) words, "The crown of a great inheritance is mine." And it would give girls a well-founded sense of pride in their heritage, since knowledge of the "wondrous deeds" of Jewish heroines of old would, as educator Minnie D. Louis (1841–1922) explained, highlight the fact "that Jewish women, single and married, wielded a potent influence" on the course of Jewish history that they could emulate.[31]

31. Mrs. F. Noot, "The American Jewess," *JM*, March 7, 1890; Ella Jacobs, "The American Jewess II," *JM*, March 14, 1890; Fanny Binswanger, "The American Jewess III," *JM*, March 21, 1890; Helen K. Weil, "The American Jewess II," *JM*, March 14, 1890; Martha Morton, "The American Jewess," *JM*, March 7, 1890; Minnie D. Louis, "The American Jewess III," *JM*, March 21, 1890.

Fig. 55. Hebrew Sunday School confirmation class, Temple Israel, Columbus, Ohio (1888). (Courtesy of The Jacob Rader Marcus Center of the American Jewish Archives, Cincinnati, Ohio).

Such grand pronouncements in 1890 made clear the widespread support for girls' religious education; or, at least, that it was as widespread as the support for Jewish education more generally (Fig. 55). Certainly, there were families in America who either prioritized boys' Jewish education or viewed girls' religious training outside the home as unnecessary or even forbidden. However, by the late nineteenth century most American Jews probably would have agreed with the larger point of Isaac Mayer Wise's 1898 *American Israelite* editorial reviewing the history of Jewish women's education: "the neglect and exclusion of the female sex in school and place of worship are not Jewish" but an accretion from the many places Jews lived that discriminated against women and discounted their religious and intellectual abilities.[32] Virtually no one viewed religious education as any kind of threat to American identity or status. On the contrary, in

32. Editorial, *AI*, March 24, 1898.

a country still saturated with religion, ignorance of Judaism might make Jews more, not less, suspect.[33]

The question then became not whether to offer religious education to Jewish girls but how best to do so. Not until the early twentieth century was this question addressed in any systematic way beyond the Hebrew Sunday School system, which a new generation of Jewish educators condemned as unprofessional and unsuccessful even as they shared their predecessors' vision of religious education as a means of community preservation. As Samson Benderly (1876–1944), then a teacher with the Hebrew Education Society of Baltimore, wrote in 1903, "Jewish education is characterized by lack of method and efficiency." His colleague Henrietta Szold (1860–1945) agreed (Fig. 56). Like Rosa Sonneschein, she was the daughter of a rabbi who had carefully overseen her religious education. She warned that "the Jewish girl's Jewish education is no better taken care of in a land of golden opportunities than in a crowded Jewry of the East, where she at least lives an intense Jewish life with its manifold educational influences." For both Benderly and Szold, the current status of Jewish education was untenable. Not enough children in America received any kind of Jewish education, and even those who did typically faced what Szold called the "sterile, ineffectual" format of weekly Sabbath school classes taught by unqualified teachers or confirmation classes that reached only a small number of adolescents affiliated with Reform synagogues.[34]

Benderly supported a new model of Jewish education, the Talmud Torah, which would be supplementary to public education but would still provide a rigorous curriculum in nearly daily classes taught by trained, knowledgeable educators. As eventual director of the Board of Jewish Education in New York, Benderly was in a position to establish networks of schools independent of synagogues and staffed by a growing cadre of both male and female disciples who worked to integrate the progressive educational philosophy of the day into Jewish education across the United States. This mission became all the more important in the wake of the mass migration of eastern European Jews, many of whom had their own ideas about appropriate religious education for their children and sought an approach that could combine tradition with innovation.[35]

33. For overviews of Jewish education in America, see Sarna, "American Jewish Education in Historical Perspective," and Melissa R. Klapper, "The History of Jewish Education in America, 1700–2000," in *The Columbia History of Jews and Judaism in America*, ed. Marc Lee Raphael (New York: Columbia University Press, 2008), 189–216.

34. Samson Benderly, "The Jewish Educational Problem," *Jewish Comment*, June 12, 1903; Henrietta Szold, "The Education of the Jewish Girls," *Jewish Comment*, June 12, 1903.

35. On the Benderly network, see Jonathan Krasner, *The Benderly Boys and American Jewish*

Fig. 56. Henrietta Szold (*left*) with her sisters Bertha, Rachel, Sadie, and Adele, 1888. (The Jewish Museum of Maryland, Baltimore).

At no point in American history did a majority of Jewish children receive a formal religious education of any kind. Still, there were continuous discussions of what Jewish education should be like, and it is important that the discourse, if not always the practice, generally took for granted that girls should be included. No one involved in the various late nineteenth-century debates over Jewish education thought that religious training would be anything but a benefit to girls and young women seeking to identify themselves at once as American, Jewish, and female. As Szold put it, "the salvation of Jewish girls as Jewesses and ... as fine specimens of [American] womanhood depends upon a proper alignment of their Jewish education with their secular education."[36]

Education (Waltham, Mass.: Brandeis University Press, 2011). For useful surveys of American Jewish education during this period, see Klapper, *Jewish Girls Coming of Age*, chap. 4, and Laura Tomes, "Reforming Religion: Sabbath Schools and the Negotiation of American Jewish Education, 1873–1923" (Ph.D. diss., Georgetown University, 2014).

36. Szold, "Education of the Jewish Girls."

The growing interest in Jewish schooling for girls at the end of the nineteenth century found a counterpart in expanding religious educational opportunities for women. The Jewish Chautaqua Society (1893) sponsored publications, reading circles, and summer assemblies that provided adult education in Jewish history and literature that was as popular with women as men. New organizations like the American Jewish Historical Society (1892) were open to women, though they rarely occupied positions of leadership in the early years, and the Jewish Publication Society (1888) published books by women and sometimes targeted a female audience.[37] The Jewish Women's Congress held in conjunction with the Chicago World's Fair in 1893 gave numerous women a platform for delivering learned papers on such subjects as "Jewish Women of Biblical and Medieval Times," "Influence of the Discovery of America on the Jews," and "Charity as Taught by the Mosaic Code."[38] When the NCJW was founded as a direct result of this meeting, religious education was part of the original resolution, which promised to "organize and encourage the study of the underlying principles of Judaism; the history, literature and customs of the Jews, and their bearing on their own and the world's history."[39] Throughout its run, the *American Jewess* offered Jewish educational content alongside its other features. For women who sought it out, religious education was increasingly accessible, often through outlets that by their very names—*American Jewess*, American Jewish Historical Society, National Council of Jewish Women—explicitly urged the integration of American and Jewish identities.

If religious education functioned as a mechanism for combining American and Jewish identities and interests, women's activism both inside and outside the Jewish community provided the opportunity to highlight their gender interests as well. The post–Civil War era ushered in new opportunities for women to become involved in activities outside their homes. The kinds of benevolent institutions that had drawn in many American Jewish women before the war, such as Jewish orphanages and sewing circles, Hebrew Sunday Schools, and women's rights groups, continued; but the organizational abilities that ambitious

37. On the many new American Jewish organizations founded in the late nineteenth century, see Jonathan D. Sarna, "A Great Awakening: The Transformation That Shaped Twentieth-Century American Judaism," in *American Jewish Women's History: A Reader*, ed. Pamela S. Nadell (New York: New York University Press, 2003), 43–63.

38. *Papers of the Jewish Women's Congress, Held at Chicago, September 4, 5, 6, and 7, 1893* (Philadelphia: Jewish Publication Society, 1894).

39. Quoted in Rogow, *Gone to Another Meeting*, 23.

women had shown during the war in agencies like the U.S. Sanitary Commission contributed to the growth of reform movements in number, constituency, and ambition. American Jewish women were swept up in these movements, with several paths open to them.

Some concentrated their efforts within the Jewish community, as Henrietta Szold did when she founded a night school in 1889 to help eastern European Jewish immigrants in Baltimore learn English and otherwise acclimate to their new home. Szold, widely acknowledged as one of the most Jewishly educated women in the United States, also participated in nondenominational organizations, such as the alumni association of Baltimore's Western Female High School. However, she spent much of her time working on behalf of the Jewish community through institutions like the Jewish Publication Society and the Federation of American Zionists, and she eventually established Hadassah in 1912, which developed into the largest Jewish women's organization in the world.[40]

Other Jewish women, like Hannah Greenebaum Solomon (1858–1942) and Maud Nathan (1862–1946), began their reform careers within their elite social circles (Fig. 57). Solomon and her sister were the first Jewish women invited to join the exclusive Chicago Women's Club, which grew increasingly political over the last decades of the 1800s as it pursued citywide improvement projects like sanitation systems and the expansion of public education in the face of huge population surges in Chicago.[41] Nathan was drawn into the National Consumers' League when she began to search for meaningful work after her daughter died tragically young. By the end of the nineteenth century, both Nathan and especially Solomon had also become national figures in Jewish women's organizations, with Solomon serving as the first president of the NCJW upon its

40. For a take on the Russian Night School by someone who knew Szold, see Benjamin Hartogensis, "The Russian Night School of Baltimore," *Publications of the American Jewish Historical Society* 31 (1928): 225–28. The classic Szold biographies are Irving Fineman, *Woman of Valor: The Life of Henrietta Szold, 1860–1945* (New York: Simon & Schuster, 1961), and Joan Dash, *Summoned to Jerusalem: The Life of Henrietta Szold* (New York: Harper & Row, 1979). A new account is Dvora Hacohen, *To Repair a Broken World: The Life of Henrietta Szold, Founder of Hadassah*, trans. Shmuel Sermoneta-Gertel (Cambridge, Mass.: Harvard University Press, 2021). Representative books on Hadassah, founded too late to be a focal point of this essay, include Mira Katzman-Yungman, *Hadassah: American Women Zionists and the Rebirth of Israel*, trans. Tammy Berkowitz (Oxford: Littman Library, 2012); Mary McCune, *"The Whole Wide World Without Limits": International Relief, Gender Politics, and American Jewish Women, 1893–1930* (Detroit: Wayne State University Press, 2005); and Erica B. Simmons, *Hadassah and the Zionist Project* (Lanham, Md.: Rowman & Littlefield, 2006).

41. On the Chicago Women's Club, see Maureen A. Flanagan, *Seeing with Their Hearts: Chicago Women and the Vision of the Good City, 1871–1933* (Princeton: Princeton University Press, 2002).

Fig. 57. Maud Nathan. (Courtesy of The Jacob Rader Marcus Center of the American Jewish Archives, Cincinnati, Ohio).

founding in 1893. Neither ever gave up involvement in reform organizations outside the Jewish community, finding ways to balance their commitments. Both supported women's enfranchisement and attended the 1904 founding meeting of the International Woman Suffrage Alliance in Berlin, with Nathan becoming the most prominent American Jewish woman suffragist. As she explained, she did not want her life to be "bounded by the walls of the synagogue," though she remained involved in numerous Jewish women's groups.[42]

Still other American Jewish women became prominent reformers outside the Jewish community. Lillian Wald (1867–1940), a pioneer of the settlement house movement, worked with both poor Jewish immigrants and wealthy Jewish supporters at her internationally famed Henry Street Settlement, yet she rarely paid much attention to her Jewish identity. She never denied her Jewishness, but neither did she foreground its importance in her life of reform. This choice remained firm even in her later work with the peace movement, which involved larger numbers of Jewish women motivated by what they saw as their Jewish responsibility to the world.[43] Similarly, Annie Nathan Meyer (1867–1951), Maud Nathan's sister, committed herself to the cause of women's higher education and was a founder of Barnard College in 1889. Like Wald, she did not hide the fact that she was Jewish, but she also did not register much in the way of protest when Barnard showed signs of discrimination against Jewish students.[44]

All these women were native-born Americans, and some, like the Nathan sisters, boasted American roots extending back to the colonial period. Already as young women in the 1880s, all were active in a variety of causes and had achieved a certain renown, and as they matured, they became leaders and influencers among reform-minded Americans in general and women in particular. Whatever their personal attachments to Judaism, which ranged from the Szold's more traditional observance to Solomon's embrace of Reform Judaism to Wald's

42. Maud Nathan, *Once Upon a Time and Today* (New York: G. P. Putnam's Sons, 1933), 49. Joyce Antler provides a useful capsule biography of Nathan in *The Journey Home: How Jewish Women Shaped Modern America* (New York: Schocken, 1997), chap. 2, as does Pamela S. Nadell for Solomon in *America's Jewish Women: A History from Colonial Times to Today* (New York: Norton, 2019), chap. 2.

43. On Wald, see Marjorie N. Feld, *Lillian Wald: A Biography* (Chapel Hill: University of North Carolina Press, 2009), and Sklar, *Florence Kelley and the Nation's Work.*

44. On Meyer's involvement in founding Barnard, see Lynn D. Gordon, "Annie Nathan Meyer and Barnard College: Mission and Identity in Women's Higher Education, 1889–1950," *History of Education Quarterly* 26, no. 4 (1986): 503–22. On antisemitism at Barnard in the early twentieth century, see Helen Lefkowitz Horowitz, *Alma Mater: Design and Experience at Women's Colleges from Their Nineteenth-Century Origins to the 1930s* (New York: Knopf, 1984).

general disinterest in religion, they all knew themselves to be models for American Jewish women. All were frequently interviewed and profiled in the American Jewish press. Like Gratz before them, Szold and Wald never married, and both Nathan sisters lost their only children at a young age. Among these community leaders, only Solomon raised a family while launching a reform career, something made possible by a supportive husband and financial security (Fig. 58). Except for Szold, all of these women came from very comfortable homes and elevated class status. In these ways, they were not representative of American Jewish women, especially once migration irrevocably changed the demographics of American Jewry, but they did represent the overwhelming number of American Jews who followed their lead and took up all manner of reform causes at the end of the nineteenth century.

Those efforts were clearly on display in the 1890 *Jewish Messenger* symposium. When asked what they would prescribe for the American Jewess, the contributors responded with a chorus of suggestions that went beyond religious education. One group prioritized connection to Judaism and Jewishness. Belle Minzesheimer insisted that, "above all things, the Jewess of to-day should be imbued with a more decided faith in her religion." Another group emphasized the importance of patriotism and the development of American identity, an increasingly contested theme in the wake of ever-growing numbers of immigrants whom the established Jewish community expected to acculturate as quickly as possible. As educator Minnie D. Louis insisted, "An American is an American whether professing Catholicism, Protestantism, Judaism, or Atheism." A third group focused on the consonance of American and Jewish womanhood, with teacher Julia Richman (1855–1912) pointing out that, even though the American Jewess was "first, a woman," that description meant something different in the modern world of the New Woman than it had for traditional Jewish women of the past. Of all the contributors, only Annie Nathan Meyer distanced herself altogether from the discussion, stating flatly, "I do not know that I advise any particular training for Jewish young ladies beyond the best that can be had for all young ladies." For everyone else, the modern American Jewish woman would productively combine American, Jewish, and female identity, especially through activism.[45]

In 1890 not all American Jewish women felt comfortable embracing the political ramifications of female identity and labeling themselves as suffragists, even

45. Belle Minzesheimer, "The American Jewess," *JM*, March 7, 1890; Minnie D. Louis, "The American Jewess III," *JM*, March 21, 1890; Julia Richman, "The American Jewess II," *JM*, March 14, 1890; Annie Nathan Meyer, "The American Jewess," *JM*, March 7, 1890.

Fig. 58. Hannah Greenebaum Solomon (*left*) and her family, 1904. Plate facing page 118 of her autobiography, *Fabric of My Life.* (New York, 1946). (Princeton University Library).

though women's reform activities in so many areas were leading more of them to recognize the importance of formal political participation. And even when Jewish women's organizations were led by supporters of women's enfranchisement, the issue was not always front and center. When Solomon assumed the presidency of the NCJW, for example, she was already a committed suffragist, but the issue was not part of the NCJW's original religious and educational mission, regardless of the opinions of the organization's leaders and members. Nathan's activism with the Consumers' League led her to believe firmly that the vote was necessary to improve working women's lives. Wald, however, a staunch suffragist herself, thought that bread and butter economic issues and union organizing would be more relevant for the immigrant women she encountered in tenements and settlement houses, though she did not discount the importance of giving those women a political voice.[46] Annie Nathan Meyer, reliably contrarian,

46. On American Jewish women and suffrage, see Melissa R. Klapper, *Ballots, Babies, and Banners of Peace: American Jewish Women's Activism, 1890–1940* (New York: New York University Press, 2013), chap. 1.

achieved parallel distinction within the anti-suffrage movement to her sister Maud's prominence in the suffrage movement. It remains unclear why a founder of Barnard and a champion of women's education would oppose suffrage. It is possible that longstanding personal animosity between the sisters, who entertained the public with their opposing appearances on debate stages and dueling letters to the editor, offers at least a partial explanation. Meyer herself explained her opposition as skepticism about what she referred to as "spreadhenism," the idea that enfranchised women would somehow purify politics and reform the world by dint of voting.[47] Maud Nathan ridiculed such ideas and insisted that suffrage was both a right and a privilege of citizenship that women were entitled to no less than men. In addressing Jewish audiences, she also drew upon biblical figures of female leadership such as Miriam, Deborah, and Esther to justify the special support she believed Jewish audiences should offer the cause.[48]

For many American Jews, Nathan's arguments rang truer than those of Meyer, yet they still showed some reluctance to support suffrage. For middle-class and native-born American Jewish women in particular, the problem was not generally the righteousness of the cause but the unwelcoming nature of the movement, which at least as far back as Ernestine Rose's day had shown disconcerting flashes of antisemitism. In 1869 the suffrage newspaper *The Revolution* published an article referring to Jews as "a useless portion of society," a statement for which editors Susan B. Anthony (1820–1906) and Elizabeth Cady Stanton apologized, but only halfheartedly.[49] Anna Howard Shaw (1847–1919), doctor, minister, and president of the National American Woman Suffrage Association from 1904 to 1915, had been known to say negative things about Jews, and the growing social antisemitism of the late nineteenth century infected other reform movements as well.[50] The publication of Stanton's *Woman's Bible* in 1895, which

47. "Annie Nathan Meyer, Wife and Mother, Opposes Woman Suffrage," *American Hebrew*, June 12, 1914. For more on Meyer's anti-suffragism, see Antler, *Journey Home*, chap. 2; Susan Goodier, *No Votes for Women: The New York State Anti-Suffrage Movement* (Urbana: University of Illinois Press, 2013); and Susan E. Marshall, *Splintered Sisterhood: Gender and Class in the Campaign Against Woman Suffrage* (Madison: University of Wisconsin Press, 1997).

48. See, for example, "Mrs. Nathan on Suffrage Issue," *New Haven Union*, October 25, 1912.

49. Lori D. Ginzberg, *Elizabeth Cady Stanton: An American Life* (New York: Hill & Wang, 2009), 135–36. On antisemitism in the women's rights movement more generally, see Elinor Lerner, "American Feminism and the Jewish Question," in *Anti-Semitism in American History*, ed. David A. Gerber (Urbana: University of Illinois Press, 1986), 305–28.

50. Trisha Franzen, *Anna Howard Shaw: The Work of Woman Suffrage* (Urbana: University of Illinois Press, 2014), offers an overdue modern biography of Shaw but engages much more with her purported racism than antisemitism. For another example of Jewish women's sometimes

in parts directly blamed Judaism for the patriarchy and misogyny of human history, exacerbated the situation. Mainstream suffragists, horrified by the *Woman's Bible*'s attacks on organized religion, hastily distanced themselves, but never by publicly denouncing the radical text's antisemitism. And when a delegation of Jewish women visited Stanton to protest, she turned them away—in her own telling, at least—by citing the traditional morning prayer by which Jewish men thank God for not making them women. The damage was done.[51]

During state-level campaigns in the early twentieth century, many of which failed, suffrage leaders like Carrie Chapman Catt (1859–1947) and Harriet Stanton Blatch (1856–1940), Stanton's daughter, publicly blamed immigrants and especially Jews for the setbacks, even though, as Wald and others pointed out, the strongest support for the failed 1915 referenda in New York, Massachusetts, and Pennsylvania came from the most heavily Jewish districts.[52] Given this background, it is not surprising that major Jewish women's organizations like the NCJW, Hadassah, and the National Federation of Temple Sisterhoods (founded 1913) formally endorsed women's enfranchisement only at the last minute or not at all, despite the individual support of most of their members and the widespread Jewish communal enthusiasm for suffrage evident in sermons, periodicals, and local activism.[53]

Whatever their members' feelings toward suffrage, these Jewish women's organizations had plenty of other causes to support. Like many American women's clubs and societies, Jewish women's organizations at end of the nineteenth century participated in a generalized shift from the charitable and cultural pursuits that had justified a certain amount of participation in the public sphere to the reform and educational movements that swiftly—and irrevocably—eroded the distinctions between public and private that had relegated women to domesticity. In an age of mass migration, extreme poverty, horrific urban living and working conditions, and both voluntary and coerced Americanization, women's

---

fraught relationship with reform organizations, see Marni Davis's discussion of the Women's Christian Temperance Union in *Jews and Booze: Becoming American in the Age of Prohibition* (New York: New York University Press, 2012), 41ff.

51. On the *Woman's Bible* and Jewish responses to it, see Kathi Kern, *Mrs. Stanton's Bible* (Ithaca: Cornell University Press, 2001), 66, 157–58, 168, 208.

52. Ellen Carol DuBois, *Harriot Stanton Blatch and the Winning of Woman Suffrage* (New Haven: Yale University Press, 1997), 41, 148–49. Elinor Lerner analyzes Jewish support for suffrage in "Jewish Involvement in the New York City Woman Suffrage Movement," *American Jewish History* 70, no. 4 (1981): 442–61.

53. Klapper, *Ballots, Babies, and Banners of Peace*, 51–54.

organizations became the engine of a more "scientific" philanthropy that eventually led to new fields like social work and public health.[54]

Increased contact with Jewish immigrant women, many of whom arrived in the United States accustomed to economic and political activity, also encouraged American-born Jewish women to continue expanding their roles in the public sphere. Just as middle- and upper-class American women supported working-class women through organizations like the Women's Trade Union League, American-born members of the NCJW and synagogue sisterhoods supported immigrant Jewish women by setting up any number of social service programs.[55] NCJW members met solo women immigrants at the docks and saw them safely to their final destinations in an effort to keep them out of the pernicious networks of "white slavery" that had sprung up around immigration.[56] Synagogue sisterhoods funded institutions such as the Hebrew Technical School for Girls in New York.[57] Jewish women's organizations of all kinds resisted anti-immigrant measures like the literacy tests proposed repeatedly during the late nineteenth and early twentieth centuries.[58] Numerous young, middle-class Jewish women

54. There is a large scholarly literature on this shift. Key works include Paula Baker, "The Domestication of Politics: Women and American Political Society, 1780–1920," *American Historical Review* 89, no. 3 (1984): 620–47; Karen J. Blair, *The Clubwoman as Feminist: True Womanhood Redefined, 1868–1914* (New York: Holmes & Meier, 1979); Flanagan, *Seeing with Their Hearts*; Martha S. Jones, *All Bound Up Together: The Woman Question in African American Public Culture, 1830–1900* (Chapel Hill: University of North Carolina Press, 2007); and Daniel J. Walkowitz, "The Making of a Feminine Professional Identity: Social Workers in the 1920s," *American Historical Review* 95, no. 4 (1990): 1051–75. For the impact of the shift on Jewish women's organizations, see William Toll, "A Quiet Revolution: Jewish Women's Clubs and the Widening Female Sphere," *American Jewish Archives Journal* 41, no. 1 (1989): 7–16; Linda Gordon Kuzmack, *Woman's Cause: The Jewish Woman's Movement in England and the United States, 1881–1933* (Columbus: Ohio State University Press, 1990); Beth Wenger, "Jewish Women and Voluntarism: Beyond the Myth of the Enabler," *American Jewish History* 79, no. 1 (1989): 16–36; Klapper, *Ballots, Babies, and Banners of Peace*; and Nadell, *America's Jewish Women.*

55. The classic work on the Women's Trade Union League remains Nancy Schrom Dye, *As Equals and As Sisters: Feminism, the Labor Movement, and the Women's Trade Union League of New York* (Columbia: University of Missouri Press, 1980). See also Vapnek, *Breadwinners.*

56. On efforts to keep Jewish women out of the hands of traffickers, see Kuzmack, *Woman's Cause*, and Edward J. Bristow, *Prostitution and Prejudice: The Jewish Fight Against White Slavery, 1870–1939* (New York: Schocken, 1983).

57. See Jenna Weissman Joselit, *Aspiring Women: A History of the Jewish Foundation for Education of Women* (New York: Jewish Foundation for Education of Women, 1996), and Melissa R. Klapper, "Jewish Women and Vocational Education in New York City, 1885–1925," *American Jewish Archives Journal* 53, no. 1–2 (2001): 113–46.

58. See Jeanne D. Petit, *The Men and Women We Want: Gender, Race, and the Progressive Era Literacy Test Debate* (Rochester: University of Rochester Press, 2010).

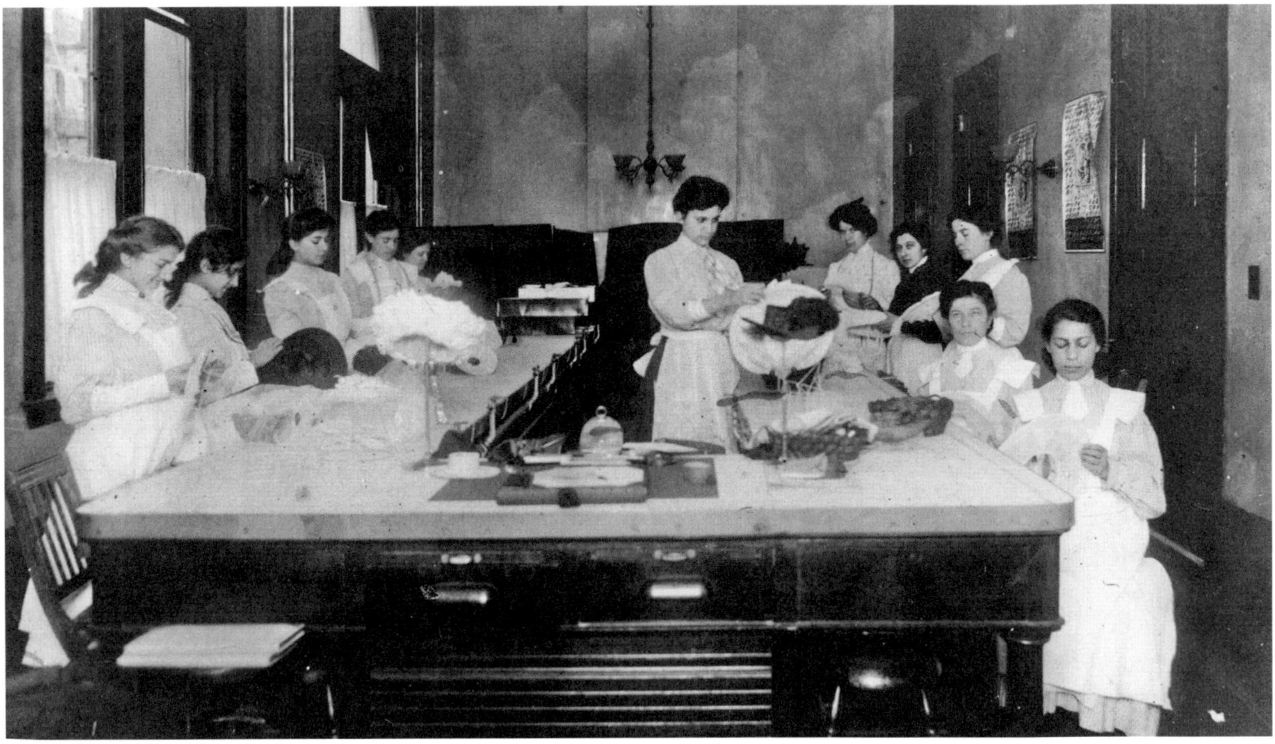

Fig. 59. Millinery class at the Clara de Hirsch Home for Working Girls in New York, ca. 1900. (92nd Street Young Men's and Young Women's Hebrew Association Archives, New York).

worked at institutions like the Young Women's Union in Philadelphia or the Esther Hellman Settlement House in San Francisco as residents dedicated to hands-on communal work. They often continued to run educational and vocational programs there after leaving for marriage and their own domestic lives (Fig. 59).[59]

There was undoubtedly an element of social control and self-protection on the part of the "benefactors" within these cross-class relationships. Established American Jews' concerns over the antisemitism they feared mass migration was provoking exacerbated the heavy-handed expectations of swift Americanization that some organizations demanded as a price for aid, a price that some politically radical Jewish immigrants refused to pay. Immigrant Jewish women

59. On the Young Women's Union, see Klapper, *Jewish Girls Coming of Age*, and Elizabeth Rose, "From Sponge Cake to 'Hamentashen': Jewish Identity in a Jewish Settlement House, 1885–1952," *Journal of American Ethnic History* 13, no. 3 (1994): 3–23. On the Esther Hellman Settlement House, see Miriam Heller Stern, "Ladies, Girls, and Mothers: Defining Jewish Womanhood at the Settlement House," *Journal of Jewish Education* 69, no. 2 (2003): 22–34.

were perfectly capable of standing up for themselves, as they vividly displayed during the 1902 kosher meat riots and the 1917 cost-of-living protests in New York, not to mention the hugely significant role played by Jewish immigrants in the American labor movement of the early twentieth century.[60] Yet it is also the case that Jewish immigrants willingly flocked to institutions like the Henry Street Settlement in New York or the Chicago People's Institute and made their own decisions about what would benefit them and how much they were willing to acculturate to their new environments.

A certain level of gender solidarity enabled women of many class and ethnic (if not racial) backgrounds to find at least some common ground amid social tension, and much of American Jewish women's activism during the latter years of the nineteenth century focused on such issues. Shared concerns about motherhood, in particular, sparked a maternalism in reform and politics that gave women a common vocabulary and basis for increasingly public action. In some ways, rhetoric about maternalism even allowed Jewish women more entry into general American associational life than their male counterparts. And even though American-born and immigrant Jewish women encountered each other across gulfs of language, politics, nationality, religious observance, and life experience, many of them nonetheless recognized in each other mutual interest in strengthening Jewish family and community life in America.

As editor of the *American Jewess*, Rosa Sonneschein explicitly set out to provide a literary home for readers who shared the goal of bettering the lives of American Jewish women (Fig. 60). She sometimes solicited weighty essays from rabbis and other communal leaders on this subject. Among the prominent men who published pieces on the ideal American Jewish woman were Henry D. Berkowitz (1857–1924), Emil G. Hirsch, Adolph Moses (1840–1920), and David Philipson (1862–1949), all major players in the American Reform rabbinate

60. See Paula E. Hyman, "Immigrant Women and Consumer Protest: The New York City Kosher Meat Boycott of 1902," *American Jewish History* 70, no. 1 (1980): 91–105, and Dana Frank, "Housewives, Socialists, and the Politics of Food: The 1917 New York Cost-of-Living Protests," *Feminist Studies* 11, no. 2 (1985): 255–85. There is an enormous literature on Jewish participation in the American labor movement. For a mix of representative classic and recent scholarship, see Alice Kessler-Harris, "Organizing the Unorganizable: Three Jewish Women and Their Union," *Labor History* 17, no. 1 (1976): 5–23; Susan Glenn, *Daughters of the Shtetl: Life and Labor in the Immigrant Generation* (Ithaca: Cornell University Press, 1990); Annalise Orleck, *Common Sense and a Little Fire: Women and Working-Class Politics in the United States, 1900–1965* (Chapel Hill: University of North Carolina Press, 1995); and Daniel Katz, *All Together Different: Yiddish Socialists, Garment Workers, and the Labor Roots of Multiculturalism* (New York: New York University Press, 2011).

Fig. 60. *The American Jewess* 4, no. 2 (November 1896). (Princeton University Library. Gift of Leonard Milberg).

who were well-placed to observe the American Jewish women who filled their synagogue pews.[61] But Sonneschein turned to far more women than men for contributions to the *American Jewess* and used her editorial position to encourage American Jewish women to expand both their literal and their figurative boundaries, whether that meant seeking out deep knowledge of Jewish history, visiting sites of Jewish interest abroad, or engaging in the politics of the day, from suffrage to Zionism. Her target audience was primarily American-born, but she recognized that the gendered experiences of women writers might also appeal to those immigrant Jewish women who sought conventional social and economic mobility.

In 1898 Sonneschein published her own essay on "The American Jewess," which served as both a review and a rallying cry ahead of the coming twentieth century. She claimed that only in the last thirty years had the appellation "American Jewess" even been a possibility, since before that time different groups of Jews had "clustered together in accordance with their nativities" and "failed to assimilate in America religiously as well as socially." The Jewish woman of yesteryear, in this retelling, could never become fully American until she liberated herself from "nightmares of a dark past, out of place in the glorious light into which she had emerged." In this essay Sonneschein sided entirely with the Reform movement's disavowal of a lachrymose Jewish identity more appropriate to the "Ghetto Jewess" than the "liberty-loving American Jewess" who no longer had any reason to fear prejudice and persecution. The open American environment called for a new Jewish woman who "prefers to be a part and parcel of humanity rather than a chattel of her religion," whether she was American-born or a recent arrival. This new American Jewish woman embraced her religious heritage and still strongly preferred a Jewish husband and home life, but her spiritual energies, buoyed by her new educational and professional opportunities, called for an expansion of activities beyond the traditional. She would insist on a modern approach to Judaism, she would take her place in the public world of culture and philanthropy, she would be of sound body and mind, she would accept her daughters' even greater independence, and she would work tirelessly on behalf of her country and her sister citizens, Jewish or not.

61. Emil G. Hirsch, "The Modern Jewess," *AJ* 1 (April 1895): 10–11; Adolph Moses, "The Position of Woman in America," *AJ* 1 (April 1895): 15–20; Henry D. Berkowitz, "Woman's Part in the Drama of Life," *AJ* 1 (May 1895): 63–66; and David Philipson, "The Ideal Jewess," *AJ* 4 (March 1897): 257–62. On women in late nineteenth-century synagogues, see Karla A. Goldman, *Beyond the Synagogue Gallery: Finding a Place for Women in American Judaism* (Cambridge, Mass.: Harvard University Press, 2000).

Whereas less than twenty years earlier Sonneschein had hesitated even to include the word "Jewish" in her history of the Pioneers, by the very end of the nineteenth century she was ready to proclaim that the "American Jewess" was not only a possibility but a reality worth celebrating. "Rachel, the mother in Israel, need not weep for her American daughters," Sonneschein proclaimed. The new American Jewish woman "remains Jewish in spirit, in feeling, in faith and in conviction."[62] There are problems with Sonneschein's version of American Jewish history, which acknowledged neither the diversity of past experiences nor the major changes happening in her own day in light of the hundreds of thousands of eastern European Jewish immigrants arriving yearly. But her vision of American Jewish life did speak both to American-born Jews and to the new immigrants who believed in the exceptional promise of the United States. That vision had animated earlier arrivals as well, providing a through line for the Jewish experience in the United States that encompassed many tensions among dissimilar groups with diverse experiences at different times but also structural similarities in terms of acculturation to new lives.

Jewish women provided a good example of this dynamic. Different gender roles in western and eastern Europe led to different immigrant experiences in the United States, but in every case gender provided an important matrix of acculturation.[63] And many of the same kinds of experiences challenged American Jewish women across the decades. The frequent discussion of girls' religious education did not lead to much other than its fairly widespread acceptance by the end of the nineteenth century, but during the early twentieth century a new cadre of professional educators began to establish standards and schools that would provide systematic Jewish education to more children, including girls, than ever before. They shared the ambitions of the antebellum visionaries like Rebecca Gratz, who saw in religious schooling a means of ensuring Jewish continuity and growth. The rapid expansion of Jewish women's organizing at the turn of the twentieth century, from the NCJW to Hadassah to synagogue sisterhoods to *landsmanschaftn* to unions, gave women political, social, and cultural power both inside and outside the American Jewish community. Like their antebellum counterparts before them and their twentieth-century counterparts after them, the new Jewish women of the late nineteenth century demonstrated that there need not be a stark choice between gender, religious tradition, and civic activism.

62. Rosa Sonneschein, "The American Jewess," *AJ* 6 (February 1898): 205–9.

63. Hyman, *Gender and Assimilation in Modern Jewish History.*

THE AMERICAN EDUCATION OF ABRAHAM CAHAN: JEWISH ENGAGEMENT WITH AMERICAN EDUCATION AND INTELLECTUAL CURRENTS IN THE LATE NINETEENTH CENTURY

DANIEL SOYER

ABRAHAM CAHAN arrived in America on June 6, 1882, a month before his twenty-second birthday (Fig. 61). Disembarking at Philadelphia, he quickly took the train to New York, where he lived the rest of his life. Cahan thus arrived at the very beginning of the mass immigration of east European Jews that over the course of the next four decades transformed the American Jewish community into the largest in the world. Getting in on the ground floor, so to speak, Cahan himself played an important role in building that community, in interpreting America for the immigrants, and in explaining the immigrants to America. He is best known as editor of the *Jewish Daily Forward* (*Forverts*), the most widely read Yiddish newspaper in the world, and as author of the English-language novel of immigrant life, *The Rise of David Levinsky*, still in print over a century after it first appeared. Cahan thus served as a bridge between the immigrants' east European Jewish culture and the American cultural, intellectual, and political worlds with which he became familiar with remarkable speed and thoroughness.

Cahan was born in Podbereze (Paberžė, Lithuania) and grew up there and in the nearby city of Vilna (Vilnius), then in the Russian empire. From a typical Yiddish-speaking family, he received a traditional Jewish education. But as a teenager, Cahan set out to learn Russian and, it seems, as much as possible to *become* Russian. He was extraordinarily successful at absorbing the spirit of Russian high culture, especially its literature and intellectual currents, whose sensibilities he later brought to his engagement with American culture. While a student at Vilna's Jewish teachers' institute, he was drawn into revolutionary activities and, after working briefly as a teacher, fled Russia and made his way to the United States. There, Cahan continued his radical activities and helped lay the groundwork for the Jewish labor movement and Yiddish journalism.

Cahan, the Yiddish- and Russian-speaking immigrant, may thus seem a strange

Fig. 61. Abraham Cahan at a young age. (Courtesy of The Forward Association, Inc., New York).

choice as a lens through which to view Jewish involvement with American intellectual life in the last third of the nineteenth century. But, just as he had thoroughly absorbed the Russian language and culture, Cahan set out aggressively, and successfully, to learn English and enter American culture. Over his first decade in the country, he came into contact with the American educational system as a student at the elementary and university levels, and as a teacher in public evening schools. He also began a career as an English-language journalist, started writing fiction in English, and joined the American socialist movement. All these activities pulled him into American Jewish and non-Jewish circles of educators, intellectuals, writers, and activists. Even if Cahan was not exactly typical, his experiences show just how porous were the barriers between immigrant culture, the culture of well-established American Jews, and that of Americans in general.

Between 1926 and 1931, Cahan published *Bleter fun mayn leben* (*Leaves from My Life*), an autobiography that even in five volumes reaches only to 1914. In truth, the book is a sprawling and inelegantly written work, its language a mix of Cahan's native Lithuanian Yiddish, Germanisms that Cahan admits to having absorbed from the German American socialist movement, and Americanisms that Cahan espoused as being representative of the real Yiddish spoken by the immigrants. Cahan himself could have used an editor. But by that time, he was the most powerful person in Yiddish journalism, and perhaps in Yiddish letters in general. No one was going to tell him how to write or what to cut. Maybe this expansive power turned out to be a good thing, because *Bleter* contains fascinating details not only of immigrant life and the *Forward*, but also of all the American and Jewish sectors with which Cahan came into contact. This essay takes as its starting point parts of volumes 2–4, which deal with the author's first two decades in America.[1]

When Cahan first arrived, he later recalled, he found America to be "a new world—in the literal meaning of the words!" He felt uncomfortable, but also energized, as by "the strong, healthy smell of a freshly plowed field." And very quickly, he wrote, "it seemed to me that, unwittingly, I was also becoming a different person." He actively pursued this transformation by learning English from "Appleton's grammar," which he describes as a textbook for Germans to

1. Abraham Cahan, *Bleter fun mayn leben*, 5 vols. (New York: Forward Association, 1926–1931). For an abridged English translation of the first two volumes, see *The Education of Abraham Cahan*, trans. Leon Stein, Abraham P. Conan, and Lynn Davison (Philadelphia: Jewish Publication Society, 1969). Volume 4 continues into the second decade of the twentieth century.

learn English. Within a short period, Cahan was giving English lessons to other immigrants, though his own knowledge of the language was "theoretical—put more simply, very little."[2]

Cahan decided that the only thing to do was to learn English like a real American boy and go to school. So he talked the principal of a local public school into allowing him to sit in on a class of boys ages twelve to fourteen. The mass Jewish immigration was just beginning, and Cahan estimated that only about a third of his classmates in this school in the heart of the Lower East Side were Jewish, and about half of those were the children of German-Jewish immigrant parents. The students in Mr. Farrell's class indeed gained a thoroughly American education by use of *McGuffey's Fifth Eclectic Reader.*

The graded series of McGuffey's readers was (and continues to be) enormously successful, selling tens of millions of copies and helping to standardize the language, set the moral tone, and influence the literary tastes of generations of Americans. Originally composed by Presbyterian minister William Holmes McGuffey and evolving through many editions, the McGuffey readers appealed through their extensive illustrations and short excerpts from Anglo-American literature, which were meant to be read aloud. They originally promoted a distinctly and explicitly Protestant Christian sense of morality, often drawn directly from the Bible, and not without a dose of antisemtism. The explicit religious content faded over time, but the essentially Calvinist morality remained. Because the South provided an important market for the textbooks, however, such moral and political issues as slavery and the recent Civil War were not discussed. It is not clear what Cahan thought of the readers' evolution. What he remembered was the phonetics lesson: "The bobolink, the bobolink, spink, spenk, spink." Perhaps this exercise was responsible for his later interest in bird watching.[3]

By the 1880s, American Jews were just beginning their long "passionate love affair with public schooling."[4] As Mary Antin, the famous immigrant memoirist, put it, immigrant Jewish parents brought their children to school as if it were an "act of consecration."[5] Like the McGuffey readers that they used, the public schools aimed to inculcate in children, and perhaps especially immigrant

2. Cahan, *Bleter fun mayn leben,* 2:100, 113, 118.

3. *Ibid.,* 2:118–22; Samuel J. Smith, "McGuffey Readers" (September 2008), Liberty University, Faculty Publications and Presentations, https://www.academia.edu/8323076/McGuffey_Readers; Clarence William Perkins Jr., "Moral Culture in the McGuffey Readers, 1836 to 1901" (Ed.D. diss., Teachers College, Columbia University, 2011).

4. Cahan, *Bleter fun mayn leben,* 2:91.

5. Mary Antin, *The Promised Land* (Boston and New York: Houghton Mifflin, 1912), 205.

children, a common sense of American citizenship and a common American culture. Jews certainly hoped that this sense of Americanness would be broad enough to include them as Jews as well as Americans. The schools were thus to be, as Kansas City Rabbi Henry Berkowitz argued, the "great equalizer."[6] But although American public schools were meant to be "nonsectarian," through much of the nineteenth century this idea simply meant that they did not discriminate between Protestant sects. Like the McGuffey readers, they were in truth Christian and Protestant.

Only slowly did the public schools give up their Protestant Christian character, making possible the true consummation of the love affair. In struggles to make the schools really nonsectarian, Jews sometimes benefited from Catholic efforts to root out Protestant elements in the curriculum, such as readings from the King James Bible. In New York, Archbishop John Hughes led the fight, but what he really hoped for was public funding for Catholic parochial schools. Jews, on the other hand, flocked to the public schools. Some already played leadership roles on local school boards—including Rabbi Isaac Mayer Wise, who served on Cincinnati's board of examiners for new teachers. Although the influx of Jewish women into the teaching profession came only in the twentieth century, some Jews, and in some places even some rabbis, began to teach in the public schools as well.[7]

Although it was not so evident when Cahan went to school briefly in the early 1880s, schooling was undergoing curricular reform in the last two decades of the century. Public schools had been characterized by large classes and rigid curriculum. Now, educational reformers borrowed from the ideas of European pedagogues such as Johann Pestalozzi, Johann Herbat, and Friedrich Froebel to push American schooling away from rote memorization to child-centered learning. Drawing also from the psychology of G. Stanley Hall and William James, they sought to make "school fitted to the child" and more relevant to the child's life outside the classroom. Moreover, schools were now to be tools for social betterment.

6. Cahan, *Bleter fun mayn leben*, 2:91.

7. Gerald Sorin, *A Time for Building: The Third Migration, 1880–1920* (Baltimore: Johns Hopkins University Press, 1992), 106; Naomi W. Cohen, *Encounter with Emancipation: The German Jews in the United States, 1830–1914* (Philadelphia: Jewish Publication Society, 1984), 91–92; Hasia R. Diner, *A Time for Gathering: The Second Migration, 1820–1880* (Baltimore: Johns Hopkins University Press, 1992), 152–53; Stephen F. Brumberg, *Going to America, Going to School: The Jewish Immigrant Public School Encounter in Turn-of-the-Century New York City* (New York: Praeger, 1986), 61, 67; Jacob Rader Marcus, *United States Jewry 1776–1985*, vol. 3, *The Germanic Period, Part 2* (Detroit: Wayne State University Press, 1993), 300.

In New York, several Jews played important roles in instituting these reforms. Dr. Joseph Mayer Rice, for example, was a Philadelphia-born physician turned school reformer. Reviewing the state of schools in New York, Rice declared that the "school has been converted into the most dehumanizing institution that I have ever laid eyes upon." "Do what you like with the child," the system's motto seemed to him to be. The emphasis was on efficiency, not learning: "immobilize him, automatize him, dehumanize him, but save, save the minutes." He proposed to reorganize the system's structure and pedagogy. Louisiana-born Adolph Sanger, a lawyer and politician allied with Tammany Hall, had even more direct influence. A champion of kindergarten, against those who saw it as a foreign imposition, Sanger became president of the Board of Education in 1893. He "injected a new spirit into the board," promising "more teaching and less reciting." Under the influence of reformers, schools took on many roles in caring for children of diverse backgrounds, establishing libraries, health clinics, and recreational programs, though not all of the innovations enacted in principle made it into operation in the classroom.[8]

While men headed up the system, the teaching staff consisted increasingly of women. By 1888, 63 percent of American teachers were women, 90 percent in urban areas. In the late nineteenth century, many of them were Irish or Irish American, representatives of the last great wave of immigration, who would educate and Americanize the children of the new wave. Jewish women, who in the twentieth century would come to dominate the teaching force in New York, were only just entering the profession. One of the pioneers was Julia Richman, the daughter of Bohemian Jewish immigrants and herself partly the product of New York City public schools. Graduating from the city Normal School (later Hunter College) in 1872, Richman began her career in public education at the age of eighteen. Ten years later she was an assistant principal, and two years after that the first Jewish woman and the first Normal School graduate to become a principal. Richman's renown as an educator came after the turn of the century, when she was named the first female district superintendent and became a widely read author on issues of education. But even early in her career she was an innovator, developing a system of "flexible promotion," which was supposed to allow children to advance at their own speed, and "homogeneous grouping," or tracking, whereby the "brightest material, medium material, and

8. Diane Ravitch, *The Great School Wars: A History of the New York City Public Schools* (1974; repr. Baltimore: Johns Hopkins University Press, 2000), 110–14, 124–30, 167–69, 172; Cyrus Adler and Abram S. Issacs, "Sanger, Adolph, L.," http://www.jewishencyclopedia.com/articles/13177-sanger-adolph-l.

poorest material" were put into separate classes. Richman was also an ardent Americanizer, seeing the school as standing between the "alien of today and the citizen of tomorrow." Although she herself was involved in a number of Jewish causes, the perceived harshness of her Americanizing methods sometimes led to conflicts with the immigrant community she served.[9]

Morris Raphael Cohen's experiences in the 1890s illustrate both the difficulties that Jews still faced in the public schools and the promise those schools held out to them. Cohen, who later became a renowned professor of philosophy at the City College of New York, arrived in New York from Belarus in 1892 at the age of about twelve and was promptly placed with younger children in the beginners' "ABC class" to learn English. He was steadily promoted, though he recalled later barely understanding what was going on around him. But he soon learned to read and write English, and when he won an essay contest, he was promoted to grammar school, the next level up. In Brooklyn, though his teacher instructed pupils to recite the Lord's Prayer and told one boy not to "walk like a sheeny," Cohen impressed her and continued to win more prizes for his writing. Later, in a college prep class, he was caught reading Emerson on the sly. The teacher "chased me around the room with his stick until he became somewhat winded. Thereupon he demoted me to the foot of the class, which made me much more comfortable. There I could read more freely and without his frequent interruptions, which I considered as irrelevances."[10]

Mary Antin was another success story of the American public school, and someone who had a much less ambivalent relationship to it. After arriving in Boston in 1894, she too was put in the "baby class" to learn English at the age of thirteen. Like Cohen, she was instructed to recite the Lord's Prayer with her class, until admonished not to by the Jewish boy sitting next to her. But she adored her teachers "as superior beings" and soon became the "show pupil of the class." Above all, school wrought the "miracle" that turned her, almost literally as she tells it in her memoir, into a brand new person—an American citizen, equal to George Washington himself, able to lay claim to Boston's

9. Ruth Jacknow Markowitz, *My Daughter, the Teacher: Jewish Teachers in the New York City Schools* (New Brunswick: Rutgers University Press, 1993), 10–12; Martha Kransdorf, "Julia Richman's Years in the New Public Schools, 1872–1912" (Ph.D. diss., University of Michigan, 1979), esp. 63–64, 72; Selma Berrol, "Julia Richman," in *Jewish Women in America: An Historical Encyclopedia*, ed. Paula Hyman and Deborah Dash Moore, 2 vols. (New York: Routledge, 1997): 2:1148–49; Irving Howe, *World of Our Fathers* (New York: Harcourt Brace Jovanovich, 1976), 278.

10. Morris Raphael Cohen, *A Dreamer's Journey* (Boston: Beacon Press, 1949), 70–84. The exact date, and even year, of Cohen's birth are uncertain. See David Hollinger, "Cohen, Morris Raphael," *American National Biography* (New York: Oxford University Press, 2000).

Puritan fathers as her spiritual ancestors. At her grammar school graduation she was held up by a visiting member of the school board as the model of what the school could do for the immigrant and what the immigrant could do for the school. Later, in her famous memoir, she essentially did the same, joining the debate over immigration by presenting herself as an example of what might become of the immigrants if they were given the chance.[11]

For many years Cahan taught English in an evening school for immigrants, part of a wide-ranging culture of adult education that many Jews participated in as organizers, teachers, and students. This culture of evening lectures and classes for working people had its heyday in the mid-nineteenth century, when most of the patrons were working-class Anglo-Americans and German immigrants. But Jews extended it well into the twentieth century. Independent societies sponsored many of these programs, but in New York, at least, the Board of Education undertook a "massive educational extension effort" beginning in 1888 and expanded it under the leadership of Henry Leipziger from 1890. Born in Manchester, England, to German-Jewish parents, Leipziger arrived in New York in 1865, graduated from City College, taught public school, and earned a law degree. A member of Temple Emanu-El, the flagship Reform Jewish congregation, Leipziger was influenced by Reform Judaism's emphasis on ethics, uplift, and the compatibility of science and religion. Under his leadership, the Board of Education's programs were enormously popular. In 1897–1898, more than half a million people attended lectures on such topics as "How to Breath," "The Times of the Roman Emperors," "Through the Light Portions of the Dark Continent," "Practical Electricity," "Money and How to Make It," "Pictures from a Hindoo Life," and "Indians as Folks."[12]

While the Board of Education lectures avoided politics and aimed at Americanization in the most conventional sense, others were overtly political and oppositional. Cahan was himself one of the most popular lecturers on the socialist circuit. Socialist lecturers sought to enlighten the working class in order to better equip its members to engage with the world and change it. Cahan, anarchists like Emma Goldman, and others spoke on such topics as "The Development of Private Property," "The Necessity of Education," "Socialism from A to Z," "The Origin of Rights," "History as Science," and "What Is Trade Unionism." Two itinerant Scottish immigrant intellectuals also took Jewish immigrants under their wings. Edward King, a type-founder by trade, was a Comtean Positivist

11. Antin, *Promised Land*, esp. 204–40, 281.

12. Cahan, *Bleter fun mayn leben*, 2:155; Brumberg, *Going to America, Going to School*, 148–56.

with "leftist politics" and, according to Cahan, "like an uncle" to the immigrant intelligentsia. The university-educated Thomas Davidson, on the other hand, was a radical individualist opposed to socialism. Morris Raphael Cohen remembered him as a major intellectual influence through his philosophy classes at the Educational Alliance and other venues.[13]

American radical circles in the late nineteenth century were motley indeed. German immigrants were the main constituency of both the socialist and the anarchist movements, and Cahan and other early Yiddish-speaking radicals attended German meetings and read the German-language socialist press (Fig. 62). As for the movement's "real Americans," Cahan characterized them as a mix of real socialists (Marxists), freethinkers, Greenbackers, single taxers, temperance activists, and all sorts of "cranks." Many combined their socialism with Spiritualism, including the librarian at the "American" branch of the Socialist Labor Party (SLP), then the main socialist organization in the United States, who regularly communicated with deceased relatives and animal familiars. On a trip to Boston, Cahan met Edward Bellamy, the author of the utopian novel *Looking Backward* (1888), which promoted a system that Bellamy called "nationalism" but was really a form of socialism. A network of Nationalist Clubs grew up to advocate for Bellamy's ideas, drawing many adherents from the social elite. Although the clubs soon faded, some were transformed into units of the SLP. Daniel DeLeon, a law professor at Columbia University who was beginning to explore Marxism, joined one of these clubs. Born in Curaçao of Sephardic Jewish background, DeLeon became one of the most articulate American interpreters of Marxism, though his sectarian temperament led to the decline of the SLP once he became its leader.[14]

In contrast to Marxism, which remained marginal, the single-tax doctrine of the homegrown social philosopher and economist Henry George briefly gained some traction among radicals and reformers. Searching for an explanation for the social inequality of the Gilded Age, George argued that a monopoly of land ownership was the root of nearly all evil. By favoring rent values over productive use, it established an economic stranglehold over the entire economy, not only encouraging speculation but also blocking initiative, depressing wages, and exacerbating urban overcrowding. The remedy was to place a nearly confiscatory

13. Tony Michels, *A Fire in Their Hearts: Yiddish Socialists in New York* (Cambridge, Mass.: Harvard University Press, 2005), 74–91; Howe, *World of Our Fathers*, 231; Cahan, *Bleter fun Mayn Leben*, 2:159–62; Cohen, *Dreamer's Journey*, 103–22.

14. Cahan, *Bleter fun mayn leben*, 2:87–89, 306–15; 3:247–55, 281–84.

Fig. 62. "In these cafés they meet after the theatre or an evening lecture." Illustration by Jacob Epstein for Hutchins Hapgood, *The Spirit of the Ghetto* (New York, 1902), p. 41. (Library of Congress).

tax on land not used for productive purposes. Ultimately, without doing away with the free market or private ownership, this policy would lead to a cooperative society in which the fruits of labor would be more equitably shared. George was not exactly a socialist, but when he ran for mayor of New York in 1886 in a campaign that constituted a remarkable popular revolt against both political and social elites, socialists like Cahan supported him enthusiastically. Later, though, George broke with his socialist comrades and stressed the reformist aspects of his program.[15]

As opposed to both socialism and George's single-tax philosophy, what came to be called Social Darwinism justified the emerging social hierarchies by associating them with apparently "natural" processes. As developed by British thinker Hebert Spencer and filtered through the writings of his American popularizers, Social Darwinist thought pervaded American society. Andrew Carnegie, the steel magnate and "philosopher of wealth," argued that inequality was a necessary condition for human progress, indeed for civilization itself. Any attempt to interfere with this inequality—or with the rule of the rich and powerful—would be disastrous, bringing down civilization to the common ruin of all classes. But these ideas were not limited to the likes of Carnegie. Cahan encountered Social Darwinism in the person of a crank who went by the name of Professor Gunton, who showed up at socialist meetings to defend capitalism. "His chief weapon," wrote Cahan, "was Darwinism—the usual argument that is put forward against socialism." On the other hand, some anarchists considered themselves followers of Spencer as well, perhaps drawn by his application of scientific principles to social problems in ways that challenged traditional pieties. To better refute Social Darwinist arguments, Cahan decided to study up on Spencer. He intended to write a systematic critique, but never completed it.[16]

The founders of the settlement houses that dotted the immigrant neighborhoods offered an alternative to Social Darwinist thought and important venues for educational activities. Cahan explained what a "settlement" was:

15. Edward T. O'Donnell, *Henry George and the Crisis of Inequality: Progress and Poverty in the Gilded Age* (New York: Columbia University Press, 2015), 48–56, 258–59, 277–78; Cahan, *Bleter fun mayn leben*, 2:251–73.

16. "Social Darwinism," in *The Reader's Companion to American History*, ed. Eric Foner and John A. Garraty (Boston: Houghton Mifflin, 1991), 999–1000; Bernard Lightman, "Spencer's American Disciples: Fiske, Youmans, and the Appropriation of the System," in *Global Spencerism: The Communication and Appropriation of a British Evolutionist*, ed. Bernard Lightman (Leiden: Brill, 2016), 123–48; Andrew Carnegie, "Wealth," *North American Review*, 148 (June 1889): 653–64; Cahan, *Bleter fun mayn leben*, 2:354–55, 419–20.

> Educated American university graduates settle in a poor neighborhood with the goal of instilling an intelligent and refined life in the children, to give them a place to spend time in a respectable way, and thereby to separate them from bad company. Instead of running around in the street and associating with degenerate children, perhaps with criminals, they have the society of respectable and educated people, who accustom them to reading good books, discussing interesting issues, and to engage in sports and other pastimes in a respectable way.

But Cahan's definition was a little too narrow. The settlement house offered all sorts of uplifting activities—classes, clubs, recreational facilities, libraries, even sometimes cafés and residences—to their "neighbors" of all ages. Cahan himself lectured at New York's University Settlement on socialism (a lecture attended by Seth Low, president of Columbia University) and on the Russian revolutionary movement. He compared the Russian movement to the settlements, but concluded that the latter were ultimately "satisfied" with the "inequalities and injustices" of capitalist society. Emma Goldman agreed with Cahan on this point. "Teaching the poor to eat with a fork is all very well," she said, "but what good does it do if they have not the food?" As far as Goldman was concerned, the settlements did "more harm than good"[17]

Lilian Wald, New York's leading settlement activist, clearly disagreed with both Cahan and Goldman. Like many settlement workers, Wald drew inspiration from the Christian Social Gospel movement, stressing its vision of "universal belonging" and brotherhood that would transcend narrow divisions. This was hardly the conservative vision that Cahan and Goldman implied. Rather, the Social Gospel drew on Christian sources to call for a "new social order on earth ... the City of God"—perfection in this world, not just in the next. With this goal in mind, Wald set out to counter the "dehumanizing and uncivilized" inequality she found on the Lower East Side, where she had settled. To the Social Gospel, she added a measure of maternalism, a belief that it was women's duty to safeguard the morals of society and the well-being especially of women and children. And it is true that as a trained nurse she focused first on providing practical assistance to her neighbors. But, like Jane Addams in Chicago, Wald also recognized that poverty could not be alleviated solely by teaching people to eat with a fork, and so she took part in movements for wide-ranging social reform.

In a movement led largely by women, Wald was also the most prominent Jew,

17. Cahan, *Bleter fun mayn leben*, 3:274–80; Emma Goldman quoted in Marjorie N. Feld, *Lillian Wald: A Biography* (Chapel Hill: University of North Carolina Press, 2008), 76.

though she strenuously played down this identity. Hailing from a well-off German Jewish family in Rochester, New York, she absorbed an assimilationist and universalist ethos. Nevertheless, despite her public disavowal of her Jewishness, her social networks were largely Jewish. When she founded the Nurses' Settlement (later Henry Street Settlement) in 1893, her main benefactor was Jacob Schiff, who instructed her in the religious sensibilities of her clients. She was also friendly with the Lower East Side's Yiddish intellectual elite, and even allowed some Yiddish plays to be produced at Henry Street. But however much she tried to be sensitive to the Jewish immigrant community's particularity, she remained committed to a process of liberal Americanization.[18]

If the settlement houses aimed to educate recent immigrants, the Jewish Chautauqua Society's prime audience consisted mostly of middle-class Americanized Jews. Founded in 1893, the society was modeled on the adult education movement that was a "composite" of "college ... summer resort ... [and] religious assembly," originating at Chautauqua in western New York. The most characteristic features of the Chautauqua movement were its annual summer encampments at Chautauqua itself or at one of the many independent offshoots, where participants could combine their country vacations with uplifting lectures and artistic programs. Methodist in its original inspiration, the Chautauqua movement evolved toward liberal Protestant nondenominationalism informed, like the settlement houses, by the Social Gospel. At the end of the nineteenth century and the beginning of the twentieth, Chautauqua was tremendously popular, with Theodore Roosevelt calling it the "most American thing in America." After he had begun his career as an English-language author, Cahan once lectured at such an encampment. But he did not seem nearly as impressed as Roosevelt. "People run from lecture to lecture," he wrote sarcastically. "The place looked like a fair (*yarid*)." By the 1920s, when the movement was already in decline, most high-brow intellectuals agreed with Cahan that Chautauqua was hopelessly provincial.[19]

But in the 1890s, Chautauqua impressed Catholics and Jews enough that they formed their own counterparts. The energetic Reform rabbi Henry Berkowitz, who had special interests in Jewish education and interfaith relations, founded

18. Feld, *Lillian Wald*, esp. 5–7, 13–14, 20–27, 36–38, 40–44, 55, 65, 72–73, 79.

19. Andrew Rieser, *The Chautauqua Moment: Protestants, Progressives, and the Culture of Modern Liberalism* (New York: Columbia University Press, 2003), 5, 12, 133; Cahan, *Bleter fun mayn leben*, 4:207. Cahan recalled that he had spoken at Chautauqua, Pennsylvania. He was either mistaken as to the location, or he spoke at one of the many independent offshoots of the original New York camp.

the Jewish Chautauqua Society with the blessing and assistance of the original body. Berkowitz's society was officially nondenominational, but in fact aligned with Reform Judaism, striving to harmonize Judaism with mainstream American culture. In addition to its own summer convocations, the society sponsored reading circles, correspondence schools, and teacher workshops. It published study guides on Judaism, Jewish history, Hebrew language, and other topics. The programs were especially popular among women, who had fewer educational outlets than men, and among Jews in rural areas and small towns, who otherwise had few opportunities to partake in Jewish culture in general. The society also undertook to educate non-Jews about Judaism, equated with modernity and moral reform, as a way of combating antisemitism. The Jewish Chautauqua Society could even boast Roosevelt among its visiting lecturers.[20]

Despite all this grassroots intellectual ferment, Cahan experienced a certain amount of frustration with the educated native-born Americans with whom he had contact. With their shallow thinking and conservative outlook, they simply did not measure up to the standards of the radical intellectual Russian youth Cahan had known and against whom he measured all things intellectual, literary, political, and cultural. When he discussed socialism with Emanuel Kurscheedt, an organizer of the YMHA's evening classes, Kurscheedt would simply mumble, "Crazy, crazy, crazy." Likewise, during occasional dinners at his school's principal's house, the principal and his family would take the Social Darwinist position that there would always be social classes as long as there were differences in human capabilities. Cahan also joined a debating society of young graduates of City College—mostly teachers, and mostly "Christians" and "real Americans." But although they might debate the merits of capitalism and socialism, to Cahan's frustration all they really cared about was honing their speaking and arguing skills, not the issue itself.[21]

Cahan soon had his own brief encounter with higher education. Convinced by some comrades that he could be useful to the movement as a lawyer, he entered Columbia Law School in 1888. At the time, Jewish students were a rarity, and Cahan was the only Russian Jew in the class. Most of the students were "real Americans, German-Americans, or Irish-Americans—all American born." Some

20. Marcus, *United States Jewry*, 3:547–49; Lila Corwin Berman, *Speaking of Jews: Rabbis, Intellectuals, and the Creation of an American Public Identity* (Berkeley: University of California Press, 2009), 24–26; Peggy Kronsberg Pearlstein, "Understanding through Education: One Hundred Years of the Jewish Chautauqua Society, 1893–1993" (Ph.D. diss., George Washington University, 1993); Rieser, *Chautauqua Moment*, 125.

21. Cahan, *Bleter fun mayn leben*, 2:155–56, 316–20.

came from elite families. Though some were university graduates, many were not, and in any case no degree or exam was required. Though he bonded with one classmate, a fellow atheist, over a pamphlet by the prominent freethinker Robert Ingersoll, Cahan once again found that the American students did not measure up—"they laughed at ideals, nothing like Russian students." The study of Blackstone reminded him of Talmud study from his brief time in the yeshiva. But disgusted at the hypocrisy of the law, and finding he lacked the temperament for it anyway, Cahan dropped out after a year.[22]

Like his experience with American primary education, Cahan's brush against American professional education came at a time when it was undergoing significant changes. The idea that someone would prepare for a legal career by attending law school, instead of apprenticing in an attorney's office, was a relatively new one that emerged around the time of the Civil War. And different law schools took different approaches. When future Supreme Court Justice Louis Brandeis attended Harvard Law School between 1875 and 1877, it was already pioneering the idea that the law should be treated as an academic discipline, a "science" that "should be studied as such." While at Harvard, Brandeis, who lacked a college degree, found himself in what to him was an exciting intellectual milieu that drew on circles well beyond the law school. In Cambridge and Boston, he heard lectures and attended receptions with the likes of Ralph Waldo Emerson, Henry Adams, and John Greenleaf Whittier. On the other hand, though Columbia too developed a new, rigorous approach to the study of law as a coherent body of knowledge, it took a more strictly vocational approach, offering a path to a successful career. This choice did not seem to bother future Jewish communal leader Louis Marshall, who crammed the two-year course into one year of study in 1875–1876, but left without a degree. Marshall established a close relationship with the school's dominant personality, Dean Theodore William Dwight, and excelled at memorization, which Dwight prized. There is no record of whether Marshall and Cahan ever discussed their differing impressions of Columbia Law School.[23]

Undergraduate education was similarly undergoing a transformation. Until the last couple of decades of the nineteenth century, American colleges were largely

22. *Ibid.*, 2:342–43.

23. Philippa Strum, *Louis D. Brandeis: Justice for the People* (Cambridge, Mass.: Harvard University Press, 1984), 18–24; M. M. Silver, *Louis Marshall and the Rise of Jewish Ethnicity in America: A Biography* (Syracuse: Syracuse University Press, 2013), 10–16; Thomas Bender, *New York Intellect: A History of Intellectual Life in New York City, from 1750 to the Beginnings of Our Own Time* (New York: Knopf, 1987), 274.

finishing schools for the children of the elite. Most students were preparing for careers in the law, medicine, or the ministry. But a degree was seldom required for entry into business, especially the family business, or even the professions, so only a few people attended college, and many of them failed to complete the course. Many universities had some sort of Christian denominational affiliation, and the curriculum emphasized classical languages, rhetoric, and natural philosophy. Universities were hardly hotbeds of intellectual innovation or even of particularly deep thinking. But in the decades after the Civil War, American higher education responded to the need for a more highly trained managerial and technical workforce in modern industry and commerce, to the advancing standardization of fields such as engineering, medicine, and law, and to a growing interest in finding solutions for the social problems created by industrialization and urbanization. The new German model of the modern research university began to make inroads, and new universities such as Johns Hopkins in Baltimore made advanced research a central part of their mission. Some older schools followed suit.[24]

The Jewish college experience also changed—and not always for the better. Even as new nonsectarian schools were established, as older ones very slowly downplayed their religious roots, and as many became more serious about intellectual pursuits, student life came to revolve more and more around sports and a social life from which Jews were frequently excluded. Students often disdained intellectual pursuits, as well as what they perceived as Jewish (and Chinese) intellectual precociousness. This trend does not seem to have affected Arkansas-born Cyrus Adler much, however, when he attended the University of Pennsylvania between 1879 and 1883. He begins his recollections of his college years with a description of sports, class fights, pranks, and drinking beer. He then apologizes for doing so … before returning to these very subjects. It probably did not hurt the Jewish cause at Penn that a Jewish classmate was a boxer and footballer. As for compulsory chapel, Adler demanded to be excused on the grounds that he was a Jew. As soon as he got permission not to attend, he started to go regularly.[25]

Adler took advantage of the new emphasis on research in American universities, earning a Ph.D. in Semitics at Johns Hopkins University—perhaps the

24. Bender, *New York Intellect*, 280–90; Sherry Gorelick, *City College and the Jewish Poor: Education in New York, 1880–1924* (New Brunswick: Rutgers University Press, 1981), 47–57.

25. Diner, *A Time for Gathering*, 166–67; Bender, *New York Intellect*, 279, 287; Dan A. Oren, *Joining the Club: A History of Jews at Yale* (New Haven: Yale University Press, 1985), 11–21; Cyrus Adler, *I Have Considered the Days* (Philadelphia: Jewish Publication Society, 1941), 22–32.

first person to take a doctorate in that subject at an American school. But in his choice of fields, Adler was perhaps typical of the few Jews to make careers in American academia in this period. Most taught in "the realm of Judaically oriented subjects of the classical curriculum": Hebrew, Semitics, Bible, rabbinics. Some taught foreign languages, particularly German. Even in the emerging new curriculum, it was easier for Jews to get jobs in languages or the sciences than in culturally sensitive areas like American history and English literature, where Jews were still often regarded as foreign interlopers. The new field of psychology seems to have been one field in which Jews were permitted to take leadership roles; Joseph Jastrow even became president of the American Psychological Association in 1900.[26]

Though Adler seems to have had no trouble personally, his experience may be instructive as to why more Jews did not advance in the chummy world of academia. As he later recalled, faculty social life was an only slightly more erudite version of its undergraduate counterpart. At the Johns Hopkins faculty club, each member had his own beer stein, and the singing of bawdy songs in English, German, and Latin was a favored pastime. Adler also roomed for a time with his mentor, Paul Haupt, an intimate arrangement that certainly would be frowned on today. Even, or maybe especially, then, Jewish integration into these kinds of social worlds was more difficult than the establishment of strictly business or intellectual relationships.[27]

Given that so many American institutions of higher education had Christian denominational origins and affiliations, it is not surprising that some Jewish leaders thought of establishing a Jewish college or university. Even before the Civil War, Rabbi Isaac Mayer Wise expressed interest in "an educational institute somewhere in the West ... in the interest of science and Judaism." Wise pushed the large Jewish fraternal order B'nai B'rith to undertake such a project, and indeed, the order saw education as one of its primary missions—a mission both particularly Jewish and, at the same time, universal. As one B'nai B'rith leader put it, "*Science* is the *Messiah* of the human race, leads to human happiness and leads toward the realization of the brotherhood of man."[28] With Wise's backing, Grand Saar (President) Benjamin Franklin Peixotto introduced

26. Marcus, *United States Jewry*, 3:301–3, 318–19; Diner, *A Time for Gathering*, 166–67; Adler, *I Have Considered the Days*, 48–64; Oren, *Joining the Club*, 113.

27. Adler, *I Have Considered the Days*, 51–52, 59.

28. Deborah Dash Moore, *B'nai B'rith and the Challenge of Ethnic Leadership* (Albany: SUNY Press, 1981), 20–21, 28.

a resolution at the order's 1866 convention to found a "Jewish school of higher education." Such a school, Peixotto argued, would "give to the now vacant pulpits and shepherdless flocks of Israel in America, in due time and at the moment when most required for the rising generation, Jewish ministers qualified in the language and rhetoric of the land, while learned in the laws of Judaism ... and develop the spiritual happiness of Israel."[29]

But the delegates voted down the motion to create a Jewish college, and the school's stated purpose provides a clue as to why. Wise, and apparently Peixotto, envisioned the proposed institution as at least partly a rabbinical seminary. Such a school, undoubtedly, would not contribute to science in a way that would satisfy some members, and it would inevitably involve its sponsor in American Jewry's emerging denominational quarrels, something B'nai B'rith's leaders hoped to avoid. Furthermore, not all B'nai B'rith members were convinced that the "spiritual happiness of Israel" lay in the synagogue at all. It seemed better to direct the order's resources toward building an orphanage, something both necessary and less controversial. An 1895 proposal again urged B'nai B'rith to undertake a university "dedicated to the people of the United States as an imperishable evidence of the gratitude of the Jews of America for the blessings we enjoy under a free and enlightened government." But it failed too. No secular university under Jewish auspices was established until the twentieth century.[30]

The several Jewish institutions of higher learning that were established in the nineteenth century had a purely religious character, training rabbis and teachers. Isaac Leeser, a defender of traditional Judaism who nonetheless wanted to see it adapt to American conditions, founded Maimonides College in 1867, but it closed in 1873, five years after Leeser's death. Hebrew Union College (HUC) opened in Cincinnati in 1875 and soon evolved into the preeminent seminary for the training of Reform rabbis. The Jewish Theological Seminary (JTS), which aimed to serve the "Jews of America faithful to Mosaic law and ancestral tradition," opened in 1887; the Rabbi Isaac Elchanan Theological Seminary (RIETS), serving the more conservative Orthodox Jewish community, launched in 1897; and Gratz College, a teachers' seminary that accepted women as students, arose in 1893. But, "in the sense that the Germans abroad understood the concept, the

29. Edward Grusd, *B'nai B'rith: The Story of a Covenant* (New York: Appleton-Century, 1966), 52–53.

30. Grusd, *B'nai B'rith*, 50–53, 94–95, 116–17; Cornelia Wilhelm, *The Independent Orders of B'nai B'rith and True Sisters: Pioneers of a New Jewish Identity, 1843–1914*, trans. Alan Nothnagle and Sarah Wobick (Detroit: Wayne State University Press, 2011), 84–100.

Hebrew Union College [in its early years] was not a scholarly institution." And the same could have been said about the other schools. HUC, JTS, and RIETS (as Yeshiva University) later became full-fledged academic institutions, but that transformation took place in the twentieth century.[31]

But not all scholarship, Jewish or otherwise, took place in the emerging research universities. Adler, for example, who did much to inject Jewish studies into the American intellectual mainstream, did so from his position at the Smithsonian Institution. Brought on board to bolster what he called "the older learning and the humanities," because of the Smithsonian's strength in the sciences, he found a congenial perch. When first offered the job as librarian, he almost turned it down because he thought himself inappropriate for the role as a Sabbath-observing Jew. But he was told that this strict observation was no obstacle, that he could set his own hours. The atmosphere at the Smithsonian was certainly a scholarly one, with "a group of men much larger and more eminent than that of any two faculties of our greatest universities," but also one interested in bringing scientific learning to the public. Adler did so, not only at the Institution, but also at the Chicago Exposition of 1893, where he helped to organize the ethnographic exhibits.[32]

Adler also helped to organize the American Jewish Historical Society (AJHS) in 1892, one of a number of ethnic historical societies that arose around that time in response to growing ethnocentrism and racial nativism among the Anglo-American elite. As "old stock" Americans increasingly defined true patriotism as an inheritable trait, buttressed by an increasing number of genealogical and historical societies, it seemed to some observers that the best way to present a counterargument was to prove that one's own group—Irish, Germans, Swedes, Jews, and so on—had been in America just as long as anyone else and had contributed just as much to building the country. So it was with the AJHS, many of whose founders hoped it would help to combat rising antisemitism. Even Professor Charles Gross of Harvard, a historian of medieval England and one of the very few Jews with an academic position in history, agreed that by promoting knowledge of the Jewish role in building America, "we shall be able to remove a great deal of the prejudice that still remains among the people of this country against the Jews." In addition to collecting materials, the society

31. Jonathan D. Sarna, *American Judaism: A History* (New Haven: Yale University Press, 2004), 80, 138, 184, 192; Marcus, *United States Jewry*, 3:95–96, 551–53; Jeffrey S. Gurock, *The Men and Women of Yeshiva: Higher Education, Orthodoxy, and American Judaism* (New York: Columbia University Press, 1988).

32. Adler, *I Have Considered the Days*, 179–85; Cohen, *Encounter with Emancipation*, 207.

held an annual conference, the proceeds of which it then published. In keeping with the society's aims, much of what it published was filiopietistic, apologetic, or bibliographic in nature. Adler himself was not entirely happy with this state of affairs. He would have liked to have seen more rigorous and dispassionate scholarship; and indeed, this tension between filiopiety and professionalism persisted in the society well into the twentieth century. In the meantime, the society managed to achieve some recognition from such major American historians as Herbert Baxter Adams, who, despite his own contributions to the racial conception of American history, hoped to consolidate the entire historical field into the recently organized American Historical Association.[33]

Besides museums, expositions, and historical societies, scholarly knowledge was transmitted to the general public through encyclopedias. These, along with other reference books, were important consumer goods in an emerging mass market in the middle of the nineteenth century. They provided the information that Americans craved and found "useful" in an era when industrialization, a revolution in transportation, and the expansion of education combined to make knowledge of the wider world seem both more necessary and more accessible through print. People could use the knowledge they gained from reference books in business, school, or individual self-improvement. But these works also came to signify "middle-class respectability" and "learnedness." Abraham Cahan certainly aspired to learnedness, if not exactly middle-class respectability, so one can imagine his excitement, when once,

> walking on Fourth Avenue, I spotted in the window of a bookstore an encyclopedia of 15 volumes, with a tag on which was written, "18 dollars"—a very cheap price. I went in and examined the books. I don't remember the name of the encyclopedia. I only remember that it was a popular work. The print was crisp, but very small, and the lines were thickly packed. But an encyclopedia! And cheap too: 18 dollars for fifteen very large and thick books.

Cahan dragged them home and proudly placed them on a shelf with a couple of dozen English and Russian books and various socialist pamphlets.[34]

33. John Appel, "Immigrant Historical Societies in the United States, 1880–1950" (Ph.D. diss., University of Pennsylvania, 1960); Jeffrey S. Gurock, "Introduction" to the special issue "From *Publications* to *American Jewish History*: The Journal of the American Jewish Historical Society and the Writing of American Jewish History," *American Jewish History* 81, no. 2 (1993/1994): 155–72; Jeffrey S. Gurock, "Signposts: Cyrus Adler's Vision of American Jewish Historical Writing," *American Jewish History* 101, no. 4 (2017): 489–99.

34. Ann K. Johnson, "The People's Book: Making, Selling, and Reading of Reference Works in Nineteenth-Century America" (Ph.D. diss., University of Southern California, 2014), 3, 7, 167, and *passim*; Cahan, *Bleter fun mayn leben*, 2:173–74.

Cahan did not remember which encyclopedia he had purchased. If it was D. Appleton & Company's *American Cyclopedia*, he already knew one of the editors. Appleton was one of the country's leading reference book publishers. From its six-story New York headquarters, its staff of writers and editors could easily consult the holdings of the nearby Astor and Mercantile libraries. The entire fourth floor of the building was given over to the *Cyclopedia*, the staff of thirty-two men sitting at a large desk in the middle of a room "bursting with books." There they edited contributions, revised articles for yearbooks and new editions, and checked facts. In addition to these generalists, Appleton, like other encyclopedia publishers, tapped into the growing corps of university-trained specialists. The headquarter's ground floor held a retail bookshop, but many of Appleton's sales came from itinerant salesmen and agents who spread its wares beyond the city to rural areas, as well as to schools across the country.[35]

Michael Heilprin worked on Appleton's fourth floor, one of four associate editors of the *American Cyclopedia*. Born in Poland to an "old-fashioned" Yiddish-speaking Jewish family, Heilprin, according to Cahan, dressed in a traditional long coat and wore *peyes* (side locks) into adulthood. But his father read German philosophy, and Michael himself moved to Hungary and became a supporter of Lajos Kossuth, the leader of the fight for Hungarian independence in the failed revolutions of 1848. Eight years later, he arrived in the United States, where he spoke out against slavery and, like some other '48ers, remained "the liberal, the fighter for freedom, the radical partisan." Cahan met Heilprin through the latter's social work with the more recent Jewish immigrants. Cahan describes Heilprin as a "spiritual aristocrat in the finest sense of the term," who radiated "education, refinement, and gentleness" and looked like a "professor or a musician." In those days, Cahan notes, such men were rare in New York, and Heilprin attracted attention. With a knowledge of Polish, Hungarian, German, French, English, and Hebrew, as well as a phenomenal memory, Heilprin was a natural encyclopedist: "He himself was a living encyclopedia. He used to look through all of the articles. When there was some error in a figure or a fact, it could not escape his eye." Nevertheless, Heilprin had no interest in socialism and therefore "was not a thinker" in Cahan's eyes. "His rare abilities were inclined toward disciplines (*visnshaftn*) that required memory."[36]

Heilprin himself contributed a number of articles to the encyclopedia, including ones on classical topics ("Cyrus," "Media" [*sic*]) and modern European

35. Johnson, "The People's Book," 37–50, 54, 88, 99–106, 119–20, 167, 169–70.
36. Cahan, *Bleter fun mayn leben*, 2:69, 131–38; Marcus, *United States Jewry*, 3:19.

history and events, some of which he had himself participated in ("Hungary," "Kossuth"). He also wrote the long entry on "Hebrews." Contrary to Cahan's charge that Heilprin was simply an excellent reciter of facts, a charge that was consistent with many encyclopedias' own boasts that they were objective by being "passionless," "thorough," and "just," Heilprin's entry clearly approaches its subject from a distinct perspective. More or less explicitly, he makes a number of points. First, the Hebrews (or Israelites, or Jews) are a distinct people originating at the "very dawn of the history of mankind" and continuing in an unbroken chain to the present day; modern Jews are thus the same people as the ancient Hebrews. Second, the national and the religious elements in Jewish history cannot be separated; given this intertwining and the fact that the Jews continued as a nation even after dispersion, Jewish history is unique. Third, Jewish history is essentially secular. Heilprin does not say, for example, that God bestowed upon Abraham a divine mission or that God exiled the Jews from their homeland for their sins; rather, Abraham "is recorded as acting under divine mission," and a series of cultural and political failures led to exile. Fourth, the Jews have been unjustly persecuted, especially given their contributions to civilization. Finally, in modern times internal Jewish enlightenment and emancipation from without have combined to enable the Jews to make even greater contributions to the nations among whom they live and to human civilization in general. Gentile Americans reading the *New American Cyclopaedia*, therefore, were given a sympathetic account of Jewish history and culture, one that would encourage them to identify their Jewish neighbors favorably with the Hebrews of the Bible.[37]

American Jews also undertook a number of publishing projects themselves. Work on the *Jewish Encyclopedia* did not begin until 1898, and the first volumes did not appear until 1901. By that time, though, the Jewish Publication Society (JPS) had been in business for over a decade, formed in 1888 after a number of earlier false starts. Like the encyclopedia, and like the AJHS and the Jewish Chautauqua Society, the JPS had its non-Jewish precedents; one call for its organization cited the Episcopalian Publication Society, the Methodist Book Concern, and the Presbyterian Tract Society. The JPS can also be understood as part of a surge in Jewish religious and cultural expression, and as a reflection of a growing sense of confidence among American Jews that they could take over from Germany as the main western center of Jewish creativity. Among its goals

37. Michael Heilprin, *Selection of Articles Contributed to the New American Cyclopaedia* (n.p., ca. 1890); Johnson, "The People's Book," 78.

were to "improve community relations" by publishing materials that reflected well on Jews and Judaism, and to keep Jewish youth in the fold by issuing engaging high-quality literature in English.[38]

The secretary of the publication committee, and for many years the JPS's only full-time employee, was Henrietta Szold, later most famous as the founder of Hadassah, the women's Zionist organization. The daughter of a prominent Baltimore rabbi, she served an apprenticeship in Jewish scholarship with her father. Moving to Philadelphia in 1893 to assume her position at the JPS, Szold found herself "evaluating manuscripts, copyediting, proofreading, indexing, working with the printer, keeping track of manuscripts, and corresponding with authors, as well as preparing publication committee minutes."[39] To this list might be added writing, translating, and editing manuscripts for content. In fact, she did everything connected with not only the administrative but also the intellectual work of the JPS, guiding it into the twentieth century.

The JPS set out to publish a wide range of history and literature, but the choice of specific works remained a bit of a quandary. The desire to stand above Jewish sectarian squabbles made it difficult to settle on religious books. And although the JPS did put out a full English translation of Heinrich Graetz's five-volume *History of the Jews*, its members argued over the balance between scholarship and popularity. Even as the JPS hoped to promote American Jewish writing, many of its early publications were translations from German, originally British, or both, that is, British translations of German works. Fiction posed a similar dilemma. How serious should it be? To what extent should it be allowed to offer a critical view of Jewish life? One work by Emma Wolf was rejected because it included "immoral" characters and an irreligious rabbi.[40]

When the JPS recruited the acclaimed British-Jewish author Israel Zangwill to contribute what became *Children of the Ghetto*, his novel of life among both immigrant and acculturated Jews in Britain, Mayer Sulzberger, chairman of the publication committee, admonished him to keep it light, "studiously avoid the deep distress of tragedy," and not "harrow the feelings much." Zangwill worried that his work would be rejected because it "told the truth," but *Children of the Ghetto* became the "most talked about book of the season" when it appeared in 1892. Zangwill may have paved the way for realist writing about Jewish immigrant life. But when Sulzberger, during negotiations with Cahan, warned him

38. Jonathan D. Sarna, *JPS: The Americanization of Jewish Culture, 1888–1988* (Philadelphia: Jewish Publication Society, 1989), 1–27.

39. *Ibid.*, 30–31, 47–50.

40. *Ibid.*, esp. 34–39, 44, 74–82, 88–91.

against "selecting ugliness as the ideal," Cahan concluded that "the gulf between the tastes and views of your organization and my own seems to be impassable." He did not publish with the JPS.[41]

Cahan met Zangwill when the latter visited New York in 1898. The occasion was a celebration in honor of the seventieth birthday of the great Russian writer Leo Tolstoy. As Cahan recalled, not many important American writers or critics attended because, first of all, Tolstoy was not well known then in America, and second, because Tolstoy's non-aristocratic persona was not to their liking. Zangwill arrived straight from the boat, was given a place of honor, and made a well-received and humorous speech. Cahan later showed the guest around New York's Jewish ghetto, and Zangwill explained to his guide that although critics in England praised his work, they never included him in lists or overviews of important British writers. When Zangwill suggested that perhaps they considered his work "esoteric," Cahan suggested that maybe a better word would be "exotic." In any case, they agreed that there might be a bit of antisemitism involved in Zangwill's exclusion from the English canon. They complimented each other's work.[42]

By that time, Cahan had begun to gain some renown as an author of English-language realist fiction about Jewish immigrant life in New York, and he was sometimes compared to Zangwill. In this and other ways, Cahan served as an interpreter between the Yiddish-speaking and English-speaking worlds. But Americans' taste for light and romantic writing—always with a happy ending—frustrated Cahan, who considered Russian literature to be far deeper, truer to life, and of much greater social significance. The prominent American realist William Dean Howells, who had befriended Cahan, warned him that it might be hard to find an outlet for his work, and he was right. American editors felt that art must always be about beautiful things and that the lives of working-class immigrants did not qualify. As one editor put it, referring to Cahan's first story, *Yekl*: "Our male and female readers want a novel about richly dressed cavaliers and ladies, a love that develops between them as they play golf on the meadows. How can a novel interest them that concerns a Jewish immigrant, a blacksmith turned tailor, who comes to despise his ignorant wife?"[43]

More than simply an aesthetic judgment, the editor's comments reflected a deep conservatism among established American intellectuals. After the Civil War, in a period of intense class conflict, the intellectual elite worried over the

41. *Ibid.*, 39–42, 80.

42. Cahan, *Bleter fun mayn leben*, 4:221–24.

43. *Ibid.*, 4:37–38.

very survival of "culture" and "democracy." The former they associated with themselves, and the latter they distrusted. In either case, Cahan's working-class immigrants, whether as fictional characters or as real people, had no legitimate part. Culture should, intellectual leaders believed, be somewhat divorced from and stand on a higher plane than politics. But in fact, their cultural views were closely connected to their politics. And as they expressed their opinions in a new crop of magazines, as well as in books, they zealously guarded their status as arbiters of American culture and argued for a "purified" and laissez-faire democracy run by "gentlemen." Cahan, of course, believed the opposite—that the true task of literature was to be engaged, even subversive.[44]

Cahan found common ground on these issues with Howells, the dean of American letters, who in this period moved from Boston to New York and broke ranks with his elite peers. Awakened to the dismal conditions in America's factories and tenements, Howells turned "traitor to the brownstone class." In his writing, he looked to go beyond "love affairs" and began to endorse a "vague kind of socialism" while exploring the shadows of urban industrial life. Already America's most prominent advocate and practitioner of literary realism, Howells also read and promoted the new Russian literature. In this context, Howells sought to connect with the immigrant intelligentsia, searched out Cahan, and arranged to meet with him.[45]

Certainly, meeting Howells in 1892 was important for Cahan, and if Cahan is to be believed, he influenced Howells as well. The two met at Howells's Stuyvesant Square home, where "the perfume of spiritual refinement" permeated. They conversed about Russian and American writers and about socialism, and Howells proudly showed his guest a letter he had received from Ivan Turgeniev praising his work. Cahan had the feeling that much of what he himself had to say about Russian culture and about politics was new to Howells, and that the older man found it very interesting. Howells viewed Cahan as a significant new talent and encouraged him to focus more on English-language fiction writing. For his part, Cahan saw Howells as a great writer, closer to the Russian spirit than any other American author. Still, Cahan thought Howells did not go far enough, that he was too careful not to offend puritanical American sexual sensibilities.[46]

But American culture was changing with the rise of a new bohemian intellectual and artistic class that started its own magazines and published its own books to challenge the established elite and bourgeois culture. The bohemians sought

44. Bender, *New York Intellect*, 171–85, 207–9.

45. *Ibid.*, 191–95, 215.

46. Cahan, *Bleter fun mayn leben*, 4:21–28, 32–37.

to revolutionize artistic and literary expression, as well as gender relations and norms of social behavior. Some even discovered socialism. From Greenwich Village, it was only a short walk to the Lower East Side, and a number of Anglo-American intellectuals looked there for the intellectual and cultural spirit they found lacking in mainstream America. The immigrant Jewish quarter was especially linked in their minds not only with Jews but also with Russia, whose literature they had begun reading and whose revolutionary movement they had heard about. Cahan, of course, was perfectly situated to become one of the leading guides to this world, shepherding visitors through the neighborhood's cafés and discoursing on Russian culture. But if Cahan helped to open new vistas for his bohemian friends, they too opened new worlds for him. Invited to the Lanthorn Club on William Street, he found the walls decorated with art and the rooms furnished in such a way that the "the entire appearance of the place tasted of 'artistic temperament' and with artistic 'freedom from ceremony.'" There, "American literati, journalists, painters and sculptors" drank whiskey, ate sandwiches, made speeches, and talked about their forthcoming work. Cahan met Stephen Crane there, and they discussed the problems of writing realistic fiction for an unappreciative American audience.[47]

But while Cahan sometimes aspired to creative writing, he was continually pulled back into journalism in both English and Yiddish. American journalism was undergoing a revolution during the 1880s and 1890s, led partly by immigrant and second-generation Jews. Cahan's first English-language article appeared in the *New York World*, which had been recently bought by Joseph Pulitzer, a Hungarian immigrant who had gotten his journalistic start in the German-language press in St. Louis. When Pulitzer took over the *World* in 1883, it had a circulation of 15,000. By the end of the century, it was selling 600,000 copies daily by emphasizing the sensational, by employing stylistic innovations such as illustrations and large headlines, by undertaking crusades on various issues, and by relentlessly promoting itself. But it also sought to cover the "marvels and mysteries" of urban life, becoming a guide to the modern American city for a largely immigrant and second-generation readership. Pulitzer wanted the *World* to be, as he put it, "both a daily school-house and a daily forum—both a

47. Christine Stansell, *American Moderns: Bohemian New York and the Creation of a New Century* (New York: Metropolitan Books, 2000), 1–39; Bender, *New York Intellect*, 220–21, 230; Tony Michels, "The Lower East Side Meets Greenwich Village: Immigrant Jews, Yiddish, and the New York Intellectual Scene," in *Choosing Yiddish: New Frontiers of Language and Culture*, ed. Lara Rabinovitch, Shiri Goren, and Hannah S. Pressman (Detroit: Wayne State University Press, 2013), 69–86; Cahan, *Bleter fun mayn leben*, 4:61–63.

daily teacher and a daily tribune." Pulitzer's background was at least partially Jewish, though it is not clear how cognizant he was of that fact. Others were. Cahan thought he had a "true Jewish face" and a "true Jewish nervous temperament," and that he had been "born with a Jewish entrepreneurial spirit." Pulitzer's adversaries were also aware of his Jewish background and did not shrink from pointing to it when they wanted to discredit him.[48]

Adolph Ochs took a different tack after purchasing the *New York Times* in 1896, turning the newspaper into the voice of elite respectability by emphasizing the *Times*'s "conservatism, decency, and accuracy," and by adding business news. The *Times* would be, Och's proclaimed, "a high-standard newspaper, clean, dignified and trustworthy"; it would present the "news impartially, without fear or favor." Soon after he took control, the *Times* adopted its famous motto, "All the news that's fit to print." The formula was a successful one, and although the *Times* could not compete with the *World* for circulation, its readership had economic, political, and cultural power, and so it became, according to one later observer, "the world's most influential newspaper." Born of German-Jewish immigrant parents, Ochs grew up in Tennessee, entered the newspaper world as a teenage "chore boy and printer's devil," and worked his way up from there. Married to the daughter of Rabbi Isaac Mayer Wise, Ochs remained active in Reform Jewish circles. But fearing that the *Times* might be labeled a Jewish paper, he generally kept it aloof from Jewish issues. In all, Ochs made the *Times* a paper that respectable people, or those with aspirations to respectability, would not be embarrassed to read.[49]

Still another strategy was employed by the New York *Commercial Advertiser* under the guidance of its young city editor, Lincoln Steffens, beginning in 1897. Steffens took a stodgy and little-read newspaper, known as "Grandma," and turned it into a lively sheet with high literary standards. Like Pulitzer's *World*, the *Commercial Advertiser* under Steffens favored the "story" over "information"; but unlike its competitor, it resisted sensationalism by hiring college graduates and aspiring writers to describe real life "simply, honestly, and directly." Steffens saw the immigrant neighborhoods as representative of this reality and as an antidote to the Victorian stuffiness that inflicted American literary culture. Cahan joined the staff and became its chief guide to the Lower East Side and

48. Michael Schudson, *Discovering the News: A Social History of American Newspapers* (New York: Basic Books, 1978), 91–105; Annie Polland and Daniel Soyer, *The Emerging Metropolis: New York Jews in the Age of Immigration, 1840–1920* (New York: New York University Press, 2012), 230; Cahan, *Bleter fun mayn leben*, 2:131, 333–35.

49. Schudson, *Discovering the News*, 107–16; Polland and Soyer, *Emerging Metropolis*, 231–32.

the immigrant world. With Cahan's help, the *Commercial Advertiser* provided its educated readers with sympathetic and respectful reportage about working-class immigrants. In heated discussions at the paper's offices, Cahan also guided his colleagues toward an appreciation of the Russian literature and literary aesthetic that he constantly tried to promote. He paid the highest compliment to his colleague Hutchins Hapgood by calling him the "closest to the intelligent Russian type" of any American he had met. Cahan brought his experience at the *Commercial Advertiser* with him when he returned to Yiddish journalism at the helm of the *Forward.*[50]

The *Forward,* which became in the twentieth century the country's leading Yiddish daily, was just part of the multilingual Jewish press that got its start well before Civil War. Publications such as Isaac Leeser's *Occident* and Isaac Mayer Wise's *American Israelite* helped bind highly mobile Jews in far-flung places to each other and to a virtual community, even as they debated the merits of Reform (*Israelite*) versus Orthodoxy (*Occident*). Wise also founded the German-language *Die Deborah* to promote German cultural identity and a sense of moral, home-based Judaism with a central role for the women who were the publication's intended audience. In 1879 the *American Hebrew* appeared as part of an ongoing Jewish revival movement. Its youthful American-born editors pledged "untiring endeavors to stir up our brethren to pride in our time honored faith." Harbingers of Conservative Judaism, they admitted that "our proclivities ... are toward 'reformed' Judaism and yet our disposition is toward orthodoxy." In addition to these national publications, a growing number of Jewish communities boasted their own local weeklies.[51]

A Yiddish-language press arose with the arrival of the masses of Yiddish-speaking immigrants in the last decades of the nineteenth century. Many early Yiddish newspapers and magazines came and went, but the most stable were the weekly *Yidishe gazeten* and the daily *Yidishes tageblat,* both published by the earliest Yiddish press magnate, Kasriel Sarasohn. The *Gazeten* and *Tageblat* were both conservative and pro-Orthodox newspapers, but the immigrant

50. Abraham Cahan, *Grandma Never Lived in America: The New Journalism of Abraham Cahan,* ed. Moses Rischin (Bloomington: Indiana University Press, 1985), xx–xxii; Polland and Soyer, *Emerging Metropolis,* 232; Cahan, *Bleter fun mayn leben,* 4:72–121.

51. Sarna, *American Judaism,* 68, 87, 136–38; Shari Rabin, *Jews on the Frontier: Religion and Mobility in Nineteenth-Century America* (New York: New York University Press, 2017), 37, 49, 60–61, 106; Kenneth Libo, "A History of Jewish Journalism in America," in *A People in Print: Jewish Journalism in America,* exh. cat. (Philadelphia: National Museum of American Jewish History, 1987), 34–39; Benjamin Maria Baader, "*Die Deborah,*" *Jewish Women's Encyclopedia,* https://jwa.org/encyclopedia/article/die-deborah.

community's radical sector, of which Cahan was part, also issued a series of newspapers and magazines advocating various brands of socialism or anarchism. Publications in Hebrew and Russian also began to appear. In 1897, the *Jewish Daily Forward* (*Forverts*) was founded, with Cahan as its editor-in-chief. He soon left, but when he returned several years later after having worked at the *Commercial Advertiser*, he brought with him the spirit of the American new journalism. By 1910, the *Forward*, with its mix of socialist earnestness and American sensationalism, had become the premier Yiddish daily in the world.[52]

The last third of the nineteenth century, and especially its last two decades, saw a tremendous expansion of the American Jewish community and, with it, an expansion of American Jewry's cultural creativity. But Jews never created their culture in a vacuum. Rather, they were profoundly influenced by the culture around them as they sought to define a way of being Jewish that was compatible with their surroundings. Jews, whether they were well-established English speakers or spoke German or Yiddish, came into contact with a variety of American institutions and absorbed American ideas. Sometimes they set up their own parallel institutions, and sometimes they participated in general ones. Sometimes they influenced the general culture. As Abraham Cahan's autobiography shows, it is impossible to draw clear lines between sectors of the Jewish community or between Jewish and American culture.

52. Moses Rischin, *The Promised Land: New York's Jews, 1870–1914* (1962; repr. Cambridge, Mass.: Harvard University Press, 1977), 117–30.

THE JEWS AND MEDICINE IN AMERICAN CULTURE

ALAN M. KRAUT

EPIDEMICS of disease are social stress tests, events of broad significance that recast the lives of those who survive them, not unlike wars. And, as in the case of wars, survivors sometimes leave personal accounts of their experiences that illuminate not only the battle with disease but also the import of the epidemic and those who fought it in the broader history of American medicine and public health. Such a document is Abraham E. Frankland's handwritten "History, Yellow Fever Epidemic: Memphis 1873," which opens a window not only on a specific public health crisis but also on the role that medicine and public health, more generally, played in the history of the Jews in the United States between the end of the Civil War and the turn of the twentieth century. While Frankland's account is not a disinterested chronicle of events, it offers a perspective on the crisis from one who battled the epidemic and was proud of the service he and other Jews could offer the residents of Memphis.[1]

When Southerners fired on Fort Sumter to begin the Civil War in 1861, the Jewish population of the United States numbered approximately 150,000. Four years later, among the tens of thousands of bedraggled soldiers in blue and gray who tramped home were 8,000 to 10,000 Jews, including 2,000 who had fought for the Confederacy. Jews had thrived in Southern port cities like Savannah and Charleston since the colonial era. Later they settled in river ports where economic opportunities were abundant. One such commercial center on the Mississippi River was Memphis, Tennessee.

As did many hubs, Memphis had a modest Jewish population, approximately 400 Jewish men, women, and children out of a total population of 22,623 in 1860.[2]

1. A. E. Frankland, "History, Yellow Fever Epidemic: Memphis 1873" (May 1874), a 171-page handwritten manuscript in the Abraham E. Frankland Papers (MS 464), box 1, folder 2, Jacob Rader Marcus Center of the American Jewish Archives, Cincinnati. I previously treated Frankland and his manuscript in a documentary analysis. See Alan M. Kraut, "A. E. Frankland's History of the 1873 Yellow Fever Epidemic in Memphis, Tennessee," *American Jewish Archives Journal* 59, no. 1–2 (2007): 89–98. Excerpts from the manuscript were printed in a 14-page pamphlet, A. E. Frankland, *Report … on the Yellow Fever Epidemic in Memphis, Tenn., 1873* (Memphis: Price, Jones & Co., 1873), a copy of which is in the Hebrew Union College Library, Cincinnati.

2. Selma S. Lewis, *A Biblical People in the Bible Belt: The Jewish Community of Memphis, Tennessee,*

Memphis Jews had been loyal to the Confederacy during the war. Frankland, a leader of that community and a partner in a firm of auctioneers and commission merchants who dealt in "negroes" as well as real estate, furniture, and other commodities in the antebellum era, had a ready explanation for the pro-Confederate sentiments: "As was quite natural, they [the Jews] sided with the section that was their birthplace and their home."[3]

A. E. Frankland was born in England in 1831. He immigrated to the United States with his family, settling in New York and later moving to Nashville, Tennessee, in 1845. An ambitious young man, he relocated to Memphis, where his energy and industriousness in commerce were amply rewarded. As did many Jews who settled in the South and found business opportunities there, Frankland supported secession enthusiastically and joined the struggle to preserve the institution of slavery. During the Civil War, Frankland conducted espionage for the Confederate military, an endeavor to which he proudly alluded in a satirical essay, "Kronikals," written in what historian Jonathan Sarna has characterized as "pseudo-Biblical language."[4] The manuscript, preserved but not published until 1957, also offered a devastating denunciation of the merchants, many of them Jews from Cincinnati and other commercial centers, who descended upon Memphis after it was captured by Union forces to engage in profiteering. Frankland acknowledged that Southern merchants also sought to take advantage of wartime conditions, but his contempt for Northerners who speculated in cotton exceeded his dislike of fellow Southerners who did the same. These "merchant princes" and their nefarious schemes to wring profits from the South's misfortune struck Frankland as especially repugnant. He and his compatriots understood all too well how these business dealings reinforced antisemitism, yet even the pleas of Rabbi Simon Tuska of Memphis could not dissuade Jewish traders from arriving in droves from the North.[5]

After the war, Frankland stood with Southerners seeking to reinstate the old

---

1840s–1860s (Macon, Ga.: Mercer University Press, 1998), 60; Goldring/Woldenberg Institute of Southern Jewish Life, "Encyclopedia of American Jewish Communities—Memphis Tennessee," https://www.isjl.org/tennessee-memphis-encyclopedia.html.

3. A. E. Frankland, "Fragments of History," *American Jews' Annual for 5650* (Cincinnati: Bloch, 1890), 93. The "negroes" bought and sold by Frankland are mentioned in an advertisement quoted in Lewis, *A Biblical People in the Bible Belt*, 35.

4. A. E. Frankland, "Kronikals of the Times: Memphis, 1862," ed. Maxwell Whitman, *American Jewish Archives Journal* 9 no. 2 (1957): 83–125; Jonathan D. Sarna, *When General Grant Expelled the Jews* (New York: Nextbook/Schocken, 2012), 42.

5. Sarna, *When General Grant Expelled the Jews*, 42; Bertram W. Korn, *American Jewry and the Civil War* (Philadelphia: Jewish Publication Society, 1951), 152.

order, including the subjugation of African Americans. A thirty-third-degree Scottish Rite Mason, Frankland joined a vocal group of Freemasons who were also former Confederate officers in opposing members of Tennessee's postwar state government who sought to grant freed slaves the right to vote. He supported the formation of the Ku Klux Klan and did not oppose the use of violence and intimidation to oppress the freedmen.[6]

By the time the yellow fever epidemic erupted in 1873, Frankland had turned his business interests exclusively to real estate. He was also a Jewish community leader, especially interested in providing his Memphis neighbors with medical assistance. In addition to his leadership of the International Order of B'nai B'rith lodge in Memphis, Frankland was a founder and the president of the Hebrew Hospital Relief Association, which served the sick and especially the poor. Although many Memphis residents fled the city in the face of the epidemic, Frankland did not. Instead, he daily risked his life to save others—Jew and Gentile alike—events chronicled in his priceless handwritten account of the crisis. Just as he stood with his white Southern neighbors in the Civil War, denouncing his Northern coreligionists who sought to exploit them during the conflict, now Frankland sought to demonstrate that he, a Jew, could join with non-Jews in battling the disease that menaced everyone.

In the decades following the Civil War, yellow fever outbreaks periodically ravaged communities in the Southeastern states. Residents of the region knew the signs of the pestilence all too well. It began with a mosquito bite. The incubation period was three to six days, after which the victims ran a fever of 102–104 degrees. Their pulses grew rapid, but soon slowed as their faces grew flushed. The eyes appeared sunken, the tongue ringed in red and furred at the center. Not long after, there was nausea, vomiting, and constipation. Now the skin was tinged yellow, and the vomit darkened because it was mixed with blood. The smell was unmistakable. Many of yellow fever's victims died within a week.[7] Memphis was no stranger to epidemics, including yellow fever, which had swept through the region in 1855, when 250 cases and 134 deaths were

6. Whiteman, introduction to Frankland, "Kronikals of the Times," 83–84.

7. Two important volumes on yellow fever in the South are Margaret Humphreys, *Yellow Fever and the South* (New Brunswick: Rutgers University Press, 1992), and John H. Ellis, *Yellow Fever and Public Health in the New South* (Lexington: University of Kentucky Press, 1992). See also Khaled J. Bloom, *The Mississippi Valley's Great Yellow Fever Epidemic of 1878* (Baton Rouge: Louisiana State University Press, 1993), and Jo Ann Carrigan, *The Saffron Scourge: A History of Yellow Fever in Louisiana, 1796–1905* (Lafayette: University of Southwestern Louisiana Press, 1994).

recorded.[8] The year 1873 began badly for the city. Its horse and mule populations were stricken by epizootic meningitis, paralyzing the transportation system. A severe freeze suspended river traffic for a month, causing great financial loss. A smallpox epidemic swept the city in the first months of the year, followed by a wave of Asiatic cholera. When yellow fever descended in September, the city was already reeling.[9] The epidemic was catastrophic. Yet, the local Jewish community found in it an opportunity to demonstrate generosity of spirit. The Jewish community's battle with the disease drew them closer to each other and to their non-Jewish neighbors.

Epidemics are events not trends. Historian of medicine Charles Rosenberg has described epidemics as following a theatrical arc that includes a beginning, middle, and end.[10] A. E. Frankland would have agreed. In his account of the yellow fever epidemic, written to document his own efforts and those of his coreligionists, Frankland likened its beginning to a drama's first act. When the curtain went up, Frankland learned that one friend or acquaintance after another was falling ill.[11] He noted with contempt the desire of many in the business community to downplay the spreading sickness so as not to damage public confidence and commerce. He was especially infuriated by the indifference to the suffering of the poor: "what was the life of the poor to them compared to their money making and money getting...."[12]

Frankland's own response was to offer aid to both Jews and Gentiles. Nor was he the only Jew in Memphis to render such service. In his account, Frankland praised the heroism of Rabbi Max Samfield, "even at the dying bed of the Prostitute, Jew, or Gentile no difference to him[;] he was everywhere. Even at the dead hour of midnight you could have found him amidst the lurid glare of the pine torch reciting the burial service while the rain poured down in torrents and the sobs of remaining friends, broken, by retracing our steps from the resting place of the dead."[13] At a moment when many of the community's secular leaders, including its political leadership departed for the safety of themselves and their families, Rabbi Samfield stayed and served his neighbors.

Frankland labored tirelessly among the sick, from early morning until mid-

8. Marcus J. Stewart and William T. Blacker Jr., eds., *History of Medicine in Memphis* (Memphis: Memphis and Shelby County Medical Society, 1971), 24–26.

9. *Ibid.*, 26.

10. Charles E. Rosenberg, "What Is an Epidemic? AIDS in Historical Perspective," in Rosenberg, *Explaining Epidemics and Other Studies in the History of Medicine* (Cambridge: Cambridge University Press, 1992), 279.

11. Frankland, "History, Yellow Fever Epidemic," 6–14.

12. *Ibid.*, 21–22.

13. *Ibid.*, 76–77.

night most days. In addition to distributing funds and attending to other administrative tasks, he was at the bedside of those stricken, many of whom he described as "the poorest of the poor, but respectable and hardworking." At one point 135 individuals were sick and required daily visits for weeks. Some were frightened of doctors and had to be persuaded or forced to get treatment.[14]

When the disease finally subsided, Frankland had survived, but his beloved son Walter, who also helped care for patients, had succumbed to it. Frankland pursued solace in Judaism. He wrote that "God [had] seen fit to take him and we dare not repine. 'What HE does is well done,' we have said it so often to others. We must practice it ourselves now. He [Walter] is better off removed from this sphere of suffering and trials. Who shall not say his spirit has its rewards?"[15] Overall, the Memphis Jewish community was reduced to 300 by departure or death. Based on internments at the Reform and Orthodox cemeteries, respectively, Frankland calculated that 94 Jews had died, leaving behind 31 widows, 11 widowers, and 181 orphans.[16] Frankland's altruism had saved lives and achieved for him and his Jewish colleagues the gratitude and acceptance of his Gentile neighbors. Ultimately, Frankland came to hold leadership positions in both Jewish and non-Jewish aid organizations. The epidemic had been an engine of social integration in Memphis.

The yellow fever epidemic in Memphis and other such episodes are reminders of how interconnected medicine, migration, and upward mobility were in the American Jewish experience during the second half of the nineteenth century and beyond. Although most Jewish immigrants did not achieve the financial success of A. E. Frankland, many of the German Jews who arrived in the decades before the Civil War and the two decades after the war aspired to commercial success. They took up peddling, hoping eventually to acquire enough capital to open a store or engage in trade on a larger sale as had Frankland. After arrival in the United States, they gravitated to commercial hubs on the coast such as New York, Philadelphia, or Baltimore. River ports such as Cincinnati and St. Louis, or cities on lakes, such as Chicago or Buffalo, became increasingly popular. Peddlers purchased goods and traveled by horse or horse-drawn wagon to sell their wares to residents of small towns and farmers' families, returning home only to replenish stock and visit with family.[17]

14. *Ibid.*, 86. 15. *Ibid.*, 93–96. 16. *Ibid.*, 86.

17. The best volume on Jewish peddlers is Hasia R. Diner, *Roads Taken: The Great Jewish Migrations to the New World and the Peddlers Who Forged the Way* (New Haven: Yale University Press, 2015).

Peddlers' peripatetic existence and poverty limited their access to many services, including medical attention. Those who consulted local physicians or treatment in hospitals often encountered antisemitism, especially in institutions that had been founded by a Christian denomination. Jews in need of care often found the medical environment devoid of spiritual support in the Jewish religious tradition. Too often Christian caregivers made their help contingent upon religious conversion. The Jewish response to poverty and the unwanted attention of missionaries in the medical environment was typically institutional. Just as Roman Catholics founded hospitals where the rites and rituals of Catholicism could be offered to patients, protecting them from Protestants seeking souls, so did Jews. Jewish hospitals provided spiritual support in times of illness with religious services, celebrations of Shabbat and other holidays, the pastoral care of rabbis, and kosher food for the observant.

Preventing the Jewish poor from becoming dependent on public resources was seen as a means to diminish antisemitism. Likewise, building Jewish hospitals provided places to train Jewish doctors and nurses, circumventing the barriers encountered at institutions controlled by non-Jews. Larger cities like Cincinnati, New York, Newark, New Orleans, Baltimore, Philadelphia, San Francisco, and Chicago had Jewish hospitals by the late nineteenth and early twentieth centuries that cared for both Jewish patients and non-Jews. Their Jewish founders often regarded them as a gesture of appreciation for acceptance into the largely non-Jewish communities where they resided. Burgeoning populations had increased the healthcare needs of cities. Sectarian hospitals shifted some of the burden of that challenge from municipal shoulders to those of private organizations. By accepting non-Jewish patients, the Jewish medical establishment helped diminish antisemitism and ease the way for upward mobility in the community.[18]

Epidemics were catalysts in the creation of Jewish hospitals in the United States. The first were institutional responses to urban epidemics of cholera and yellow fever in the mid-nineteenth century.[19] The 1849 cholera epidemic

18. Alan M. Kraut and Deborah A. Kraut, *Covenant of Care: Newark Beth Israel Hospital and the Jewish Hospital in America* (New Brunswick: Rutgers University Press, 2007), 2–9.

19. An overview of the Jewish hospital in the United States is Ethan Bridge, "The Rise and Development of the Jewish Hospital in America" (Rabbinical thesis, Hebrew Union College, 1985). There have been a number of individual hospital studies. Notable published volumes are Dorothy Levenson, *Montefiore: The Hospital as Social Instrument, 1884–1984* (New York: Farrar, Straus and Giroux, 1984); Arthur J. Linenthal, *First a Dream: The History of Boston's Jewish Hospitals, 1896 to 1928* (Boston: Beth Israel Hospital in association with the Francis A. Countway Library of Medicine, 1990); Kraut and Kraut, *Covenant of Care*; Frederic Krome, *The Jewish Hospital and Cincinnati Jews in Medicine* (Charleston, S.C.: History Press, 2015); Candace

in Cincinnati, a commercial city populated by German Jewish merchants and craftspeople, spurred the establishment of Jewish Hospital in 1850. Its founders intended to provide care for the nearly 4,000 Jews who resided in the city, as well as impoverished and homeless peddlers who roamed the Midwest and clung to their Jewish identities. New York City, ravaged by repeated onsets of cholera, chartered the Jews' Hospital in 1852 (renamed Mount Sinai Hospital in 1866). After three years of fundraising, much of it personally guided by businessman Sampson Simson, the hospital opened its doors in 1855 for the purpose of, in the words of its constitution, "affording surgical and medical aid, comfort and protection in sickness to deserving and needy Israelites for all purposes appertaining to hospitals and dispensaries, a benevolent, charitable, and scientific hospital."[20] Jews in New Orleans founded a hospital when yellow fever infested the city in 1868. It was named for businessman Judah Touro who, decades earlier, had used some of his considerable wealth to establish an infirmary for sailors suffering from yellow fever. The hospital bearing Touro's name became the largest free hospital in Louisiana. Following an epidemic of typhoid fever, the German Jews who had settled in San Francisco as shopkeepers and peddlers during the Gold Rush of the 1850s founded the Mount Zion Hospital Association. In Chicago, the great fire of 1871 necessitated the rebuilding of the city, which included construction of Michael Reese Hospital, named for the Bavarian-born businessman whose surviving family donated the fortune he had amassed in San Francisco.

Although almost all the physicians who had been denied privileges or medical training in non-Jewish institutions were men, the vision and organizational acumen to raise funds for Jewish medical facilities almost always originated with local Jewish women who sought to protect their communities from the twin menaces of disease and antisemitism. In Denver, the Hebrew Ladies' Benevolent Society, under the leadership of Frances Wisebart Jacobs, helped establish the National Jewish Hospital for Consumptives in 1899, though a nonsectarian institution, many of its tuberculosis patients were impoverished eastern European Jewish workers sent by their labor unions, or *landsmannschaftn* (immigrant benevolent societies).[21] After 1900, more Jewish hospitals would be founded in congested cities to care for industrial workers and their families.

*

O'Connor, *A Legacy of Caring: The History of Barnes-Jewish Hospital* (St. Louis: The Foundation for Barnes-Jewish Hospital), 2018.

20. Jews' Hospital in New York, *Constitution* (New York, [1852]).

21. Milton Anfenger, *The Birth of a Hospital: The Story of the Birth of the National Jewish*

The themes of medicine, migration, and upward mobility so apparent in Memphis in 1873 were echoed later in the careers of Jews who found in medical careers a path up the socioeconomic ladder. Father and son physicians Aaron and Henry Friedenwald practiced in the busy port of Baltimore, which had 10,000 Jews by the 1880s. Aaron Friedenwald, son of immigrant entrepreneur Jonas Friedenwald, was born in Baltimore in 1836 and received his medical degree from the University of Maryland in 1860. He took advanced training in Berlin, Prague, Vienna, and Paris. He had returned to Baltimore by 1862, where he established a practice in ophthalmology, receiving a professorship at the Baltimore College of Physicians and Surgeons. Admired by his colleagues, Friedenwald served a term as president of Maryland's state medical society. Friedenwald was among those Jewish physicians who used his reputation and financial means to play a broader role in Jewish life via philanthropy. Concerned with the abuse and persecution of Jews in Europe, Friedenwald channeled his efforts into Jewish resettlement, presiding over local branches of the Baron de Hirsch Committee and the Alliance Israélite Universelle.[22]

Aaron's son, Dr. Harry Friedenwald, followed in his father's footsteps as a well-respected ophthalmologist. After receiving his medical degree from the Baltimore College of Physicians and Surgeons, Harry studied in Germany, and, like his father, deplored the oppression of European Jewry. He wrote to his father that he hoped to liberate them from their "dens in Russia and Poland." Feeling a responsibility to render aid and assistance, he wished to see his European coreligionists "under the care and protection which their brethren and the [United States] afford." Harry became an associate professor at the Baltimore College of Physicians and Surgeons in 1890, succeeding his father there as a full professor in 1902.[23] As the children and grandchildren of German Jewish migrants became more prosperous, many followed this pattern of journeying abroad to acquire advanced medical training in European institutions and then assisting Jews who were still suffering oppression in Europe.

Hospital in Denver, Colorado (Denver: National Jewish Hospital, 1943), and Mary Ann Fitzharris and Jeanne Abrams, *A Place to Heal: A History of National Jewish Medical and Research Center* (Denver: National Jewish Medical and Research Center, 1978).

22. Solomon R. Kagan, *Jewish Contributions to Medicine in America, 1656–1934* (Boston: Boston Medical Publishing Company, 1934), 29–30; Cyrus Adler and Harry Friedenwald, "Friedenwald," jewishencyclopedia.com/articles/6366-friedenwald; Harry Friedenwald, *Life, Letters, and Addresses of Aaron Friedenwald, M.D.* (Baltimore: Lord Baltimore Press, 1906).

23. Kagan, *Jewish Contributions to Medicine in America*, 273; the quotations are from Alexandra Lee Levin, *Vision: A Biography of Harry Friedenwald* (Philadelphia: Jewish Publication Society of America, 1964), 80.

Still, in the second half of the nineteenth century, pathbreaking advances in theoretical medical knowledge were not the products of American minds. Robert Koch in Germany and Louis Pasteur in France articulated the germ theory of disease that transformed medicine. Surgeons were learning from England's Joseph Lister that antiseptic and aseptic techniques in the surgical suite saved lives. Although these breakthroughs were crossing the Atlantic, in America heroics were more often found in operating rooms than in laboratories.

Jewish physician Dr. Howard Lilienthal, a native of Albany, New York, studied medicine at Harvard University and, following graduation in 1887, joined the house staff at Mount Sinai Hospital in New York, where he remained from 1892 to 1940. In 1887, the staff there was split into medical and surgical divisions, and Lilienthal became the first trainee to select surgery as his primary focus. A thoracic surgeon, he rose to become the first chief of the Surgical Division at Mount Sinai in 1914. He was also on staff at Bellevue Hospital from 1909 to 1940, and after 1917 was on the clinical surgery faculty at Cornell University Medical College. During World War I he was in the Medical Corps of the U.S. Army Reserve and was director of the Mount Sinai Hospital Unit in France. A bold surgeon, Lilienthal performed the first successful pulmonary lobectomy for inflammatory disease of the lungs in 1914. He published prodigiously and was an innovator in medical instrumentation and operative and diagnostic techniques. Among his innovations was a portable operating table and an improved rib retractor. His most notable pioneering efforts were in the nascent field of thoracic surgery. He developed operations for pulmonary tuberculosis, lung suppuration, and carcinoma of the lung and esophagus. Of his many books and article, his textbook *Thoracic Surgery* (1925) was the standard work for many years and is considered by many surgeons to be a classic. Among the organizations in which Lilienthal was active, he was a founder of the American Cancer Society.[24]

Some surgical innovators owed their insights to their experience as Civil War surgeons. Jacob da Silva Solis-Cohen, a Sephardic Jew, was born in New York in 1838 and studied medicine at Jefferson Medical College and the University of Pennsylvania. He was trained as a general surgeon but became fascinated with laryngoscopy. Considered to be the pioneer in that field in the United States, Solis-Cohen gained much of his expertise in the Union Army during the Civil War. Two years following the war, he performed the first laryngectomy on a laryngeal cancer patient.[25]

24. Ronald L. Eisenberg, *Jews in Medicine: Contributions to Health and Healing Through the Ages* (New York: Urim Publications, 2019), 429–30.

25. *Ibid.*, 373.

Solis-Cohen had a distinguished academic career, teaching physiology and hygiene of the voice at the National School of Elocution and Oratory in Philadelphia, where he gathered material for his book, *The Throat and the Voice* (1879). In 1870, he was appointed lecturer on laryngoscopy and diseases of the throat and chest at Jefferson Medical College, earning promotion two years later to professor of laryngology. He was a founder of the American Laryngological Association and was elected its second president. Solis-Cohen's textbook, *Diseases of the Throat and Nasal Passages* (1872), became the standard volume in the field and remains among the classics in the field of laryngology. A meticulous and ambitious researcher, his "Croup in its Relations to Tracheotomy" (1874) was based on data from 5,000 cases, a large study for that era.[26]

Beginning in the 1880s, the themes of medicine, migration, and upward mobility resonated loudly in the American Jewish experience once again as the lives of many Americans were transformed by industrialization, urbanization, and mass immigration from southern and eastern Europe. Between 1880 and the early 1920s, more than 23.5 million newcomers arrived; 2.25 million were eastern European Jews. Unlike the Reform Jews who had emigrated from the German states earlier in the nineteenth century and were often assimilated into European society, these newcomers were, for the most part, impoverished, Yiddish-speaking Orthodox Jews. Even as these less fortunate seekers arrived, Jewish migration from the German states continued. German Jewish physicians, especially those who had received excellent medical training abroad, sought to assist these less secular Jews, hoping that their numbers and needs would not occasion an escalation in antisemitism in the United States. Some were inspired to help the poor and vulnerable become upwardly mobile because of their own affiliation with European radical traditions.

Perhaps no immigrant Jewish physician of the period 1865–1900 achieved greater eminence and upward mobility in the United States than Dr. Abraham Jacobi (Fig. 63), a pioneer in the field of pediatrics and a reformer committed to radical social and political change. Born in 1830, a child of a poor Westphalian family, Jacobi studied medicine at the universities of Greifswald, Göttingen, and Bonn, receiving his medical degree from the latter institution in 1851. Politically active in the revolutionary movement of 1848, he was convicted of treason and imprisoned until 1853. After his release he went to England, where he stayed with both Karl Marx and Friedrich Engels until he traveled to New

26. *Ibid.*, 373–74.

Fig. 63. Abraham Jacobi at City College, New York, 1912. (Library of Congress).

York, where he started a medical practice. Jacobi never abandoned his radical beliefs, continued to correspond with Marx and Engels, and founded the New York Communist Club in 1857.[27]

In 1860, Jacobi joined the staff of Jews' Hospital (Mount Sinai), where he established the first pediatric department in a general hospital in New York City. He was appointed professor of childhood diseases at New York Medical College in 1861, and from 1867 to 1870, he chaired the medical department at the New York Medical College. Jacobi taught at Columbia University's College of

27. Martin Kaufman, Stuart Galishoff, and Todd L. Savitt, eds., *Dictionary of American Medical Biography*, 2 vols. (Westport, Conn.: Greenwood Press), 1:389–90; Eisenberg, *Jews in Medicine*, 387; Kagan, *Jewish Contributions to Medicine in America*, 140–43.

Physicians and Surgeons from 1870 to 1902. He remained on Mount Sinai's staff until his death in 1919, serving as the president of the medical board from 1884 to 1919. He was also associated with the German Hospital (later Lenox Hill Hospital) for many years and with several institutions devoted to the welfare of children, including the Hebrew Orphan Asylum and the Infant Hospital on Randall's Island. His leadership was much sought after. In 1882 he was elected president of the New York State Medical Society and, in 1885, president of the New York Academy of Medicine. From 1868 to 1871 he coedited the *American Journal of Obstetrics and Disease of Women and Children.* Always the activist, Jacobi fought for birth control and civil service reform in the United States.

In 1873, Abraham Jacobi married Dr. Mary Putnam, who had received her medical degree in 1864 from the Female Medical College of Pennsylvania. Mary Jacobi (Fig. 64), who was not Jewish, was an accomplished author and a pioneer in gynecology. She established her own medical practice and lectured at the newly established Women's Medical College of the New York Infirmary and Mount Sinai Hospital. She became only the second woman member of the Medical Society of the County of New York and was the first woman allowed membership in the American Medical Association. In 1876, she received the Boylston Prize from Harvard for her influential essay, "The Question of Rest for Women During Menstruation." Her research refuted the position of many male and female doctors who argued that women could not assume the same professional responsibilities as men because menstruation weakened their constitutions. A radical like her husband, Mary Jacobi was an active suffragist and one of the six founders of the League for Political Education. Committed to medical research, Mary Jacobi conscientiously documented her own brain tumor and published a paper on the matter, "Descriptions of the Early Symptoms of the Meningeal Tumor Compressing the Cerebellum, From Which the Writer Died, Written by Herself." Mary Putnam Jacobi did in fact die later in 1906.[28]

Even as Jewish physicians educated wholly or partly abroad were contributing to the development of American medicine, there was increasing concern about the inferior training that many medical students were receiving in the United States. The most pointed criticism emerged from the pen of a Jewish educator without formal medical training. Abraham Flexner held up a mirror to medical education in the United States so that Americans might see the many imper-

28. Kaufman et al., eds., *Dictionary of American Medical Biography,* 1:390–91. The best biography of Jacobi is Carla Bittel, *Mary Putnam Jacobi and the Politics of Medicine in Nineteenth-Century America* (Chapel Hill: University of North Carolina Press, 2009).

Fig. 64. Mary Putnam Jacobi. Frontispiece to *Life and Letters of Mary Putnam Jacobi*, ed. Ruth Putnam (New York, 1925). (Wellcome Library, University of London).

fections and pursue reform. His survey of medical schools was critical in the transformation of the United States from a backwater to the vanguard of medical education in the world.[29]

Flexner was born in 1866 in Louisville, Kentucky, the sixth of nine children of Moritz Flexner, a German immigrant haberdasher, and Esther Abraham, a seamstress. Although the family lost its savings in the financial panic of 1873, the assistance of an older brother allowed Abraham to spend two years at Johns

29. Abraham Flexner, *Abraham Flexner: An Autobiography*, rev. ed. (New York: Simon and Shuster, 1960); Thomas Neville Bonner, *Iconoclast: Abraham Flexner and A Life of Learning* (Baltimore: Johns Hopkins University Press, 2002).

Hopkins, where he earned a B.A. in classics. Financially unable to continue his education, Abraham returned to Louisville, where he taught Latin and Greek at a high school and later founded his own school to test his ideas about education. In 1896, he married one of his former students, Anne Laziere Crawford, whose success as a playwright allowed Flexner to pursue a master's degree in psychology at Harvard and to spend a year abroad at universities in Berlin and Heidelberg.

Flexner's intellectual focus was on the role of higher education in America and the character of the American university. His unflattering portrait, *The American College: A Criticism* (1908), attracted the attention of the Carnegie Foundation for the Advancement of Learning. The foundation had been invited to conduct an investigation of medical schools by the American Medical Association after its own in-house report found that many did not meet its standards. Although Flexner was not a physician, he was selected to conduct the study by Henry Pritchett, the president of the Carnegie Foundation, who admired Flexner's ability as a writer and his criticism of traditional patterns of education. The foundation commissioned Flexner to assess 155 medical schools for *Medical Education in the United States and Canada*, known as the *Flexner Report*.[30] Published in 1910, it initiated a wave of reform in medical education.

Some change was already underway. Following the Civil War, increased funding, fresh leadership, and innovative ideas were transforming the classroom. Some of these improvements occurred at new institutions. When the Baltimore merchant Johns Hopkins died in 1873, he left $7 million for the construction of a hospital and a university. At older universities like Harvard, a generation of traditional educators committed to the classics was giving way to a new generation trained in European methods of research and science. But students often arrived at these college classrooms with minimal preparation, sometimes without even a high school diploma. Students took medical courses in any order they pleased, following a two-year program that often lacked an established sequence. In European universities, especially those in Germany, laboratory sciences such as physiology, chemistry, histology, pathological anatomy, and later, bacteriology placed students on the cutting edge of medical progress. Not so in the United States, where few schools had laboratories or encouraged research among their faculty. In the United States, apprenticeship was the means for educating many young healers. Educational standards were flexible even at Harvard Medical

30. Abraham Flexner, *Medical Education in the United States and Canada: A Report to the Carnegie Foundation for the Advancement of Teaching* (New York: Carnegie Foundation, 1910).

School, where students needed only to pass most of the exams. Moreover, most medical education was not conducted at great universities but occurred in commercial institutions. Even revised state licensing laws promoting higher standards had not eliminated the huge imbalance in the quality of medical education.

The *Flexner Report* made an indelible mark on physician training in the United States. In his evaluation, Flexner applied standards established by the Council on Medical Education of the American Medical Association (AMA). The council's minimum standard for physician education mandated four years of high school, four years of medical training, and successful results on a licensing test. The AMA's preferred standard asked for five years of medical school, including one year of basic science, which later became part of the premedical curriculum in undergraduate school, and a sixth year of hospital internship. By the time Flexner completed his report in 1910, the number of medical schools was already in decline, sinking from 162 in 1906 to 131 in 1910, the result of rising requirements by state licensing boards and other authorities. Many schools simply could not bear the financial burden of increasingly high standards. Flexner's assessment was the nail in the coffin of many others, especially proprietary schools that tried to save themselves through fraud and misrepresentation.[31]

Flexner conducted onsite visits of medical schools. His descriptions were detailed and sometimes seasoned with sharp thrusts of humor. There were medical libraries with no books and faculty members who never taught but sought wealth through private practice. Laboratories were often rooms with a few test tubes. Admission standards were waived for those who could afford the fees. Flexner's conclusions were stark. Top schools must be strengthened, with institutions such as Johns Hopkins as the model. A few from the middle ranks could be raised to the Hopkins standard. However, the majority must be closed. Some schools merged. By 1915, the number of schools had declined from 131 in 1910 to 95, and the number of medical graduates from 5,440 to 3,536 annually. Flexner's report led to the closure of underfunded medical schools in almost every region of the United States and all but two African American medical schools. Flexner's biographer, although somewhat critical of the rigid standards Flexner insisted upon, characterized him as "the severest critic and the best friend American medicine ever had."[32]

*

31. Paul Starr, *The Social Transformation of American Medicine: The Rise of a Sovereign Profession and the Making of a Vast Industry* (New York: Basic Books, 1982), 116–41.

32. Thomas Neville Bonner, "Searching for Abraham Flexner," *Academic Medicine* 73 (February 1998): 160–66.

The kaleidoscope of medicine, migration, and upward mobility was profoundly refocused by demographic changes in the Jewish population of the United States during the last decades of the nineteenth century. While many Jewish medical students and physicians were attracted to medical specialization and innovation, others were inspired to enlist in the expanding efforts to address public health problems resulting from mass migration and the evolution of urban life in the United States. And once again, epidemics were catalysts in transforming the experience of Jewish migrants.

As crowding and poor municipal sanitation led to an uptick in epidemics, Americans were quick to blame the newcomers. Eastern European Jewish migrants of the late nineteenth century were suspected of bringing diseases that endangered the lives and health of their hosts. Fear of disease became the rationale for nativists who wished to exclude as many Jews as possible from the United States. Quarantine became an instrument for the expression of such antisemitism. The federal government only gradually assumed quarantine inspection prerogatives from state officials. In 1892, the same year that Ellis Island opened its doors as a federal immigration inspection station in New York harbor, Jewish immigrants found themselves targeted by New York State quarantine officers as a threat to the public's health.

That year an outbreak of typhus in New York City was blamed on 268 Russian Jewish passengers who had arrived on the *SS Massillia* and on those with whom they had come into contact. Jewish immigrants were quarantined on North Brother Island. Soon quarantine detention was extended to include all Russian Jewish newcomers, without the slightest evidence that typhus was present on the ships they had arrived on. Eventually, thanks to a bond offered by the United Hebrew Charities Organization, all but twenty-three of the detained *Massillia* immigrants were released and found new homes in the United States. The twenty-three not admitted were sent back, not because of disease, but for economic reasons. Officials determined that they were likely to require charity from public coffers to survive.[33]

Shortly after the typhus scare abated, public fears were once again inflamed when cholera threatened New Yorkers. Officials suspected that Jewish immigrants passing through Hamburg on the *SS Moravia* had brought the microorganism *Vibrio cholerae* with them. President Benjamin Harrison directed that all passengers traveling steerage on every arriving ship undergo a twenty-day quarantine. Cabin passengers holding first- or second-class tickets were exempt.

33. The best source on this episode is Howard Markel, *Quarantine! East European Jewish Immigrants and the New York City Epidemics of 1892* (Baltimore: Johns Hopkins University Press, 1997).

If Harrison hesitated to push for broader restriction, or to mention Russian Jews as a special threat, state and municipal officials were much less reluctant to denounce the newcomers as a health menace. Pressure from frightened Americans persuaded Congress to pass the Quarantine Act in 1893, separating the controversial issue of immigration restriction from quarantine. The law, to be administered by the U.S. Marine Hospital Service, called for a national system of quarantine regulations, immigrant inspection procedures, and health standards aimed at protecting the American population from disease rather than wielded as a weapon of exclusion by immigration's opponents. Because the epidemics of typhus and cholera were short-lived, so, too, was the backlash against Jewish immigrants, who entered the United States in increasing numbers until the restrictive legislation of the 1920s.[34]

Once immigrants—Jews and Gentiles—set foot on American soil, their lives were made vulnerable by a variety of public health challenges. In the crowded streets and congested tenements of immigrant neighborhoods, such as New York's Lower East Side, disease was rampant. In sweatshops and factories, injuries from the machinery of production were frequent. Respiratory disorders from inhaling the noxious fumes of industrial chemicals and lead poisoning were too often the price of job opportunities. A new generation of Jewish reformers and physicians rose to address the suffering and, in the process, enhanced their own careers. Again, the connections among medicine, migration and social mobility were evident.

One public health crusader was Lillian D. Wald (Fig. 65), a trained nurse who created New York's Henry Street Settlement to serve the health needs of the poor in one community and the Visiting Nurse Service to bring medical assistance into the homes of those most in need, first in New York and later in communities across the country.[35] Wald was born in 1867 in Cincinnati, Ohio, one

34. *Ibid.*, 27, 173–82.

35. There is no definitive biography of Lillian Wald. Her autobiography, *The House on Henry Street* (New York: Henry Holt, 1915), remains the best published source for insight into her perceptions of her early career. Among studies of Wald are Beatrice Siegel, *Lillian Wald of Henry Street* (New York: Macmillan, 1983); Doris Groshen Daniels, *Always a Sister: The Feminism of Lillian D. Wald* (New York: Feminist Press of the City University of New York, 1989); Marjorie N. Feld, *Lillian Wald: A Biography* (Chapel Hill: University of North Carolina Press, 20009); Paul Kaplan, *Lillian Wald: America's Great Social and Healthcare Reformer* (New York: Pelican, 2018). Some useful correspondence is published in Clare Coss, ed., *Lillian D. Wald, Progressive Activist* (New York: Feminist Press of the City University of New York, 1989). A fresh look at the Henry Street Settlement and its legacy is Ellen M. Snyder-Grenier, *The House on Henry Street: The Enduring Life of a Lower East Side Settlement* (New York: New York University Press, 2020).

Fig. 65. Lillian Wald. Undated photograph by Harris & Ewing. (Library of Congress).

of Max Wald and Minnie Schwartz Wald's four children. Both parents' families were descended from rabbis and merchants in Germany and Poland. The families arrived in flight from European political unrest in 1848. By 1878, they had relocated first to Dayton, Ohio, and then to Rochester, New York. Wald was not raised in a religious home, nor did she receive a Jewish education. Hers was a secular home nourished by books and music. Young Lillian attended an English/French boarding and day school in Rochester and then traveled widely after being rejected for admission to Vassar because, at sixteen, she was too young. She worked briefly as a journalist, but an encounter with a young nurse inspired Wald to attend nursing school in New York City.

At the age of twenty-two Wald was admitted to the Women's Medical College of the New York Infirmary to study medicine, while working at the New York Juvenile Asylum and assisting with a class on home nursing for poor immigrant families on the Lower East Side. Wald was galvanized by the poverty and dislocation she witnessed and decided to dedicate her life to bringing affordable health care to the poor. Leaving medical school, Wald and her friend and colleague, Mary Brewster, moved to the College Settlement House on Rivington Street, then to a Jefferson Street tenement, and finally to 265 Henry Street, a building purchased for them by philanthropist Jacob Schiff, where the two young ladies founded the Nurses' Settlement in 1895, later renamed the Henry Street Settlement. Even before they moved into the house on Henry Street, Brewster and Wald founded the New York Visiting Nurse Service. Lillian Wald pioneered the concept of "public health nursing," a term she coined to describe the notion that the nurse's "organic relationship with the neighborhood" should mark the starting point of effective healthcare.

Beginning in 1893, Wald and Brewster ventured into the apartments of their poor neighbors at the behest of physicians, charitable agencies, and individuals reaching out for care. Wald established a sliding fee scale to accommodate the needy. These nurses were committed to ministering to the ill, but they were also expected to educate the poor and foreign-born in good health habits and proper hygiene, all the while serving as models of moral rectitude. Wald's nurses worked eight to ten hours a day, six to six and a half days a week. They visited eight to twelve apartments per day and confronted a wide variety of ailments, often infectious and highly contagious diseases, almost always complicated by poverty and, among immigrants, lack of familiarity with the language and culture of their new country. On warm summer days in the 1890s, the nurses wore large straw hats and long skirts which they lifted with one hand, holding a medical bag in the other, as they climbed over tenement rooftops to get from one building to the next. Conserving energy was vital.[36]

Wald's service had no affiliation with any larger institution until 1909, when the Metropolitan Life Insurance Company subsidized some of Wald's nurses to attend to its policyholders. Because so many of Wald's patients were Jews newly arrived from eastern Europe, Jewish philanthropists, many of them German Jews, were in the forefront of Wald's supporters. Jacob Schiff and his mother-in-law, Betty Loeb, underwrote Wald's early efforts. Wald and Brewster jointly received $120 per month for living expenses and nursing supplies, with additional funds provided for projects as required. Later, the names of prominent

36. Wald, *House on Henry Street*, 28.

German Jewish philanthropists such as Warburg and Lewisohn would appear on Wald's contribution lists.

Nathan Straus was another German Jewish philanthropist who used his fortune to improve the medical condition of newly arrived eastern European Jews, especially children (Fig. 66). Born in Otterberg in the Palatinate, Kingdom of Bavaria, in 1848, Nathan Straus was the third child of Lazarus and Sara Straus.[37] The family immigrated to the United States in 1854, settling in Georgia. The Civil War brought the Straus family to financial ruin, so they moved to New York City, where Nathan's father started L. Straus & Sons, selling crockery and glassware. One of their customers was the R. H. Macy & Company department store. By 1888, the three Straus brothers became partners in Macy's and co-owners by 1896. Around the same time, Nathan and his brother Isidor purchased an interest in another dry goods business, which became the renowned Brooklyn department store Abraham & Straus.

As Nathan Straus's wealth increased, so did his philanthropy and public service. From 1889 to 1893, he served as New York City Parks Commissioner and in 1898 became commissioner of New York City's Department of Health. He and his wife, Lina, had a special interest in children's health. Aware that many youngsters from impoverished families lacked access to nutritious food, especially wholesome milk, they privately funded the Nathan Straus Pasteurized Milk Laboratory and opened milk stations where fresh milk could be distributed without charge. The pasteurized milk provided to children was a major weapon in the battle against infant mortality from typhoid, scarlet fever, diphtheria, and tuberculosis, as well as malnutrition. Inadequate access to nutritious food contributed mightily to the high rate of infant mortality in the United States. In part because of the generosity of Straus and other philanthropists and reformers, infant mortality in the United States declined from 25 percent in 1890 to 15 percent in 1903. In New York, it had declined to 7 percent by 1900, reflecting the success of public health reformers such as Straus.[38]

Straus's philanthropy was not confined to undernourished children. During the economic panic of 1893, Straus sold coal at the very low rate of five cents per twenty-five pounds so poor New Yorkers need not suffer the cold; those unable to pay got their coal without charge. He also funded lodging houses and subsidized 50,000 meals for one cent each. He retired from business in 1914 to devote his time to philanthropy. Some of his notable contributions that im-

37. Kaufman et al., eds., *Dictionary of American Medical Biography*, 2:723.

38. Nathan Straus, *Disease in Milk: The Remedy, Pasteurization*, ed. Lina Straus (New York: E. P. Dutton, 1913).

Fig. 66. Nathan Straus. Undated photograph by Bain News Service. (Library of Congress).

proved health in the United States included serving 1,135,731 penny meals for the unemployed from the milk depots he had established earlier in New York City. During World War I, he raised money from the sale of his yacht to feed war orphans. When American servicemen returned from Europe after World War I, some of those docking in New York enjoyed their first meal in their home country in Battery Park thanks to Straus's largesse.

Straus died in 1931. An ardent Zionist who established the Jerusalem Health Center and for whom the Israeli city of Netanya was named, Nathan Straus was memorialized in many ways for his contributions to health in the United States, including the renaming of Rutgers Square on New York's Lower East Side to Straus Square. Nathan Straus linked his Judaism to his deeds with a remark he made at a dinner held in his honor, "Humanity is my kin, to save babies is my religion."[39]

In addition to reformers such as Wald and Straus, a new generation of American-born Jewish physicians was drawn to public health. The intersection of medicine, migration, and upward mobility in American Jewish life is reflected in their careers. Milton Joseph Rosenau was born in Philadelphia in 1869 to Nathan Rosenau and Mathilde Blitz, German Jewish immigrants (Fig. 67). Nathan received his medical degree from the University of Pennsylvania twenty years later and enlisted in the U.S. Marine Hospital Service (USMHS, later renamed the U.S. Public Health Service), a uniformed federal agency created by President John Adams in 1798. When Milton Rosenau joined the USMHS, the Surgeon General in charge was Walter Wyman. In 1893, Congress added to the duties of the Surgeon General the responsibility of preventing the spread of contagious and infectious diseases from one state or territory to another. It fell to Wyman to set up a system of quarantine regulations and to organize some of his physicians into a squad to battle epidemics in areas under the purview of the service.[40]

In 1895, the twenty-six-year-old Rosenau was sent to Eagle Pass, Texas. Agents of Mexico's Tlahualilo Company had lured approximately 1,000 African Americans from Alabama and Georgia to farm cotton and corn in the Mexican state of Durango. The grueling work, poor diet, and unhealthy living facilities left the workers ill with what the employers called "cotton pox." Many began returning to the United States. When they reached the border, the citizens of Eagle Pass met them with hostility and quarantine, fearing that they might be carriers of communicable diseases. The Texas State Department of Health diagnosed these workers with the dreaded disease smallpox and asked the U.S. Surgeon General for help. Wyman sent several physicians, including Rosenau, to supervise a two-hundred-bed field hospital. Guards sent to assist Rosenau divided the group into two camps, one for the sick and the other for the well. Tents were sent so that the facilities used for the sick could be burned afterward. Rosenau named the area where the tents were erected Camp Jenner in honor

39. Quoted at "Nathan Straus," http://www.jewage.org/wiki/ru/Article:Nathan%20Straus%20-%20Biography?embedded=true&textonly=1.

40. Kagan, *Jewish Contributions to American Medicine*, 387–89; Eisenberg, *Jews in Medicine*, 419–20.

Fig. 67. Milton J. Rosenau wearing the uniform of the U.S. Public Health Service, ca. 1900. (National Library of Medicine).

of Dr. Edward Jenner, the English physician who first developed the smallpox vaccine in the late eighteenth century.[41]

Rosenau inspected the workers twice a day, and persons with new cases of the disease were moved to the hospital tent. Between August 11 and October 21, when the camp closed, no new cases were diagnosed. Overall, 178 cases of smallpox were treated, and 60 deaths recorded, 51 from smallpox, a very high mortality rate of 28.7 percent, but perhaps low under the circumstances. The survivors were transported to their former homes in Alabama and Georgia.

41. The episode is best explored in John Mckiernan-González, *Fevered Measures: Public Health and Race at the Texas-Mexico Border, 1848–1942* (Durham: Duke University Press, 2012), 103, 104, 109, 110, 114, 120, 162, 278–79.

Rosenau's efforts avoided a much larger disaster and earned him respect within the USMHS for his work in what one scholar has characterized as a "transnational social field."[42]

Between 1899 and 1909, Milton Rosenau directed the Hygienic Laboratory, a diagnostic facility that supported the quarantine work of the USMHS. This experience and his earlier role as an epidemic fighter armed him to do battle against the 1918 influenza pandemic. Lieutenant Commander Rosenau had three collaborators: Lieutenant W. J. Keegan of the Navy, Assistant Surgeon General Gleason C. Lake of the Public Health Service (PHS), and PHS officer and medical detective Dr. Joseph Goldberger, the conqueror of pellagra. Together they conducted two sets of experiments using human subjects.

Rosenau speculated that the cause of the influenza was an organism so minute that it could pass through a laboratory filter. Conducting work at the Chelsea Naval Hospital in Boston, Rosenau and his collaborators were determined to learn whether the immense suffering was caused by a filterable virus. Using naval volunteers, Rosenau sought to induce the virus in healthy men and to determine its course of incubation after infection. From the various inoculations, the investigators concluded that influenza could be transmitted with secretions of the upper respiratory passages of patients in the early stages, usually within less than twelve hours of the disease's onset. However, the results were inconclusive because the criteria for a positive diagnosis of influenza were not well defined. Many volunteers came down with clear cases of streptococcal tonsillitis. Only a few of them got influenza, and the investigators speculated that, "being young male adults in a region where epidemic influenza had recently prevailed," they might have acquired "more than average resistance."[43] By the time the pandemic burned out between 1919 and 1920, more than 500,000 Americans had died, but the precise nature of the organism killing them remained a medical mystery. Rosenau spent the rest of his career at Harvard and the University of North Carolina training a new generation of public health advocates.

Epidemics were not the only threat to life in an increasingly urban and industrial America. In factories and sweatshops, workers strained their backs in poorly

42. *Ibid.*, 279.

43. M. J. Rosenau, W. J. Keegan, Joseph Goldberger, and G. C. Lake, "Experiments upon Volunteers to Determine the Cause and Mode of Spread of Influenza, Boston, November and December, 1918" and "Experiments upon Volunteers to Determine the Cause and Mode of Spread of Influenza, Boston, February and March, 1919," *Hygienic Bulletin*, no. 123 (Washington, D.C.: Government Printing Office, 1921), 5–53 and 55–97.

ventilated and inadequately lighted spaces to roll cigars or sew garments. Others bent over their kitchen tables, twisting wires to construct artificial flowers. Accidents with machinery or fires that overtook workers with no avenue of escape made every workplace a possible death trap. Jewish laborers and their families were among the victims of such conditions, but Jews were also prominent among the physicians and activists who protested for change. Their public lives echoed the confluence of medicine, migration, and upward mobility.

George Moses Price was born in 1864 in Poltava, Russia, and immigrated to the United States in his youth.[44] At the age of twenty-one, Price took a job as an inspector for the New York City Bureau of Sanitary Inspection. Scraping together money from his salary and, later, a variety of odd jobs, Price financed his own medical education, receiving his medical degree from New York University Medical College in 1895. The year before he received his degree, Price became an inspector for the Tenement Commission; with degree in hand, he was employed by the New York Board of Health.[45]

In 1910, garment industry workers conducted a major strike, which ended with all parties signing on to the "Protocols of Peace," crafted by the young attorney Louis Brandeis. Among the provisions was the formation of a Joint Board of Sanitary Control to remedy the unhealthy and unsafe factory conditions that had compelled workers to protest so vigorously. Dr. Price was chosen to chair the board, which was comprised of union representatives, employers, and the public. Under Price's leadership, the board initiated regular inspections of shop conditions, monthly fire drills, and ongoing educational campaigns to improve sanitation and public health. The year after the settlement, the board conducted the first of a series of annual surveys.[46] It found what the *New York Times* described as "extreme and widespread fire dangers."[47] Where emergency exits even existed, many had been blocked.

Such was the case for one of the deadliest industrial disasters in U.S. history, the Triangle Shirtwaist Factory fire. Located on the eighth through tenth floors of an industrial building in Greenwich Village, the company followed the

44. Leo Shpall, "The Diary of Dr. George M. Price," *Publications of the American Jewish Historical Society* 40, no. 2 (1950): 173–81; Leo Shpall, "The Memoir of Doctor George M. Price," *Publications of the American Jewish Historical Society* 47, no. 2 (1957): 101–10; and George M. Price and Leo Shpall, "The Russian Jews in America: Second and Final Installment," *Publications of the American Jewish Historical Society* 48, no. 2 (1958): 78–133.

45. "Dr. G. M. Price Dies; Foe of Sweatshop," *New York Times*, July 31, 1942, 15.

46. Richard A. Greenwald, *The Triangle Fire, the Protocols of Peace, and Industrial Democracy in Progressive Era New York* (Philadelphia: Temple University Press, 2005).

47. Dr. G. M. Price Dies," *New York Times*, July 31, 1942, 15

common practice of locking all doors during work shifts, to prevent unauthorized breaks and theft. When a fire broke out on March 25, 1911, workers could not escape. Some died of smoke inhalation, some burned to death, and some leapt from windows. In all, 146 garment workers died—123 women and girls and 23 men. Most were Jewish and Italian immigrants, mostly between the ages of fourteen and twenty-three.

In response, the state legislature created the Factory Investigating Commission to examine workplace safety and health conditions, and because of his experience and outstanding record, George Price directed the sanitary investigations. Among the actions he took was a recommendation that the garment industry move from the dilapidated lofts of the Lower East Side to cleaner, roomier quarters in midtown Manhattan.[48] The Joint Board under Price's leadership abolished the roller towels and common drinking cups often associated with the spread of tuberculosis, conducted studies of ventilation, air purity, and temperature of workplaces, insisted on clean windows and proper artificial lighting to protect workers' eyesight, and mandated that first aid and nursing services had to be accessible to workers. Still, tuberculosis and other health menaces prevailed. Price's solution was the formation of a Union Health Center, which opened its doors in 1913 in a single room near Union Square in lower Manhattan. By 1921, the need for such services motivated Price to move the center to a four-story building on Seventeenth Street; later it moved to Seventh Avenue in the heart of the garment district.

Price had a special concern for Jewish immigrant workers. Four years before he earned his medical degree, he had published a book in Yiddish filled with advice for eastern European Jews headed for the United States, *Di Yuden in Amerika* (1891). A moving passage might well have served as a eulogy for Dr. Price when he died in 1942, but also for many other Jewish immigrants who pursued careers in medicine:

> Hold fast, this is most necessary in America. Forget your past, your customs, and your ideals. Select a goal and pursue it with all your might. No matter what happens to you, hold on. You will experience a bad time, but sooner or later, you will achieve your goal.... A bit of advice for you: Do not take a moment's rest. Run, do, work and keep your own good in mind.... A final virtue is needed in America—called cheek.... Do not say, "I cannot; I do not know."[49]

48. Alan M. Kraut, *Silent Travelers: Germs, Genes, and the "Immigrant Menace"* (New York: Basic Books, 1994), 188–90; David Von Drehle, *Triangle: The Fire That Changed America* (New York: Atlantic Monthly Press, 2003), 212–13.

49. George M. Price, *Di Yuden in Amerika* (Odessa, 1891), 12. Translated and cited in Moses

Besides allowing the unsafe conditions that resulted in injuries of the kind Dr. George Price sought to prevent, sweatshops and crowded tenements harbored disease. One of the greatest threats to the health of newcomers in America was tuberculosis (TB). The tubercle bacillus thrived in the congestion of urban industrial life in both Europe and the United States. Because so many Jews found jobs in American cities, some non-Jews came to call TB the "tailor's disease" or the "Jewish disease."[50] Although data suggest that Jews in the United States did not suffer and die from TB disproportionately, those who suffered from the disease, and their families, attracted the attention of Jewish physician Dr. Charles Spivak. As a doctor and medical institution builder, Spivak was inspired by a radical political vision not unlike that of Abraham Jacobi.

Born Chaim Dovid Spivakofski in 1861 in Krementshug, Russia, Charles Spivak began his adult life as a revolutionary socialist and by 1882 was forced to flee his country (Fig. 68). Eight years later, Spivak earned his medical degree with honors from the Jefferson Medical College in Philadelphia, and by 1895 he was chief of gastrointestinal diseases at the Philadelphia Polyclinic. His wife's ill health, very likely TB, caused Spivak to move his family to Denver, where he taught and practiced medicine. By the 1890s, Denver had become the destination of choice for many TB sufferers who were assured by their physicians that the cool, dry climate would help heal them.[51] In 1904, Spivak helped found the Jewish Consumptive Relief Society (JCRS) in Denver to offer culturally sensitive medical treatment to Jewish TB sufferers. While Spivak administered an institution that catered to the ritual needs of Orthodox Jews, such as kosher cuisine, as a physician, he sought to reconcile those needs with state-of-the-art medicine.[52] Following the rules of *kashrut* made it more likely that his observant patients would eat the large portions of wholesome food that the medical understanding of the day equated with treating TB.[53] The sanatorium had only six men and one woman as its first patients, who were housed in wooden

Rischin, *The Promised City: New York's Jews, 1870–1914* (Cambridge, Mass.: Harvard University Press, 1970), 75.

50. Kraut, *Silent Travelers*, 155.

51. Jeanne E. Abrams, *Charles David Spivak: A Jewish Immigrant and the American Tuberculosis Movement* (Boulder: University Press of Colorado, 2009).

52. Charles Spivak, "The Genesis and Growth of the Jewish Consumptives' Relief Society," part 2, *The Sanatorium* 1 (March 1907): 26. Issues of this journal are located among the papers of the Jewish Consumptive Relief Society Records at Denver University.

53. Dr. Adolph Zederbaum, "Kosher Meat in Jewish Hospitals and Sanatoria," *The Sanatorium* 2 (November 1908): 275.

Fig. 68. Charles Spivak. (Western States Jewish History Association).

tent cottages. However, demand increased quickly, and by World War I, almost three thousand patients had "chased the cure" at JCRS. Open to consumptives whatever their race or religious faith, the JCRS accepted patients in all stages of TB at no charge.[54]

Another eastern European Jewish immigrant whose medical reputation derived from his engagement with TB was Dr. Maurice Fishberg. Born on August 16, 1872, in Kamnetz Podolsk, Ukraine, Fishberg immigrated to the United States in 1890. In 1897, he received his degree from the Medical College of New York

54. Charles Spivak, "The Genesis and Growth of the Jewish Consumptives' Relief Society," part 1, *The Sanatorium* 1 (January 1907): 6–7.

University. His first significant professional post was as the medical examiner for the United Hebrew Charities. His assignment was to ensure that the charitable dollars of the Jewish philanthropic community were being wisely spent to keep Jewish immigrants healthy and sufficiently productive to support themselves and their families. In 1905, he returned to Europe as a consultant to the U.S. Bureau of Immigration to investigate the condition of immigrants headed to the United States. Between 1915 and 1928, he was a professor of clinical medicine at the University and Bellevue Hospital Medical College. He was also the chief physician of the Montefiore Hospital and its Bedford Sanatorium, and maintained a long association with New York's Beth Israel Hospital.[55]

A prolific author, Fishberg wrote medical textbooks, scientific papers, and monographs. His *Pulmonary Tuberculosis*, published in 1921 and reprinted in many editions, was the most thorough and comprehensive volume on the disease written to that point, covering both theoretical and practical understandings of a disease that was the great killer of the nineteenth century. Although effective drug treatment was decades in the future, Fishberg suggested how home care, carefully planned and executed, could be as effective as sanatorium and climatic treatment, offering hope to physicians pursuing control of the disease among those who could not afford institutional treatment. A decade after the book was published, one physician wrote, "This classical book provides the general practitioner with the latest and most thorough knowledge of the pathogenesis, diagnosis, prophylaxis and treatment of pulmonary tuberculosis in all its phases. It is recognized as the most authoritative and complete presentation of the subject in any language, is of great value to both general practitioners and specialists and has won him recognition as a leading authority in tuberculosis. He paved the way for further studies in this subject."[56]

Interested in anthropology as well as medicine, Dr. Fishberg was committed to refuting nativist charges that Jews were a separate and physically inferior people, inherently prone to tuberculous, a slander that Fishberg refuted with data collection and analysis. He conducted his research with calipers, taking skull measurements of five hundred of his United Hebrew Charities patients. Although he initially thought that Jews demonstrated a homogeneity of cranial

55. "Dr. M. Fishberg Dies of Heart Attack at Home," Jewish Telegraphic Agency, https://www.jta.org/archive/dr-m-fishberg-dies-of-heart-attack-at-home; Kagan, *Jewish Contributions to Medicine in America*, 73–75.

56. Quoted in Kagan, *Jewish Contributions to Medicine in America*, 74. For a most valuable discussion of Fishberg and TB, see Mitchell B, Hart, *The Healthy Jew* (New York: Cambridge University Press, 2007), 143–72.

type greater than other groups, he eventually concluded that Jews were not of pure Semitic descent, but exhibited extensive racial intermixture. He asserted his belief that European Jews had been so changed by intermarriage with other groups that they retained no relationship at all with a pure Semitic or African type. Moreover, they were no different physically from the non-Jewish Europeans who were their neighbors. Minor differences in appearance or patterns of behavior were responses to environmental conditions. According to Fishberg, centuries of segregation and persecution born of bigotry had caused Jews to adopt distinctive postures, such as a stooped spine or dour facial expressions. Patterns of discrimination had forced Jews into some trades or professions and cultivated patterns of social behavior. Fishberg elaborated upon his views about the centrality of environment in his comprehensive 1911 volume, *The Jews: A Study of Race and Environment.*[57] Fishberg's emphasis on environment to explain differences among Jews from around the world echoed the findings of an even more renowned Jewish anthropologist, Columbia University's Franz Boas.[58]

As a physician concerned with the Jewish immigrant community's physical and mental health, Fishberg wrote prodigiously for widely circulated Jewish publications such as the *Menorah*, offering advice on how best to stay well and raise healthy children in the United States.[59] Cleanliness was essential. He contended that, "of the homes of the poor population of the city, the Jewish home is the cleanest."[60] He argued that cleanliness was central to Jewish culture, sacred and secular. He mentioned the ritual bath, or *mikva*, as well as the steam baths so popular among Russian Jews. Fishberg declared that the food consumed by Russian Jews was "considered to be above reproach, even by those who are prejudiced." Fishberg was referring to the dietary laws of *kashrut*, which demanded a "thorough inspection as to the health of the animal killed."[61] However, Fishberg could not help but agree with nativists that the bodies of eastern European Jew-

57. Maurice Fishberg, *The Jews: A Study of Race and Environment* (New York: Charles Scribner's Sons, 1911).

58. Franz Boas, *Changes in Bodily Form of Descendants of Immigrants* (New York: Columbia University Press, 1912).

59. Fishberg's series of essays in the *Menorah* between July and September 1902, "Health and Sanitation of the Immigrant Jewish Population," describes general health conditions among Russian Jewish immigrant populations. Most of these articles were later republished verbatim in Maurice Fishberg, "Health and Sanitation: New York," in Charles S. Bernheimer, *The Russian Jews in the United States: Studies of Social conditions in New York, Philadelphia, and Chicago, with a Description of Rural Settlements* (Philadelphia: John Winston Co., 1905).

60. Fishberg, "Health and Sanitation of the Immigrant Jewish Population of New York," *Menorah: A Monthly Magazine for the Jewish Home* 33 (August 1902): 74

61. *Ibid.*, 76.

ish immigrant children were "greatly retarded."[62] Rather than a sign of inherent inferiority, he attributed the condition to insufficient exercise during childhood in both Europe and the United States. He advocated rigorous exercise for all, especially the young. He wrote in one of his 1902 articles about the Jewish poor of New York's Lower East Side, "I want to state right here that what the East Side needs most is gymnasiums.... Gymnasiums ... should be multiplied and the younger generation be attracted to enjoy the benefits."[63]

Fishberg was not alone among Jews from eastern Europe who were born between 1865 and 1900 and made major contributions as physicians to the health and safety of their fellow immigrants. These physician-activists embraced the notion that environment outweighed genetics. Living and working conditions seemed to be at the root of the ill health that many immigrants suffered. That conclusion was in sharp contrast to the belief of many non-Jewish physicians that some physical conditions were inherent to Jews. One such popular diagnosis offered by clinicians to describe the highly agitated state of emotional instability they saw in their Jewish patients was "Hebraic debility." Such a broad and derogatory theory of the difference between Jewish immigrants and the pioneering American stock of old threatened to limit opportunities for upward mobility in the United States.

Dr. Richard Cabot, an unusually reflective Boston memoirist of English ancestry, was typical in his contempt for the Jews who "shuffled" up to him with "bent back and deprecating eyes." He loathed what he described as "nervous complaining, whimpering" Jews. When he found before him a Jewish male "with his beard upon his chest and the inevitable dirty black frock-coat flapping about his knees," Cabot confessed that he did not "see *this* man at all," merging him in the background of the average Jew."[64]

Just as Dr. Maurice Fishberg offered data in refutation of the notion that TB was the "Jewish disease," in 1907 a young physician, Dr. Hyman Morrison, published an article refuting the "Hebraic debility" diagnosis. He did not contest claims that there was a higher incidence of nervous disorders among Boston's

62. Maurice Fishberg, "Health Problems of the Jewish Poor," a paper read before the Jewish Chautauqua Assembly, July 27, 1903, reprinted in *American Hebrew* (New York: Press of Philip Cowen, 1903), 15.

63. Maurice Fishberg, "Health and Sanitation of the Immigrant Jewish Population," *Menorah: A Monthly Magazine for the Jewish Home* 33 (July 1902): 39.

64. Richard C. Cabot, *Social Service and the Art of Healing* (New York: Moffat, Yard and Company, 1909), 4–5.

eastern European Jewish community than among the general population.[65] However, he did find that the spike of nervous disorders among Jews was transitory, produced by the stresses of external circumstances and treatable.

Some of Morrison's fifty-one subjects said they were "strong and ruddy" when they arrived in America but were ground down by unrelenting labor and poor living conditions. One woman described how she "lived with strangers and worked from morning till night in a poorly lighted and poorly ventilated shop, with only a small, dry lunch for a mid-day meal." The result? "I soon began to grow weak; my eyes became dim, and my head commenced to ache, my teeth grew poor, and since then I have had stomach trouble." Morrison concluded, "This is to be expected, considering the stress and strain incidental to establishing oneself in a strange land." "Hebraic debility" was not a disease of the Jew, but an ailment shared by all who felt the stress of migration and relocation.

As one physician engaged with the history of medicine observed, "Medicine belongs to humanity at large and no nation, race, or group can claim the entire credit. Medical science is the cumulative work of all ages and all mankind and hence it is universal."[66] Medicine was a large tent, and Jews, too, could reside there. In the United States from 1865 to 1900, their place in that tent expanded. Increasingly, Jewish men and women who engaged in healing found themselves at a busy crossroads where medicine, migration, and yearnings for social access and status intersected. From A. E. Frankland's care for yellow fever's victims in 1873 to Jewish physicians' and reformers' struggles with tuberculosis and industrial injury and ailments, Jews embraced the role of healer. Leonard Dinnerstein has characterized the period 1865–1900 as the time when antisemitism was in flower in American society.[67] Jewish healers diminished the virulence of antisemitism; at other times, their medical careers paved for them a path to upward mobility. Poised on the rim of a new century, Jews engaged with the healing arts were among the vanguard of those who in the century ahead would propel the United States to world leadership in medical research and the conquest of disease. The drama of their achievements can still be found in the pages of reports, journal articles, textbooks, and memoirs, valuable addenda to the chronicle of the Jewish experience in America.

65. Hyman Morrison, "A Study of Fifty-One Cases of Debility in Jewish Patients," *Boston Medical and Surgical Journal* 157 (December 19, 1907): 816–19.

66. Kagan, *Jewish Contributions to Medicine in America*, xi.

67. Leonard Dinnerstein, *Antisemitism in America* (New York: Oxford University Press, 1994), 35–57.

"RAILROADED AND STEAMBOATED AWAY": TECHNOLOGY, SCIENCE, AND THE AMERICAN JEWISH IMAGINARY, 1850–1914

NOAH EFRON

HOW FAR the world has come, and Jews with it, in just a century! That was the point of an essay called "Progress," printed in the New York Jewish newspaper *Asmonean* in the dog days of summer 1853. The piece originated in Leipzig as the lead article in the May 17 edition of the *Allgemeine Zeitung des Judenthums.*[1] It was translated into elegant English by Rabbi Isaac Mayer Wise, who would soon rise to become the revered leader of America's Reform movement, eventually establishing the great institutions of that movement: the Union of American Hebrew Congregations and Hebrew Union College. But he was now just nine years off the boat from Radnitz, Bohemia, still finding his way on American soil. "What a short time it is—but as yesterday," the essay continued, "and verily we must be surprised at the gigantic paces of progress which mankind have achieved in that short period." Although the eighteenth century was a time of great men—"the age of Fredric the Great, Mendelssohn, Lessing and Voltaire"—so much had gotten better since. "Then was yet the time of personal servitude in all Europe, the most abominable spirit of dividing into class; the tolls imposed on Israelites were still in existence; then was yet the mighty barrier of caste not only in external affairs, but in weighty and important matters; ... there was not even equality before the tribunals of justice." Now the world had opened to Jews: "The abolition of the tolls, the opening of the Ghettoes—although shut again in some places—the liberty of settling where one chooses, and of earning a living by any honorable employment, the right of possessing real estate, and in many countries, the full privileges of citizenship ..., are the tokens of a progress which one hundred years ago neither Jew nor Gentile would have dreamed of."[2]

1. "Der Fortschritt," *Allgemeine Zeitung des Judenthums,* May 17, 1853, 253–54.
2. Isaac Mayer Wise, "Progress," *Asmonean,* July 22, 1853, 113.

Behind all this progress, the essay goes on, is a great leap forward for science and technology.

> [W]hat a progress in production, in factories and in all technical arts; in roads, railroads, telegraphs, printing presses, in the communication of nations, exchange of produces, navigation and application of steam. Is it necessary to remind our readers as to the progress of science during the last century? We only need look at ... physics, which was seventy years ago but in its infancy.... [W]e look on the material advantages, and we find a development of commercial systems, principles and means, and a system of monetary transactions, of which they at that period had not as much as an idea, also our ordinary mode of living betrays a mighty progress.

Gains in scientific knowledge enabled the introduction of technologies in great factories that produced undreamed-of wealth. Owing to these advances, the world had escaped a "low and partial state of miserable egotism" and "ascended the summit of unity and equality." Jews, too, had emerged from *their* low and partial state:

> [I]gnorance has given way to a full measure of science and arts; and the want of taste has made way for education, elegance and luxury. Also on the field of science, the most rigid road for progress, time has achieved a thorough acknowledgment of its demands; the religious ideas and the spirit have conquered against the dead form, benumbed ordinances and outworn ceremonies; the rigid yoke of old is no more; superstitions have been discarded; mere presentments have been thrown aside in favor of pure consciousness; and even the outside of Synagogues and of the ceremonials have been accommodated to the demands of the time. What a mighty progress!

Here the Leipzig essay ends. Wise endorsed it, no doubt—why else would he trouble to translate it and bring it to print?—but not without adding a long addendum that began, "The *Allgemeine* has forgotten, or was compelled not to mention, that the past century has brought the independence of America." In all that pertains to progress, Wise went on, America "far outweighs" Europe. Here,

> an asylum has been thrown open to the oppressed and suffering of all nations, and the thirst for liberty has been heightened by the practical demonstration of the prosperity and progress of a democratic republic. Liberty of conscience has been proclaimed for the first time, which at once condemns the history of fifteen bloody centuries and all nations were invited to meet and fraternize on this virgin soil, not defiled by the blood of Jews and heretics. This is the mightiest progress of the past century, for it is an entire new phase in the social development of mankind.... The American States [rest] ... on the new basis of absolute justice—the institute of slavery excepted, which was a given circumstance when the consti-

> tution was framed—and upon the results of experience. This basis is an entirely new one! All ancient and modern history is at once done away with; and thence comes the most powerful progress of the last century.

In America in the middle of the nineteenth century, Wise wrote, the weight of history is released. All is new, and new lives could be lived. There was no better sign of this liberation than science and, especially, the technologies that science brought. These were appearing in a torrent, Wise wrote, and they released men and woman from their toils, creating wealth and altering space and time by linking far-off places by steamship and rail and allowing news made in Washington to reach New York and San Francisco in an instant by wire.

Fig. 69. The masthead of *The Asmonean*, vol. 1, no. 2, for the week ending November 2, 1849. (New York Public Library).

The essay "Progress" would not surprise regular readers of the *Asmonean*, who found on the pages of the first Jewish weekly in America a pulsing enthusiasm for science and technology (Fig. 69). Almost every edition included a description of a new laboratory discovery or technological wonder. An *Asmonean* subscriber between 1851 and 1856 would have read about fire annihilators, hot air balloons, shoe-cleaning machines, steamships, telegraphs, elevated railways, sweeping machines, sewing machines, whirlpool gold separators, grain elevators, power looms, weaving machines, textile uptake machines, cropping machines, calculating machines, ice-making machines, portable refrigerators, crushing and amalgamating machines, gas lighting, mechanical ventilation, miners' safety lamps, bevel sawing machines, ruling machines, polychromatic printing presses, quartz crushing machines, corn shellers, type-casting machines, leather polishing machines, book page turners, safety locks, iron safes, dredging machines, antifriction boxes, dying apparatuses, barrel-making machines, stave-jointing machines, crozing machines, spark arresters, fat distillery apparatuses, winnowing machines, printers' friskets, harvester cutters, high-speed shoe and boot makers, double-acting force pumps, clover hullers, hat body felters, window-washing machines, stave machines, sheet metal folding machines, curvilinear sawing machines, soda water generators, serpentine spinner fishing reels, street-sweeping machines, boiler incrustation preventers, solid-shank anchors, and a good many more inventions.[3]

There was a reason all this new-fangled and scientific technology turned up in a Jewish newspaper, one that might be called *ideological*.[4] As Robert Lyon, its

3. W. H. Phillips, "The Fire Annihilator," *Asmonean*, December 26, 1851, 3; "Our Weekly Budget," May 2, 1851, 14; "Progress of the Electric Telegraph," September 23, 1853, 7; "The Crystal Palace," October 28, 1853, 13; "New Costume for the Ladies," June 20, 1851, 4; "Singer's Patent Sewing Machine," July 9, 1852, 7; "Wants of the Gold Miners," October 8, 1852, 4; "Samples of Uncle Sam's Cuteness," October 22, 1852, 273; "The Power-Loom," September 30, 1853, 193; "Shawls," October 29, 1852, 16–17; "It Is Erroneously Stated," August 22, 1851, 145; "Preserved Meats and Meat-Biscuits," January 28, 1853, 175–76; "Conrad Hill Mine, North Carolina," July 15, 1853, 107; "Gas Light, Its Inventors and Improvers," June 5, 1851, 2 (also see "The Crystal Palace," October 28, 1853, 13); "Ventilation of Mines," November 18, 1853, 39; "Miners Safety Lamp," January 13, 1854, 99; "New Patents Issued," April 7, 1854, 195; "List of Patents," June 23, 1854, 75; "Foreign Items," September 1, 1854, 159; "New Patents Issued," February 9, 1855, 135; "New Patents Issued," June 22, 1855, 58; "List of Patents," April 4, 1856, 199; "Weissenborn's Patent Boiler Incrustation Preventer," June 13, 1856, 71; "Improvements in Anchors—Metalic Castings," November 11, 1853, 7. The high-speed boot maker was devised in Prague by a Jewish shoemaker named Bush. "The Emperor witnessed the making of a pair of boots, which occupied but a few minutes, and expressed himself highly pleased with the proceedings." The emperor also made a large donation to the Jewish hospital. "Foreign Items," *Asmonean*, September 1, 1854, 159.

4. There was also a practical reason. Robert Lyon, the paper's editor, was by 1852 also publishing another paper every Tuesday and Friday, the *New York Mercantile Journal and Financial Recorder*. Written for businessmen, merchants, and financiers, the *Mercantile Journal* reported as a matter of course—alongside the price of such commodities as beeswax, gunny cloth, gunpowder, saltpeter, twine, and rags—on developments in shipping, rail, communications, and manufacture, all of which might matter to men who made or traded things for a living. And what mattered to these men might also matter to the Jews who read the *Asmonean*. *Asmonean* subscribers included men prominent in trade and finance, who might find reports of new inventions useful in their businesses. Owing to both practical and ideological reasons, almost 30 percent (29.3 percent, to be precise) of the paper's articles covered "non-Jewish items," according to a coded content analysis. A good portion of these items dealt, directly or indirectly, with new discoveries and inventions, especially those relevant to manufacture, transportation, and com-

editor, wrote in the inaugural issue, the *Asmonean* aimed to remove "the prejudices of darker times" and to promote a Judaism "free from the trammels of the schools of casuistry." Science and technology shared these aims and could help to achieve them.[5] The paper's masthead was a dense pastiche of American and Jewish symbols and slogans, with an eagle bearing a shield of David over the Stars and Stripes, and carrying a banner reading, "Two are better than one," above a second banner reading, "A Threefold cord is not quickly broken." Centered at the bottom, between the volume number and the name and address of the publisher, was the paper's slogan, "Knowledge is Power," an aphorism commonly (if not entirely accurately) attributed to Sir Francis Bacon, a father of empirical natural science.

Lyon published the *Asmonean* until he died in 1858. The decades that followed were ones of change, fast and momentous, both for Jews in America and for science and technology. In the second half of the nineteenth century and the first quarter of the twentieth, American Jews and American science both established themselves on new foundations, growing rapidly, setting up new institutions, and revising both how they saw themselves and how others saw them. Along the way, Judaism in America and science and technology in America were linked in unexpected ways. Science and technology became mixed up in wrangles among American Jews about what it meant to be a Jew in America and what it ought to mean. Jewish leaders arguing in favor of religious reform of all sorts adduced the discoveries of modern science as evidence that one or another change was needed. Those arguing against reform did the same. Science and technology got tangled up in how Jewish religious leaders described the relationship their religion bore to the Christian faith of most other Americans. And, most of all, science and technology played a part in Jewish notions of what sort of place America could and should be—and *needed* to be for Jews to thrive there. These debates were true especially during the great immigrations of Jews from eastern Europe that ebbed and mostly flowed from 1881 to 1924.

Science and Technology, Reform and Tradition

When Isaac Mayer Wise published "Progress" in 1853, the notion of progress was very much on his mind. In that same year, Wise wrote about the "Exhibition of the Industry of All Nations," New York's version of the London Exhibition

---

munication. Barbara Straus Reed, "Unity, Not Absorption: Robert Lyon and the *Asmonean*," *American Journalism* 7, no. 2 (1990): 89–92.

5. Robert Lyon, "To Our Subscribers," *Asmonean*, October 26, 1849, 1.

of 1851. As the *Asmonean* eagerly reported, a grand iron-and-glass crystal palace had been constructed, illuminated by the glare of "five thousand burners, a larger number than in the streets of New York and Brooklyn together ... which almost blinds the eye of the visitor with its sudden and intense brilliancy."[6]

While the exhibition was under construction, the *Asmonean* devoted to it a full broadsheet page, with a reproduction of a lavish etching of the "largest and most beautiful construction in the country."[7] As the exhibition approached completion, Wise satirically detailed his expectations:

> In the department of optics, we should like to see a microscope powerful enough to detect therewith the beneficial results of the secret societies lately sprung up in our midst foreign to Judaism, and an impediment to the cause of progress.... [W]e should wish to see in that department a metallic mirror in which the orthodox could truthfully see their own forms so that they should no longer oppose reforms, and a telescope by which that party could look into futurity and see the result of inactivity; and a *camera obscura* in which they could see the demands of the age in their true light. Such are the articles which we should like to see in the Crystal Palace, then we would take a season ticket, even if it cost twice as much as now.[8]

Wise's point was that, just as science was showing the world in its true form and obliterating false and primitive beliefs, a similar revolution could bring forth a truer form of Judaism, sweeping clean centuries of benighted dogma. When, in 1854, Wise started his own paper, the *Israelite*, he wrote in its first issue that the publication "declares war against error, superstition, prejudice, ignorance, arrogance, hypocrisy and bigotry." What's more, he wrote, it "will favor enlightenment, education, a moderate and rational progress, ... will cherish the spread of knowledge, the progress of learning, and the triumph of truth, will respect liberty of conscience, thought and speech." Judaism "is destined to become *the religion* of the civilized world." For this project to come to pass, Wise wrote, it is necessary to sidestep the "past-talmudical rabbinical literature, in which the bright glare of a hair-splitting sagacity vies with a childish casuistry, ... a barren mountain of books entombing the putrefactions of ten centuries ... cultivated by a dozen or more of obscure men who lack the scientific preparation necessary to make the matter accessible or useful to the community."[9]

6. "The Crystal Palace," *Asmonean*, October 28, 1853, 13.
7. "New-York Crystal Palace for the Exhibition of the Industry of All Nations," *Asmonean*, November 19, 1852, 57.
8. Isaac Mayer Wise, "What We Should Like to See at the World's Fair," *Asmonean*, August 14, 1853, 113.
9. Isaac Mayer Wise, "To the Reader," *Israelite*, July 15, 1854, 4.

For Wise, science was closely linked to religious reform. He wrote that Judaism had descended "into the minutiae of casuistry" and "the delusions of Cabalah" because the rabbis had strayed from "all secular science except medicine and mathematics and all closer intercourse with the world outside of the Ghetto."[10] In modern times, science revealed such primitive religion for what it was: "Copernicus, Keppler [*sic*], and Galileo, and after them, Isaac Newton, revolutionized all former conceptions of the universe.... Theology at the beginning of the seventeenth century, being actually destroyed in its basis, a new philosophy was bound to come."[11] And science would renew Judaism: "Jewish reform signifies in principle an appeal to philosophy and science in the exposition of scriptures, especially in regard to law and doctrine."[12]

It was not just science, but new technology too, that required Judaism to place itself on a new foundation. One lesson of technology in modern times, Wise believed, is that change is inevitable. Technology *drove* change, as he later insisted in lectures and sermons: "With the discoveries of steam and electricity as motive powers, a new philosophy in the schools and a new creed in the churches have taken hold upon the minds."[13] Time and again, Wise celebrated the fact that new technologies swept away old theologies and philosophies. After an 1855 train trip, Wise wrote in a reverie:

> Nothing can demonstrate to better advantage the immense powers of man, than the rail-way between Wheeling and Baltimore. Tunnels, bridges, viaducts and artificial plains interchange in such a rapid succession, that admiration and surprise have a complete mastery over the traveler; there rocks are split and removed or excavated, precipices are filled up, hills are leveled, rivers are bridged, narrow vallies [*sic*] are widened.... Let the Baltimore and Ohio Railroad speak and put your doctrines to shame.
>
> ... We fly to distant territories on the wings of fire and water, we speak into distant lands by the terrible force of lightning, we enlist the sun in our service to paint our pictures, we propel cities across the ocean in as short time as our fathers went from Dan to Jerusalem ... ; still we are required to think and feel as our good forefathers did, what nonsense! Distant nations have come in close contact, exchanged ideas, revolutionized each other's thoughts, feelings and conceptions, the superstitions between nations are *railroaded* and *steamboated* away,

10. Isaac Mayer Wise, "Reformed Judaism," in *Selected Writings of Isaac M. Wise*, ed. David Philipson and Louis Grossmann (Cincinnati: Robert Clarke Company, 1900), 293.

11. Isaac Mayer Wise, "Spinoza's Metaphysics," *Israelite*, July 24, 1868, 4–5.

12. Wise, "Reformed Judaism," 265.

13. Isaac Mayer Wise, "The Messiahship of Jesus Was of Foreign Origin," *American Israelite*, January 20, 1882, 236.

> the partition wall between man and man, totters and falls, we already look over the old superstructure and recognize each other; but our poor philosophers maintain, that it is wickedness to think differently from our forefathers, to remove the old and tottering wall of separation, to think on a more enlarged field than our old men did; how pitifully narrow, how little touched by the spirit of our age are those men if they are honest; we pity them.... Progress is the will of the Lord; rapid progress is the spirit of ours.[14]

With "ideas," "conceptions," and "superstitions" being "*railroaded* and *steamboated* away," and with technological progress defining the spirit of the age, reform was necessary and inevitable. Failure to adapt meant extinction.

Wise's belief in technological progress, and the good it could do for society, grew stronger through the Civil War. This expectation was not inevitable. For some, the new technologies of transportation, communication, armament, and photography made war ever more destructive and brought it closer to home, tamping their enthusiasm. Sermonizing on the first Yom Kippur after the war ended, the most solemn day of the year, to his congregation at Bene Yeshurun Temple of Cincinnati, Wise countered that all the "strife, war, oppression and vice" the country had seen lately was not the result of the new technologies and ideas. Rather, these innovations had not spread fast enough or far enough: "All the progresses achieved, all the enlightenment spread, ... reached after all but a small fraction of the human family.... Darkness covers the earth and gross darkness the people." Jews must embrace technological advances with greater resolve: "Hold out at the portals of reason, where God has placed you to guard the heavenly fire, fear no sacrifice, for the glory of the Lord shineth upon thee, thy rationality will triumph; ... philosophy and science, progress and invention have come to thy assistance."[15]

In 1867, Wise published a speech he heard in Cincinnati by the Reverend Amory Dwight Mayo, the preacher of the city's Unitarian Church of the Redeemer. After each paragraph, Wise interpolated his own criticism, adding comments like "[t]his paragraph of Mr. Mayo contains a considerable mistake." Wise concluded,

14. Isaac Mayer Wise, "A Tour to the East," *Israelite*, May 25, 1855, 364. Wise returned time and again to the progress he witnessed when he looked out the window of a train car. Traveling over the Allegheny Mountains in 1857, for instance, he wrote that "every rock which was removed or excavated, every viaduct from hill to hill, every bridge across the wild precepices [*sic*], or a rolling stream" bore witness to him that "the mind of man is so entirely different from every other creature on this sublunary globe, that it is so much superior, so highly exalted above all things around him." Wise, "Editorial Correspondence," *Israelite*, October 23, 1857, 130.

15. Isaac Mayer Wise, "The Sacrifices for Judaism," *Israelite*, October 6, 1865, 108–9.

> Clergymen insist upon feeding their flock on the spiritual Manna, which fell, not from heaven, but from the synods, conferences, papal bulls, and scholastic lyceums in the ages of darkness, or at the morning dawn of civilization, and then wonder at the misfortune, that the flock starves.... But the people and the character of the people are radically changed. Since those days, steam and electricity wiped out the old servitude, criticism and natural science upset all the medieval elements, the progress of constitutional liberty made free men of the blind tools of princes and priests, the spread of useful information and its close connection with the daily bread set people to think and philosophize, the world moves rapidly onward and the churches stand still as a lifeless rock; therefore, the congregations decline.[16]

What was true for Christians was true too for Jews. "I am a reformer," Wise wrote elsewhere, "because I am convinced that none can stop the stream of time, none can check the swift wheels of the age."[17]

Wise saw himself as a moderate, revising Judaism only insomuch as the stream of time and the swift wheels of the age required. "I have always the *Halakha* for my basis, I never sanction a reform against the *Din*," he wrote. "I never urge my principles upon another, nor do I commence to start a reform in a synagogue."[18] Not surprisingly, reformers more radical than Wise shared his view that new technologies and advancing science signaled a sort of progress that was both a spur and a prooftext for Jewish reform. After a trans-Atlantic telegraph cable was successfully laid, David Einhorn—a German-born rabbi driven from Baltimore to Philadelphia for his sharp condemnation of slavery—did not shy from calling for radical reform: "Ceaselessly the word of God reveals itself in the advancing knowledge of His works, in the shaping of history! ... [A] time like the present, in which human research has given birth to a giant straddling the ocean, is not merely as filled, but in an incomparably greater degree more filled with God than was gray antiquity."[19] In finding support for reform in such

16. Isaac Mayer Wise and Amory Dwight Mayo, "A Speech to Cincinnatians about Cincinnati," *Israelite*, December 13, 1867, 4.

17. Isaac Mayer Wise, "Letter of Dr. Wise," *Occident and American Jewish Advocate* 6, no. 12 (March 1849): 616.

18. *Ibid.* In his day, there were those who saw Wise as a radical whose conciliatory pronouncements aimed to prettify his iconoclasm, and there are scholars today, too, who hold this assessment. The first full-throated statement of this view was Aryeh Rubinstein's, more than a generation ago: "Isaac Mayer Wise is invariably portrayed as a proponent of moderate Reform in Judaism.... Wise was a radical Reformer, not a moderate." Aryeh Rubinstein, "Isaac Mayer Wise: A New Appraisal," *Jewish Social Studies* 39, no. 1/2 (1977): 53.

19. Quoted in Michael A. Meyer, *Response to Modernity: A History of the Reform Movement in Judaism* (Detroit: Wayne State University Press, 1995), 246. Einhorn preached to his congregants that "Radical Reform wants a Judaism that bears the royal messianic mantle; moderate Reform—a Judaism swathed in Orthodox and reformist rags." Quoted in *ibid.*, 249.

achievements as a telegraph cable, Einhorn was expressing an attitude shared by almost all reformers, radical, moderate, and in between. The very *meaning* of technology seemed to be that change is for the better. For this reason, technology and science were almost natural metaphors for religious reform, and reformers were quick to press them into service in essays and sermons. Moreover, technology and science were changing the country before the eyes of Americans; to survive such rapid change, reformers argued, it was necessary for American Judaism to change, too. From "the researches of modern times," Rabbi Emil G. Hirsch, Einhorn's son-in-law and himself a champion of radical reform, told his congregants at Chicago's Temple Sinai, "we may learn that Reform is not arbitrary."[20] Rabbi Max Lilienthal, who, beginning in 1855, held the pulpit of Cincinnati's Bene Israel congregation and frequently collaborated with Wise, made this same argument in an open letter to Isaac Leeser, a traditionalist who fretted over how quickly certain longstanding Jewish practices were being jettisoned by reformers:

> You are entirely wrong in ascribing the present movement of Jewish reform to a mere temporary invention of some eccentric heads, and not, on the contrary, to the logical consequence of "the spirit of the age," in which we are living.... [Being] justified before the tribunal of our reason, our religious life in its totality has to undergo the same critical trial, to experience the same revolutions as all other departments of our society, —if Judaism shall not remain behind the movements of the time.[21]

Lilienthal was piqued that traditionalists like Leeser maligned Reform leaders who used new scientific ideas and inventions to justify their views. It was a common knock against reformers. As Rabbi Samuel Myer Isaacs wrote in his own journal, "Because science does not see the reason why an Israelite should

20. Emil Gustav Hirsch, "Evolution in Religion," *Jewish Advance*, May 6, 1881, 5.

21. Max Lilienthal, "The Spirit of the Age; Letters on Reform Addressed to the Rev. I. Leeser by Dr. Lilienthal, Letter III," *Israelite*, December 19, 1856, 189. Eighteen years later, in an 1874 speech praising the incipient opening of Hebrew Union College, Lilienthal declared that the "trodden paths of antiquated theology will not do any longer. The natural sciences, justified criticism and restless skepticism have undermined many of its foundations.... Free investigation and free inquiry, sanctioned by reason, though discredited by systems of blind faith, must rule supreme." Quoted in Bruce Ruben, "Max Lilienthal: Rabbi, Educator, and Reformer in Nineteenth-Century America" (Ph.D. diss., City University of New York, 1997), 284. Leeser was the strongest voice of traditionalism among American Jews from the late 1820s to the late 1860s; although never ordained, he long served as the *Hazzan* (cantor) and de facto rabbi of Philadelphia's storied Mikveh Israel synagogue (before American soil was home to even a single rabbi). His monthly journal, the *Occident and American Jewish Advocate*, begun in 1843, was widely seen as a voice of Jewish traditionalism.

not indulge in so rich a culinary delicacy as bacon, the positive injunction in Holy writ 'is opposed to the spirt of the age' and may be disregarded with impunity. Because the superior wisdom of modern times has failed to discover in the Decalogue any mention of the street railroads, of course it is perfectly right to employ one of those useful vehicles in going to and from the Synagogue."[22] In an essay criticizing the "Reform Creed," Samuel Bruel, a Cincinnati hatter and traditionalist community leader, wrote that reformers are "puffed up with superficial notions" and that, for them, "the truths of science, statistics and progression are now the order of the day." These reformers are enchanted by the newest technologies, and Bruel agreed that "Judaism ... deserves to enjoy in practice the benefits. ... " But the reformers learned the wrong lesson from technology and science: "Of course, say they: 'we are wiser than our predecessors; having their experience and their study as our guides, we are therefore better enabled to appreciate natural philosophy than they were; we have penetrated as far as knowledge can reach, and opened the forbidden tracts for future development, and as a legitimate result, we can comprehend the essence of revealed religion in a manner more acceptable to the spirit of the age.'"[23] Bruel's dispute with reformers was not that they found inspiration in steamships, railroads, telegraphs, and labor-saving machines. These things are astonishments, Bruel admitted, but they demonstrate the opposite of what the reformers think they do. They prove not that reform is *needed*, but that it is *unnecessary*. If anything, the miracles of technology are prooftexts for *traditional* Judaism:

> Can it be shown that science or statistics conflict with the historical account narrated in Genesis? Does science, &c, gainsay any of the precepts of the law of Moses as revealed to him? From what source are all the various materials obtained? the iron to build the machinery and railroads? and who infused the spirit of wisdom into the mind of mankind to construct them all? Whence is the fuel obtained to generate the steam and gas? what market supplies the table from which all living creatures on this earth are fed, and who provides the material from which we are

22. Samuel Myer Isaacs, "Is Reform a Success," *Jewish Messenger*, September 4, 1861, 35. Isaacs wrote repeatedly about the technological wonders of his age, which he admired while still worrying that they would turn the heads of the Jews of his day, reform and traditionalist alike. In a despondent 1857 essay he wrote, "We live in a very remarkable age, in a period distinguished for its rapid advancement in art, science and enterprise. We know more than our ancestors, live better than they did, have more lofty ideas than they had, earn more, spend more, dress better, travel faster ... we have certainly advanced with gigantic strides." This new plentitude, Isaacs continued, did not translate to spiritual advance for reformers or for the Orthodox. Samuel Myer Isaacs, "Orthodoxy," *Jewish Messenger*, May 8, 1857, 80.

23. Samuel Bruel, "The Reform Creed and Temple Worship," *Occident and American Jewish Advocate* 22, no. 1 (April 1864): 29–30.

clothed? and lastly, what bank furnishes the gold to pay for them?—*We* answer, that these invaluable productions are the gift of the Almighty God to mankind, for their use, comfort, and happiness. And now, O Israel, what doth the Lord thy God request of thee in return for these bountiful gifts? Merely to fear Him, to walk in all His ways, to serve Him with love in all thy heart and soul, to keep His commandments, His statutes, and His judgments, and above all, diligently to perform them (Deut. x. 12).[24]

Isaac Leeser, the publisher of the *Occident*, where Bruel's essay appeared, had for years argued that science and technology fit best with a *traditionalist* approach to Judaism. As early as 1841, in a sermon called "Religious Education," Leeser preached that the sciences "can well be blended with the study of religion; and do not imagine that the teaching of the former will be hurtful to the latter, or that careful study of the Bible and commentators will retard the progress in science. They who tell you the opposite are either not acquainted with general knowledge or ignorant of the language and tendency of Scripture."[25] In Leeser's view, it was a mistake to interpret scientific and technological progress as a spur to modernize religious traditions and traditional Jewish beliefs. He complained from the pulpit of a "strange inconsistency":

[T]hose very ones that speak so much of the incompatibility of religion with the light of science never examined the doctrines of faith for themselves; they are ignorant of the Bible, and, more strange to say, of the very sciences which they profess to venerate so much; and all their haranguing about the absurdity of belief is founded upon hearsay, or upon the assumption that it is unwise to suppose that laws enacted three thousand years ago should be useful still. It is marvelous how little reason there is for infidelity, how weak the grounds are upon which unbelief rests for support, and how the contrary of the foregoing assertions is true; for all science tends to confirm the truth of the law of God.[26]

Leeser returned to this point many times. In "Our Motto" he posited: "Some have imagined that the pursuit of science is inimical to religion. This is certainly true when a man rises from his secular studies with a soul of pride and a heart of presumption ... and sets himself up as an arbitrator of God's holy revelation."[27] As Leeser saw it, reformers looked upon the progress of technology and science as a warrant to believe that, just as people have reshaped God's

24. *Ibid.*, 30.

25. Isaac Leeser, "Religious Education," in *Discourses, Argumentative and Devotional, on the Subject of the Jewish Religion*, 3 vols. in 2 (Philadelphia: Haswell and Fleu, 1837–1841), 3:230–31.

26. Isaac Leeser, "The Blessings of Revelation," in *Discourses, Argumentative and Devotional*, 2:53.

27. Isaac Leeser, "Our Motto," *Occident and American Jewish Advocate* 1, no. 3 (June 1843): 110.

works, they can and should reshape God's words and God's commandments. This presumption, Leeser believed, was a vanity. Instead, Leeser insisted that technology and science showed that reform of Judaism was unneeded and ill informed: unneeded because traditional Judaism was, by its nature, well suited to absorb all that is good about modernity; and ill informed because reformers assumed that there were conflicts between what scientists found to be true and what Jews had long known to be true, and that these conflicts could be resolved only by bringing Judaism into line with science.[28]

Technology and science were invoked constantly by American rabbis and Jewish intellectuals in arguments over reform and tradition in the second half of the nineteenth century. What is most remarkable is that almost everyone who was engaged—moderate reformers, more radical reformers, moderate traditionalists, and more avid traditionalists—found evidence to confirm their various positions. For reformers, technology and science were irrefutable demonstrations that the spirit of the age was one of progress and reform. Each *clack-clack-clack* of wheels on rail was a signal that America was changing and that only a Judaism capable of change would thrive. For traditionalists, Judaism needed no revision to meet the new world.[29]

Darwin

One may search in vain among the letters, essays, books, and sermons of nineteenth-century American Jews for disparagements of steamships, railways, telegraphs, and other new technologies, or of new findings in chemistry and physics. Charles Darwin and his theories, however, were different. Starting in the early 1860s, the theory of evolution by natural selection was singled out for criticism, often energetically philosophical, especially by rabbis committed to reform. In the 1870s and 1880s, there were rabbis who rejected Darwinian evolution, those who embraced it, and those who remained ambivalent about it. By the 1890s, almost all American Jewish rabbis and writers had made their peace with Darwin. For some, especially in the Reform movement, grappling with Darwin left a lasting impression on their theology. Indeed, as intellectual

28. Isaac Leeser, "Scriptural Predictions," in *Discourses on the Jewish Religion*, 3d ser., vol. 6 (Philadelphia: Sherman & Co., 1867), 264.

29. There were, Leeser would later write, "those who wished to preserve Judaism [and] dreaded to be brought in contact with an education [in science] which necessarily had such pernicious effects. It requires no demonstration on our part to prove ... there is no necessary connection between liberal knowledge ... and infidelity." Isaac Leeser, "Progress," *Occident and American Jewish Advocate* 24, no. 11 (February 1867): 485.

historian Daniel R. Langton has observed, "ideas related to evolution ... coalesced constructively to provide a new foundation for the Jewish religious imagination" among Reform leaders, essentially giving shape to "the apparent incoherence of the reforming agenda."[30]

Jewish criticism of evolution by natural selection, such as it emerged in the years just after Darwin published his theory, was almost always expressed alongside a celebration of science itself. When the Reverend Dr. Jacob Mayer, a close colleague of Wise and an outspoken supporter of reform, criticized Darwin in an 1867 lecture at the Temple of Cincinnati, he opened with an encomium: "Our age of progress and enlightenment, in which on the field of exact science great and important discoveries succeed each other with astonishing rapidity; and reasonable doubts shake the old fabric of superstition and credulity, so much so as to cause the entire removal of blind submission to the opinion of others, by the all-powerful yearning for convincing truth."[31] Darwin, Mayer went on, "maintains that under the impression of exterior influence, which governs the living world and consequently changes it, man, too, from an inferior creature changed into his actual appearance and condition." And it is true, Mayer agreed, that theories of this sort "may *possibly* be right; *certainly* they are ingenious." But, he asked, "does that suffice?"

Mayer's answer was that it does not. This is not to say that Mayer dismissed science. Of Darwin and Charles Lyell, he asked, "Are these men, however, the only authorities of science?" He answered his own question with another: "Is there not also Alexander V. Humboldt—our Alexander the Great, who we may be proud of?" Humboldt, Mayer wrote, studied the nature of the Americas, and he reached conclusions different from those of Darwin, ones more in line with a "Mosaic cosmology." He concluded that the greater evidence supported Humboldt over Darwin—a confirmation of the methods of science itself.

In the fall and winter of 1874 and 1875, Isaac Mayer Wise delivered a series of twenty-two evening lectures to his congregation at Bene Yeshurun Temple in Cincinnati, criticizing Darwin and setting out an alternative, nonmaterialist sort of evolution. It was the most extensive refutation of Darwinian theory that had ever been offered to American Jews, from the most renowned rabbi in the land. It was also a love song to science. Of Darwin himself, Wise said:

30. Daniel R. Langton, *Reform Judaism and Darwin: How Engaging with Evolutionary Theory Shaped American Jewish Religion* (Berlin: De Gruyter, 2019), 105–11.

31. Jacob Mayer, "The Origin and Education of Men: Lecture Delivered in the Temple of Cincinnati," *Israelite*, May 3, 1867, 4.

> I admire Mr. Darwin as an eminent biologist, whose hypotheses deserve a careful consideration. He displays more originality of thought in his particular branch than many prominent men, and his research is vast and wonderful. Men like Darwin are very rare, few and far apart. He deserves our admiration.[32]

Still, Wise went on, in his theories of evolution, and especially *human* evolution, Darwin had strayed from science. *Descent of Man,* Wise said, "is the most unscientific book he did write," and it amounts to "a momentary aberration of the human mind, a sporadic and epidemic disease of an over-loaded age, as was at its respective time alchemy, astrology, phrenology, and exploded exorcism." What troubled Wise was that Darwin offered pseudoscience as if it were real science. In this way, Darwin was no better than "prejudiced sectarians [who] expound Bible passages."[33]

When the lecture series was about halfway done, on December 10, 1874, Theresa Wise died after a long, wasting disease. She was, Wise wrote in the preface, "my wife, my dearly beloved companion in this eventful life, the mother of my children, the faithful partner of my joys and my sufferings."[34] Most everyone in the audience—Wise's congregation, after all—surely knew of their rabbi's tragedy. More than two thousand mourners attended the funeral, and many more read the heartsick coverage in the paper.[35] After the last lecture, Wise offered his audience "a parting word":

> When I was young, I chose a bride, the fairest of all maidens, and to her I made the sacred vow of fidelity. She always loved, cherished, encouraged and inspired me with confidence, boldness and fortitude.... Eternally young, bright, kind, forbearing, affectionate and mild, she always was the same angel of consolation.

Finally, Wise concluded:

> Again, in the days of my sorrow, in affliction and distress, I have sought her and found her again. Again she has taken me by the hand and taught me the great principle, a man must be stronger than his grief. This immortal bride, this matchless angel, friends, is—SCIENCE, PHILOSOPHY.... One Eureka! at a discovered truth outweighs years of patience, anxiety and suffering.[36]

32. Isaac Mayer Wise, *The Cosmic God: A Fundamental Philosophy in Popular Lectures* (Cincinnati: Office American Israelite and Deborah, 1876), 55.

33. *Ibid.*, 55–57, 62–63.

34. *Ibid.*, 4.

35. "Theresa," *American Israelite*, December 18, 1874.

36. Wise, *The Cosmic God*, 180–81. Wise's pairing of science and philosophy is telling, especially in a lecture series and book using philosophy to challenge the most celebrated (and controversial) scientific theory of the day. Perhaps the concept Wise was trying to convey was the

Week after week, as his wife lay dying and then afterward, Wise had attacked Darwin for his materialism, a "brutalism" that left life empty of meaning. And still, his final word on the subject was an oddly affecting endorsement of science. Wise's circumstances were extreme, and so was the passion of his response to them. But, like Wise, almost all Jewish leaders who criticized Darwin cushioned their denunciation with admiring approval of science.

The first mention of Darwin that traditionalists found in Isaac Leeser's *Occident* was buried in a reprinted 1863 review by British geologist Samuel Rowles Pattison, in which the "theories of Prof. Huxley and Mr. Darwin [that] regard man as a creature gradually developed out of an ape" are dismissed in passing as "a fancy." The review is apologetic, eager above all to demonstrate that Lyell's geology does not conflict with the Bible and concluding that "in all this, there is nothing absolutely hostile to Scripture."[37] One historian has written that, for Jews in the final decades of the nineteenth century, a "dangerous challenge came from science, Darwinian theories in particular."[38] In fact, even for those most disturbed by the theory of evolution, debating Darwin offered a chance to endorse science, and they unfailingly did.

Moderate reformers like Wise, more radical ones like Einhorn, and traditionalists like Leeser were of one mind: there was no antagonism between their religion and science. What they disagreed about was the sort of Judaism needed in order to prevent such antagonism from taking root. Historian Marc Swetlitz succinctly observed that disagreements about matters of science "among American Jews were often debates about the nature of Judaism." It proved equally true that *agreement* about the easy compatibility of science and Judaism served as a basis for debate about the nature of Judaism.[39]

German notion that has no good analogue in English, *Wissenschaft*, which means something rather like systematic and objective research into any topic, and of which philosophy and empirical sciences are prime examples. Still, the lectures and book leave no room to doubt Wise's affection for natural science and his belief that science, rightly pursued, and philosophy, rightly pursued, will settle into peaceable harmony. This, in fact, was the premise of *The Cosmic God.*

37. Samuel Rowles Pattison, "The Antiquity of Man," *Occident and American Jewish Advocate* 21, no. 5 (August 1863): 216–17.

38. Naomi W. Cohen, *What the Rabbis Said: The Public Discourse of Nineteenth-Century American Rabbis* (New York: New York University Press, 2008), 22.

39. Marc Swetlitz, "American Jewish Responses to Darwin and Evolutionary Theory, 1860–1890," in *Disseminating Darwinism: The Role of Place, Race, Religion, and Gender*, ed. Ronald L. Numbers and John Stenhouse (New York: Cambridge University Press, 1999), 234.

Jews and the Warfare of Science with Theology in Christendom

From the middle of the nineteenth century, rabbis and writers across the wide spectrum of Jewish beliefs put forward technology and science to argue that Judaism was, in ways, superior to Christianity. In part, this effort was a reaction to Christian missionaries, who saw in Jews natural candidates for conversion. It was also an answer of sorts to needling disparagements that issued from pulpit and lectern. Wise wrote in his *Reminiscences* that in the 1850s, "every pastor and every insignificant little preacher, every common jester, and every political rogue raised blows upon the Talmud and the Jews.... [T]hese things disgusted me.... [I] wrote articles filled with fire and brimstone instead of with becoming and polite words."[40] Amid the blows and brimstone, technology and science became part of ongoing Jewish apologetics.

In 1864, the *Jewish Messenger* ran a long review of a lecture on the history of medicine delivered before the New York Academy of Medicine by John Draper, president of New York University Medical School. Ten years later, Draper would publish his most famous book, a jeremiad against Christian (Catholic, most of all) hostility toward science, *History of the Conflict between Religion and Science.* Already in his speech to the academy, Draper attacked what he saw as a brutal superstition that reigned in Christian Europe: "There were fairies in the moonshine, ghosts in the darkness, apparitions in the twilight, goblins in the kitchen, spectres in the garret." Cosmopolitan Jewish physicians with training from the excellent medical colleges of Salerno and Montpellier (institutions that "carried on very much in the manner that medical colleges are now") paid a horrible price for the hateful ignorance of their Christian patients, who saw in their doctor's helpful ministrations a "sinister" magic. The reviewer applauded Draper and approved his estimation giving Jewish physicians of the Middle Ages "the eminence in the profession[,] which might well be expected from an impartial student of history." The report left readers to conclude that in the war waged by the Church against medical science, Jews were on the side of science.[41]

40. Isaac Mayer Wise, *Reminiscences*, trans. and ed. David Philipson (Cincinnati: Leo Wise & Company, 1901), 272.

41. "Literature and Art," *Jewish Messenger*, February 26, 1864. A decade later, the *Jewish Messenger* lavished praise on Draper's *History of the Conflict between Religion and Science*, complimenting its "accurate scholarship," its "patient investigation," its "thorough-going frankness of statement," and its infliction of a "crushing blow at the Papacy." Further: "The history of scientific investigation is presented with clearness and candor, and the errors and the crimes committed by Church and State in the interest of religion are pointed out so forcibly and so impartially, that the reader is irresistibly impelled to admit the full extent of the wrong done to civilization

Emma Lazarus said as much outright in an 1882 essay, "Judaism: The Connecting Link between Science and Religion." Lazarus wrote that "the Christian search" was encumbered by the irrational "doctrines of the Trinity, Resurrection, supernaturalism and asceticism," articles of faith that are "crumbling to ruin" as they are confronted by "all the revolutions of modern science." But Judaism, "capable of infinite expansion and subtilization, may go hand in hand with science, strong and steadfast as herself, to the very brink of the unknowable and unthinkable."[42]

Seeing conflict between religion and science as *Christian* conflict, misappropriated at times by misinformed Jews to tragic effect, was by this time a mainstay of traditionalist Jewish thought. Writing in the *Occident* in 1867, Isaac Leeser argued that reformers who believed that science was at odds with traditional Jewish learning and ritual wrongly assumed that Judaism suffered from a problem that was, in fact, *Christian* in nature:

> The evident errors of Christian dogma, which we have always rejected, these pretenders affected to think were inherent in Judaism also, and they thus made themselves merry over the simplicity of their fathers and less enlightened companions who still adhered to the requirements of Scriptural Judaism.... [T]he upheaving in the Christian world, and the unsettling of dogmas which in themselves cannot be understood or proved, were alone the cause of the rise of new opinions among us.... All moral diseases are contagious equally with physical ones; and so is the mental obliquity which will credit nothing that is incapable of ocular demonstration when it has been taken hold of by a learned class.[43]

Leeser argued that Judaism, thoroughly understood and properly practiced, embraced science. It was only when their faith was tinctured with Christianity that Jews became convinced that hostility governed the relationship between their religion, on the one hand, and their rationality and science, on the other.

Leeser believed that Jews who argued to reform their religious practices and beliefs had grown confused between Judaism and Christianity, a result of their imprudent infatuation with the religion of the Americans among whom they lived. This point had special importance for Leeser because, as he saw it, the whole reform project was based on precisely the sort of error that allowed Jews

---

in impeding the pursuit of knowledge." What's more, Draper sets out "the services rendered to science by the Jews at Alexandria, at Rome, in Spain, and in Arabia," a contrast to Christians who were their contemporaries. "Church and Science," *Jewish Messenger*, December 18, 1874, 4.

42. Emma Lazarus, "Judaism: The Connecting Link Between Science and Religion," *American Hebrew*, September 1, 1882, 28.

43. Isaac Leeser, "Progress," 485–87.

to think that their religion (like Christianity) was at war with science. In refashioning Judaism in the mold of American Protestantism—a process exemplified by forsaking Hebrew prayer for English, entertaining the notion that Sunday ought to be the Jewish Sabbath instead of Saturday, debating whether to introduce the organ into the sanctuary, and more—reformers would achieve the unintended consequence of drawing Jews *away* from rationality and toward dogmatism, *away* from peaceful embrace of science and toward the belligerent obscurantism of dogmatic Christianity. For Leeser and other traditionalists, the lesson to be drawn from the rejection of science by Christians was that Jews must stick steadfast with the Judaism of their fathers and grandfathers, a Judaism at ease with science by its nature. To reform Judaism was to introduce unwittingly the same "moral disease" that spurred Christian hostility toward science.

Not surprisingly, reformers saw matters differently, although important elements of Leeser's recurred in their own views. Wise wrote in his newspaper in 1873 that Christianity, by its nature, is belligerent toward "philosophy, science, and criticism," whereas Judaism, by its nature, is "in profound peace" with them:

> Christianity, in any of its known forms, cannot maintain itself beyond the current phase of civilization.... Therefore, the perpetual warfare of the Church against the onward march of progressive and irresistible liberty in all parts of the civilized world, by the Pope and his prelates on the one hand, by the established churches of England and Prussia on the other, and by the fragments thereof in our own country.... [A]ll dogmatism finds its grave in the spirit of free research and the feeling of personal independence which may be termed the chief characteristics of the nineteenth century. Philosophy, science, and criticism overthrow all dogmas wherever found.... The feeling of personal independence and the pride of philosophy revolt against ... priestly arrogance, which places man's dignity and reason far below a conglomerate of dead-letters. Therefore, the war of the Church against philosophy and science, is as old as the Church herself.[44]

In its doomed war on science and philosophy, Christianity "in any of its known forms" did not represent *religion.* A religion without dogma and without "priestly

44. Isaac Mayer Wise, "The Religion of Future Generations," *Israelite,* November 28, 1873, 4. Twenty years earlier, Wise had poked fun at the irrationality with which Christian Americans approached their religion, "the more absurd, the more revolting against human reason, and the more ridiculous the marvelous mystery is, the better it will succeed in securing the favor and admiration of the thousands.... The great doctrines of the millennium, of Mormonism, of spiritual rapping and knocking, of conversing with the spirits of the departed, and other things of such a sublime nature have filled the lunatic asylums with unhappy inmates." "But," Wise added, "there are no Israelites among them, they cannot be deluded by impostors nor by that which is inexplicable at the first sight." Isaac Mayer Wise, "Religion and Inquiry," *Asmonean,* July 22, 1853, 112.

arrogance," one in which "every man define[s] Deity to himself, as may be in his power to do so," would survive and thrive. Such a religion, Wise continued, "is Judaism."[45]

Like the best battlefield reporters, in his dispatch from "the war of the Church against philosophy and science," Wise found grand themes in the hostilities he described.[46] In repudiating science and philosophy, and the new spirit that animated them, the Church stood opposed to "the progress of justice and equality" and "the self-evident truths [that are] ... deeply rooted in the minds of this country." Wise wrote that the Church's hostility toward science was inseparable from its larger crusade, "the warfare of the church against the onward march of progressive and irresistible liberty in all parts of the civilized world."[47] "Make

45. Wise, "The Religion of Future Generations," 4.

46. The responses to the putative conflict between religion and science that were framed in the second half of the nineteenth century served as enduring patterns for similar responses through the first decades of the twentieth century as well. Pittsburgh's Rabbi Rodolph Coffee wrote in 1900 that during the Middle Ages, "all ideas and thoughts were sifted through the channels of the Established Church before they reached the outside world. Science was utterly crushed, and the man who attempted to prove truths contrary to accepted teaching was either compelled to cease, as Roger Bacon, or put to death, as Bruno." The position of Jews "in this vexing question of religion and science" is clear: "[Religion and science] are not forces in direct antithesis to one another, ... nor is it at all necessary to make a sharp line of demarcation between the two." Rodolph I. Coffee, "The Conflict Between Religion and Science," *American Hebrew*, August 3, 1900, 318. Two years later, Rabbi Barnett Elzas of Charleston wrote that John Draper's *The Conflict between Science and Religion* "discloses no such conflict. It merely describes the conflict between science and the Roman Catholic theologians—which is a very different matter. Religion and science have never been in conflict." Barnett A. Elzas, "The Conflict between Science and Religion," *American Israelite*, January 30, 1902, 4 (emphasis in original). In 1908, the *American Hebrew* could declare flatly that "the 'Conflict between Religion and Science' has no terrors for us." "The Charity Jew," *American Hebrew & Jewish Messenger*, July 3, 1908, 200. The similarity of these statements—and many more nearly identical ones can be found—tends to veil the fact that in these years, attitudes among American Jews toward science were changing in fundamental ways. Like new wine in old vessels, the rejection of the notion of a war between religion and science, though it was often expressed in the same ways, came to take on new meaning and new urgency as the nineteenth century gave way to the twentieth.

47. To his acolytes, Wise became a symbol of these views. Rabbi Henry Berkowitz recalled that as a student he had this encounter with Wise: "One day, in his office, I saw him reach across his desk, setting to one side a great mass of theological and other papers, and selecting for perusal a leading American scientific journal. 'What!' I asked in surprise, 'Do you find time to read a journal of this kind, too?' With his genial smile he replied that he could better afford to neglect all the other periodicals than this which brought to him the real revelations of God's work in the world. This reply was peculiarly significant, for it revealed an attitude of mind towards the new scientific school of thought quite at variance with that which was general." Henry Berkowitz, *Intimate Glimpses of the Rabbi's Career* (Cincinnati: Hebrew Union College Press, 1921), 157–59.

this country Catholic, Episcopalian, Presbyterian or Evangelical in any sense," Wise wrote, "and free government is at an end."[48] In this, Wise and Leeser agreed.[49]

America, a Land of Science

Jews of all sorts in America cared about "the onward march of progressive and irresistible liberty," all the more so in the last decades of the nineteenth century and the first decades of the twentieth. These were years of upheaval for Jews in America. To the fewer than one-quarter million who lived in the United States in 1881, almost two million immigrants were added by 1914, a tenfold increase.[50] In New York City, the population swelled from 80,000 to 1,400,000.

48. Wise, "The Religion of Future Generations." Not long after Wise published these words in Cincinnati, Samuel Myer Isaacs wrote in the same spirit in his New York paper. Isaacs opened with the complaint that, owing to poor Jewish education, "our young ones enter the public life or continue to pursue the study of the sciences" innocent of the "intrinsic value and sublime nature of Judaism." As a result, "many views and principles, taught at the religious schools, appear to be refuted or contradicted by the light of modern science." In fact, Isaacs wrote, the war between religion and science is a Christian war. "Christianity has from its earliest times appeared in antagonism to science, and with unfavorable eyes viewed modern progress." In contrast, "in the Jewish religion, the freest investigation was not only allowed and encouraged, but also exercised most unrestrictedly." By way of illustration, Isaacs continues, "the hypothesis brought forth by Darwin, which engages the attention of the learned world, was asserted by a rabbi and appears in the religious book *Ikkarim* of the orthodox Rabbi Joseph Albo, who lived at the beginning of the fifteenth century." The fact "that Darwin was anticipated by a Jewish scholar, and at the same time, that these theories were by no means considered antagonistic to our creed [demonstrates that] the Jewish religion has not to fear the light of science." Samuel Myer Isaacs, "Judaism and Darwinism," *Jewish Messenger*, March 20, 1874. Only a week before this article appeared, another widely respected Reform rabbi, Solomon Hirsch Sonneschein of St. Louis, published a very similar essay, "The Theory of Evolution Manifested 450 Years Before Darwin by a Jewish Philosopher," *Israelite*, March 13, 1874, 4.

49. The two men had found common language and common cause in 1847, when Leeser published two of Wise's lectures in the *Occident*, and soon thereafter they worked together to convene representatives of the country's main congregations and organize them into a union. The initiative failed, as the gap between traditionalists and reformers had grown too large to bridge. Bruce L. Ruben, *Max Lilienthal: The Making of the American Rabbinate* (Detroit: Wayne State University Press, 2011), 108–11. In 1855, the two men did convene a general synod of American Jewish rabbis and lay leaders under the slogan "Shalom 'al Yisrael" (Peace be upon Israel). The event was effectively boycotted by both radical reformers and conservative traditionalists. "Cleveland Assembly of 1855," *Encyclopedia of Cleveland History*, https://case.edu/ech/articles/c/cleveland-assembly-1855.

50. Simon Kuznets, "Immigration of Russian Jews to the United States: Background and Structure," *Perspectives in American History* 9 (1975): 35–124; Andrew Godley, *Jewish Immigrant Entrepreneurship in New York and London, 1880–1914: Enterprise and Culture* (New York: Palgrave

So vast an increase posed challenges both for the immigrants and for the communities that absorbed them.

These same years were a time of extravagant expansion and change in American science. America's first research university, Johns Hopkins, opened its doors in 1876. In 1905, the steel magnate Andrew Carnegie set up the foundation bearing his name, with the intention of advancing higher learning, especially in the sciences.[51] John D. Rockefeller incorporated his foundation in 1910, aiming to "advance the civilization of the peoples of the United States ... and of foreign lands in the acquisition and dissemination of knowledge, and in the promotion of any and all the elements of human progress."[52] Around this time, *Science* reprinted a long speech given by Yale physicist Henry A. Bumstead at the opening of the Carnegie Science Building at Arcadia University in Pennsylvania. Elaborating on "the place of scientific studies in the education of the individual," Bumstead said that the sciences were creating a new American type: "they think more of facts and less of words; they are more cautious in reaching conclusions and in defining the probability of the correctness of their results; they are more careful to guard against being prejudiced by external circumstances and implications; they get as near to first hand evidence as they can."[53] Science in America at the turn of the century was producing new institutions and new researchers, embracing new values to generate advanced knowledge and technologies, and doing it all in abundance and without precedent.

American Jews and American science, each growing and changing in character, became linked in the first decades of the twentieth century in ways that continue to exert an impact on both up to this day. Science had long been *associated* with progress; now it was seen as the main motor of progress, not just in the laboratory and on the factory floor, but also in schools, courtrooms, statehouses, churches, prisons, stock exchanges, and every other institution

---

Macmillan, 2001), 78; "Jewish Statistics," *American Jewish Year Book* 1 (1899–1900): 283; H. S. Linfield, "Statistics of Jews," *American Jewish Yearbook* 28 (1926–1927): 379–428.

51. "The Carnegie Foundation," *Science*, n.s., 21, no. 540 (May 5, 1905): 716. In his founding letter to his trustees, Carnegie directed that universities, colleges, and technical schools that are "under control of a sect" or that require their officers, faculty, or students "to belong to any specified sect, or which impose any theological test, are to be excluded" from his largesse.

52. "The Rockefeller Foundation," *Science*, n.s., 31, no. 793 (March 11, 1910): 379. The foundation was not successfully incorporated until 1913.

53. H. A. Bumstead, "The Functions of a University Laboratory," *Science*, n.s., 31, no. 793 (March 11, 1910): 365.

that mattered. The *ethos* of science, which the pioneering Jewish sociologist of science Robert Merton (whose given name was Meyer Robert Schkolnick) would decades later say is characterized by "intellectual honesty, integrity, organized skepticism, disinterestedness, [and] impersonality," demanded that researchers be judged not by where they came from, to what God they prayed, or by what accent tinged their prayers, but instead solely by the quality of their contributions.[54] This ethos fit with a certain view of an America in which all were welcome and success or failure was not predetermined by background or creed.[55] Science appeared to be hostile to old elites for two reasons. Its ideals were meritocratic, looking beyond, at least in principle, social-club status and power passed down from parent to child. Also, as new research centers opened, as universities formed new science departments (or expanded old ones beyond recognition), and as hospitals established modern research labs of their own, these new institutions were not encrusted with traditions and norms about the sort of workers they ought and ought not to employ.[56]

For all these reasons, enthusiasm for science among American Jews swelled at the start of the twentieth century, figuring in the sermons of rabbis, the editorial choices of Jewish journalists, the curricula of night classes for immigrants and of schools for their children, the calculations of philanthropists, and the deliberations of the leaders of Jewish organizations. Science also intruded into efforts toward the "Americanization" of immigrants. As some Jew achieved renown in science, their successes were enlisted as prime demonstrations of the contributions Jews had and would make to America. Science was enlisted as a tool to parry the claims of antisemites and to demonstrate the superior enlightenment of Jews and Judaism. In all these ways, science came to be at the heart

54. Robert K. Merton, "Science and the Social Order," *Philosophy of Science* 5, no. 3 (1938): 321–37.

55. Of course, matters were not that simple. By World War I, roughly half of New York University students were Jews, a quarter of Columbia students, one in five Harvard students, and one in eight Yalies. But a backlash would come. In 1914, Frederick Keppel, dean of Columbia College, asked, "Isn't Columbia overrun with European Jews, who are most unpleasant persons socially?" Harvard bacteriologist Richard Clark Cabot polled his students in 1922 about whether the university ought to limit attendance by certain races. See, for instance, William T. Ham, "Harvard Student Opinion on the Jewish Question," *Journal of Education* 96, no. 11 (September 28, 1922): 293; "Exclusion from College," *Outlook*, July 5, 1922, 406. For an overview, see Stephen Steinberg, *The Academic Melting Pot: Catholics and Jews in American Higher Education, report prepared for the Carnegie Commission on Higher Education* (New York: McGraw-Hill, 1974).

56. A similar explanation has been offered for the surprising prevalence of Jews (in the same years, more or less) in Hollywood. Neal Gabler, *An Empire of Their Own: How the Jews Invented Hollywood* (New York: Crown, 1988).

of an American Jewish *imaginary*—a picture of what Jewish life in the country could and should be like.[57]

Immigrants as a Problem to Be Solved

The great swell of immigrants came for the reasons immigrants always come: they were fleeing danger and persecution, seeking to improve their circumstances, or, usually, both at once. Their first challenge was to make a living, keep a roof over their heads, and maintain their health in neighborhoods that were, as William Dean Howells wrote in 1896, "more densely populated than any other area in the world." Their "fate is hard," he continued, their houses are "horrible," and they themselves are "desperately poor" and live in "filth" and "stench," less like humans than "wild beasts."[58]

Among the immigrants were Jews of every description. Most fit one or more of the three types historian Jonathan Sarna has identified. There were "pious Jews" eager "to transplant their East European practices and institutions to the new world." Others were "hustler[s]" who came to America "to make a fortune." And some were "freethinking radical[s]." Many immigrants were some mix of these types, observing what rituals they could, trying to make it in America, and showing sympathy for progressive politics. "They struggled," Sarna writes, to balance "their ancient faith, their economic aspirations, and their utopian ideologies."[59]

These Jewish immigrants were a problem to be solved.[60] They were a problem for sympathetic Americans, like Howells, who fretted about their impoverished

57. The crucial notion that certain "imagined forms of social life and social order" center on a particular vision of science and technology was first proposed by Sheila Jasanoff in "Future Imperfect: Science, Technology, and Imaginations of Modernity," in *Dreamscapes of Modernity: Sociotechnical Imaginaries and the Fabrication of Power*, ed. Sheila Jasanoff and Sang-Hyun Kim (Chicago: University of Chicago Press, 2015).

58. William Dean Howells, "An East-Side Ramble," in *Impressions and Experiences* (New York: Harper, 1896), 127–49. The Jewish immigrants Howells describes are law-abiding, generally of good cheer, and possessed of remarkable energy and drive. His description of their circumstances is dire, but his portrayal of their character is appreciative.

59. Jonathan D. Sarna, *American Judaism: A History* (New Haven: Yale University Press, 2004), 158–59.

60. And they were widely discussed as such. Journalist Burton Hendrick, who wrote extensively and with florid ambivalence about "the Jews in America," declared flatly that the year 1881 "marks the beginning of the American Jewish 'problem,' as that word is commonly understood.... The transplantation of millions of Jews from their mediaeval home in Central Europe—a transplantation which was perhaps not at first deliberate and conscious, but which is becoming increasingly so—forms not only the most startling migration in the history of Israel,

state, the suffering it caused, the disease it spread, and the social disorder it created. Immigrant Jews were a problem, too, for less sympathetic Christian Americans, who worried they might permanently injure the character of the country. At this time that, as historian Hasia Diner notes, "the American popular press ... was taking a decidedly racist turn," publishing lurid exposés claiming that Jews were behind prostitution, theft, graft, disease, and many other ills.[61] Such reports had an impact: by the end of the nineteenth century "Immigration Restriction Leagues" were operating coast-to-coast.[62]

The waves of new Jewish immigrants were not just a problem for Christian Americans who worried about the Christian character of country. The rise in

---

but gives the United States its great 'Jewish problem.'" Burton J. Hendrick, *The Jews in America* (Garden City, NY: Doubleday, Page & Company, 1923), 27–30.

61. Hasia R. Diner, *The Jews of the United States, 1654 to 2000* (Berkeley: University of California Press, 2006), 169. A renowned example of this yellowjournalism is George Kibbe Turner, "The Daughters of the Poor: A Plain Story of the Development of New York City as a Leading Center of the White Slave Trade of the World, Under Tammany Hall," *McClure's Magazine* 34 (November 1909): 45–61. Turner describes a massive Jewish "machine" that ensnares young girls, transforming some into prostitutes for the local market and sending most, as "white slaves," to destinations across the country and around the world. The essay is credited with having spurred Congress to pass the 1910 Mann Act outlawing the transport of women across state lines "for immoral purposes."

62. In 1894, a group of young, patrician Harvard graduates—among them a future Harvard president, a future Massachusetts governor, and a future U.S. senator—set up the Immigration Restriction League (IRL) in Boston, an organization that soon had branches across the country, from New York to San Francisco. By 1896, there was a National Association of Immigration Restriction Leagues. The groups' concern was that waves of immigration from eastern and southern Europe—Jews and Catholics—were causing an "alien degradation of American character." Immigration Restriction League, "Various Facts and Opinion Concerning the Necessity of Restricting Immigration" (Boston, 1894), quoted in Erika Lee, *America for Americans: A History of Xenophobia in the United States* (New York: Basic Books, 2019), 135. Some critics saw the threat posed by Jews in racial terms. Madison Grant, an IRL leader, progressivist lawyer, and zoologist, declared that "the cross between any of the three European races and a Jew is a Jew." Madison Grant, *The Passing of the Great Race: Or, The Racial Basis of European History* (New York: Charles Scribner's Sons, 1918), 15–17. Others saw the threat as cultural. Sometimes the two analyses met, as when sociologist E. A. Ross argued in *The Old World in the New* that the "pioneer breed" of Anglo-Saxon Americans was being "swamped and submerged by an overwhelming tide of latecomers from the old-world hive"; quoted in Lori Jirousek, "Mary Antin's Progressive Science: Eugenics, Evolution, and the Environment," *Shofar* 27, no. 1 (2008): 61. The matter was debated not just on the pages of magazines and in social clubs, but also in the halls of Congress. In 1896, Henry Cabot Lodge, a Boston Brahmin then newly elected to the U.S. Senate, introduced legislation requiring prospective immigrants to pass an English literacy exam. When it failed, similar bills were proposed in 1898, 1902, 1906, 1913, and 1915. Diner, *Jews of the United States*, 183.

anti-Jewish sentiment and legislation also troubled Jews who had come long before these immigrants or had been born in America and had established themselves. Behind this worry was complicated ambivalence. On the one hand, the antisemitism aroused by the masses of immigrants was a threat to all Jews in America. On the other, as American Jews saw it, criticisms of the immigrants were not entirely baseless. As one contemporary wrote of Jews long established in the United States: "No descendant of the Mayflower is prouder of his American origin than the Jew whose ancestors have lived in this country for two or three generations. It is impossible to say an unkinder thing to such an American aristocrat than to confuse him indiscriminately with the recent arrivals from Poland and Russia."[63] For established Jews, the old-country religious orthodoxy of many of the new immigrants, the political extremism of a small but loud group of them, their refusal to leave behind Yiddish and the accents that made their English laughable, their dingy clothes, and the crassness of their peddling—all these things made the "greenhorns" (as the new immigrants were disparagingly known) uncomfortably *un-American*.[64]

The challenges created by the immigrants, and the wish to show that Jews not long off the boat would not forever remain alien in American life, gave shape and energy to what one historian has called "the political project of American Jews" in the last decades of the nineteenth century and the first decades of the twentieth.[65] The project had two aspects, both reformist in nature. One was to "Americanize" the new immigrants, reforming them to fit their new circumstances. The other was to ensure that Jews could operate freely in the public square by reforming exclusionary aspects of America's society and economy.[66] Science had a role to play in both sorts of reform.

Reforming Jews

For some Jewish leaders and philanthropists, "Americanizing" (sometimes they called it "civilizing") Jewish immigrants was an urgent task. Arrangements

63. Hendrick, *Jews in America*, 5–6.

64. Gerald Sorin, "Mutual Contempt, Mutual Benefit: The Strained Encounter Between German and Eastern European Jews in America, 1880–1920," *American Jewish History* 81, no. 1 (1993): 34–59.

65. Diner, *Jews of the United States*, 172.

66. In this respect, as David A. Hollinger rightly points out, Jews were hardly alone, finding common cause with Catholics ("de-Christianization," in early twentieth-century America, amounted principally to "de-Protestantization"), secular Protestants, many mainline Protestants, and "freethinkers" of a great variety of backgrounds. David A. Hollinger, "Jewish Intellectuals and the De-Christianization of American Public Culture in the Twentieth Century," in *Science,*

were made to spread Jews in small numbers to more authentically American locales, like farms from New Jersey to Oregon.[67] Charitable organizations devised programs operating within Jewish neighborhoods to speed the assimilation of immigrants. The National Council of Jewish Women sponsored Jewish settlement houses around the country, where immigrant children might be introduced to the Boy Scouts, learn American folk songs, receive instruction in nutrition, or otherwise acquire the basic skills and concepts of American life. These programs show concern for the welfare of newly arrived Jews facing a harsh reality, but they also reveal anxiety on the part of "uptown Jews" that the masses of "downtown Jews" might diminish their own hard-won status as Americans.[68] The Jewish press printed disparagements of the immigrants—of their "wretched abodes," "festering filth," "filthy little butcher shops," "dissipated men," "cursed child wives," "vile diseases," "dense ignorance," "abject misery," and "strident, piercing voices that strike the ear most unpleasantly"—concluding that "they must be Americanized, in spite of themselves."[69] Here, science could help. Joseph Jacobs, the polymath folklorist, told the gathered members of the Harvard Menorah Society that college-educated Jews, trained in such "abstract study" as mathematics or physics, would "raise the tone" of American Jewry. Jews schooled in rational pursuits could "represent in the Jewish

---

Jews, and Secular Culture: Studies in Mid-Twentieth-Century American Intellectual History (Princeton: Princeton University Press, 1996), 17–41.

67. Leonard G. Robinson, "Agricultural Activities of the Jews in America," *American Jewish Year Book* 14 (1912–1913): 57–108.

68. The difference in the polish of the cultural patina of well-established Jews of German origin and greenhorn eastern Europeans was pondered with concern not only by Jews. In *Jews in America,* journalist Burton Hendrick warned about the hordes of "Polish" Jews (by which he meant Ostjuden) who had darkened the docks, streets, and slums of New York: "The process of 'Americanization' is going to be slow and more difficult with this class of immigrants than with any other, except perhaps the Southern Italians. The million and a half Jews—probably more—that crowded into the New York tenements are by no means digested. This does not mean they never will be. The completeness with which the Sephardic and German Jews have been absorbed into the national life, the high standard of patriotic citizenship they have evinced, and the services they have rendered in education, science, letters and other activities, show that there is nothing in the Jewish nature that necessarily dooms him to forever be alien. But the task with the Polish Jew is going to be a longer and more difficult one. That there are hundreds of thousands in New York's Polish Jew population who do not align themselves with these radical movements, and to whom American history and American institutions mean much, is clear. The unpleasant fact, however, is that there is an uncomfortable remainder who do" (170–71).

69. "The New York Ghetto: A Reform Needed," *Jewish Messenger,* August 28, 1891, sec. Little Folks Page, 5; "Our Ghetto: A Remedy Required," *Jewish Messenger,* September 4, 1891, 4; "The New York Ghetto: Views of the Board of Health," *Jewish Messenger,* September 11, 1891, 4.

community the highest ideal."[70] Pursuit of science would *refine* immigrant Jews who, Jacobs recognized, might display a "greed for power" and a regrettable tendency to "force their way to the front."[71]

Americanizing was not just something that established Jews hoped to do to immigrants; the word is also *reflexive*, something immigrants hoped to do to themselves and, especially, their children. It is a complicated thing to remake yourself in a new image, and it is a complicated thing to raise children who see their parents as greenhorns. Here, too, science could help. In an effort to narrow the gap between the cultures they came from and the culture they came to, Jewish immigrants not only flooded night school English classes; they also attended all sorts of learned lectures, haunted library reading rooms, and eagerly sent their girls and boys to public schools and universities, as well as to Jewish schools where science and technology were at the heart of the curriculum.[72]

The Hebrew Technical Institute was established in New York in 1884 with the aim of teaching sciences to "the poorer Jewish children of the metropolis" in order "to make them good, practical mechanics," as *Scientific American* reported. The school gave students training that would lead to a job, but its emphasis was on instilling the "underlying principles" of science, for which it was fitted out with laboratories for chemistry, physics, and biology.[73] Sixteen years later, in an article about technical education, a writer for the *Jewish Messenger* assured readers that "he who perfects machines to lessen human toil and increase useful production is truly serving civilization, and the educated mechanic does more to hasten the world's progress than the combined wisdom of all its statesmen."

70. Joseph Jacobs, "The Academic Jew," *American Hebrew & Jewish Messenger*, April 30, 1909, 668–69. Jacobs was once called "one of the most learned and brilliant of the Jews who migrated to the United States from Europe in the last years of the last century"; "Review: Jewish Contributions to Civilization, An Estimate," *Advocate of Peace* 81, no. 9/10 (September 1, 1919): 300. He was an editor of the monumental *Jewish Encyclopedia*, the *American Jewish Year Book*, and the *American Hebrew*, while at the same time directing the Bureau of Jewish Statistics of the American Jewish Committee and serving as a professor at the Jewish Theological Seminary.

71. Jacobs, "The Academic Jew."

72. It was hoped that these schools, as the great early twentieth-century Jewish educator Alexander Mordecai Dushkin later remembered, would reflect "the two universal ideas which have profoundly affected all of our modern life, namely, Science as a Method and Democracy as an Aim." Dushkin, *Living Bridges: Memoirs of an Educator* (Jerusalem: Keter Publishing House, 1975), 15.

73. "The Hebrew Technical Institute," *Scientific American* 52, no. 26 (June 27, 1885): 405. See, too, "Hebrew Technical Institute," *New York Times*, January 14, 1889, 8. Most of the money to build the institute came from the Baron de Hirsch Fund, whose president at the time was Myer Isaacs, the eldest son of Rabbi Samuel Myer Isaacs. Myer Isaacs was a judge, publisher of the *Jewish Messenger*, a philanthropist, and an exemplar of an established Jew eager to help immigrants settle and acculturate in America.

The great achievement of the Hebrew Technical Institute was that it promoted such progress by training "our unfortunate persecuted brethren," making them fit citizens, able to contribute "[w]here lands are to be surveyed, roads to be constructed, ships to be built and navigated, soils of every kind and under every variety of climate to be cultivated, and manufactures with their labor-saving machinery to be established."[74] Jacob Riis wrote that "the great Hebrew Institute, with its scope 'Americanizing, educational, social and humanizing,' is a vast net in which the youth of the dark East Side tenements are caught and made into patriots and useful citizens."[75] Mastering science, and the machines it made, could transform immigrants into American patriots pushing America forward.

Most American Jews looked to the laboratories then being installed in public schools to make this transformation. Benjamin Gruenberg was nine in 1883 when he moved with his parents to New York City from Russia, and after studying biology in city schools, he returned to teach biology, rising to head the biology and science departments of the New York City school system from 1902 to 1920 (and completing his Columbia University doctorate in genetics in 1911). Such education, Gruenberg later reflected, serves "to free the people from various provincialisms and superstitions and fears which they had accumulated through centuries."[76] With the same aim, Jewish libraries stocked science books in great numbers. A 1900 census of Philadelphia's Knesset Yisrael circulating library listed almost two science books for every three books of Judaica.[77] A public librarian said that while most borrowers gravitate to novels and travel books, "It is different with the Jews; they always want books that contribute to their intellectual development: often a little fellow of fifteen or sixteen is offended if you offer him tales of adventures. He prefers a work on science or political economy."[78] Among new Russian immigrants, a Cincinnati rabbi reported, "the great men whose birthdays are to be celebrated" included Aristotle, Archimedes, Copernicus, and Darwin, while it was "quite impossible to find a Jewish name deserving of a place in this galaxy."[79]

74. Peter Friedman, "Technical Education," *Jewish Messenger*, June 19, 1900, 5.

75. Jacob Riis, "The Jews of New York," *Review of Reviews* 13 (1896): 58–62.

76. Gruenberg's remembrances appear in an essay he wrote with his wife, Sidonie Gruenberg, "Crosscurrents in the Rearing of Youth," *Annals of the American Academy of Political and Social Science* 236 (November 1944): 67–73.

77. Robert Singerman, "Books Weeping for Someone to Visit and Admire Them: Jewish Library Culture in the United States, 1850–1910," *Studies in Bibliography and Booklore* 20 (1998): 106.

78. Anatole Leroy Beaulieu, "Jewish Immigrants and Judaism in the United States," *American Hebrew & Jewish Messenger*, June 9, 1905, 39.

79. E. Schreiber, "Random Thoughts," *Jewish Review*, December 24, 1897, 7.

Not just children were Americanized through science; their parents were, too. The first director of the Hebrew Technical Institute, Henry M. Leipziger, an immigrant himself, left to start a public lecture series for adults—what he called a "university for all the people"—under the banner of the New York Public Library and the New York Board of Education.[80] The *American Hebrew* reported in 1900 that immigrants came in droves to learn what they needed to "achieve fruitful results for civilization and mankind." They heard lectures on "physiology and hygiene, ... electricity, heat, sound, light and color, photography, microscopy, technology, astronomy, navigation, the science of weather and the wonders of modern science."[81] There were also lecture courses on history, art, and literature, but science was at the heart of the project. In 1900, half a million immigrants came to the free lectures, and in 1915, more than one and a quarter million attended.[82] Whatever else appeared on the syllabus, the lectures offered what Leipziger called "democratic culture" and "the development of citizenship."[83]

The notion that science holds a key to citizenship was by then commonplace among American Jewish leaders. Describing the patriotism of Jews in the *North American Review* in 1905, Abram Isaacs, a rabbi in Patterson, New Jersey, and professor at New York University, found Jewish fitness for America in the "spirit that moves a poor peddler in a New York Jewish quarter to study Kant's philosophy while on his rounds, or to read in faithful translations Herbert Spencer on Darwin."[84] Already in 1893, the rabbi of New York's Temple Emanu-El, Joseph Silverman, wrote in the *American Hebrew* that "industrial and moral progress" are fundamentally linked, in a way that made science a valuable tool in absorbing immigrants:

> The industrial spirit has broadened men's views.... They begin to see how little theological opinions has [*sic*] to do with mechanical laws, with the results of arithmetical calculations and are led to realize the necessity of liberality in theological discussions and philosophical debates.... The application of exact sciences to all such practical purposes as bring to us the comforts and delights of

80. "Dr. H. M. Leipziger, Educator, Is Dead," *New York Times*, December 2, 1917, 44.

81. S. D. McCormick, "The Free Lecture Course," *American Hebrew*, February 16, 1900, 466.

82. S. T. Willis, "Free Lectures in New York Schools," *Forum*, May 1900, 332–34. Also see Nelson R. Beck, "The Use of Library and Educational Facilities by Russian-Jewish Immigrants in New York City, 1880–1914: The Impact of Culture," *Journal of Library History* 12, no. 2 (1977): 133; Henry M. Leipziger, "Education for Adults Through Public Lectures in New York City," *Annals of the American Academy of Political and Social Science* 67 (September 1916): 212.

83. Leipziger, "Education for Adults Through Public Lectures," 213.

84. Abram S. Isaacs, "The Jew in America," *North American Review* 181 (November 1905): 682.

> modern civilization has taught us a higher philosophy and almost revolutionized our religion and morals.... There are two types of immigrants. The one comes to this country and contents himself with making cheap music in the streets for the amusement of little children, and to catch a few stray pennies. The other comes here and at once seizes every opportunity to develop his physical powers and industrial instincts.... The practical trades, arts and sciences tend to build up strong character and noble citizenship. The Jew has always been a prominent factor of civilization, because he was an agriculturist, a mechanic, a tradesman, merchant and scientist.[85]

Science in the first years of the twentieth century also offered evidence that Jews were fit to be Americanized. Starting in 1908, the Jewish chair of anthropology at Columbia, Franz Boas, sent "a small army of serious, scholarly looking young men [into] the homes of tenement dwellers," equipped with measuring tape and craniometers, with the aim of recording the shapes of their skulls. He hoped to answer the question of whether immigrants "retain tenaciously their physical and mental characteristics, and therefore [are] unfitted for ultimate absorption in the coming American race. 'You may educate them,' we have been told; 'you may teach them English, send them to the public schools, even give them the ballot. But can you undermine the inheritance of centuries? Can you change the shape of a man's skull?'" Boas's crew measured 30,000 heads and found that the answer is yes, the "American environment [spurs] an improvement for the Jew," whose head grows "longer" in the New World, his body taller, his chest fuller, and his mind more supple. "If ... it is possible, in a single generation, to give the child a different shaped skull from his parent, it is likewise possible to fill it with high ideals—to make him, which his father was not and probably never can become, an intelligent, self-respecting, industrious American."[86]

Reforming America

For some immigrants, the harsher aspects of life in America—discrimination, depredation, disparagement, shunning—meant that America failed to live up to its own high-minded ideals. Some were drawn to progressivism, criticizing the rigidity of the divide between rich and poor in the United States, and between Blacks and whites. Of the white people who took part in the 1909

85. Rev. Dr. Joseph Silverman, "Industrial and Moral Progress," *American Hebrew*, May 19, 1893, 84.

86. Burton J. Hendrick, "The Skulls of Our Immigrants," *McClure's Magazine* 35 (May 1910): 36–50.

founding the National Association for the Advancement of Colored People, half were Jews, and Jews were prominent supporters of the establishment of the National Urban League in 1911. Immigrant Jews took leading roles in labor unions, which swelled in the first decades of the century. Jews were also leading lights in the American socialist movement, which grew more or less in lockstep with the increasing population of Jewish immigrants.[87] When the National Progressive Women's Suffrage Union was formed in New York City in 1907, "its main bases of support were Jewish garment workers on the Lower East Side and in Harlem."[88]

The attempt to reform America by fighting for civil rights, a better deal for workers, votes for women, medical care for everyone, and more became entangled with an effort to "de-Christianize American public culture," as historian David A. Hollinger memorably put it.[89] The 1913 charter of the Anti-Defamation League (ADL) defined the organization's goals: to "secure justice and fair treatment to all citizens alike and to put an end forever to unjust and unfair discrimination against and ridicule of any sect or body of citizens."[90] Jews in these years faced discrimination in many realms. There were homes they could not rent, neighborhoods that did not welcome them, firms that would not hire them, clubs that would not have them. In a cause célèbre, Jacques Loeb, a French-born New York Jewish biologist who stunned the world when he induced parthenogenesis by chemical stimulus, was in 1913 kept out of New York's exclusive Century Club because he was a Jew. J. McKeen Cattell, the Columbia psychology professor who proposed Loeb's membership, was outraged: "There are not in the United States twenty scientific men more eminent; there are not among the members of the Century Club twenty men more distinguished.... You have rejected Dr. Loeb, even though you would not dare admit it, because he descends from and has the traits of that race which before and since the birth of Christ has supplied in proportion to its numbers more men of genius, the Greeks only excepted, than any other."[91] Loeb poked fun at the "snobocracy" that kept him out of the

87. Will Herberg, "The Jewish Labor Movement in the United States," *American Jewish Year Book* 53 (1952): 10–15, 25.

88. Elinor Lerner, "Jewish Involvement in the New York City Woman Suffrage Movement," *American Jewish History* 70, no. 4 (1981): 444.

89. Hollinger, "Jewish Intellectuals and the De-Christianization of American Public Culture," 17–41.

90. Leon L. Lewis and Sigmund Livingston, "Anti-Defamation League," *American Israelite*, November 20, 1913, 4.

91. "Resents Rejection of Loeb," *Boston Evening Transcript*, May 14, 1913, 7. See, too, "Rejection of Loeb Stirs Century Club," *Fulton Sun* (Missouri), May 14, 1913, 6. The issue occupied

club, predicted that old elites would soon "degenerate," and anticipated that science would win the day.[92]

Loeb's vision for science was one he had long held. In 1909, he advised President Theodore Roosevelt that "the transition of the past to modern statesmanship is marked by the substitution of fertile science for sterile bureaucracy."[93] Later, Loeb wrote that, in the modern world, good government "consists in the application of the results of the exact sciences to the improvement of the lot of humanity." Science "will free the minds from all those forms of ignorance, superstition and fanaticism which are the culture medium of mob emotionalism." What is needed, Loeb declared, is "a new type of statesmen, who are familiar with and follow the development of the *exact*—i.e., the experimental and quantitative—sciences, and who are willing and capable of applying the results of exact science to the intellectual, moral, physical and economical uplift of the masses."[94] Not only is the "conception of life" provided by scientists "compatible with ethics: it seems the only conception of life which can lead to an understanding of the source of ethics."[95]

Among the many American Jews (and, of course, non-Jews) who believed, like Loeb, that science could prod their country to adhere more fully to the ideals that they took to be the *American* values of equality of opportunity and nondiscrimination was immigrant rights activist Mary Antin. In her 1912 autobiography, *The Promised Land*, she wrote that since America was established,

---

Cattell for a long time; as late as 1927, he wrote: "it is science that has led the way to true freedom of thought.... Those with the power, whether in state or church, have ever been ready to impose their creeds and their control upon others.... The methods of science, slowly gaining in force and volume through the centuries, will in the end bring truth and reason into all our beliefs and actions." J. McKeen Cattell, "Science, the Declaration, Democracy," *Scientific Monthly* 24, no. 3 (1927): 201.

92. Charles Rasmussen and Rick Tilman, "Loeb on Racism, Zionism and Ethnocentrism," in Rasmussen and Tilman, *Jacques Loeb: His Science and Social Activism and Their Philosophical Foundations* (Philadelphia: American Philosophical Society, 1998), 137. The *American Israelite*, reporting on the scandal, wrote: "The Hebrews can get along without the Century Club. The Century Club, if it is to live up to its pretense of being an association of men of achievement, cannot get along without the Hebrews." "Honor and Insult: Rhode Island Honors a Jew While New York Insults One," *American Israelite*, May 22, 1913, 4.

93. Rasmussen and Tilman, *Jacques Loeb*, 86. Five days later, Roosevelt sent an appreciative reply. The president was "particularly pleased by your scientific basis for the belief that we are justified in our optimism" that society is improving. *Ibid.*, 87.

94. Jacques Loeb, "Biology and War," *Science* 45, no. 1152 (January 26, 1917): 76.

95. Jacques Loeb, *The Mechanistic Conception of Life: Biological Essays* (Chicago: University of Chicago Press, 1912), 31.

> the greatest achievements ... have been in the accumulation of scientific knowledge. But all this knowledge is useless until it is applied to daily life, both public and private.... If scientists find that heredity and environment are equal factors in shaping a man, then the legislatures shall pass such laws as will insure to every future American the best possible birth and the finest possible nurture.... The inspiration of the legislatures shall be the laboratory, not the counting-room. The man of wisdom shall not be elbowed out of the law courts by the man of means. The law of the land, in every instance, shall be the law of nature.[96]

This notion that the "law of nature" can create a society more fair and more decent than the tradition-bound and discriminatory laws of man was pervasive among Jews in the first decades of the twentieth century (and remained pervasive past mid-century). It suffused sermons on Friday evenings and Saturday mornings, as when Rabbi Montague N. A. Cohen preached to Temple Beth Israel in San Diego that "scientific enlightenment ... is a philosophy and a scientifically proved fact, as well as a true theory, justified by natural science.... Its ethical force will gently guide us."[97] It was there when Rabbi Henry Berkowitz set the curriculum of the Jewish Chautauqua Society, an organization sprung from the Chautauqua Literary and Scientific Circle, offering courses, lectures, reading circles, and pamphlets to bolster the educations of Jewish youth and adults, with the aim of "character building." For this purpose, "arithmetic and algebra, geography and the sciences, art and aesthetics, history and literature are all alike to be made effective in strengthening the moral fiber of the growing generation." What is needed is a "spiritualizing of knowledge" to "illuminate the pathways of progress."[98]

The idea that science led to social progress and increased democracy was shared, too, by philanthropists seeking to improve the lot of Jews in America. Jacob Schiff, a financier and philanthropist who made a good deal of his fortune by backing railway expansion, funded departments at Harvard, bankrolled scientific expeditions, gave extravagantly to New York's Museum of Natural History, served on the board of the Bronx Zoo, built hospital wings and laboratories, and funded medical research. When Schiff died in 1920, the *New York Times* reprinted his will in full. Large legacies went to the New York Public Library; to the research budgets of Montefiore Hospital, the "Baby's Hospital"

96. Mary Antin, "A Woman to Her Fellow-Citizens," *Outlook*, November 2, 1912, 485. About Antin, see Lori Jirousek's fascinating "Mary Antin's Progressive Science," 58–79.

97. Montague N. A. Cohn, "Ethical Materialism," *B'nai B'rith Messenger*, August 1, 1913, 9.

98. Henry Berkowitz, "Some Tendencies of Modern Education," *American Israelite*, July 30, 1908.

of the City of New York, and the Tuberculosis Preventorium for Children; to New York University, Harvard, and the Tuskegee Institute; and to a Jubilee Fund to research deafness.[99] Schiff's pattern of giving was repeated by dozens and dozens of Jewish philanthropists in the first decades of the twentieth century.[100] When a Philadelphia bacteriologist, Louis Gershenfeld, catalogued the leading lights of "Jewish Philanthropy in Science," he took note of sixty-four families that had "made large contributions for scientific endeavor" throughout the country, building laboratories, endowing university departments, starting science museums, planetariums, and zoos, sponsoring scientific conferences, and supporting hospital research in New York, Newark, Pittsburgh, Los Angeles, San Francisco, Chicago, Boston, Olympia, New Orleans, Cincinnati, St. Louis, Milwaukee, Philadelphia, Atlantic City, Baltimore, Detroit, and Houston.[101]

The Jewish Scientist as Role Model

By the first years of the twentieth century, Jewish scientists had become role models and were regarded, often, as heroes. They were in demand at high-society evenings like one staged in November 1908 by an organization called "The Judaeans." Top Jewish doctors, biologists, and historians discussed "The Jew and the Prevention and Relief of Disease" before Jewish worthies at the posh Hotel Astor, in a banquet hall decorated with artifacts chosen by the Museum of Natural History in consultation with the Ethnological Bureau in Washington, D.C.[102] What scientists did in and outside their laboratories was eagerly

99. "J. H. Schiff's Will," *New York Times*, October 6, 1920, 15. Schiff also gave to Hebrew Union College, the Jewish Theological Seminary, the Jewish Philanthropic Societies in the City of New York, the Federation for the Support of Jewish Philanthropic Societies, the Israelitische Waisenanstaldt of Frankfurt, Germany, and other Jewish causes, as well as to the Metropolitan Museum of Art. Most of the causes Schiff supported were in science and medicine.

100. As the years passed, greater emphasis was put on modern scientific research. "Older forms of gifts," noted one report on a new Jewish foundation, "almost invariably took the shape of buildings or beds, [which] effected little towards the improvement of preventive medicine." True "medical progress ... is only possible by the improvement of medical knowledge and methods by such foundations as that of Mr. Adolph Lewisohn." "The Adolph Lewisohn Foundation," *American Hebrew & Jewish Messenger*, January 27, 1911, 385.

101. Louis Gershenfeld, *The Jew in Science* (Philadelphia: Jewish Publication Society, 1934), 217–19.

102. "The Jew and the Prevention and Relief of Disease," *American Hebrew & Jewish Messenger*, November 27, 1908, 105; "The Jews and the Prevention of Disease," *American Hebrew & Jewish Messenger*, December 11, 1908, 157. On the Hotel Astor, see Fremont Rider, *Rider's New York City and Vicinity, Including Newark, Yonkers and Jersey City* (New York: H. Holt and Company, 1916), 171.

covered by Jewish papers. The San Francisco *Hebrew* reported in 1900 that Albert Michelson had lately won first prize "in natural philosophy" at the Exposition universelle in Paris for his "invention of the echelon spectroscope ... by means of which the length of rays of light can be measured." The *American Israelite* reprinted the story of this Jewish "gentlemen who is attracting decided attention in the scientific world."[103] After the physicist became the first American scientist to win the Nobel Prize, in 1907, for something as stirring to the imagination as measuring the speed of light (using instruments he invented), Michelson was a hero, and he stayed a hero well after he died in 1931. The honors heaped on him, the prizes he won, and even the trips he took were tracked with enthusiasm; when Christiana University of Sweden conferred an honorary degree, the readers of Jewish papers knew about it.[104] As a contemporary wrote of him, "every scientific society, every large university in England, Germany, France, Italy, South America that has any honors, medals, cash prizes to offer had made Michelson the recipient of them at some time or another."[105]

Another hero was Simon Flexner. Jewish papers followed him starting just weeks after he graduated as "an honored student at Johns Hopkins University, ... one of the most successful students of this renowned institution."[106] Every stage of his career was documented, the jobs he took, the societies he joined, the lectures he gave, the trips he made, the receptions he attended as the guest of honor, and the awards he received. Cyrus Adler recounted his achievements in an entry in the 1906 *Jewish Encyclopedia.* After John D. Rockefeller hired Flexner in 1902 to organize operations and direct the laboratories at the new Rockefeller Institute for Medical Research, he became one of the best-known scientists in the country, the subject of articles with headlines like "How Science May Save Thousands of Children's Lives" and "Rockefeller Institute for Med-

103. "A Rising Light in Science," *American Israelite*, September 20, 1900, 5.

104. "About People," *American Israelite*, October 12, 1911, 6.

105. Herman Jacobsohn, "Albert A. Michelson," *Los Angeles Times*, August 12, 1923, magazine, 37.

106. "Louisville, Ky.," *American Israelite*, June 4, 1891, 3. The paper then reported when Flexner returned to Hopkins to begin postgraduate studies (September 24, 1891, 2), when he received his first university appointment (June 16, 1892, 2), when he sailed "to spend some time at the Universities of Strasburg, Berlin and Vienna" (March 30, 1893, 5), and when the Philadelphia Pathology Society threw a reception in his honor (May 3, 1894, 2). The early interest the American Israelite showed in Flexner was due in part, perhaps, because he grew up in Louisville and passed as a local boy to the editors of the Cincinnati paper. Soon, though, Jewish papers around the country were following his rising career. The *Jewish Messenger* reported when Flexner won a fellowship at Hopkins (June 12, 1891, 2).

ical Research to Be Best in the World."[107] When Flexner announced in 1907 that he had created a serum to treat an epidemic of meningitis, he was praised "as not only one of the world's foremost scientists, but as a real benefactor of all his race."[108] Among the scientists Flexner recruited for the Rockefeller Institute were men who themselves soon became heroes in the Jewish community: Samuel Meltzer, Phoebus Levene, and Jacques Loeb (who, not many years later, would be rejected by the Century Club).

The great renown of leading Jewish scientists was not lost on other American Jews. In some years, the only "Decorations, Honors and Distinctions Awarded to Jews" that were recorded in the *American Jewish Year Book* were those going to scientists.[109] An analysis of "Jews of Prominence in the United States," based on *Yearbooks* from 1903 to 1918, found 395 doctors, chemists, engineers, zoologists, bacteriologists, and other scientists, a number far higher than all the rabbis, lawyers, politicians, teachers, and soldiers combined.[110] Newspapers reported the accomplishments of great Jewish inventors, who "have been connected with some of the greatest inventions of the age," as Joseph Jacobs wrote in a 1914 survey. Jews had a hand in the technologies that did the most "to make modern civilization": the telephone, airship, automobile, and photograph.[111]

Alongside the constant praise, however, there was disquiet over the fact that few of the Jews who made names for themselves in the laboratory or workshop showed much interest in Judaism. In his 1911 Yom Kippur eve sermon to the congregation of the Free Synagogue, gathered at Carnegie Hall, Stephen S. Wise praised "the dean of the practice of medicine in American, great alike as physician and as citizen, Abraham Jacobi; a Jewish scientist of world-wide fame

107. "How Science May Save Thousands of Children's Lives," *Chicago Daily Tribune*, August 7, 1904, 2; "Rockefeller Institute for Medical Research to Be Best in World," *Chicago Daily Tribune*, August 28, 1904, 1.

108. "A Cure for Meningitis: Discovered by Dr. Flexner, Head of the Rockefeller Institute," *New York Times*, August 6, 1907, 1; "Dr. Flexner's Serum," *Courier-Journal* (Louisville, Ky.), August 11, 1907, 4. For Flexner's first announcement of the serum, see Simon Flexner, "Concerning a Serum-Therapy for Experimental Infection with Diplococcus Intracellularis," *Journal of Experimental Medicine* 9, no. 2 (March 14, 1907): 168–85.

109. The 1903 edition, for example, recounted honors awarded to Flexner, to biochemist Lafayette Mendel, to Samuel Bloomstein, a researcher of childhood diseases, and to Harry Friedenthal, an expert in diseases of the eyes and ears. "Decorations, Honors, and Distinctions Awarded to Jews, August 27, 1902, to August 25, 1903," *American Jewish Year Book* 5 (1903–1904): 214.

110. I. George Dobsevage, "Jews of Prominence in the United States," *American Jewish Year Book* 24 (1922–1923): 110.

111. Joseph Jacobs, "Count Zeppelin and David Schwarz," *American Hebrew & Jewish Messenger*, November 20, 1914, 80.

and world-wide service, Simon Flexner; a Jewish scholar, one of the foremost physicists of our time, Albert Michelson." He went on: "Every one of the men whom I have named is as truly Jewish in birth and blood as I am." But these men, "our greatest sons," are "errant from and alien to the household of Israel, which needs them, their power, their consecration, their genius, as truly as any cause, however high, that claims their lives!"[112]

Wise was not alone in his vexation that among the most famous American Jews were scientists, physicians, and inventors who were Jewish in birth and blood but in few, if any, other ways. For others, however, the lightness with which the mantle of religion rested on successful scientists was part of their appeal. These scientists were seen to embody a certain ideal of citizenship, forged in the image of science itself, in which Jews could be full-fledged and equal Americans and human beings. Journalist Herman Jacobsohn brought to a close a *Los Angeles Times* profile of Albert Michelson with this flourish:

> In the Swedish Academy of Science, he is considered a German. He was born in Germany and came to America a grown boy. The Germans claim that it was they who gave him his passion for thoroughness, accuracy, and love of work for its own sake. The Jews claim that he is not a German but a Jew, a man belonging to a race whom official Germany has always haunted [*sic*] like a mad dog. America declares that she has given him his education in the high schools of San Francisco and in the United States Naval Academy. More, she has afforded him a field in which to exercise his genius. But while such squabbles afford big themes for little men, big men are not touched by them. We have the genius and his work. Establishing his exact nationality will not add a single iota to the world's scientific treasures. And while it is fine to be a German, a Jew, or an American, it is still finer to be a man.[113]

Part of the appeal of science, technology, and medicine for Jews at the start of the twentieth century was that these avenues promised to put Jews on a path toward recognition as humans and to lead America to become a place where a Jew could be, above all, a human.

112. "Rabbi Wise Calls for Jewish Leaders," *New York Times*, October 2, 1911, 11. Disappointment with Michelson, in particular, may have been piqued by the fact that, as Jonathan Sarna has shown, he owed the appointment to the U.S. Naval Academy that led to his brilliant career to the fact that he was Jewish. In recommending Michelson's appointment to President Ulysses S. Grant, Congressman Thomas Fitch wrote that "these people [the Jews] are a powerful element in our politics, the boy who is uncommonly bright and studious is a pet among them, and I do most steadfastly believe that his appointment at your hands, would do more to fasten these people to the Republican cause, than anything else that could be done." Jonathan D. Sarna, *When General Grant Expelled the Jews* (New York: Nextbook/Schocken, 2016), 89n.

113. Jacobsohn, "Albert A. Michelson," 37.

Conclusion

At the start of World War I, the proud assertion that Jews could be found at the forefront of American science, medicine, and invention rested on a few outstanding examples—Michelson, Flexner, and Loeb, above all others. In the decades that followed, the number of Jews renowned in these fields grew spectacularly. Children of immigrants who sought science degrees in American universities were joined by established scientists who emigrated as conditions in Europe became less hospitable to Jews. Albert Einstein, when he moved once and for all to the United States in 1933, taking the first position at the Institute for Advanced Study newly established by Simon Flexner's brother Abraham, was at once the most famous scientist and the most famous Jew in the world. By then, a new chapter in the history of American Jews and American science had begun; several decades later, one in four physicists in America was Jewish, and one in five mathematicians, bacteriologists, biochemists, and physiologists.[114] Among the American Nobel Prize winners, these percentages were higher still.[115]

By this time, science and technology were an important part of the self-image of many American Jews, part of what it meant to be a Jew in America and what it meant for America to be a safe home for Jews.[116] Still, fundamental elements

114. Stephen Steinberg, *Academic Melting Pot.*

115. Statistics like these are unreliable and crude. It is hard—maybe impossible, probably pointless, and certainly distasteful—to come up with criteria that establish who is and is not Jewish (self-identification? Jewish parents or grandparents? Halakhic matrilineality?). Still, the basic trend that these numbers reflect would be hard to deny: Jews—by any definition—succeeded in science, medicine, and invention far more than their raw numbers would have predicted. For thoughtful and persuasive discussions of this point, see Seymour Martin Lipset and Everett Carll Ladd Jr., "Jewish Academics in the United States: Their Achievements, Culture, and Politics," *American Jewish Yearbook* 72 (1971): 89–128, and Paul R. Mendes-Flohr, *Divided Passions: Jewish Intellectuals and the Experience of Modernity* (Detroit: Wayne State University Press, 1991), 23–53.

116. This pattern would later be repeated, to a degree, by other immigrants to America, especially immigrants from East Asia. A 2014 study shows that immigrants from China, India, and Vietnam are well over twice as likely to be employed in science, technology, or medicine as native-born Americans. Pyong Gap Min and Sou Hyun Jang, "The Concentration of Asian Americans in STEM and Health-Care Occupations: An Intergenerational Comparison," *Ethnic and Racial Studies* 38, no. 6 (2015): 845–47. Some of the same considerations that drew Jewish immigrants to science a century earlier may be part of what draws these immigrants to science, technology, engineering, and medicine today, such as an association of science with ideals of democracy and meritocracy. What was perhaps most extraordinary about the rush of Jews toward science at the start of the twentieth century was that it coincided with the most accelerated growth and institutionalization of science in all of human history. Modern American Jewry and modern American science burgeoned and flourished at the same time, and their histories are inextricable.

of the attitudes of American Jews toward science, medicine, and invention had already been established long before, by men like Rabbi Isaac Mayer Wise in the middle of the nineteenth century. Even then, Wise had seen in the success of science a sure sign that the world—and America above all—was opening to Jews in new ways, representing a sort of "progress" that might make Jews more fit for America and America more fit for Jews. Already, Wise had argued that science had the power to raise Jews from their benighted state in the ghettos of Europe and to refashion both Jews and Christian society until "the partition wall between man and man totters and falls." He believed that "natural science upset all the medieval elements" and all the hidebound traditions and prejudices that might keep Jews apart from other Americans. Wise had predicted that the success of the scientific ethos would lead to an America in which liberty of conscience and justice were unassailable, and were extended to Jews as surely as they were available to Christians.

Wise had seen that science and invention were engines of progress that would refashion both Jews and America, leaving them more perfectly suited one for the other. A new order was coming. It had to come, as the old order, thankfully, had been *railroaded* and *steamboated* away.

THE AMERICAN RABBINATE ON THE CUSP OF CHANGE: GUSTAV GOTTHEIL'S SEVENTIETH BIRTHDAY DINNER IN 1897

JONATHAN D. SARNA

NEW YORK's foremost Reform rabbi, Gustav Gottheil (1827–1903) of Temple Emanu-El, reached the venerable age of seventy on May 28, 1897. Two days earlier, to mark the occasion, the city's Board of Jewish Ministers hosted a lavish dinner for him at the Tuxedo, a hall located at Madison Avenue and 59th Street. Rabbis, family members, and the editors of local Jewish newspapers all attended the event, which won mention in major Jewish newspapers. In addition, one of the newspaper editors, Jacob Philip (J. P.) Solomon (1838–1909), produced and circulated ("among friends") a privately printed pseudonymous satire inspired by the evening's speeches, *The Chronicles of the Rabbis: Being an Account of a Banquet Tendered to "Episcopus" by the Rabbis of New York City upon the Anniversary of his 70th Birthday.*[1] Together, the event and the satire shed light on hierarchy and discord within New York Judaism as the nineteenth century wound down, and particularly on four themes of enduring significance: (1) the emergence of new models of the rabbinate; (2) the uneasy relationship between rabbis and unordained lay leaders; (3) the growing chasm between classically trained European-born rabbis and those educated in the United States; and (4) the widening tension between Orthodoxy and Reform.

Gustav Gottheil

Gustav Gottheil (Fig. 70), who upon his death would be described as New York Judaism's "most prominent official figure," was born in a small unprepossessing Prussian town named Pinne (today, Pniewy, Poland). He received a traditional Jewish education, attested to and likely overseen by the town's highly respected rabbi and preacher, Joseph Chayyim (J. Heimann) Caro (1800–1895), renowned for his fluency in Hebrew, knowledge of German literature, and love of Zion.[2] He

1. Ben F. Rayim (J. P. Solomon), *The Chronicles of the Rabbis* (New York: Hebrew Standard, 1897).

2. Richard Gottheil, *The Life of Gustav Gottheil: Memoir of a Priest in Israel* (Williamsport, Pa.: Bayard Press, 1936), 2–3, 329–30; Ephraim E. Urbach, "Le-Demuto shel Harav Yosef Hayyim Caro," *Sefer Wloclawek: Wloclawek and Vicinity Memorial Book* (Tel Aviv: Ahdut Press, 1967), 133–43 (available online through the Digital Public Library of America); Louis Ginzberg and

also attended the yeshiva in Posen, where he presumably studied under Rabbi Shlomo Eger, the son of Caro's own teacher, Rabbi Akiva Eger. At some point in the 1840s, Gottheil attended the short-lived Berlin Jewish Teachers Seminary, receiving a certificate signed by the renowned Jewish scholars Leopold Zunz, Moritz Steinschneider, and Fürchtegott Lebrecht.[3] He also acquired a thoroughly modern German education, including the study of Latin, Greek, French, philosophy, and biblical exegesis, leading to a degree from the University of Jena granting him the much-coveted title of "Doktor."[4] He was thus "equally the product of the Yeshiva as of the German University."[5] This dual training, along with his liberal inclinations, led to his appointment, in 1855, as a teacher and occasional preacher in the religious school of the radical reformer Rabbi Samuel Holdheim in Berlin.

Gottheil felt insufficiently appreciated by the trustees of Holdheim's congregation and in 1860 accepted a position at the Manchester Congregation of British Jews, the community's new Reform synagogue, founded in 1857 and located at Park Place (where a Nazi bomb destroyed it in 1941). There his "powers as a leader and a spokesman" emerged. He learned English rapidly and became a powerful orator. He acquired "the clerical bearing and technique" of an English minister. He introduced "American-style" reforms, including a revised liberal liturgy, mixed seating, and an organ. He taught German on the side at Owens College (later the University of Manchester). And he established warm ties with Christian clergy and academics as well as with Orthodox members of the city's Great Synagogue, where on at least one occasion he preached. His success as a bilingual preacher, pastor, liberal activist, educator, and friend to Jews and non-Jews alike in his community came to define his rabbinate. He employed many

---

Peter Wiernik, "Caro, Joseph Hayyim B. Isaac Selig," *Jewish Encyclopedia*, 12 vols. (New York: Funk & Wagnalls, 1901–1906), 3:588–89.

3. Gottheil, *Life of Gustav Gottheil*, 12. Richard Gottheil describes the school as a "rabbinic seminary," but it was actually a Jewish teachers' seminary (judische Schullehrer-Seminarium), which lasted from 1840 to 1850. See Andreas Brämer, "'Making Teachers ... Who Do Not Treat Their Profession as an Occasional Business': Leopold Zunz and the Modernization of the Jewish Teacher Training in Prussia," *European Journal of Jewish Studies* 7, no. 2 (2013): 151–70, and Ismar Schorsch, *Leopold Zunz: Creativity in Adversity* (Philadelphia: University of Pennsylvania Press, 2016), 61–63, 175–77. Gottheil's claim that his father studied at the "rabbinic seminary" while teaching at Holdheim's congregation is impossible. Given the signatories on his certificate, he must have studied there as a teenager in the 1840s.

4. Gottheil, *Life of Gustav Gottheil*, 6–8.

5. Rabbi I. S. Moses, "Eulogy on Dr. Gustave [*sic*] Gottheil," *Year Book of the Central Conference of American Rabbis* 13 (1903): 362–63, reprinted in Gottheil, *Life of Gustav Gottheil*, 508.

Fig. 70. Gustav Gottheil. Rochester, 1895. With inscription "Noch ein trauernder Jude" ("Yet another Jew in mourning"). (Jewish Theological Seminary).

of these same techniques when he accepted an offer to become rabbi of Temple Emanu-El and moved to New York in 1873.[6]

Temple Emanu-El, when Gottheil arrived, was one of the foremost Reform congregations in the world. Founded in 1845, it boasted a membership of four hundred families who represented, according to the trustees, "the very Elite of the Jewish Community in this country."[7] It took pride both in its wealth and in its generosity to the less fortunate. Its Moorish home, at the corner of 5th Avenue and 43rd Street, was described as "perhaps the most costly and ornate of any erected in this country for religious purposes."[8] And it compensated its clergy handsomely. In June 1875, the trustees raised Gottheil's salary to $10,000 per annum—about $236,000 in today's money—where it remained until he retired.[9] Many of his contemporaries in the late nineteenth-century American rabbinate earned about one-twentieth as much.[10]

The high salary paid to Gottheil was not merely conspicuous consumption on the congregation's part. While his son apologetically explained that "the Board of Trustees desired him to live in a style befitting the representative of the Congregation Emanu-El" and that rents in New York were "out of all proportion to income," in reality, as historian Michael A. Meyer recognized, the American

6. Gottheil, *Life of Gustav Gottheil*, 11–22; Bernard Drachman, *The Unfailing Light: Memoirs of an American Rabbi* (New York: Rabbinical Council of America, 1948), 42–43; Bill Williams, *The Making of Manchester Jewry 1740–1875* (Manchester: Manchester University Press, 1976), 295–96, 421 n.206. Gottheil succeeded the scholarly Rabbi Dr. Solomon Marcus Schiller-Szinessy. For a brief history of the congregation by David Hoffman, see https://www.jacksonsrow.org/our-history/.

7. Board of Trustees of Temple Emanu-El to Gottheil, December 26, 1872, reprinted in Gottheil, *Life of Gustav Gottheil*, 27.

8. *New York Observer*, September 17, 1868, reprinted in Gottheil, *Life of Gustav Gottheil*, 23. See Myer Stern, *The Rise and Progress of Reform Judaism* (New York: Myer Stern, 1895), 63, and Rachel Wischnitzer, *Synagogue Architecture in the United States: History and Interpretation* (Philadelphia: Jewish Publication Society of America, 1955), 72–77.

9. Gottheil, *Life of Gustav Gottheil*, 36–37, 306. The salary seems to have been common knowledge among his colleagues. The calculation in 2019 dollars is based on https://westegg.com/inflation/.

10. Kimmy Caplan, "In God We Trust: Salaries and Income of American Orthodox Rabbis, 1881–1924," *American Jewish History* 86, no. 1 (1998): 77–106; Daniel Judson, *Pennies for Heaven: The History of American Synagogues and Money* (Waltham, Mass.: Brandeis University Press, 2018), 91–99. The great Protestant preacher Henry Ward Beecher earned $15,000, but the average ministerial salary amounted to some $574. See E. Brooks Holifield, *God's Ambassadors: A History of the Christian Clergy in America* (Grand Rapids, Mich.: Eerdmans, 2007), 179, and James Hudnut-Beumler, *In Pursuit of the Almighty's Dollar: A History of Money and American Protestantism* (Chapel Hill: University of North Carolina Press, 2007), 76–96.

social context "deemed acquisition of riches a mark of superior achievement and the necessary prerogative for exercising power."[11] Perhaps above all, Gottheil's lofty salary reflected his unique and remarkable combination of talents. In addition to his pastoral skills, dignified bearing, and fine sense of humor, he was also among the first professional rabbis in New York to serve as a "representative Jew"—an ambassador to non-Jews, as well as a visible symbol of those values that his congregants held dear. He preached eloquently in two languages: German, which the immigrant generation still revered, and English, for everybody else. As a preacher and speaker, he numbered among the top ranks of New York's clergy and ably represented the entire Jewish community on state occasions. In addition, he displayed erudition, including deep familiarity with both Jewish and general culture in German, English, and Hebrew. "The spirit of Jewish scholarship always hovered around him," a colleague recalled.[12]

Gottheil also reached out to female members of his temple. He established a renowned (and widely emulated) Sisterhood of Personal Service that enlisted women to aid the less fortunate. And he played a key role in the creation of a short-lived Ladies' Hebrew Seminary for training "lady teachers" for Jewish schools.[13] Beyond that, he befriended Christian colleagues and was even invited to speak, as a Jew, from their pulpits. On one well-remembered occasion, he occupied the official chair of the esteemed Episcopal bishop of New York, Henry C. Potter; the two men were friends. He likewise enjoyed friendships with many other Christian leaders; they considered him the "bishop of the Jews." Though sometimes accused of kowtowing to those Christians, he and many of his lay leaders felt that familiarizing church leaders with Jews and Judaism worked to combat prejudice and bigotry.[14]

Gottheil likewise maintained cordial ties with a wide range of Jewish colleagues, including those who did not subscribe to his own Reform tendencies. "My Father always believed that Jews of all shades of opinion and religious convictions

11. Gottheil, *Life of Gustav Gottheil*, 36; Michael A. Meyer, *Response to Modernity: A History of the Reform Movement in Judaism* (New York: Oxford University Press, 1988), 282.

12. Rabbi Joseph Friedlander, *American Hebrew*, May 1, 1903, reprinted in Gottheil, *Life of Gustav Gottheil*, 506.

13. Felicia Herman, "From Priestess to Hostess: Sisterhoods of Personal Service in New York City, 1887–1936," in *Women and American Judaism: Historical Perspectives*, ed. Pamela S. Nadell and Jonathan D. Sarna (Hanover, N.H.: Brandeis University Press, 2001), 148–81; David Kaufman, "Jewish Education as a Civilization: A History of the Teachers Institute," in *Tradition Renewed: A History of the Jewish Theological Seminary of America*, ed. Jack Wertheimer, 2 vols. (New York: Jewish Theological Seminary of America, 1997), 1:572.

14. Gottheil, *Life of Gustav Gottheil*, 115–45, 505.

should stand together," his son Richard recalled. On the second day of Jewish holidays, which Reform Jews do not observe, his father often took Richard to "festival services in the most orthodox congregations in East Broadway and Hester Street," where immigrants worshiped. "Not only did he wish to worship with his brethren," Richard explained. "He wished to train his son to feel as he did—that whatsoever affected the Jews anywhere must affect him also."[15]

Gottheil's broad-minded view of the rabbinate led him to cofound, in 1881, the New York Board of Jewish Ministers (renamed in 1946 the New York Board of Rabbis). Open to "qualified, recognized Rabbis of Greater New York and its vicinity"—an indication that those deemed unqualified could be excluded—the board embraced "orthodox and reform Rabbis alike." The Orthodox rabbi David de Sola Pool, who wrote the board's early history, explained that it promoted "the spirit of fraternal cooperation among the Rabbis of the city," organized discussions of "practical, theological and ritual questions," and furthered "communal interests."[16] Gottheil played a key role in all of these areas, once chiding his colleagues for wasting "much time in conversations and resolutions" and then boldly setting forth seven innovative projects that he encouraged them to take up and address.[17]

Gottheil was perhaps the foremost representative in New York of the new rabbinic ideal that emerged in the United States in the second half of the nineteenth century. As in Germany, the new class of "rabbi-doctors" possessed earned university degrees in addition to formal rabbinic ordination. Many of them, like Gottheil, preferred to be called "Doctor" rather than "Rabbi," accentuating their general learning over their religious credentials.[18] Both titles distinguished them from earlier prayer-leading *hazzanim* (prayer readers or cantors), often

15. *Ibid.*, 97.

16. David de Sola Pool, "The New York Board of Jewish Ministers," in *The Jewish Communal Register of New York City 1917–1918*, 2d ed. (New York: Kehillah (Jewish Community) of New York City, 1918), 294–300; Alvin Kass "Watchman for the Community: A History of the New York Board of Rabbis," in *The American Rabbi: A Tribute on the Occasion of the Bicentennial of the United States and the Ninety-fifth Birthday of the New York Board of Rabbis*, ed. Gilbert S. Rosenthal (New York: KTAV Publishing House, 1977), 9–22. Gottheil also helped found, and in 1897 presided over, a regional rabbinic organization known as the Jewish Ministers' Association of America, which later became part of the Central Conference of American Rabbis. See *American Hebrew*, November 5, 1897, 24, and Gary Phillip Zola, "Southern Rabbis and the Founding of the First National Association of Rabbis," *American Jewish History* 85, no. 4 (1997): 353–72.

17. Gottheil, *Life of Gustav Gottheil*, 243–47.

18. Meyer, *Response to Modernity*, 281. Max Lilienthal, who arrived in New York in 1845, helped set the pattern for the new class of rabbi-doctors; see Bruce L. Ruben, *Max Lilienthal: The Making of the American Rabbinate* (Detroit: Wayne State University Press, 2011), esp. 70.

denominated "Jewish ministers" in the United States, who sometimes lacked any credentials whatsoever. The new titles bespoke the growing professionalization of the rabbinate in the post–Civil War era. Like law, medicine, and other "professions," the rabbinate introduced selective training schools, formal membership organizations (like the Board of Jewish Ministers), standard uniforms, and bureaucratic rules.[19]

The best rabbi-doctors, like their Protestant counterparts, excelled in the priestly, prophetic, and pastoral aspects of their positions. They became local celebrities, "princes of the pulpit." Their demeanor, their posture, and even their height commanded attention.[20] They were self-consciously manly: they knew how to dress and how to comport themselves. They delivered elegant English-language sermons, impressing non-Jews as well as Jews, women and men alike. Their resounding voices filled large halls. Newspapers regularly quoted them. Politicians befriended and engaged them. Congregants basked in their reflected glory.[21]

Besides Gottheil, only a handful of English-speaking American rabbis came close to measuring up to this ideal. Morris J. Raphall (1798–1868), of New York's B'nai Jeshurun, who held a doctorate from the University of Erlangen and presided at the Birmingham Synagogue in England before immigrating to the United States in 1849, was the first such "glamour rabbi" in America. He

19. Samuel Haber, *The Quest for Authority and Honor in the American Professions, 1750–1900* (Chicago: University of Chicago Press, 1991); Donald M. Scott, *From Office to Profession: The New England Ministry, 1750–1850* (Philadelphia: University of Pennsylvania Press, 1978); Thomas L. Haskell, *The Emergence of Professional Social Science: The American Social Science Association and the Nineteenth-Century Crisis of Authority* (Urbana: University of Illinois Press, 1977); Burton J. Bledstein, *The Culture of Professionalism: The Middle Class and the Development of Higher Education in America* (New York: Norton, 1976).

20. Simon Tuska's "feeble voice and small stature" eliminated him as a candidate for New York's Temple Emanu-El in 1860, according to Isaac M. Wise; see Abraham J. Karp, *Jewish Continuity in America: Creative Survival in a Free Society* (Tuscaloosa: University of Alabama Press, 1998), 130. The fact that Rabbi Max Samfield of Memphis was known as "The Little Man with a Big Heart" underscores how important a factor height usually was in determining a rabbi's success; see Memorial Volume to Rabbi Max Samfield of the *Jewish Spectator* (Memphis), 1915 (SC-8210x), Jacob Rader Marcus Center of the American Jewish Archives, Cincinnati.

21. See, generally, Ismar Schorsch, "Emancipation and the Crisis of Religious Authority: The Emergence of the Modern Rabbinate," in Schorsch, *From Text to Context: The Turn to History in Modern Judaism* (Hanover, N.H.: Brandeis University Press, 1994), 9–50; Holifield, *God's Ambassadors*, 120–21, 145–81; Zev Eleff, *Who Rules the Synagogue? Religious Authority and the Formation of American Judaism* (New York: Oxford University Press, 2016), 159–81; Naomi W. Cohen, *Encounter with Emancipation: The German Jews in the United States, 1830–1914* (Philadelphia: Jewish Publication Society of America, 1984), 190–94.

was distinctive, too, in his promotion of a modernized Orthodoxy on the Anglo-Jewish model. In his day, he commanded "the highest remuneration then offered to an American rabbi," won appreciation from Christians for his learning and preaching, was the first Jew ever invited to deliver a prayer before the U.S. Congress, and became mired in controversy when, in 1861, he defended slavery on the basis of his literal reading of the Bible. By the time Gottheil arrived in New York, Raphall had passed away.[22] Among Gottheil's contemporaries, rabbis like Max Lilienthal and Isaac M. Wise in Cincinnati, Emil G. Hirsch in Chicago, Elkan Cohn in San Francisco, and Kaufmann Kohler in New York embodied this same rabbinic ideal. Hebrew Union College, founded by Wise in 1875 in Cincinnati, looked to train many more professional rabbis in their image.

Gottheil's Seventieth Birthday Dinner

The kosher dinner tendered to Gottheil by the Board of Jewish Ministers for his seventieth birthday in 1897 reflected the esteem in which its members held him for exemplifying this beau ideal. It arouses some surprise, however, that they honored him with a *kosher* dinner. Lance Sussman, after all, has shown that mainstream Reform Judaism had broken with the Jewish dietary laws almost two decades earlier. The great banquet in Cincinnati in 1883 marking the tenth anniversary of the Union of American Hebrew Congregations and the first ordination from Hebrew Union College, which Gottheil attended, became known as the *trefa* banquet precisely because it was so obviously *not* kosher. Indeed, Reform Judaism's 1885 Pittsburgh Platform explicitly disavowed "all such Mosaic and rabbinical laws as regulate diet."[23] Foodways, by the late nineteenth century, served as a visible and ideological marker between Reform Jews and their non-Reform brethren. Nevertheless, at least in New York, gatherings that brought Orthodox and Reform rabbis together continued to uphold the Jewish dietary laws. That policy helped to keep posh establishments with kosher kitchens, like the Tuxedo, in business.[24] Even though only a minority of the members of the Board of Jewish Ministers kept kosher—five of seventeen—they

22. Bertram Wallace Korn, *Eventful Years and Experiences: Studies in Nineteenth-Century American Jewish History* (Cincinnati: American Jewish Archives, 1954), 40–41, 98–124; Jonathan D. Sarna, *American Judaism: A History*, 2d ed. (New Haven: Yale University Press, 2019), 95–96. Raphall's salary, though equivalent in 1850 to what his best-paid Protestant contemporaries earned, was, in purchasing power, only about a quarter of Gottheil's subsequent salary.

23. Lance J. Sussman, "The Myth of the Trefa Banquet: American Culinary Culture and the Radicalization of Food Policy in American Reform Judaism," *American Jewish Archives Journal* 57, no. 1–2 (2005): 29–52.

24. "The New Tuxedo," *American Hebrew*, September 12, 1902, 475.

would be accommodated with food they could eat.[25] J. P. Solomon's satire of the evening confirms this decision. "The feast," he observed, "did not provide any of the creeping things and other abominations with which the Rabbis who had forsaken the laws of their forefathers delighted in." Although most Reform banquets in New York did feature seafood, the celebration's organizers, knowing more traditionally observant members would "not eat of the abominations of the idols," asked themselves, "why should we offend them?"[26]

The five who likely cared about kosher food and might have been offended had it not been served were: Henry Pereira Mendes (1852–1937), the esteemed Sephardic rabbi of Shearith Israel, who, by coincidence, had earlier ministered to the Sephardic community in Manchester; his older brother, Frederick de Sola Mendes (1850–1927), the rabbi of Shaaray Tefillah congregation (now the West End Synagogue), who started out as an Orthodox rabbi and gradually transitioned his congregation to Reform; Bernard Drachman (1861–1945) of Congregation Zichron Ephraim (now the Park East Synagogue), a pupil of Gottheil's at Temple Emanu-El who became an Orthodox rabbi; Falk Vidaver (1845–1909), rabbi of Congregation Beth Israel Bikur Cholim, an Orthodox synagogue that had recently introduced an organ and choir; and Adolph Radin (1848–1909), the Jewish chaplain of New York and Brooklyn penal institutions.[27] The Mendes brothers and Drachman not only kept kosher, they also taught at the small traditionalist Jewish Theological Seminary, which had opened its doors a decade earlier for "Jews of America faithful to Mosaic law and ancestral tradition."[28]

25. For this number, see *American Hebrew*, October 29, 1897, 765. Four members had recently died: Adolph Huebsch, Henry S. Jacobs, Alexander Kohut, and Aaron Wise; *American Hebrew*, July 2, 1897, 269.

26. *Chronicles of the Rabbis*, 1.

27. For the attendees, see *American Hebrew*, June 4, 1897, 136, and *Chronicle of the Rabbis*. On H. P. Mendes, see Eugene Markovitz, "Henry Pereira Mendes: Architect of the Union of Orthodox Jewish Congregations of America," *American Jewish Historical Quarterly* 55, no. 3 (1966): 364–84; on Frederick de Sola Mendes, see Moshe Davis, *The Emergence of Conservative Judaism: The Historical School in 19th-Century America* (Philadelphia: Jewish Publication Society of America, 1965), 349–51; on Drachman, see Bernard Drachman, *Unfailing Light*, 40, 164, and Jeffrey S. Gurock, "From Exception to Role Model: Bernard Drachman and the Evolution of Jewish Religious Life in America, 1880–1920," *American Jewish History* 76, no. 4 (1987): 456–84; on Vidaver, see *New York Times*, December 16, 1895, 3, and October 6, 1909, 9; and on Radin, see Nathan Stern, "Obituary Address—Adolph Moses Radin," *Year Book of the Central Conference of American Rabbis* 19 (1909): 424–31.

28. Robert E. Fierstien, *A Different Spirit: The Jewish Theological Seminary of America, 1886–1902* (New York: Jewish Theological Seminary of America, 1990), 54. See also Hasia Diner, "Like the Antelope and the Badger: The Founding and Early Years of the Jewish Theological Seminary, 1886–1902," in *Tradition Renewed*, ed. Wertheimer, 1:3–42.

Richard Gottheil, a supporter, like his father, of Hebrew Union College, had polemicized against the new seminary soon after it opened, declaring it to be "a crying wrong that one cent of money should be given to this hotbed of exclusiveness and of down-right bigotry."[29]

Now, with Gustav Gottheil being honored, the seminary looked to be declining. Its most famous faculty member, Alexander Kohut, had passed away, and its president, Sabato Morais, lay dying. The seminary failed to graduate even a single rabbi in 1896 or 1897.[30] What nobody knew was that just days prior to the dinner, the renowned Jewish scholar Solomon Schechter, in Cambridge, had been asked whether he would "care to come to New York to take charge of the Chancellorship of the Jewish Theological Seminary."[31] His arrival in 1902 would change the course of American Judaism.

Meanwhile, a host of other rabbis in New York who respected the traditional Jewish dietary laws found no place at the Gottheil dinner. Most of them were "downtown" immigrant rabbis from Russia and Hungary. Even if Gottheil occasionally visited their synagogues on the second day of Jewish holidays, they remained unaffiliated with the uptown Board of Jewish Ministers and operated within their own Orthodox universe. No English-language Jewish newspaper even noticed when several Orthodox rabbis and lay leaders founded, on February 26, 1897, a tiny rabbinical school grandly named the Rabbi Isaac Elchanan Theological Seminary "to promote the study of the Talmud and to assist in educating and preparing students of the Hebrew faith for the Hebrew Orthodox Ministry." Years later, as part of Yeshiva University, it would become one of the largest and most influential Orthodox rabbinical seminaries in the world.[32] Not invited either, apparently, were better-known Orthodox rabbis like Chief Rabbi Jacob Joseph (1840–1902), by then incapacitated by a stroke, Philip (Hillel) Klein of Oheb Zedek Congregation (1849–1926), Leopold Zinsler of Shaari Zedek (1856–1922), and Moses Maisner of Adath Israel (1838–1918).[33] Because

29. Quoted in Fierstien, *A Different Spirit*, 75.

30. *Ibid.*, 96.

31. Schechter to Mayer Sulzberger, May 9, 1897, as quoted in Karp, *Jewish Continuity in America*, 135; Mel Scult, "Schechter's Seminary," in *Tradition Renewed*, ed. Wertheimer, 1:48.

32. The Certificate of Incorporation is reprinted in Gilbert Klaperman, *The Story of Yeshiva University: The First Jewish University in America* (Toronto: Macmillan, 1969), 244–45; for its history see 48ff.

33. On Joseph, see Sarna, *American Judaism*, 182–83, and works cited there, as well as Yonah Landau, *The Rav Hakolel and His Generation: A Biography of Yaakov Yosef Chief Rabbi of New York 1888–1902 and His Battles for Yiddishkeit at the Turn of the Century* (New York: privately published, 2016); on Klein, see Nancy Isaacs Klein, *Heritage of Faith: Two Pioneers of Judaism in*

the board was known to be "made up largely of Reformers," and likely also for social, economic, and linguistic reasons, east European Orthodox rabbis preferred to associate with those of their own kind.[34] So for all that the Gottheil dinner looked to display rabbinic unity, with kosher food and the presence of Orthodox rabbis like Mendes and Drachman, that appearance was, upon closer inspection, somewhat illusory. By 1897, New York's Jewish community had fractured.

Women too were missing from the dinner. Press accounts listed neither Gottheil's wife, Rosalie (Wollman), nor his daughters; only his son and son-in-law attended. Like so many formal dinners of the time, the rabbinical dinner was a stag affair, restricted to men.

Beyond issues of unity and inclusiveness, the press descriptions of the dinner echoed what one might expect: an abundance of food, much discussion of the "doings and sayings of American Judaism," a formal ("eloquent") address by the renowned Rabbi Kaufmann Kohler, a "feeling" response by Gottheil, six shorter speeches, two Hebrew poems, rhyming couplets in English, a "nursery ode," a jolly version of the Passover hymn "Dayenu" rewritten to extol Gottheil's merits, and a formal closing grace. The dinner displayed the Jewish learning expected of rabbis, their simultaneous embrace of general culture, and their light-heartedness. Every speaker, according to the *American Hebrew*, whether in "raillery" or in "honest earnestness," addressed the same basic theme: "Dr. Gottheil's prominent merits in the field of American Judaism."[35]

Between the lines, though, differences among the rabbis peeked through. The two Hebrew poems, for example, were both read by immigrant rabbis (Vidaver and Radin) known to be sympathetic to Zionism. Gottheil too favored Zionism, and within a few months would agree to become founding vice president of New York's Federation of Zionist Societies (his son Richard served as president and subsequently presided over the Federation of American Zionists).[36] Gottheil

---

America (Hoboken, N.J.: KTAV Publishing House, 1987), 5–61; on Zinsler, see *American Jewish Year Book* 5 (1903–1904): 108; and on Maisner, see *American Jewish Year Book* 5 (1903–1904): 77, and Drachman, *Unfailing Light*, 179.

34. *American Hebrew*, March 12, 1897, 509. Klein, Maisner, and Zinsler would all join what came to be known as the Union of Orthodox Jewish Congregations when it organized in 1898; *New York Times*, June 10, 1898, 12 (misspelling both Maisner and Zinsler). The New York Board of Jewish Ministers had encouraged the creation of an Orthodox Union earlier that year; see *American Hebrew*, April 1, 1898, 640.

35. "Dr. Gottheil's 70th Birthday," *American Hebrew*, June 4, 1897, 156.

36. Richard Gottheil ascribed his father's conversion to Zionism to the 1881 pogroms in Russia, the rise of antisemitism (including in the United States), the publication of Theodor Herzl's *The Jewish State* in 1896, and the First Zionist Congress a year later. Gottheil, *Life of Gustav Gottheil*,

was one of the few prominent early Reform rabbis to embrace Zionism. Most of his Reform colleagues, in keeping with their movement's 1885 Pittsburgh Platform and the uncompromising resolutions of the Central Conference of American Rabbis (1897) and the Union of American Hebrew Congregations (1898), vehemently opposed it. Indeed, the featured speaker at the dinner in Gottheil's honor, Kaufmann Kohler (1843–1926), the son-in-law and successor of the radical Reform leader David Einhorn at Temple Beth El, New York's other flagship Reform temple (it would merge with Emanu-El in 1927), had attacked the "folly of the Zionist movement" in print just a few weeks earlier. He vehemently protested "against the insinuation that we are not with every fibre of our heart American citizens" and characterized Theodor Herzl and his supporters as "madmen."[37] Understandably, the dinner papered over these stark differences between the city's best-known and most-admired Reform rabbis. Kohler diplomatically addressed the "age, experience and ripe wisdom" of Gottheil instead.[38]

The dinner also papered over differences between Gottheil and his assistant and heir apparent, Joseph Silverman (1860–1930). Born in Cincinnati, Silverman was ordained at Hebrew Union College, where he had mastered the outer forms of the new rabbinic ideal, though his actual knowledge of rabbinic literature was weak. He possessed no European training and was reputedly the first American-born rabbi to serve in New York City. Silverman looked like a Tem-

---

190–91. However, Bernard Drachman, who studied with Gottheil in the 1870s, described Gottheil as being a closet supporter of a return to Zion much earlier, influenced, perhaps, by his teacher, Caro. Drachman recalled Gottheil saying, "I am sometimes asked by Gentiles, clergymen and others, what is my attitude on the question of the return of the Jews to Palestine. In such cases I examine the personality of the questioner. If I think he is a *rosho* (a Jew-hater) and his secret motive a desire to see Jews expelled from Western Lands, I say, 'We Reform Jews have given up that doctrine. What we believe in and want is equal rights of citizenship in all lands in which we dwell.' But if I think he is a sincere seeker after knowledge, who desires merely to know what Jews believe and feel, then I say, 'This is a very precious doctrine and very dear to millions of Jews. Perhaps God, in His mercy, will re-establish our ancient state and restore our ancient glory. Should that happen, all Jews would rejoice.'" Drachman, *Unfailing Light*, 43. On the controversy attending Gottheil's role, as a Reform rabbi, in the Zionist movement, see Evyatar Friesel, *The Zionist Movement in the United States 1897–1914* (Tel Aviv: Kibbutz Hameuchad, 1970), 28–31 (in Hebrew). On Reform Judaism and Zionism, see, especially, Michael A. Meyer, "American Reform Judaism and Zionism: Early Efforts at Ideological Rapprochement," *Studies in Zionism* 4, no. 1 (1983): 49–64, and Jonathan D. Sarna, "Converts to Zionism in the American Reform Movement," in *Zionism and Religion*, ed. Shmuel Almog et al. (Hanover, N.H.: Brandeis University Press, 1998), 188–203.

37. Kaufmann Kohler, "Communications: Folly of the Zionist Movement," *American Hebrew*, May 14, 1897, 38.

38. *American Hebrew*, June 4, 1897, 156.

ple Emanu-El rabbi—tall, handsome, and gifted with a sonorous voice—but Richard Gottheil recognized that he was "in no way a learned man, either in Jewish or non-Jewish lore."[39] Indeed, in many ways he was Gustav Gottheil's antithesis. The trustees hired him without consulting their senior rabbi, and relations between the two remained frosty. They publicly disagreed over Zionism and held different conceptions of the role of the rabbi and of what was appropriate to speak about from the pulpit.[40] On one notorious occasion in 1895, Gottheil discoursed on "Priest and People," while Silverman—a proponent of "New Pulpit" ideas advocating that ministers should be in touch with "the life of the day" and that "the Pulpit should have something to say about every novel that has a run"[41]—preached on "The Moral Influence of Fiction in General and of Trilby in Particular," a sermon based on George du Maurier's bestselling 1895 novel featuring a wicked Jewish hypnotist named Svengali and the beautiful model whose singing voice he controlled.[42] The episode underscored the yawning generational and cultural gap between Gottheil and Silverman. Silverman's words at Gottheil's birthday dinner are not preserved, but when Temple Emanu-El memorialized Gottheil following his death in 1903, the family tellingly requested that Silverman not deliver the eulogy.[43]

The Chronicles of the Rabbis

The communal fractures and rabbinic disputes that the banquet in Gottheil's honor sought to obscure found expression in an extraordinary satire, *The Chronicles of the Rabbis.* The purported author of the sixteen-page pamphlet was one "Ben F. Rayim," a play on the Hebrew for "among friends." It was dedicated to "Episcopus," a reference to Gottheil himself, who, as we have seen, both befriended and emulated the Episcopal bishop of New York. And it was printed at the press of the *Hebrew Standard.* Before long, the satire came to be known as the work of J. P. Solomon, the *Hebrew Standard*'s editor.[44]

39. Gottheil, *Life of Gustav Gottheil,* 147, 263–64. For a more sympathetic view, see Edna Nahshon, "The Pulpit and the Stage: Rabbi Joseph Silverman and the Actors' Church Alliance," *American Jewish History* 91, no. 1 (2003): 5–27.

40. Sarna, "Converts to Zionism in the American Reform Movement," 191. In the 1920s, following his retirement, Silverman toured Palestine and became an ardent Zionist.

41. H. R. Haweis, "The New Pulpit," *North American Review* 160 (February 1895): 172–84, esp. 180; Nahshon, "The Pulpit and the Stage," 9–10.

42. *American Hebrew,* February 21, 1895, 469, and November 29, 1895, 107.

43. Gottheil, *Life of Gustav Gottheil,* 263–64.

44. *American Jewish Year Book* 6 (1904–1905): 190. Israel Davidson, *Parody in Jewish Literature* (New York: Columbia University Press, 1907), 247 (no. 306), first attributed the pamphlet

Described by a friend as "a lawyer, sincerely pious Jew, and learned in Hebrew lore, disposed over a mind of unusually brilliant power, with a tendency toward pungent humor,"[45] Solomon was born in Manchester, where he studied at the Jewish Free School. He immigrated to the United States in 1854 (so he and Gottheil never overlapped in Manchester), attended Franklin College and Notre Dame in Indiana, and received a law degree from Columbia in 1864, the same year that he was admitted to the New York bar.[46] By then he had established a reputation in journalism and in politics, where he staunchly supported the Democratic Party.[47] He also delivered lectures in various local Orthodox synagogues. Indeed, "laymen like Mr. Solomon, who have adopted another profession than that of the ministry, but who possess the ability and inclination to expound the general duties of Israel and to remind [Jews] … of what is apt to be forgotten in the indifference of the hour" won high praise from the Orthodox-leaning New York *Jewish Messenger* in 1863.[48] Solomon maintained a "large and successful" law practice in New York from 1865 to 1902; led multiple general and Jewish fraternal organizations, including the Orthodox Kesher Shel Barzel, which he served as "Grand Saar"; delivered periodic lectures on Jewish history and religion; and stepped in as "lay preacher" at B'nai Jeshurun when its pulpit stood vacant.[49] From September 23, 1882, until his death in 1909, he edited the *Hebrew Standard,* a widely read New York Jewish weekly characterized by the *Jewish Encyclopedia* as "strongly conservative," "of Orthodox tendencies," Democratic in its politics, and "the first attempt at the issue

---

to Solomon. The copy at Hebrew Union College, annotated with the help of J. P. Solomon's son William (comptroller of Central Synagogue), confirms the attribution and identifies most of the satire's "Dramatis Personae."

45. Albert M. Friedenberg, "Main Currents in American Jewish Journalism," *Reform Advocate,* May 27, 1916, 511. On Friedenberg (1881–1942), see Edward D. Coleman and Alexander Marx, "A Selected Bibliography of the Writings of Albert M. Friedenberg," *Publications of the American Jewish Historical Society* 35 (1939): 115–37.

46. *American Jewish Year Book* 6 (1904–1905): 190; New York Times, May 20, 1864, 2.

47. See Solomon's "The Law Concerning Chaplains," in *Israelite,* November 29, 1861, 172, and his Hebrew-language election circular on behalf of Judge Albert Cardozo in 1867, reproduced in *Publications of the American Jewish Historical Society* 34 (1937): 285–88.

48. *Jewish Messenger,* October 9, 1863, 111; see also the tribute to him from the president of Congregation Beth Israel Bikur Cholim in *Jewish Messenger,* June 23, 1865, 195.

49. *Jewish Exponent,* June 4, 1909, 7; *American Hebrew,* May 28, 1909, 91; *New York Times,* May 27, 1909, 9; *American Jewish Year Book* 6 (1904–1905): 190. For reports of his lectures, see *Israelite,* May 16, 1873, 2, and June 20, 1873, 4; *Jewish Exponent,* April 17, 1896, 7. For his work as lay preacher, see Israel Goldstein, *A Century of Judaism in New York: B'nai Jeshurun, 1825–1925* (New York: Congregation B'nai Jeshurun, 1930), 160.

of a cheap, popular Jewish newspaper in the English language."[50] In 1897, the *Hebrew Standard* promised "a guaranteed circulation exceeding that of all the other New York City Jewish newspapers combined" (Fig. 71). That prominence probably explains why Solomon was invited to the dinner in Gottheil's honor.[51]

Solomon deployed his "pungent humor" to great advantage in his satirical depiction of that dinner. An unusual nineteenth-century American Jewish example of religious satire written in English,[52] *Chronicles of the Rabbis* employed language and allusions from the Bible to skewer the vanities, follies, and hypocrisies of "the Rabbis of the City of Gotham." It offered particularly harsh critiques of Reform rabbis, focusing on religious deviations, perceived ignorance, and bloated salaries. Through sarcasm, parody, and wit, it aimed to speak a layman's idea of truth to rabbinic power. In addition, like Gilbert and Sullivan's comic operas, so popular at the time, it mocked unqualified people in positions of august authority. The opening lines set the scene:

> Now it came to pass when Episcopus [Gottheil] was the chief ruler of the Rabbis of the City of Gotham.

50. Albert M. Friedenberg, "Hebrew Standard," *Jewish Encyclopedia*, 6:311. The paper also often characterized itself as "conservative" in its religious stance, which at that time was simply the opposite of liberal; the terms "Orthodox" and "conservative" were often used interchangeably. J. D. Eisenstein, in his *Ozar Zikhronothai* (New York, 1929), 117, claims that the paper was "established on an Orthodox basis." Solomon's sister Jane was married to an Orthodox *hazan*, the Reverend Jacob Kantrowitz; see *American Hebrew*, August 18, 1893, and *American Israelite*, October 10, 1912, 2.

51. Friedenberg, "Hebrew Standard," 311; Friedenberg, "Main Currents in American Jewish Journalism," 511. George Batten's *Directory of the Religious Press of the United States* (New York, 1892), 94, credited the *Hebrew Standard* with 27,500 subscribers, while counting only 14,000 for the *American Hebrew*. An 1897 ad for the *Hebrew Standard*, bound in with Solomon's pseudonymous *Chronicles of the Rabbis*, promised the "guaranteed circulation." Other New York Jewish newspapers of the day included the *American Hebrew*, the *Jewish Messenger*, and the *Hebrew Journal*.

52. For a history of religious satire, see Terry Lindvall, *God Mocks: A History of Religious Satire from the Hebrew Prophets to Stephen Colbert* (New York: New York University Press, 2015). Davidson's *Parody in Jewish Literature*, 209–63, lists more than four hundred Jewish parodies, many published in (and dealing with) America, but only a handful in English. Samuel B. H. Judah's *Gotham and the Gothamites: A Medley* (New York, 1823) was the first social satire written by an American Jew; see Jonathan D. Sarna, "Subversive Jews and American Culture: Notes on the Leonard Milberg Collection of Early American Judaica," in *By Dawn's Early Light: Jewish Contributions to American Culture from the Nation's Founding to the Civil War*, ed. Adam D. Mendelsohn (Princeton: Princeton University Library, 2016), 192–94. For a subsequent English-language satire composed by early twentieth-century Reform rabbinical students, see Joan S. Friedman, "The Pilgrim Rabbis: Reform Rabbis Behaving Badly in a Lost Satire," *American Jewish Archives Journal* 70, no. 1–2 (2018): 69–116.

> And the Rabbis were pious servants of the Lord, and their love for each other exceeded that of the love of David and Jonathan [1 Samuel 18], and jealousy and envy were unknown between them.
>
> And they said one to another: Behold the number of the years of our chief, even Episcopus, will soon be three score and ten, and for piety he standeth like Saul the son of Kish, head and shoulders above all the other Rabbis of the congregation of Israel [1 Samuel 9:2].
>
> Now let us gather and prepare a banquet in his honor, whose splendor shall exceed the feast of Ahashverosh which he made unto all his princes and servants, even in the third year of his reign [Esther 1:3–5].[53]

Having thus backhandedly poked fun at the rabbis for their jealousies, envies, and penchant for extravagance, Solomon directly addressed, albeit in a humorous way, what he and lay leaders of his kind felt most distinguished the new rabbis from their predecessors: their salaries surpassed their piety. Into the mouth of the ideologically somewhat spineless "Frederick the tiller of the soil"—a play on Frederick de Sola Mendes—he placed the following soliloquy:

> Some people may belie us,
> And think we're not as pious
> As Rabbis surely ought to be.
> That we preach but do not practice,
> While all know the simple fact is
> That we must draw our salary.[54]

Solomon, as he admitted in his *Chronicles*, had "no regard for the servants of the Lord, and respecteth neither their pulpits nor their salaries."[55] Having grown up in an era when most ministers earned modest salaries and cowered before congregational lay leaders, and having made the personal decision to adopt a profession other than the rabbinate, he looked to cut rabbis like de Sola Mendes down to size. Nor was he alone. At the founding of the Jewish Publication Society in Philadelphia, back in 1888, East Coast Jewish lay leaders like Mayer Sulzberger, Cyrus Adler, Simon Wolf, Benjamin F. Peixotto, and Simon Rosendale tried to exclude all rabbis (including Gottheil) from the executive committee. "There seemed to be but one opinion prevailing about the rabbis," the Baltimore physician Aaron Friedenwald wrote at that time, "and it was not a very flattering one. Apparently their influence is at a low ebb."[56] In 1892, at the establishment of the American Jewish Historical Society, tensions between

53. *Chronicles of the Rabbis*, 1. 54. *Ibid.*, 5. 55. *Ibid.*, 3.

56. Quoted in Jonathan D. Sarna, *JPS: The Americanization of Jewish Culture, 1888–1988* (Philadelphia: Jewish Publication Society, 1988), 22.

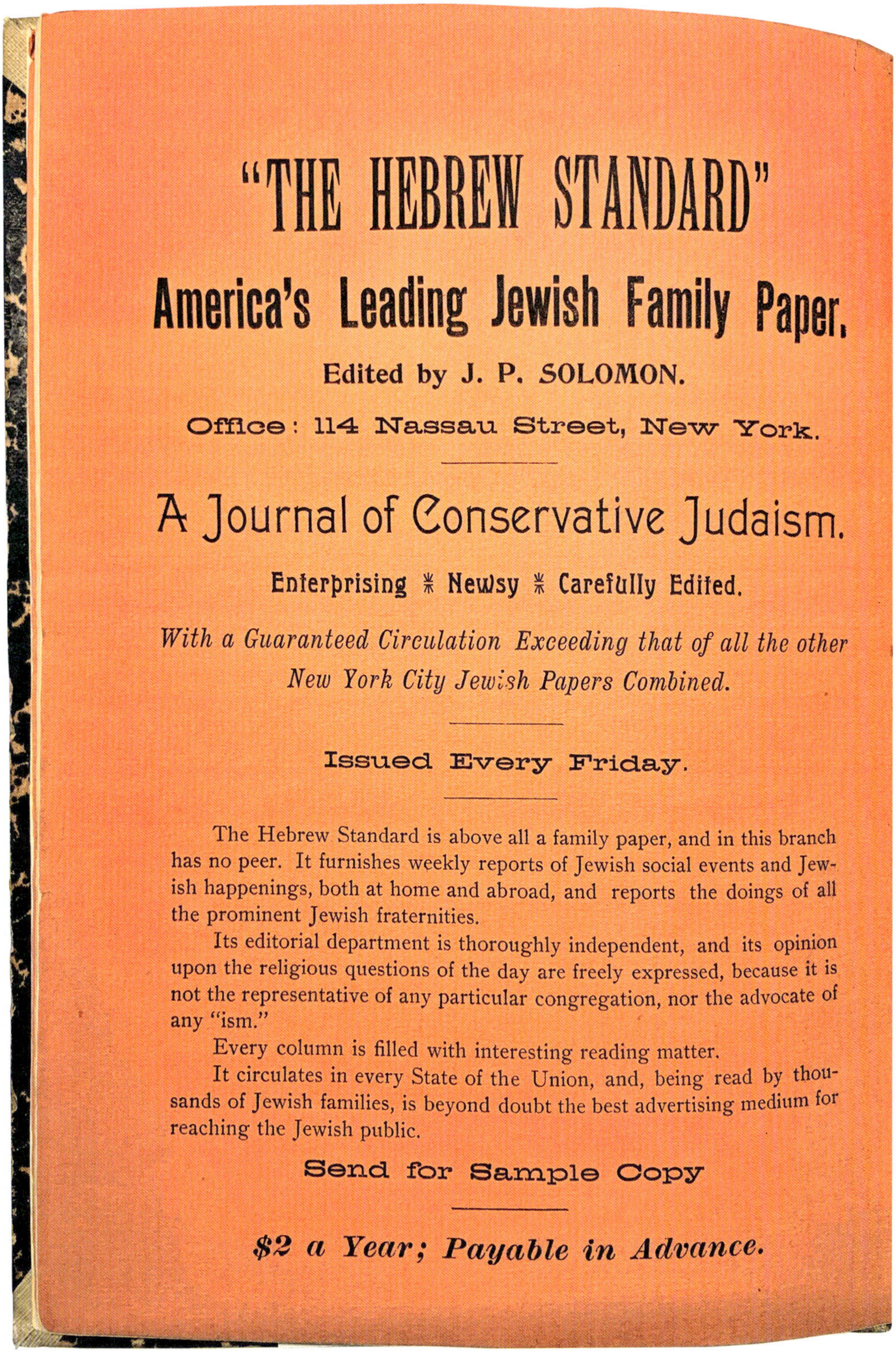

"THE HEBREW STANDARD"

America's Leading Jewish Family Paper.

Edited by J. P. SOLOMON.

Office: 114 Nassau Street, New York.

A Journal of Conservative Judaism.

Enterprising * Newsy * Carefully Edited.

With a Guaranteed Circulation Exceeding that of all the other New York City Jewish Papers Combined.

Issued Every Friday.

The Hebrew Standard is above all a family paper, and in this branch has no peer. It furnishes weekly reports of Jewish social events and Jewish happenings, both at home and abroad, and reports the doings of all the prominent Jewish fraternities.

Its editorial department is thoroughly independent, and its opinion upon the religious questions of the day are freely expressed, because it is not the representative of any particular congregation, nor the advocate of any "ism."

Every column is filled with interesting reading matter.

It circulates in every State of the Union, and, being read by thousands of Jewish families, is beyond doubt the best advertising medium for reaching the Jewish public.

Send for Sample Copy

$2 a Year; Payable in Advance.

Fig. 71. Announcement for the *Hebrew Standard* on the final page of *The Chronicles of the Rabbis* (New York, 1897). (Center for Jewish History, New York).

the laity and the clergy flared again when rabbis once more found themselves excluded from leadership. "Clergymen simply are treated by the Jews in a way that they must feel as if the pew and the pulpit are in antagonism," Kaufmann Kohler angrily protested at that time. While rabbis complained that Jews "instinctively" feared "clerical rule," lay leaders faulted the new class of rabbis for their foreignness, ignorance, pomposity, and most of all, their alleged inability to work together for the sake of the Jewish community.[57]

Philadelphia, long a center of Quaker anticlericalism, became the center of Jewish anticlericalism.[58] One of the city's foremost lay leaders, the lawyer, businessman, and politician Moses Aaron Dropsie (1821–1905), in an anti-Reform screed entitled *On Deform in Judaism* (1895), excoriated the rabbis of his day even more harshly than Solomon would, though the substance of their indictments ran parallel:

> Most of the rabbis who have studied in the United States possess a superficial education in Judaism, many of them appear to be excellent business men who have assumed the clerical profession because it is pecuniarily more profitable, or because they deem it more dignified and influential. Instead of discoursing upon and explaining the Scriptures and descanting on the doctrine and history of Judaism, and its great heroes and sages, they entertain their flocks with novelties, and emanations of wild imaginations, undisciplined by mental culture, and discourse eloquently or glibly on most any subject matter, which they borrow from the writings of eminent or popular authors, to whom they give no credit.[59]

Rather than advance the education of rabbis, Dropsie, through his will, created a secular college, long known as Dropsie College, "for the promotion of and instruction in the Hebrew and cognate languages and their respective literatures and in the Rabbinical learning and literature." Tellingly, he established the college to train a wide range of students without "distinction on account of creed, color, or sex." Not one of those he named as governors of the new college was a rabbi.[60]

57. Nathan M. Kaganoff, "AJHS at 90: Reflections on the Oldest Ethnic Historical Society in America," *American Jewish History* 71, no. 4 (1982): 473–74. For other sources on Jewish anticlericalism in this period, see Sarna, *JPS*, 302nn37–40.

58. Jonathan D. Sarna, "The Making of an American Jewish Culture," in *When Philadelphia Was the Capital of Jewish America*, ed. Murray Friedman (Philadelphia: Balch Institute Press, 1993), 151. Scult, "Schechter's Seminary," 55–56, notes that "anticlericalism was widespread among most of the 'conspirators' who founded the new Seminary" in 1902, including Philadelphians Solomon Solis-Cohen, Mayer Sulzberger, and Cyrus Adler.

59. Moses A. Dropsie, *On Deform in Judaism, and on the Study of Hebrew* (Philadelphia: Billstein & Son, 1895), 2.

60. "Last Will and Testament of Moses A. Dropsie" (1905), copy in the possession of the au-

While anticlericalism would continue to factor in American Jewish life, especially in Philadelphia, by 1897 leaders and journalists like Solomon understood that in New York, learned laymen like himself would never actually dislodge rabbinic authority figures. He personally liked and admired Temple Emanu-El's Gottheil and opened the pages of the *Hebrew Standard* to him.[61] Even though his newspaper might continue to satirize and "chronicle" rabbinic pretensions, he conceded, through the voice of "Frederick the tiller of the soil," that rabbis would remain a permanent fixture on the American Jewish scene:

Let the press then waste its paper,
It's only mere passing vapor
That quickly fades away.
It may laugh at our Judaism
Overwhelm us with its criticism
We're here to stay—for pay.[62]

Yet, even as he acknowledged that rabbis were "here to stay," Solomon vented against the "Amhaaratzim" (Hebrew/Yiddish for ignoramuses), those who had not studied, as Gottheil and Kohler had, at traditional yeshivot and European universities. Because he, like his fellow lawyer Dropsie, possessed substantial Jewish learning, he considered rabbinic ignorance particularly unforgivable. As he put it, he "despised the Amhaaratzim, having sworn in his wrath: I will utterly put out the remembrance of every Amhaaretz Rabbi from under heaven."[63] He failed to appreciate that, in America, multiple models of the ministry existed, some focused on education and scholarship, some on social justice and organizational talent, and some on pastoral skills and "genius for friendship."[64] Among Jews, as among Protestants, the latter two models were gaining in popularity, while learned scholars often failed in the pulpit.

Solomon singled out for attack the jovial Rabbi Maurice H. Harris (1859–1930) of Temple Israel, who, he alleged, not only "belonged to the tribe of the Amhaaratzim," but was also "a chief thereof." Harris, whom Gottheil had ordained in New York, was the son of a British rabbi and had transformed his New York

---

thor. For the politics surrounding the creation of Dropsie College, see Herbert A. Parzen, "New Data on the Formation of Dropsie College," *Jewish Social Studies* 28, no. 3 (1966): 131–47.

61. See the German poem published in the *Hebrew Standard*, July 3, 1885, reprinted in Gottheil, *Life of Gustav Gottheil*, 148.

62. *Chronicles of the Rabbis*, 5.

63. *Ibid.*, 11, employing the language used in Deuteronomy against the wicked Amalekites; see Deut. 25:19.

64. Holifield, *God's Ambassadors*, 158–64.

congregation from the Orthodox Hand in Hand Synagogue to the Reform Temple Israel.[65] Solomon believed that Harris "knew within his soul that he was a transgressor of the statutes and ordinances which the Lord had given unto his forefathers." He also claimed that Harris was ignorant of "the language of the Jews" (that is, Hebrew). For his part, Harris called upon Jews to boycott the *Hebrew Standard*, earning him the sobriquet "Maurice the Chief of the boycotters" in the *Chronicles*. As if to underscore the chasm that yawned between rabbis of the Harris type and learned European-trained scholarly rabbis like Kaufmann Kohler, Solomon imagined a conversation between them:

> [KOHLER:] Canst thou love the Torah when thou disregardest its precepts, or know aught of its wisdom, when thou art unable to read it, for art thou not of the Amhaaratzim?
>
> [HARRIS:] Verily, thou art of the past, and darkeneth counsel by words without knowledge.
>
> As the yoke of bondage was removed from our fathers when they went up out of the land of Egypt, even so has the yoke of the Torah been removed from us, the Rabbis of to-day, by the magic spell of Reform.
>
> Why should we study the Torah, when we believe not in its commands?[66]

Harris, in Solomon's telling, went on to remind Kohler that his own reforms, such as deriding the "sacred word" of God through biblical criticism, changing the Sabbath day from Saturday to Sunday, and describing circumcision as a "relic of barbarism," lay the groundwork for the road that younger rabbis now traveled. "If we have sinned," he told Kohler, "we have but followed thy example; if we are ignorant of the Law and the language of our fathers, it is because thou and thy school of prophets declare, that the Torah in this land has lost its significance and that Hebrew in our prayers is unnecessary." Kohler, at least in the satire, conceded the point. He "smote his breast and exclaimed, 'I have sinned!'"[67]

The tension between "learned" European-trained rabbis and "ignorant" American-trained ones who promoted new models of the rabbinate played out across the United States in the late nineteenth century, particularly as young English-speaking graduates of Hebrew Union College bid to succeed retiring European-trained rabbis, most of whom (unlike Gottheil) had never mastered

65. "The Rev. Dr. Maurice H. Harris of New York," *Israel: The Jewish Magazine* 3 (1900): 127–29; "Harris, Maurice Henry," *Universal Jewish Encyclopedia*, 10 vols. (New York: Universal Jewish Encyclopedia, Inc., 1939–1943), 5:219.

66. *Chronicles of the Rabbis*, 8.

67. *Ibid.*, 9.

English. Dropsie's fulminations against "rabbis who have studied in the United States" reflected that tension. The noted Baltimore rabbi Benjamin Szold was pensioned off in 1892 because younger members of his congregation felt "that the services of an English-speaking rabbi, trained in this country, would be preferable."[68] Philadelphia's Rabbi Marcus Jastrow was forced to retire that same year, likewise in favor of an English-speaking, American-trained rabbi far less learned than himself (the much beloved Henry Berkowitz of the first graduating class of Hebrew Union College).[69] Where leading urban congregations once prided themselves on the erudition and scholarly accomplishments of their rabbis, now an increasing number sought just what some reformers associated with Hebrew Union College looked to produce: "sensible, practical, American men who would understand the people."[70]

This same tension, of course, was playing out in Temple Emanu-El of New York between the aging Gustav Gottheil and the young Joseph Silverman. Though carefully hidden in official accounts of the dinner, Solomon gave it substantial play. He dubbed Silverman "Joseph the Trilbyite," recalling the rabbi's infamous sermon, and dismissed "Joseph" as both ignorant and contentious. Into his mouth he placed a satirical defense of New Pulpit ideas, couched in a love poem to the enchanting Trilby herself:

> Why should I preach upon religious themes,
> Which are at best but foolish dreams,
> Why speak of heaven or talk of Paradise,
> When thou standeth lovely before my eyes?
>
> Why not inhale the fragrance of thy roses
> Nor waste the time to sermonize on Moses,
> Is not the remembrance of thy own sweet Alice,
> Better far than those of Tsitsis or of Tallis?[71]

Solomon did not lambast all of the young rabbis he mentioned in his *Chronicles*. The young Stephen S. Wise, at age twenty-three then serving as rabbi at

68. Alexandra Lee Levin, *The Szolds of Lombard Street: A Baltimore Family, 1859–1909* (Philadelphia: Jewish Publication Society of America, 1960), 280.

69. Michal Galas, *Rabbi Marcus Jastrow and His Vision for the Reform of Judaism: A Study in the History of Judaism in the Nineteenth Century* (Brighton, Mass.: Academic Studies Press, 2013), 126–28, 205–8.

70. Rabbi Max Heller, as quoted in Michael A. Meyer, "A Centennial History" in *Hebrew Union College–Jewish Institute of Religion at One Hundred Years*, ed. Samuel E. Karff (Cincinnati: Hebrew Union College Press, 1976), 50.

71. *Chronicles of the Rabbis*, 13–14.

B'nai Jeshurun, and thirty-year-old Rudolph Grossman, the rabbi of Rodeph Sholom (where he succeeded Stephen Wise's father, Aaron Wise, upon his death in 1896), received far better treatment at his hands. Solomon portrayed Wise ("Stephen the Younger"), even if but a mere "stripling," as an effective organizer, diplomat, and peacemaker. To Grossman ("Rudolph the Rodefer"), a graduate of Hebrew Union College, he offered even higher praise, describing him as "a young man of passing merit and of great understanding."[72] The fact that both men were born abroad, children of learned, European-trained rabbis, and, in 1897, still conservative in their religious orientations likely influenced these judgments. Later, both men moved into the Reform camp.[73]

The gallant hero of Solomon's account was the Orthodox Bernard Drachman ("Bernhard the Zichronite"). Drachman, who was American-born and thoroughly at home in the English language, "did not walk in the ways of Joseph the Trilbyite," Solomon admiringly noted. He instead represented a synthesis of Orthodoxy and modernity: he held degrees from Columbia University, the Jewish Theological Seminary of Breslau, and the University of Heidelberg. His Orthodox congregation, Zichron Ephraim (today the Park East Synagogue), founded in 1890 and located on New York's Upper East Side, demonstrated by its very existence that Orthodoxy and bourgeois American life could march hand in hand. Drachman had studied under Gottheil as a teenager, his further education in Germany had been supported by Temple Emanu-El, and he was a proud member of the New York Board of Jewish Ministers, so it was understandable that he attended the kosher dinner in his teacher's honor. Yet, when he stood up to praise "Episcopus" in an eight-stanza poem sung to the tune of "Tit-Willow" in Gilbert and Sullivan's wildly successful 1885 comic opera, *The Mikado*, he found himself, Balaam-like, condemning the honoree for abandoning so much of Jewish tradition. The final chapter and single longest poem in Solomon's *Chronicles* found "Bernhard the Zichronite" pondering (but leaving unresolved) the paradox of how Gottheil could break the Sabbath, cut off "all the troublesome things in the law," relish oysters, "smile for the Gentile," "pocket ten thousand a year," and yet be such a "good fellow." A characteristic stanza seethes:

72. *Ibid.*, 4.

73. On the young Stephen Wise and his father, Aaron Wise, see Robert D. Shapiro, *A Reform Rabbi in the Progressive Era: The Early Career of Stephen S. Wise* (New York: Garland, 1988), 10–40. On Ignatz Grossman, see Morris A. Gutstein, *A Priceless Heritage: The Epic Growth of Nineteenth-Century Chicago Jewry* (New York: Bloch, 1953), 123, and for his family, Charles Reznikoff, "Grossman, an American Family of Rabbis," *Universal Jewish Encyclopedia*, 5:105–6.

The tallis like poison or Hebrew he shuns.
Good fellow, good fellow, good fellow:
And all hats are removed by this biggest of guns,
This good fellow, good fellow, good fellow.
In his temple he teaches his numerous band.
Bare-neck'd and bare-faced and bare-headed to stand.
Like the Goyim that visit each church in the land.
Good fellow, good fellow, good fellow.[74]

Solomon concluded *Chronicles of the Rabbis* with the fantasy that Gottheil, at seventy, would renew his vigor and become "like unto a young man." A jesting compliment, the phrase also reflected a deep truth: the post–Civil War New York Jewish community that both men had known for most of their adult lives stood on the cusp of change. Massive east European Jewish immigration, generational change, the widening gap between religious conservatives and liberals within Judaism, the Americanization of the rabbinate pitting European-trained rabbis against those trained in the United States, changing conceptions of what a rabbi should be, the debate over Zionism, and the ongoing tensions between rabbis and lay leaders fractured and transformed Judaism in New York over the next generation. Looking back, the dinner celebrating Gustav Gottheil's seventieth birthday in 1897 marked the end of an era.

74. *Chronicles of the Rabbis*, 14–15.

APPENDIX

The Chronicles of the Rabbis

BEING AN ACCOUNT OF A BANQUET TENDERED
TO "EPISCOPUS" BY THE RABBIS OF
NEW YORK CITY UPON THE
ANNIVERSARY OF HIS
70TH BIRTHDAY

BY

"BEN. F. RAYIM."

DEDICATED TO "EPISCOPUS"

1897

HEBREW STANDARD PRINT.

DRAMATIS PERSONAE[1]

(Written by "Ben F. Rayim," J. P. Solomon, Editor of the "Hebrew Standard.")

Episcopus — Gustave Gottheil.

Joseph the Trilbyite — Joseph Silverman. "Trilby" was the text of a Sabbath sermon.

Frederick the Tiller of the Soil — Frederick de Sola Mendes, a gentleman farmer at New Rochelle.

Falk the Bikur-Cholemite — Falk Vidaver of Congregation Beth Israel Bikur Cholim.

Bernard the Zichronite — Bernard Drachman of Congregation Zichron Ephraim.

Maurice the Chief of the Boycotters — Maurice H. Harris of Temple Israel.

Kaufman the Bethelite — Kaufman Kohler of Temple Beth-El.

Raphael the Benjamite — Raphael Benjamin of Shaar Hashomayim (now Central Synagogue).

Western Pope — Isaac Mayer Wise.

Rudolph the Rodefer — Rudolph Grossman of Temple Rodeph Sholem.

William the Chief Musician of the Temple — William Sparger, Cantor of Temple Emanu-El.

Adolph of the Assuremites — A. H. Radin.

Stephen the Younger — Stephen S. Wise.

(All the above, with the exception of Isaac Mayer Wise, were occupants of pulpits in or near New York City in 1897 when these "Chronicles" were written.)

---

1. This typed page appears only in the copy at Hebrew Union College–Jewish Institute of Religion, Cincinnati, where it was pasted in. Some of the spellings in the list do not match those used in the text. In handwriting at the top of the page, the following was scrawled: "Compiled by Rabbi Saul P. Appelbaum with the expert help of Wm. J. Solomon, son of J. P. Solomon and former publisher of the 'Hebrew Standard' and Comptroller of Central Synagogue, New York." Many thanks to Dr. David Gilner for making a scan available to me.

CHAPTER I.

1. Now it came to pass when Episcopus[2] was the chief ruler of the Rabbis of the City of Gotham.[3]
2. And the Rabbis were pious servants of the Lord, and their love for each other exceeded that of the love of David and Jonathan,[4] and jealousy and envy were unknown between them.
3. And they said one to another: Behold the number of the years of our chief, even Episcopus, will soon be three score and ten, and for piety he standeth like Saul the son of Kish,[5] head and shoulders above all the other Rabbis of the congregations of Israel.
4. Now let us gather and prepare a banquet in his honor, whose splendor shall exceed the feast of Ahashverosh which he made unto all his princes and servants, even in the third year of his reign.[6]
5. That our hearts be made glad while we eat of the fat of the land,[7] and our souls be made merry with wine and strong drink.[8]
6. And the thing seemed good in their eyes; and they said unto Joseph the Trilbyite[9] and unto the young man Stephen,[10] and unto Frederick the tiller of the soil:[11] Prepare ye unto us a banquet that we may do honor unto Episcopus; and they enjoined upon them that the drinking be without compulsion, to do according to the pleasure of every man.[12]
7. And straightways they prepared the feast, but did not provide any of the creeping things and other abominations with which the Rabbis who had forsaken the laws of their forefathers delighted in.
8. For they said each unto the other, Behold Pereira of the house of Mendes,[13] and Falk the Bikurcholemite[14] and Bernhard the Zichronite[15] will not eat of the abominations of the idols, why should we offend them? And the thing seemed good in their eyes.

2. Gustav Gottheil (1827–1903); see Richard Gottheil, *The Life of Gustav Gottheil: Memoir of a Priest in Israel* (Williamsport, Pa.: Bayard Press, 1936).

3. "Gotham" ("goat town") was an Anglo-Saxon name for New York City popularized by Washington Irving. Residents of the original Gotham, near Nottingham, England, were considered "wise fools" in the Middle Ages. Irving used the name to suggest a city of self-important but foolish people. See Irving Lewis Allen, "Gotham," *The Encyclopedia of New York City*, ed. Kenneth T. Jackson (New Haven: Yale University Press, 1995), 475.

4. 1 Samuel 18.

5. 1 Samuel 9:2.

6. Esther 1:3–5.

7. Genesis 45:18.

8. Deuteronomy 14:26.

9. Joseph Silverman (1860–1930); see Edna Nahshon, "The Pulpit and the Stage: Rabbi Joseph Silverman and the Actor's Church Alliance," *American Jewish History* 91, no. 1 (2003): 5–27. *Trilby*, George du Maurier's bestselling 1894 novel, features a wicked Jewish hypnotist named Svengali and the beautiful model Trilby, whose singing voice he controlled; Silverman delivered a sermon on that novel.

10. Stephen S. Wise (1874–1949); on his early career, see Robert D. Shapiro, *A Reform Rabbi in the Progressive Era: The Early Career of Stephen S. Wise* (New York: Garland, 1988).

11. Frederick de Sola Mendes (1850–1927); see Moshe Davis, *The Emergence of Conservative Judaism: The Historical School in 19th-Century America* (Philadelphia: Jewish Publication Society, 1965), 349–51.

12. Esther 1:8.

13. Henry Pereira Mendes (1852–1937) of Congregation Shearith Israel, New York, a founder of the New York Board of Jewish Ministers; see Eugene Markovitz, "Henry Pereira Mendes: Architect of the Union of Orthodox Jewish Congregations of America," *American Jewish Historical Quarterly* 55, no. 6 (1966): 364–84. Like Gottheil, Mendes served a congregation in Manchester, England, before being called to the United States, but they did not overlap.

14. Falk Vidaver (1845–1909); see *New York Times*, December 16, 1895, 3, and October 6, 1909, 9.

15. Bernard Drachman (1861–1945); see his autobiography, *The Unfailing Light: Memoirs of an American Rabbi* (New York: Rabbinical Council of America, 1948), and Jeffrey S. Gurock, "From Exception to Role Model: Bernard Drachman and the Evolution of Jewish Religious Life in America, 1880–1920," *American Jewish History* 76, no. 4 (1987): 456–84.

9. And when the tidings reached Maurice the chief of the boycotters,[16] he lifted up his voice and exclaimed, "Rot!"; for he knew within his soul, that he was a transgressor of the statutes and ordinances which the Lord had given unto his forefathers.
10. And unto Episcopus, it was as the savor of sweet frankincense, and his soul rejoiced that he should be chosen as the man whom his brethren delighted to honor.
11. And he communed within himself in the silent watches of the night[17] and said: Wherewith shall my stomach be satisfied, for the food which they will set before me is strange unto me, and of which I have not partaken for years, and my heart delighteth not therein.
12. But Episcopus was wise in his generation and kept his own counsel.

CHAPTER II.

1. And when the Rabbis heard of the feast, some of them were in sore travail, for they said: Whence shall come my help,[18] for I have neither gold nor silver, and my lot is cast among those who have not been blessed with an abundance of riches. How can I go up unto the feast when there are no shekels in my purse?
2. But, nevertheless, they put on a bold face and clothed themselves in clean shirts and went unto the feast, for they said, "The Lord will provide."[19]
3. And there assembled all the Rabbis of Gotham and the City of Churches,[20] both great and small, from Kaufman the Bethelite,[21] who was learned in the books and writings of the Jews, to Alexander[22] of the tribe of Amhaaratzim[23] who knew not the difference between one Hebrew letter and another.
4. And they washed their hands and sat around the table, and Raphael the Benjaminite[24] broke bread and made a blessing.
5. Now Raphael the Benjaminite, was the handsomest Rabbi in the city, and the daughters of Zion worshiped him for his beauty, and he was the desire of their souls, even as the hart panteth after the water brooks,[25] so they longed after him.
6. And he was white and ruddy, distinguished among ten thousand, and the Rabbis were envious of his beauty.
7. His head was bright as the finest gold, and his locks were once like waving foliage tinged with the brightness of the sun at the going down thereof.

16. Maurice H. Harris (1859–1930); see "The Rev. Dr. Maurice H. Harris of New York," *Israel: The Jewish Magazine* 3 (1900): 127–29, and "Harris, Maurice Henry," *Universal Jewish Encyclopedia*, 10 vols (New York: Universal Jewish Encyclopedia, Inc., 1939–1943), 5:219.

17. For the history of this phrase, see https://en.wikipedia.org/wiki/Watches_of_the_Night.

18. Psalms 121:1.

19. Genesis 22:14 (King James translation).

20. New York was one of a number of cities that bore this moniker. It was bestowed by journalist James D. McCabe Jr., *Lights and Shadows of New York Life, or, The Sights and Sensations of the Great City* (Philadelphia: National Publishing Company, 1872), 491. In 1890, the New York City Directory listed 450 churches and synagogues.

21. Kaufmann Kohler (1843–1926); see his "Personal Reminiscences," in his *Studies, Addresses and Personal Papers* (New York: Bloch, 1931), 469–80, and Joseph L. Blau's introduction to the reprint edition of Kohler's *Jewish Theology, Systematically and Historically Considered* (New York: KTAV, 1968), xi–xli.

22. Louis A. Alexander (1853?–1913); in 1897 he served as the rabbi of Atereth Ts'bi (Ateres Zwie) congregation in Manhattan. He subsequently held numerous East Coast pulpits and is best remembered as the first Jew to serve as a chaplain in a Massachusetts penal institution; see *Jewish Advocate*, January 2, 1914, 1.

23. Hebrew/Yiddish for "ignoramuses."

24. Raphael Benjamin (1846–1906); see *Universal Jewish Encyclopedia*, 2:185.

25. Psalms 42:2.

8. His cheeks were as a bed of spices, as turrets of sweet perfumes; his lips, like lilies, dropping with fluid myrrh.[26]
9. And he said unto himself, I will bare my head that they may see my manly brow, and their souls be eaten up with envy of my beauty. And he uncovered his head before making the blessing over the bread.
10. And Bernhard the Zichronite waxed wroth when he saw it, for it was not seeming in his eyes and was an offense unto him, but Episcopus winked the other eye.[27]
11. And they feasted and made merry, and stuffed themselves with stuffed squabs,[28] and sweetened their palates with sweetbreads.
12. While yet they were eating, the countenance of Kaufman the Bethelite fell, and he was consumed with anger, and he said unto Joseph the Trilbyite and Stephen the young man and Frederick the tiller of the soil, who had prepared the feast according to the commands given unto them: Is it not enough that we have a Western Pope,[29] why make ye now unto yourselves strange gods and set them up that the people may make obeisance?
13. And they were sorely distressed, for they wot not what sin they had committed, and they said unto him: wherewith have thy servants offended, my lord, and why is thine anger enkindled against us?[30]
14. And Kaufman the Bethelite, put his hand within his bosom, and took therefrom a menu card, on which was written what was to be eaten, least[31]—as Joseph the Trilbyite and Stephen the young man and Frederick the tiller of the soil, unto whom was entrusted the preparation of the feast—said, the Rabbis might over-eat themselves and be unable to expound the Law, as is their custom upon the Sabbath.
15. And he showed them the words, "Sorbet a la Cardinal"[32] written thereon, and with a loud voice and with exceeding wroth said: "Have we then a Cardinal among us, who shall go forth before the people with garments dyed red even as Edom?"[33]
16. And Stephen the young man came near unto him, and said: "Pardon, my lord, let thy servant, I pray thee, speak a word in my lord's ears, and let not thy anger burn against thy servants; for thou art greater than Episcopus.[34]
17. The sorbet is but a cooling portion, to cool the fierce fire of the Rabbis, who burn to study the Law, and thou knowest, that Episcopus burneth neither for the Law nor for the Prophets.

26. Song of Songs 5:11–13.

27. "Wisdom may smile, but Cunning can't | She winks the other eye"; see *Punch*, October 24, 1891, 204.

28. For the history of squab (pigeon) in Jewish cuisine, see "pigeon" in Gil Marks, *Encyclopedia of Jewish Food* (New York: John Wiley, 2010), 460–61.

29. Isaac Mayer Wise (1819–1900) of Cincinnati; see Sefton D. Temkin, *Isaac Mayer Wise: Shaping American Judaism* (Liverpool: Littman Library, 1992).

30. A play on lines from *The Confessions of Ste. Augustine, Bishop of Hippo*, translated and annotated by J. G. Pilkington (Edinburgh: T. & T. Clarke, 1876), 99 (chap. 10).

31. i.e., lest (?)

32. Sorbet à la cardinal, or cardinal sherbert, was a popular turn-of-the-century dessert made with raspberry pulp; it was the approximate color of a Catholic cardinal's *zucchetto*. For the recipe, see Adolphe Meyer, *The Post-Graduate Cookery Book* (New York: Caterer Publishing Company, 1903), 269.

33. "Edom" means red in Hebrew. According to the Bible, Edom is Esau, who was ruddy from birth (Genesis 25:25, 36:1).

34. Genesis 44:18. The passage hints at rivalry between Kohler and Gottheil, the city's foremost Reform rabbis.

18. Let this thing pass, I pray thee, for if it be told to Solomon the scribe,[35] (exterminated be his name and remembrance!)[36] we shall soon become as a proverb and a byword to the people; for his pen stingeth like a scorpion and biteth like an adder,[37] and he has no regard for the servants of the Lord, and respecteth neither their pulpits nor their salaries.["]
19. And Stephen the young man became unto him like unto the one who appeased the destroying angel upon the threshing floor of Ornan the Jebusite.[38]
20. And the anger of Kaufman the Bethelite disappeared, even as the passing cloud upon the face of the heavens, and he sat himself once more among his brethren.
21. Now are not all these things written in the Chronicles of the Rabbis even unto this day?[39]

35. Jacob Philip (J. P.) Solomon (1838–1909), editor of the *Hebrew Standard* and author of these *Chronicles*. By inserting himself into his own narrative, Solomon made clear that he knew what many a rabbi thought of him.

36. On this curse, usually applied to enemies of the Jewish people, see https://en.wikipedia.org/wiki/Yimakh_shemo.

37. Proverbs 23:32.

38. 1 Chronicles 21:15.

39. 1 Kings 15:7.

CHAPTER III.

1. Now it came to pass that when the feast was nigh ended, that Rudolph the Rodefer[40] arose from his seat among the brethren and said: Young am I in days, and ye are very old; therefore I hesitated and feared to show you what I knew.
2. I had said, Days shall speak, and multitude of years shall make wisdom known.[41]
3. Not those rich in years must always be wise; neither do the aged constantly understand what is just.
4. Therefore do I say, Hearken unto me, for inasmuch as it is written that in the multitude of counsel there is wisdom,[42] so likewise in the multitude of Rabbis there should be some piety.
5. Let us therefore return thanks unto the Lord for the good things we have eaten, for the strong drink wherewith we have strengthened ourselves, and for Episcopus whom we have honored.
6. And Episcopus communed within himself and said: Verily, this is a young man of passing merit and of great understanding.
7. And when Maurice the boycotter heard the words of Rudolph the Rodefer, he lifted up his voice and exclaimed, "Rats!" for he was afraid that he might be called upon to pronounce the blessing, and he knew not the language of the Jews in which it should be spoken, for he belonged to the tribe of the Amhaaratzim and was a chief thereof.
8. And Stephen the young man went unto Pereira of the

40. Rudolph Grossman (1867–1927); see Charles Reznikoff, "Grossman, an American Family of Rabbis," *Universal Jewish Encyclopedia*, 5:105–6.

41. Job 32:7.

42. Proverbs 11:14.

house of Mendes, and he answered and said: The Rabbis do not understand the speech of their forefathers, verily they are as the Ephraimites, who fought against Jephthah in his battle with the Midianites at the crossing of the fords of the river Jordan, and cannot frame their tongues to pronounce the words, and he refused.[43]

9. And Stephen the younger went to Bernhard the Zichronite, and he answered and said: Is thy servant a Chazan[44] that he should do this thing? and he also refused.

10. And Stephen the younger went to William the chief musician of the Temple,[45] and he consented to *bensch*.[46] And Maurice the boycotter said to him, "Cut it short," for his soul within him fretted, for it was to him as a strange tongue, for he was not learned in the seventy languages[47] taught by the Western Pope in his school at Porkopolis,[48] being of the Amhaaratzim.

11. And William the chief musician of the Temple also uncovered his head when he said the blessing, that they might gaze upon his locks and see his beauty, but the Rabbis, from Kaufman the Bethelite even unto Alexander of the tribe of the Amhaaratzim, exclaimed with accord: There is none like Raphael the Benjaminite for comeliness and beauty, and William the chief musician of the Temple bowed his head for shame, and mourned and refused to be comforted.[49]

CHAPTER IV.

1. Now after these things had happened,[50] Frederick the tiller of the soil, and Falk the Bikurcholemite, and Alexander of the tribe of Amhaaratzim took their harps in their hands.
2. And Adolph of the Asuremites,[51] took also his manicure.
3. And all the Rabbis surrounded them like bees and said unto them, O sing to us a new song that we may make ourselves merry, sing unto us of the glories and greatness of Episcopus;[52] for they were known to be of the sweet singers of Israel.[53]
4. And Frederick the tiller of the soil, sat at the head of the table, and taking his harp in his hands, lifted up his voice and sang:

> Somewhat of a poet,
> Although you may not know it,
> And my thoughts run readily into rhyme.
> Why, even in my slumbers,

43. Judges 12:6.

44. "Cantor" (Hebrew).

45. William Sparger (1860–1904), cantor and music director at Temple Emanu-El in New York; see Neil W. Levin, "William Sparger," https://www.milkenarchive.org/artists/view/william-sparger/.

46. Literally "to bless" (Yiddish), but when used without any qualifier, as here, implies to say the grace after meals; see http://www.balashon.com/2006/11/bensch.html.

47. Jewish tradition, based upon Genesis 10, holds that there are seventy nations and languages in the world; see "Nations and Languages, The Seventy," *Jewish Encyclopaedia*, 12 vols. (New York: Funk & Wagnall's, 1901–1906), 9:188–90.

48. Harris had not attended Hebrew Union College in Cincinnati (by coincidence, the largest pork-producing city in the world for several decades prior to the Civil War), but was ordained instead by Gottheil. On Porkopolis, see Liz Gray, "Porkopolis: Cincinnati's Pork-Producing Past," https://www.greatamericancountry.com/places/local-life/porkopolis-cincinnatis-pork-producing-past.

49. Psalms 77:3. Sparger may have suffered from bipolar disorder. He attempted suicide in fall 1903 and subsequently disappeared; see the *Philadelphia Inquirer*, October 18, 1903, 1, and *New York Times*, November 6, 1903, 1.

50. See, for example, Ezra 7:1.

51. Adolph M. Radin (1848–1909); among other posts, he served as chaplain of all penal institutions in New York and Brooklyn. "Asurem" derives from the Hebrew word for "prisoners" or "captives"; on Radin, see Nathan Stern, "Obituary Address—Adolph Moses Radin," *Year Book of the Central Conference of American Rabbis* 19 (1909): 424–31.

52. Psalms 95:1, 96:1.

53. 2 Samuel 23:1.

I dream in rhythmic numbers
As the golden stairs I climb.

And while I make no pretensions
To tenses and declensions,
I'm quite at ease with tropes.[54]
Although a Rabbi by profession
I must make you this confession
That I know full well the ropes.

Some people may belie us,
And think we're not as pious
As Rabbis surely ought to be.
That we preach but do not practice,
While all know the simple fact is
That we must draw our salary.

Whether Union Prayer Book or Tefillah,[55]
Sefer Torah, Tehillim or Megillah,[56]
They're all alike to me.
That its better to doff the Tallis[57]
Then continually cope with "dalles,"[58]
With me you must agree.

Let the press then waste its paper,
It's only mere passing vapor
That quickly fades away.
It may laugh at our Judaism
Overwhelm us with its criticism
We're here to stay—for pay.

While we mount our swift Pegasus
With the Parnass to Parnassus,[59]
How the Kehillah[60] nods and becks,
They know not what we believe,
But we all laugh in our sleeve,
For we all believe in cheques.

The pattern on the Mount
Is surely no account
To the Rabbi of modern days.
Episcopus' example
To us is full and ample
How a big salary to raise.

5. And when Frederick the tiller of the soil had ended his song, a shout of great joy went up from the Rabbis,
6. For they knew not that his voice was as sweet as the droppings of honey from the honey comb.[61]

54. Tropes are traditional musical notations for chanting the various biblical books; see https://en.wikipedia.org/wiki/Hebrew_cantillation.

55. The Reform *Union Prayer-Book for Jewish Worship* (1895) and the Orthodox prayer book, *Tefilot Yisra'el* (1848/9); see Sharona R. Wachs, *American Jewish Liturgies* (Cincinnati: Hebrew Union College Press, 1997).

56. Pentateuch, Psalms, Scrolls—books in the Hebrew Bible.

57. Traditional prayer shawl, discarded by many Reform congregations by the late nineteenth century.

58. Poverty (Hebrew/Yiddish).

59. The winged horse Pegasus, in Greek mythology, lives on Mt. Parnassus, the home of poetry, music, and learning. Parnass is the traditional Hebrew name for the congregational president.

60. Congregation or community (Hebrew).

61. Song of Songs 4:11.

7. And they exclaimed with a loud voice: Great is Frederick the tiller of the soil.
8. And he answered and said, Nay, brethren, none is great but Episcopus.
9. And Episcopus smiled, and pulled down his vest.

CHAPTER V.

1. And Frederick the tiller of the soil, again lifted up his voice[62] and said unto his brethren, unloosen your girdles and be merry, for this is the night dedicated to Episcopus, let us rejoice therein.[63]
2. From the fat meadows have I come unto you, and my hair is yet wet with early dew.[64]
3. Like the waters flowing from Kedron[65] doth my soul murmur with delight, yea even as the banks of the Jordon overfloweth when the windows of heaven are opened and the rain descendeth therein, so doth my heart overflow with gladness.
4. Happy are ye, o ye teachers in Israel, yea thrice happy art thou, o Episcopus, in the sunshine of whose smiles we are permitted to bask.
5. Like unto the mighty cedar of Lebanon art thou, o Episcopus, for all the teachers in Israel look up unto thee.[66]
6. Like unto the lily of the valley[67] art thou, o Episcopus, for thy fragrance rejoiceth the earth.
7. Thou art verily a "Sun and Shield"[68] to thy brethren, yea even a moon and a firmament full of stars and a buckler[69] to those who know thee.
8. The Western Pope feareth thee, even Emil the son of Samuel,[70] hangeth his head in confusion when thy name is uttered.
9. (While he was yet speaking, Maurice the boycotter plucked the sleeve of his neighbor, even the sleeve of Henry the Sing-Singer,[71] and whispering in his ear said: "He is giving the old man guff.)"
10. And Frederick continued his parable and said: O, Episcopus! The field of the Lord is rich with the harvest of piety from the seed thou hast sown.
11. The Sabbath of the Lord thou wouldst transfer to the first day of the week, and what Rabbi among us did say thee nay?[72]
12. Thou wert the first to preach Christology from the Jewish pulpit[73] and no Rabbi dared lift up a voice against thee, for thy pomposity is as great as the tower of Babel,[74]

62. 2 Chronicles 5:13.
63. Psalms 118:24.
64. Song of Songs 5:2.
65. Kedron is often rendered Kidron or Qidron. It refers both to a valley marking the eastern boundary of Jerusalem and to a brook or wadi there; see 2 Chronicles 29:16.
66. Song of Songs 5:15.
67. Song of Songs 2:1.
68. A play on Gottheil's *Sun and Shield: A Book of Devout Thoughts for Every-Day Use* (New York: Brentano's, 1896).
69. 2 Samuel 22:31; a "buckler" is a small, round shield.
70. Emil G. Hirsch (1851–1923), leading Reform rabbi of Chicago; see Tobias Brinkmann, *Sundays at Sinai: A Jewish Congregation in Chicago* (Chicago: University of Chicago Press, 2012).
71. Henry M. Speaker (1868–1935), chaplain at Sing Sing prison (1895–1898) and later the principal of Gratz College; see *American Jewish Year Book* 6 (1904–1905): 192.
72. Temple Emanu-El introduced "Sunday lectures" in 1888, but pledged that "the observance of the Sabbath services, as heretofore practiced in the Temple," would be "continued inviolate." Subsequently, Gottheil concluded that Sunday services "infused new life into our congregations." See Myer Stern, *The Rise and Progress of Reform Judaism* (New York: Myer Stern, 1895), 84; Gottheil, *Life of Gustav Gottheil*, 155.
73. As early as 1876, Gottheil preached on "Certain Contrasts and Comparisons of Judaism and Christianity"; see Gottheil, *Life of Gustav Gottheil*, 128.
74. Genesis 11:4–9.

thy self-conceit even as the brazen serpent that was set up in the wilderness.[75]

13. For all that thou hast done we praise thee, for the regularity with which thou hast drawn thy salary, we admire thee.
14. Though art as meek as Moses, as zealous as Elijah, as modest as Hillel.
15. And Maurice the boycotter said unto himself, "Nit."[76]
16. And Joseph the Trilbyite and Stephen the young man took a tallis and covered the face of Episcopus, for his face shone with a brightness even as the face of Moses which when he descended from the mount, was covered with a veil.[77]
17. Now when Adolph the Assurimite beheld the brightness of the countenance of Episcopus, and being full of juice, he clothed himself in a white ephod[78] and placing a garland of flowers upon his head, took up his manicure, and standing on a high seat continued the parable of Frederick the tiller of the soil, saying: As the appearance of the rainbow in the midst of the clouds; and the Rabbis exclaimed with one voice: So is the face of Episcopus.[79]
18. As the lightning preceding from the splendor of the holy *Hayoth*;[80] and the Rabbis exclaimed with one voice: So is the face of Episcopus!
19. As the celestial blue thread in the Tallis of Rudolph the Rodefer;[81] and the Rabbis exclaimed with one voice. So is the face of Episcopus!"
20. As the rose in the midst of a delightful garden, as the diadem placed upon the head of the king, even as the transcendental beauty of Raphael the Benjaminite; and the Rabbis exclaimed with one voice: So is the face of Episcopus!
21. And when Episcopus heard the sweet voice of Adolph the Assurimite and the praise bestowed upon him, he smiled beneath the Tallis that covered his face, and the Rabbis each filled their cups with wine and strong drink and smiled with him.

CHAPTER VI.

1. Then arose Rudolph the Rodefer and said,
2. Hear my words, O ye wise men, and give ear unto me, ye that have knowledge.[82]
3. For the ear trieth words, as the mouth tasteth meat.[83]
4. Let us choose to us judgement; let us know among ourselves what is good.[84]

75. Numbers 21:9.
76. German for "not."
77. Genesis 9:23; Exodus 34:29–33.
78. A priestly garment; see Exodus 28:6–12, and Yehoshua M. Grintz and S. David Sperling, "Ephod," in *Encyclopaedia Judaica*, ed. Fred Skolnik and Michael Berenbaum, 2d ed., vol. 6 (New York: Thomas Gale, 2007), 455–56.
79. This and the following lines play on the exhilarating high holiday hymn "Mar'eh kohen," describing the appearance of the High Priest (here compared to "Episcopus") as he left the Holy of Holies. See Morton M. Leifman, "Mar'eh kohen," https://www.milkenarchive.org/music/volumes/view/golden-voices-in-the-golden-land/work/mareh-kohen/, and Jonathan Saks, *The Koren Mahzor Yamim Nora'im Rosh Hashana & Yom Kippur* (Jerusalem: Koren, 2010), 1192.
80. The four creatures accompanying the divine chariot described in Ezekiel 1:5–12 and 10:15. For their place in Jewish and Christian tradition, see https://en.wikipedia.org/wiki/Living_creatures_(Bible).
81. Rabbi Rudolph Grossman apparently adhered to the Hasidic practice, championed by the grand rebbe of Radzyn, Gershon Chanoch Henech Leiner (1839–1890), to add a specially dyed blue threat to his prayer shawl, as per Numbers 15:38 and Rabbi Leiner's (controversial) analysis of how *tekhelet* was produced. For a brief history and illustration, see https://en.wikipedia.org/wiki/Tekhelet.
82. Job 34:2.
83. Job 34:3.
84. Job 34:4.

5. For hath it not been said by the wise men in Israel: Where three are eating at one table, and they do not discourse upon the words of the Law, it is as though they had partaken of the offerings of the dead.[85]
6. And the words of Rudolph the Rodefer seemed good in their sight, and they cast their eyes upon Alexander of the Amhaaratzim, upon Joseph the Trilbyite, and upon Maurice the boycotter, and said unto them: Speak ye unto us of the Law.
7. And Kaufman the Bethelite laughed and said: these men know as much about the Law and its precepts as the bramble in the parable of Jotham, knew of Abimelech the son of Jerubbaal;[86] verily they are all sons of Belial.[87]
8. And Maurice the boycotter whispered in the ear of his neighbor, even the ear of Alexander of the Amhaaratzim: He thinks he is the only pebble upon the Rabbinical beach.
9. And Kaufman the Bethelite overheard the words of Maurice the boycotter and waxed exceedingly wroth, and he arose from his place and with fierce anger pointed his finger at him and said unto him: Thou son of Belial, knowest thou not what is written: Whoso keepeth the fig tree shall eat the fruit thereof; so he that waiteth on his master shall be honored.[88]
10. Do figs grow upon thistles[89] and can copper be brought out from the bowels of the earth without the sweat of the brow?[90]
11. Canst thou behold the sweet influences of Pleiades, or gaze upon the bands of Orion when thine eyes are closed with blindness.[91]
12. Canst thou love the Torah when thou disregardest its precepts, or know aught of its wisdom, when thou art unable to read it, for art thou not of the Amhaaratzim?
13. And Maurice the boycotter replied unto him and said: Verily, thou art of the past, and darkeneth counsel by words without knowledge.
14. As the yoke of bondage was removed from our fathers when they went up out of the land of Egypt, even so has the yoke of the Torah been removed from us, the Rabbis of to-day, by the magic spell of Reform.
15. Why should we study the Torah, when we believe not in its commands?
16. Was thou not the first to deny its inspiration?[92]
17. Verily, thy voice was heard among the loudest at the gates of the city, that the Law was for our forefathers, and not for us.

85. Mishnah Avot 3:3.

86. Judges 9:7–21.

87. Deuteronomy 13:14, meaning scoundrels, worthless or depraved people.

88. Proverbs 27:18.

89. A New Testament allusion (Matthew 7:16) befitting Kohler, who, as Solomon knew, studied Christianity.

90. Job 28:2.

91. Job 38:31.

92. An oblique reference to Kohler's daring doctoral dissertation, *Der Segen Jacob's* (Berlin, 1867), which applied the methods of biblical criticism to the study of Jacob's blessing in Genesis 49. Reputedly, the dissertation disqualified Kohler for any central European congregation and led to his immigration to the United States; see Robert F. Southard, "The Theologian of the 1885 Pittsburgh Platform: Kaufmann Kohler's Vision of Progressive Judaism," in *Platforms and Prayer Books: Theological and Liturgical Perspectives on Reform Judaism*, ed. Dana Evan Kaplan (Lanham, Md.: Rowman & Littlefield, 2002), 61–79.

18. Was it not thy influence that abrogated the ancient prayers of Israel and substituted in its place that unclean thing called the Union Prayer Book?[93]
19. Why clothest thou not thyself in a Tallis? Where are thy phylacteries and thy fringes, where the signs upon the door-posts of thy house?[94]
20. Verily, I say to you, o Kaufman the Bethelite, that thy sin is greater than my ignorance, for with thy knowledge of the Torah and the wisdom of the sages of Israel that thou possessests, thou are like unto Jeroboam the son of Nebat, who not alone sinned himself, but caused others to sin also, which was evil in the sight of the Lord.[95]
21. Did I ever deride the sacred word of God as thou didst in thy book, "Der Segen Jakob's?"
22. Did I ever desire to change the Sabbath of the Lord from the seventh unto the first day, even the Sabbath of the Gentiles, to please the publicans and the money lenders?[96]
23. Have I ever proclaimed from the housetops, in the hearing of the multitudes of Israel that the covenant God made with Abraham, is a "relic of barbarism?"[97]
24. Verily, I say unto thee, O Kaufman the Bethelite that thy sins against Judaism are without number, even as the stars of the heavens and the sands which are on the seashore.
25. If we have sinned, we have but followed thy example; if we are ignorant of the Law and the language of our fathers, it is because thou and thy school of prophets declare, that the Torah in this land has lost its significance and that Hebrew in our prayers is unnecessary.
26. Verily, thy words are "bosh" (which signifieth in the vernacular, the expressions of foolish men).
27. And Kaufman the Bethelite smote his breast and exclaimed, "I have sinned!"

CHAPTER VII.

1. Now Falk the Bikurcholemite, was well versed in the language of the Hebrews and in the learnings of the sages of Israel, and he meditated upon the law day and night[98]—whenever he had time.
2. And he sat at the feast, and his soul rejoiced at the good things which Frederick the tiller of the soil and Joseph the Trilbyite and Stephen the young man had prepared, and he drank of the wine and strong drink which had been set before him.

93. Kohler was the editor of the 1895 *Union Prayer-Book.*

94. Deuteronomy 6:8–9.

95. 1 Kings 12:25–33.

96. Kohler introduced Sunday services at Chicago's Sinai Congregation in 1873; see Brinkmann, *Sundays at Sinai.*

97. The phrase may previously have been uttered by the president of Chicago's Sinai Temple in 1885, but Kohler expressed the same sentiments at the Pittsburgh rabbinical conference, where he sought to abolish mandatory circumcision of adult converts; see *American Israelite,* May 15, 1885, 4, and the *Proceedings of the Pittsburg* [sic] *Rabbinical Conference November 16, 17, 18, 1885* (Richmond, Va.: Old Dominion Press, 1923), 16.

98. Joshua 1:8.

3. And when he beheld that Kaufman the Bethelite had confessed his sin against Judaism and its precepts, he was sorely troubled, but rejoiced greatly that he had escaped by the skin of his teeth, for he communed within himself and said: Peradventure, if I had received his salary, I might also have had to confess my evil doings.
4. And while the strength of the wine was yet upon him, he arose from his place and said: My brethren, the spirit of prophesy came upon me and said unto me: Son of man, write; and I said: What shall I write?[99]

99. Ezekiel 2:2.

5. And the spirit took me by the hand and led me to the river, even the East River, and I sat upon the banks thereof, and the spirit placed a pen in mine hand and set a scroll before me and said unto me: Write the praises of Episcopus, and his greatness, and his wondrous works.
6. And Bernhard the Zichronite said to Maurice the boycotter: It must have been the same lying spirit that went into the mouth of the Micaiah the son of Imlah, when he prophesied before the King at Ramoth Gilead, when he went forth to battle.[100]

100. 1 Kings 22.

7. But Maurice the boycotter understood him not, for he had never read the Book of Kings, wherein it is written—being of the Amhaaratzim.
8. And behold, this is what I have written; and he placed the scroll in the hands of Frederick the tiller of the soil, who was the ruler of the feast and sat at the head of the table, that he might read it before them.
9. And Frederick the tiller of the soil read it aloud; and save Pereira of the house of Mendes, Kaufman the Bethelite, Adolph the Assurimite and Episcopus, none who were at the feast understood what was read, for it was in the language of the Hebrews, and they were of the tribe of the Amhaaratzim.
10. And Maurice the boycotter and the others said unto Falk the Bikurcholemite: Give it unto us in United States (which in the vernacular meaneth: in plain English).
11. And Falk the Bikurcholemite took his harp in his hand and sang:

> Awake up my glory; awake psaltery and harp:
> I myself will wake up early[101]—for I won't go home till morning.

101. Psalms 57:9.

> Lift high the glass, sing loud his praise,
> Episcopus! Episcopus!
> Long life to him and happy days,
> Episcopus! Episcopus!

The brightest flower in the field
All to his prescience now must yield,
For who can beat his "Sun and Shield?"[102]
Episcopus! Episcopus!

102. See note 68 above.

His sermons are like precious gold,
Episcopus! Episcopus!
Delighting all, both young and old,
Episcopus! Episcopus!
From North to South, from East to West,
He is the greatest and the best,
And singing birds cry from their nest
Episcopus! Episcopus!

The Western Pope may loudly boast,
Episcopus! Episcopus!
But reckons now without his host,
Episcopus! Episcopus!
No "smeecha"[103] sweet has touched his lips
Nor does he fear the Papal whips,
From Torah's wine alone he sips,
Episcopus! Episcopus!

103. Hebrew for rabbinic ordination. Some questioned whether Gottheil, or for that matter Isaac M. Wise, possessed formal ordination. With professionalization and a new focus on "credentials" in the late nineteenth century, questions like this took on new urgency; see Samuel Haber, *The Quest for Authority and Honor in the American Professions, 1750–1900* (Chicago: University of Chicago Press, 1991).

Then drink to him, here's to his health,
Episcopus! Episcopus!
Long life to him, and peace and wealth,
Episcopus! Episcopus!
Long may he be with us to teach
By his example, and to preach
To all whome'er his voice can reach.
Episcopus! Episcopus!

12. And his voice was as the voice of thunder, and the cups and earthen pitchers, the works of the hands of the potter, and the brazen vessels upon the table shook at the sound thereof.
13. And the children of Episcopus who were at the feast quaked with fear and dismay, and their limbs trembled at the sound of his voice, for they had never heard anything like unto it, for it was even as the rushing of the trees in the wilderness of Kadesh when the thunderstorm passeth over.[104]
14. And his voice became as a parable in the mouths of the Rabbis, for it is recorded in their books, that thereafter, when one went to Episcopus, to inquire whether it was permissible to eat of the food declared to be unclean according to the laws of Moses, as was the custom of some of the Rabbis, he answered and said unto them:

104. Psalms 29:8.

Go to thunder; which meaneth, go and inquire of Falk the Bikurcholemite.

CHAPTER VIII.

1. Now Stephen the young man was of the house of Jeshurun, and being a stripling had not waxed fat, and therefore was unable to fulfill the words of the Scriptures, as it is written: And Jeshurun waxed fat and kicked.[105]
2. And though his side whiskers were curious to behold, they were nevertheless marvelous in their beauty: his eyes as the eyes of doves by the rivers of waters, washed with milk and fitly set.[106]
3. And the daughters of Judah mourned and refused to be comforted when they beheld him, and they said one unto another: Verily, evil days have come upon us, this is a reproach unto us and unto all Israel, that he taketh not unto himself a wife.
4. But Stephen gave no heed to their murmurings, and when a damsel approached him he closed his eyes and passed over unto the other side, that his soul might not become rebellious when he gazed upon her.[107]
5. And he assisted Frederick the tiller of the soil in the preparations of the feast, and he wrote invitations to Solomon the scribe and to the other scribes, and sealed them with the seal of Episcopus, bidding them to come up to the banquet, that they might write down all the honors paid to Episcopus and his glories.
6. That his piety and modesty should be remembered and kept through every generation, every family, every province and every city; and that his eating a kosher supper and repeating Hebrew prayers should not fail from among the Jews, nor the memorial of them perish from their seed.[108]
7. But Stephen the younger, forgot to place the invitations in the hands of the messengers by posts on horse-horseback [*sic*], and riders on mules, camels and young dromedaries, as did Haman the son of Hamadatha, when he sought the destruction of the Jews.[109]
8. And when Solomon the scribe, and Abraham the messenger of glad tidings at three dollars a year,[110] and Joseph of the house of Davis,[111] and Philip the soft soaper,[112] heard of the mishap, they were sorely afflicted; and they rent their garments and clothed themselves in sack cloth, and put ashes on their heads and even plucked their beards in anger,[113] for Episcopus was dear unto Solomon

105. Deuteronomy 32:15. Wise served as the rabbi of B'nai Jeshurun.

106. Song of Songs 5:12. Wise was single in 1897; he married Louise Waterman in 1900.

107. An oblique hint that Wise was known to be something of a "ladies' man."

108. Esther 9:28.

109. Esther 3:1, 9.

110. Abram Isaacs (1851–1920), the editor of the *Jewish Messenger*; see Joshua Bloch, "Abram Samuel Isaacs," *Publications of the American Jewish Historical Society* 31 (1928): 265–66.

111. Joseph Davis (1826?–1905) was the editor of the *Hebrew Journal*, published in New York; see *American Israelite*, January 26, 1905, 1.

112. Philip Cowen (1853–1943) was the editor of the *American Hebrew*; see his autobiography, *Memories of an American Jew* (New York: International Press, 1932), and *New York Times*, April 21, 1943, 25.

113. Esther 4:1.

the scribe even as the apple of his eye, but he despised the Amhaaratzim, having sworn in his wrath: I will utterly put out the remembrance of every Amhaaretz Rabbi from under heaven.[114]

114. Deuteronomy 25:19.

9. And there was enmity between them, and they tried to boycott him; whence cometh the name, "Maurice the boycotter," but the people flocked to his "Standard" and they strengthened his hands even as the hands of Moses were stayed by Aaron and Hur when Joshua discomfited Amalek and his people with the edge of the sword.[115]

115. Exodus 17:8–13.

CHAPTER IX.

1. Now Stephen the young man, as he assisted at the feast, noticed that the countenance of Joseph the Trilbyite was cast down and his appearance was as of one who was sorely troubled.
2. And he went to him as he sat at the feast and said: What aileth thee, o, my brother, why art thou sad and what evil hath befallen thee?
3. Is there bitterness in thy meat or wormwood and gall in thy cup? Verily, is it not written: A merry heart doeth good like medicine, but a broken spirit drieth the bones.[116]

116. Proverbs 17:22.

4. And Joseph the Trilbyite answered and said: There are no flies on me, neither is there any fly in mine ointment.
5. Although affliction cometh not forth of the dust, neither doth trouble spring out of the ground,[117] yet is my soul weary and mine anguish greater than I can bear.

117. Job 5:6.

6. And when Stephen the younger strongly urged upon him to declare himself, he told him that he had prepared a speech in honor of Episcopus, and that he was sorely pressed down with its weight and prayed to be speedily delivered thereof.
7. And Stephen girded up his garments about his loins, and ran with haste to Frederick the tiller of the soil who sat at the head of the table, and told him of the grievance of Joseph the Trilbyite, for his bowels of compassion moved for him—having been there oft before—and that he was waiting to be called upon to speak words of wisdom and counsel to the assembled Rabbis, that he might have a safe and a speedily deliverance.
8. And straightwise Frederick the tiller of the soil arose and said: O ye cedars of Lebanon, ye ornaments of the Law! Give hear to my voice and hearken to the words of my lips.[118]

118. Psalms 5:2–4.

9. Is it not written in the words of Amos, who was among the herdsmen of Tekoa:

"They drink wine in bowls
And anoint themselves with the chief ointments,
But they have not grieved
For the affliction of Joseph."[119]

10. Behold, Joseph the Trilbyite suffereth, let us remove the weight from his stomach, even as Jacob rolled the stone from the mouth of the well that we the sheep of Israel may drink of the spiritual waters with which he is filled to overflowing.[120]
11. And Joseph arose and made obeisance to Episcopus and said:
12. I am the first of the Trilbyites, and thanks to the power of Solomon the scribe, the name of "Reb Trilby" is known from Dan to Beersheba,[121] from Squedonk[122] to Yuba Dam.[123]
13. And Pereira of the house of Mendes, said unto his neighbor, Verily, the young man is a son of Belial, because he talketh profanely.
14. And Joseph continued and said: my soul is bound up in the soul of Episcopus, for he ever leadeth me in the pleasant places of Emanuel.[124]
15. Verily he hath been to me even as a "Sun and Shield,"[125] and when I say my prayers before lying on my couch, no longer do I say as when a child: "Before me is Uriel and behind me Rafael,"[126] but by plenary indulgence of the Western Pope I now say, "behind me is Uriel, and before me is Rafael," (for Rafael meaneth in the vernacular of the Ashkenazim, "Gottheil"),[127] for he is ever before me as my pattern.
16. And Maurice the boycotter and Alexander of the Amhaaratzim gazed upon each other with wonder and astonishment, that Joseph the Trilbyite should know so much Hebrew.
17. And he said further: No longer should we be slaves to the past. Verily I say unto you, the outstretched "hand" is a relic of Orthodox bondage—it is the "foot" which is a fitting emblem of this age of our redemption from the yoke of the Shulchan Aruch.[128]
18. The "foot" of progress upon the neck of Rabbanism; oh, how beautiful upon the mountains are the "feet" of the messenger[129] that has brought the glad tidings of Reform to all young Rabbis who, otherwise, could never have entered a Jewish pulpit.

119. Amos 6:6.
120. Genesis 29:10.
121. Judges 20:1.
122. Equivalent to Podunk, an insignificant, out-of-the-way, or completely fictitious place.
123. Alludes to a joke about the consequences of saying "Yuba Dam." "Talketh profanely" in the next line refers to this same folkloristic motif; see http://www.fresnostate.edu/folklore/ballads/RcYubaDa.html.
124. Psalms 23:2. Silverman served as Gottheil's associate and heir apparent at Temple Emanu-El.
125. See note 68 above.
126. The traditional Jewish prayer before retiring to rest at night, *Kri'at Shema 'al ha-mittah*, includes a thrice-repeated reference to these protective archangels; see Joseph H. Hertz, *The Authorised Daily Prayer Book* (New York: Bloch, 1948), 1004.
127. The earliest known Gottheil ancestor "took on the family-name at the time when family-names were forced upon the Jews, translating the Hebrew *Raphael* into the German Gottheil (i.e. healing comes from God)"; Gottheil, *Life of Gustav Gottheil*, 1.
128. The Code of Jewish Law by Joseph Caro, first published in 1565.
129. Isaiah 52:7.

19. No longer the "hand" of friendship, but the "foot" upon the tender errand of mercy; no longer the "hand" to welcome those who are not with us, but the "foot" to spurn those who fail to do homage to the Western Pope, and after him to Episcopus.
20. (And while he was yet talking, Maurice the boycotter whispered in the ear of his neighbor, even the ear of Alexander of the Amhaaratzim: Did I not tell thee that "Joe's a Kicker," meaning in the vernacular, that he was of a contentious spirit.[130])
21. Who is there like unto Trilby? and where in the heaven above, or on earth beneath, or in the water under the earth, is there anything as beautiful as the "tootsie wootsies" of Trilby's (meaning in the vernacular, her feet.)[131]
22. The songs of Miriam and Deborah[132] are things of the past. Hannah and Esther are antiquated relics, but the echo of the voice of Trilby shouting "milk," shall ring through countless ages, typical of the milk of human kindness; of the milk and honey which floweth in the treasuries of congregations that have no mortgages upon their Temples.
23. And Alexander of the Amhaaratzim cried aloud, "he's off," and Pereira of the house of Mendes reproved him, saying: nay, he is not off, for verily he standeth.
24. And Alexander of the Amhaaratzim replied, "I mean he is off his base," but Pereira of the house of Mendes understood him not, for he was as guileless as a lamb.
25. Then Joseph sang:

Oh, Trilby! Oh Trilby! so beautiful and sweet,
In soldier's jacket and unslippered feet,
I, thy Svengali,[133] will awaken thy lyre
And touch men's hearts with thy celestial fire.

Why should I preach upon religious themes,
Which are at best but foolish dreams,
Why speak of heaven or talk of Paradise,
When thou standeth lovely before my eyes?

Why not inhale the fragrance of thy roses
Nor waste the time to sermonize on Moses,
Is not the remembrance of thy own sweet Alice,[134]
Better far than those of Tsitsis or of Tallis?

Let us then meet the problem face to face,
"Progress and Reform" is the motto of our race.[135]
For sure as pie, the universal religion will be
The worship of feet, of thy feet, Oh, fair Trilby.

130. The relationship between Gottheil and Silverman was known to be frosty. When Temple Emanu-El memorialized Gottheil following his death in 1903, the family tellingly requested that Silverman not deliver the eulogy; see Gottheil, *Life of Gustav Gottheil*, 147, 263–64.

131. Exodus 15:11. Solomon implies that instead of worshiping God, Silverman worships the Irish model Trilby O'Ferrall, heroine of George du Maurier, *Trilby* (New York: Harper, 1894).

132. Exodus 15 and Judges 5.

133. The Jewish villain of *Trilby*, Svengali, used his hypnotic powers to control Trilby. The term "Svengali" soon came to be applied to anyone who exercises a controlling influence on another, especially for a sinister purpose.

134. A reference to one of the most famous lines in Trilby: "Oh, don't you remember sweet Alice, Ben Bolt?" See https://victorianweb.org/art/illustration/dumaurier/trilby/99.html.

135. "Progress and Reform" was associated both with the Progressive movement in American politics and with the Reform movement in Judaism.

CHAPTER X.

1. Now Bernhard the Zichronite did not walk in the ways of Joseph the Trilbyite, and when he heard his words, his wrath was enkindled against him.[136]
2. And his anger shone with brightness from his eyes, even as the precious stone which he wore upon the bosom of his shirt, which was a delight to his congregation and all Israel.
3. And his voice, was as the cooing of the turtle dove when the singing time of the birds is heard in our land.[137]
4. But Episcopus was a thorn in his side, for he had strayed from the paths of his fathers and had gone after the inclinations of his own heart and after the desire of his own eyes.
5. Nevertheless, he went up early to the feast, least it might be said of him: "He is a kicker in Israel."[138]
6. And when Joseph the Trilbyite had ended his song, he arose from his place at the table and said: I have neither harp nor manicure, yet will I sing unto you, that your hearts be made glad while ye are merry with wine.
7. And then he took a bone out of his throat, and drank of the cup of wine which Stephen the young man brought to him and requesting the Rabbis to join in the chorus of praise, sang:

(Air: "Tit-Willow," in "The Mikado."[139])
I will sing of a rabbi whom all of you deem,
A good fellow, good fellow, good fellow:
For all must confess he does certainly seem
A good fellow, good fellow, good fellow.
And you know whom I mean, tho I mention no name.
For I see by the praise that you pay to his fame
That you rightly regard him, and plainly proclaim
A good fellow, good fellow, good fellow.

This rabbi, you know, is the friend of his race,
Good fellow, good fellow, good fellow.
And these words are writ large on his unctuous face:
"Good fellow, good fellow, good fellow."
He studies the cash and the comforts of men,
If they happen to be of the uppermost ten,
And he uses for them both his tongue and his pen,
This good fellow, good fellow, good fellow.

The Hebrew he ranks 'mong the barbarous tongues,
Good fellow, good fellow, good fellow:

136. 2 Chronicles 32:25.

137. Song of Songs 2:12.

138. See chapter 9, line 20, above.

139. "Air" in the sense of "tune." Gilbert and Sullivan's *The Mikado* (1885) satirized British politics and institutions, disguising them as Japanese, and was the most successful comic opera of its time in both England and the United States.

To save money and time and men's teeth and their lungs,
Good fellow, good fellow, good fellow.
Of the troublesome Sabbath he breaketh the spell.
And its suffering victims he kindly does tell,
That a service on Sunday will do quite as well—
This good fellow, good fellow, good fellow

On each feature his smile for the Gentile it plays.
Good fellow, good fellow, good fellow;
And he tells all his people to mimic his ways,
Good fellow, good fellow, good fellow.
Their past as a nightmare he bids them forget,
Nor think of their Zion with pangs of regret,[140]
For America sure is their "Zion," you bet,
Good fellow, good fellow, good fellow.

He freely makes use of his surgical saw,
Good fellow, good fellow, good fellow;
Cutting off all the troublesome things in the law,
This good fellow, good fellow, good fellow
To the Jews, like a savior, salvation he brings,
For gone is their yoke of rabbinical things
Through the favor and grace of this kindest of kings,
This good fellow, good fellow, good fellow.

Trefa dishes, he says, is ju-dicious to eat,
Good fellow, good fellow, good fellow.
He relishes oysters and all sorts of meat
This good fellow, good fellow, good fellow.
He advises each rich and respectable Jew
To follow the best of philosophers true
And "Bacon" and "Cant" he should never eschew,
Good fellow, good fellow, good fellow.

The Tallis like poison or Hebrew he shuns,
Good fellow, good fellow, good fellow;
And all hats are removed by this biggest of guns,
This good fellow, good fellow, good fellow.
In his temple he teaches his numerous band
Bare-neck'd and bare-faced and bare-headed to stand,
Like the Goyim that visit each church in the land,
Good fellow, good fellow, good fellow.

Most noble and brave, he forgetteth himself.
Good fellow, good fellow, good fellow.
He hateth low profits and loathes vile pelf,
Good fellow, good fellow, good fellow.

140. Actually, Gottheil supported Zionism, one of few Reform rabbis of his time to take this stance; see Gottheil, *Life of Gustav Gottheil*, 190–94, and above p. 449, n. 36.

Though he tolls in God's vineyard from love not for gain
With martyr-like meekness and grace he does deign
To pocket ten thousand a year with much pain.
This good fellow, good fel'ow, good fellow.

8. And when Bernhard the Zichronite had ended his song, Pereira of the house of Mendes arose and embraced him, and kissed him upon the cheek, and said to him: "Verily, thou art a daisy."[141]
9. For when he heard the words of praise of Pereira, his eyes shone with a lustre exceeding that of the precious stone which he wore upon the bosom of his shirt.
10. And they feasted and sang and made merry, and the neighbors marvelled greatly at the noise.
11. And when the night was about spent and they were full of wine and heavy with sleep, Rudolf the Rodefer, arose and said: "Rabbosaynu, it is time to read the morning Shemang."[142]
12. And Maurice the boycotter said: That is something I have not done since the days of my youth, but Episcopus kept his own counsel.
13. And when the daybreak came, they arose and girded themselves about the loins and took their staffs in their hands and went to their dwelling places.
14. And when Stephen the young man arose the next morning, his head was greatly swollen and he came nigh perishing with thirst; for he was but a stripling and unaccustomed to the drinking of much wine.
15. But Maurice the boycotter continued in the land as an Amhaaretz, and the people gazed with astonishment at the immensity of his gall, that he should appear before them as a Rabbi.
16. And after this Episcopus renewed his vigor, and became like unto a young man.
17. Now the acts of his strength and of his might and the exposition of his greatness, behold they are written in the book of the "Chronicles of the Rabbis," even unto this day.[143]

ת׳ ו׳ ש׳ ל׳ ב׳ ע׳[144]

141. A humorous poem of the day, "The School Marm," satirized a teacher who applied a "mighty hand," a switch, and a ruler to a young schoolboy and then brightly exclaimed, "Thou art a daisy"; see Thomas W. Handford, comp., *Elmo's Humorous Speaker* (Chicago: Belford-Clarke, 1890), 217.

142. The Passover haggadah famously recounts the story of five rabbis who spent the whole night discussing the exodus from Egypt, until their students came and said to them, "Rabbis ('Rabbosaynu'), it is time to read the morning *Shema* (Deuteronomy 6:4–9)"; see Philip Birnbaum, *The Birnbaum Haggadah* (New York: Hebrew Publishing Company, 1976), 64–66. *Shemang*, rather than *Shema*, reflects a Sephardic pronunciation that preserves the guttural form of the Hebrew letter ʻayin.

143. Esther 10:2.

144. Traditional Jewish books piously conclude with praise of God. These six Hebrew letters form an acronym for *Tam venishlam shevakh le-El borei olam*, "I complete this with praise for God, Creator of the world."

THE GREAT NINETEENTH-CENTURY PURIM REVIVAL

ZEV ELEFF

BY HIS OWN admission, Myer Samuel Isaacs was not diligent about recording his memories and musings in his diary.[1] He had resolved, at times, to be more conscientious, but routinely confessed to his personal journal that his obligations distracted him from logging daily entries. Nonetheless, the incomplete diary is a historical treasure, revealing much about New York Jewish life and a young man who possessed strong connections to the elite classes of New York and its Jews.

The two categories were not always mutually exclusive. Isaacs was the eldest son of Rabbi Samuel Myer Isaacs, the religious leader of Shaaray Tefila and editor of a popular Jewish weekly newspaper, the *Jewish Messenger*. Rabbi Isaacs was one of the rare Orthodox ministers to maintain his high standing among America's Jews and was a mainstay in a myriad of institutions. The younger Isaacs was twenty years old when he started journaling. He was a past valedictorian of New York University and then enrolled in that institution's law school. Myer, wrote his younger brother Abram, "received a full measure of parental guidance, and the labor was lightened by his studious disposition and the love of learning which made the acquisition of Hebrew and secular knowledge a comparatively easy task."[2] He kept a wide circle of well-to-do friends and socialites, associations that would later help him as a lawyer, Republican-aligned diplomat, and activist. In his diary, Isaacs wrote about synagogue rivalries and local gossip. He penned political commentary on President Abraham Lincoln and reviewed theater performances, most of them negatively, except for scenes that featured the promising young stage actor named John Wilkes Booth. Isaacs also detailed more personal points, like his courtship of his future wife, Maria, family

1. On Myer Isaacs, see Abram S. Isaacs, "Myer S. Isaacs: A Memoir," *American Jewish Year Book* 8 (1906–1907): 19–33. On the broader Isaacs family, see Adam D. Mendelsohn, "The Sacrifices of the Isaacs: The Diffusion of New Models of Religious Leadership in the English-Speaking Jewish World," in *Transnational Traditions: New Perspectives on American Jewish History*, ed. Ava F. Kahn and Adam D. Mendelsohn (Detroit: Wayne State University Press, 2014), 11–37.

2. Isaacs, "Myer S. Isaacs," 19.

Passover preparations, and his pivotal leadership in the Purim Association of New York.[3]

Isaacs was very proud of his role in founding and furthering the Purim Association and its annual masquerade ball charity event. The affair drew hundreds—later thousands—of Jews and non-Jews among the upper crust of Gotham and the middle class that aspired to join and act like the higher classes.[4] Depending on the year, the proceeds supported a Jewish orphanage, hospital, or local benevolent society. The ball's theme added an exotic flare and was in keeping with the Purim tradition of costumes and conviviality. Young women and men looked forward to the judges' decision on the best-dressed guest. Some came for the lampoon routine performed by members of the organizing committee and to receive a copy of the humorous *Purim Gazette.*[5] Others attended for the grand orchestras commissioned to perform at the ball.

Before the inaugural Purim ball held in March 1862, Isaacs investigated local German Liederkranz societies and spoke with professional "floor managers" to determine how best to choreograph the flow of a gala social event.[6] On occasion, he complained that the "Purim ball is engrossing rather too much of my thoughts and time." Isaacs assumed a large share of the responsibilities because the other organizers, he claimed, were "boys still." Having recently graduated beyond his teenage years, Isaacs considered himself much more mature than his peers, who had "too little stability and knowledge of the world." He regretted that one other Purim ball leader engaged in the business for the wrong reasons—because of the "senseless adulation inflicted on him by 'the girls.'"[7] Isaacs persevered, however. The second Purim ball in 1863 was, in his estimation, "in every respect a grand success": "Nothing to equal it had ever

3. On the Purim Association, see Philip Goodman, "The Purim Association of the City of New York (1862–1902)," *Publications of the American Jewish Historical Society* 40, no. 2 (1950): 135–72.

4. See, for example, Beverly Gordon, "Victorian Fancywork in the American Home: Fantasy and Accommodation," in *Making the American Home: Middle-Class Women and Domestic Material Culture, 1840–1940,* ed. Marilyn Ferris Motz and Pat Browne (Bowling Green, Ohio: Bowling Green State University Popular Press, 1988), 63–64.

5. On the reception of the Purim Association's *Purim Gazette,* see, for example, "The Purim Festivities," *Jewish Messenger,* March 17, 1865, 91.

6. "The Purim Ball," *New York Daily Herald,* March 29, 1867, 10. On the German variation in American life, see Heike Bungert, "'Feast of Fools': German-American Carnival as a Medium of Identity Formation, 1854–1914," *Amerikastudien/American Studies* 48, no. 3 (2003): 325–44.

7. Entry for February 18, 1863, Myer S. Isaacs Diary (SC-5452), Jacob Rader Marcus Center of the American Jewish Archives, Cincinnati. I am very grateful to Adam Mendelsohn for alerting me to this fascinating text and graciously sharing his notes with me.

before been witnessed in the city." Then the triumphant Isaacs declared that his event was, "in point of fact, the first successful masquerade ever given in this country."[8]

The Isaacs diary entries on Purim betoken a spirit of renewed interest in Jewish holidays in the United States during the latter half of the nineteenth century among both laypeople like Isaacs and rabbinic leaders. For instance, Rabbi Isaac Mayer Wise, America's leading Reform rabbi, took stock of Jewish holiday observance in the pages of the newspaper he had founded in Cincinnati during the 1850s. Some occasions, like Rosh Hashanah and Yom Kippur, loomed too large to wither. In addition, Wise claimed, the "Passover Feast has preserved itself." He figured that Hanukkah, Purim, and Shavuot required significant rabbinical effort to persevere in the New World. Referring to the latter's English nomenclature, Wise surmised that "Pentecost has been revived by the reformers, who made of it confirmation day." He expressed some worry for Sukkot, the third (along with Passover and Shavuot) of the yearly biblical festival holidays, and regretted that "our very orthodox spokesmen are ready to let the Succoth go out of existence among us."[9]

Like Isaacs's diary, Wise's accounting of Jewish holiday observance reflected the rising interest in preserving traditional occasions in American Jewish life. It also signaled Wise's understanding that some occasions required creativity to help laypeople find meaning in them, just like Myer Isaacs's Purim balls. This trend paralleled cultural changes and the spike in observance of Christmas and Easter among American Christians.[10] The preservation of the Hebrew calendar, both its observance and the production of physical copies of it for practical use, had been a longstanding method for Jews to keep their coreligionists in the fold. The strategy was first deployed in Europe and then, in the 1800s, by rabbis in North America.[11] In the latter half of the nineteenth century, a clique of Jewish newspapers reminded readers of upcoming holidays in their weekly calendars

8. Entry for March 12, 1863, Myer S. Isaacs Diary.

9. "The Succoth Feast," *American Israelite*, October 12, 1883, 4.

10. See Leigh Eric Schmidt, *Consumer Rites: The Buying and Selling of American Holidays* (Princeton: Princeton University Press, 1995), 191–95.

11. See Elisheva Carlebach, *Palaces of Time: Jewish Calendar and Culture in Early Modern Europe* (Cambridge, Mass.: Harvard University Press, 2011), 5–27, and Zev Eleff, "They Who Control the Time: The Orthodox Alliance of Abraham De Sola and Jacques Judah Lyons and the Nineteenth-Century Jewish Calendar," in *Neither in Dark Speeches nor in Similitudes: Reflections and Refractions between Canadian and American Jews*, ed. Barry Stiefel and Hernan Tesler-Mabé (Waterloo, Ontario: Wilfrid Laurier University Press, 2016), 95–110.

and sold advertising space to merchants marketing items—matzah and etrogs, for instance—that were needed to perform holiday rituals properly.[12]

The heightened interest in Jewish holiday observance during this epoch is not an unknown subject. Around the turn of the twentieth century, folklorist Beatrice Weinreich studied the "Americanization of Passover" among eastern European migrants.[13] More recently, historians have noted the revival of Hanukkah. Historian Jonathan Sarna has written about the laypeople who formed the Keyam Dishmaya group that sought to reinvigorate interest in traditional Jewish life and culture. This small circle of young people focused much of its energies on the eight-day wintertime festival. Keyam Dishmaya's program at the Young Men's Hebrew Association in New York in December 1879 garnered much attention from Jews and non-Jews.[14] In addition, historian Dianne Ashton has singled out religious leaders such as Rabbi Max Lilienthal of Cincinnati, who started his campaign to elevate Hanukkah among youngsters in the 1860s. Hanukkah-themed children's literature and holiday pageants held in synagogues gained traction in subsequent decades.[15] In assessing the various dimensions of the Festival of Lights renaissance, Ashton surmised that "Hanukkah emerged as a newly meaningful holiday for nineteenth century American Jewish leaders because its story provided images and lessons useful to clergy and lay leaders on all sides of a heated debate about how Judaism should adapt to America."[16]

In this chapter, I focus on the rejuvenation of Purim in the United States. To some extent, balls and other notice paid to this rabbinic festival anticipated the efforts exerted for Hanukkah. In fact, in the 1880s Jewish journalists interpreted

12. See Shari Rabin, "People of the Press: The *Occident*, the *Israelite*, and the Origins of American Judaism," in *By Dawn's Early Light: Jewish Contributions to American Culture from the Nation's Founding to the Civil War*, ed. Adam D. Mendelsohn (Princeton: Princeton University Library, 2016), 75–82, and Jonathan D. Sarna and Zev Eleff, "The Etrog Trade in the New World," in *Be Fruitful!: The Etrog in Jewish Art, Culture, and History*, ed. Warren Klein, Sharon Liberman Mintz, and Joshua Teplitsky (Jerusalem: Mineged Press, 2022), 195–211.

13. Beatrice S. Weinreich, "The Americanization of Passover," in *Studies in Biblical and Jewish Folklore*, ed. Raphael Patai, Francis Lee Utley, and Dov Noy (Bloomington: Indiana University Press, 1960), 341–55.

14. See Jonathan D. Sarna, "The Late Nineteenth-Century American Jewish Awakening," in *Religious Diversity and American Religious History: Studies in Traditions and Cultures*, ed. Walter H. Conser Jr. and Sumner B. Twiss (Athens: University of Georgia Press, 1997), 1–25.

15. See Dianne Ashton, *Hanukkah in America: A History* (New York: New York University Press, 2013), 74–104.

16. *Ibid.*, 70.

the Keyam Dishmaya's Hanukkah campaign and the Purim balls as accomplishing the very same goal.[17] The rise of Purim has two parts. First, laypeople like Myer Isaacs popularized Purim balls in New York and then in large and small Jewish hubs throughout the United States. For this reason, the balls typically took place in private halls rather than in synagogues. Purim balls redounded to the Jewish contribution to American high-society culture. To be sure, rabbis tended to disapprove of these events, accusing their supporters of stripping a holiday of its religious components for the sake of social climbing. Lay leaders like Isaacs, however, deflected these criticisms, explaining that masquerade and merriment had always stood at the center of Purim and that their reconstruction of the holiday had drawn to Judaism young people who would otherwise be far removed from such Jewish spaces as, say, the synagogue. That Purim balls also proved to the general public that Jews could entertain themselves and their non-Jewish neighbors in good style was in the 1860s—and most other epochs—crucially important for a minority group in the United States to establish its American bona fides.

In time, rabbinic leaders also saw in the Purim holiday an opportunity to engineer a religious revival. They focused their attention more squarely on the Purim story, popularizing the biblical tale of Queen Esther and the sinister Haman. Rabbis of all stripes were anxious to recruit young Jews back to the emptied synagogues and therefore used clever license to repurpose the Purim narrative to target Jewish women, tasking them with the Esther-like role of ushering their fathers, husbands, and sons back to Jewish life.

The Invention of the Purim Ball

In January 1860, the women of Congregation B'nai Jeshurun in New York rented space in a nearby hall to hold a social. "A very pleasant evening was spent by all," according to the *Jewish Messenger*.[18] The occasion was not unusual for Manhattan's Jews, who expected a handful of annual banquets and musical fundraisers on behalf of several very good causes. For some reason, however, the good tidings received from the B'nai Jeshurun program supplied Myer Isaacs with an idea or, rather, "a suggestion, which in our opinion is a pretty good one." In the pages of his father's newspaper, Isaacs proposed that "Purim night should be selected as the occasion of a good fancy dress ball, the proceeds to be devoted to charity." Isaacs figured there was room in his coreligionists' busy wintertime

17. "The Purim Ball," *American Hebrew*, February 27, 1880, 22.
18. "New York City," *Jewish Messenger*, January 13, 1860, 14.

calendar. "We think that a respectable sum would be realized; at any rate, there is no harm in thinking about it."[19]

Isaacs's assumption about the association of a classy event with fundraising was typical of the "charity market" among Victorian elites. Philanthropy was an exchange: the donor obtained an "experience"—musical concerts or theater performances, for example—for his or her generous contribution. In a period marked by class distinction, particularly in the United States and England, the charity market provided the affluent with an opportunity to purchase virtue while also solidifying, quite publicly, their place atop the social ladder.[20] Purim, Isaacs figured, was an ideal candidate for this sort of ritual enhancement because one of its traditions was charitable giving. Moreover, the rabbinically ordained holiday was physically and socially less onerous than Passover or Rosh Hashanah. Purim occurs for just a single day, and Jewish law does not require adherents to remain in synagogue for long periods or to change their diets or other behaviors. To the contrary, Purim is a holiday of general cheerfulness, incorporating the distribution of food gifts to friends and the needy and participation in a festive meal featuring wine and a public reading of the Book of Esther.

More than a month later, two weeks before Purim, Isaacs was "sorry to perceive that our suggestion in regard to a Purim Ball has not yet been carried out." However, there was still time, he urged, "to make all arrangements for a grand Fancy Dress Soiree on Purim night." Isaacs noted that Jews in Mobile and New Orleans had successfully adapted masquerade-themed affairs for their Purim celebrations, in keeping with the French-styled carnival culture that had gained a considerable foothold in the American South.[21] To his disappointment, no preparations for a ball were initiated. He tried again the following year, positing that Purim ought to be treated, for Hebrews, as a national holiday, "nearly equivalent to the Fourth of July."[22] Once again, to Isaacs's chagrin, nothing came of his idea.

Myer Isaacs assumed more responsibility for Purim as the holiday approached in the winter of 1862. The twenty-year-old assembled a small group of young men to organize the event at Irving Hall, decorating the space with ornaments

19. *Ibid.*

20. See Sarah Roddy, Julie-Marie Strange, and Bertrand Taithe, *The Charity Market and Humanitarianism in Britain, 1870–1912* (London: Bloomsbury Academic, 2019), 50–53.

21. "Purim," *Jewish Messenger*, February 24, 1860, 60. On masquerade culture in the American South, see Jennifer Atkins, "'Using the Bow and the Smile': Old-Line Krewe Court Femininity in New Orleans Mardi Gras Balls, 1870–1920," *Louisiana History* 54, no. 1 (2013): 5–46.

22. "The Festival of Purim," *Jewish Messenger*, February 22, 1861, 60.

and plenty of pageantry. The committee members were all Isaacs's age or somewhat younger. Like Myer Isaacs, they were first-generation Americans with something to prove about their aspirations to appear on a routine basis in the New York society columns. They claimed membership to literary societies and other programs that put on respectable mixers that put them into contact with young women in genteel contexts.[23] New York statutes forbade masquerades, so Isaacs publicized the event as a "Fancy Dress Ball." The guests intuited the meaning and came dressed as Little Red Riding Hood and Shakespearean figures such as Romeo and Hamlet. No one appeared as Esther, Mordecai, or other Jewish personalities. Isaacs hired the Seventh Regiment Band to entertain the higher classes of New York until 4 a.m.[24] The affair was very well received, compelling Isaacs to galvanize friends and formalize the Purim Association of the City of New York to ensure that the newfound tradition would persist.

The New York Purim ball straddled the line between a Jewish ritual and a New York society event. Yet, it hewed in the direction of the latter. The Purim Association did not hold the gala on the actual date of Purim—usually the day after or in the subsequent week—allowing Jewish Gothamites to observe Purim with its more traditional and less extravagant trappings. Decoupling the Purim ball from the ritual of Purim indicated to interested parties that the ball was meant to signify the Jewish community's contribution to Manhattan culture rather than a narrower Jewish event—or, as Isaacs put it, to "come off in such a way as to justify the suggestion that all New York is celebrating Purim."[25] Each year, members of the Purim Association were charged to "use their influence" to persuade a wider swath of society to attend the event.[26]

The New York Purim ball's second installment was upgraded to the Academy of Music. The Purim Association distributed eight hundred invitations, which turned out to be quite insufficient. In all, three thousand women and men attended the ball in March 1863. A report published in the *New York Times* declared that a "more brilliant affair has never been witnessed at the Academy." The article focused on two aspects: elegance and decorum. Emphasizing the purported ethnic features of the Jewesses present, the newspaper complimented the "black-eyed beauties" in attendance: "So many pretty faces have never before been seen at one occasion." They dressed in decidedly non-Jewish costumes as Joan of Arc, Mother Goose, Pocahontas, and Anne Boleyn: "Many of the dresses

23. Goodman, "Purim Association of the City of New York," 140–42.
24. See J.S.R. "The Purim Ball," *Jewish Messenger*, March 21, 1862, 88–89.
25. "The Purim Ball," *Jewish Messenger*, March 22, 1867, 4.
26. See, for example, Society, "The Purim Ball," *Jewish Messenger*, February 14, 1879, 2.

were exceedingly rich and displayed great taste."[27] Mention was also made of the fine musical composition, which solidified the Purim ball's standing as a culturally serious enterprise, not just a well-planned party. The Purim Association counted on these favorable reviews; the organizers furnished a press room for journalists, where they could write and enjoy complimentary snacks.[28]

The masquerade theme might have fit into Jewish tradition, but Isaacs intended for it to appeal to all New Yorkers. Routinely, the top-priced seating boxes went to couples with surnames such as Seligman, Rosenwald, Schiff, and Guggenheim.[29] The Purim Association spared no expense on the music. On several occasions, composers of high caliber such as Claudio Grafulla tested their works in progress on the crowds. Isaacs noted that Matthew Arbuckle's military band tended to excite the audience and complement other musical guests in the galleries. Needing to meet raised expectations year after year, the Purim Association arranged in the 1880s for appearances by Her Majesty's Orchestra along with members of various British ballet companies. The Purim Association floor committee took it upon itself to engage the opulent population in regimented dancing. Another committee worked hard before the event to make certain that "even Paris itself could not present a more beautiful picture." A correspondent for the *Jewish Messenger* described one Purim ball scene:

> The decorations were in the best of taste; the usual bareness of the stage was set off by a rustic bridge, covered with flowers and evergreens, and surmounted by a gas jet, blazing with the words "merry Purim." Under the bridge, a waterfall flowed through a bed of lilies and roses. From the large centre chandelier, were suspended drapings of various colors, which were connected with the balcony boxes, while the proscenium boxes were decorated with beautifully designed floral devices, bearing the monograph of the society. In the lobby there were plants and flowers in profusion, and a delicate perfume pervaded the air. Added to this, a dozen electric lights shed their dazzling lustre on the scene.[30]

The guests could be counted on to add to this splendid atmosphere, embracing the evening's unique masquerade feature (Fig. 72). The outfits displayed at the annual affair were the types of costumes that a Mr. Parodi, a preferred patron for the Purim ball, had for rent in his shop.[31] In one report of a masquerade ball, a Miss Plato won a prize for impersonating the "Queen of Hearts," but there was

27. "The Purim Ball," *New York Times*, March 7, 1863, 2.
28. J.W., "New York," *American Israelite*, March 23, 1883, 315.
29. "The Purim Ball," *American Hebrew*, March 16, 1883, 5.
30. "The Purim Ball," *Jewish Messenger*, March 18, 1881, 5.
31. "Purim Ball," *Jewish Messenger*, March 10, 1865, 79.

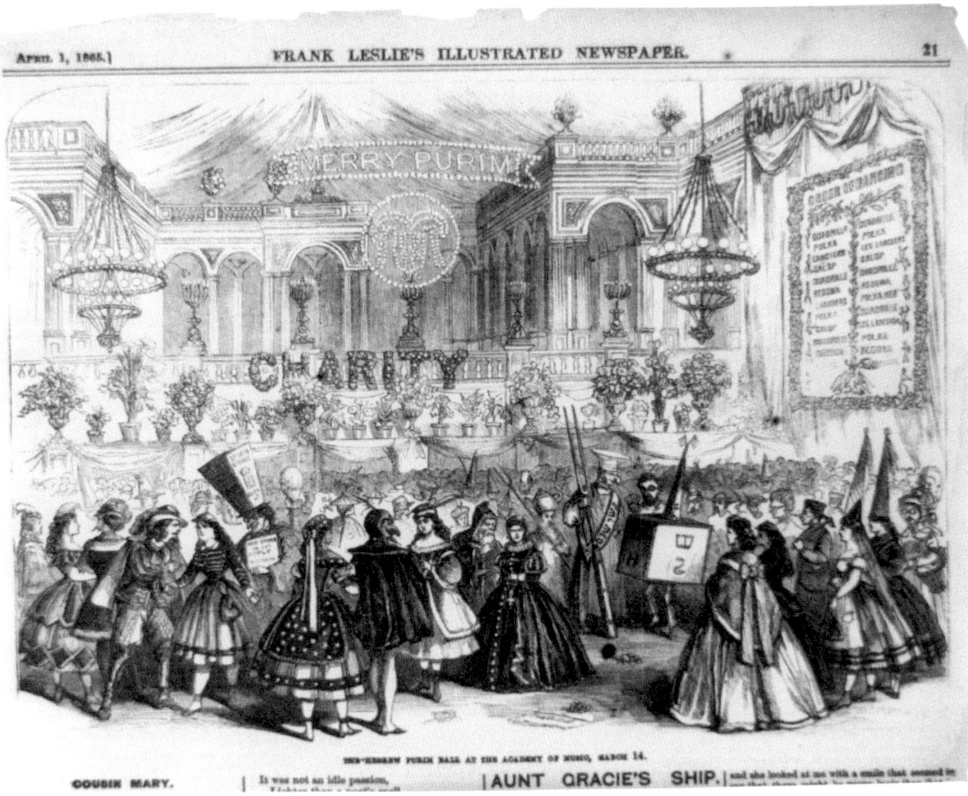

Fig. 72. "The Hebrew Purim Ball at the Academy of Music, March 14." *Frank Leslie's Illustrated Newspaper*, April 1, 1865, p. 21. (Library of Congress).

no mention of a single Queen Esther entered into the costume competition.[32] Subsequent iterations of the grand celebration included more Purim-themed pageantries but still maintained a cool embrace of Esther and the Jewishly focused Purim narrative.[33] Decades later, Queen Esther started to appear among the costume varieties. In the 1880s, an actress reportedly dressed like a Persian-attired Esther took her cue from the orchestra to "descend from her throne" and commence the dancing.[34] Still, the heroine of the Purim tale more often came up short against the popularity of other royals like the Queen of Sheba.[35]

Isaacs was likely just as pleased to see mention of societal correctness maintained at the affair. At the 1863 Purim ball, "[t]he most perfect order prevailed,

32. "That Purim," *Jewish Progress*, March 6, 1885, 4.

33. The exception proves the rule. In 1866, one journalist reported that the "essentially Hebrew character of the affair, was in itself a pleasant surprise." See "Purim Suggestions," *Jewish Messenger*, March 9, 1866, 1.

34. "The Purim Ball," *Jewish Messenger*, March 9, 1883, 2.

35. "The Purim Ball," *Jewish Messenger*, March 2, 1888, 2.

and every arrangement, police, supper, hat and cloak, and whatever, was perfect and unmarred by the slightest accident." The journalist confessed that the "usual variety of absurdities" was exhibited, but most everything redounded to the graceful production of the Purim ball.[36] The fine and effusive reviews were sufficient for Isaacs to declare that the Purim ball had emerged, by its second iteration, as a Manhattan "institution," an affair "naturalized in New York."[37] After almost two decades of service, Isaacs started to entrust others to arrange the finer details of the yearly masquerade. "To say that the Purim Association will conduct the affair," he once wrote in valedictory tones, "is to indicate that it will be a credit to New York."[38]

One particular episode emphasizes Isaacs's concern for the public relations of his grand event. In 1868, a group of young Jewish women and men was arrested during a brief social visit on their way to the Purim ball. They were escorted to a police station and arraigned for violating New York City's law against donning masks in public. The charges were dropped, but Isaacs's outrage lingered. It was evident that these people were celebrants on their way to the marquee Purim ball and not conspirators in some insidious plot of hooliganism. Isaacs pointed out that city officials, including the chief of police, were regular guests of the annual soirée and could themselves testify to the innocence of the occasion. As Isaacs wrote in the *Jewish Messenger*, "Purim masquerades have never in our city, in a single instance, given rise in any consequence more disastrous than a severe cold, a violent headache, or an incurable disease of the heart."[39] However, at least one New York newspaperman disagreed. An editorial in the *New York Observer* averred that the "law forbidding persons to go about with masks on is a good one." The writer rejected Isaacs's reasoning and reduced the Purim ball to a Jewish affair, a problematic event arranged by a "foreign" element:

> If it were understood that the Jews had one night in a year when they were allowed to disregard the law, every thief and robber who wished to wear a mask would turn Jew for that night at least. All these foreigners who come among us must understand that good laws cannot be repealed or violated to suit their manners and customs. They must do as other people have to do; and if they are not satisfied, they can go back again.[40]

36. "The Purim Ball," *New York Times*, March 7, 1863, 2.

37. See "The Purim Ball," *Jewish Messenger*, March 13, 1863, 6, and "The Purim Ball," *Jewish Messenger*, March 6, 1868, 4.

38. "The Purim Ball," *Jewish Messenger*, February 14, 1879, 4.

39. "Law and Order," *Jewish Messenger*, March 13, 1868, 1.

40. "Editorial," *New York Observer*, March 19, 1868, 94.

Isaacs recorded his indignation at the "contemptible paragraph," a not uncommon threat to strip his coreligionists of their American citizenship and him of his station among the higher classes of New York. He wrote an "angry letter" to the publisher of the offending newspaper, but nothing under his name appeared in subsequent issues.[41] In his own newspaper, Isaacs reproduced the anti-Jewish editorial, comparing its sentiments to Ulysses S. Grant's General Orders No. 11, which expelled Jews from his military territory during the Civil War. Isaacs focused his rebuke on the epithet "foreigner," reminding his readers that most traditions and rituals practiced in the relatively young United States were imported from overseas. Isaacs surmised that, like his intentions for the Purim ball, it was the role of the Jew in this situation to educate and cultivate the surrounding population: "If, in educating the world, he is compelled to expose the ignorance, illiberality and fanaticism of those who pretend to form public opinion, he cannot decline the contest he has the power to meet successfully."[42]

The episode proved to be just a minor distraction, with no material impact on the Purim Association and its costume ball. "Refinement and social culture," pundits continued to agree, "dominated the vast assemblage."[43] New York socialites—otherwise involved in business, theater, and politics—continued to gravitate to the event, looking forward to the Purim ball after the series of more "reckless" socials conducted by German societies concluded by mid-February.[44] Tickets for the event did not last long on the open market, especially the preferred theater boxes.[45] In the early 1890s, the Purim Association rented a larger space in Madison Square Garden and held an auction for the choicest seats in the vestry room of Temple Emanu-El.[46] In the first two decades of the Purim Association's activity, the ball's proceeds usually netted a sizeable sum, about $18,000 (today, $480,000). The funds were distributed to the local Jewish hospital, benevolent society, or orphan asylum.[47] By the 1880s, the galas several times accrued more than $150,000 (today, $4 million).[48] In the final decades of the century, a significant portion of the funds was concentrated toward

41. Entry for March 19, 1868, Myer S. Isaacs Diary.
42. "Israelites on Sufferance," *Jewish Messenger*, March 27, 1868, 1.
43. "The Purim Ball," *American Hebrew*, March 8, 1889, 66.
44. "The Purim Ball," *Jewish Messenger*, February 12, 1869, 4.
45. See, for example, "New York Letter," *American Israelite*, March 12, 1875, 5, and "The Purim Ball," *American Hebrew*, February 4, 1887, 200.
46. "The Purim Ball," *American Hebrew*, February 24, 1893, 556.
47. See finances listed in "The Purim Ball," *Jewish Messenger*, February 27, 1880, 5.
48. See "The Purim Ball," *Jewish Messenger*, March 18, 1881, 5.

assisting the wave of eastern European immigrants settling in the United States, a preferred cause of Myer Isaacs later in life.[49]

The success of New York's Purim ball inspired emulation. Charleston's Jews held a two-part program, catering first to children and later in the evening to adults.[50] St. Louis's Jews were very proud of their "well-regulated" masquerade ball, which, they claimed, was "one of the most enjoyable affairs in the society world."[51] In New Orleans, where the tradition predated the New York incarnation, festivities continued into the last decades of the century and were enhanced by "elegant and costly costumes" and pageants that competed with the best local Christmas scenes.[52] Each locale fashioned the event according to its own milieu. The Purim program held at Philadelphia's Young Men's Hebrew Association, much influenced by the local Jewish aristocracy, was orchestrated more like a debutante ball.[53]

Purim balls were also effective programs for Jews in smaller enclaves. The balls were replicated in Montgomery, Alabama, and Wilkes-Barre, Pennsylvania.[54] The annual galas in Orangeburg, South Carolina, drew local conservative Christians as well as Jewish visitors from relatively larger communities in Charleston, Savannah, and Augusta.[55] With orchestra accompaniment and room to spare at the upscale Centre Square Hall, the Purim ball in Allentown, Pennsylvania, was so highly regarded that reservations were placed by "leading society people from Philadelphia, New York and Baltimore."[56]

As in New York, Purim balls across the United States attracted Jews and non-Jews. For example, the Hebrew Ladies' Benevolent Society in Atlanta held a Purim ball to support the local orphanage and recruited guests from "all persuasions of our citizens."[57] The Purim balls in Chicago were expanded in the 1890s for the many "visiting strangers."[58] The Hebrew Benevolent Society of Brooklyn arranged a Purim ball for "well-to-do citizens without regard to race

49. See "The Purim Ball," *Jewish Messenger*, March 3, 1882, 5.

50. Minnie, "Purim Ball," *American Israelite*, April 5, 1878, 5.

51. "The Purim Ball of the Ladies' Hebrew Relief Society," *Jewish Free Press*, March 19, 1886, 4.

52. "The Purim Ball," *American Israelite*, March 21, 1884, 2.

53. "Hebrew Assembly," *Philadelphia Inquirer*, March 6, 1891, 2.

54. See "The Purim Ball," *Daily Dispatch* (Montgomery), March 5, 1886, 8, and "Purim Ball," *Sunday News Dealer* (Wilkes-Barre), March 4, 1883, 8.

55. "Purim Ball," *Times and Democrat* (Orangeburg), March 25, 1886, 9.

56. "The Purim Ball," *Morning Call* (Allentown), January 5, 1885, 1.

57. "The Purim Ball," *Goldsboro Daily Argus*, February 25, 1898, 4.

58. Sholem, "Ligonier, Ind.," *American Israelite*, March 20, 1890, 1.

or religious prejudices."[59] In Spokane, Washington, Christians attended the ball even though it coincided with the restrictive observances of Lent.[60] The *Weekly Banner* in Brenham, Texas, reported that the Purim programs produced there by the Young People's Hebrew Benevolent Society "have always been very popular and are attended by citizens generally."[61] About a hundred miles away, another grand ball was arranged on a yearly basis by the Ladies' Hebrew Aid Society in Waco.[62] Similarly, the Jewish community of Texarkana, Arkansas, opened the main parlor doors of the local Harmony Club around 10 p.m. for a "grand march." The multireligious attendees danced and enjoyed the Purim ball long past midnight.[63]

The balls in each location shared some similar characteristics. Full of pageantry but light on Jewish content, the events were cultural and entertaining, and usually featured music and dancing. Their late-evening start times provided an added dimension of high-class social consumption for adults, Jewish or not, who valued an elegant soirée (Fig. 73, a–f). Finally, Purim balls were, in the main, organized by laypeople. In New York, the Purim ball was prepared by young men, usually unmarried and aspiring to the most elevated rungs of Manhattan's social scene. Elsewhere, women's benevolent groups assumed responsibility for the Purim pageants. Excluded from synagogue boardrooms, Jewish women were eager to handle these arrangements and took pride in the much-anticipated event.

Purim balls rarely took place in the synagogue. Religious leaders like Rabbi Isaac Mayer Wise expressed displeasure with the Purim ball phenomenon, and perhaps revealed more than a modicum of jealousy in their vituperations against the popular and usually lay-led events. In March 1875, Wise supposed that Myer Isaacs would be "in his glory this week" after another Purim ball and the adoration and acclaim that came to him in the New York society pages. "Please don't expect me to do the same," wrote Wise in his own Cincinnati newspaper, "for the spectacle of hundreds of ladies dressed in all the colors of the rainbow, the hundreds of gentlemen all wearing the depressing swallow-tail, and all dancing, flirting or promenading."[64] Isaacs was unrepentant. Rabbinic elites like Wise

59. "The Purim Ball," *Brooklyn Daily Eagle*, March 7, 1884, 4.
60. "The Purim Ball," *Spokane Review*, March 15, 1892, 5.
61. "Purim Ball," *Brenham Weekly Banner*, February 6, 1880, 3.
62. "Waco, Tex.," *American Israelite*, February 17, 1898, 3.
63. "Texarkana, Ark.," *Jewish Voice*, March 22, 1895, 6.
64. "New York Letter," *American Israelite*, March 26, 1875, 4.

P
MERRY PURIM
Mr Jenkins receives an invitation to the Purim Ball.

(*a*)

COSTUMES.
He selects a costume
a la, Chinois.

(*b*)

(*c*)

Fig. 73 (*a–f*). A suite of sequential pencil sketches by John Avery, Jr. (1830–1883), dating from the 1860s. (Princeton University Library. Gift of Leonard Milberg);

(*facing, a–b*)*:* (*a*) "Mr. Jenkins receives an invitation to the Purim Ball"; (*b*) "He selects a costume *à la Chinois*";

(*above, c*): (*c*) "He executes a *pas de chin chin*";

(*overleaf, d–f*): (*d*) "Imminent mirth of the fairy who tied their tails together"; (*e*) "The result—when they got up to dance"; (*f*) "And what followed—."

MERRY PURIM
Innocent mirth of the fairy who tied their tails together –

(*d*)

The result – when they got up to dance –

(*e*)

And what followed –

(*f*)

"condemn us for attributing so much consequence to a mere social assemblage," he wrote about the charge that the Purim ball minimized the Jewish aspects of the holiday. But Isaacs was proud that an emerging generation of American Jews had come to look forward to the holiday. What is more, he argued, the "Purim festival, as celebrated here and in other cities during the past few years, has been the means of creating a kindly and favorable impression of the Jewish community in the eyes of their neighbors."[65] He well understood that the success of the Purim ball contrasted with the present soporific state of the synagogue. Isaacs pressed a challenge to the rabbinical class of American Jewish leadership to step up and recast Purim as they saw fit, but in a light that shown bright enough to attract the rest of American Jewry's attention.

Rabbis and Religious Declension

In November 1885, Rabbi Samuel Hirsch of Philadelphia's Keneseth Israel pleaded with his Reform rabbinical colleagues to redouble their efforts to "imbue [holidays] with life."[66] Hirsch was among a handful of rabbis who attended a much-discussed conference to write and vote on a set of religious planks.[67] He feared that much of the group's business would be to dispatch with traditions that appeared to them outmoded, and he beseeched his colleagues to consider reorientation rather than rejection.

The American rabbinate had read much commentary from laypeople in the newspapers complaining that religious elites spent too much energy on tinkering with the ritual prescriptions of the Sabbath and not enough time on holidays. A Jew from Bowling Green, Kentucky, for example, testified that "holidays pass with little or no observance, and such observance as exists is merely a form whose significance is unthought of or forgotten: a custom to the old, a compulsion to the young."[68] Another writer, likely Hirsch's son, Rabbi Emil G. Hirsch, lamented the attitudes festering in his local community. "Chicago has been slandered," offered the anonymous writer, "the report is rife in the land that we care but little for the Jewish holidays."[69] In response to these appeals

65. "The Purim Ball," *Jewish Messenger*, April 5, 1867, 4.

66. "Authentic Report of the Proceedings of the Rabbinical Conference," *Jewish Reformer*, January 22, 1886, 3.

67. On the Pittsburgh Conference, see Jonathan D. Sarna, "New Light on the Pittsburgh Platform of 1885," *American Jewish History* 76, no. 3 (1987): 358–68.

68. N.M.B, "Correspondence," *Jewish Reformer*, April 16, 1886, 7.

69. Radical, "Our Chicago Letter," *Jewish Reformer*, March 26, 1886, 6.

to animate a listless Jewish calendar, rabbis in the United States called for a reexamination of holiday messaging and rituals.[70] The multiple perspectives offered in newspapers and other religious outlets represent the complex ways in which American Jews sought to leverage and augment their traditions and rituals for the sake of a Jewish revival in the United States.

In the 1870s, the religious condition of American Judaism was in sorry shape. To help remedy the situation, Jewish religious elites looked to women to inspire themselves and their husbands and children to return to the religious fold. During the prior decades, the Civil War had an unusual impact on Jews. On the one hand, America's Israelites had been in a very good position in the garment industry to profit from the need for uniforms and, later, the desire among veterans to reenter civilian life dressed in the latest styles.[71] The influx of wealth into the American Jewish community resulted in a synagogue boom. In addition, the war's lessons in moral authority and the powerful image of Abraham Lincoln combined to impress the need for strong top-down leadership structures. Both of these "determinants of change" increased the stature of the American rabbinate.[72] Yet, the expansion of rabbinic authority and the appearance of cavernous and unfamiliar synagogue buildings also tended to alienate the rank-and-file from religious life.

This discontent was particularly true among the rising generation of American Jews in the 1870s.[73] A pundit in New York feared that "young Israelites do not manifest that love for the synagogue which their fathers and forefathers showed."[74] Another in Philadelphia noted that among the local synagogues he frequented, it was evident that a "large proportion of the children of congregants is not present."[75] In Baltimore, a journalist opined that synagogue attendees were better off without the younger crowd. "There are a great many young persons whose behavior during services is really scandalous," complained David Binswanger. "Talking, giggling, and a general want of attention are not only very annoying to the worshippers and disrespectful to the officiating ministers, but they are positively sacrilegious in violating the properties of the House of

70. See, for example, L. Kleeberg, "The Rationality of the Progressive Movement," *Jewish Reformer*, March 12, 1886, 9.

71. See Adam Mendelsohn, "Beyond the Battlefield: Reevaluating the Legacy of the Civil War for American Jews," *American Jewish Archives Journal* 64, no. 1–2 (2012): 83–111.

72. On "determinants of change," see Zev Eleff, *Who Rules the Synagogue? Religious Authority and the Formation of American Judaism* (New York: Oxford University Press, 2016), 129–58.

73. *Ibid.*, 167–74.

74. "Hebrew Rabbinical Education," *New York Herald*, June 11, 1872, 5.

75. "Why Are They Absent?" *Jewish Record*, February 14, 1879, 4.

God." Binswanger claimed that he was in receipt of "several communications calling attention to the want of decorum," testimonies that supported his grim report of Jewish religious life.[76] Binswanger's brother in St. Louis similarly lamented that Jews in his community disregarded the Sabbath and other prescriptions of Jewish law in the synagogue and in the home. His coreligionists "believe in Saturday as the day of rest," bemoaned Augustus Binswanger, "but not as a holy day."[77] All this evidence pointed to a religious downturn and the need for a collective search for ways to rescue Jewish life from this nadir.

One popular prospective savior was the Jewish woman. Americans of all kinds viewed wives and mothers as the most powerful forces in their homes.[78] Rabbis surmised that women could use that influence to direct more traffic to the synagogue. Since the colonial era, the congregation was the core institution of American Jewish life. Organizations like the Young Men's Hebrew Association, cultural societies, and education-minded institutions challenged the synagogue's hegemony. Rabbis hoped that by appealing to Jewish women, they could maintain the status quo. For example, Rabbi Kaufmann Kohler suffered terrible attrition at his synagogue in Chicago.[79] In his struggles to bring "business men, and chiefly the young people," to religious services, he called on the "Jewish woman, who best represents the heart of the household," to support his cause.[80] Kohler was a staunch advocate of a traditional view of the "delicate" woman who cultivates those domestic virtues that produce "robust" men and ensure Jewish life within and without the home.[81] In Kohler's words, "women's responsibility stands uppermost in fashioning the character of men. Not only at home, but also in society at large."[82]

76. David Binswanger, "Behavior in the Synagogue," *Jewish Chronicle*, February 9, 1875, 5.

77. See Augustus Binswanger, *An Address before Shaare Emeth Congregation, St. Louis, MO. March 4th, 1887* (Chicago: Occident, 1887), 7.

78. See, for example, Richard L. Bushman, *The Refinement of America: Persons, Houses, Cities* (New York: Knopf, 1992), 100–38.

79. "Too Many Rabbis," *Daily Inter-Ocean* (Chicago), June 20, 1879, 3.

80. Kaufmann Kohler, *The Origin of the Sabbath* (Chicago, 1876), 19–20.

81. Kaufmann Kohler, *Esther or the Jewish Woman*, vol. 5 of 20 Lectures Delivered at Temple Beth-El (New York: Stettiner, Lambert & Co., 1888), 2; the series is available at the American Jewish Historical Society. On Kohler's view of Jewish womanhood, see Karla Goldman, "The Ambivalence of Reform Judaism: Kaufmann Kohler and the Ideal Jewish Woman," *American Jewish History* 79, no. 4 (1990): 477–99. Kohler argued that his view of women's roles was different from earlier perspectives. The Old World, maintained Kohler, "dresses the young woman for the marriage market … building a golden cage around her to make her look upon her life as a mere pleasure ground and play, until life's solemn duties take her by surprise and disappoint her in her false and foolish expectations." See Kohler, *Esther*, 7.

82. Kohler, *Esther*, 6.

To be sure, women were also affected by the far-reaching religious malaise. One Jewess in Gotham put her rabbis on notice that, unless they improved their craft, she and her friends would continue to quench their intellectual curiosities at the Sunday lectures given by the Ethical Culturalist and self-proclaimed heretic Felix Adler:

> We like to be instructed on subjects with which we sympathize. We prefer to listen to all sermons on Saturdays; but if our rabbis decline to leave the beaten track and cull flowers for us in the open fields, do not blame us for figuring among the Sunday audiences. Besides, many of us young ladies are not long from school—a foreign accent, and occasional breaches of grammar grate upon our ears.[83]

This case notwithstanding, Kohler and other rabbinic elites continued to look to women to persuade their husbands and brothers to return to Judaism. Much of his evidence was inferred from biblical interpretation. He pointed to Miriam and Deborah, who, as Kohler interpreted their stories, exercised leadership by inspiring Moses and Barak to act.[84] Yet, both examples appeared as sidebars in a published sermon that focused on Queen Esther of the Purim tale. Kohler approved of Esther's integrity, her acceptance of Mordecai's guidance, and her appeal to Ahashverosh to exercise his monarchical powers to vanquish Haman and support Jewish interests. These were lessons that ought to have resonated in Kohler's time. "Women's idealism may redeem the commonest of men from his coarseness and lift him to purer and nobler views and habits," he preached. "She can by her finer tact elevate the tone of conversation, and by her glow of enthusiasm and sympathy charm the silliest man into reverence of the truly good and pure and perfect; and again, by levity and flippancy drag the loftiest aims of men down into the mire of selfishness and vulgarity."[85]

The "Queen Esther" Revival

Kaufmann Kohler's sermon from the late 1880s reflected the emergence of Queen Esther in American Jewish discourse. Decades earlier, she was none too popular. Esther had intermarried when she wed King Ahashverosh, an arrangement

83. Sylvia, "A Hint to Our Preachers," *Jewish Messenger*, March 28, 1877, 5. Felix Adler was the scion of a prominent Reform rabbinic family and leader of the religiously agnostic Ethical Culture Movement. See Benny *Kraut, From Reform Judaism to Ethical Culture: The Religious Evolution of Felix Adler* (Cincinnati: Hebrew Union College Press, 1979).

84. See Karla Goldman, *Beyond the Synagogue Gallery: Finding a Place for Women in American Judaism* (Cambridge, Mass.: Harvard University Press, 2000), 164.

85. Kohler, *Esther*, 6.

frowned upon by American Jewish leaders who worried about assimilation. Moreover, her story concludes with vengeful battles and gruesome executions, elements that did not sit well with the genteel attitudes of the Victorian Age. For this reason, the English novelist Grace Aguilar downplayed the gory vengeance and instead highlighted Esther's "woman's work," namely, her "strength of prayer."[86] Aguilar tried her very best to portray Esther as Victorian, not at all "in a vindictive and unfeminine light," gaining the approval of Solomon da Silva Solis, an American Jewish intellectual who had a hand in bringing Aguilar's publications to the United States.[87] But even more than Esther's intermarriage and role as the leader of a "bloodthirsty" band of Hebrews, the total absence of God from the narrative did much to push the Book of Esther down in the biblical power rankings.

American Jews possessed a surfeit of Jewish heroines. In addition to the classical matriarchs of Genesis, they touted Ruth and Deborah. Ruth was the "outsider" who observed the best of Judaism and converted her way into "insider" status.[88] Along with Rebecca, Deborah was the inspiration for several Jewish periodicals in the United States and Europe.[89] Esther, freighted with complicated baggage, was therefore expendable. Some Jews did not bother to defend Esther, even as Purim reemerged as a popular Jewish holiday. When discussed, commentators described Esther with apologetic overtones. For example, several mid-nineteenth-century rabbinic writers in the United States published essays around Purim time that called into question the historical accuracy of the Book of Esther, pointing out the tale's absence from Persian texts.[90] Christians also paid little attention to Esther. Protestant and Catholic theologians struggled to make meaning out of a text that makes not a single reference to

86. See Grace Aguilar, *The Women of Israel*, vol. 1 (London: R. Groombridge, 1845), 146–47.

87. *Ibid.*, 151; and S. Solis, "Remarks on Miss Aguilar's 'Women of Israel,'" *Occident* (May 1846): 88.

88. See Zev Eleff, "For Insiders or Outsiders? The Book of Ruth's American Jewish Reception," in *Gleanings: Interdisciplinary Reflections on Ruth*, ed. Stuart W. Halpern (New York: Yeshiva University Press, 2019), 195–209.

89. See Maria T. Baader, "From 'the Priestess of the Home' to 'the Rabbi's Brilliant Daughter': Concepts of Jewish Womanhood and Progressive Germanness in *Die Deborah* and the *American Israelite*, 1854–1900," *Leo Baeck Institute Year Book* 43 (January 1998): 50–52. My thanks to Jonathan Sarna for alerting me to this important article.

90. See, for example, Isidore Kalish, "Prefatory Remarks to the Book of Esther," *Israelite*, February 23, 1855, 261; M.E.M., "Remarks on the Book of Esther," *Israelite*, March 28, 1862, 310; and "Authenticity of the Book of Esther," *Jewish Messenger*, September 9, 1864, 73.

91. See Jo Carruthers, *Esther Through the Centuries* (Malden, Mass.: Wiley-Blackwell, 2008), 21–49.

God.[91] Some Jews lobbied unsuccessfully for Esther to enter the public ranks of Joan of Arc, Madame Roland, Maria Theresa, or even Cleopatra.[92] Other Jews, still beholden to the sacred book, preferred to focus on the self-assured Mordecai, who admonished the timid Esther to do the right thing on behalf of her people.[93]

Esther became more useful in the 1870s as her narrative seemed to fit better into the exigencies of American Jewish life. Jews in postbellum America looked to the Book of Esther for inspiration to grapple with an increasing awareness of growing antisemitism, what one historian has described as the "emergence of a full-fledged antisemitic society."[94] To be sure, Jews since the colonial era had been cognizant of their "outsider" status in some realms of American life.[95] Yet, events during and after the Civil War focused their consciousness and elevated the stakes.[96]

Eventually, American Jews found the Purim tale useful to cope with this sad reality. Situated in Persian exile, Esther's story, as Scott Langston has argued, simultaneously contains warnings of bigotry in a host nation and the support that American Jews might experience in a "foreign" land.[97] Fittingly, Jews cast Ulysses Grant as a Haman figure after he issued General Orders No. 11 in 1862 and again six years later when he ran for president.[98] In 1872, Rabbi Leopold Wintner of St. Paul, Minnesota, wrote about growing bigotry toward Jews that characterized them as a "class" apart from other Americans. Wintner also alluded to Lincoln, who rescinded Orders No. 11, when he praised the modern spirits that checked Grant-like personalities and the rising instances of antisemitism. "[L]ike the first Haman," Wintner assured his readers, "who found his doom through the agency of the [*sic*] Queen Esther, so will also the Hamans of our

92. "Esther," *Jewish Messenger*, March 14, 1862, 78.

93. "Our Old Hero," *Jewish Messenger*, March 6, 1868, 1.

94. Leonard Dinnerstein, *Antisemitism in America* (New York: Oxford University Press, 1994), 35.

95. For a survey of American Jewry's encounter with intolerance and openness, see Zev Eleff, "The Jewish Encounter with Discrimination, Tolerance and Pluralism in the United States," in *Interpreting American Jewish History at Museums and Historic Sites*, ed. Avi Y. Decter (Lanham, Md.: Rowman & Littlefield, 2016), 161–78.

96. See Jonathan D. Sarna, *When General Grant Expelled the Jews* (New York: Nextbook/Schocken, 2012), 3–23.

97. See Scott M. Langston, "Reading a Text Backward: The Book of Esther and Nineteenth-Century Jewish American Interpretations," in *The Book of Esther in Modern Research*, ed. Leonard J. Greenspoon and Sidnie White Crawford (London: T&T Clark International, 2003), 20–16.

98. See Sarna, *When General Grant Expelled the Jews*, 49.

days fall before that beautiful and illustrious Queen—Civilization!"[99] Another Jewish writer found similarities between Esther and Jews in the United States, like the diplomat Oscar Straus, who worked alongside benevolent rulers and governments that halted hatred. Jews could take a lesson from Esther and "help perpetuate the republic."[100] Others envisioned the orphaned Esther as the immigrant Jew on New York's Lower East Side who required ennobling support from her government.[101]

Religious leaders were in the vanguard of efforts to reposition Esther. Rabbi Kohler and others concerned about the languishing religious condition seized on her narrative to preach on the feminine role in Jewish revival. Importantly, obedience and compromise were familiar tropes for Reform Jewish leaders deploying Esther as their scriptural lodestar. Rabbi Julius Goldammer of Cincinnati, for example, praised Esther as that "noble and generous woman" who risked her life, not to mention royal luxury, for her people.[102] Also in the Queen City, Rabbi Isaac Mayer Wise praised Esther's willingness to obey the sagacious Mordecai.[103] On a different occasion, the pragmatic Wise compared himself to Mordecai and his progressive rabbinical school's much-needed benefactors to Esther, who gave pause to her "busy life of plenty" and "cast a glance at the misery of [her] poor brethren who are being inhumanly maltreated and outraged."[104]

Orthodox Jews also celebrated "our Esthers [who] do good for the cause of our faith when some of the sterner sex are careless."[105] In fact, the increased popularity of Purim inspired one commentator to pray that in the "mirth and glee of Purim wit and humor, all the scathing wounds of life's dire battle, all the sore controversies and quarrels between Orthodox and Reform ... be forgotten."[106] Whether or not the prayer was answered, the sentiments from all spectrums of American Judaism aligned. One of the leading Orthodox exponents, Rabbi Henry Pereira Mendes of Shearith Israel in New York, produced a Purim play that took certain liberties with the tale of Esther to admonish the

99. "The Hamans of History and of Our Days," *Israelite*, April 12, 1872, 8. See also "In the King's House," *American Hebrew*, March 3, 1893, 576.

100. Judaeus, "What Would You Do If You Were a Rabbi?" *Jewish Messenger*, April 18, 1890, 3. On Straus and antisemitism, see Naomi W. Cohen, *A Dual Heritage: The Public Career of Oscar S. Straus* (Philadelphia: Jewish Publication Society of America, 1969), 67–73.

101. "Merry Purim," *Jewish Messenger*, March 14, 1884, 3.

102. "The Story of Esther," *Israelite*, March 18, 1870, 8.

103. "Mordecai Richly Rewarded," *American Israelite*, November 29, 1878, 4.

104. "The Good and Wise Mordecai," *American Israelite*, January 27, 1882, 244.

105. "Purim," *Jewish Messenger*, March 19, 1875, 4.

106. "The Purim Festival," *Jewish Reformer*, March 19, 1886, 1.

women in the audience to look after their husbands' spiritual well-being. In archaic prose, Mendes imagined Mordecai upbraiding the Jewish maidens of Shushan and blaming them for the miscreant behavior of young men and the "irreligion" spreading throughout their land:

Oh, ye young women! Ye have much
To do with irreligion such
As now has seized on our young men!
You countenance their folly when
They mock what's holy, just to please
Their fancies. If you'd only seize
Each opportunity to say
You scorn the man who throws away
Respect and duty, quickly he
To his religion true would be![107]

Mendes did not hold back, peppering Mordecai's rebuke with contemporaneous religious infractions. Like Kohler, Mendes pointed out the low regard in which American Hebrews held the Sabbath. More concerned with traditional Jewish practice than his Reform colleagues, Mendes added to his script transgressions against the kosher dietary laws:

For shame ye maidens! Yours the fault,
Whose echoes reach high heaven's vault!
Refuse to smile upon the man
Whose coward, dastard spirit can
Incite him thus to sin, and ye
Will find our faith will honored be!
Ye join them when on Sabbath nights,
They seek unsanctified delights!
Ye join them when, in faithless mood,
They sit and eat forbidden food.
Ye join them when they dare refuse
To own that they by birth are Jews![108]

Mendes's remedy, issued through Mordecai, was clear: "Set good example, you, the maids, and never shall portentous shades of coming punishment be seen approaching."[109] Like his rabbinic counterparts, Mendes was convinced that women must play a role in reviving Jewish life by rousing their languishing menfolk. Queen Esther, more than any other female biblical personality, set

107. H. Pereira Mendes, *Esther: A Purim Play* (New York: Philip Cowen, 1899), 14.
108. *Ibid.*, 15.
109. *Ibid.*

the example. All these considerations helped to elevate the Book of Esther in American Jewish discourse. By June 1880, a rabbi in Evansville, Indiana, could confidently expect of his listeners that the "history of Esther is undoubtedly familiar to every one of you."[110] Through Esther, then, the American rabbinate found its own ecclesiastical way to elevate Purim and reach the rank-and-file.

"The Opposite Happened" (Esther 9:1)

In time, the strategies of lay and rabbinic leaders influenced one another. Synagogue leaders recognized the utility of the Purim ball for social and financial purposes. In March 1898, a Brooklyn reporter who had attended the annual Purim ball held at Beth Elohim found it to be "among the most notable events that have taken place this season in Jewish circles."[111] The "old-style orthodox" congregation on Crown Street in Philadelphia was "gaining friends in the community" because of a grand "Hebrew Charity Ball" that was host to "eight hundred joyous faces, intent on fun and frolic."[112] Some of the newspaper reports indicated the more pragmatic purposes of these affairs. For example, to raise funds for a new fire escape, Boston's Congregation Ohabei Shalom rented space in a nearby fraternity hall to accommodate a large guest list for its Purim ball.[113]

The Esther rebound that started atop rabbinic lecterns made headway within lay circles. In 1881, in an issue of the *Purim Gazette* distributed at the New York Purim ball, the journalist Moritz Ellinger wrote about contemporary Esthers who secured "family life" with doses of "gentleness." The attitude reflected the Purim Association's newfound embrace of Esther.[114] Tracing the "Esthers" of Jewish history, Ellinger drew a straight line from Queen Esther through her spiritual heirs—including Gracia Mendes Nasi of Portugal in the sixteenth century and Rebecca Gratz in the United States of the mid-1800s—to the major task before current American Jewish women.[115] In some instances, Jewish women

110. "Mordecai a Type of Israel," *American Israelite*, June 4, 1880, 5. Not everyone joined the Esther cause. For instance, see Emil G. Hirsch, "The Story of Esther," *Reform Advocate*, March 9, 1895, 39–40. Hirsch much preferred the Hanukkah story over Esther's.

111. "Annual Purim Ball," *Brooklyn Daily Eagle*, March 9, 1898, 12.

112. Damocles, "Philadelphia News," *Israelite*, March 20, 1874, 6.

113. Bostonia, "Purim Ball," *American Israelite*, March 24, 1882, 309.

114. On the reception of the Purim Association's *Purim Gazette*, see, for example, "The Purim Festivities," *Jewish Messenger*, March 17, 1865, 91.

115. "A Few Jewish Women," *Purim Gazette* (1881): 9–10. I am grateful to Elisa Ho of the Jacob Rader Marcus Center of the American Jewish Archives for supplying me with a digital copy of this rare publication. Ellinger's essay was apparently well received and republished in

embraced the rabbis' presentations of Esther and advised other Jewesses to apply that wisdom to their lives. In Mobile, Alabama, Annie Jonas Moses published a Purim play in the 1870s that aimed to disabuse erstwhile Esther detractors and underline the virtues of the protagonist's femininity (Fig. 74). In Moses's rendering, Esther resisted intermarrying but, in the end, deferred to the far-thinking advice of Mordecai: "It is thy faith, Esther, that bids me urge thee still. Think of thy people, their sufferings and their degradation." To further assuage Esther's doubts, Mordecai urges her, "Seek then this power that may be granted thee! Endeavor to relieve or assist your brethren in affliction." Similarly, the Southern playwright downplayed the Jewish vengeance. King Ahashverosh applauds the Jews: "They have acted wisely and generously! They fought only when necessitated and have spared the homes and substance of those made desolate." What is more, in response to Jewish military ethics and Esther's sacrifice of her own Jewish identity, a Persian messenger relays that "many of the people of the land became Jews." Esther is gladdened and reports to Ahashverosh, "Thy Queen is but a humble representative of the virtues of her people."[116] Eve Davieson of Chicago concluded her own Purim poem in a similar vein:

> Esther knelt once more
> To save her people through her eloquence.
> Then, with a pure devotion, meekly turned
> And lifted up her heart and hands to God.[117]

Both authors gained admirers. Davieson's poetry was syndicated within the expanding Jewish press.[118] Likewise, Moses's play was featured in many synagogues and received top billing at a Purim ball in Petersburg, Virginia.[119] The demand for Moses's work was such that she revised and reissued the Purim play sixteen years after the appearance of the first edition.

The warm sentiments for Queen Esther trickled down to America's Jewish children. For instance, Jennie Morris of the New York Hebrew Free School won an essay prize for her "Esther" composition. After rehearsing the broad themes of the Book of Esther, the young lady beseeched "every girl" to "bear

---

a New York Jewish newspaper as "A Few Jewish Women," *American Hebrew*, April 1, 1881, 78. See also "The Purim Ball," *Jewish Messenger*, March 18, 1881, 5.

116. [Annie Jonas Moses], *Esther: A Drama in Five Acts* ([Mobile, 1871]), 10, 21, 22.

117. Eve Davieson, "Esther," *Reform Advocate*, March 7, 1896, 55.

118. For a detailed description of the rise of Jewish newspapers in this period, see Richard Gottheil and William Popper, "Periodicals," *Jewish Encyclopedia*, vol. 9, ed. Isidore Singer (New York: Funk & Wagnalls, 1905), 611–12.

119. "Petersburg, Va.," *American Israelite*, March 27, 1885, 2.

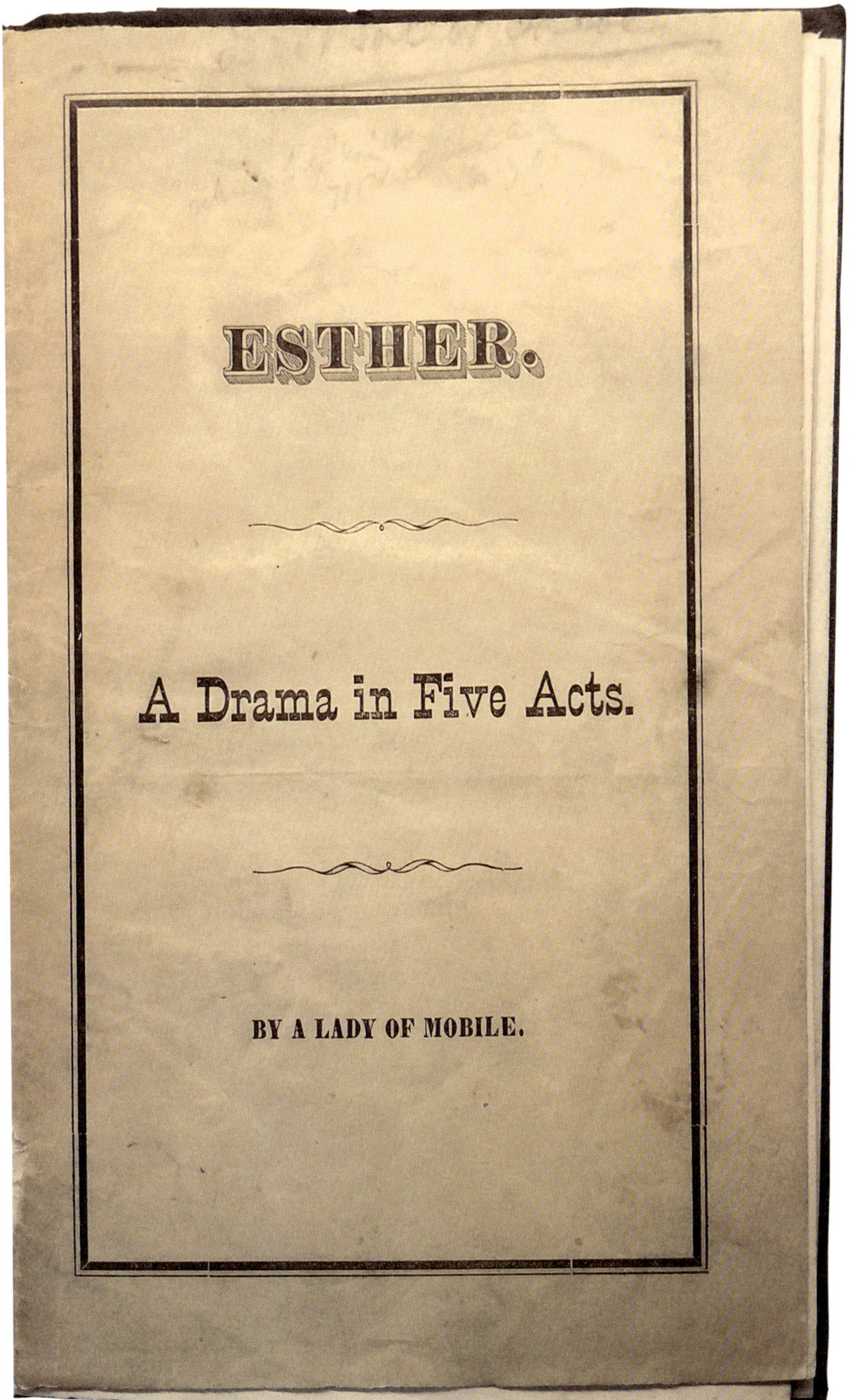

Fig. 74. [Annie Jonas Moses], *Esther. A Drama in Five Acts* ([Mobile, Ala., 1871]). (American Jewish Historical Society).

in mind that she has the power of influencing those around her by her sincere, religious and modest conduct." For Jewish males—"every boy and man"—the Free School's star student advised them to remain open to the "elevating and refining influence of those who follow the faithful and sincere conduct of women, who also go in the way of women such as Ruth and Queen Esther."[120]

These portrayals of a feminine Esther resonated best with the Jewish women whom Jacob Rader Marcus had in mind when he wrote that, "with very few exceptions, the American Jewesses of the postbellum years were apparently satisfied with their lot in life."[121] Then again, they were also agreeable to others who recognized that women's roles were in significant flux. These Jews desired an Esther who challenged the status quo. During the 1890s, Jewish women—like the individuals who founded the National Council of Jewish Women in 1893—became more aware of their capacity as laypeople to shape synagogue life and to promote causes like suffrage and immigrant care.[122]

One such exemplar was Rosa Sonneschein, the editor of the *American Jewess.* She used her magazine to advocate for women in religious life and in the political sphere. On one occasion, Sonneschein depicted Esther as a model for the modern Jewish woman. Borrowing from an antisemitic trope, Sonneschein admitted "that Israel is still pursued and persecuted by living Hamans," but "so also do we believe in the existence of many Esthers." For Sonneschein, Esther was political and bold, daring and, in Sonneschein's rendering, independent. Sonneschein also wrote of an Esther of old and new, "who in time of trial and danger would sacrifice life and happiness for God and family, for Israel and its adherents."[123]

This laywoman also provided space to members of the rabbinate to issue their own appeals. Rabbi David Philipson's essay on "The Ideal Jewess" drew on the Book of Esther to illustrate his charge for Jewish women on the brink of the twentieth century. "The story tells us that the *man* Mordecai could not accomplish the task of deliverance without the aid of the *woman* Esther," wrote Philipson. "Is this not in a sense typical? Is not woman the saving influence in the finer life of man?" He averred that the "time [has] come again when it

120. Jennie Morris, "Esther," *American Hebrew*, February 29, 1884, 40.

121. Jacob R. Marcus, *The American Jewish Woman, 1654–1980* (New York: KTAV, 1981), 66.

122. See Goldman, *Beyond the Synagogue Gallery*, 195–96; Melissa R. Klapper, *Ballots, Babies, and Banners of Peace: American Jewish Women's Activism, 1890–1940* (New York: New York University Press, 2013), 1–8; and Panela S. Nadell, *America's Jewish Women: A History from Colonial Times to Today* (New York: W. W. Norton, 2019), 101–7.

123. Rosa Sonneschein, "Editorial: Queen Esther," *American Jewess* 6 (March 1898): 296.

appears as though the mainstay of our faith is woman." Philipson sympathized with and encouraged the expansion of women's rights in many sectors, but not at the cost of losing her leadership in the home:

> Men are frequently heard to say, my wife, my daughters are the religious members of the family, they represent me. Is salvation again to come to the Jews through woman? Can Esther in this sense be regarded as a type? … As far as external rights go, let woman have them all as long as they do not endanger her womanliness; let her have all the advantages of education, of developing mind and heart; let her have a directing hand in all the institutions of our modern life, but let her be shielded from all the influences that shall make her merely like man and less than woman.[124]

Philipson's editorial was emblematic of the collective attempt by Jewish leaders to deploy a very particular strategy for the sake of American Judaism. From Kohler to Philipson, theirs was a keen understanding of the role of Jewish holiday observance in facilitating a Jewish revival, and a shared vision for how that renaissance might be catalyzed through their female coreligionists. It started as an alternative to the lay-driven Purim ball. Sometimes the two groups were in direct competition. Yet, by the close of the nineteenth century the strategies complemented and cross-pollinated one another. American Jews came to understand their collective strengths and the power of Purim.

124. David Philipson, "The Ideal Jewess," *American Jewess* 4 (March 1897): 257–59.

IN SEARCH OF THE MODERN JEW

MICHAEL P. KRAMER

Where shall we look for the great modern Jews?
—EMMA LAZARUS, "Was the Earl of Beaconsfield a Representative Jew?" (1882)

Prelude

ON THE CUSP of the mid-twentieth-century breakthrough of Jewish American literature, still under the long, tenebrous shadow of the Holocaust, the literary and cultural critic Leslie Fiedler took to the pages of *Commentary* with a provocative call to "re-examine our literary heritage as Jewish writers and readers of English."[1] *Our* literary heritage: his pronoun deserves attention. Fiedler was plainly addressing his ethnic and intellectual cohort—Alfred Kazin, Irving Howe, Lionel Trilling, Philip Rahv, Saul Bellow, Isaac Rosenfeld, among others. Like him, they were second-generation east European immigrants, children of the huddled masses who began to arrive through the sunset gates in the closing decades of the nineteenth century and changed forever the image of the Jew in America.[2] They were educated in America's public schools, taught to admire, indeed to revere, the classics of English and American literature, to assign to them moral as well as aesthetic value. They came of age wanting to, expecting to enter "the temple of culture" proudly, not as acolytes but as priests.[3] They would master the literary tradition as critics, join its ranks as writers. This achievement, Fiedler explained, was the two-century-old

This research was supported by the Israel Science Foundation (grant number 1061/16).

1. Leslie Fiedler, "What Can We Do About Fagin? The Jew-Villain in Western Tradition," *Commentary* (May 1949): 411–18.

2. In response to Fiedler's essay, *Commentary* published a two-part symposium in September and October 1949 on "The Jewish Writer and the English Literary Tradition," which included many of the cohort. On the history of *Commentary*, see Benjamin Balint, *Running Commentary: The Contentious Magazine That Transformed the Jewish Left into the Neoconservative Right* (New York: Public Affairs, 2010). For more on the relation of the mid-century cohort to Jewish American literary history, see my "Acts of Assimilation: The Invention of Jewish American Literary History," *Jewish Quarterly Review* 103, no. 4 (2013): 556–79.

3. See Jonathan Freedman, *The Temple of Culture: Assimilation and Anti-Semitism in Literary Anglo-America* (New York: Oxford University Press, 2000).

promise of the Enlightenment: the creation of a neutral, secular zone where modern Jews and Christians could together rid themselves of religious dogma, of stifling superstition, of prejudice and bigotry, and work together to forge a universal and universalist human culture. For his part, the modern European Jew emerged "from the ghetto to stand beside his Gentile brother, to accept European culture and to modify it." They had done their job well, Fiedler thought. Think Marx, Freud, Kafka. Now it was the turn of American Jews like themselves. *Our* literary heritage: it was not the Gentiles' alone, Fiedler asserted, but ours as well. After all, T. S. Eliot had been "a profounder influence on a good many of us than the Baal Shem Tov or the author of Job."[4]

But Hitler had given Fiedler reason to question their assumptions about Enlightenment promises and even to doubt American opportunity. Was the tradition really *ours*? Now, when he considered the long history of Anglo-American literature, he could not see past the horrifying image of the "Jew-villain." Everywhere he turned, there he was, in countless works, well known and obscure. Most disheartening, there he was in works penned by some of the most respected authors of English literature—Geoffrey Chaucer, Christopher Marlowe, Alexander Pope. And not just in the pre-Enlightenment past. There he was in William Wordsworth, Charles Dickens, D. H. Lawrence, Ezra Pound, and even T. S. Eliot. Most disheartening of all, there he was in Shakespeare, the model writer (in Matthew Arnold's words) "in whom sweetness and light, and all that in human nature is most humane, were eminent."[5] There he was, Shylock, "the Usurer, the Jew with the Knife, the Jew as Beast."[6]

He had always been there, of course. Over the span of the nineteenth century, his presence had been analyzed and criticized by Jewish writers from Isaac Harby to Emma Lazarus and Emma Wolf.[7] Still, to Fiedler and his cohort he was

4. Fiedler, "Jew-Villain," 411.

5. Matthew Arnold, *Culture and Anarchy*, ed. J. Dover Wilson (Cambridge: Cambridge University Press, 1971), 57–58.

6. Fiedler, "Jew-Villain," 412.

7. See Isaac Harby, "The Merchant of Venice," in *A Selection from the Miscellaneous Writings of the Late Isaac Harby, Esq.*, ed. Henry L. Pinckney and Abraham Moïse (Charleston, S.C.: Printed by James S. Burgs, 1829), 262–67, and Lazarus, "Was the Earl of Beaconsfield a Representative Jew?" *Century* 23 (April 1882): 939–42. On Emma Wolf's account of a performance of *The Merchant of Venice* in *Other Things Being Equal* (1892), see below pp. 551–554. For an overview of the image of Shylock in American culture before Fiedler's generation, see Michael N. Dobkowski, "Gilded Age Images: Shylock Revisited," in Dobkowski, *The Tarnished Dream: The Basis of American Anti-Semitism* (Westport, Conn.: Greenwood Press, 1979), 78–112. See also Ellen Schiff, "Shylock's *Mishpocheh*: Anti-Semitism on the American Stage," in *Anti-Semitism in American History*, ed. David A. Gerber (Urbana: University of Illinois Press, 1987), 79–99.

hidden in plain sight, obscured by an abiding belief in the redemptive promise of Arnoldian "culture" and, plainly, by their personal literary ambitions. But this vile and violent image of the Jew could no longer be ignored. It was not an aberration. Shakespeare's Shylock was "familiar, at least as a name and a vague terror, to almost everyone." And he had many incarnations. "A compulsive image," Fiedler understood, "he haunts the English imagination; a creature of fear and guilt, he exists before and beneath written literature, an archetype inhabiting the collective unconscious of the English-speaking peoples." The figure of the Jew-villain is "central to our whole culture, before which as Jews we are embarrassed, dumb." To embrace the Anglo-American literary tradition—a desire Fiedler refused to relinquish—the post-Holocaust Jew had to confront the bogeyman of that tradition, that "symbol of darkness whose name we share."[8]

Compare the grotesque image of the Jew-villain of Anglo-American literary tradition conjured by Fiedler in *Commentary* to the image of the Jew—long wronged, yet noble and resilient—represented in a textbook published in Philadelphia a half century earlier by the Jewish Publication Society of America (JPS). Unpretentiously entitled *Readings and Recitations for Jewish Homes and Schools*, it was compiled by Isabel Emanuel Cohen, scion of a prominent, eminently respectable Sephardic German Philadelphia family, older sister to Dr. Solomon da Silva Solis-Cohen, "a physician and a litterateur," who was instrumental in the founding of the JPS and served as a member of its publication committee (Fig. 75).[9] The volume comprised a compendium of poems and prose excerpts drawn primarily from the same Anglo-American literary tradition feared and revered by Fiedler. But her selections, she writes in the preface, were "suitable for reading and recitation in Sabbath-schools and Sunday-schools, at entertainments of Jewish societies, and in the home circle."[10] *Suitable*, inoffensive to its primary audience of Westernized, modern American Jews like herself, not a single incarnation of Shylock to be found, hidden in plain sight.

Suitable, too, as it addressed the JPS's primary goals, even though the society

8. Fiedler, "Jew-Villain," 412–13.

9. Henry Samuel Morais, *The Jews of Philadelphia: Their History from the Earliest Settlements to the Present Time* (Philadelphia: Levytype Company, 1894), 352, 178. For a genealogy of the Solis-Cohen family, see the "Binswanger/Solis-Cohen Collection" at http://dla.library.upenn.edu/dla/pacscl/ead.pdf?id=PACSCL_UPENN_CAJS_USUSUSPUCJSCJSARCMS18 (accessed February 10, 2021).

10. Isabel E. Cohen, comp., *Readings and Recitations for Jewish Homes and Schools* (Philadelphia: Jewish Publication Society of America, 1895), 3.

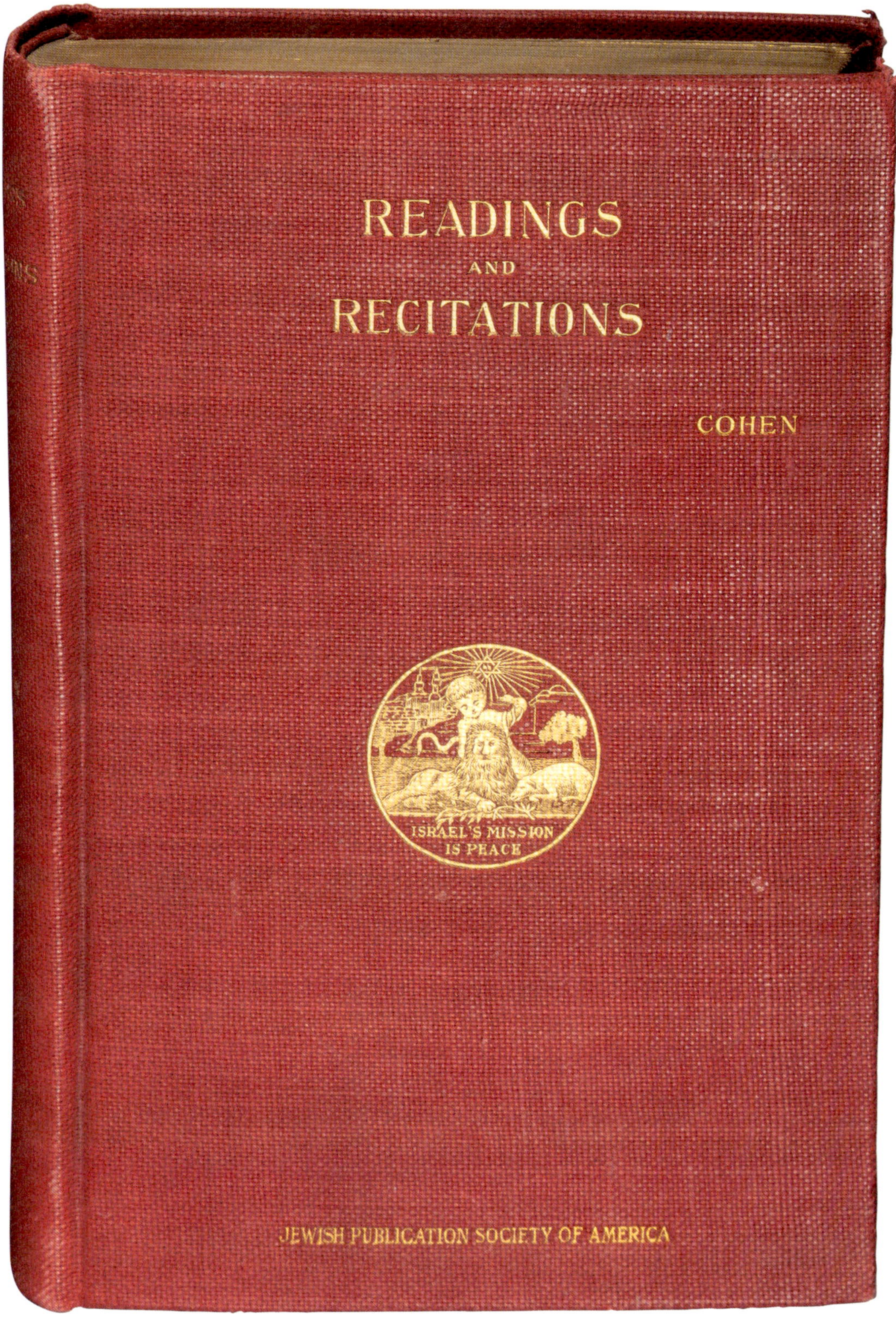

Fig. 75. Front cover of Isabel E. Cohen's compilation of *Readings and Recitations for Jewish Homes and Schools* (Philadelphia, 1895). (Princeton University Library).

published textbooks only "grudgingly."[11] Founded seven years earlier, the society had committed itself "to publish works on the religion, literature, and history of the Jews" with the twofold goal of cultivating Jewish literacy among an American Jewish community in serious need of it—a repeated complaint of Jewish leaders over the course of the nineteenth century—and of providing "our neighbors" with an appropriate account of Jewish accomplishments past and present, that is, to counter antisemitism.[12] Hence, Cohen's statement in the preface that her selections were chosen "to illustrate some phases of Hebrew history and character." An understatement, to be sure, since, taken together, her selections present a narrative that limns the long arc of Jewish history, from biblical through medieval to modern times, making her textbook something of a companion volume to the formal histories previously published by the JPS, Lady Magnus's *Outlines of Jewish History* and Heinrich Graetz's *History of the Jews.*[13] But the textbook did not present the long arc of Jewish *literary* history, at least not in the narrow sense. Although the JPS had published that same year an English translation of Gustav Karpeles's *Jewish Literature and Other Essays*, which offered "a bird's eye view of the whole course of our literature," demonstrating the unflagging creativity and productivity of Jewish writers over the millennia, Cohen's strategy was different.[14] Even though her volume was expressly meant for Jews, and even though it presents numerous selections from Jewish writers (including translations from Yehuda Halevi, selections from Isaac and Benjamin Disraeli, several poems by Emma Lazarus, and two poems by her brother Solomon), she chooses to tell the story of the Jews, to offer sympathetic images of the Jews, mostly in the words of non-Jews.

Several pragmatic factors may explain Cohen's editorial strategy, dictated by the requirements of the JPS.[15] But Cohen had a more substantive, ideological goal as well. As she writes in the preface, her purpose was "to show the influence for good that the Bible of the Jews has had upon the history and literature of English-speaking peoples."[16] Cohen's decision to take selections from the

11. Jonathan D. Sarna, *JPS: The Americanization of Jewish Culture, 1888–1988* (Philadelphia: Jewish Publication Society, 1989), 77–78.

12. *Ibid.*, 25.

13. Lady Katie Magnus, *Outlines of Jewish History, from B.C. 586 to C.E. 1890* (Philadelphia: Jewish Publication Society of America, 1890); Heinrich Graetz, *History of the Jews*, 5 vols. (Philadelphia: Jewish Publication Society of America, 1891–1895). See Sarna, *JPS*, 29–39.

14. Gustav Karpeles, *Jewish Literature and Other Essays* (Philadelphia: Jewish Publication Society of America, 1895), 9. On Karpeles and the JPS, see Sarna, *JPS*, 56–58.

15. See Sarna, *JPS*, 25.

16. Cohen, *Readings and Recitations*, 3.

great Anglo-American writers was not so much fawning as proprietary. It was, she might have said, *our* literary heritage. Not adopted by the Jews, as Fiedler understood it, but spawned by them. David's kingdom may have been defeated, but in the words of Lord Byron (selection 2), "David's lyre grew mightier than his throne!" Indeed, "the whole history of the world to this day is in truth one continual establishing of [an] Old Testament revelation," according to Matthew Arnold (selection 97), "and its importance is so immense, that the people to whom it was given, and whose record is in the Bible, deserve fully to be singled out as the Bible singles them." The opening selection of the volume, an excerpt from David Kaufmann's *George Eliot and Judaism*, offers an even more radical version of the argument: "Destroyed as the national independence of Judea was by Rome, a solitary Jewish idea sufficed, in its disfigurement, to shatter the Roman Mythology in all its splendour [and] arose to unimagined power." Christianity itself was a Jewish idea, its success a feather in the cap of the Jews. And "even after men had inhumanly and treacherously sought to deprive [the Jews'] mental life of light and air," Kaufmann continues, they are still "able to enrich every literature of the world from its treasures." What better way to shore up Jewish self-respect, rhapsodized one reviewer of Cohen's compilation, "for none will lay it aside without feeling that a religion which could ... inspire such bards has every claim upon the intelligent reverence of those in its household born."[17] To embrace the Anglo-American literary tradition, Cohen's volume argues, is to reap in joy what Jews have sown in tears.

Recent scholars have often remarked upon the "dual image" of the Jew in Anglo-American literature, "both noble and ignoble, black and white ... Saint or Devil."[18] But the observation has deeper roots. In 1882, for instance, Emma

17. Anonymous review in the *Reform Advocate*, September 21, 1895, 496.

18. Harold Fisch, *The Dual Image: The Figure of the Jew in English and American Literature* (London: World Jewish Library, 1971), 5–6. See also Louise A. Mayo, *The Ambivalent Image: Nineteenth-Century America's Perception of the Jew* (Rutherford, N.J.: Fairleigh Dickinson University Press, 1988). Louis Harap's encyclopedic work, *The Image of the Jew in American Literature: From Early Republic to Mass Immigration* (Philadelphia: Jewish Publication Society of America, 1974), generally follows the same pattern. For an early, nuanced approach, see Lionel Trilling, "The Changing Myth of the Jew," *Commentary* (August 1978): 24–34; the essay was originally composed in 1931. For recent work that critiques the pattern, see Bryan Cheyette, *Constructions of the "The Jew" in English Literature and Society: Racial Representations, 1875–1945* (Cambridge: Cambridge University Press, 1993), and Sharon B. Oster, *No Place in Time: The Hebraic Myth in Late-Nineteenth-Century American Literature* (Detroit: Wayne State University Press, 2018). For a theoretical critique of the antisemitism/philosemitism distinction, see Zygmunt Bauman,

Lazarus saw the ostentatious self-presentation of Benjamin Disraeli as representative of the duality observable in the Jewish character, combining the "powerful imagination and mathematical precision in argument" of Spinoza with the "astuteness, the sarcasm, the pathos, the egotism, and the cunning" of Shylock.[19] In 1889, in the earliest book-length account of the image of the Jew in Anglo-American literature, Rabbi David Philipson noted "the various guises [the Jew] has been made to assume, running the whole length, from the villainy of [Marlowe's] Barabbas to the ideal nobleness of [George Eliot's] Mordecai."[20] Surely, both Cohen and Fiedler were aware of the duality. But each chose to focus exclusively on a single image, to take control of the image of Jews and Judaism, each from a different sociopolitical position and with a different polemical purpose. By highlighting what came to be called "the Jewish contributions to civilization," Cohen wanted to overshadow the vile medieval image of the Jew inherited by the nineteenth century, to move the modern emancipated Jew from questionable margin to confident mainstream, to claim the bourgeois American respectability that she and her community had earned for themselves, and no doubt as well, to shore up the elevated image in the face of the new wave of east European immigration that threatened it.[21] Fiedler, defiant child of those immigrants, wanted nothing of Cohen's middle-class respectability, had no desire to cover over the fearsome image of the "Jew-villain" but set out to *kidnap* it, to harness its power, to transform its marginality into a critical contrarianism, to look forward, as many of his cohort did, to the emergence of a different kind of modern Jew, to "the day when the [alienated] Jew will come to seem the central symbol, the essential myth of the whole Western world."[22]

"Allosemitism: Premodern, Modern, Postmodern," in *Modernity, Culture and "The Jew,"* ed. Bryan Cheyette and Laura Marcus (Cambridge: Polity Press, 1998), 143–56.

19. Lazarus, "Earl of Beaconsfield," 939–40.

20. David Philipson, *The Jew in English Fiction* (Cincinnati: Robert Clark & Co., 1889), 5. I will have more to say about Philipson below. Philipson's survey makes clear that the treatment of Jews in British literature provided a significant context for their treatment in American literature. For lack of space, I have focused in this essay almost wholly on the American scene.

21. See, for example, Joseph Jacobs, *Jewish Contributions to Civilization: An Estimate* (Philadelphia: Jewish Publication Society of America, 1919), and Cecil Roth, *The Jewish Contribution to Civilization* (London: Macmillan, 1938). For a critique of this phenomenon, see Jeremy Cohen and Richard I. Cohen, eds., *The Jewish Contribution to Civilization: Reassessing an Idea* (Oxford: Littman Library of Jewish Civilization, 2008). On the defensive reaction of Jewish American literary historians to the new immigration, see my "Against the Tide: Re-Discovering Early Jewish American Literary History," *Studies in American Jewish Literature* 33, no. 1 (2014): 1–12.

22. Fiedler, "Jew-Villain," 416, 418.

These two divergent Jewish views of Anglo-American literary history are each predicated upon the anomalous position of the post-Enlightenment, emancipated Jews who were their respective audiences. Both Fiedler and Cohen had to negotiate the dual image of the Jewish characters, the vile villains and virtuous victims who inhabit the history they claimed as their heritage, and to fashion a usable past that would shore up their very different visions of a modern Jew. In so doing, they also had to reconcile the fundamental fact of their modernity, of their sense of having broken from the Jewish past, of having sloughed off significant elements of the religious and cultural characteristics of the historical Jewish community, of having reformed their ideas about what Jews believe and what their role in the world should be, of having assumed the culture of their contemporaries and championed the idea of America—had to reconcile all of this with their insistence that they were nevertheless standard bearers of Jewish tradition. When Jewish American writers began in earnest to produce a literature of their own after the Civil War, they were faced with this anomaly.

But not only Jewish writers. Christian writers, too, were confronted with the idea of a Jew who refused to fit neatly into the paradigms of the past but did not slip unproblematically into the new and had to imagine how to incorporate the new Jew into their imaginative worlds in ways that made sense to them. What follows immediately are brief excursions into three novels by Christian writers that take a Jew as their major or titular character. Much has been written about American antisemitism in the years between the Civil War and World War I, and there are antisemitic stereotypes in each of these novels.[23] But what is central to the narrative strategy of each is how the stereotypes serve as foils for the depiction and conceptualization of a different kind of fictional character, a modern Jew.

23. For a brief overview of American antisemitism, see Jonthan D. Sarna, "Antisemitism in the United States," in *The Cambridge Companion to Antisemitism*, ed. Steven T. Katz (forthcoming). Studies of this particular period include: Naomi W. Cohen, "Antisemitism in the Gilded Age: The Jewish View," *Jewish Social Studies* 41, no. 3–4 (1979): 187–210; Naomi W. Cohen, "Antisemitic Imagery: The Nineteenth Century Background," *Jewish Social Studies* 47, no. 3/4 (1985): 307–12; Dobkowski, *Tarnished Dream*; Leonard Dinnerstein, *Antisemitism in America* (New York: Oxford University Press, 1994), 35–78; and John Higham, *Send These to Me: Jews and Other Immigrants in Urban America* (New York: Atheneum, 1975), 116–95. For a more sanguine view, see Oscar Handlin, "American Views of the Jew at the Opening of the Twentieth Century," *Publications of the American Jewish Historical Society* 40, no. 4 (1951): 323–44. For a response, see Robert Rockaway and Arnon Gutfeld, "Demonic Images of the Jew in the Nineteenth Century United States," *American Jewish History* 89, no. 4 (2001): 355–81.

Religion and Romance

The often fraught relationship between Christians and Jews is rooted in the fact that the two religions with which they identify are intricately, even inextricably related historically and theologically. While the Jews have rejected the central claims of Christianity, they have not been able to ignore Christianity altogether, at least not in the West, where it defines the larger world in which they have lived for more than a millennium. The tension persists even in tolerant America under a government "which to bigotry gives no sanction, to persecution no assistance—but generously affording to all Liberty of conscience, and immunities of Citizenship."[24] Both Fiedler and Cohen recognized this. The images of Jews they invoke are retoolings of the stereotypes through which Christians have viewed them. In an even more fundamental way, the Christian imagination cannot rid itself of the Jews, not without erasing or significantly modifying an essential element of itself. Would the New Testament be new, argued Rabbi Gustav Gottheil, "without its foundation of the Old Testament"?[25] Only by virtue of the fact that the Jews' "fathers did eat manna in the wilderness, and are dead" can Jesus declare, "I am the living bread which came down from heaven" (John 6:49–51). Paradoxically, the otherness of the Jews is both exacerbated and ameliorated by this vital, genealogical relation. Their survival as a people, despite the remarkable ascendancy of Christianity and the centuries of dispersions suffered and aspersions cast, has been a persistent irritant to the Christian imagination and as such, oyster-like, a spur to creativity. The Jews' embrace of modernity over the course of the nineteenth century complicated the relation even more. What to make of the Jews? What to make of the modern Jew?[26]

The young adult novel *Rebecca the Jewess* (1879) is one sort of response to this question. The author, Harriette Newell Woods Baker (writing under the pen-name Mrs. Madeline Leslie), had impressive Protestant bona fides (Fig. 76). She was the daughter of the founder of Andover Theological Seminary, wife of a Congregationalist minister, and mother to four Episcopal clergymen. Her own

24. Moses Seixas to George Washington, August 17, 1790, in Madison C. Peters, *Justice to the Jew: The Story of What He Has Done for the World* (New York and London: F. Tennyson Neely, 1899), 36–37.

25. Gustav Gottheil, "Jesus and the Jews," quoted in *ibid.*, 262.

26. For a fuller overview of the relationship between Christianity and Judaism in modern times, see Susannah Heschel, "Jews and Christianity," in *The Cambridge History of Judaism*, vol. 8, *The Modern World, 1815–2000*, ed. Mitchell Hart and Tony Michels (New York: Cambridge University Press, 2017), 1063–92.

"Pictorial Wagner" (1899); "Anton Seidl" (1899); "Songs and Song Writers" (1900); "History of Musical Instruments" (1909); "Success in Music and How it is Won" (1909); and "Grieg and His Music" (1909). This last shows that Grieg, far from being a minor musician, was a composer of the first rank and a fertile melodist at the time when melody seemed to become extinct. His books on travel include "The Pacific Coast Scenic Tour" (1890); "Spain and Morocco" (1891), and "Lotos Time in Japan" (1898). They stamp their author as an accomplished traveler with rare powers of observation, who knows how to see and then to tell what he has seen. He is also the author of "Primitive Love and Love Stories" (1900), a work of enormous research, in which he elaborates his theory that romantic love is a modern sentiment, unknown to savages, as well as to the Greeks, Hebrews, and other civilized ancients. Numerous articles relating to his travels, to beauty, to woman suffrage, to gastronomic and psychological topics and music have been written by him for the leading magazines, and for more than two decades he has lectured on the history of music in the National Conservatory, New York; also at the Master School of Music in Brooklyn. Mr. Finck was married Oct. 17, 1890, to Abbie Helen, daughter of H. M. Cushman of New York. She is also an excellent writer on musical topics.

BAKER, Abijah Richardson, clergyman and author, was born at Franklin, Norfolk co., Mass., Aug. 30, 1805, son of Capt. David and Jemima (Richardson) Baker. He was graduated at Amherst College in 1830, and then became principal of Dorchester (Mass.) Academy. While studying theology at Andover Theological Seminary he became so proficient in Hebrew, that he was requested to correct the proof sheets of Prof. Stuart's "Hebrew Grammar." He was graduated in 1835, taught in the English department of Phillips Academy, Andover, and in 1838 was settled over the Congregational Church at Medford, Mass. He had grown to be remarkably liberal in his religious ideas and expressions, so much so that during his pastorate at Medford a Baptist, a Methodist and Universalist Church were formed by his advice and assistance from his own congregation, and still the numbers of the latter were so great that the church building had to be twice enlarged. Mr. Baker remained in Medford for thirteen years. Accepting a call from Lynn, he organized the Central Congregational Church, and raised most of the means to build its handsome house of worship. In 1855 he became pastor of the Congregational Church at Wellesley, Mass., and in 1863 of the E Street Church in South Boston. He remained in South Boston until 1866, when he retired from the active service of the ministry to devote himself to the completion of a commentary on the "Sermon on the Mount." During his settlement in Medford and Lynn Mr. Baker prepared a work for Sunday schools entitled "The Catechism Tested by the Bible," which was translated into six languages. He received the degree of D.D. from Austin College, Texas. He was naturally gifted for the profession of teacher, not only having a mind of great clearness, but possessing the power to enable others to see things as clearly as he did. While teaching at Andover and Lynn he prepared a "School History of the United States" which combined geography with history. With his wife's assistance, he edited two magazines: "The Mother's Assistant" and the "Happy Home." He also edited an American edition of Cobbin's "Childs' Commentary" and treatises on various religious subjects. He was married, at Andover, Mass., Oct. 1, 1835, to Harriette Newell, daughter of Rev. Leonard Woods, D.D., and had six sons. Of these one died in infancy, four entered the Episcopal ministry, and the other became professor of gynecology in the Harvard medical school. Dr. Baker died in Dorchester, Mass., April 30, 1876.

A. R. Baker

BAKER, Harriette Newell Woods ("Mrs. Madeline Leslie"), author, was born at Andover, Mass., Aug. 19, 1815, daughter of Dr. Leonard and Abby (Wheeler) Woods. Her father was the first professor in Andover Theological Seminary, and afterward president of that institution. Endowed with a lively imagination, she began to write stories when a child, and at the age of ten sent one to the "Youth's Companion." In return she received a silver dollar and a request for other contributions, which she furnished from time to time, without informing the editor of her youthfulness. She was educated at Abbot Female Seminary and at an academy in Catskill, N.Y., and then studied at home until she was twenty, when she became the wife of Rev. Abijah R. Baker, a teacher in Phillips Academy. Her married life was passed chiefly in Medford, Lynn and South Boston, Mass., where her husband was pastor of Congregational churches, and there she continued her literary work, performed the duties of a minister's wife, and brought up six sons. Not less than two hundred works were the product of her pen, most of them being tales for Sunday-school and general reading. They attained great popularity, and several were republished in England, and were translated into German, French and Bohemian. Included in the list are the "Silver Lake," "Golden Spring," "Brookside" and "Tim" series, and the "Leslie" stories. "Tim: The Scissors Grinder," was her most popular book, and (in the form of a cheap reprint) was sold or given away by thousands in England. Some of these were published over the pseudonyms "Mrs. Madeline Leslie" and "Aunt Hattie." Others, such as "The Courtesies of Wedded Life" (1855; new ed., 1869), and "Cora and the Doctor," were published anonymously. Her characters are well drawn, and so strikingly true to life that one recognizes them among his daily acquaintances. Her style is simple, chaste, often elegant; her plan is natural and progressive; and many of her scenes are picturesque and impressive, and charged with the power and pathos that belong to the great masters of fiction. Moreover, her writings are all of the purest moral tone, without cant or mawkish sentimentality, but displaying a keen insight into the spiritual nature of man and woman, and a proper sense of their relations as moral and accountable beings. Mrs. Baker died in Brooklyn, N. Y., April 26, 1893.

Harriette N. Baker

KING, James Gore, lawyer, was born in New York city, June 6, 1868, son of Edward and Isabella Ramsay (Cochrane) King, and a descendant of John King, who came to America in 1702, settling at Boston; his wife was Mary Stowell, of Newton, Mass., and the line of descent is traced through

Fig. 76. Entry for Harriet Newell Woods Baker in *National Cyclopedia of American Biography*, vol. 14 (New York, 1917), p. 154.

religious proclivities were channeled into literature. She was a prolific writer of moralistic and religious books for young Christians looking for leisure-time entertainment that would tamely titillate but confirm their beliefs, gratify their expectations, inspire their own evangelism, and perhaps, in the case of *Rebecca the Jewess*, convince their parents to donate money for missionary activities—a cause to which the novel makes explicit reference.[27] In her "Prefatory Note," however, Baker fancies a wholly different kind of reader: "some beloved child of Israel who is groping in the dark among types and symbols, in vain expectation that Shiloh will come," who, upon reading the novel, will "come to believe that Jesus Christ is indeed the Messiah promised of old."

Rebecca the Jewess is built upon the frame of a conventional, sentimental romance: a beautiful young orphaned heiress is aggressively pursued by an unsuitable suitor who hoodwinks her guardians and threatens her virtue (Fig. 77). The heroine is eventually rescued by a handsome young hero who unmasks the scoundrel as a fraud, and yes, reader, she marries him.[28] Baker layers onto this formulaic structure a conversion narrative that is foreshadowed in the prefatory image of her ideal reader. Rebecca Stickney, the beautiful heiress, is a "beloved child of Israel," daughter and granddaughter of strictly observant rabbis (Fig. 78). The danger she experiences, besides that of the villainous suitor, is a spiritual despair caused by her "groping in the dark" of Old Testament prophecies—"Our sceptre and lawgivers have departed from Judah," she worries, musing on Genesis 49:10, "and yet Shiloh has not come"—and the attendant

27. Mrs. Madeline Leslie, *Rebecca the Jewess* (Boston: Ira L. Bradley, 1879), 196. On her life, see [Harriette Newell Woods Baker], *The Autobiography of a Very Remarkable Woman*, ed. Walter Baker (London: A. T. Roberts, 1894). Various obituaries are collected on pp. 227–32.

28. For a general introduction to the form of the sentimental novel, see Janet Todd, *Sensibility: An Introduction* (London: Methuen, 1986). On the figure of the Jewess in contemporaneous British fiction, see Nadia Valman, *The Jewess in Nineteenth-Century British Literary Culture* (Cambridge: Cambridge University Press, 2007). No doubt, standing behind Baker's *Rebecca* is the Rebecca of Walter Scott's *Ivanhoe* (1820), although her relation to Judaism and Christianity is markedly different. For a contemporaneous account, see Philipson, *The Jew in English Fiction*, 70–87, and see the excerpts from Scott's novel in *Essential Papers on Jewish-Christian Relations in the United States: Imagery and Reality*, ed. Naomi W. Cohen (New York: New York University Press, 1990), 26–27 and 187–99. For more on Scott's character, see, for example, Rachel Schulkins, "Immodest Otherness: Nationalism and the Exotic Jewess in Sir Walter Scott's *Ivanhoe*," *Nineteenth-Century Gender Studies* 12, no. 1 (2016): 111–31; Judith Lewin, "The 'Distinction of the Beautiful Jewess': Rebecca of 'Ivanhoe' and Walter Scott's Marking of the Jewish Woman," *Jewish Culture and History* 8, no. 1 (2006): 29–48; and Valman, *The Jewess in Nineteenth-Century British Literary Culture*, 20–34. On the possible Jewish-American origin of Scott's character, see Judith Lewin, "Legends of Rebecca: *Ivanhoe*, Dynamic Identification, and the Portraits of Rebecca Gratz," *Nashim: A Journal of Jewish Women's Studies and Gender Issues*, no. 10 (Fall 2005): 178–212.

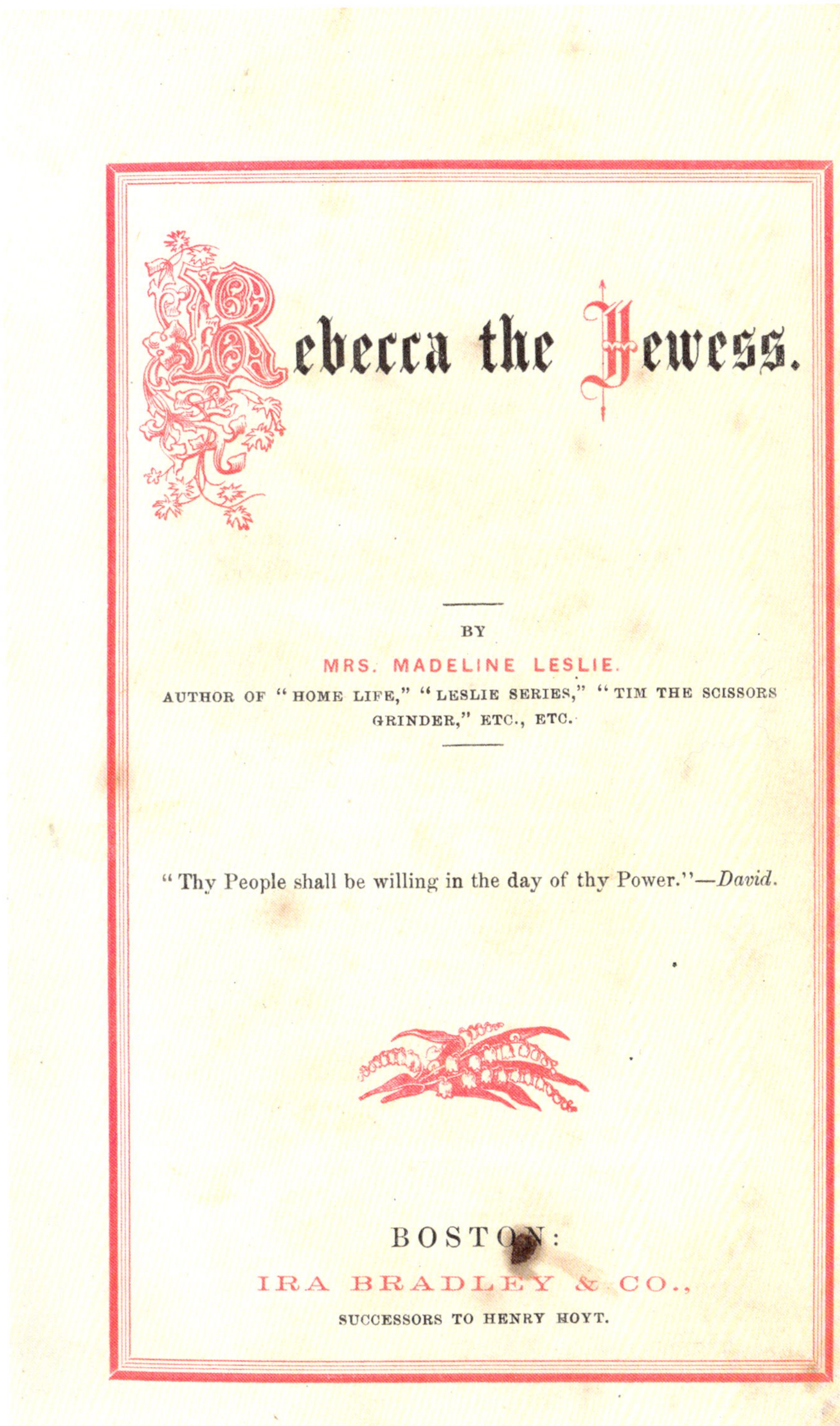

Rebecca the Jewess.

BY

MRS. MADELINE LESLIE.

AUTHOR OF "HOME LIFE," "LESLIE SERIES," "TIM THE SCISSORS GRINDER," ETC., ETC.

"Thy People shall be willing in the day of thy Power."—*David.*

BOSTON:

IRA BRADLEY & CO.,

SUCCESSORS TO HENRY HOYT.

Fig. 77. Title page of Mrs. Madeleine Leslie [Harriet Newell Woods Baker], *Rebecca the Jewess* (Boston, 1879). (Ohio State University).

guilt she feels about abandoning the faith of her fathers.[29] The handsome hero is George Livermore, an Episcopal minister, who benevolently guides her out of the darkness toward the belief "that Jesus Christ is indeed the Messiah promised of old," convincing her that by accepting Christ she fulfills her destiny as a Jew. He then joins her at the altar.[30]

The movement in the novel from darkness to light, from Rebecca lost to Rebecca saved, is facilitated by reading. Just as Baker hopes her imagined Jewish reader will read *Rebecca the Jewess*, so Rebecca the Jewess furtively reads a memoir entitled *The Converted Jew*. More significant, she reads the New Testament and learns how to understand the Old Testament typologically, to see its figures and events as adumbrations of Christ, as, for instance, when Jesus explains to his disciples that the manna that sustained the Israelites in the wilderness prefigures himself as "the living bread" that will sustain believers spiritually. The characters spend much time in the novel reading the Bible, querying its prophecies, interpreting its types. Livermore preaches that from the moment of "the advent of our Messiah ... all types and symbols, used beforehand to predict his coming, ceased," that after the crucifixion, the ultimate sacrifice, the antitype, "there was no longer need of bulls and goats to atone for sin."[31] No need to fret anxiously why Shiloh has not come, for the promise has already been fulfilled. Crucially, in Livermore's theology, the fulfillment of the types does not abolish God's promise to "the descendants of Abraham." To Rebecca, he expresses his gratitude "for the blessings that have come to me, a Gentile, through you," for Moses, for David, and, most of all, for "Jesus Christ, born of a Jewish mother, of the line of Abraham and David." In the novel's world, Jews are not despised and their dispersion is not a punishment for rejecting Jesus. Even modern Jews, by virtue of their genealogical distinction, retain their status in the history of salvation as "God's chosen race."[32]

Livermore's words echo those of the popular contemporaneous evangelist Dwight L. Moody: "When I meet a Jew, I can't help thinking of the promise that God made to Abraham. I can't help having a profound respect for them,

29. Leslie, *Rebecca the Jewess*, 16.

30. On the conversion novel and, especially, its relation to the sentimental novel, see Michael Ragussis, *Figures of Conversion: "The Jewish Question" and English National Identity* (Durham: Duke University Press, 1995), 15–56.

31. Leslie, *Rebecca the Jewess*, 126–27. The classic introduction to typology is Erich Auerbach, "Figura," trans. Ralph Manheim, in Auerbach, *Scenes from the Drama of European Literature* (Manchester: Manchester University Press, 1984), 11–78.

32. Leslie, *Rebecca the Jewess*, 126–27.

FRONTISPIECE. Chap. 1.

Fig. 78. Frontispiece of *Rebecca the Jewess.*

for they are God's people."[33] Livermore's rapprochement with the Jews in *Rebecca the Jewess* evinces no trace of the overarching historical vision of Moody's dispensationalism, the belief that fueled the work of many nineteenth-century American missionaries, that the Second Coming was imminent and will be preceded by the conversion of the Jews and the reestablishment of a Jewish polity in the Holy Land. But it does share in the appreciation and reverence for Jews *as Jews* embedded in that theology, even as it aims to convert them. Most Jews in the novel are imagined in this mold.

While the author claims that many of the incidents in the novel "are strictly true," *Rebecca the Jewess* reads like a wish-fulfillment fantasy. Rebecca is presented as, to use Jonathan Sarna's term, "the Jew next door," wholly modern save for her religious views, but it is unclear how well acquainted Baker was with the reality of Jewish social and religious life in 1870s America or how much she withheld or distorted.[34] The novel presents no Shylocks or Fagins (it is not clear whether the rejected suitor is actually Jewish or simply pretending to be), but it is not free from time-worn stereotypes that delineate by negation Rebecca's path from the Judaism of the past to its modern fulfillment in Christianity. We are told that Rebecca's late father was a rabbi who "was distinguished even among his own brethren for his great learning, and the rigor with which he held fast to the minutest ceremonies of the ancient Jews," demanding adherence from others as well. At the same time, he was a successful businessman who did not allow his observances to interfere with his financial dealings, "even though these plans embraced the oppression of the poor and needy." Through this image of the father and an "irascible" Rabbi Ben Ezra who serves as Rebecca's bugaboo, traditional Judaism is presented as a religion of stubbornness, intolerance, cruelty, and greed.[35]

The only available alternative in the unidentified and unidentifiable city in which the novel is set is the benevolent Christianity of Mr. Livermore, toward which Rebecca turns, along with a seeming cascade of others. To be sure, missionary efforts had been ongoing in America since the early nineteenth century, but the opposition from the Jewish pulpit and the proliferating Jewish

33. Dwight L. Moody, "Christ in the Old Testament," in Moody, *To All People*, ed. Joseph Cook (New York: E. B. Treat, 1877), 354. On Moody's attitude toward the Jews, see Yaakov Ariel, *An Unusual Relationship: Evangelical Christians and Jews* (New York: New York University Press, 2013), 63–67.

34. See Jonathan D. Sarna, "The 'Mythical Jew' and the 'Jew Next Door' in Nineteenth-Century America," in *Anti-Semitism in American History*, ed. Gerber, 57–78.

35. Leslie, *Rebecca the Jewess*, 24–25, 163, 187.

community had also been unyielding. The first number of Isaac Leeser's *Occident and American Jewish Advocate* devoted an article to castigating and ridiculing the efforts of the American Society for Meliorating the Condition of the Jews, warning that "we shall keep a watchful eye on their movements."[36] By the time *Rebecca the Jewess* was published, Isaac Mayer Wise's *American Israelite* had been in circulation for twenty-five years, waging unflagging battle against "the demoralizing influence of the apostatizing missionary."[37] No mention at all is made of a Reform Judaism that was poised to reject outright the ceremonial law and the notion of a return to Zion, and certainly not of those who claimed that Reform Judaism was to be the religion of the future and called on Christians to join them. By all accounts, the persistent efforts of missionaries such as Moody were largely ineffectual. "The Inquisition could not make Christians of us," Josephine Lazarus wrote in her universalist *Spirit of Judaism*, "nor can all the mild but zealous efforts of the Presbyterians ever make a single honest convert."[38] Still, the image of the "beloved child of Israel" longing to be saved was one to which many Christians clung with sincere fervor, one that defined for them the ideal modern Jew.

Baker's *Rebecca the Jewess* domesticates the exotic, channeling its eponymous heroine through the conventions of the sentimental novel, filtering out the negative Jewish traits (those attributed to her father and rabbi), and drawing her refined Jewish self into the modern Christian mainstream. In *Joseph the Jew*, popular novelist Virginia Wales Johnson textualizes the Jewish problem differently (Fig. 79).[39] To begin with, she prefers her titular character to remain exotic, "a stranger" who travels through a series of romantic landscapes peopled by "a curious mixture of nationalities"—in an embedded tale, even an Indian rajah

36. *Occident and American Jewish Advocate* 1, no. 1 (April 1843): 47.

37. *American Israelite*, July 4, 1879, 4.

38. Josephine Lazarus, *The Spirit of Judaism* (New York: Dodd, Mead, and Company, 1895), 91. See Lincoln A. Mullen, "Sincerity: Jewish Converts and Resistance to Missions," in Mullen, *The Chance of Salvation: A History of Conversion in America* (Cambridge, Mass.: Harvard University Press, 2017), 173–220. See also Jonathan D. Sarna, "The American Jewish Response to Nineteenth-Century Christian Missions," in *Essential Papers on Jewish-Christian Relations in the United States*, ed. Cohen, 21–42. For more on the missionary movement during the period, see Yaakov Ariel, *Evangelizing the Chosen People: Missions to the Jews in America, 1880–2000* (Chapel Hill: University of North Carolina Press, 2000), 9–76.

39. Virginia Wales Johnson, *Joseph the Jew: The Story of an Old House* (New York: Harper and Brothers, 1874). For more on the author, see the entry by Sarah G. Bowerman in *Dictionary of American Biography*, vol. 5 (New York: Scribner's, 1933), 124.

plays a role—all painted in broad strokes of colorful ethnic commonplaces. We glimpse, for instance, "placid, blond Englishmen" and "merry careless negroes," encounter an old woman with "passionate Minorcan blood" and another whose Native American traits are so marked, the author tells her readers, that there was "no need to ask her nationality."[40] In this heterogenous literary environment, the Jews, too, take their assigned place—if more fully and sympathetically drawn. Joseph Rost is a Danish Jew, the younger son of a family of diamond dealers. The Rosts are clannish, secretive, suspicious of outsiders, and obsessed with wealth, but "with an instinct to avoid display"—traits, the author makes clear, that were developed "of necessity" and "taught by cruel oppression." And they are devoted to their faith. Whereas Baker denigrates ritual observance as Old Testament legalism, a symptom of spiritual ossification, Johnson describes Jewish religious customs in respectful and picturesque (if not always wholly accurate) detail. For instance, she details the Rosts' Passover preparations:

> For three days before Pesach, glass utensils were immersed in water, copper and iron vessels purified by fire, and the whole house cleansed. The appointed fasts had been kept, and the second day—Enf [Erev?] Pesach—sacredly observed, because on that day the Lord slew the first-born of Egypt, and Israel was spared. The previous night Solomon Rost had passed through every room with a wooden bowl and quill to detect stray morsels of food. Aunt Martha took care that he should find some scraps in his progress, as that was expected. At dark the family gathered around the table, where the Paschal Lamb was served with unleavened bread and bitter herbs.

Indeed, Johnson comments, with admiration, "There had never been a backslider from the faith of their fathers among the race." Nor would there be. Even during his adventures in the American hinterland, relying on others for food and shelter, Johnson remarks on "Joseph's entire rejection of bacon" and his proud refusal to swear on a cross.[41] Rebecca Stickney epitomizes Jewishness by becoming a Christian; Joseph Rost, by steadfastly remaining a Jew.

But Joseph Rost is no ordinary Jew, neither the mythical Jew of Christian culture nor the American Jew next door. Johnson casts him as the swashbuckling hero of a modern American adventure romance. Yet he is not a typical American romance hero either, not a Natty Bumppo in the American wilderness, not an Ishmael on a whaling voyage. It is important for Johnson that he is not American at all, that he is a "stranger" and a Jew. While the novel is set during the recent American Civil War, it begins on foreign soil, in the Rost

40. Johnson, *Joseph the Jew*, 29, 19, 38, 31.
41. *Ibid.*, 18, 12, 15, 32, 38.

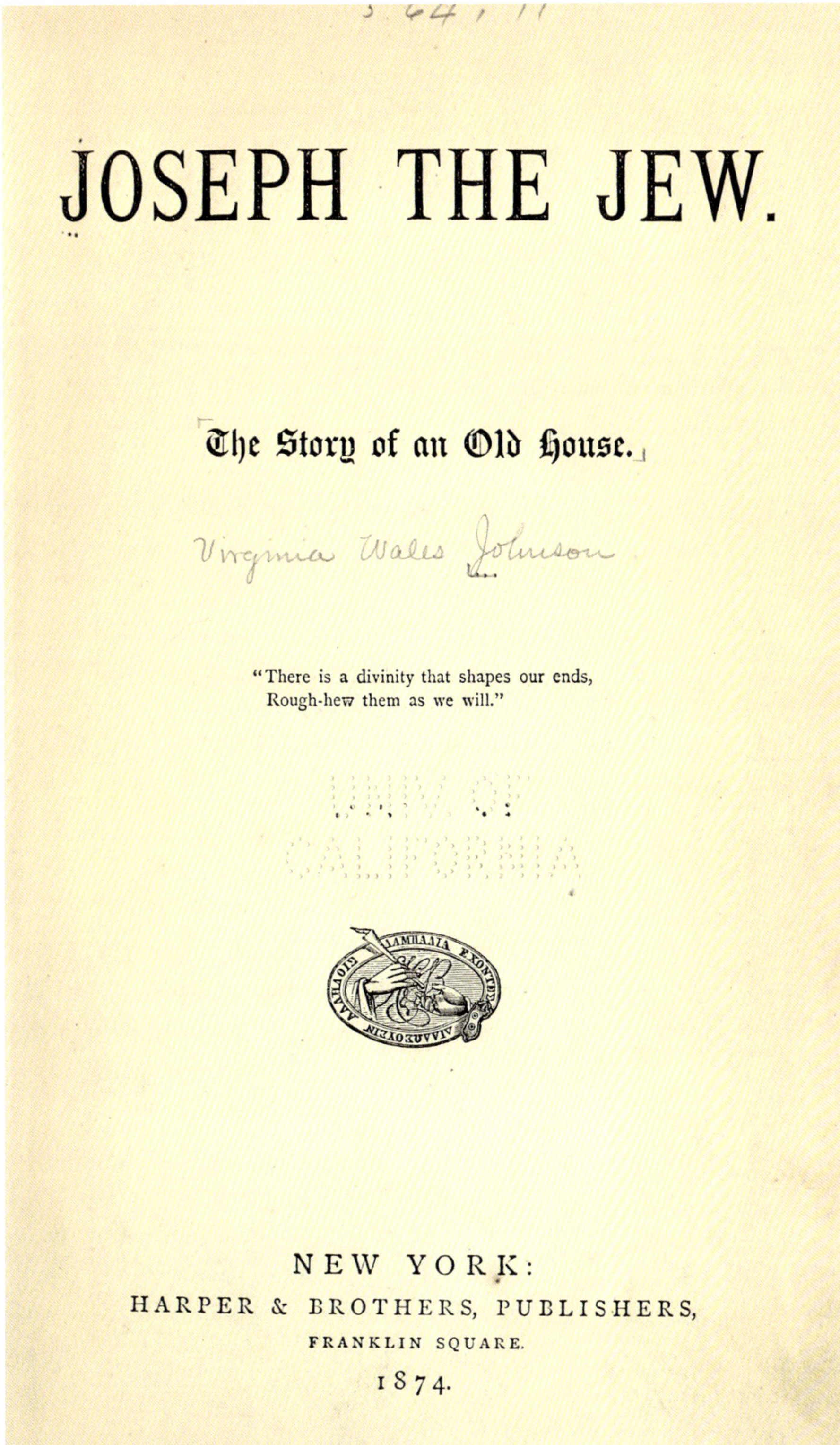

JOSEPH THE JEW.

The Story of an Old House.

Virginia Wales Johnson

"There is a divinity that shapes our ends,
Rough-hew them as we will."

UNIV. OF CALIFORNIA

NEW YORK:
HARPER & BROTHERS, PUBLISHERS,
FRANKLIN SQUARE.
1874.

Fig. 79. Title page of [Virginia Wales Johnson], *Joseph the Jew* (New York, 1874). (University of California).

home in Denmark, where Joseph's uncle recounts a tale of piracy on the high seas. Joseph's late grandfather was on a voyage home from a business journey to the Far East when his ship was raided and his valuable goods stolen, along with those of others on the ship. Joseph overhears his family's plan to send his older brother to search for and retrieve the jewels in America, and, anxious to prove his manhood, Joseph takes the grandfather's papers and leaves for the war-torn New World in his brother's stead. What follows is an action-packed yarn: a hairbreadth escape, attempted murder, naval blockade running, a hunt for hidden treasure, a haunted old mansion, violent Civil War battles, a family buried alive, treachery and heroism, and a plethora of queer characters of various races. These include an unctuous, ignoble, fox-faced Jew named Ruben Wentzel, who shadows Joseph, hoping for a share (or more) of the lost treasure, and against whom Joseph's admirable Jewishness is measured. All this action in the first third of the novel, when Joseph is abruptly and inadvertently killed. As if to underscore Joseph's abiding distinctiveness, Johnson has Ruben say kaddish over his fallen body. The familiar "stock situations" of the genre are defamiliarized by Joseph's religious and cultural alterity.[42]

Joseph the Jew's active role as the protagonist of the narrative ends with his death. What follows is an American sentimental novel—Johnson herself calls it a "domestic drama"—a stark and deliberate generic shift.[43] Played out against the background of the Civil War, the novel skirts the issues of the conflict itself and offers instead the tale of the Hearns, a family fallen on hard times after the father's disgrace and disappearance following a financial speculation gone awry. His sickly wife, two daughters—one beautiful but flighty, one plain but faithful—a brainy but impractical son, and a mysterious Black housekeeper are left to fend for themselves. Their story becomes enmeshed with those of two other families—the Raines, upper class with European pretensions, and the Thornes, headed by a strict Calvinist father—out of which flirtations, love triangles, jealousies, betrayals, and acts of self-sacrifice ensue, with more twists and turns peppered with American cultural commentary than can be summarized here. Joseph the Jew is mentioned in passing only a handful of times in these scenes, which comprise the bulk of the novel. Still, in a profound way, the novel remains emphatically his. When Joseph is about to die, he is discovered by two soldiers, who turn out to be Nicholas Hearn, the bright son of the absent father, and Nelson Thorne, the handsome son of the Calvinist father. Joseph passes on

42. See Helen Hughes, *The Historical Romance* (New York: Routledge, 1993), 2–3.
43. Johnson, *Joseph the Jew*, 86,

to them his grandfather's documents and an account of his treasure hunt. The events of the sentimental novel and the intertwining of the families commence only after this crucial scene. In the closing chapters, the adventure tale briefly returns, the two soldiers discover the treasure, and even more significant, it is revealed that Nelson Thorne's grandfather was the pirate who had stolen the jewels and that Nicholas Hearn's grandfather was the captain of the ship and, apparently, the true owner of the pirated jewels. In short, the treasure returns to its rightful owners; the disgraced father's debt is paid, and he returns home; the pirate's sin is expiated, and his grandson marries the captain's plain but faithful granddaughter.

For Johnson, these unlikely connections and resolutions are meant to suggest more than mere coincidence, the stuff of popular romance. The novel's epigraph is taken from the closing scene of Hamlet: "There's a divinity that shapes our ends, | Rough-hew them how we will." The divinity that the Prince of Denmark recognizes in his story, Johnson implies, is what shapes the modern drama in which the Jew of Denmark is destined to play a determinative role. When Joseph absconds with his grandfather's papers, the author writes, he "crossed the line of the future," a future that he could not have predicted, one that is not even his own, but one that, as rough-hewn as it seems, he is fated to facilitate. To be sure, Johnson wears her theology lightly. Most characters do not see the hand of God in the unfolding of events. Only Nelson Thorne's Calvinist father comments, "It is the providence of God, my son." The sins of the fathers are visited upon their posterity. But in the divinity-shaped plot Johnson has devised, "the coming of the Jew" brings redemption to the American Christian characters—notably, after the trauma of the Civil War. The final line of the novel reads: "Joseph the Jew has fulfilled his allotted task."[44] In effect, he has died for their sins. In the language of biblical typology, his story is fulfilled in the story of the Americans.

When Nelson Thorne searches for the treasure in the old haunted house described in Joseph Rost's papers, he encounters the same apparition seen earlier by the Jew, but Nelson notices in perplexed wonder that the ghost closely resembles his own Calvinist father. Nelson relates the adventure to his father, hoping for an explanation. Although the father soon surmises that the apparition was the pirate grandfather's ghost, he initially ridicules the son's improbable tale. "Oh, an admirable serial story!" he mocks. "Close of the number, apparition of old man appears to wandering Jew—for such I take your hero to be—and the

44. *Ibid.*, 18, 116, 18, 131.

reading public left with hair standing on end."[45] Of course, Joseph was not *the* Wandering Jew, the legendary figure who is said to have cruelly mocked a weary Jesus on the way to Calvary and is condemned to wander the world without respite until the Second Coming.[46] Johnson imagines a different literary role for her Jew. But her character's quip speaks to the currency of the figure in nineteenth-century America. Americans could find accounts of recent sightings of the millennia-old Jew in the newspapers or read a proto-muckraking novella of political corruption called *The Wandering Jew in America*, or enjoy dime novels with titles such as *Monte Cristo Afloat, or, The Wandering Jew of the Sea* and *Buffalo Bill's Death Deal, or, The Wandering Jew of the West*.[47] They could find in Eugene Field's "Holy Cross" a mawkish tale of the ancient Jew's suffering and salvation in the Southwest of the Conquistadores; experience in Herman Melville's *Clarel* a masque performed by the monks of the Mar Saba monastery about "the Jew | Who wanders ever ... hungering also for the day | Whose dawn these weary feet shall stay"; or, in *The Innocents Abroad*, visit with a sardonic Mark Twain "the veritable house where the unhappy wretch once lived who has been celebrated in song and story for more than eighteen hundred years."[48]

At its root, the story of the Wandering Jew, in all its various and varied renditions, symbolized the collective fate of the Jewish people, their rejection of Jesus as the justification for centuries of exile and oppression. It was this core understanding that prompted Isaac Mayer Wise to overhaul and rehabilitate the figure, to modernize him, to transform exile into divine mission, to reimagine the Wandering Jew (that is, the Jews as a people) as the avatar of civilization, the harbinger of human progress, the enlightener of mankind. "The grand drama of the Wandering Jew will continue," Wise declares, "until there shall be no more

45. *Ibid.*, 116.

46. For an encyclopedic account of the Wandering Jew, see George K. Anderson, *The Legend of the Wandering Jew* (Providence: Brown University Press, 1965). See also Galit Hasan-Rokem and Alan Dundes, eds., *The Wandering Jew: Essays in the Interpretation of a Christian Legend* (Bloomington: Indiana University Press, 1986).

47. William Macon Coleman, *The Wandering Jew in America: A Novel* (Washington, D.C.: J. G. Hester, 1875); Prentiss Ingraham, *Monte Cristo Afloat, or, The Wandering Jew of the Sea*, Beadle's New York Dime Library, no. 399 (1886), and Ingraham, *Buffalo Bill's Death Deal, or, The Wandering Jew of the West*, Beadle's New York Dime Library, no. 1004 (1897). See also Harap, "American Journeys of the Wandering Jew," in Harap, *Image of the Jew*, 239–58, and Rudolf Glanz, "The Wandering Jew in America," in *The Wandering Jew*, ed. Hasan-Rokem and Dundes, 105–18.

48. Eugene Field, *The Holy Cross, and Other Tales* (Chicago: Stone and Kimball, 1893), 13–35; Herman Melville, *Clarel: A Poem and Pilgrimage in the Holy Land*, ed. Walter E. Bezanson (New York: Hendricks House, 1960), 349–50; Mark Twain, *The Innocents Abroad, or, The New Pilgrim's Progress*, 2 vols. in 1 (New York: Harper and Brothers, 1922), 2:319.

superstition, no ignorance and no intolerance, no hatred, no self-delusion and no darkness among sects."[49]

When Lew Wallace (Fig. 80), the author of *Ben-Hur*, considered using the Wandering Jew as the "active agent, the *Deus ex Machina*" of *The Prince of India*, his historical romance about the fall of Constantinople to the Turks in 1453, he, too, imagined him as a religious reformer, a would-be dispeller of darkness, speculating that this Jew's "more than fourteen centuries of life, spent in every corner of the globe, have enriched him with more than human attributes of knowledge, learning, foresight, with more than human ability for dealing with men and with affairs" (Figs. 81 and 82). To be sure, he is not Wise's unabashed and unqualified hero, and in the end "he brings about the catastrophe" that is the fall of Constantinople.[50] Wallace's Wandering Jew is a complex figure, a sophisticated thinker and passionate actor, both tortured and egotistical, principled and loyal, but also subject to jealousies and resentments that bring him to Shylock-like vengeance. Still, the purpose Wallace assigns him is not wholly unlike that which Wise sees as the reformist mission of the Jews.

Wallace poured the imaginative foundation of *The Prince of India; or, Why Constantinople Fell* between 1881 and 1884, when he served as American minister to Turkey. He conceived of fifteenth-century Constantinople as a "picturesque" landscape, colorfully Oriental and cosmopolitan, still medieval. "Knights in armor course through my pages," he reported to his sister-in-law, "feats of individual valor and personal prowess enliven them."[51] Romantic episodes abound: grave looting in Tyre, the Hajj in Mecca, Christian pageantry in Constantinople, a storm on the Bosporus, a royal love triangle, religious intrigue, abduction of a beautiful maiden, *damnatio ad bestias*, a devastating conflagration, disguises and deceptions, and, of course, an extended account of the famous battle that led to the fall of the Byzantine capital and the end of the empire. But the theme that runs through all this is the plan of the Wandering Jew to bring a purified religion "pleasing in the sight of the Lord God of Solomon" to a severely sectarian world, a world scarred not only by the Crusades but also by schisms both within Islam and, more central to the narrative, within Christianity.[52] To say that the Jew fails in his mission is, first, to recognize that, generically, while historical

49. Isaac Mayer Wise, *The Wandering Jew: A Lecture* ([Cincinnati, 1877]), 12.
50. Lew Wallace, *An Autobiography*, 2 vols. (New York: Harper and Brothers, 1906), 2:982.
51. *Ibid.*
52. Lew Wallace, *The Prince of India, or, Why Constantinople Fell*, 2 vols. (New York: Harper and Brothers, 1893), 1:23.

Fig. 80. Gen. Lew Wallace (1860). (Brady-Handy Photograph Collection, Library of Congress, Prints and Photographs Division).

THE PRINCE OF INDIA

OR

WHY CONSTANTINOPLE FELL

BY

LEW. WALLACE

AUTHOR OF "BEN-HUR" "THE BOYHOOD OF CHRIST"
"THE FAIR GOD" ETC., ETC.

Rise, too, ye Shapes and Shadows of the Past
Rise from your long-forgotten graves at last
Let us behold your faces, let us hear
The words you uttered in those days of fear
Revisit your familiar haunts again
The scenes of triumph, and the scenes of pain
And leave the footprints of your bleeding feet
Once more upon the pavement of the street

LONGFELLOW

VOL. I.

NEW YORK
HARPER & BROTHERS PUBLISHERS

Fig. 81. Title page of Lew Wallace, *Prince of India* (New York, 1893). (University of California).

romance welcomes the fictional and the fantastic, it cannot abide the counterfactual. In the end, history is history. But it is also to recognize, thematically, the depth of the discord within Byzantium itself and the role of internecine evils in the fall of the capital. In Wallace's narrative, although the Jew is instrumental in encouraging the Muslim conquest, Constantinople does not fall because of him. It falls despite him.

"Nothing is more dangerous," writes historian Steven Runciman, "than to try to be eirenical in matters of religion."[53] But this is precisely what the Wandering Jew intends, hoping thereby to dispel his curse and be released "from this too long life." Disguising himself as the titular Indian prince who has studied all the world's scriptures, he pleads the case that "faith is a natural impulse" but that "there can be no reform or refinement of faith except God be its exclusive subject." Of course, neither the Moslems nor the Christians of *The Prince of India* look kindly on the idea of "lopping off all parasitical worships such as are given to Christ and Mahomet."[54] For Christians in particular, and they are the novel's focus, the Great Schism of 1054 still divides East and West, the Council of Florence's attempt at reconciliation has failed, and each side still holds tenaciously to its Christ-centered theological positions. Wallace calls attention repeatedly, for instance, to the Azymite controversy, whether the bread of the Eucharist—representing the body of Christ—should be unleavened or leavened, the term being used with utter contempt to refer to the Western church by the Eastern.[55] To question the divinity of Christ in such an atmosphere, no matter how eirenic the intentions, is to court disaster. Frustrated by Christian intransigence (and angry at their failure, in one of the novel's romantic subplots, to rescue his kidnapped step-daughter), the Wandering Jew leaves the Byzantine capital, joins the Moslem side (still as the Prince of India), and the conquest begins.

The fact that Wallace gives a mission of peace and reconciliation to the Wandering Jew, however foolhardy and futile, is noteworthy. His fundamental sympathy with his character's theology is clear, if not from the novel itself, then from the author's account of his personal beliefs at the opening of his autobiography. Wallace was never "a member of any church or denomination"; and while he did "believe absolutely in the Christian conception of God," he insisted that Jesus was a human being—divine only in the sense that his "divinity was the Spirit

53. Steven Runciman, "The Schism Between the Eastern and Western Churches," *Anglican Theological Review* 44 (1962): 337.

54. Wallace, *Prince of India*, 1:54.

55. See John H. Erickson, "Leavened and Unleavened: Some Theological Implications of the Schism of 1054," *St. Vladimir's Theological Quarterly* 14 (1970): 155–76.

Fig. 82. Lew Wallace, *The Prince of India.* (Courtesy of Between the Covers, Gloucester City, N.J.)

[of God] within him."[56] Moreover, Wallace conceived of the Wandering Jew's mission as ongoing, having planned before his death a sequel to *The Prince of India* in which the Jew leaves the Constantinople of 1453 and makes his way to the court of Ferdinand and Isabella in 1492. He would "sail with Columbus in search of a new world, there to find the end of controversy, to try the universal brotherhood of man, and found the religion of the one God."[57] The Wandering Jew was to become the modern American reformer.

Assimilation and Aesthetics

A half century before Leslie Fiedler's half-abashed encounter with the "Jew-villain" in the English literary tradition, Rabbi David Philipson published *The Jew in English Fiction* with the express purpose of "correcting the false impressions ... regarding Jews and Judaism" that readers may very well have acquired by reading English literature "from the time of Elizabeth to our day."[58] Like Fiedler, he takes a stern look at Marlowe's Barabbas, Shakespeare's Shylock, and Dickens's Fagin. Unlike the post-Holocaust critic, however, Philipson is not flustered by the ubiquity of the Jew-villain, even as he notes that "the prejudices of an early day have not yet died out." *Not yet*: Philipson limns a literary history that is broader and more sanguine than Fiedler would allow, charting a range of sympathetic, even fawning images of Jews, from Richard Cumberland's Sheva in 1794 to George Eliot's Mordecai in 1876, and he looks forward with "unquenchable optimism" to a time "when hatred and oppression shall be no more, and justice, love and peace shall rule among men."[59]

Not coincidentally, this forward-looking literary history parallels the emergence of Reform Judaism in Europe and America over the course of the nineteenth century, which Rabbi Philipson called "the most striking Jewish religious phenomenon of modern times." After centuries of breathing the stifling atmosphere of the ghetto and of exclusion "from all sympathetic concern with the culture of the world," Jews were now turning a probing eye toward Judaism, subjecting it "to searching examination in the light of the broader culture," making critical distinctions between nationality and religion and, within religion, between the ceremonial law and "the universal commands implanted in

56. Wallace, *Autobiography*, 1:1–2.

57. *Ibid.*, 2:1002.

58. Philipson, *The Jew in English Fiction* (1889), 1, 5.

59. David Philipson, *The Jew in English Fiction*, 4th ed., enl. (New York: Bloch Publishing Company, 1918), 207.

the heart of man."[60] A new type of Jew was emerging, a modern figure who, for Philipson, raises the cardinal question of whether or not "the Jew" should or could any longer serve as "proper material for the novelist." If cultural particularity and local color are what attract the attention of readers and writers, as Philipson maintains, then "the Jew" as a fictional character was effectually becoming a thing of the past. Nowadays, he argues, "when the Jew ... has stepped out of the Ghetto into the free light and air; when he has dropped his traditional distinguishing marks; when he in all has become like his neighbor—thinking like thoughts, indulging the same ideals, no longer a stranger in a strange land ... but filled with patriotic feeling for the welfare of whatever country he may inhabit; when, in all but religion, he is like unto all—every representation of the modern Jew, except in the religious light ... is a mark of gross ignorance, ... evil and injustice."[61] Confident in Reform ideology, Philipson cannot, or will not, imagine the pressures as well as the possibilities—social, cultural, and religious—that might make modern Jews, assimilated in all but religion, objects of interest to writers, both Jewish and non-Jewish. In fact, by the time he published the first edition of *The Jew in English Fiction*, efforts at depicting the modern Jew *qua* modern Jew—not as sentimental heroine, swashbuckling hero, or mythic figure, and not in the service of a Christian metanarrative—had already begun.

Bavarian-born physician Nathan Mayer wrote several Jewish historical romances, published serially in Isaac Mayer Wise's *Israelite* in the 1850s.[62] Then the Civil War broke out. Mayer served in the Union army, where, as a surgeon, he attained the rank of brigadier general. In the immediate postbellum period, his literary imagination turned from the past to the contemporary Jewish world and the war he knew intimately. His novel *Differences* appeared first serially in the *Israelite* in 1867 and then in book form that same year (Fig. 83). Philipson may not have known of Mayer's novel (it is not mentioned in the first edition of *The Jew in English Fiction*), but, strikingly, it can serve as a test case for Philipson's contentions about the fictional representations of modern Jews and the Reform ideology upon which they are built.[63]

60. David Philipson, *The Reform Movement in Judaism* (New York: Macmillan, 1907), v, 5, 7.

61. Philipson, *The Jew in English Fiction* (1889), 10, 12.

62. See Harap, *Image of the Jew*, 275. Mayer's antebellum fiction includes: *The Count and the Jewess, or, The Magic Cave of Wilbuka: A Tale of the Sixteenth Century* (1856); *Persecution at Frankfurt: A Tale of Vincent Fettmilch* (1856); *The Fatal Secret, or, Plots and Counterplots: A Novel of the Sixteenth Century* (1858); and *The Last of the Asmoneans* (1859).

63. In the 1918 edition of *The Jew in English Fiction*, Philipson includes a "Bibliography of Jewish Life in English Fiction" compiled by Rebecca Schneider, which lists Mayer's *Differences*.

The protagonist of *Differences* is Louis Welland, a German Jewish immigrant to the United States. In a deliberate rhetorical move, however, neither the other characters nor readers are initially made aware that he is anything but German, which is how the author refers to him on the very first page and consistently throughout.[64] And by German, the narrator means high-minded, cultured, and poetic. ("To some extent," the author remarks, "all Germans are poets.") A passing reference to an obscure physical marker is the only hint of ethnic difference: "His face proved that his descent was not purely Teutonic, but that there mingled with his blood a Southern or Eastern current."[65] Still, nothing marks him overtly as being Jewish. Much of his backstory we learn later. Educated at a German university and a veteran of the 1848 revolutions on the rebel side, he was wrongly and deceptively deprived of his patrimony because he is a Jew; he then immigrated to the Unites States, trained as a government land surveyor in New York, and was sent on assignment to Tennessee months before the outbreak of the Civil War. We meet him *in medias res*, on his journey south, where he enters the lives of the Southern aristocracy, including the Goldman family, described by the author as being "of Hebrew descent, and firmly attached to a rational interpretation of their religion." Yet not even they discern that he is a Jew. In an exquisitely ironic scene at the Goldman home, some forty pages into the novel, the estate manager bemoans the fact that a turkey has been incorrectly slaughtered, at which the matriarch of the family explains to Welland, "We are a Hebrew family, sir ... and it is a religious custom." When Welland responds, "I know [the custom] madam ... and have the honor of professing the same faith," there is, "a pause of astonishment," emphatic if only momentary.[66] After which, the narrative dispassionately moves on. Similar scenes of revelation, followed by another character's brief and passing disbelief, appear at significant moments later in the novel as well. Mayer's point is plain. In fiction as in life, when a Jew has assimilated culturally—when, to use Philipson's words, he has "dropped his traditional distinguishing marks"—his Jewishness ceases, or should cease, to define him presumptively as different.

By calling his novel *Differences*, Mayer telescopes his intention to interrogate the general question of distinctions among people—differences of religion, to be sure, but also of class, race, nationality, gender, character, and above all, the political differences that led to the secession of the Southern states and the Civil

64. See Michael A. Meyer, "German-Jewish Identity in Nineteenth-Century America," in *The American Jewish Experience*, ed. Jonathan D. Sarna (New York: Holmes & Meyer, 1986), 45–61.

65. Nathan Mayer, *Differences: A Novel* (Cincinnati: Bloch and Company, 1867), 4, 5.

66. *Ibid.*, 34, 47.

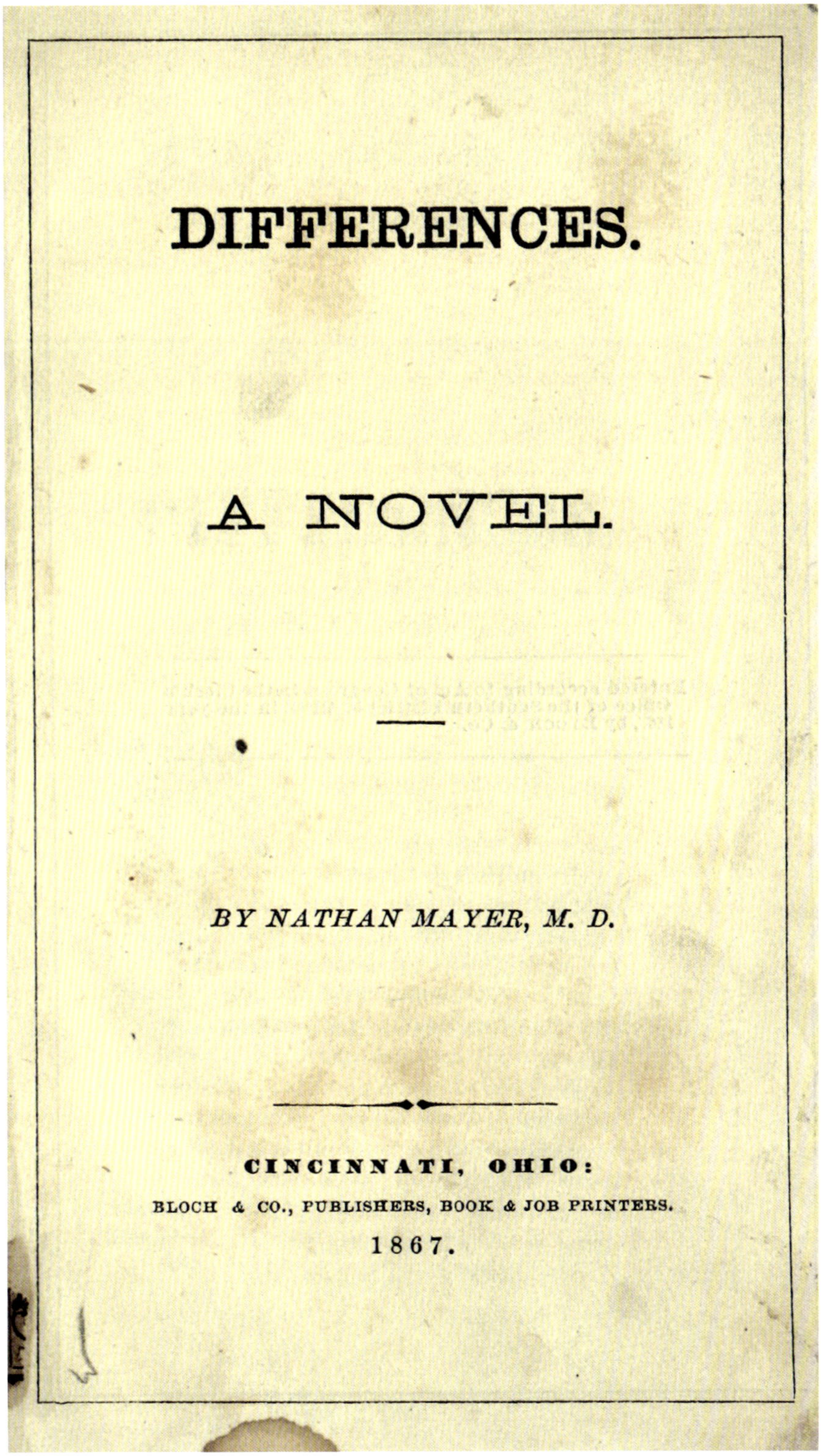

DIFFERENCES.

A NOVEL.

BY NATHAN MAYER, M. D.

CINCINNATI, OHIO:

BLOCH & CO., PUBLISHERS, BOOK & JOB PRINTERS.

1867.

Fig. 83. Title page of Nathan Mayer, *Differences* (Cincinnati, 1867). (University of North Carolina).

War. Mayer takes the conventional love plot formula—boy meets girl, boy loses girl, boy gets girl back again—and fleshes it out through the interplay of these sets of differences. Welland meets bright, blond, and beautiful Antonia Goldman. Both are Jews, although this fact seems to have little significance to either. Otherwise, they are very different: he is a poor Northerner with liberal political sympathies; she is a rich Southerner with the attendant traditional values. But they fall in love over discussions of German literature. As hostilities approach, a scoundrel from Welland's past colludes with a rival suitor (a Southern landowner of French descent and questionable morals) to spread a rumor that Welland is a Union spy. He is forced to escape ahead of an angry lynch mob of poor whites, but not before the couple declare their love and their intent to marry. Welland joins the Union army, for which he fights nobly, rising in the ranks. Meanwhile, misinformation reaches Antonia that Welland has forsaken her and is betrothed to another. A loyal daughter of the South, she accepts his Southern rival's proposal of marriage as he goes off to join the Confederate forces. Differences divide the lovers, the war divides the country, and all these events transpire with barely more than passing mention of the characters' religion.

The Civil War is the climax of Mayer's drama of differences and its consummate symbol. But as the novel moves toward its denouement, the war recedes behind the marriage plot, the political differences fall behind the religious ones, and the modern Reform Jew takes center stage, offering the possibility of reconciliation on all fronts, becoming, in effect, an avatar of amity. The scene moves to New York City, and Jews and Judaism become thematically more significant. Antonia's brother Charles Goldman is there, at first tending to matters of the family business and later convalescing after being injured fighting for the Confederacy. Through him, we meet other Jews, all shaped in various ways by the long history of antisemitism, foils for the modern Jew. In a cameo appearance we are introduced to "a type of the noblest class of medieval Jews," kind and benevolent but insular, a vestige of older times, when "the harsh bigotry of the Gentile" caused Jews to rely only on each other. More prevalent is the commercial Jew, whose standard of judgment for all matters, including matters of the heart, is pecuniary. Locked into an exilic mentality, skeptical even of American liberalism, he explains, "Our country is our money, and the power and influence it gives us; these are our only acknowledged rights."[67]

Charles is yet another sort of Jew, "a moral coward" afraid to "face continually

67. *Ibid.*, 383, 377. See Barry E. Supple, "A Business Elite: German Jewish Financiers in Nineteenth-Century New York," in *American Jewish Experience*, ed. Sarna, 73–88.

the charges, just or unjust, which society has been in the habit of bringing against those of the Jewish ... faith." He has fallen in love with a beautiful dark-haired Gentile but is loath to reveal his Jewishness to her or her father, fearing rejection on that account. In this context, Welland, though he has himself been affected by antisemitism, refuses to be defined by it and emerges as an agent of accord, espousing an ideology that effects a delicate balance between ethnic self-assertion and assimilation. On one hand, he rebukes Charles for his pusillanimity: "You might as well tear the nose from your face as endeavor to solve your connection with your people." On the other, he maintains that Jewish difference is hardly different at all. He advises the Goldmans not to scruple about Charles marrying a Christian, as the prohibition is "merely a custom." And he counsels Emma, Charles's Gentile betrothed, not to scruple about converting to Judaism. "God is God, whether adored in the Jewish, Christian or Mohammedan manner," he tells her. "The dogmas, moral teachings, and social precepts are the same in spirit."[68] The differences are only ceremonial, and conversion is strictly formal, so she might as well pacify Charles's family. The marriage of Charles and Emma is the penultimate scene in Mayer's novel of differences, enacting the union of Jew and Christian and the reunion of North and South. In the final lines, Antonia and Welland reconcile and declare, for themselves, for America, and for liberal religion, "United in love ... despite former differences.... United forever."[69]

Had David Philipson known of Mayer's novel, he may have celebrated it as an early model of a new Jewish literature yet to come, in which the modern Jew, assimilated in all but religion, would display, as he writes in the peroration to the final edition of *The Jew in English Fiction*, the "larger outlook" that comes from "the light of freedom," a harbinger of a day "when hatred and oppression shall be no more, and justice, love and peace shall rule among men."[70] Four decades later, flush with the successes of the mid-century breakthrough of Jewish American writing and the emergence of a new kind of Jewish hero—alienated rather than assimilated, tormented rather than triumphant—Leslie Fiedler limned an edgier trajectory for Jewish American literature and pointed to a more vexed and ironic origin. "It is self-evident," he wrote in his survey of *The*

68. Mayer, *Differences*, 219, 220, 452–53. To put Welland's position into context, see Benny Kraut, "Reform Judaism and the Unitarian Challenge," in *American Jewish Experience*, ed. Sarna, 89–96.

69. Mayer, *Differences*, 462.

70. Philipson, *The Jew in English Fiction* (1918), 207.

Jew in the American Novel (in effect, a follow-up to his earlier Jew-villain essay), that "the Jewish American novel in its beginnings must be a problem novel," that "its essential problems must be those of identity and assimilation," and that its "obsessive theme," illustrative of that problem, would be "intermarriage with its ambiguous blending of the hope of assimilation and the threat of miscegenation."[71] Fiedler locates those beginnings not in Mayer's *Differences*, where assimilation is hardly a challenge and the objections to intermarriage are whisked away with a wave of Reform universalism and an offhand invitation to convert, but in the work of a non-Jew, Henry Harland's dark, angst-ridden *The Yoke of the Thorah*, in which the hope and threat of intermarriage wrestle with melodramatic fury within the body of the novel's protagonist, Elias Bacharach (Figs. 84 and 85).[72]

When we are introduced to him, Elias appears to be a model modern Jew, much like Mayer's Louis Welland. Which is to say, he is young, cultured, artistic (he's a painter), and, except for his telltale name, not noticeably Jewish. Like Welland, he falls in love with a blonde and beautiful young woman amid a romantic swirl of shared literature, art, and music. But here the similarities end. Unlike Antonia Goldman, Elias's young woman, Christine Redwood, is not Jewish. Neither regards this difference as an issue, not because they see the fundamental compatibility of modern Judaism and liberal Protestantism—as Welland counsels in *Differences*—but because they are indifferent to religion, or seem to be. What matters is the elite modern culture they share, and they decide to marry. Neither does Elias's being a Jew matter to Christine's Universalist father, who, in his gruff way, says to Elias, "You're a perfect gentleman; and you can't help it if you were born a Jew. You don't look like one, and you don't act like one."[73] But Elias's uncle, the Orthodox rabbi Felix Gedaza, is far from indifferent. Portrayed as a mysterious, scheming Gothic villain, he scorns Elias, preying upon his psychological and physical weaknesses—the memory of his Orthodox upbringing and a genetic propensity to epilepsy—that together induce a physical collapse just as the couple are about to exchange vows. Elias may have appeared to be a modern Jew, may have sloughed off ceremonial rites

71. Leslie Fiedler, *The Jew in the American Novel* (New York: Herzl Press, 1959), reprinted in Fiedler, *To the Gentiles* (New York: Stein and Day, 1972), 75.

72. See Harap, "The Strange Case of Henry Harland," in Harap, *Image of the Jew*, 455–71. For a reading of Harland's novel different from mine, see Stephanie Foote, "Ethnic Plotting: Henry Harland and the Jewish Writer," *American Literature* 75, no. 1 (2003): 119–40.

73. Sidney Luska [Henry Harland], *The Yoke of the Thorah* (New York: Street and Smith, 1900), 85. The novel was originally published in 1887.

Fig. 84. Henry Harland in his London home. *Booklovers Magazine* 3. no. 3 (March 1904). (Princeton University Library).

and believed himself to have transcended exclusivist Judaism, but he finds himself unable to throw off the yoke of the Thorah. Convinced by his uncle that his collapse was an act of God rescuing him from the curse of intermarriage, he forsakes Christine and is coerced into marrying the daughter of a crass (if also good and kind) nouveau riche German Jewish family with whom he shares little more than ethnic origin. He does not love her. Although she is a fine musician, she does not share (to use Philipson's words) Elias's "sympathetic concern for the culture of the world." The idyllic new world of the beginning of the novel, in which aesthetic assimilation prevails over religious and ethnic differences, crumbles into emotional chaos and the tortured protagonist's untimely death.

In his brief preface to the first edition of *The Jew in English Fiction*, Philipson cites but summarily dismisses *The Yoke of the Thorah* as representative of a recent spate of novels "whose only claim to public attention was the fact that their author introduced Jews as prominent personages, and affected to give true pictures of Jewish life and sentiment." Philipson's reluctance to comment further on the novel only underscores his disdain for what he felt was Harland's stilted depiction of "Jewish life and sentiment." Elias Bacharach is not the modern Jew Philipson postulated. He is not comfortably assimilated, not wholly at home in modernity. Nor has he Louis Welland's religious confidence, his Reform belief in a Judaism that can embrace both assimilation and religious self-assertion, intermarriage and Jewish integrity. Such Jews do not exist in *The Yoke of the Thorah*. The novel imagines its modern Jewish protagonist as the helpless victim in a clash of irreconcilable opposites, of "rationalism" and "common sense" on one hand, and of "superstition" and "the most reactionary sort of orthodoxy" on the other. He must choose between stark opposites, the humanistic openness and cultural refinement he envisions in Christine and the ethnic atavism and bourgeois vulgarity that characterize the German Jewish community in which he lives. Harland's preferences are clear. When Elias decides that his love for Christine transcends his ethnic ties and religious obligations, Harland writes, "The man had got the better of the Jew." When he considers religious allegiance above Christine, Harland writes, "The Jew had got the better of the man."[74] As Philipson's rabbinic colleague Kaufmann Kohler wrote in a scathing review of the novel, "A Jew must either brave the curses and execrations of the law and of all the authorities and representatives of Jewish life in order to be 'a man,' independent and free, or remain under the curse, an object of pity and compassion

74. *Ibid.*, 85–86, 83, 68.

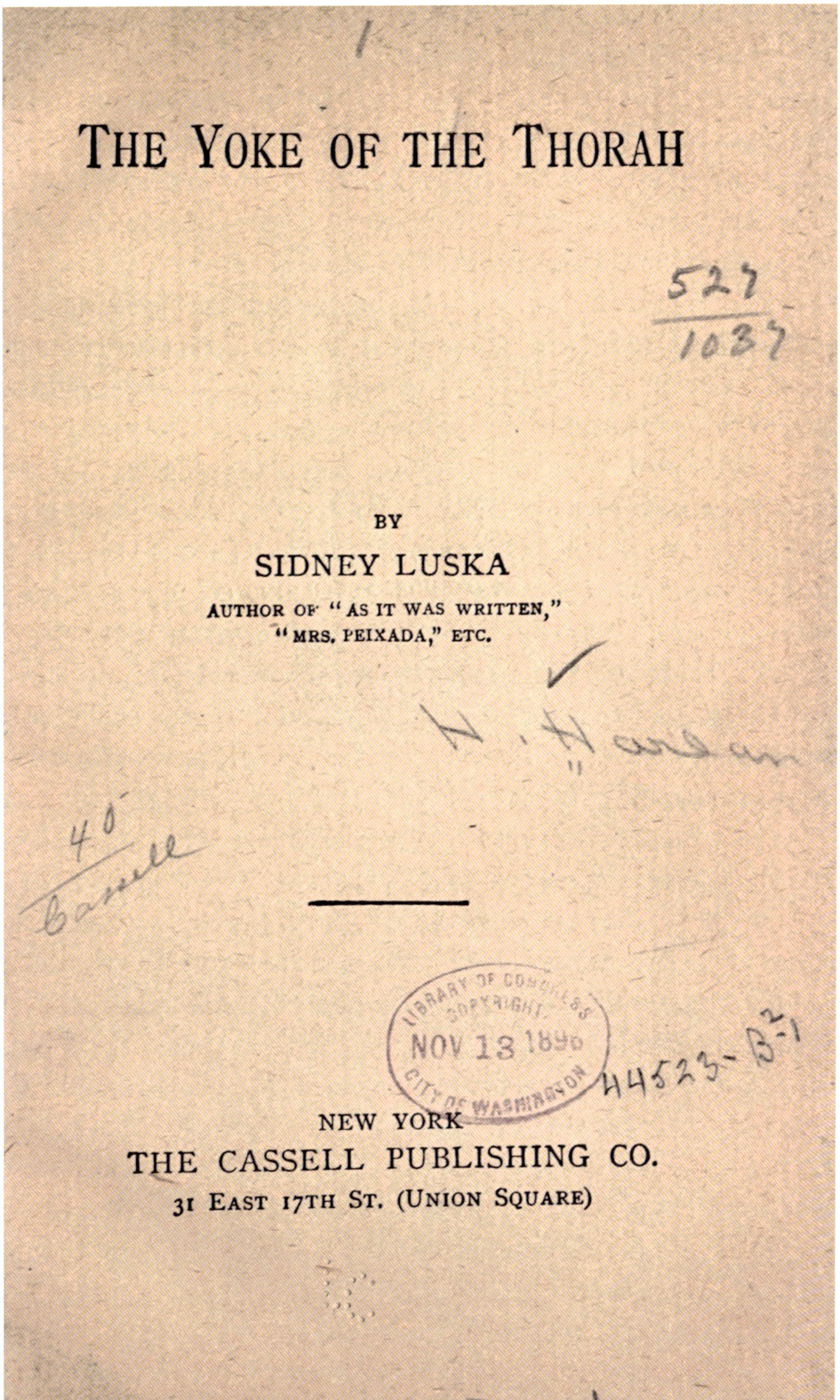
THE YOKE OF THE THORAH

BY

SIDNEY LUSKA

AUTHOR OF "AS IT WAS WRITTEN," "MRS. PEIXADA," ETC.

LIBRARY OF CONGRESS COPYRIGHT NOV 13 1896 CITY OF WASHINGTON

NEW YORK
THE CASSELL PUBLISHING CO.
31 EAST 17TH ST. (UNION SQUARE)

Fig. 85. Title page of Sidney Luska [Henry Harland], *The Yoke of the Thorah* (New York, 1896). (Library of Congress).

in the eyes of humanity." Either man or Jew: there is no middle ground, no room for reconciliation. "In the author's opinion," Kohler writes, "the Thorah is nothing less than a declaration of perpetual war of clannish, exclusive, bigoted, intolerant and superstitious Judaism against largehearted, broad and vigorous humanity." The novel displays nothing more, Kohler concludes, than the author's "utter ignorance about the Jewish religion which he is bent upon denouncing."[75] The criticism is understandable. For Kohler, as for Philipson, the novel's excluded middle is the Reform Judaism they espoused, their model for a modern, equitable society. But it may not have been ignorance alone that shaped the novel's polarized portrayal of Judaism. Harland was an aspiring young writer who, while living in Manhattan, claimed to have "circulated almost exclusively among the Jews" for several years. Taking them on as a subject and adopting the ethnic pseudonym of Sidney Luska, he hoped to advance his career by attracting Jewish readers who would buy his books "for the sake of seeing what New York can produce in the way of a truly Jewish story."[76] However, he was also a devotee of Felix Adler and the Ethical Culture Society and was poised to see the Jewish community, and Kohler and Philipson's Reform, through that radically critical lens. He no doubt knew of Adler's deep disappointment with Reform Judaism's failure to live up to "the great anticipations which were connected with the movement in its earlier stages" and his lamenting "the stubborn vitality which seems to inhere in the hoary superstitions of the past," including, and most relevant here, in regard to "the propriety of intermarriage between Jews and Christians."[77] Harland understood that his portrait of Rabbi Gedaza was grotesque and exaggerated, explaining in a footnote that he was well aware that "among the better-educated and more intelligent Jews in America, orthodoxy of this stripe is not common." Still, he argued, even the most liberal, free-thinking Jews "retain their prejudice against intermarriage, and even their superstitions anent its consequences."[78] Like Adler, Harland sees the liberalism of Reform Judaism as a cover for a stubborn ethnocentrism. The rabbi's insidious, demonic behavior, his fierce and bigoted opposition to Elias's marriage with a Gentile, is

75. Kaufmann Kohler, "'The Yoke of the Torah': A Critique and a Protest," *Menorah* 3 (September 1887): 144.

76. Henry Harland to Edmund Clarence Stedman, quoted in Foote, "Ethnic Plotting," 121.

77. Felix Adler, *Creed and Deed: A Series of Discourses* (New York: Published for the Society for Ethical Culture by G. P. Putnam's Sons, 1880), 239, 51. See Benny Kraut, *From Reform Judaism to Ethical Culture: The Religious Evolution of Felix Adler* (Cincinnati: Hebrew Union College Press, 1979), esp. 214–26, for an analysis of his critique of Reform Judaism.

78. Harland, *Yoke of the Thorah*, 65–66.

the melodramatic representation of these stubborn, vestigial beliefs, and Elias's fall is their tragic consequence. What offended Kohler in *The Yoke of the Thorah* is precisely what attracted Fiedler: the image of a tormented modern Jew, educated and cultured, an artist, helplessly ensnared in a web woven of "the hope of assimilation and the threat of miscegenation."

In 1897, musing in Philadelphia's *Jewish Exponent* on how the Jew might be depicted in the fiction of the future, Mrs. Albert Berkowitz reasoned that it would be the responsibility of Jewish writers—writers who have inherited a "fervid Jewish spirit" but have been raised in "a more aesthetic culture"—to "create [Jewish] characters and portray life that are the results of the new emancipated conditions of to-day." Contra Philipson, Berkowitz suggests that, for all their similarities, modern Jews remained different, that realistic representations of the modern Jew served a unique purpose, to reflect "all the pathos of centuries of darkness, of fidelity and hope, and at last triumphant and justified faith." By thus embodying "the Jewish ideal of human life," fiction about modern Jews would have universal appeal, not only interesting to Jews but also inspiring to all "human hearts." It was obvious to her as well that "in America was the future Jew to be realized" and that women would be instrumental in realizing her vision. She noted that a "young American Jewess, Miss Emma Wolfe [*sic*]," had already begun down this path, taking as the subject of her fiction "one of the problems which new social conditions have developed." But, she demurred, "her solution may not be accepted as the correct or final one."[79]

Berkowitz was referring to Emma Wolf's novel *Other Things Being Equal* (Fig. 86), an examination of modern Jewish life in contemporary San Francisco, and the specific problem she refers to is that of Jewish-Christian intermarriage. But the larger issue is: Does the modern Jew ultimately have a future at all—not simply in fiction, as Philipson suggested, but in life? As the title suggests, Wolf's novel is premised upon the liberal society dreamed of since the Enlightenment—wistfully recalled by Fiedler in his "Jew-Villain" essay—a society in which Jews and Christians are culturally commensurate and freely intermingle. And yet, Wolf notes, a residual resistance to full integration, fueled by ethnic pride and a lingering resentment of historical wrongs, demands that Jews keep to a "narrowly conventional Jewish pathway" and, if nothing else, marry

79. Mrs. Albert [Clara Landman] Berkowitz, "The Jew in the Fiction of the Future," *Jewish Exponent*, January 15, 1897, 1–2.

80. Emma Wolf, *Other Things Being Equal* (Chicago: A. C. McClurg, 1892), 102. For more on Wolf, see Lori Harrison-Kahan, "'A Grave Experiment': Emma Wolf's Marriage Plots and the

strictly among themselves.[80] Of course, these contending forces are present in Mayer's *Differences* and Harland's *The Yoke of the Thorah* as well, and even in *Rebecca the Jewess*—and, as Fiedler suggested, they form a characteristic plot element in much of the Jewish American fiction that is to come.[81] But in *Other Things Being Equal*—a novel either unknown or uninteresting to Fiedler—the problem created by the fundamental ambivalence of the modern Jew is given an ideological hearing with a candor that the other novels do not achieve. One commentator called that candor "courageous," but it gave Mrs. Berkowitz pause.[82]

Wolf's protagonist is Ruth Levice, the only daughter of a wealthy, liberal-minded Jewish couple who have raised her to be a proud Jew but "to believe that every broad-minded man of whatever sect will recognize and honor the same quality in any other man." When confronted by her cousin with the feeling that their Christian acquaintances looked down on them, Ruth responds dismissively. After all, the social world she moves in is not Christian per se but secular. "We all dance and talk alike," she argues. "We have had the same schooling, speak the same language, read the same books, are surrounded by the same elements of home refinement." Ruth is, in her father's words, "a perfect type of what culture and refinement can give."[83] Or, in Philipson's words, "in all but religion ... like unto all," at least, like all of her wealthy class. So when she falls in love with an equally broad-minded Christian man—especially one whose Christianity closely resembles her liberal Judaism—she sees no reason not to accept his proposal of marriage. Still, her father objects, insisting on Jewish difference. Every Jew is, by birth, "invested with certain hereditary traits that are unconvertible," he argues, bearing "in his blood the glory, the triumph, the misery, the abjectness of Israel." Inevitably, these Jewish traits will manifest in certain unpalatable behaviors, if not in the Levices themselves, then among other Jews with whom they associate, prompting antisemitic reactions that would drive a wedge between his daughter and the world, ending in her unhappiness. The

---

Deghettoization of American Jewish Fiction," *American Jewish History* 101, no. 1 (2017): 5–34, and Jessica Kirzane, "Women, Love, and the Reform Jewish Mission: Jewish-Christian Marriage in Emma Wolf's *Other Things Being Equal* and Its Literary Successors," *American Jewish History* 104, no. 2–3 (2020): 289–322.

81. See Adam Sol, "Longings and Renunciations: Attitudes Towards Intermarriage in Early Twentieth Century Jewish American Novels," *American Jewish History* 89, no. 2 (2001): 215–30.

82. Anonymous, "American Women of the Jewish Faith Who Have Distinguished Themselves in Literature, Drama, Music, Philanthropy and Society," *Sentinel*, February 13, 1913, 9.

83. Wolf, *Other Things Being Equal*, 10–11, 175.

OTHER THINGS BEING EQUAL

BY

[Miss] EMMA WOLF

CHICAGO
A. C. McCLURG AND COMPANY
1892

LIBRARY OF THE UNIVERSITY OF CALIFORNIA.

Fig. 86. title page of Emma Wolf, *Other Things Being Equal* (Chicago, 1892). (University of California).

objections raised by Ruth and her suitor—a doctor of impeccable character and reputation—do not address her father's passionate yet vague objection but go straight to the heart of the ambivalent aims of the modern Jew. "It was a great oversight on your part," the doctor complains, "when you threw your daughter, equipped as she is, into Christian society—put her in the way of loving or being loved by any Christian, knowing all along that such a state of affairs could lead to nothing." Indeed, he says, "it was cruel." For her part, although she insists that she would never renounce her Judaism, she argues that the religion itself had become so attenuated that there was essentially nothing she would have to abjure. "On our New Year I should still feel that a holy cycle of time had passed," she argues, "but I live only according to one record of time, and my New Year falls always on the 1st of January." She would still attend services on the Day of Atonement, but she and her father had already agreed that fasting was "mere sham and pretence." She had been taught "contempt for all but a few" forms and asks her father, "wherein does our religion show itself?"[84] The modern Jew's desire to assimilate in all but religion, to maintain (in Mrs. Berkowitz's terms) a "fervid Jewish spirit" while participating fully in "a more aesthetic culture," seems to Wolf to verge on equivocation at best, hypocrisy at worst.

In her representation of the modern Jew, Wolf does not ignore the history of antisemitism or, more particularly, the image of what Fiedler called "the Jew-villain in Western tradition." In fact, she strategically inserts a performance of Shakespeare's *Merchant of Venice* into the narrative to help put into relief her conception of the modern Jew. Immersed as she is in the cultural world of her class, Ruth is an avid theatergoer and a particular devotee of the actor Edwin Booth, who has come to San Francisco and will be performing the role of Shylock (Fig. 87). Ruth has seen other performances of *Merchant* and is well aware of the gamut of interpretations of Shakespeare's Jew. She "had seen one who made Shylock merely a fawning, mercenary, loveless, blood-thirsty wretch" and "another who presented a man of quick wit, ready tongue, great dignity, greater vengeance, silent of love, worthy of hate." Now, she is eager to judge for herself Booth's interpretation of the character and, significantly, is escorted to the theater by her Christian suitor-to-be. After viewing the play, she admires the fact that "Booth, without throwing any romantic glamour on the Jew, showed him as God and man, but mostly man, had made him: an old Jew, grown bitter in the world's disfavor through fault of race ... now turned fiend,

84. *Ibid.*, 175, 174, 178.

Fig. 87. Victor Moblard, *Edwin Booth as Shylock.* Watercolor and pencil, late nineteenth century. (Folger Shakespeare Library).

[who] endeavors with tooth and nail to wreak the smouldering vengeance of a lifetime upon the chance representative of an inexorable persecution."[85] Fiedler had judged the play "the key to the degraded picture of the Jew" throughout history.[86] But Ruth, deeming Booth's performance "all quite natural," appears to feel no connection between the Jew-villain of old Venice and the modern Jews of San Francisco—he is of the past, she is of the present—even as her

85. *Ibid.*, 77, 72. For a history of interpretations of Shylock, see John Gross, *Shylock: A Legend and Its Legacy* (New York: Simon and Schuster, 1992). On Edwin Booth and Shylock, see pp. 138–44.

86. Fiedler, "Jew-Villain," 417.

appearance at the theater with a Christian raises the eyebrows of other Jews and Christians at the performance. Pointedly, her most passionate reaction to the play transcends the fact that Shylock is a Jew, "at least," she says, "according to the modern idea." What moves Ruth most is not the Jew's treatment by the play's Christians but the old man's misery, brought on by his "wretched little" daughter, Jessica. Ruth is outraged by Jessica's heartless betrayal of her father, stealing his ducats and running off with her Christian lover. She "detests" the daughter and feels boundless sympathy for "the weary, heartbroken old man."[87] And with this reaction, Wolf foreshadows Ruth's own crisis, having to choose between her father and her Christian lover.

A half-century later, Fiedler will reclaim Shylock as a Jew, embracing his threatening otherness and transforming it into cultural critique. But at this point in time, Wolf looks expectantly beyond the vestigial ethnocentrism (as she sees it) of Reform theology, shifting our gaze from the particularity of Shylock's persecution to the universality of his aggrieved fatherhood. Ruth accedes to her father's wishes, not because she comes to accept his arguments, which she does not, but as a renunciation of Jessica, as an expression of unconditional filial devotion, because of a love that transcends their individual differences as well as her own happiness. For his part, her father is moved by the selflessness of her love and haunted by the sadness he has brought upon her, and so relents. Crucially, unlike his daughter, his change of heart is accompanied by a thoroughgoing change of mind. Wolf has him experience, as death approaches, an epiphany of universal brotherhood. "Below me surged a black mass of crowding, jostling, hurrying beings," he recalls, and while "I knew they were all so different ... I felt, poised thus above them, that they were creatures of the same God."[88] In her effusive review of *Other Things Being Equal* in her universalist polemic, *The Spirit of Judaism*, Josephine Lazarus extols "the rare tenderness and pathos with which the subject is treated" in the novel and extends the logic of its narrative. Interfaith marriage is merely a trope for a larger social and spiritual movement. Lazarus challenges her readers, "Let us take our Judaism fearlessly out into the world, to be put to any test, but, above all, freely to be used, not in its own service, but in the service of the God in whom it believes, the universal Father of all." To meet this challenge, the modern Jew "must be rid of self, of this intense pre-occupation to survive in any form, as race, creed or nation, this desperate struggle to exist in name if nothing else."[89] To be true to the spirit

87. Wolf, *Other Things Being Equal*, 79, 86.

88. *Ibid.*, 255.

89. Josephine Lazarus, *The Spirit of Judaism*, 84, 88–89.

of Judaism, to fulfill its historical mission, she argues, modern Jews must be willing not only to intermarry but also to cease being Jews.

Coda

The search for the modern Jew in American literature does not end here, of course. Most Jews, even the most staunchly Reform, were not ready to pick up the radical gauntlets thrown down before them by Josephine Lazarus or Felix Adler, were content to hold their particularism and universalism in suspension. Besides, other things were not equal in America. Antisemitic publications continued to appear, among others, Telemachus Timayenis's virulent hodgepodge of stereotypes in *The American Jew* or Gordon Clark's invocation of the Jew-villain and recurrent condemnation of "Jew-bankers" in his critique of the financial system, *Shylock.*[90] Not to mention the ubiquity of repulsive Jewish characters in American literature, from the lustful, nouveau-riche Simon Rosedale in Edith Wharton's *House of Mirth* to the greedy, murderous junk dealer Zerkow in Frank Norris's *McTeague*, to the fictitious carpetbagger Jew in W. E. B. Du Bois's *Souls of Black Folk*, the "heir of the slave-baron," who "squeeze[s] ... blood from debt-cursed tenants."[91] To be sure, there were non-Jewish countervoices as well—Zebulon Vances's popular *The Scattered Nation*, for instance, or Madison Peters's *Justice to the Jew*—voices that took upon themselves the task of promulgating positive images of the Jew.[92] Moreover, the masses of East European Jews had already begun to enter America's harbors, appearing to observers from the haughty Henry James to the ambivalent Jacob Riis as alien and uncouth, anything but equal, anything but modern.[93] The arrival of

90. [Telemachus Timayenis], *The American Jew: An Exposé of His Career* (New York: Minerva Publishing Company, 1888); Gordon Clark, *Shylock as Banker, Bondholder, Corruptionist, Conspirator* (Washington, D.C.: Author's Publisher, 1894). On Timayenis, see Leonard A. Greenberg and Harold J. Jonas, "An American Anti-Semite in the Nineteenth Century," in *Essays on Jewish Life and Thought: Presented in Honor of Salo Wittmayer Baron*, ed. Joseph L. Blau et al. (New York: Columbia University Press, 1959), 265–83.

91. W. E. B. Du Bois, *The Souls of Black Folk: Essays and Sketches* (Chicago: A. C. McClurg, 1903), 126–27. On the literary uses of the Jew in Du Bois's volume, see my "W. E. B. Du Bois, American Nationalism, and the Jewish Question," in *Race and the Production of Modern American Nationalism*, ed. Reynolds J. Scott-Childress (New York: Garland, 1999), 169–94.

92. Zebulon Baird Vance, *The Scattered Nation* (New York: Marcus Schnitzer, 1918); Peters, *Justice to the Jew.*

93. See Henry James, *The American Scene* (New York: Harper and Brothers, 1907), 126ff., and Jacob Riis, "The Jews of New York," *Review of Reviews* 13 (January 1896): 58–62. On Henry James and the Jews, see, for example, Leo B. Levy, "Henry James and the Jews: A Critical Study,"

the newcomers prompted the established American Jews of the previous waves of immigration to found the American Jewish Historical Society and the Jewish Publication Society of America, to publish the multivolume Jewish Encyclopedia, to produce works such as Isaac Markens's *The Hebrews in America* (1888), Max Kohler's edition of Charles P. Daly's *The Settlement of the Jews in North America* (1893), Henry Samuel Morais's *The Jews of Philadelphia* (1894), and Simon Wolf's *The American Jew as Patriot, Soldier and Citizen* (1895)—all efforts to take stock of their own accomplishments and keep the image of the modern, cultured Jew in the public eye.

As for the immigrants themselves, some imagined them in the buoyant terms of their predecessors—casting them not only as modern Jews but also as representative Americans. Israel Zangwill, the most significant Anglo-Jewish literary figure of the time (and an admirer of Emma Wolf), gave to America its most potent universalist metaphor in *The Melting Pot*, a melodrama of interfaith romance between two recent immigrants, a Jewish survivor of the Kishinev pogrom and the Russian daughter of its aristocratic instigator. In the play, the "Jew-immigrant" outflanks his effete native American rival, assumes the mantle of America for himself, and, standing beside his Christian lover, declares in a prophetic, universalist ecstasy how in America "the Great Alchemist melts and fuses [all the different peoples, of all different faiths] with his purging flame," and that it will be the immigrants who will "all unite to build the Republic of Man and the Kingdom of God."[94] Mary Antin, a disciple of Josephine Lazarus, introduces her multilayered immigrant autobiography, *The Promised Land*, as a conversion narrative, not from Jew to Christian, but from medieval to modern, from past

Commentary 26 (September 1958): 243–49; Harap, *Image of the Jew*, 359–76; and Jonathan Freedman, "Henry James and the Discourses of Anti-Semitism," in Freedman, *Temple of Culture*, 117–54. On Jacob Riis and the Jews, see Louis Fried, "Jacob Riis and the Jews: The Ambivalent Quest for Community," *American Studies* 20, no. 1 (1979): 5–24.

94. Israel Zangwill, *The Melting Pot: A Drama in Four Acts* (New York: Macmillan, 1909), 91, 199. On Zangwill's admiration for Emma Wolf, see Harrison-Kahan, "'A Grave Experiment.'" In his day, Zangwill was more well known among Jews for his ghetto fiction. For a contemporaneous account of Zangwill's position in American Jewish culture, see Philipson, "Zangwill's 'Children of the Ghetto' and Others," in *The Jew in English Fiction* (1918), 161–208. For recent accounts, see Erik Marc Greenberg, "A Prophet and His People: Israel Zangwill and His American Public, 1892–1926 and Beyond" (Ph.D. diss., UCLA, 2012); Joseph H. Udelson, *Dreamer of the Ghetto: The Life and Works of Israel Zangwill* (Tuscaloosa: University of Alabama Press, 1990), esp. 81–109; and Sarna, *JPS*, 39–42. For more on Zangwill, assimilation, and the melting pot metaphor, see my "The Art of Assimilation: Ironies, Ambiguities, Aesthetics," in *Modern Jewish Literatures: Intersections and Boundaries*, ed. Sheila E. Jelen, Michael P. Kramer, and L. Scott Lerner (Philadelphia: University of Pennsylvania Press, 2011), esp. 313–22.

to future, from the insular world of the Russian ghetto to the optimistic vistas of America. "I began life in the Middle Ages," she gushes, "and here am I still, your contemporary in the twentieth century, thrilling with your latest thought." She understands that her own coming of age recapitulates the evolution of the human race, from the lower form of particularities and division to the higher form of democratic inclusiveness, discovering in her personal American immigration "an interpretation of the universal life."[95]

Other immigrants were less captivated by these heady versions of Americanization, less interested in representing the new immigrants as versions of Louis Welland or Ruth Levice. Most prominent among them, and most influential on Fiedler's generational cohort, was Abraham Cahan. In his fiction, as in his journalism, the densely populated, gritty world of the east European ghetto is presented unapologetically, naturalistically, the immigrants themselves depicted as caught in an ironic play of forces they cannot control and barely understand. "Nor is there a tenement house," he writes in his first book, *Yekl*, "but harbours in its bosom specimens of all the whimsical metamorphoses wrought upon the children of Israel of the great modern exodus by the vicissitudes of life in this their Promised Land of to-day." Their exodus might be modern, but their journey to modernity is unpredictable. Cahan's illiterate protagonist, Yekl (who has taken to calling himself Jake), has sloughed off the ritual trappings of Judaism and, his coworkers comment mockingly, "thinks that shaving one's mustache makes a Yankee," but he is no Reform Jew, not assimilated in all but religion, no paragon of modernity. His transformation—as far as it goes—is superficial and painful.[96] In Fiedler's words, Cahan "treats with art and candor the facts of Jewish life in the United States," and his willingness to maintain a critical stance even toward the Jewish establishment makes him "the model for all serious Jewish-American novelists" as they remodel the image of the modern Jew.[97]

95. Mary Antin, *The Promised Land* (Boston and New York: Houghton Mifflin, 1912), xii–xiii. The dedication page reads: "To the Memory of Josephine Lazarus, Who lives in the fulfillment of her prophecies." For more on Antin's autobiography, assimilation, and place in Jewish American literary history, see my "Assimilation in The Promised Land: Mary Antin and the Jewish Origins of the American Self," *Prooftexts* 18, no. 2 (1998): 121–48.

96. Abraham Cahan, *Yekl: A Tale of the New York Ghetto* (New York: D. Appleton, 1896), 29, 12.

97. Fiedler, *The Jew in the American Novel*, 77.

DEFENDER OF HER SEX AND HER PEOPLE: NINA MORAIS COHEN

PAMELA S. NADELL

> [Woman's] revolution has been tardy because her household Tyrannus has riveted closer chains than the political one.
> —NINA MORAIS, "The Limitations of Sex" (1881)

> The Hebrew wishes no allowance for his faults. He desires merely to be accepted or rejected as a man.
> —NINA MORAIS, "Jewish Ostracism in America" (1881)

MORE THAN a quarter of a century ago the distinguished historian Leonard Dinnerstein declared, "From the end of the Civil War until the beginning of the twentieth century, the United States witnessed the emergence of a full-fledged antisemitic society."[1] Nina Morais (later Cohen) came of age as that antisemitic society was aborning (Fig. 88). A gifted teacher and ardent activist, a woman of considerable intellect and a writer of penetrating analysis, named among the most prominent Jewish authors of the day, she weighed in on the great issues of her age: the woman's problem and the Jewish problem.[2]

I thank Jonathan Sarna for suggesting Nina Morais's "Jewish Ostracism in America" for this chapter, and Jack Cunningham for research assistance.

1. Leonard Dinnerstein, *Antisemitism in America* (New York: Oxford University Press, 1994), 35. Significant works discussing the period considered in this chapter include: John Higham, "Social Discrimination against Jews in America, 1830–1939," *Publications of the American Jewish Historical Society* 47, no. 1 (1957): 1–33; David A. Gerber, ed., *Anti-Semitism in American History* (Urbana: University of Illinois Press, 1986); Michael N. Dobkowski, *The Tarnished Dream: The Basis of American Anti-Semitism* (Westport, Conn.: Greenwood Press, 1979); Naomi W. Cohen, "Antisemitism in the Gilded Age: The Jewish View," *Jewish Social Studies* 41, no. 3–4 (1979): 187–210; David S. Koffman, Hasia R. Diner, Eric L. Goldstein, Jonathan D. Sarna, and Beth S. Wenger, "Roundtable on Anti-Semitism in the Gilded Age and Progressive Era," *Journal of the Gilded Age* 19, no. 3 (2020): 473–505.

2. She was one of nine Jewish writers of verse named by the Reverend Madison Clinton Peters in *Justice to the Jew* (1899); see Jonathan D. Sarna, "The Forgetting of Cora Wilburn: Historical Amnesia and *The Cambridge History of Jewish American Literature*," *Studies in American Jewish Literature* 37, no. 1 (2018): 73–87. Others noted her national reputation; see "Hebrew Money Kings:

Fig. 88. Nina Morais Cohen illustrated in *Congress of Women Held in the Woman's Building, World Columbian Exposition, Chicago, U.S.A., 1893* (Kansas City, 1894), p. 113. (Princeton University Library).

Born in Philadelphia in December 1855, Bonina (Tobah) was the eldest child of Sabato and Clara Morais. Her father, the Italian-born minister-*hazzan* of the city's oldest synagogue, Mikveh Israel, urged his congregation to stand as a bastion of tradition against the reforms then sweeping across American Judaism. In 1886, dismayed by Reform Judaism's radical theological turn, he led the way to founding the Jewish Theological Seminary of America, the future training ground for Conservative rabbis. He became the seminary's first president. His wife, Clara Esther Weil Morais, born in Philadelphia to a German Jewish immigrant father and a mother descended from refugees of the Inquisition, had taught at the Hebrew Education Society, a school combining secular education with instruction in Hebrew language and literature.[3]

Their first child, who went by Nina, dated her earliest memories to the Civil War: hanging lanterns to celebrate Union victories and sitting with the women as they scraped lint to make dressings for wounded soldiers.[4] She was educated at public and private schools and at Girls' Normal School, Philadelphia's first female public secondary school. Like another rabbi's eldest daughter, Baltimore's Henrietta Szold, much of her education took place in the home. Mothers taught their daughters the arts of sewing, canning, pickling, preserving, marketing, dusting, gardening, baking, and cooking. Nina would also have learned the tasks necessary to help care for the six babies that arrived after her.[5]

Meanwhile, her father taught her Italian, Hebrew, and more. Years later, when Nina Morais observed that "[i]t is undoubtedly true that the more enlightened the father the more capable the daughter," she was surely speaking of her own experience. He also taught her to stand up for her convictions. Sabato Morais's

---

Jewish Millionaires of New York Plan a Great Fair," *Buffalo Sunday News*, December 1, 1889, 9. On Nina Morais Cohen, see W. Gunther Plaut, *The Jews in Minnesota: The First Seventy-Five Years*, American Jewish Communal Histories (New York: American Jewish Historical Society, 1959); Judith E. Endelman, "Nina Morais Cohen," in *Jewish Women in America: An Historical Encyclopedia*, ed. Paula E. Hyman and Deborah Dash Moore (New York: Routledge, 1997); Diane Lichtenstein, *Writing Their Nations: The Tradition of Nineteenth-Century American Jewish Women Writers* (Bloomington: Indiana University Press, 1992), 47, 51, 75–76, 80, 88–89, 101–2, 131.

3. Mikveh Israel Jewish Congregation, certificate of birth, no. 238, December 6, 1855. See also Pamela S. Nadell, *Conservative Judaism in America: A Biographical Dictionary and Sourcebook* (New York: Greenwood Press, 1988), 191–93; Henry S. Morais, *The Jews of Philadelphia: Their History from the Earliest Settlements to the Present Time; A Record of Events and Institutions, and of Leading Members of the Jewish Community in Every Sphere of Activity* (Philadelphia: Levytype Co., 1894), 154–58.

4. Nina Morais Cohen, "Nationality and the Jews," *Menorah* 12 (January 1892): 30–37.

5. On Szold, see Pamela S. Nadell, *America's Jewish Women: A History from Colonial Times to Today* (New York: Norton, 2019), 65.

controversial stances on national and Jewish communal issues had caused him to "suffer," so his daughter wrote. His opposition to slavery led his synagogue to issue a gag order on his preaching. Nina also remembered slights from her schoolmates for her opinions. When her father died in 1897, he was translating Jeremiah for the Jewish Publication Society's planned English-language Bible. She completed the work.[6]

But long before her father's death, Nina's world was rent asunder when her mother died at the age of thirty-nine. Nina had turned sixteen just three months before. Her youngest brother was only two. Sabato Morais never remarried. Instead, his eldest child took over the care of the children and the running of the household.[7] As the children grew and needed less of her time, she followed in her mother's footsteps, becoming a teacher and then a superintendent at Philadelphia's Hebrew Sunday School.

She pursued literary and intellectual interests that had been nurtured not only by her father and her formal education, which was uncommon in an era when few girls and boys went beyond elementary school, but also in the literary circles of the city's Jewish elites. In 1877, she won a prize from the Young Men's Hebrew Association, an organization founded two years before, for her essay "Circumstances as a Factor." Here she defended what the *American Israelite* called an "unpopular" position, arguing that unfortunate circumstances can be conquered by will. "The weak will bewail his fate," she wrote, "the strong will make adversity subservient to his purpose." Perhaps her own fate following her mother's death shaped her stance.[8]

6. Nina Morais, "Little Wandering Swallow," *American Hebrew*, December 26, 1884, 104 (translations of Italian poetry); N. Morais, "Jewish Ostracism in America," *North American Review* 133 (September 1881): 265–75; N. M. Cohen, "Nationality and the Jews"; Arthur Kiron, "A Renaissance of Jewish Readers in Victorian Philadelphia," in *Jewish Renaissance and Revival in America: Essays in Memory of Leah Levitz Fishbane*, ed. Eitan P. Fishbane and Jonathan D. Sarna (Waltham, Mass.: Brandeis University Press, 2011), 71–110, 76; Nina Morais to Henry Morais, April 24, 1898, Henry S. Morais Papers, box 2, folder 40, pp. 19–24, Yeshiva University Archives. On the preparation of the Jewish Publication Society's *Holy Scriptures*, see Jonathan D. Sarna, *JPS: The Americanization of Jewish Culture, 1888–1988* (Philadelphia: Jewish Publication Society, 1989), 95–115.

7. Nina's brother Henry, four years her junior, reported these events in his *Jews of Philadelphia*, 319.

8. "Sunday School: The Hebrew Sunday School Society of Philadelphia," *American Hebrew*, January 9, 1880, 90; "Correspondence: Our Philadelphia Letter," *American Hebrew*, October 19, 1883, 110; Kiron, "Renaissance of Jewish Readers"; "Philadelphia Letter: Dance to the Death Hebrew Instruction," *American Israelite*, November 16, 1877, 2. Only part of the essay was published in the *American Israelite* because, the article says, it was published in its entirety elsewhere.

Not until her youngest brother was sixteen did Nina marry. Emanuel Cohen, born in Carbondale, Pennsylvania, came to Philadelphia to learn law. He and his future wife shared a love for literature and writing. He too had won an essay prize from the Young Men's Hebrew Association.[9] In December 1886, they wed and set off for Minneapolis.

Three decades earlier, Minneapolis had just begun to grow from a frontier settlement into a town. As its population multiplied ten times over between the end of the Civil War and 1880 and as Minneapolis became the "twin city" of neighboring St. Paul, the Jewish population grew, too. In 1856, a handful of families had founded the first synagogue in the Upper Midwest. By the beginning of the twentieth century, 8,500 Jews lived in the Twin Cities.[10]

In Minneapolis, Emanuel Cohen joined a law firm with his name on its letterhead and became a successful insurance lawyer and leader in Jewish affairs. He represented the Baron de Hirsch Fund, which supported Jewish agricultural ventures and was vice chair of the local committee for the American Jewish Congress. His religious sensibilities, more liberal than those of his father-in-law, led to his membership in Shaarai Tov, a synagogue that had veered to Reform by the time the Cohens arrived and where he taught religious school. Embracing the idea of a Jewish community center as the successor to the settlement houses that had served the immigrants, he left, at his death in 1920, a substantial bequest to build one in Minneapolis. It became the Emanuel Cohen Center.[11]

By the time Emanuel and Nina Morais Cohen arrived in Minneapolis, a "silken curtain" had fallen, separating Jewish and Christian society. In the 1850s and 1860s, when Minneapolis was not yet a bustling city, Jews and Christians had socialized in glee clubs, literary circles, and even their homes. But that world was long gone. With law partners named Kitchel and Shaw and with powerful reputations that had preceded them, Emanuel Cohen and his wife became the exceptions, the rare Jews welcomed across the divide. Cohen was one of the few Israelites admitted to the exclusive Minneapolis Club. He served on the board of directors of the Athenaeum, a private subscription library, which later partnered with the Minneapolis Public Library. In 1919, he successfully lobbied the Minnesota state legislature to prohibit real estate transactions from discriminating against anyone because of religious faith or creed.[12]

9. Morais, *Jews of Philadelphia*, 317–20.

10. Plaut, *Jews in Minnesota*, 33–39, 284, 317; Jacob Rader Marcus, *To Count a People: American Jewish Population Data, 1585–1984* (Lanham, Md.: University Press of America, 1990), 105.

11. Plaut, *Jews in Minnesota*, 147–48, 229, 250.

12. Kirsten Delegard and Penny Peterson, "Emanuel Cohen and the Battle against Anti-

Meanwhile, in their new home, his wife pursued her longstanding interests: teaching, civic engagement, and writing. The couple never had children. Nina Morais Cohen skipped the Jewish Women's Congress in September 1893 at the Chicago World's Fair. She had gone to the fair in May as a delegate from the literary club Coterie to attend the General Federation of Women's Clubs meeting at the Congress of Representative Women. Coterie's members dedicated themselves to deepening their knowledge of a single topic each year. When Morais Cohen went to the world's fair, the ladies of Coterie were just finishing their study of the Johnsonian Age. Coterie's members not only discussed books, they also researched and wrote papers to present to the group. This program was similar to that of the St. Louis Pioneers, a literary association founded by another rabbi's daughter, Rosa Fassel Sonneschein.[13] While attending the national meeting of the General Federation of Women's Clubs, Morais Cohen also read a paper at the Congress of Representative Women. Her reputation as a poet already established, her subject was "Homer and His Poems."[14]

Had Morais Cohen returned to Chicago in September for the Jewish Women's Congress, she would surely have appeared on its program, and there would have been no need to read her letter of support for the new National Council of Jewish Women at its founding meeting.[15] Her father called the council's establishment a "great event in the history of Judaism in America."[16] His daughter agreed. In the summer of 1894, she launched its Minneapolis section, remained its president until 1907, and also headed the Minnesota division. For a quarter of a century, the council, her chief vehicle for leadership and service to the Jewish community, merged her passions for Jewish literature and history, teaching,

---

Semitism in Minneapolis," https://www.tptoriginals.org/emanuel-cohen-and-the-battle-against-anti-semitism-in-minneapolis/; Plaut, *Jews in Minnesota*, 270–71; Chapter 188, H.F. No. 913, *Laws of Minnesota* (1919).

13. Jane Cunningham Croly, *The History of the Woman's Club Movement in America* (New York: General Federation of Woman's Clubs of America/Henry G. Allen & Co., 1898), 739; Pamela S. Nadell, "The Pioneers," *Paper Brigade* 3 (2019): 187–88.

14. Nina Morais Cohen, "Homer and His Poems," in *The Congress of Women: Held in the Woman's Building, World's Columbian Exposition, Chicago, U.S.A., 1893: With Portraits, Biographies and Addresses*, ed. Mary Kavanaugh Oldham Eagle (Chicago: W. B. Conkley, 1894), 113–22. See note 4, where she was called a "writer of verse." I have found only one of her poems, "The Oriole Sings." Its text appears in Plaut, *Jews in Minnesota*, 148.

15. Helen Kahn Weil, "Jewish Women of Modern Days," in *Papers of the Jewish Women's Congress* (Philadelphia: Jewish Publication Society of America, 1894), 26-42, 41, 265. Many sources report that she attended this meeting.

16. *Proceedings of the First Convention of the National Council of Jewish Women, 1896* (Philadelphia: Jewish Publication Society, 1897), 307.

and social service.[17] As the council's president, Nina Morais Cohen invited members to her home on Saturday afternoons for classes on the Bible, Jewish history, literature, and culture. Her deep learning and her joy in teaching drew dozens to what was effectively a school for female leadership. Not only did many of the future leaders of Minneapolis's women's organizations attend, but among its "graduates" was Fanny Brin, a future president of the National Council of Jewish Women.[18]

Outside of the council, Nina Morais Cohen, like her husband, parted that "silken curtain" dividing Jew and Gentile. Her reputation as a writer and her ardent advocacy for woman's suffrage preceded her arrival in Minneapolis and opened doors across the divide. The founding meeting of the Minneapolis Woman's Club took place in her parlor.[19] When the National American Woman Suffrage Association met in the City of Lakes in 1901, she welcomed its honorary president, Susan B. Anthony, and vice president, Anna Howard Shaw, to her home.[20] Having lectured as an elocutionist in Philadelphia before her marriage, she taught for the University of Minnesota extension courses on literature at the Athenaeum, where her husband sat on the board.[21] Her love for poetry led to her fundraising for a memorial to the poets Shelley and Keats in Rome.[22] Meanwhile she continued to write, using the new byline, uncommon for that day, Nina Morais Cohen.

Before she married, Nina Morais's reputation as a writer and commentator on affairs of her day was well established thanks to her articles in the *North American Review.* Founded in 1815 and edited in the early 1870s by Henry Adams of the storied family that gave America two presidents, the magazine was then

17. Plaut, *Jews in Minnesota*, 147–51. The Minneapolis chapter early endeavors included immigrant aid, Sabbath school classes, and a camp for mothers and children on the shores of Lake Minnetonka.

18. *Ibid.*, 150; Mary Dillon Foster, *Who's Who Among Minnesota Women: A History of Woman's Work in Minnesota from Pioneer Days to Date, Told in Biographies, Memorials and Records of Organizations* ([St. Paul]: Mary Dillon Foster, 1924), n.p.; Croly, *History of the Woman's Club Movement*, 739; Hyman Berman and Linda Mack Schloff, *Jews in Minnesota* (St. Paul: Minnesota Historical Society, 2002); "National Council of Jewish Women: Committees, Speakers, Etc.," *American Hebrew*, November 6, 1896, 5.

19. Foster, *Who's Who Among Minnesota Women*, n.p.

20. *Ibid.*; Ida Husted Harper, *The History of Woman Suffrage*, vol. 6 (New York: National American Woman Suffrage Association, 1920), 317.

21. Foster, *Who's Who Among Minnesota Women*, n.p.; Croly, *History of the Woman's Club Movement*, 739; Berman and Schloff, *Jews in Minnesota*; Delegard and Peterson, "Emanuel Cohen and the Battle against Anti-Semitism in Minneapolis."

22. Plaut, *Jews in Minnesota*, 151.

little more than the private journal of Boston-bred elites. Adams, seeking his successor in 1876, was terrified that it would either die "or go to some Jew."[23] Instead, the wealthy Mayflower descendant Allen Thorndike Rice bought it, transplanted it to New York, and transformed it into a leading voice on contemporary affairs. In 1879, the *North American Review* waded into the debate over women's right to vote, publishing, among others, the respected suffragists Lucy Stone, who had refused to take her husband's name when she married, and Elizabeth Cady Stanton, who had the minister delete the phrase "promise to obey" from her marriage vows.[24]

Rice published divergent opinions in the pages of the *North American Review.* In July 1880 a Boston woman declared that it was dangerous to give women, so obviously inferior to men, the vote. M. A. Hardaker, who grew up in Maine, spent time in Germany, and read philosophy, argued that men "*think* more than women" and that their thought process, based on reason and knowledge, "is of a better quality." Women's smaller brains, she averred, limited their intelligence. But Hardaker did concede that women had contributed to civilization by feeding and clothing their families, caring for the sick, and bringing beauty to dress, decoration, and household arts.[25]

Twenty-six-year-old Nina Morais, then still single and living in Philadelphia, rose to Hardaker's challenge. Convinced that when "a cultivated woman" rails against expanding women's sphere she must be taken seriously, Morais rebutted the antisuffragist's points one by one. No scientific evidence had ever proved that brain size equals brain power or that differences in male and female brains exist. Instead, Morais asserted that disparities between the sexes rested on their different educations and preparations across all societies. A woman's "household Tyrannus" exercised power through "her fear of bodily torture, of privation … of loss of love." But, Morais exulted, the revolution, though slow

23. Quoted in Daniel Okrent, *The Guarded Gate: Bigotry, Eugenics, and the Law That Kept Two Generations of Jews, Italians, and Other European Immigrants Out of America* (New York: Scribner, 2019), 38.

24. Julia Ward Howe, Thomas Wentworth Higginson, Wendell Phillips, Lucy Stone, Elizabeth Cady Stanton, "The Other Side of the Woman Question," *North American Review* 129 (November 1879): 418–46.

25. M. A. Hardaker, "The Ethics of Sex," *North American Review* 131 (July 1880): 62–74. Little is known about the author. For another of her articles, see M. A. Hardaker, "A Study in Sociology," *Atlantic Monthly* 50 (August 1882): 214–21. For an article based on an interview with her, see "A Maine Girl: Who Leads the Party of Advanced Ideas in Boston and Who Is One of the Principals of the Society Which Has Substituted Science for Scripture," *Memphis Daily Appeal*, April 1, 1881.

in coming, was finally underway, in part thanks to the lengthening "intervals between motherhood" that permitted women to expand their horizons and opportunities. "Equality, intellectual and moral, is the key to the sexual problem," she closed.[26]

The essay was praised and even excerpted in newspapers as far away as Helena, Montana. Two years later, Morais again championed women's rights and woman suffrage in the *North American Review.* Proud to stand for women's rights alongside Antoinette Brown Blackwell, the first woman ordained by a mainstream Protestant church, she argued that because women pay taxes, they deserve the same rights as the American colonists who had revolted against taxation without representation. Perhaps thinking of her own experience as a twenty-eight-year-old unmarried woman who had won acclaim for her writing and who gave public recitations and readings, she insisted that expanding women's education and opportunities to earn a living would "prevent marriages that are not unions of respect and affection."[27]

Before that second article appeared, Nina Morais had taken up another challenge, this time in defense of her people. In September 1881, she published "Jewish Ostracism in America" in the *North American Review.* This time she wrote of the array of prejudices Jews faced in the nation she called "the scrap-bag of the world," which, under the Constitution, had no right to discriminate against her people.[28] Her forthright essay provides a snapshot of a moment when that full-fledged antisemitic society of the Gilded Age was coming into view.

Morais opens "Jewish Ostracism" with the observation that antipathy to foreigners is an "instinct of the human heart." The "Aryan countries" of Europe, where a wave of antisemitism had erupted in Germany in 1879, offered proof. At the court of Kaiser Wilhelm I, Adolf Stoecker, the court chaplain, was attacking Jews in his sermons, blaming them for emptying the churches, while his Christian Socialist Workers' Party made anti-Jewish agitation the center of its platform. Wilhelm Marr founded the Antisemitic League to lead the Teutonic struggle against the threat from the Jewish race and coined the

26. Nina Morais, "The Limitations of Sex," *North American Review* 132 (January 1881): 79–95.

27. "Limitations of Sex," *Helena Weekly Herald,* February 24, 1881, 1; H. Morais, *Jews of Philadelphia,* 320; Lillie Devereux Blake, Nina Morais, Sara A. Underwood, Clemence Sophia Lozier, "Dr. Hammond's Estimate of Woman," *North American Review* 137 (November 1883): 495–519, 506. Blake and Lozier were active in the suffrage movement. Nothing is known about Sara Underwood.

28. Morais, "Jewish Ostracism in America," 266.

term "antisemitism." The eminent historian Heinrich von Treitschke lent his respectability, criticizing the Jews for their contempt for Germans and their undue influence over the press. He justified the antisemitic agitation—which spawned a petition for restricting Jewish influence that gathered a quarter of a million signatures—as German nationalists' understandable reaction "against an alien element which has usurped too much space in our life." To the east, pogroms had broken out in Russia in the spring of 1881 in the wake of the assassination of Tsar Alexander II.[29] Some of the victims had already made their way to New York. Although Morais mentioned American antipathy to Jewish immigrants, aversion to foreigners across the ocean was not the driving force behind her essay. Instead, she wrote about the host of social and institutional barriers American Jews confronted, among them the "provident hotel-keeper [who] avoids the contact of the Hebrew purse."[30]

The opening salvo in what the *New York Herald* called "the war against the Jews" in hotels was launched in 1877, when, at the start of the summer, the Seligman family arrived in Saratoga Springs, New York, for their annual vacation.[31] Judge Henry Hilton, manager of the Grand Union Hotel, informed the banker Joseph Seligman—one of the nation's wealthiest men and a friend of Presidents Lincoln and Grant—that they were no longer welcome to stay at the hotel where they had previously summered. Hilton had decided to refuse rooms to "Israelites," anticipating that like-minded vacationers, preferring to socialize among their own kind, would flock to the Grand Union.[32]

29. Michael A. Meyer, "Great Debate on Antisemitism: Jewish Reaction to New Hostility in Germany, 1879–1881," *Leo Baeck Institute Year Book* 11, no. 1 (1966): 137–70; Paul R. Mendes-Flohr and Jehuda Reinharz, eds., *The Jew in the Modern World: A Documentary History*, 3d ed. (New York: Oxford University Press, 2011), 320; I. Michael Aronson, "Geographical and Socioeconomic Factors in the 1881 Anti-Jewish Pogroms in Russia," *Russian Review* 39, no. 1 (1980): 18–31.

30. Morais, "Jewish Ostracism in America," 269.

31. *New York Herald*, July 23, 1879, reprinted in *Coney Island and the Jews: A History of the Development and Success of This Famous Seaside Resort, Together with a Full Account of the Recent Jewish Controversy* (New York: G. W. Carleton & Co., 1879), 20.

32. This episode has been recounted frequently. John Higham framed it as an instance of social discrimination in "Social Discrimination against Jews in America." Recently, Britt Tevis has argued that this exclusion constituted legal discrimination; Britt P. Tevis, "'Jews Not Admitted': Antisemitism, Civil Rights, and Public Accommodations Laws," *Journal of American History* 107, no. 4 (2021), 847–870. On Grant's friendship, see Jonathan D. Sarna, *When General Grant Expelled the Jews* (New York: Nextbook/Schocken, 2012), 61–62, 126. It is possible that the rejection may have been made in person since Seligman dated his letter to Hilton, reprinted in the press, "Clarendon Hotel, Saratoga, June 1, 1877"; see "War Among the New York Princes," *American Israelite*, June 22, 1877, 6.

Thanks to the prominence of its protagonists, the Seligman Affair, as the event came to be known, generated considerable publicity around the country. But exclusion from elite watering holes was not news to Jews. For more than a decade, the American Jewish press had reported that certain hotels barred Jews.[33] What was new was the publicity and the escalation of the war. Two years later, Austin Corbin, owner of Coney Island's Manhattan Beach Hotel, announced that he would not permit a single Israelite to stay at his opulent summer playground. Corbin insisted, "We cannot bring the highest social element to Manhattan Beach if the Jews persist in coming. … They are contemptible as a class. …"[34]

Morais knew that banishment from hotels and from boardinghouses that advised "Jews need not apply" was only the most recent flagrant example of the discriminations Jews faced. They encountered animus at an early age, when "the little child in school finds no room for the Jew in the game at recess."[35] Perhaps she was thinking back to her own experiences or to those that her brothers and sisters brought home at the end of their school day. At some point, they had likely heard this popular children's ditty:

> I had a piece of pork, I put it on a fork,
> And gave it to the curly-headed Jew.
> Pork, Pork, Pork, Jew, Jew, Jew.

In "Jewish Ostracism," Morais echoed its taunt. "Jew, Jew, Jew," she wrote, "is the one all-comprehensive charge." Was it she or one of her sisters who suffered this humiliation: "'I am sorry for you,' said a teacher to her best pupil, placed at the end of the class; 'it is your misfortune, not your fault, that you are a Jew.'"[36] Morais observed that school districts marked Jewish children truant when they stayed home on the Jewish holidays. Some even deliberately scheduled exams for those days. Restrictions and quotas in private schools, colleges, and universities

33. Naomi W. Cohen mentions a report as early as 1864; see Cohen, "Antisemitism in the Gilded Age," 188. The *American Israelite* repeated in 1877 that such exclusions were not new; see Julian Werner, "New York Letter," *American Israelite*, June 29, 1877, 2.

34. *Coney Island and the Jews*, 20–21. See also Herbert N. Eaton, *An Hour with the American Hebrew: Including … Remarks on the Hitlon-Seligman Affair, and the Late Misunderstanding at Manhattan Beach* (New York: Jesse Haney & Co., 1879), 78–79; Leonard A. Greenberg, "Some American Anti-Semitic Publications of the Late 19th Century," *Publications of the American Jewish Historical Society* 37 (1947): 421–25.

35. Morais, "Jewish Ostracism in America," 269.

36. Jonathan D. Sarna, "The Pork on the Fork: A Nineteenth Century Anti-Jewish Ditty," *Jewish Social Studies* 44, no. 2 (1982): 169–72; Morais, "Jewish Ostracism in America," 270.

lay in the future when she wrote "Jewish Ostracism." Yet already Greek letter fraternities at the City College of New York excluded Jews.[37] But America's schoolrooms did even more to harm Jewish children: they instilled prejudice. Sabato Morais's predecessor at Mikveh Israel, Isaac Leeser, had warned that American public schools were "essentially Christian." Rabbi Henry Berkowitz recalled how "out of place" he felt in his Pittsburgh schoolroom as the students bowed their heads to say the Lord's Prayer. The future Jewish communal leader Louis Marshall was not disturbed by daily New Testament readings in class; but when Easter came and the teacher read the story of the crucifixion, he heard "contempt" and "hatred" each time she uttered the word "Jew." His classmates heard it, too. For days afterward, recess meant vicious name-calling and even blows.[38]

Morais understood that much of the animosity toward Jews stemmed from that Easter story, that the Jews, having murdered the Christian Savior, failed to accept Jesus as the messiah and were eternally punished for their crime. That message was conveyed not only through New Testament readings and Christian prayers but also throughout the school day. American public schools were not sectarian; they did not favor one particular denominational church. But they were decidedly Protestant. Morais wrote of school mistresses teaching that the "invention of the press is the result of Christian civilization; the geography of India is the triumph of Christian progress; the science of morals is inseparable from Christian dogma." The McGuffey readers, widely used from the nineteenth century until well into the twentieth, confirmed her impressions. They taught that salvation could be achieved only through Jesus Christ. Prejudices against the Jews, she wrote, were "wrought in the very woof of Christianity," woven into the fabric of Western civilization.[39]

The summer she was writing "Jewish Ostracism," the *American Israelite* published an essay condemning the "aggressive" Christianity then on display in Germany and Russia. Court Chaplain Stoecker, calling for "a return to the Christian faith," preached to large crowds that Jews were a "cancer" threatening to Judaize the "German spirit." The pogroms were the handiwork of marauding

37. Marcia Graham Synnott, "Anti-Semitism and American Universities: Did Quotas Follow the Jews?" in *Anti-Semitism in American History*, ed. Gerber, 233–71, 237.

38. Naomi W. Cohen, *Jews in Christian America: The Pursuit of Religious Equality* (New York: Oxford University Press, 1992), 82; Lloyd P. Gartner, "Temples of Liberty Unpolluted: American Jews and Public Schools, 1840–1875," in *A Bicentennial Festschrift for Jacob Rader Marcus*, ed. Bertram Wallace Korn (New York: KTAV Publishing House, 1976), 157–89.

39. Morais, "Jewish Ostracism in America," 269; William H. Jeynes, *A Call for Character Education and Prayer in the Schools* (Santa Barbara, Calif.: ABC-CLIO, 2009), 178.

Russian Orthodox mobs.[40] This aggressive Christianity was also on the march in the United States. Commemorating the centennial of America's birth in 1876, Rabbi David Einhorn heard its drumming. The Declaration of Independence, he wrote, never once mentioned the word Christian. But now a vociferous cry, "The United States is a Christian country," rang out across the nation. On this side of the Atlantic, according to the *American Israelite*, "the Jew being damned, must be proselytized, coaxed or bought for the Church ... the last phase of Christian love." [41] By the time Nina Morais published "Jewish Ostracism," there were many signs that American Christians were demonstrating that love.

The catastrophe of the Civil War convinced some observers that the calamity occurred because of what the Constitution had omitted. The preamble, "We the People of the United States, in Order to form a more perfect Union," had established the government but failed to "ordain" the new nation as a Christian one. The solution was to amend the Constitution to recognize "Almighty God as the source of all authority and power in civil government" and to acknowledge Jesus Christ as the "Governor among the nations." [42] Although never likely to succeed, lobbyists for a Christian amendment continued their efforts across the nineteenth century and beyond. Support came from those disturbed by the enormous changes underway in American life, the result of expanding industrialization, urbanization, immigration of non-Protestants, and secularization. The movement's leaders singled out anyone who opposed Christ as enemies.

In "Jewish Ostracism" Morais did not to respond directly to the drive for the Christian amendment, which, during the 1870s, was spearheaded by the National Reform Association, whose president was the retired Supreme Court Associate Justice William Strong, a devout Presbyterian. But she addressed the issue obliquely by the attention she paid to the Constitution. She wrote that the American Revolution had forged a nation of foreigners into a union. The Constitution, designed to protect them, gave all men the right to "the claim of the American citizen." Nevertheless, the First Amendment, "Congress shall make no law respecting an establishment of religion, or prohibiting the free exercise

40. Mendes-Flohr and Reinharz, eds., *The Jew in the Modern World*, 318; Cohen, "Antisemitism in the Gilded Age."

41. Quoted in Cohen, *Jews in Christian America*, 76. Naomi Cohen first remarked on this aggressive Christianity of the Gilded Age; see Cohen, "Antisemitism in the Gilded Age." See also "The Cause of Persecution," *American Israelite*, July 1, 1881, 4. The anonymous author refers to the writings of the evangelical German pastor Theodor Christlieb.

42. Quoted in Morton Bordon, "The Christian Amendment," *Civil War History* 25, no. 2 (1979): 156–67, 160.

thereof," had not precluded states from legislating religious bias. Not until the year after the centennial, she informed the *North American Review* audience, had New Hampshire, the last state with a religious test for office, struck down the requirement that its governor and assemblymen be Protestants.[43]

But religious tests for office were not the only legal disabilities affecting Jews in America. Sunday laws were another. By the end of the 1870s, the National Reform Association had expanded its agenda to forge a coalition with those who sought to enforce Sabbath observance and to save America from the dangers of intoxication.[44] In 1879, the association launched a drive for a federal Sunday law. States had long imposed their own Sunday "blue laws"; Pennsylvania's dated to colonial times. In 1866, when a Jewish defendant was accused of breaking them, the state court ruled that those observing the Jewish Sabbath must still obey civil laws enforcing the Christian Sabbath: "This has been repeatedly decided."[45]

Nina Morais knew of her father's opposition to Sunday laws, his conviction that they violated the Founding Fathers' decision to separate church and state. When Philadelphia's Centennial Exposition opened on May 10, 1876, Methodist Episcopal Bishop Matthew Simpson declared not only that the United States was a Christian nation, but that the exposition would close on Sundays.[46] Now, she drew the attention of *North American Review* readers to this problem. Most would have been unaware of the implications of Sunday laws for Sabbath-observant Jews, how they lost a full day's work each week, how the courts could summon them on their holy day, how they were barred from recreation on a day they did not hold sacred. These readers would not have heard of the debates among American rabbis about the best recourse. Could states exempt from penalty those who honored the Jewish Sabbath if they worked quietly in their homes? At the time Morais was writing, a battle for such an exemption,

43. "William Strong," Supreme Court Collection, https://library.cqpress.com/scc/document.php?id=bioenc-427-18169-979555&v=43cb73cbfaef9449; Morais, "Jewish Ostracism in America," 267.

44. Cohen, *Jews in Christian America*, 66–72. The National Reform Association, the umbrella organization for this Christian crusade, did not disband until 1945; Bordon, "Christian Amendment."

45. J. Thomas Jable, "The Pennsylvania Sunday Blue Laws of 1779: A View of Pennsylvania Society and Politics During the American Revolution," *Pennsylvania History* 40, no. 4 (1973): 412–26; Albert M. Friedenberg, "Jews and American Sunday Laws," *Publications of the American Jewish Historical Society* 11 (1903): 101–15.

46. Naomi W. Cohen, *What the Rabbis Said: The Public Discourse of Nineteenth-Century American Rabbis* (New York: New York University Press, 2008), 39-40; Cohen, *Jews in Christian America*, 75; "Washington Letter: All Israelites Are Brethren, Civilized Barbarism," *American Israelite*, May 12, 1876, 2.

underway in Pennsylvania for the past five years, was just one vote short of passage in the state legislature. Objecting to Sunday laws and to all regulations that in any way disenfranchised America's Jews, she charged, "The musty odor of colonial charters and Puritanical laws still clings to the halls of American legislation."[47]

The appearance in Philadelphia in December 1875 of Dwight Moody, the most popular evangelist of the last third of the nineteenth century, brought into view another manifestation of the era's aggressive Christianity. Moody had relocated the revival meetings of the countryside to America's cities. There he transfixed tens of thousands of ostensible sinners, promising them salvation if they would repent and accept Christ as their personal Savior. Preaching the classic tropes of Christian anti-Judaism, he reminded his audiences that the Jews had condemned Jesus to save the criminal Barabbas and that they were eternally punished for refusing to accept Christ as Lord. But in Philadelphia he voiced another charge, that at a meeting in Paris, a thousand Jews had boasted of killing the Christian God. Sabato Morais was incensed. "None of us would have believed," he thundered, "that the attempt to inflame the passions of multitudes against law-abiding Hebrews would have been tried ... two days before the Centennial year was ushered in."[48]

Another signpost of Christianity ascendant was the establishment in 1874 of the Woman's Christian Temperance Union (WCTU). Its founding president, Annie Wittenmyer, had organized kitchens to feed sick and wounded soldiers during the Civil War. After the war, in Philadelphia, she secured Bishop Simpson's approval to organize a Methodist Women's Home Missionary Society. Steadfastly bringing material and spiritual aid to the poor, its missionary women visited 50,000 homes around the country during the centennial year.[49] In her almost eight-hundred-page history of the WCTU, Wittenmyer wrote of the thousands of prayer and public meetings held across the land. In Philadelphia, crowds followed marching bands parading through the streets and called upon citizens to save America from "the dangers of the rum-shop." Even the women

47. Morais, "Jewish Ostracism in America," 268; Cohen, *Jews in Christian America*, 72–79.

48. Quoted in Cohen, "Antisemitism in the Gilded Age," 193–94.

49. Frances Elizabeth Willard, *Woman and Temperance, or, The Work and Workers of the Woman's Christian Temperance Union* (Chicago: Woman's Temperance Publication Association, 1883), 160–67; Annie Wittenmyer, *History of the Woman's Temperance Crusade: A Complete Official History of the Wonderful Uprising of the Christian Women of the United States against the Liquor Traffic, Which Culminated in the Gospel Temperance Movement* (Philadelphia: The Christian Woman, 1878), 491–504.

of Philadelphia's Congregation Rodeph Shalom were inspired to encourage the mayor to pursue ever more strict enforcement of the prohibition against selling liquor on Sundays. Wittenmyer knew that "in the by and by," when temperance would triumph, "the kingdom of heaven will come."[50] Although Wittenmyer wanted women to preach in the pulpit, her opposition to incorporating woman suffrage into the aims of the WCTU propelled Frances Willard to its presidency in 1879. Brandishing the banner of temperance, suffrage, and other reforms, she led the union to become the largest woman's organization of its era, a powerhouse in the story of Christianity triumphant in late nineteenth-century America.[51]

Morais gave but a single sentence to the "patronizing, pitying spirit of the Christian missionary" as expressed in the last phase of Christian love: "the Jew being damned, must be proselytized" and brought to the light to be saved. The first organized missions, the Female Society of Boston and the Vicinity for Promoting Christianity among the Jews and what became the American Society for Meliorating the Condition of the Jews, were established in 1816.[52] Across the nineteenth century, they and others spent considerable sums trying to bring American Jews to Jesus. In the last quarter of that century, more churches entered into missionary work. Six missionary stations were established between 1880 and 1899 to entice prospective converts, especially among the east European Jewish immigrants flooding into America after 1881. They mounted industrial training, kindergarten, and English classes, along with Sunday schools, open-air meetings, lantern-slide lectures, and summer camps. Jewish leaders strenuously battled the missionaries over the course of the century. Still, in the end, Christian missions to the Jews "posed only a petty threat to American

50. Marni Davis, "'No Whiskey Amazons in the Tents of Israel': American Jews and the Gilded Age Temperance Movement," *American Jewish History* 94, no. 3 (2008): 143–73; American Experience, "Annie Turner Wittenmyer," https://www.pbs.org/wgbh/americanexperience/features/grant-wittenmyer/; Robert F. Martin, "Wittenmyer, Sarah Ann 'Annie' Turner," The Biographical Dictionary of Iowa, http://uipress.lib.uiowa.edu/bdi/DetailsPage.aspx?id=415; Willard, *Woman and Temperance*, 160–67; Wittenmyer, *History of the Woman's Temperance Crusade*, 491–504.

51. American Experience, "Annie Turner Wittenmyer"; Willard, *Woman and Temperance*, 160–67; Wittenmyer, *History of the Woman's Temperance Crusade*, 491–504.

52. Morais, "Jewish Ostracism in America," 271–72; Jonathan D. Sarna, "The American Jewish Response to Nineteenth-Century Christian Missions," *Journal of American History* 68, no. 1 (1981): 35–51; Jonathan D. Sarna, "American Christian Opposition to Missions to the Jews, 1816–1900," *Journal of Ecumenical Studies* 23, no. 2 (1986): 225–38. On Christian love as a tool for conversion, see Jonathan D. Sarna, "Jewish-Christian Hostility in the United States: Perceptions from a Jewish Point of View," in *Uncivil Religion: Interreligious Hostility in America*, ed. Robert N. Bellah and Frederick E. Greenspahn (New York: Crossroad Press, 1987), 5–22.

Jewry." One report counts just 1,265 baptisms by American missions for the entire nineteenth century.[53]

But Christianity's anti-Judaism was not the only form of Judeophobia that Morais addressed. She knew that what made the Jewish race so objectionable was its "shrewdness and questionable dealings in trade," its members' all-consuming interest in "the key-note of the dollar." The stereotypes of Jews' absorption with money and their unscrupulous ways of getting it dated to the Middle Ages and became personified for all time in Shylock, the moneylender in Shakespeare's *The Merchant of Venice*, the second most frequently performed of his plays (after *Hamlet*) on the New York stage in the second half of the nineteenth century.[54] In childhood, boys and girls heard about Jewish tricksters in Mother Goose tales:

> Jack sold his egg
> to a rogue of a Jew
> Who cheated him out of half of his due.
> The Jew got his goose,
> Which he vowed he would kill,
> Resolving at once
> His pockets to fill.[55]

During the Civil War, Jews were frequently accused of profiting unscrupulously from the conflict. In one of the best-known anti-Jewish episodes in American history, General Ulysses S. Grant expelled from the Department of Tennessee the "Jews, as a class, [for] violating every regulation of trade established by the Treasury Department." At war's end, a series of fires in Jewish clothing businesses led seven major insurance companies, convinced that crooked Jews burned down their own properties for the insurance money, to collude to refuse

53. Max Eisen, "Christian Missions to the Jews in North America and Great Britain," *Jewish Social Studies* 10, no. 1 (1948): 31–66; Sarna, "American Jewish Response to Nineteenth-Century Christian Missions," 51. In July 1903, Henry Zeckhausen reported 12,394 baptisms of Jews by missionary societies in the nineteenth century, but the statistics came from missionary societies in London, Scotland, Germany, the Baltics, Russia, Sweden, Holland, and France; American societies were credited with only 1,265. Henry Zeckhausen, "Awakening of the Church to Its Due Responsibility to the Jew, or An Historical Retrospect of Missions to the Jews," in *The Minutes of the First Hebrew-Christian Conference of the United States* (Pittsburgh, 1903), 39; Eisen, "Christian Missions to the Jews," 55.

54. Harley Erdman, *Staging the Jew: The Performance of an American Ethnicity, 1860–1920* (New Brunswick: Rutgers University Press, 1997), 21.

55. Cited in Dobkowski, *Tarnished Dream*, 104. Not until the 1930s was this rhyme excised from most editions of *Mother Goose.*

to insure any Jewish concerns.[56] Reports from the business credit rating firm Dun & Bradstreet for the middle decades of the nineteenth century assumed that Jews defrauded their creditors. After the Cincinnati clothing wholesale business Bernheimer, Einstein and Co. expanded to Philadelphia, Dun & Bradstreet's correspondent wrote that they were "doing excellent business … character and habits good … but they are Jews and their ancestors took Jewels of the Egyptians when they left Egypt and never returned them."[57] In their writings, Nina Morais's more famous contemporaries Herman Melville and Henry James echoed similar depictions of devious Jews obsessed with mammon. She did not mention them, but she did see in *Oliver Twist*'s pickpocket Fagin the prejudice of the ages brought forth.[58]

Morais also addressed a variation on this theme of money-obsessed Jews that took hold in the 1870s. For some Jews who had immigrated to the United States in the middle decades of the nineteenth century from German states and lands like Moravia and Bohemia (among them Joseph Seligman), America had delivered on their dreams of prosperity. Now they dared to presume that their new-found wealth would allow them entrée into society, just as it allowed them to purchase the "large diamonds and flashy clothes" that Morais observed them wearing. Their "ostentation," she wrote, "shocks refined people."[59] These parvenus, she knew, were the reason social and professional clubs blackballed Jews. The blacklisting of Theodore Seligman, the son of Joseph's brother Jesse, at New York's Union Club, which Jesse had helped found and where he had been a vice president for twenty years, lay ahead. But the literary society at Columbia University had already snubbed the future U.S. commerce secretary Oscar Straus, and the New York Bar had refused to admit a candidate because he was a Jew.[60]

56. Sarna, *When General Grant Expelled the Jews*, 7; Leonard Dinnerstein, *Antisemitism in America* (New York: Oxford University Press, 1994), 36–37. See also Britt P. Tevis, "The Construction of Arson as a Jewish Crime in Nineteenth-Centuy America," paper presented at the Annual Conference of the Association for Jewish Studies, San Diego, December 2019.

57. Cited in Stephen G. Mostov, "Dun and Bradstreet Reports as a Source of Jewish Economic History: Cincinnati, 1840–1875," *American Jewish History* 72, no. 3 (1983): 333–53, 350. On the firm, see Stefan Rohrbacher, "From Wurttemburg to America: A Ninteenth-Century German-Jewish Village on Its Way to the New World," *American Jewish Archives* 41, no. 2 (1989): 143–71; Dobkowski, *Tarnished Dream*, 86–87.

58. Morais, "Jewish Ostracism in America," 272.

59. *Ibid.*, 269.

60. The Union Club episode occurred in 1893. For an interesting retrospective a year later, see "New York: A Slap at the Union League," *American Israelite*, December 13, 1894, 2. See also Dinnerstein, *Antisemitism in America*, 39. The episode at the New York Bar is mentioned in Stephen Birmingham, *"Our Crowd": The Great Jewish Families of New York* (New York: Harper

Morais internalized the criticism directed at these upstarts. She admitted that "the body of rich Jews in America fails to display the culture that wealth demands … the Jew does not always present a pleasing appearance." She wished that such men would understand that "the Jew is never judged as an individual, but as a specimen of a whole race." Every time one of these arrivistes breached etiquette, he offered "the back of every Jew to the lash of prejudice."[61]

Antipathy to these nouveau riche would continue to grow. In 1886, another Jewish woman, Alice Hyneman Rhine (later Southern), described the "Race Prejudice at Summer Resorts." Less than a decade after the opening battle in the hotel "war against the Jews," cottages in the Catskills had become divided into those for Jews and those for Christians. Added to the charges about lack of refinement, vulgarity, and social climbing, she noted that Jews were now criticized for bargaining over rooms rates and affronting Christians by playing cards on Sundays in those rooms with the doors open.[62]

Even before "Jewish Ostracism" appeared, these arrivistes were being grotesquely caricatured in cartoons in American magazines and newspapers. *Puck* responded in 1879 to Austin Corbin's intransigence by publishing a full-color cartoon, "Hints for the Jews.—Several Ways of Getting to Manhattan Beach." A few take to an air balloon named "Aaron-out," trying to land at the sea gate guarded by a constable. At a side gate, the hotel's bandmaster near-sightedly admits a troupe of grinning, hook-nosed, bandy-legged, trombone and trumpet players. At the main entrance, a sign announces that "applicants for admission must sign and partake of the following bill of fare." A couple whose son sports a yarmulke stands near the maître d', nose in the air, pointing to the menu: ham sandwiches, pig's cheeks, bacon, sausages, and pigs pudding. Behind them are guillotine-inspired contraptions. Above one, a sign reads, "Kinky hair must positively be straightened out, per order of Corbin." Its victim, his legs pulled down by weights, his hair clamped into a vise, shrieks as a pulley yanks him heavenward. At the other, signed "parabolic noses must be trimmed down to Christian style," a man kneels, the tip of his enormous nose between the blades. An inset alludes to Corbin's assertion to the *New York Herald* that when he

& Row, 1967), 178. The original source may have been "Editor's Easy Chair," *Harper's New Monthly Magazine* 54 (July 1877): 300.

61. Morais, "Jewish Ostracism in America," 270–71. An earlier Jewish suffragist, Ernestine Rose, defended her nation from the "Christian lash" in her exchange with the *Boston Investigator's* editor, Horace Seaver, in 1837; Bonnie S. Anderson, *The Rabbi's Atheist Daughter: Ernestine Rose, International Feminist Pioneer* (New York: Oxford University Press, 2017), 129.

62. Alice Hyneman Rhine, "Race Prejudice at Summer Resorts," *Forum* 3 (July 1887): 523–31.

said, "Personally I am opposed to Jews," he meant that he "never knew but one 'white' Jew in my life."[63]

Others ostracizing the Jews claimed that Jews, not they, were the ostracizers. "The Israelite is said to avoid Christian society," preferring the "racial exclusiveness of the Hebrew," Morais argued for them. Jews did not invite those they did business with into their homes; Hebrews herded together at their own resorts.[64] Morais knew why. First, she said, Jews feared rejection based on experiences of the past, "born amid the fires of persecution." When Hebrews could see their extended hands accepted without reservation, this fear would dissipate.[65]

But the other reason for exclusiveness, "Jewish marriage restrictions," must, in her opinion, remain. Morais, the daughter of the "leader of America's moderate Traditionalists," stood firmly on the side of Jewish endogamy. The problem of intermarriage had come up in America long before. In 1743, the great letter writer of colonial Jewry, Abigaill Levy Franks, confessed privately to her son across the seas her deep despair over the intermarriage of his sister Phila. More than a century later, when Helen Wise, daughter of leading Reform rabbi Isaac Mayer Wise, married the Christian attorney James Moloney, it was front-page news in the *New York Times*.[66] Cognizant of the pain caused by broken hearts, Morais argued, "The infusion of Aryan blood into Jewish veins would be suicidal for Judaism; it would in a short time remove prejudice by doing away with the object." For the young, for the unmarried, "the social amalgamation of Jew and Christian must measurably be incomplete." But blaming the parvenus and Jewish endogamy diverted attention from those laying the groundwork for anti-Jewish prejudice: the mothers singing nursery rhymes of Jewish vices to their babes and the Sunday school catechisms preaching hatred of the Jew.[67]

What Morais did not tackle was a group of men in the vanguard of the bigotry against her people. They came from America's disaffected elites, distraught and

63. Cartoon by Joseph Keppler, *Puck*, July 30, 1879; John J. Appel, "Jews in American Caricature: 1820–1914," *American Jewish History* 71, no. 1 (1981): 103–33; John Appel and Selma Appel, *Jews in American Graphic Satire and Humor: From the Collection of John and Selma Appel* (Cincinnati: American Jewish Archives, 1984); Eaton, *An Hour with the American Hebrew*, 78–79.

64. Morais, "Jewish Ostracism in America," 271.

65. *Ibid.*

66. Cohen, *What the Rabbis Said*, 34; *The Letters of Abigaill Levy Franks, 1733–1748*, ed. Edith B. Gelles (New Haven: Yale University Press, 2004), 123–31; Anne C. Rose, *Beloved Strangers: Interfaith Families in Nineteenth-Century America* (Cambridge, Mass.: Harvard University Press, 2001), 77–78; "A Clandestine Marriage," *New York Times*, May 31, 1878; "Our Gossip," *American Hebrew*, June 6, 1878, 1.

67. Morais, "Jewish Ostracism in America," 271.

disempowered by the emerging modern industrial society. Boston's Brahmins, the physical and metaphorical descendants of the Mayflower, found themselves displaced, losing their positions of influence and prestige amidst massive economic and social changes. One of them, Henry Adams, looked back years later on his situation in 1868. He saw that the Jews who had come to America, reeking of the stench of the ghetto, had brought with them "a keener instinct, an intenser energy, and a freer hand" than he and his Brahmin compatriots could counter. Adams concluded that the Jews had defeated him, this "American of Americans, with Heaven knew how many Puritans and Patriots behind him." Unfairly pushed out, he had to somehow get back onto the track.[68] One way to do so was to keep Jews out of society and send them back to where they belonged.

When in 1879 the American Society for the Suppression of the Jews met in Saratoga Springs, its members set out to do just that. They pledged to keep Jews out of public office, to stay away from performances where Jews wrote the music and acted, to refuse to read Jewish authors, and never to set foot on a Jewish-owned railroad or to do business with a Jewish-owned insurance company. They agreed with Austin Corbin: "The highest social element … won't associate with Jews, and that's all there is about it."[69]

But that society was short-lived. Following the fervor of Christian anti-Judaism and the nefarious stereotypes about Jews and money, the prejudices against Jews rested, so Morais wrote, on what a character in George Eliot's last novel called Christians' "abysmal" ignorance about Jews. So she gave her readers a short lesson in Jewish history and religion. From Abraham, the missionary of the one "incorporeal God," the Jews had carried their love of learning to pagan Rome and from there to the East and to the Moors. Jewish learning had paved the way for the Protestant Reformation. Contemporary Jews had made substantial contributions to modern civilization. As for Jewish religion, its teachings were universal lessons for a moral life: truth, love for thy neighbor, care of the stranger, respect for all. Morais recounted for her Gentile audience the words of Hillel the Elder. He taught the heathen who wanted to learn Judaism while standing on one foot and told them: "What is displeasing to thyself, do not unto thy neighbor. This is the law, the rest is commentary."[70]

In the end, Morais hoped that Americans would no longer do to the Jews what

68. Quoted in Dobkowski, *Tarnished Dream*, 119; *The Education of Henry Adams: An Autobiography* (Boston: Houghton Mifflin, 1918), 238.

69. *Coney Island and the Jews*, 20.

70. Morais, "Jewish Ostracism in America," 275; George Eliot, *Impressions of Theophrastus Such* (New York: Harper and Brothers, 1879).

was displeasing to themselves. She asked her readers to grant Jews "liberty" and recognize their "individuality." "Jewish development in America is yet young," she concluded. Let it develop and infuse the "particular genius of the Hebrew" into the life of this republic.[71]

"Jewish Ostracism" furthered Morais's reputation, and parts of the essay were reprinted elsewhere. The *American Hebrew* published it alongside a column praising her for fulfilling the literary promise she had shown in "Limitations of Sex" earlier that year. Like that earlier essay, this one reached a wide audience at a moment when some four million of an estimated six million Jews in the world, "a greater number ... than at any time in our history," faced prejudice.[72] The *American Hebrew* also recommended that whenever American Jews needed an eloquent advocate, they should turn to her, as the ancient Israelites had called to Deborah, the "prophetess of old ... 'Awake, awake, and utter a song.'" The editors printed the response of the New York *Evening Telegram*, which called the essay "timely and excellent"; the reviewer shared Morais's conviction that Christians knew little about Jews. What they did know came either from the Old Testament—the "mythical Jew" in Jonathan Sarna's apt phrase—or from encountering "a few of the most contemptible kind that are found on Chatham Street."[73]

Chatham Street and its environs in the notorious Five Points district was where, since the 1820s, poor immigrant Jews had first settled after landing in New York. Some of them had unfortunately made recent headlines. In 1875, Pesach Rubenstein, a pious twenty-eight-year-old whose wife and daughter remained behind in Russia and who lived on Bayard Street in the Five Points, was accused of having slashed the throat of his seventeen-year-old pregnant cousin. Until a short time before, she had been his nurse during a long convalescence. The case of the murdered Jewess and of the accused, who succeeded in starving himself to death before the state could execute him, transfixed the nation. Newspapers reported more than a thousand stories about it.[74]

71. Morais, "Jewish Ostracism in America," 275.

72. Nina Morais, "A Jewish Plea for Individual Rights," *Portland Daily Press* (Maine), September 12, 1881, 1; "Literary," *American Hebrew*, August 8, 1881, 3.

73. Jonathan D. Sarna, "The 'Mythical Jew' and the 'Jew Next Door' in Nineteenth-Century America," in *Anti-Semitism in American History*, ed. Gerber, 57–78; *American Hebrew*, August 19, 1881, 1.

74. Annie Polland and Daniel Soyer, *Emerging Metropolis: New York Jews in the Age of Immigration, 1840–1920* (New York: New York University Press, 2012), 11–13; Scott D. Seligman, "Pesach Rubenstein and the Murdered Jewess" (unpublished ms., 2017). See also Rebecca

Then, in the winter of 1880, Chatham Street's Jewish women also made headlines. They had accosted Morgan Dix, rector of Trinity Church, the historic Episcopal congregation established at the end of the seventeenth century, when he and they were the victims of a cruel hoax. Notes sent to Chatham Street's "old clothes ladies" announced that the rector would be selling his wife's clothes on the morning of February 21 and that they should come to the parsonage. On the appointed day, women and children "of Semitic profile" began ringing Dr. Dix's bell and shoving each other. They drew the attention of street urchins, who shouted: "Git onto de Sheenys! Here's de Essex Street women's rights a holdin' a convention." The police had to enforce "the exodus of the children of Israel from his window."[75]

Americans easily recognized the poor immigrant Jews of Chatham Street. Unfortunately, continued the *Evening Telegram*, they were less likely to come across "Jews of the better and best sort ... as fine specimens of manhood and womanhood as are to be found in corresponding classes among Christians."[76] How could Americans learn to overcome their prejudice? In February 1883, another American Jewish woman embarked on the project that Morais had begun of educating the country's Christian citizens about Jews. Emma Lazarus, a descendant of Jews who had trudged out of Spain to find freedom in the New World, was the poet who would soon write "The New Colossus," which after her death would welcome the "huddled masses yearning to breathe free" to the lady in New York Harbor lifting her "lamp beside the golden door." In "The Jewish Problem," which appeared in *Century*, a magazine that claimed 200,000 readers, Lazarus wrote of the trouble, "as old as history," that Jews have faced, even as it assumed a new form in each age. She firmly believed that the "life or death of millions of human beings hangs upon its solution."[77]

Lazarus presented her readers with a sweeping survey of Jewish history.

Kobrin, "'The Murdered Hebrew Maidservant of East New York': Gender, Class, and the Jewish Household in Eastern Europe and Its Diaspora," in *Gender and Jewish History*, ed. Marion A. Kaplan and Deborah Dash Moore (Bloomington: Indiana University Press, 2010), 72–87.

75. George W. Walling, *Recollections of a New York Chief of Police, with a Supplement on the Denver Police by A. Kaufmann* (1887, 1890; repr. Montclair, NJ: Patterson Smith, 1972), 309–12.

76. Excerpt from the *Evening Telegram*, reprinted in the *American Hebrew*, August 19, 1881, 2. On Jews, race, and whiteness in this era, see Eric L. Goldstein, *The Price of Whiteness: Jews, Race, and American Identity* (Princeton: Princeton University Press, 2006).

77. Emma Lazarus, "The Jewish Problem," *Century* 25 (February 1883): 602–11; Esther Schor, *Emma Lazarus* (New York: Nextbook/Schocken, 2006), 163–65.

Starting with antiquity, she wrote of slaves under the pharaoh's lash, of Jews' dispersion across the Roman empire, and of the triumph of Pauline Christianity over the Ebionite Christians who followed Jewish law and Jesus. She discussed the plight of Jews under Western Christendom, when sovereigns bought and sold them, priests preached that they murdered Christian children at Passover, and her ancestors faced massacres, riots, and expulsions. In the modern era, the French Revolution had emancipated the Jews from the ghetto. Now Jews demonstrated their patriotism wherever they lived. As for her own country, Lazarus reiterated Morais's point about the "sin of the individual" thrust upon the entire "race," how in America every Jew knew that "his security and reputation are ... bound up with those of the meanest rascal who belongs to his tribe."[78] Then she turned to that eternal prejudice rearing its ugly head in her nation, too, the country that had given her people "Freedom to love the law that Moses brought." Lazarus pointed to discriminations that Morais had highlighted: exclusion from resorts and schools, and the twisting of the noun "Jew" into a verb of "opprobrium" denoting cheating and scheming. Lazarus sensed a "profound antipathy engendered by fanaticism ... ready to break out ... at any moment." The persecution of centuries had come to this golden door.[79] Then Lazarus ventured where Morais had not in proposing a solution. Morais looked to enlightenment of her fellow Americans to solve the Jewish problem. Lazarus looked to another of George Eliot's novels for an answer. In *Daniel Deronda* the title character wants to restore a political existence to his people, to make them a nation again. Only their own nation could offer refuge and act as an intercessor to help Jews around the world facing injury and barbarity. Emma Lazarus agreed: "*They must establish an independent nationality.*"[80]

Nina Morais, soon to marry, move to Minneapolis, and settle into her new life, does not seem to have taken up her pen for this proto-Zionism. But a decade after she published "Jewish Ostracism," she returned to the subject of anti-Judaism. Her writing had brought her such acclaim that when the Jewish Publication Society was founded in Philadelphia in 1888, the *Jewish Messenger* remarked that its executive board should have recognized the position of women by including on its roster more "American Jewesses.... The proportion of one to twenty is

78. Lazarus, "Jewish Problem," 608.

79. Emma Lazarus, "In Exile," in Lazarus, *Selected Poems*, ed. John Hollander, American Poets Project (New York: Library of America, 2005); Lazarus, "Jewish Problem," 608.

80. Lazarus, "Jewish Problem," 610 (emphasis in original); George Eliot, *Daniel Deronda* (New York: Harper and Brothers, 1876).

Oriental, not American." Emma Lazarus had died less than a year before, so her name was not on its list. But Nina Morais Cohen's was.[81]

In 1892, in "Nationality and the Jew," published in *Menorah*, the journal of the fraternal order B'nai B'rith, Morais Cohen takes another snapshot of the American antisemitic society. It had now come into full view. What had changed since the publication of "Jewish Ostracism"? The Russians had come. The pogroms of 1881 were followed a year later by the May Laws, the first in a new series of restrictions making Jewish life increasingly untenable in tsarist Russia. They regulated Jewish settlement, limited business activities, and instituted quotas on the number of Jews in secondary schools and universities. In March 1891, Jews privileged to live outside the Pale of Settlement were expelled from Moscow. As a result, Russian Jews, who had constituted 0.9 percent of the immigrants arriving in America in 1881, made up 6.5 percent of the total in 1887. By one account, the community that had numbered 250,000 in 1880 had gained almost 400,000 immigrants between 1881 and 1890. Then in 1891, another 110,000 arrived.[82] No longer were poor immigrant Jews visible only on Chatham Street. In 1887, the young historian Frederick Jackson Turner found Boston's Salem Street "packed with swarthy sons and daughters of the tribe of Israel—such noises, such smells, such sights!" He was immensely relieved to leave behind "this mass of oriental noise and squalor." With ever more immigrant poor congregating in America's cities, it appeared as if the nation would never be able to absorb them. As the authors of a forum on antisemitism in the Gilded Age have observed, after 1881 the notion of Jewishness—in which immigrant status, race, and religion were inextricably fused—took up far greater space in the American imagination. More than any other group, Jews became the "receptacle for the fears and anxieties that white, middle-class Americans harbored regarding the rise of industrial capitalism" and the enormous changes it wrought.[83]

Cartoons in the 1880s depicted not only hook-nosed Jewish parvenus, but also added two sinister themes: Jews were replacing real Americans, and they were corrupting innocent American women. A series in *Judge*, a New York

81. "The Publication Society," *Jewish Messenger*, June 8, 1888, 4. The others were Minnie Louis, Henrietta Szold, and Leah Cohen Harby. The paper hyphenated the name Morais-Cohen, but I have not seen that usage repeated elsewhere. For another discussion of the founding of the Jewish Publication Society, see Sarna, *JPS*, 20–21.

82. Dinnerstein, *Antisemitism in America*, 43; Mendes-Flohr and Reinharz, eds., *The Jew in the Modern World*, 532.

83. Frederick Jackson Turner quoted in Dobkowski, *Tarnished Dream*, 144; "Introduction," in Koffman et al., "Forum on Anti-Semitism in the Gilded Age and Progressive Era."

City weekly, shows Jews taking over the city. They rename Canal Street "Levi Street," elect a Jew mayor, publish the *New Jerusalem Herald*, and revel as the sign of the city's last American business, "John Smith & Co. Dry Goods established 1820," is lowered and replaced with that of "Moses Eckstein Son & Levi." Overhead, a banner reads, "We Own the Town."[84] In the cartoon "The Slaves of the Jews," *Judge* showed a line of demur, proper American women—their noses pert, their feet dainty, their waists cinched by bustles—seeking jobs at Frankfurter and Offenbacher's Frills and Fringes sweatshop. Forced by capitalism to go out of the home to work, the flower of American womanhood parades before a hook-nosed, fleshy-lipped, grasping, bearded Jew, with his three lascivious, bandy-legged partners grinning behind him. In an inset, a group of "mashers" waits outside to prey on the women at the end of their workday. In another inset, a Jew holding an enormous key exclaims: "It vos not mine pizness if dey geds burned—dey mus' earn dose vages, und so I lock 'em in all righd." As Jonathan Sarna has shown, the diabolical messages are clear. Jews seek profit even if that means locking young American women in firetraps and enjoying not only the fruits of their labor but also the pleasures of their bodies.[85]

Beyond cartoons, the printed word increasingly characterized Jews as an unassimilable race of foreigners. In *The Modern Jew: His Present and Future*, the daughter of a U.S. senator, Anna Laurens Dawes, advocated for Jewish colonization in Palestine. Newspapers from the District of Columbia to Oregon promoted her prescription. What they did not report was the alternative she envisioned for these foreigners. If they did not colonize Palestine, they would face "extermination or a war for the supremacy to which the Jew believes himself entitled."[86]

The Greek immigrant Telemachus Timayenis achieved notoriety for popularizing racial antisemitism in three books. *The Original Mr. Jacobs: A Startling Exposé* was largely lifted from Édouard Drumont's 1,200-page *La France Juive*,

84. Jonathan D. Sarna, "Antisemitic Cartoons of the Early 1880s," in *Antisemitism Source Reader*, ed. Rebecca Kobrin (forthcoming); "The Dream of the Jews Realized," in *Judge* (1882), reproduced at Bruce A. Lesh, "Change and Continuity over Time: Historical Thinking and Images of the 'New Immigrants,'" https://centuryofprogress.org/sites/centuryofprogress.org/files/Immigration%20and%20Political%20Cartoons%20presentation.pdf. See also the color copy in the American Jewish Historical Society's Antisemitic Literature Collection (P-701), OS box 84, folder 336.

85. Sarna, "Antisemitic Cartoons of the Early 1880s"; James Albert Wales, "The Slaves of the Jews," in *Judge*, December 9, 1882, https://www.loc.gov/resource/ppmsca.05450/.

86. Quoted in Dobkowski, *Tarnished Dream*, 145; Anna Lauren Dawes, *The Modern Jew: His Present and Future* (New York: Office of the American Hebrew, 1884), 29.

a toxic stew boiling over with Christian anti-Judaism, the struggle against the Jewish race, and Jews' dangerous power over finance and capitalism. *The American Jew: An Exposé of His Career* portrayed Jews as criminals, lechers, and nefarious characters on Wall Street, in politics, and in journalism. In *Judas Iscariot: An Old Type in a New Form*, Timayenis proposed expulsion as the solution to the Jewish problem. He predicted that Americans "will turn you out of their homes, in order that you may once more take the staff of the Wandering Jew and tramp over the pathways of your ancestors."[87]

By 1890, the *American Hebrew* was so concerned about rising Judeophobia that it published a forum on "Prejudice Against the Jews," inviting some sixty prominent Americans—clergymen like the Reverend Morgan Dix of Trinity Church; educators like Elmer Hewitt Capen, president of Tufts College; and civil servants like Theodore Roosevelt, then commissioner of the U.S. Civil Service—to address the matter. Seeking to understand why Jews were barred from summer resorts, private schools, and clubs just because they were Jews, the editors asked what caused the animosity. Had their respondents any personal experience to justify this prejudice? Was its source the teachings of the Protestant or Catholic church? Had they ever seen Jews adhering to business or social standards of conduct different from those of Christians? Finally, could they suggest how to dispel the prejudice?[88]

Almost all the respondents condemned antisemitism and expressed no ill will toward Jews. But the words of several contributors brought little solace to the readers of the *American Hebrew*. The Reverend Dix wrote of teaching the historical truth of the Jews' murder of Jesus. The way to end intolerance was "to pray for God's ancient Israel ... some day [to] be 'graffed in again' and made one with us in the body of Jesus Christ." According to Unitarian clergyman Robert Collyer, churches and Sunday schools no longer preached injustice to the Jews. But he blamed the "chosen race" for separating themselves. He wanted to know what Jews were doing to break down their own prejudices. The best-selling novelist Margaret Deland reiterated the charge of Jewish "ostentatiousness," and Anna Laurens Dawes knew that "a vulgar class of Jews" caused the "whole race to suffer."[89]

The harshest words came from the president of Tufts College. According to

87. Scott D. Seligman, "He Was the Father of Anti-Semitic Publishing in America," *Forward*, February 5, 2020.

88. "Prejudice against the Jews: Its Nature, Its Causes and Remedies," *American Hebrew*, April 4, 1890, 165–74; Dobkowski, *Tarnished Dream*, 145–46.

89. "Prejudice against the Jews," 194.

Capen, anti-Jewish prejudice was caused by the "peculiar ... social characteristics of the Jews." Their manners differed from those of Americans. They refused to "assimilate like other aliens; they are always Hebrew.... They never can be Americans pure and simple." The only solution to eradicate this prejudice was the road Morais refused to take: the Jew must "take his wives from the daughters of the land," even if that meant obliterating "his characteristics as a Jew."[90]

Into this intensified fray, Nina Morais Cohen once again strode. With "Nationality and the Jews," she joined a widening discourse on the "ineradicable idiosyncrasies of race." By 1892, rabbis and writers had become increasingly comfortable claiming that the Jewish race formed "a different branch of humanity ... among the white 'family' of races." Espousing a racial definition let them assert that Jews could retain their distinctiveness even as they continued to seek social acceptance and participate in the affairs of the nation.[91] But Morais Cohen did not accept racial theory. The woman who had sought scientific evidence to debunk the superiority of larger brains knew that the notion of racial hierarchies "gives to ignorance, to greed, to prejudice a pseudo-scientific basis." Worse, the unfounded notion impedes the progress of mankind toward brotherhood. The future she envisioned would be "cosmopolitan," not "tribal." Across the ages, the Jews had pointed the way, "acting as veins and arteries between nations widely separated." Nowhere had Jews been more effective in joining themselves to the country and advancing hope for all mankind than in the United States, the land whose institutions quickly transformed the immigrant child into a native. But—and it becomes evident that this realization was the impetus for her essay—the bonds of brotherhood in America were fraying. Men shouted, "No room for aliens, none but Anglo-Saxons need apply."[92]

Now she revealed some of her own biography and that of her immigrant father, how they had claimed their place in America with their admiration for Lincoln and their patriotism. But recently the "idea of alienism, of existence by sufferance" had made America's Jews aware that even as they lived alongside the nation's citizens, they were "not of them." Then the silence of America's Christians over the horrors unleashed on her people in Russia, the banning of their survivors from America's ports because they were paupers, and a new proposal to make literacy a test for admission to America called forth her invective.[93]

90. Dobkowski, *Tarnished Dream*, 145–46; "Prejudice against the Jews," 192.

91. Goldstein, *Price of Whiteness*, 11–31, esp. 11–12, 19.

92. Cohen, "Nationality and the Jews," 34, 36.

93. *Ibid.* She thought that the new proposal was to make understanding English a requirement for admission. I assume she was referring to the possibility of a literacy test.

What had happened? In September 1891, Boston Brahmin and Republican congressman Henry Cabot Lodge published "The Distribution of Ability in the United States" in *Century* magazine. The essay should have been titled "The Distribution of Ability in the United States by Race." Lodge had sorted almost 15,000 names from a six-volume encyclopedia by birthplace, occupation, and "race-extraction." He set out to discover which nationalities and which American states had produced the greatest number of men who "have affected the history of the United States and mankind." He counted those who had governed the country, explored its terrain, fought its wars, educated its youth, inspired its thinking, advanced its science, and composed its literature. His most important finding: the Anglo-Saxons, especially his kinsmen from Massachusetts, "have produced the ability of the country."[94] His was a clarion call to preserve the dominance of the Anglo-Saxons against the rising tide of immigrant hordes.

The article supported his earlier call to restrict immigration with a literacy test. In the pages of the *North American Review*, Lodge deplored that more and more immigrants were from the "races most alien to the body of the American people and from the lowest and most illiterate classes among those races." A literacy test, he proposed, would bar those likely to lower the quality of the stock of the nation. Their "exclusion is demanded by our duty to our own citizens and to American institutions." A month later, Lodge introduced in the House of Representatives legislation promoting a literacy test for immigrants.[95] Congress did pass a new immigration act in 1891, but it did not include Lodge's literacy test. Yet he and others continued to lobby for one until it was enacted in 1917. Meanwhile, the 1891 law expanded the list of "excludables" to include "paupers or persons liable to become a public charge."

These were the developments that Morais Cohen addressed in her essay. In February 1882, she had stood on a Philadelphia wharf in the biting cold to welcome the survivors of Russian outrages. In an improvised place of refuge holding almost four hundred men, women, and children, she heard firsthand that day the stories of the survivors who saw loved ones murdered, babies flung out of third-story windows, and "nameless horrors" done to women.[96] How could her Christian neighbors remain silent in the face of such atrocities? How could the

94. Okrent, *Guarded Gate*, 36; Henry Cabot Lodge, "The Distribution of Ability in the United States," *Century* 42 (September 1891): 687–94.

95. Okrent, *Guarded Gate*, 51–52; Henry Cabot Lodge, "The Restriction of Immigration," *North American Review* 152 (January 1891): 27–37.

96. "The Refugees: Welcome to a New Home," *Philadelphia Inquirer*, February 24, 1882, 8.

nation that she loved exclude Jews whose means of making a living had been destroyed by mobs, just because they were now paupers?

But the nation was on a path toward more stringent immigration restriction. The Chinese had been excluded since 1882. An American correspondent in the Hebrew periodical *Ha-Magid* warned, "As soon as they finish with the Chinese, they will turn to the Jews and the Italians and find all kind of reasons for their exclusion.... The agitation against Jewish immigration has already taken on serious proportion. Who knows where it will end?"[97] Morais Cohen closed "Nationality and the Jews" with a bow in the direction of where she would have liked it to end: "We cannot know the ports of our destiny, but with absolute justice as our compass, we may believe that we steer aright."[98] She was, unfortunately, no prophet.

This 1892 essay seems to have been her last word on the full-fledged antisemitic society that had come into view. In the following decades, she focused on literature, teaching, and social service work. Her essay on "Homer and His Poems," delivered at the 1893 Congress of Representative Women, was published. Her father died in 1897, and she took up sorting his papers—complaining that he saved every scrap—and completing his work on Jeremiah for the Jewish Publication Society. Planning to spend time in Italy and visit relatives there, she returned to studying the language of her father. "Nationality and the Jews" may have been reprinted in 1904; an article in Philadelphia's *Jewish Exponent* quotes the essay as if it were new and bemoans the fact that her pen "has lain rusted" for too long. When, after a long illness, Nina Morais Cohen died on February 28, 1918, a few months after her sixty-second birthday, those signing her memorial appreciation were representatives of the two worlds in which she had lived: the National Council of Jewish Women, the Woman's City Club, the Minnesota Women's Suffrage Association, the Minneapolis Public Library, and the College Women's Club.[99]

In the years following her last published essay, the antisemitic society that she had brought into view for a large public became ever more firmly entrenched. The Immigration Restriction League, founded in 1894 to lobby for legislation to keep the "scum of Europe" away from American shores, included among its

97. Quoted in Abraham J. Karp, *Haven and Home: A History of the Jews in America* (New York: Schocken Books, 1985), 173.

98. Cohen, "Nationality and the Jews," 37.

99. Nina Morais to Henry Morais, April 24, 1898, Henry S. Morais Papers, box 2, folder 40, pp. 19–24, Yeshiva University Archives; "Nina Morais Cohen as Essayist," *Jewish Exponent*, July 29, 1904, 4; Plaut, *Jews in Minnesota*, 149.

members Henry Cabot Lodge and A. Lawrence Lowell, who later, as president of Harvard University, instituted a Jewish quota.[100] Even as Catholics faced anti-immigrant sentiment, their American journals preached antisemitism. After the publication of "Jewish Ostracism," Cincinnati's *Catholic Telegraph* commended Morais for treating the subject "fairly" and opined that the bonds of suffering had drawn Catholics and Jews closer in America. But one point that she had made remained true: Jews displayed "racial exclusiveness." The reviewer concluded that Jews held themselves aloof today just as they had done since the founding of the Church.[101] In the 1890s, supporters of the new Populist Party believed that Jewish influence over the economy was responsible for the financial woes of American farmers. The 1896 Democratic presidential candidate, William Jennings Bryan, famously used the crucifixion as a metaphor to conclude his speech to the nominating convention: "You shall not press down upon the brow of labor this crown of thorns, you shall not crucify mankind upon a cross of gold."[102]

At century's end, Mark Twain, wondering if Jews could do anything to eradicate this bias, wrote: "You will always be by ways and habit and predilections substantially strangers—foreigners—wherever you are, and that will probably keep the race prejudice against you alive."[103] If Nina Morais Cohen read his words, she would have despaired but not been surprised.

Living in the moment, Nina Morais Cohen took snapshots of the antisemitic society coming into view. Her essays recorded what she observed, read, and heard—how innate antipathy to foreigners erected barriers in schools, public places, businesses, and the law, and precluded Jews' full participation in American life. While blaming Christian America for the seeds of prejudice, she conceded that Jewish upstart parvenus, impoverished immigrants, and endogamy exacerbated it. But she did not ask: Why is antisemitism surging now?

Historians, however, do try to make sense of the waxing and waning of anti-Judaism and antisemitism across time and space. In his magisterial study, *Anti-Judaism: The Western Tradition*, David Nirenberg discovers this antipathy lying at the heart of Western civilization. Ancient peoples, medieval thinkers, and modern writers distilled into the figure of the Jew and Judaism whatever they

100. Dinnerstein, *Antisemitism in America*, 44.

101. *Ibid.*, 46; "Jewish Ostracism, Reprinted from *Catholic Telegraph*," *American Israelite*, September 9, 1881, 85.

102. Quoted in Dinnerstein, *Antisemitism in America*, 50.

103. Quoted in *ibid.*, 57.

found dangerous in their world at their moments in time.[104] Scholars see antisemitism as a symptom of cultural crisis. Writing in 2020 of its current wave, Steven Windmueller affirms, "Social distress and economic upheaval escalate and embolden anti-Semitic behaviors."[105]

What upheavals were rocking the nation after the Civil War, laying the foundation for rethinking Jews' place in it? At war's end, three-quarters of a million American men were dead from fighting, starvation, or disease.[106] Hundreds of thousands returned as maimed and wounded survivors. Myriads of women and children were left widowed and orphaned. The South was destroyed, its cities reduced to rubble, its countryside ravaged. Its newly freed men and women were fighting for rights as politicians argued over reconstructing the nation. They were also competing with whites for jobs as the ruined economy tried to restart.

Then an economic crisis hit. The Panic of 1873 began in Europe in the spring when prices on stocks and bonds issued to build the continent's railroads tumbled, causing runs in financial markets in Frankfurt, Berlin, and Vienna. Newly emancipated Jews, highly visible in banking and investment firms, became scapegoats. The panic hit the United States in September, when Jay Cooke & Company, overextended in railroad investments, failed. Crashing, the New York Stock Exchange shut down for ten days. Looking back on what happened, the future labor leader Samuel Gompers recalled a "primeval upheaval." Over the next three years, hundreds of banks failed. Tens of thousands of workers lost their jobs. Farmers saw profits on their crops tumble. Violent strikes followed, including a nationwide railroad strike in 1877. The panic lasted almost to the end of the decade. For the next half century, it was remembered as the "Great Depression."[107]

104. Isaac Chotiner and David Nirenberg, "How Anti-Semitism Rises on the Left and Right," *New Yorker*, January 2, 2020; David Nirenberg, *Anti-Judaism: The Western Tradition* (New York: W. W. Norton, 2013).

105. Shulamit Volkov, "Antisemitism as a Cultural Code: Reflections on the History and Historiography of Antisemitism in Imperial Germany," *Leo Baeck Institute Year Book* 23, no. 1 (1978): 25–46; Jonathan D. Sarna, "Anti-Semitism Is a Symptom," *Times of Israel*, January 1, 2020; Steven Windmueller, "The New Anti-Semitism: The Delegitimization of the Jewish People," *e-Jewish Philanthropy*, June 16, 2020.

106. Guy Gugliotta, "New Estimate Raises Civil War Death Toll," *New York Times*, April 2, 2012.

107. Scott Reynolds Nelson, "A Storm of Cheap Goods: New American Commodities and the Panic of 1873," *Journal of the Gilded Age and Progressive Era* 10, no. 4 (2011): 447–53; Edwin J. Perkins, "In the Eye of the Storm: Isaac Seligman and the Panic of 1873," *Business History* 56, no. 7 (2014): 1129–42; Nancy Lovas, "The Panic of 1873," https://www.loc.gov/rr/business/

Meanwhile, Jews began taking up greater space than ever before in America's cityscapes. Opulent synagogues sprouted in their centers: Cincinnati's B'nai Yeshurun rose on Plum Street in 1866, followed by the Moorish spires of New York's Temple Emanu-El on Fifth Avenue at 43rd Street. These were the years when the Jewish investment banking houses of Lehman Brothers (established in 1850), Kuhn Loeb (1867), Goldman Sachs (1869), and, of course, J. & W. Seligman & Co. (1864) thrived. The eight Seligman brothers' trans-Atlantic banking house weathered the Panic of 1873 undisturbed.[108]

As historian Shulamit Volkov has written about rising antisemitism in Germany in this period, "Jews were hated because they were different and poor and because they were different and rich."[109] On other city streets, more and more poor Jews were taking up space. Between 1860 and 1880, the U.S. Jewish population increased somewhere between 50 and 100 percent.[110] How many were recent immigrants, no one knows. But more of them were coming not from German lands, as Joseph Seligman had, but from farther to the east, from Russian Poland, as Pesach Rubenstein and his murdered cousin Sarah Alexander had. Speaking Yiddish, the men wearing "greasy velvet skull-caps," their wives bewigged, these "poor pedlers [*sic*], clothes-dealers, glaziers, Hebrew copyists, beggars, and hucksters" crammed into squalid tenements in neighborhoods already called ghettoes. The coming to America of these Jews, "the very lowest of the low of [t]his race," portended a frightening future.[111]

Meanwhile, Americans were also challenged by debates about the emancipation and civil rights of both African Americans and women. The Emancipation Proclamation freed the slaves in the rebellious states. The Fourteenth Amendment, ratified in 1868, made citizens of the former slaves. The Fifteenth Amendment guaranteed men, not women, the vote. The Enforcement Acts of 1870 and 1871 were passed because the Ku Klux Klan and other white nationalist groups threatened African American men's newly won rights to vote, hold office, and

---

businesshistory/September/Panic1873.html; Francois Furstenberg, "What History Teaches Us About the Welfare State," *Washington Post*, July 1, 2011.

108. David S. Koffman et al., "Forum on Anti-Semitism"; "History of Plum Street Temple," https://www.wisetemple.org/about/our-history/history-of-plum-street-temple/; Perkins, "In the Eye of the Storm."

109. Volkov, "Antisemitism as a Cultural Code," 37.

110. Jonathan D. Sarna, ed., *American Jewish Experience*, 2d ed. (New York: Holmes & Meier, 1997), 359.

111. "New York's Ghetto," *New York World*, August 3, 1874, and "The Polish Jews of New York," *New York Sun*, June 25, 1875. See Scott D. Seligman, "Pesach Rubenstein and the Murdered Jewess," 15. I thank Scott Seligman for these sources.

serve on juries. Then, in 1877, Reconstruction collapsed. It would take eighty years before the federal government enacted another Civil Rights Act.[112]

In 1860, the *New York Times* titled an article about married women's property rights "Female Emancipation." Suffragists, who had put aside their demands during the war out of loyalty to the Union, now renewed their campaigns. The National Woman Suffrage Association and the American Woman Suffrage Association were founded in 1869. As suffrage leaders tirelessly stumped across the country, the 1870s opened with the first women voting in the territories of Wyoming and Utah. But woman's rights advocates wanted more. Antoinette Brown Blackwell, who Morais later singled out in the *North American Review*, was urging women to find purposeful work outside the home.[113]

But 1873 was not only the year of the Panic. It was also the year the Comstock Law made it illegal to sell or advertise anything that would prevent conception or cause abortion and the year the lawyer Myra Bradwell lost her petition for admission to the Illinois bar. Considering her case, the U.S. Supreme Court ruled that woman's destiny, as fixed by the Creator and man, was "to fulfill the noble and benign offices of wife and mother." In 1887 women in Utah lost the right to vote.[114] It would be nearly fifty years before the Nineteenth Amendment granted women the vote, a symbol of their legal emancipation.

Americans would not speak of "Jewish emancipation" at home; they reserved the concept for the legal emancipation of Jews in Europe. But antisemitism signals the curbing of emancipation. Historian David Sorkin understands emancipation as a process of marginalized groups gaining and losing and regaining and re-losing de jure and de facto rights.[115] That is what happened to African Americans and American women in these years.

After the Civil War, Jews lived in a nation that would not unequivocally

112. The Civil Rights Act of 1957 established the Civil Rights Commission.

113. "Female Emancipation," *New York Times*, February 10, 1860, 4; Blake et al., "Dr. Hammond's Estimate of Woman," 501; Harriet Sigerman, "Laborers for Liberty: 1865–1890," in *No Small Courage: A History of Women in the United States*, ed. Nancy F. Cott (New York: Oxford University Press, 2000), 289–352, 310–11.

114. Linda K. Kerber and Jane Sherron De Hart, eds., *Women's America: Refocusing the Past*, 5th ed. (New York: Oxford University Press, 2000), 242–45; Katherine Kitterman, "'No Ordinary Feelings': Mormon Women's Political Activism, 1870–1920" (Ph.D. diss., American University, 2021). For a brief history of Utah women and the vote, see "Better Days 2020," https://www.betterdays2020.com/.

115. See, for example, "The Jewish Emancipation Bill Thrown Out," *New York Times*, May 16, 1853, 3; David Sorkin, *Jewish Emancipation: A History Across Five Centuries* (Princeton: Princeton University Press, 2019), 356.

emancipate them or African Americans or women. As Mark Twain said of the Jews at century's end and as Nina Morais Cohen observed in "Jewish Ostracism in America," Jews remained "foreigners." During the tumultuous 1870s, prejudice against foreigners and all marginalized peoples escalated in the United States. In the decades that followed, it intensified. Mark Twain called antisemitism "race prejudice." No matter the nomenclature—Nina Morais Cohen called it Judeophobia—American Jews confronted this prejudice then and would continue to face it into the next century, and alas until this very day.

THE SEARCH FOR USABLE JEWISH PASTS

BETH S. WENGER

AT THE founding meeting of the American Jewish Historical Society (AJHS) in June 1892, Harvard historian Charles Gross set forth the chief aims of the organization:

> The object of this Society should be to reveal the past of the Jews of this country, the past in all directions, but particular attention should be paid to what the Jews have accomplished as citizens of the United States. It will certainly be made evident that the Jews of this Republic have been ready to offer up life and fortune for their country, that they have been patriots in time of war and philanthropists in time of peace, that they will be patriots and philanthropists in the future as they have been in the past and as they are in the present. If we can once make that plain through the researches of the Society, it seems to me we shall accomplish a great deal.[1]

Gross, a specialist in medieval English history, was the only professional historian among the group of forty-one prominent Jews who gathered to discuss the formation of this new society, though the group contained other academics. The meeting convened at New York's Jewish Theological Seminary, home of the nascent movement of Conservative Judaism, but those who participated held a wide range of religious views and ideological perspectives. What they shared was a commitment to ensuring a Jewish communal future in the United States—a notion that undergirded their fundamental concern with documenting, chronicling, and disseminating information about the American Jewish past. This group represented an admittedly select strata of the American Jewish community; they were prominent and well-established individuals who were eager to fashion an image of Jews as unwaveringly patriotic and devoted to American democratic ideals. On that June day in 1892, these communal leaders had been brought together by their collective interest in creating an organization

1. American Jewish Historical Society, *Report of Organization, Abstract from the Minutes* (Baltimore: The Society, 1892), 8 (hereafter, Report of Organization). This published abstract is a shorter, edited version of the detailed minutes contained in the American Jewish Historical Society's archives. For a thorough account of the early years of the American Jewish Historical Society, see Jeffrey Gurock, "From 'Publications' to 'American Jewish History': The Journal of the American Jewish Historical Society and the Writing of American Jewish History," *American Jewish History*, Centennial Issue II, 81, no. 2 (1993–1994): 155–72.

designed to promote the pivotal role of Jews in the nation's founding and to underscore the vital contributions that Jews had made to American history. From mid-afternoon until well into the late-night hours, they engaged in a passionate debate about how to marshal the American Jewish past in the interests of the present.[2]

Significant scholarship has already been produced about the creation of the AJHS. Particularly intriguing are the debates recorded in the eighty-five pages of typed minutes that were excluded from the brief published report about the Society's founding. The most heated controversy erupted when the initial slate of nominees for the executive committee contained no rabbis, sparking outrage from the clergy in attendance, who considered their absence from leadership an affront to their status and authority. Responding to the perceived slight, Reform Rabbi Kaufmann Kohler at one point implored his fellow rabbis to "leave ... and abandon all work in connection with this Society."[3] But members resolved the contentious dispute by expanding the membership of the committee, ultimately adding two rabbis to the governing body. The attendees also disagreed about whether the organization ought to concentrate solely on Jewish history in the United States or extend its focus to a broader geographic region, especially the study of the Americas and the "conditions precedent to immigration to this country ... in Spain, Portugal and Holland."[4] During the course of the meeting, some of the founders argued that documenting "facts" and collecting materials about the Jewish past should be the Society's primary mission. After all, as all the attendees acknowledged, at a time when no systematic study of American Jewry existed, the task of gathering such "scattered, disjointed" material remained daunting.[5] Yet, many other founding members, such as Kohler, insisted passionately that the organization "should publish such essays, articles, or longer works that would stir the interest of the Jews and show our fellow citizens what the Jews have done in the history of culture in America."[6] Ultimately,

2. [Minutes of] Organization of the American Jewish Historical Society at the Rooms of the Jewish Theological Seminary at No. 736 Lexington Avenue in the City of New York on Monday The Seventh of June 1892, 3–4, American Jewish Historical Society Records (I-1), American Jewish Historical Society, Newton Centre, Mass., and New York, N.Y. (hereafter, Minutes).

3. Minutes, 11.

4. Report of Organization, 7. The inclusion of Portugal, Spain, and Holland reflects the founders' primary interest in documenting the first arrival of Jews in colonial and early America. It also reveals their ongoing and conscious silence about the religious, cultural, and political histories brought to the American Jewish community by the burgeoning number of east European immigrants arriving in the United States in the early years of the Society's existence.

5. Minutes, 10. 6. *Ibid.*, 31.

the founders agreed that members would present documents and papers at the Society's annual meetings; the editors of the *Publications of the American Jewish Historical Society*, the official organ of the AJHS, would then solicit these and other articles to appear in coming issues.[7] The founders fervently believed that they could secure Jewish status and combat antisemitism through the "collection of documents by which it is shown how the Jews of the United States have attained their high intellectual position, and they need not stand back in any community in this country, and they are on the highway to greater successes." They placed great faith in the hope that if the "facts" about Jewish loyalty and patriotism became more widely known, that evidence might stem the rising tide of antisemitism in the late nineteenth century. "The parent of prejudice against the Jews of America ... is ignorance," insisted Charles Gross. "If we can dispel that ignorance.... I think that will do away with a great deal of the prejudice."[8] That mission, while perhaps naïve and almost always presented as subtext rather than as strident declarations in AJHS official publications, remained foremost on the Society's agenda in its early years.

Founded in an age of nativism and rising antisemitism, the AJHS reflected a sense of both defensiveness and aspiration—fears about Jewish vulnerability combined with hope about what might be realized for Jews and others in the still evolving nation. In the closing decades of the nineteenth century, accusations of Jewish disloyalty in the Civil War, along with growing anti-immigrant sentiment, emerged on the floors of Congress, in print, and elsewhere, heightening Jewish uneasiness. These unsettling developments paralleled the mass migration of Jews from eastern Europe, exacerbating concerns among more "established" Jews about the politics and culture of their newly arrived coreligionists. Fifty years after the Society's creation, N. Taylor Phillips, one of its founders, concluded:

> [T]he Society found its origin by reason of the severe criticism of and as a protest against the mass immigration of the eighties.... This produced a reaction against mass immigration in general and against the Jewish [*sic*] in particular.... The charge for a long time had been made that this immigration would, in effect, confirm the generally age-old anti-Semitic theory that the Jews, having had nothing to do with the establishment of America or American independence, were simply parasites who would suck the blood of this Country, to the latter's detriment and, perhaps, ruin.

According to Phillips, the AJHS had been formed to establish "the early Jewish

7. Gurock, "From 'Publications' to 'American Jewish History,'" 160.

8. Minutes, 21, 14–15.

founders in their proper setting among those of other nationals and creeds."[9] In some ways, he correctly assessed the motives that animated the creation of the AJHS, linking the desire to assert belonging and legitimacy by relying on Jewish historical origins and contributions to the nation's creation.

American nativism emerged alongside a renewed concern with using history to make a rightful claim to "Americanness." Jews were hardly alone in the effort to demonstrate patriotism by showcasing their early contributions to the nation's history; the American Irish Historical Society and the German American Historical Society, created in the same era, also exhibited a preoccupation with proving their American bona fides and crafting their own histories of service to the nation.[10] The desire for communal self-defense consistently percolated within the Society's mission, as it did in other historical societies of the period. At the same time, AJHS members and the authors who submitted articles to the *Publications* never openly acknowledged antisemitic attacks or in any way questioned the nation's fundamental structures or ideals. In fact, the term "antisemitism" does not even appear in the index to the *Publications* that covers the period from the first issue until 1911.[11] As historian Adam Mendelsohn has observed, many prominent Jews of this era considered "antisemitism in America as an alien import—'legal rubbish, brought over from Europe' that was 'swept away forever' in the early nineteenth century."[12] The preferred approach to combat prejudice was to offer "proof"—evidence that would, in the hopeful minds of Society members, provide an answer to those who doubted Jewish patriotism. Oscar Straus, the Society's first president, who had served as the U.S. minister to Turkey and later as a member of President Theodore Roosevelt's cabinet, offered only the most veiled reference to antisemitism in his 1893 presidential address. He reassured the assembled members that once all Americans, and Jews themselves, better understood the history of the nation and the contributions of

9. N. Taylor Phillips, cited in "Report of the Fiftieth Annual Meeting," *Publications of the American Jewish Historical Society* 41, no. 4 (1952): 385–86.

10. John J. Appel, *Immigrant Historical Societies in the United States 1880–1950* (New York: Arno Press, 1980); John Higham, "The Ethnic Historical Society in Changing Times," *Journal of American Ethnic History* 13, no. 2 (1994): 30–44.

11. *Index to the Publications of the American Jewish Historical Society, Nos. 1–20, 1893–1911* (1914): 23.

12. Adam Mendelsohn, "'A Struggle Which Has Ended So Beneficently': A Century of Jewish Historical Writing About the American Civil War," *American Jewish History* 92, no. 4 (2004): 439. The quotations are taken from the chapter on American Jewry written by Henrietta Szold and Cyrus Adler included in an updated version of Lady Katie Magnus's *Outlines of Jewish History, from B.C. 586 to C.E. 1890* (Philadelphia: Jewish Publication Society of America, 1890).

Jews, "the better are we able to guard against the dangers that beset our growth as a nation."[13] Historian Jeffrey Gurock has described the Society's founders as "cautious defenders" whose "mode of defense" was to provide historical data in ways that bolstered present-day Jewish interests. "In its own unannounced way," he argued, "the AJHS was also a late nineteenth century American Jewish defense organization."[14] The published works and addresses delivered at the annual meetings in its early years employed selective readings of the American Jewish past to create precisely the vision for the sort of nation that the Society's founders desired and reflected the hope for Jewish belonging that they craved.

At a time when no professional field of American Jewish history existed, the creation of the AJHS represented a genuinely innovative communal endeavor. At the same time, the organization certainly had its blind spots and weaknesses. Not only did the Society publish partisan and often self-congratulatory versions of the American Jewish past, but the organization also consciously ignored aspects of American Jewish culture that did not fit the worldviews of members or the portrait of Jews they wanted to paint. For many years, the pages of its *Publications* made no mention of Zionism, organized labor, political radicalism, Yiddish culture, or basically any other aspect of east European immigrant experience. The patrician members of the AJHS offered significant charitable assistance to the newcomers but regarded them as in need of "Americanization." This loaded term included the abandonment of what more acculturated Jews viewed as antiquated practices in Judaism and the use of the "backward" language of Yiddish. It also demanded a firm rejection of radical political movements seen as disloyal, undemocratic, and in the case of Zionism, un-American in its suggestion of dual political loyalties. These attitudes, which evolved over time, grew out of genuine cultural differences but also reflected the anxieties of those Jews who feared that the ever-increasing numbers of new immigrants would only intensify antisemitism and threaten their newly won and not quite secure position in American society. While all these developments swirled around them, Society members responded by focusing on the distant Jewish past, the

13. Oscar S. Straus, "Address of the President," *Publications of the American Jewish Historical Society* 2 (1894): 3.

14. Gurock, "From 'Publications' to 'American Jewish History,'" 171. Historian Ira Robinson offers a cogent argument that the AJHS was more than an organization rooted in communal self-defense. Its agenda mirrored those of other historical societies throughout the United States in that era, and its mission reflected many similar early attempts to "professionalize" the field of history. Ira Robinson, "The Invention of American Jewish History," *American Jewish History,* Centennial Issue III–IV, 81, no. 3/4 (1994): 309–20.

contributions of Jews to America's founding, and their steadfast patriotism and staunch loyalty to the United States and its democratic ideals.

Despite its pointed agenda, the AJHS represented the first organization self-consciously devoted to discovering, documenting, archiving, and disseminating the history of Jews in the United States. The mission of the Society reflected something new in Jewish communal life, but also represented part of an ongoing emergence of Jewish historical consciousness that began to take shape in the late nineteenth century and continued in the next. In many different quarters of the community, American Jews had begun to create a shared sense of an American Jewish past. They did so in the public arena—during communal and holiday celebrations, within a myriad of organizations, and in the pages of popular histories and the Jewish press. These were not monolithic rehearsals of history, though they shared certain features. Like the AJHS's versions of American Jewish history, these multiple narratives about the American Jewish past could be self-congratulatory, self-serving, and sometimes contain a blend of fact and fiction. They often stressed the notion that Jewish experience in the United States was exceptional and represented a complete break from everything that Jews had previously encountered in their history. Needless to say, historical accuracy was not the foremost concern in these narratives, but neither were they intended as fables. Like all groups, as historian Michael Kammen has observed, Jews "reconstruct their pasts rather than faithfully record them." Furthermore, "they do so with the needs of contemporary culture in mind—manipulating the past in order to mold the present."[15] In this sense, these "histories" were always a partisan effort rather than a dispassionate undertaking. Indeed, they should not be measured against the conventions of academic scholarship, which they decidedly were not. In these years, the "facts" and discoveries of the AJHS mingled together with other popular presentations of Jewish history, renditions of the past that historian Carl Becker has called "the history that common people carry around in their heads," often full of inaccuracies and exaggerations but also delineating and crystallizing popular meanings of the past.[16] In this sense, the invention of versions of the American Jewish past was part and parcel of the creation of Jewish culture itself. The United States was tabula rasa in terms of Jewish history—a young nation with only a brief Jewish communal, intellectual, religious past. Creating a shared history with a collection of heroic figures and

15. Michael Kammen, *Mystic Chords of Memory: The Transformation of Tradition in American Culture* (1991; repr. New York: Vintage Books, 1993), 538.

16. Carl L. Becker, "What are Historical Facts?" in *Detachment and the Writing of History: Essays and Letters of Carl L. Becker*, ed. Phil L. Snyder (Ithaca: Cornell University Press, 1958), 61.

central narratives, along with a healthy dose of dissension and disagreement, provided a structure and framework that gave meaning to Jewish experience in America.

Present at the Creation

As the first president of the AJHS, Oscar Straus fervently believed that the Society should focus its efforts on "the relation of the Jews with the discovery of this continent and their participation in the early settlement of the colonies."[17] Straus had initiated the study of Christopher Columbus even before the creation of the AJHS:

> You can well understand what an important result it would have if it were historically shown that our race had a direct part of the discovery of America, how this would be an answer for all time to come to any anti-semitic tendencies in this country which doubtless will come to the surface sooner or later by reason of the large Russian immigration to our country. The grand opportunity is not often presented where historical research can contribute so directly and with such practical effect to such a noble cause as is possible in this instance.[18]

His colleagues at the AJHS concurred, and the Society devoted the overwhelming majority of its *Publications* to tracing the origins and early contributions of Jews on American soil. The papers presented at the annual meetings and those ultimately published were a mixture of primary documents and what might generously be called articles, though they often consisted of a presentation of "facts" rather than crafted or coherent arguments. In 1896, for example, Max Kohler, a prominent immigration lawyer, the son of Rabbi Kaufmann Kohler, and an AJHS founder, penned an article, "Incidents Illustrative of American Jewish Patriotism," which provided just what the title implied—a brief accounting of "several incidents in our history not otherwise connected with each other," but designed to demonstrate that "the Jew has ever been ready to battle for the cause of his adopted country."[19]

The preoccupation with establishing early Jewish origins in the United States remained crucial to the Society's core mission. As historian David Lowenthal has explained, the concern with being "first" has engaged virtually every

17. Oscar S. Straus, "Address of the President," *Publications of the American Jewish Historical Society* 1 (1893): 3.

18. Oscar S. Straus, as cited in John J. Appel, "Hansen's Third-Generation 'Law' and the Origins of the American Jewish Historical Society," *Jewish Social Studies* 23, no. 1 (1961): 10.

19. Max J. Kohler, "Incidents Illustrative of American Jewish Patriotism," *Publications of the American Jewish Historical Society* 4 (1896): 81.

minority group in every society: "Precedence evokes pride and proves title. To be first in a place warrants possession; to antedate others' origins or exploits shows superiority." That sense of defensiveness lingered within all of the Society's endeavors and lay behind many of the organization's efforts to document the Jewish role in America's founding, as Jews came to believe that "[p]riority can enshrine even a recent heritage."[20] The AJHS *Publications* focused on topics such as Jewish settlement in the West Indies and South America, as well as the early arrival and activities of Sephardic Jews in the American colonies. Indeed, the first two volumes of the *Publications* contain essays on "Jews Mentioned in the Journal of the Continental Congress" and "The Colonization of America by the Jews," along with articles about early Jewish settlement in Philadelphia, New York, Maryland, Chicago, Georgia, and Kentucky, to name just a few places.[21] In addition to disseminating information about the Jewish past, the organization also contacted the overseers of Jewish burial grounds and urged them to gather and keep "records of burials and locations of graves," stressing their "historical and genealogical importance." Leaders further resolved to "collect inscriptions in Jewish burial grounds in America prior to 1850."[22] Taken together, these various projects reflect the broader effort by the Society's founders to enhance Jewish security and prestige—and to ward off detractors—by demonstrating that American Jews were "present at the creation" and vital contributors to the nation.[23]

A variety of Jewish origin stories, propagated by both Jews and non-Jews, began centuries before the creation of the AJHS and, indeed, long before the nation's founding. The oldest of these claimed that Native Americans were descended from the ten lost tribes of Israel. The Dutch rabbi and scholar Menasseh Ben Israel was among the first to advance this theory as part of his broader argument in 1650 that the dispersal of Jews across the globe represented a harbinger of the messianic era.[24] Over the next two centuries, Jewish and Christian thinkers on both sides of the Atlantic put forward different versions of this idea. In colonial America, the lost tribes myth offered an explanation for the presence

20. David Lowenthal, *The Heritage Crusade and the Spoils of History* (1996; repr. Cambridge: Cambridge University Press, 1999), 174.

21. See *Publications of the American Jewish Historical Society* 1 (1893) and 2 (1894).

22. "Seventh Annual Meeting," *Publications of the American Jewish Historical Society* 8 (1900): viii.

23. Henry L. Feingold, "American Jewish History and American Jewish Survival," *American Jewish History* 71, no. 4 (1982): 421–31.

24. Menasseh ben Israel, *The Hope of Israel* (1650), trans. Moses Wall (1652), ed. Henry Méchoulan and Gérard Nahon (Oxford: Littman Library of Jewish Civilization, 2004).

of indigenous peoples while simultaneously lending credence to the notion of America as the New Israel, whose earliest inhabitants had descended from the ancient Hebrews. In a culture deeply embedded with biblical consciousness, such theories held enormous sway among segments of the population. Over the years, a variety of writers and observers posited parallels between the linguistic and ritual practices of ancient Hebrews and Native Americans that bolstered the lost tribes thesis.[25] While interest in the legacy of ancient Israelites often bore little connection or concern with contemporary Jews, it did paradoxically establish a Jewish foundation in America that predated the establishment of the Republic.

Although few Jews subscribed to the lost tribes theory, among them was one of the most prominent Jews of the nineteenth century, Mordecai Manual Noah. A journalist, playwright, and politician who served as U.S. consul at Tunis and as a sheriff of New York City, Noah is best known for his elaborate, though ultimately unsuccessful, attempt to create a Jewish colony on Grand Island in the Niagara River near Buffalo, New York. He purchased land in the region for his imagined Jewish "city of refuge," which he envisioned as a haven for oppressed Jews worldwide, and dedicated the cornerstone for the utopian colony in a theatrical and gaudy ceremony in 1825. He named the settlement Ararat to evoke the resting place of Noah's Ark in the Book of Genesis, and also because the name made oblique reference to him as founder. Within a year, the project had collapsed.

Despite its failure, Ararat reflected a certain faith in America's potential to provide a safe haven and refuge for Jews. At the same time, it remains noteworthy that Noah imagined Native Americans as integral to his plan; he believed fervently that they were "the lineal descendants of the Israelites," who, after escaping Egyptian bondage, "bent their course in a northwest direction, which brought them within a few leagues of the American Continent ... which they finally reached." He insisted that Native American language and rituals reflected Hebrew origins and considered it "providential" to bring the two groups together. (Yet, his otherwise romantic notions about Native peoples included, not surprisingly, a charge to "civilize" these lost Hebrew brethren.)[26] He even invited the Seneca chief Red Jacket to attend the Ararat dedication ceremony.[27] Noah's

25. Elizabeth A. Fenton, *Old Canaan in a New World: Native Americans and the Lost Tribes of Israel* (New York: New York University Press, 2020); David S. Koffman, *The Jews' Indian: Colonialism, Pluralism, and Belonging in America* (New Brunswick: Rutgers University Press, 2019).

26. "Address of Mordecai M. Noah," *Publications of the American Jewish Historical Society* 21 (1913): 249, 248, 250.

27. Mordecai Manuel Noah, *Discourse on the Evidences of the American Indians Being the*

fanciful plan to gather Jewish exiles from around the world on American soil reflected a passionate belief in the nation's freedoms, but tellingly also included a desire for reconciliation with Jews' estranged Native kin. That lofty, if likely not shared, hope repeated a common Jewish trope: such a reunion would unite "the first people in the old world [with] the rightful inheritors of the new."[28]

The AJHS's *Publications* discussed the ten lost tribes but exhibited greater concern with documenting the Jewish role in the discovery of the country and the founding of the nation. The Society's signature project, designed to "prove" Jewish belonging by virtue of precedence, came in a study of Jewish involvement in the first voyage of Christopher Columbus. By the time Oscar Straus assumed leadership of the Society, he had already contacted the Budapest rabbi and scholar Meyer Kayserling about investigating the connections between Jews and Columbus. The elite leaders of the Society commissioned Kayserling's study, believing that historical evidence would secure Jews' position among the founders of the nation and effectively answer critics and antisemites who claimed they were merely outsiders.

Published in 1894, Kayserling's *Christopher Columbus and the Participation of the Jews in the Spanish and Portuguese Discoveries* uncovered many previously unknown interactions between Jews and Columbus, including information about those who helped finance his voyage and provided him with maps and nautical instruments. We now know that Kayserling was mistaken in his assertion that four men "of Jewish stock" accompanied Columbus on his first journey; only one converted Jew was on board. Nevertheless, when his study was published in the 1890s, it provided a scholarly foundation upon which Jews could rest their claims. The book did little to diminish antisemitism, but nevertheless had a significant impact within the Jewish community. Allusions to the Jewish role in Columbus's discovery of America made their way into scores of popular books, speeches, and sermons, and gradually became an opening chapter in rehearsals of American Jewish history in all sorts of educational, communal, and cultural settings well into the mid-twentieth century.[29]

Descendants of the Lost Tribes of Israel. Delivered Before the Mercantile Library Association, Clinton Hall (New York: James Van Norden, 1837).

28. "Address of Mordecai M. Noah," 249. For more on Noah, see Jonathan D. Sarna, *Jacksonian Jew: The Two Worlds of Mordecai Noah* (New York: Holmes & Meier, 1981).

29. Moritz Kayserling, *Christopher Columbus and the Participation of the Jews in the Spanish and Portuguese Discoveries*, trans. Charles Gross (1894; repr. New York: Hermon Press, 1968). Jonathan D. Sarna discusses Kayserling's work in detail in "The Mythical Jewish Columbus and the History of America's Jews," in *Religion in the Age of Exploration: The Case of Spain and New Spain*, ed. Bryan F. LeBeau and Menachem Mor (Omaha, Neb.: Creighton University Press, 1996), 83–86.

In the nineteenth century, celebrations of Christopher Columbus took place primarily in Italian communities in the United States. But the four-hundredth anniversary of Columbus's landing in 1892 and the attendant Columbian Exposition in Chicago marked the apogee of veneration for Columbus across America. In fact, AJHS leaders had commissioned Kayserling's study with the anniversary in mind. In October 1892, commemorations of Columbus took place throughout the United States. Joining in the national mood, scores of churches and synagogues celebrated Columbus; an estimated five hundred services took place in New York City alone. Although some Jewish leaders argued that Jews should recognize the occasion in separate observances, many synagogues joined in the nationwide religious services over Columbus Day weekend.[30] Across the country, rabbis preached sermons praising Columbus's contributions and read special prayers in synagogues that had been decorated with American flags for the occasion. One rabbi used the commemoration to reinforce the notion of America as a place of shelter and refuge for Jews, declaring that "the Jewish people certainly have cause to express gratitude for the hero who founded a haven of repose for our noble race ... he discovered a country for wandering Israel."[31]

While the notion of America as a haven for Jews remained a regular theme, Columbus Day more pointedly provided an opportunity for Jews to underscore their early footprints on American soil. Across the late nineteenth century and well into the twentieth, dozens of children's stories and popular histories recounted the story of the Jews who were purportedly part of Columbus's historic voyage. Luis de Torres, the converted Jew who sailed with Columbus as his interpreter, emerged as a particular favorite in these retellings. Elma Ehrlich Levinger, one of the most popular authors of Jewish children's stories, penned a tale about the three Jews who (allegedly) sailed with Columbus. In the story, de Torres gathers with the other Jews on the ship, still fearful of the persecution they had suffered in Spain and reluctant to reveal to other crew members that "secret Jews" were on board. De Torres bemoans the fact that "the whole world [had] become a great sea of endless waves for the unhappy children of Israel." As the three men discuss their people's ongoing search for refuge, they spot land in the distance. The story closes with de Torres, "the unhappy dreamer,"

30. For a variety of opinions about why Jews should not celebrate the occasion as Jews, apart from other national celebrations, see *The American Hebrew Almanac for 5650*, September 1889–September 1890 (Cincinnati and Chicago: Bloch Publishing and Printing, 1890), 62–63.

31. Rabbi Alexander Kohut quoted in Claudia L. Bushman, *America Discovers Columbus: How an Italian Explorer Became an American Hero* (Hanover, N.H.: University Press of New England, 1992), 168.

heading for shore, unaware that "a very land of refuge and of hope for the wandering sons of Israel, lay before him across the smiling waters."[32] Levinger's story not only emphasizes that Jews had been among the first to discover and set foot on the new land but also provides an uplifting tale through the character of de Torres, who does not yet realize that he has found a new and better home for the Jewish people. As contrived as Levinger's story and others like it may have been, the tale, like the Jewish celebrations in synagogues, demonstrates that the fascination with Columbus—and with creating Jewish origin stories—was not limited to the elite membership of the AJHS. Whether or not they fully interpreted its import, many American Jews felt some need to situate themselves at the roots of the national story.

Because of the symbolic power of Columbus, his image also provided a useful tool for Jewish critiques of American life. Members of the Jewish community did not speak in a single voice on these issues, or on any others for that matter. When it came to veneration of Columbus, many Jews, especially east European immigrants, took the opportunity to employ his image in the service of their own analysis of Jewish life in America and, indeed, of America itself. In the early 1890s, just as more established members of the Jewish community and the founders of the AJHS prepared to use the four-hundredth anniversary of Columbus's voyage to claim a role in the nation's founding, some new immigrants from eastern Europe marshaled the occasion to comment on America and American Jewish culture. The physician and journalist George Price praised the efforts of Americans to "celebrate the 400th anniversary of the discovery of America by Columbus" and "to demonstrate to the Old World what the New World has accomplished." He was effusive in his admiration for American achievements, even insisting, "Not a single country all over the globe, not a single people throughout the world can boast of such progress as the United States." Yet, giving voice to the sentiments of the working class, he emphasized that the success of the United States should properly be attributed to the immigrants who built the nation, and his detailed essay provided a grim portrait of the struggle that immigrants encountered.[33] Price first published his articles on "Russian Jews in America" in the Russian Jewish periodical *Voskhod* in the 1890s. Ironically, his observations about east European immigrant life ultimately appeared in the

32. Elma Erhlich Levinger, "In the Night Watches," in Levinger, *The New Land* (New York: Bloch Publishing, 1920), 11, 13.

33. George M. Price, "The Russian Jews in America," trans. Leo Shpall, *Publications of the American Jewish Historical Society* 48, no. 2 (1958): 101 (second and final installment, continued from 48, no. 1: 28–62).

pages of the AJHS *Publications*, but not until 1958, when the Jewish community had significantly changed.

The figure of Columbus became a vehicle for articulating varying Jewish interpretations of America, often offering sharp critiques of the nation that would not be heard at the annual meetings of the AJHS. The prominent Yiddish journalist Gershon Rosenzweig, who immigrated to America in 1888 and often poked fun at the lowly state of American Jewish affairs, authored a scathing parody, *The Tractate "America"* (1892), in the midst of the Columbus quadricentennial. In the fictional Talmudic debate, "Rabbi Scribner" offers an interpretation of the country's name: "Through the astrological arts Columbus foresaw that America was destined to be a land of refuge for every scoundrel and empty-headed rake in the world, and he therefore asked mercy from God and prayed that the land not be called after him. And so, instead, they called it America—*ama reikah*, land of empty-headed rakes."[34] Just as the play on words about the naming of the nation suggests disillusionment with American culture, so, too, did the figure of Columbus serve as a device to express disappointment with the harsh conditions that new immigrants encountered in their adopted homeland.

In a fictional autobiography published in 1894, an immigrant shoemaker who had come to the United States to improve his economic lot discovered that turn-of-the-century America offered only bleak living and working conditions. Lamenting his fate, he sarcastically inquires, "Who ever asked him, Columbus, to discover America? Why did he have to bring people there, promise them all sorts of fortunes?"[35] Immigrant Jews frequently articulated their disillusionment with America by deriding Columbus. The popular Yiddish song "The Greenhorn Cousin" (*Di grine kuzine*) closes with the biting invective, "The hell with Columbus's country."[36] New immigrants did not attempt to overturn the myth of Columbus, but instead used his legacy to put forward their own reading of Jewish life in America. Granted, such sentiments would not have been articulated in any proceedings of the AJHS. Still, despite the critiques leveled, the dominant myth that positioned Jews as de facto discoverers of the nation

34. Gershon Rosenzweig, "From The Tractate 'America'" (1892), trans. David Stern, in *Jewish American Literature: A Norton Anthology*, ed. Jules Chametzsky et al. (New York: W. W. Norton, 2001), 297.

35. H. A. Yakhnuk, *In Amerike oder fun Amerike* (1894), cited in Elias Tcherikower, *The Early Jewish Labor Movement in the United States*, trans. and rev. Aaron Antonovsky (New York: YIVO Institute for Jewish Research, 1961), 122.

36. Joseph C. Landis, "Yiddish Dreams in America," in *Handbook of American-Jewish Literature: An Analytic Guide to Topics, Themes, and Sources*, ed. Lewis Fried et al. (New York: Greenwood Press, 1988), 148.

endured and could be found in sermons, articles, and children's stories well into the late twentieth century.

Judaism and Democracy

In *The Origin of Republican Form of Government in the United States* (1885), Oscar Straus boldly claimed that the ancient Hebrews—not America's founders—had first created "a government of the people, by the people, and for the people": "The children of Israel on the banks of the Jordan, who had just emerged from centuries of bondage, not only recognized the guiding principles of civil and religious liberty that 'all men are created equal,' that God and the law are the only kings, but also established a free commonwealth, a pure democratic-republic under a written constitution."[37] Just four years after the publication of Straus's book, New York's *Jewish Messenger* proclaimed, "A good faithful Jew, a Jew true to the spirit of Judaism, could not be otherwise than a patriotic American."[38] These two statements represent distinct but related corollaries that underscore one of the most ubiquitous—though completely invented—tenets of American Jewish life. The first identifies the roots of American democracy in Jewish tradition; the second insists that because of those roots, any "real" Jew is by definition a true American patriot. In American Jewish history, no theme resounds as loudly or as consistently as the perceived symbiosis between Judaism and American democracy. Yet, as one scholar has noted, "the synthesis of Judaism and Americanism is a historical fiction."[39] There is nothing inherent in either American culture or Jewish tradition to render them fundamentally compatible. Rather, American Jews themselves created this construction of American Jewish culture and repeated it endlessly in an abundance of settings until it became firmly established as a key element of Jewish identity in the United States.

Jewish clergy were fond of insisting that the nation's spiritual and legal roots lay in the Hebrew Bible. As early as 1854, in the inaugural issue of the *Israelite*, Reform Rabbi Isaac Mayer Wise proclaimed that "the principles of the constitution of the United States are copied from the words of Moses and the Prophets."[40] He reiterated those claims more than twenty years later when the

37. Oscar S. Straus, *The Origin of Republican Form of Government in the United States*, 2d ed. rev. (New York: G. P. Putnam's Sons, 1901), 117.

38. *Jewish Messenger*, April 26, 1889, 4.

39. Jerold S. Auerbach, *Rabbis and Lawyers: The Journey from Torah to Constitution* (Bloomington: Indiana University Press, 1990), x.

40. Isaac Mayer Wise, "The Fourth of July: An address delivered in the Synagogue of K.K. Benai Yeshurun," *Israelite*, July 15, 1854, 3.

nation celebrated its centennial in July 1876. That year, the Reform movement's Union of American Hebrew Congregations gathered in Washington for its third annual convention. To mark the occasion, the delegates scheduled a break from conference business and traveled to George Washington's gravesite at Mount Vernon.[41] Why, Wise asked rhetorically, "are the representatives of the Union of American Hebrew Congregations, the admirers of Moses and the prophets, assembled at the sepulcher of George Washington[?]" Answering his own question, he explained that Washington had "fulfilled in the holy cause of humanity that which Moses has written." Both men, in his opinion, had offered a sacred message of liberty, justice, and equality. Both had set the stage for the best course of human history: "Moses, the son of Amram, and George Washington are the two poles of the axis about which the history of mankind revolves."[42] With these claims, Wise neatly paralleled biblical history and American history, setting the fates of Jews and Americans on the same path (Fig. 89).

Although this rhetoric was most pervasive in Reform circles, rabbis from all three major denominations echoed the same themes. According to one Conservative rabbi, Puritanism was, "in essence, the rebirth of the Hebrew spirit in the Christian conscience."[43] Even the president of the Orthodox Yeshiva University insisted that there was no "serious conflict between our spiritual heritage and the American way of life, which is itself rooted in Hebraic spiritual values."[44] American Zionist leader Louis Brandeis often claimed that the Puritans' "constant study of the prophets" had profoundly shaped the nature of American culture, infusing it with a Jewish spirit. As one scholar has explained, "In a circuitous historical and conceptual journey, from prophecy through Puritanism, ancient Jewish ideals had become thoroughly Americanized."[45] By insisting that

41. Union of American Hebrew Congregations, *Proceedings of the Third Annual Session of the Council* (Washington, D.C., 1876), 265–76.

42. *Ibid.*, 275.

43. Abraham A. Neuman, *Relation of the Hebrew Scriptures to American Institutions* (New York: Jewish Theological Seminary of America, 1939), 6.

44. Rabbi Samuel Belkin, cited in Auerbach, *Rabbis and Lawyers*, 19, 211n37.

45. Auerbach, *Rabbis and Lawyers*, 18.

Fig. 89 (*overleaf*). Illustration of Passover by Arthur Meyer. *American Hebrew*, April 19, 1889, A180. Note George Washington's portrait in the upper right vignette and the quotation from Longfellow's "The Slave Singing at Midnight" below the main scene. (By permission of the Klau Library, Cincinnati, Hebrew Union College-Jewish Institute of Religion).

Gathering the Leavened Bread.

Taking the Afikoman.

In that hour, when night is calme
Sang he from the Hebrew Psalmist,
In a voice so sweet and clear
That I could not choose but hear.

The Seder; or the R

The Open Door.

The Passover Dishes.

gs of triumph, and ascriptions,
n as reached the swart Egyptians,
en upon the Red Sea coast
shed Pharaoh and his host. —LONGFELLOW

e Exodus from Egypt.

COPYRIGHTED, 1889, BY PHILIP COWEN.

American democracy, as Reform leader Kaufmann Kohler proclaimed, "found its classical expression in Israel's holy writings," Jews secured another path toward claiming a founding role in the creation of the nation, not merely by placing themselves temporally at the country's founding moment but also by taking credit for inventing its fundamental principles.[46]

Like many other "foundation myths," as one historian has called them, this assertion reflected both Jewish aspirations and apprehensions about belonging fully as American citizens; it elicited Jewish pride while also providing an answer to detractors—or so Jews hoped.[47] Just as the historical record of Jews who purportedly sailed with Columbus cemented the notion that Jews were, literally, here from the beginning, the insistence on a shared spiritual heritage reminded Christian America that "our values" (rooted in the Bible) are identical to "your values" (of monotheism, American liberty, and democracy). Jews employed both history and mythmaking to tell their own story about America, a story that placed Jewish contributions at the center. These filiopietistic pronouncements were indeed self-serving, but they expressed an ideal vision of America that promised a secure place for Jews while also laying the groundwork for a harmonious relationship between Jews and Christians, rooted in their mutual devotion to Scripture.

Promoting a shared biblical heritage with Christians—one in which Jews claimed the role of monotheistic progenitor—also gave Jews a claim to American spiritual belonging. The celebration of the holiday of Thanksgiving became an especially popular time for Jews to stake a claim to a mutual metahistory rooted in the Bible and to advertise their commonalities with other Americans. In the nineteenth century, Thanksgiving was regularly celebrated in churches and synagogues, and many Jews availed themselves of the chance to join "one day at least in the year in even religious communion with our fellow-citizens."[48] At special synagogue services, the singing of the national anthem and other patriotic hymns accompanied traditional psalms and prayers.[49] Rabbis not only preached their own Thanksgiving sermons during these holiday services, but often invited Christian clergy to speak from their pulpits in what became public

46. Kaufmann Kohler, "The Tocsin Call of Liberty and Democracy," in Kohler, *A Living Faith: Selected Sermons and Addresses from the Literary Remains of Dr. Kaufmann Kohler*, ed. Samuel S. Cohon (Cincinnati: Hebrew Union College Press, 1948), 113–14.

47. Orm Øverland, *Immigrant Minds, American Identities: Making the United States Home, 1870–1930* (Urbana: University of Illinois Press, 2000), 19.

48. *American Hebrew*, December 6, 1889, 124; Kammen, *Mystic Chords of Memory*, 205.

49. *American Hebrew*, November 18, 1892, 83–84.

performances of common ground. In 1879, for example, Henry Bellows, minister at New York's First Congregational Church, told the congregation gathered at Temple Emanu-El that "no people ... has had a beginning or an early history, so like the Hebrews as the American people; and the old claim of being 'a chosen people' has always been somewhat self-appropriated by our countrymen."[50] Both Jewish and Christian clergy were fond of drawing parallels between ancient Hebrews and early Americans. A 1915 American Jewish primer for teaching Bible stories compared Abraham's journey to Canaan with the voyage of the Pilgrims to the "new Canaan," explaining that both "left their homes to seek a new country, in which they could secure religious liberty."[51]

Such claims represent a cultural version of the mathematical principle of the transitive property of equality: if our texts were present and recited by the Pilgrims, then by extension we were present at the foundational moment of the nation and actually were virtual Pilgrims ourselves. One Jewish author even went so far as to argue the formula in reverse. Bestowing honorary Jewish status on the Puritans, a 1920s publication insisted that they so closely paralleled the Hebrews that "[c]ulturally they were Jews as much as non-Jews can possibly be."[52] By asserting a role equivalent to that of the Pilgrims and the Puritans, Jews reiterated (and reformulated) their own American origin story while also positing a spiritual relationship between ancient Israelite tradition and the "New Israel" that took shape on American soil.

At the same time, Jewish celebrations of Thanksgiving Day reveal just how fine a needle Jews had to thread as they staked a claim to a shared biblical heritage. While they eagerly took part in national observances, Jews also adamantly insisted on the nonsectarian nature of the Thanksgiving holiday as a time when Americans of all faiths came together to celebrate. As long as it remained religiously neutral, Jews could regard the holiday as sacred on their own terms, as an occasion to join equally in the celebration. But that vision of American society existed more in Jewish minds than in American realities. Especially in the nineteenth century, government officials from the president to governors often issued Thanksgiving proclamations that contained references to Christianity or calls to worship in churches. Year after year, Jews assailed this practice and offered searing rebukes of this sort of governmental behavior, even as they ex-

50. Henry W. Bellows, *Religious Toleration: A Discourse Given in the Temple Emanu-el, New York, on the Day of the National Thanksgiving, Nov. 27, 1879* (New York: G. P. Putnam's Sons, 1880), 9.

51. Ella Jacobs, *Methods of Teaching the Primary Grades: Course A, "Lesson X"* (Philadelphia: Jewish Chautauqua Society, 1915), 7.

52. George Cohen, *The Jews in the Making of America* (Boston: Stratford Co., 1924), 49.

tolled the virtues of America. Speaking from the pulpit in 1868, Marcus Jastrow informed his Philadelphia congregation that

> the Governor of the State has ignored the character of his office, and the character of the Constitution of the United States, by making his own particular belief the basis of a proclamation to the commonwealth, thus intimating that he wishes only such united with him in thanksgiving for the country's happiness and greatness, who may profess certain Dogmas similar to his own, and that he considers all other inhabitants under his jurisdiction unworthy to shout before their God, to serve Him with joy, to come before His presence with triumphal song, when the *country* celebrates a day of *national* importance.[53]

More than thirty-five years later, the *American Israelite* leveled the same charges. "The people know when Thanksgiving Day falls and what is the proper way of observing it," the newspaper told its readers. "The official proclamations are needless and smack too much of a union of Church and State to be to the *Israelite*'s liking."[54] These sharp critiques became standard fare at Thanksgiving, included alongside all the rhetoric about the glories of America, as Jews used the occasion not only to celebrate the nation with other Americans but also to define the parameters of the America they desired but did not actually exist. The shared history crafted by American Jews stemmed not only, and often not primarily, from the legacy of the Jewish past but also from hopes for the Jewish present and future.

Heroes and Patriots

Demonstrating the patriotism of American Jews was at the heart of the AJHS's mission. Speaker after speaker at the founding meeting reiterated the need to document and publicize Jewish loyalty to the nation. Rabbi Kaufmann Kohler declared, "The practical and theoretical aim before this society should be to get facts ... that would at once reflect credit on the Society and enhance the interest in our work by showing what the Jews of America as a body collectively and individually and as patriots and in the Jewish congregations have done for the Government, for the culture and for the entire history...."[55] Henry Leipziger, assistant superintendent of the New York public schools, implored the attendees, "As a Jew and an American I feel we must emphasize [our patriotism] more

53. Rev. Dr. Marcus Jastrow, *Sermon Delivered in the Synagogue, Rodeph Shalom, Juliana Street, on Thanksgiving Day, November 26th, 1868* (Philadelphia: R. Stein Printer, 1868), 5 (emphasis in original).

54. *American Israelite*, November 24, 1904, 4.

55. Minutes, 31.

than we have done by bringing the facts promptly and in a scholarly manner before the people."[56] In fact, the stated "Objects" of the Society, reprinted in the frontispiece of every issue of the *Publications*, proclaimed unequivocally that "a number of Jews [served] in the Continental army and others contributed liberally to defray the expenses of the Revolutionary war. Since the foundation of our government a number of Jews have held important public positions."[57] Without a hint of subtlety, the AJHS declared its partisan intent, albeit under the umbrella of scholarly inquiry.

As David Lowenthal has cogently observed, "Willingness to die for a collective cause is the supreme seal of national faith." And Jews eagerly joined in the chorus of American ethnic minorities proclaiming that faith through the sacrifices of war.[58] The need to "prove" Jewish patriotism, particularly as demonstrated by military service, had begun brewing before the Society's founding and, indeed, provided a crucial motivation for its creation. In 1891, an article in the *North American Review* mentioned the lack of Jewish loyalty during the Civil War. One veteran echoed that claim in a written response, insisting that in his year and a half in the military, he had neither seen nor heard of a single Jewish soldier. Answering the challenge from the letter's author—and from others who joined in the discussion—to produce documentation of Jewish military contributions, Simon Wolf, one of American Jewry's most prominent leaders and a founding member of the AJHS, compiled an almost six-hundred-page treatise that attempted to chronicle every Jewish soldier who had served the United States from its founding.[59] Proceeding war by war from the Revolution, cataloguing both officers and enlisted men, and documenting medals and distinguished service, Wolf refuted claims that Jews had not served their country by amassing historical evidence to the contrary. "This timely work on a

56. *Ibid.*, 29.

57. Report of Organization, Objects, n.p.

58. Lowenthal, *Heritage Crusade and the Spoils of History*, 57.

59. Simon Wolf, *The American Jew as Patriot, Soldier and Citizen*, ed. Louis Edward Levy (Philadelphia: Levytype Company, 1895), 1. The original article was by Goldwin Smith, the Regius Professor of History at Oxford University, who later assumed a position at Cornell University; he cited the escape of Judah Benjamin, a member of Jefferson Davis's cabinet, to England after the Civil War as evidence of the lack of Jewish loyalty to any country. Goldwin Smith, "New Light on the Jewish Question," *North American Review* 153 (August 1891): 129–43. The response that enraged Simon Wolf came from J. M. Rogers, "Jewish Soldiers in the Union Army," *North American Review* 153 (December 1891): 761–62. See also Sylvan Morris Dubow, "Identifying the Jewish Servicemen in the Civil War: A Re-appraisal of Simon Wolf's *The American Jew as Patriot, Soldier and Citizen*," *American Jewish Historical Quarterly* 59, no. 3 (1970): 357–69.

timely topic," declared an advertisement for the book, "called forth by recent magazine discussions regarding the position of Jewish citizens as patriots and as soldiers, contains an alphabetical register and numerous detailed notices of American citizens of the Jewish faith who have been enrolled in the armies of the country from the earliest period of American history to the present time."[60]

Founded in the comingled tributaries of communal defensiveness, pride, and the sincere if erroneous belief that "facts" might counter antisemitism, the AJHS relentlessly beat the drum about Jewish war service. The Society acquired from War Department the *Official Army Register of the Volunteer Force* in the hope of discovering numbers and activities of Jewish participants during the Civil War.[61] The organization also set out to document "the names, ranks and service of Jews who served in the Army and Navy during the Spanish-American War."[62] In its first decade, the Society's *Publications* were replete with documentation about individual Jews who served in America's wars, meticulously presenting evidence both to craft a public image of Jews as patriotic citizens and to construct a shared internal history that underscored devotion to the nation.

No Jewish patriotic figure attracted as much attention throughout the American Jewish community as Haym Salomon, perhaps because his activities took place during the Revolutionary War, linking him with the founding of the nation, and perhaps, too, because the mythology surrounding him included earnest claims that his contributions had not been properly acknowledged by the nation he served. An immigrant from Poland, Salomon arrived in the United States in the 1770s. He was reputed to have been arrested and imprisoned by the British, to have spied for the Americans, and to have helped prisoners to escape. However, no firm documentation exists to support the precise nature of his activities during these years.[63] Salomon fled to Philadelphia in 1778 and there began the much better documented phase of his career, where he earned a reputation as a successful financial broker. Salomon's skills gained the attention of Superintendent of Finance Robert Morris, and beginning in 1781, Morris resorted to Salomon regularly to secure funds for the war. By raising funds and negotiating

60. Advertising copy printed on the last page of *American Jew as Patriot, Soldier and Citizen.*

61. *Publications of the American Jewish Historical Society* 6 (1897): 163.

62. *Publications of the American Jewish Historical Society* 8 (1900): vii–viii.

63. For more on Haym Salomon's life and contributions to the Revolution, see: Jacob Rader Marcus, *United States Jewry, 1776–1985*, vol. 1 (Detroit: Wayne State University Press, 1989), 66–77; Samuel Rezneck, *Unrecognized Patriots: The Jews in the American Revolution* (Westport, Conn.: Greenwood Press, 1975); Edwin Wolf and Maxwell Whiteman, *The History of the Jews of Philadelphia from Colonial Times to the Age of Jackson* (Philadelphia: Jewish Publication Society of America, 1957), 98–113.

bills of exchange with several foreign governments, particularly the French, with whom he had conducted considerable business and established reliable contacts, Salomon contributed tremendously valuable services to the American cause. While many colonial Jews participated in international trade and finance and several worked on behalf of the Revolution, Salomon's financial prowess earned him a place of distinction in the colonial community. Robert Morris praised his efforts as "useful to the Public Interest," even allowing Salomon to publicize his business by advertising himself as "Broker to the Office of Finance."[64] Salomon died in 1785 at the relatively young age of forty-five. Largely because he had accumulated government notes of credit that had depreciated after the war, he left his family in debt. His twenty-three-year-old widow (along with three children and a fourth on the way) could claim only the household furnishings remaining from Salomon's once considerable estate.[65]

The heirs of Haym Salomon were the first to promote him as an unappreciated American hero. In 1846, at the age of sixty-one, Haym M. Salomon, his son, brought a petition for monetary compensation before Congress. In a series of petitions submitted periodically through the Civil War years, Haym M. Salomon insisted that the government repay the principal debt to his father plus interest, which he estimated at sums ranging from $300,00 to $650,000. Several congressional committees reviewed Salomon's petitions, and some bills advanced to the floor of the Senate, but all were ultimately rejected by Congress.[66]

Just a year after the founding of the AJHS, amid the burgeoning interest in documenting patriotism and forging collective histories throughout the nation, a new generation of Salomon descendants renewed the quest to gain recognition for Haym Salomon's contributions. In 1893, they petitioned not for monetary compensation but for a medal to commemorate Salomon's service to the Revolution. In a climate of heightened interest in historical commemoration and honor societies, the campaign to recognize Salomon represented a conscious effort to place Jews at the center of an emerging public memory of the American Revolution. The House Committee on the Library, a group charged primarily with overseeing the Library of Congress, did recommend that a Salomon medal

64. Rezneck, *Unrecognized Patriots*, 88, 82–89; Marcus, *United States Jewry*, 66–72.

65. She remarried a year later and resettled in the Netherlands. Rezneck, *Unrecognized Patriots*, 81–97; Marcus, *United States Jewry*, 66–77. For more on public finance and indebtedness in the colonies and early Republic, see: E. James Ferguson, *The Power of the Purse: A History of American Public Finance, 1776–1790* (Chapel Hill: University of North Carolina Press, 1961); Bruce H. Mann, *Republic of Debtors: Bankruptcy in the Age of American Independence* (Cambridge, Mass.: Harvard University Press, 2002).

66. Rezneck, *Unrecognized Patriots*, 215–16; Marcus, *United States Jewry*, 73–75.

be issued, but this venture, like previous efforts, was defeated in Congress.[67] Nevertheless, these failures marked the beginning of a process of public debate about Haym Salomon. Many of the unsubstantiated claims put forth before Congress in the nineteenth century endured for decades. As later generations of Jews resurrected Salomon in the twentieth century, he emerged as a hero instrumental to American victory in the War of Independence, who died without ever receiving monetary compensation or proper recognition from his country. But already in the closing years of the nineteenth century, Haym Salomon had become an object lesson in Jewish patriotism and a symbol of the possibilities and perils of American life.[68]

Within a span of just a few years, as some groups lobbied for congressional recognition of Haym Salomon's patriotic deeds and as the AJHS documented war service in its publications and through its collecting efforts, the first substantial campaigns to memorialize Jewish military contributions in brick and stone began to take shape. The most prolific period of monument building throughout the nation occurred between 1870 and 1910, as Americans of all stripes sought to memorialize war service and create lasting testimonies to patriotic sacrifice.[69] In the midst of a nationwide building flurry, the Jewish community dedicated its first monument to Jewish soldiers in 1904.

As other Americans began to erect memorials to Civil War soldiers, the Hebrew Union Veterans' Association (a precursor to the Jewish War Veterans) commissioned its own marker to memorialize Jewish sacrifices during the war. Erected in Salem Fields Cemetery in Cypress Hills, New York, one of the largest Jewish burial grounds, the stark monument stands fifty feet tall and is topped with a bronze eagle.[70] On the sides are four bronze tablets listing the names of Jewish soldiers. The inscription reads: "To the memory of the Soldiers of the Hebrew Faith who responded to the call of their country and gave their lives for its salvation during the dark days of its need so that the nation might live."[71] The unveiling ceremony, like many of its kind, displayed pomp and circumstance, including a parade led by the Hebrew Orphan Asylum Band, followed by two hundred marching Jewish veterans. The program featured many dignitaries,

67. Rezneck, *Unrecognized Patriots*, 215–17; Kammen, *Mystic Chords of Memory*, 218–20.

68. For more on efforts to memorialize Haym Salomon in the twentieth century, see Beth S. Wenger, *History Lessons: The Creation of American Jewish Heritage* (Princeton: Princeton University Press, 2010), 179–209.

69. Kammen, *Mystic Chords of Memory*, 115.

70. *American Hebrew*, May 12, 1905, 760–62.

71. *Ibid.*, 760.

both Jewish and non-Jewish, allowing the event to serve simultaneously as an occasion for Jewish collective pride and an opportunity to articulate a shared, interfaith commitment to the nation. The featured speaker, Nathan Straus, a leading philanthropist and co-owner of Macy's department store with his brother Isidor, denounced the evils of war; but he made a point to cite the numbers of Jews who had fought in American battles. Straus explained that during the Civil War, "the Jewish population furnished one brave soldier to every twenty-nine persons of its entire population, and more than ten thousand of the flower of its manhood enlisted in the Civil and Spanish wars."[72] Standing in one of the country's largest cemeteries, this monument became, over the years, a site used to memorialize Jewish soldiers who lost their lives in subsequent wars and a permanent testimony to Jewish loyalty and sacrifice.

American Jews certainly felt a need to "prove" their devotion through military service, even as they desired to provide a narrative of patriotism for themselves as they crafted their own versions of an American past. No matter how self-serving or defensive, American Jewish discourse about military contributions and heroism posited Jews as part of the organic fabric of the nation.

Liberty

The assertion that the mission of the AJHS was "not sectarian, but American" was first issued at the organization's founding meeting and then established as part of the Society's "Objects"; it appeared in the opening pages of each issue of the *Publications.* In his first address as president, Oscar Straus reiterated, "The uses of a society such as this, with a special line of inquiry, are in the contributions it can make to the general history of our country."[73] This declaration reflected the founders' belief that if Americans more clearly understood and appreciated the contributions of Jews, the result would be a society that recognized the value of all its citizens. At the founding meeting, Rabbi Bernard Drachman of New York's Park East Synagogue underscored this aspirational justification of the organization's work, calling the effort to document American Jewish history "an act of patriotism."[74] These high-minded and somewhat naïve objectives in fact represent a corollary to the quest for acceptance by fellow Americans and the attempt to counter antisemitic accusations. By claiming that verification of the history and activities of a minority group represented a

72. *Ibid.*, 762.

73. Oscar S. Straus, "Address of the President," *Publications of the American Jewish Historical Society* 1 (1893): 1, 4.

74. Minutes, 27.

patriotic, American endeavor, the AJHS founders made the case that the ability to maintain and recognize a distinct culture in the United States served as a litmus test for the health of American liberty and democracy. Such claims became a regular feature of Jewish communal self-definition that were tightly bound to expectations for the nation.

The veneration of American liberty, democracy, and tolerance found its most salient expression in *Religious Liberty*, a monumental sculpture created by the Jewish artist Moses Ezekiel (see Fig. 19). The statue had been commissioned by B'nai B'rith, a Jewish fraternal organization founded in 1843, as the Jewish contribution to the Philadelphia Centennial Exposition in 1876. This Jewish monument, unlike the memorial to Jewish soldiers constructed in Salem Fields Cemetery some twenty-five years later, made no specific reference to Jews. Instead, it stood as a Jewish paean to the notion of Liberty itself. The monument depicts a female figure representing Liberty, who protects the male child representing Faith. The female Liberty wears a breastplate with the shield of the United States, and in her left hand she holds the Constitution. At the base of the statue, an eagle, the symbol of America, attacks a serpent, which signifies slavery—an analogy that reflects the blind spots to racial inequality in the United States and the lack of reckoning with the nation's own collective past that characterized American and American Jewish culture in this era.

The dedication ceremony for *Religious Liberty* took place on Thanksgiving Day in 1876. This civic holiday, a favorite of Jews as noted above, proved to be a fortuitous occasion for B'nai B'rith and its members to put forward their centennial message. At the dedication ceremony, seven hundred members of the order paraded to the site of the monument, accompanied by a marching band. As the statue was unveiled, organizers of the event raised the American flag over the monument and released a multitude of miniature flags that floated over the spectators as souvenirs.[75]

Not lost in the spectacular staging of the ceremony was the unique nature of this Jewish monument. Many scholars who have studied the centennial have noted that, of the ethnic and religious associations invited to submit statues for the celebration in Philadelphia, only the Jews chose *not* to honor one of their own heroes. The Germans settled on Alexander von Humboldt; the Irish honored the teetotalist reformer Father Mathew; the Italians selected Christopher Columbus; and African Americans paid tribute to Richard Allen, founder of

75. *Report of the Executive Committee of the Constitution Grand Lodge I.O.B.B., 1875–1876* (New York: M. Thalmessinger Stationer and Printer, 1877), 2–30, 22.

the African Methodist Episcopal Church.[76] Jews decided simply to erect a testament to the idea of liberty, championing American freedom and democracy and implicitly suggesting that those American values secured rights for Jews and all other peoples. This choice reflects a typically nineteenth-century Jewish sensibility rooted in the familiar pattern of extolling liberty and democracy as fundamentally *Jewish* in origin, and in the process also defining an ideal America that ensured a secure place for Jews.[77]

In this sense, *Religious Liberty* spoke as much to Jewish self-interest as it did to faith in the United States. In the wake of the Civil War, some Christian groups insisted that the ravages of war were God's punishment for America's lack of Christian commitment. In the 1860s and 1870s, various Christian groups lobbied with increasing intensity for a constitutional amendment acknowledging the nation's dedication to Christian principles.[78] Several Jewish organizations fought vigorously to oppose the amendment, which ultimately did fail in Congress. In 1876, B'nai B'rith's decision to commission a monument to the principle of liberty was as much a Jewish political and social statement as it was a confident assertion of bedrock American values. At the dedication ceremony, the president of B'nai B'rith's Centennial Committee explicitly referred to "the unwise and unpatriotic efforts of those who would introduce sectarianism into the Constitution," and insisted that for American Jews, "this monument is our answer, and this is our protest against any unlawful encroachment upon the civil rights of American freemen."[79] *Religious Liberty*, like other monuments of its genre, asserted particular Jewish interests precisely by invoking the principles of American pluralism, tolerance, and religious freedom. Even though the centennial celebration occurred almost twenty years before the founding of the AJHS, it helps to explain the context in which a nascent Jewish community attempted to establish itself within an evolving nation and what seemed a still uncertain American future.

*

76. Richard B Nicolai, *Centennial Philadelphia* (Bryn Mawr, Pa.: Bryn Mawr Press, 1976), 69, 81; Arthur A. Goren, *The Politics and Public Culture of American Jews* (Bloomington: Indiana University Press, 1999), 36; Barbara Kirshenblatt-Gimblett, *Destination Culture: Tourism, Museums, and Heritage* (Berkeley: University of California Press, 1998), 87–88.

77. Kirshenblatt-Gimblett, *Destination Culture*, 87–88; Arthur Aryeh Goren, "Pageants of Sorrow, Celebration and Protest: The Public Culture of American Jews," *Studies in Contemporary Jewry* 12 (1996): 207, http://research.policyarchive.org/9999.pdf; Nicolai, *Centennial Philadelphia*, 69, 81.

78. Naomi W. Cohen, *Encounter with Emancipation: The German Jews in the United States, 1830–1914* (Philadelphia: Jewish Publication Society of America, 1984), 254–55.

79. *Report of the Executive Committee of the Constitution Grand Lodge I.O.B.B.*, 25.

The shared history that emerged in the decades between the Civil War and the turn of the twentieth century was born out of both the hopes and the anxieties of American Jews. The efforts to document early Jewish footprints on American soil, to chronicle every Jew who served the nation's military, and to "prove" Jewish loyalty and patriotism at every turn reveal the sense of uneasiness that lurked behind the self-congratulatory histories. Within the flurry of claims about the Jewish roots of American democracy and the enthusiastic embrace of American freedoms lay an ever-present concern with defining and shaping an American nation that made room for Jews and Judaism. At the same time, Jews also seemed to compose and collect these accounts as much for themselves as for their detractors. These retellings reflected an eagerness to define an America that Jews desired as well as to create a Jewish history in a country that had only a brief national as well as Jewish past. While often self-serving, defensive, and prideful, these narratives of Jewish experience became the foundations, however flawed and inaccurate, of Jewish collective memory and shared history in America.

Communal narratives of the American Jewish past were never monolithic, even in this period. But as the twentieth century arrived, dissenting voices and divergent interpretations of Jewish experience in America multiplied. East European immigrants, in particular, added new elements to the communal and cultural matrix of American Jewry. As they came to far outnumber the existing Jewish population in the United States, they developed their own, also value-laden, versions of an American Jewish past that suited their needs and agendas. Indeed, since the first arrival of Jews in the United States, successive generations have marshaled and selectively rewritten their histories to create and re-create their own American Jewish pasts as they navigated the needs of their time and projected visions for the future.

LOOKING AHEAD: LATE NINETEENTH-CENTURY AMERICAN JEWISH ANXIETY ABOUT THE FUTURE

M. M. SILVER

Looking Ahead to Chaos and Restoration: Rabbi Mendes's 1899 Prophecy

IN 1899, Dr. Henry Pereira Mendes, rabbi of New York's venerable Sephardic synagogue, Congregation Shearith Israel, contemplated the coming century. That year he published a prophecy, *Looking Ahead: Twentieth Century Happenings.*[1] Despite its turgid composition, the book is a fascinating mix of dystopian anxiety and utopian faith in Jewish restoration, and it is not easily classified. Two texts, one written by a Gentile journalist activist, the other by the patriarch of Jewish nationalism, are *Looking Ahead*'s ostensible counterparts; but Mendes's book is unlike them in key ways.

These two textual foils, Edward Bellamy's influential 1888 novel, *Looking Backward* (whose title is evoked by Mendes), and Theodor Herzl's program for a Zionist utopia, *The Old New Land* (*Altneuland*, published in 1902), are optimistic depictions of the future whose political agendas are neatly framed by literary conventions of plot and character.[2] In contrast, Mendes's narrative progresses from the present to the future as a kind of prophetic newscast devoid of conventional literary adornments—to call the book a "novel" would be a misnomer.

Herzl's utopia was excoriated by east European Zionists for what they viewed as its lack of Jewish cultural content,[3] but his secularized, technocratic vision of Jewish restoration nonetheless unfolded as a thoroughly "Jewish" book.[4]

1. H. Pereira Mendes, *Looking Ahead: Twentieth Century Happenings* (New York: F. Tennyson Neely, 1899).

2. For Bellamy: John L. Thomas, *Alternative America: Henry George, Edward Bellamy, Henry Demarest Lloyd, and the Adversary Tradition* (Cambridge Mass.: Belknap Press, 1983). For Herzl: Yosef Goldstein, ed., *Ahad Ha'am ve-Hertsel: ha-ma'avak al ofyah ha-politi veha-tarbuti shel ha-Tsiyonot be'tsel parashat Altnoiland* (Jerusalem: Zalman Shazar Institute, 2011).

3. See the responses collected in Goldstein, *Ahad Ha'am ve-Hertsel.*

4. Two differing interpretations of what makes a utopian novel "Jewish" are Rachel Elboim-Dror, *Ha-Mahar shel ha-etmol*, 2 vols. (Jerusalem: Ben-Zvi Institute, 1993), and Russell Jacoby, *Picture Imperfect: Utopian Thought for an Anti-Utopian Age* (New York: Columbia University Press, 2005).

The Old New Land is fixated on Jewish problems and studded with Jewish symbols (Herzl's Old New Land even includes a Third Temple, though it is misplaced in the Jerusalem landscape and rather churchlike). At least in quantitative terms, Mendes's text is not really a "Jewish" book. In the first three-quarters, Mendes, an Orthodox rabbi, makes only glancing references to Jewish topics and instead concentrates on bleak, forecasted occurrences of world history.

Such considerations attest to the idiosyncratic character of Mendes's book. If *Looking Ahead*'s compositional flaws explain its lack of success with the general public, its neglect by historians probably results from this issue of contextualization.[5] Whatever its cause, this neglect is regrettable. Mendes's odd text is a telling barometer of how late nineteenth-century Jewish leaders in America were thinking about days to come and can thus serve as the touchstone in an article about this subject.

Fin-de-siècle American Jewish society certainly had figures of greater stature and authority than this rabbi. In the religious sphere, Reform's Isaac Mayer Wise, who died in 1900, was the prominent figure. On the level of communal resources and power, Kuhn, Loeb & Company banker Jacob Schiff was in this period emerging as an imposing leader. Nonetheless, as the nineteenth century drew to a close, American Jewry lacked formal leadership niches. Mendes published his text half a decade before America Jewry attained an appreciable level of organizational solidity via the establishment of the American Jewish Committee, several years before the community's tripartite religious denominational structure became clearly evident, and also more than a decade before Zionism became a somewhat popular and effectively organized force among American Jews. In this fragmented, organizationally evolving context, Mendes had, at the moment of *Looking Ahead*'s publication, an unusual measure of formal, titular status (Fig. 90). He was the acting director of the Jewish Theological Seminary (JTS), following the death of Philadelphia rabbi Sabato Morais in 1897.[6] In 1900, when he attended the Fourth Zionist Congress in London, Mendes was vice president of the Federation of American Zionists, deputy to Richard Gottheil. (Inspired by the event, Mendes wrote a poem, "Zion's Hymn," which

5. Mention of Mendes's text can be found in: Miriam Eliav-Feldon, "If You Will It, It Is No Fairy Tale: The First Jewish Utopias," *Jewish Journal of Sociology* 25 (December 1983): 90–91; Elbiom-Dror, *Ha-Mahar shel ha-etmol*, 95–98.

6. Mendes's leadership role at the JTS ended when the institution was revamped in 1902 by, among other things, the arrival of Solomon Schechter. Later in his career, Mendes taught at the Rabbi Isaac Elchanan Theological Seminary. Eugene Markovitz, "Henry Pereira Mendes, 1877–1920" (Ph.D. diss., Yeshiva University, 1961), 130.

Fig. 90. Rabbi Henry Pereira Mendes, ca. 1900. (Courtesy of Congregation Shearith Israel, New York).

the Federation's Americanized members recited to the tune of "My Country, 'Tis of Thee.")[7]

Mendes was born in 1852 in Birmingham, England, where his father, Abraham Pereira Mendes, headed a Jewish congregation. In 1899, the year he published his prophetic text, Mendes had been at the pulpit of Shearith Israel, America's oldest congregation, for twenty-two years (his ascent to this position, after a brief period as a rabbi in Manchester, was orchestrated by his older brother, Frederick de Sola Mendes). His descent from three illustrious Sephardic families—Mendes, Meldola, and de Sola—is colorfully described in scholarly and popular sources.[8] Mendes's Orthodox orientation had a westernized cast. In his youthful years in England, Mendes never attended a yeshiva. His formative educational experience occurred at a boarding school, Northwick College, which was run by his father and featured a mixed curriculum of Jewish and general subjects.[9]

Apparently unsure at first about the durability of his position at Shearith Israel, Mendes combined medical study and ministerial duties for several years following his arrival in New York. He attained a medical degree from New York University Medical School in 1884. Relatives claimed that Mendes enrolled as a medical student in order to gain insight about *kashrut* and other Jewish practices, but the M.D. also seems to have proffered professional leverage for a few years, as Mendes ironed out sometimes tempestuous relations with Shearith Israel's small group of trustees. (After these early trials, Mendes served the congregation authoritatively for decades, becoming minister emeritus in 1920.)[10] Mendes's medical education also paid tribute to a Sephardic tradition: for centuries, Sephardic Jewish notables trained and worked as physicians.[11]

Over the last two decades of the nineteenth century, Dr. Mendes compiled an impressive record of communal activity, helping to establish and run initiatives such as the Union of Hebrew Congregations, the New York Board of Jewish Ministers, Montefiore Hospital, a New York branch of the Alliance Israélite Universelle, and organizations for hearing impaired Jewish youth and adults. He published numerous religious education texts and also contributed translations,

7. *Ibid.*, 166–67. Mendes's hymn opened with the words: "G-d we implore of thee | End Zion's misery | Send her Thy aid!" In 1898–1899 Mendes also belonged to the World Zionist Organization's administrative core, its Actions Committee.

8. *Ibid.*, 1–3; David de Sola Pool and Tamar de Sola Pool, *An Old Faith in the New World: Portrait of Shearith Israel, 1654–1954* (New York: Columbia University Press, 1955), 192–94; Stephen Birmingham, *The Grandees: America's Sephardic Elite* (New York: Harper and Row, 1971), 14–16.

9. Markovitz, "Henry Pereira Mendes," 4.

10. *Ibid.*, 11.

11. Birmingham, *The Grandees*, 23.

poems, and commentary to journalistic venues, including the *American Hebrew*.[12] Two activities on this roster merit elaboration because they relate to the rabbi's depictions of the Jewish and world future in *Looking Ahead*. These are Mendes's Zionist commitments and his outlook on interfaith activities. In the American Jewish leadership sphere, Mendes's beliefs about Jewish restoration in the Holy Land had ample precedent. The two most prominent American Jewish figures during the early and middle parts of the nineteenth century, Mordecai Noah and Isaac Leeser, lobbied for restoration, the first in a well-known oratorical appeal to Christian evangelists, the second via discussion of various farming and pioneering initiatives in his journal, *The Occident*.[13] However, Mendes's restoration enthusiasm is distinctive in that it bridges a pre-Zionist period, when such visions lacked political footing, and the post-1881 period, when Jewish nationalism organized formally in the Hibbat Zion framework and then in the Herzliyan Zionist Congress format.

Upon his entry into the United States in 1877, four years before Hovevei Zion started to establish colonies in Ottoman Palestine, Mendes lectured about the feasibility of Jewish sovereignty in the ancestral homeland, inspired by what he believed to be the impending dissolution of Turkish rule. Published in 1877 by the *New York Herald*, his restoration endorsement was suffused with contemporary frontier ethics. Jews would replace "Mohammedan apathy" with a "vigorous reign of commerce and agriculture," in keeping with a "law of progress" by which, in North America, "the white man ousts the red man."[14]

Twenty years later, a few years before the publication of *Looking Ahead*, Mendes gave a fuller exposition of his restoration outlook in a pamphlet called *The Rejuvenation of the Jew*. There he tackled anti-Zionist objections, pivoting on the issue of loyalty, which had been raised by Reform rabbis and other Jewish spokesmen.[15] Thinking of Jewish restoration in the Holy Land primarily as a spiritual process, he downplayed political loyalty anxieties. "These Hebrews in other lands will owe no duty to Palestine which can clash with the duty to their country of adoption," he declared. "Palestine can accept only spiritual loyalty."[16]

12. Pool and Pool, *An Old Faith in the New World*, 197–98.

13. Jonathan D. Sarna, *Jacksonian Jew: The Two Worlds of Mordecai Noah* (New York: Holmes & Meier, 1981); Lance J. Sussman, *Isaac Leeser and the Making of American Judaism* (Detroit: Wayne State University Press, 1995), 144–45.

14. Quoted in Markovitz, "Henry Pereira Mendes," 157–58.

15. Evyatar Friesel, *Tenuah ha-tsiyonit be-artsot ha-brit ba-shanim 1897–1914* (Tel Aviv: Hakibbutz Hameuhad, 1970), 95–104.

16. Henry Pereira Mendes, "The Rejuvenation of the Jew," *North American Review* 165 (October 1897): 487–96.

Mendes's orientation on interfaith activity was somewhat inconsistent, and it reflected the difficulties that he and other Jewish leaders faced when trying to measure the level of antisemitism in late nineteenth-century America. Mendes's arrival in the United States coincided with one of the more notorious occurrences of social antisemitism in American Jewish history, the exclusion of an eminent Jewish banker, Joseph Seligman, from the Grand Union Hotel in Saratoga Springs, New York, in June 1877.[17] Mendes's forthright expression of indignation won wide circulation: "Obnoxious Christians are denied privileges because they are not gentlemen.... If [Jews] are refused privileges it must not be because they are Jews." Yet in this response to the Seligman snub, as in other sermons and writings in this early Gilded Age period, Mendes seemed to backtrack, implicitly holding irreligious, assimilationist Jews to blame for the antisemitism that accosted them. "If the Jew would only respect" his own religious traditions, he would "be fortified against the cold winds of contempt," Mendes concluded at the close of the Saratoga affair.[18]

In the 1880s, Dr. Mendes sometimes chastised fellow Jewish clerics for what he regarded as ecumenical excess. After an incident in which Reform Rabbi Gustav Gottheil of New York's lavish Temple Emanu-El allowed a Christian group to worship at his synagogue after its church burned down, Mendes angrily remonstrated. "A house of God dedicated to the unity of God cannot without disloyalty be handed over to the worship of a Triune God," he groused.[19] In other contexts, however, Dr. Mendes cooperated with church leaders, and he sometimes published grandiose plans for interfaith projects, such as a parliament of religions in which sociopolitical challenges would be adjudicated by spiritual experts of different faiths.[20] The tension between these two visions—the promotion of Jewish chosenness in opposition to other religions versus trust in the power of interfaith cooperation to ameliorate social hardship and political wrongdoing—is embedded in *Looking Ahead.* In fact, it undergirds the book's intriguing disjunction of dystopia and messianic optimism.

Looking Ahead predicts an apocalyptic breakdown of international order caused by the feckless greed of imperial powers, economic polarization between rich and poor, political corruption, and spiritual malaise. From our standpoint, much prognostication in the book seems prescient: in Mendes's text, entangling alliances and destructive rivalries among imperial powers leads to global war during

17. Leonard Dinnerstein, *Antisemitism in America* (New York: Oxford University Press, 1994), 39.

18. Markovitz, "Henry Pereira Mendes," 61–62.

19. *Ibid.*, 63. 20. *Ibid.*, 68.

the first decades of the twentieth century, and this widespread destruction subsequently foments religious extremism, including explicitly detailed waves of Islamic jihad. On the other hand, Mendes believed that mounting global chaos would not, by the mid-twentieth century, foment antisemitic animus. Instead, he thought world disorder would propel Jews to esteemed status, both as a revived spiritual nation centered in post-Ottoman Palestine, and as international protectors of peace and justice. Here, his crystal ball shattered. Mendes's restoration faith preempted any premonition of the Holocaust.

Many details in the book are suggestive of the author's own Sephardic background. These include the list of countries (Holland, for example) that behave honorably in war and toward its victims; the relatively tolerant attitude toward Islam (despite allusions to jihad extremism, the text's Muslim spokesmen deliver eloquent disquisitions about their heritage and rights); and a revealing scene in the text's restoration conclusion, in which the messianic lineage credentials of the Jew anointed as world leader are carefully examined by a qualified religious council (this figure descends from the two remaining families, Abarbanel and Frankel, which, Mendes imagines, are rooted in the House of David).[21] The book's restoration sequence is framed as a competitive disputation among spokesmen of world faiths, each presenting arguments as to why his religion ought to be awarded control of Palestine. As such, it evokes the format of Judah Halevi's *The Kuzari*. Arguably, the overall structure of the text, featuring Jewish revival in the aftermath of unspeakable catastrophe, rests on a Sephardic sensibility about history.

Mendes's futuristic scenarios are noticeably devoid of belief in any specific twentieth-century American role in world betterment. In the text, America aligns itself within an "Anglo-Saxon Confederation." In this imperfect world, it shares power with England in an alliance that is morally superior to its rival leagues, but not irreproachable; and the basis of the confederation's moral and practical superiority appears to rest on Mendes's relatively benign racial presumptions about the inventive heartiness of the Anglo-Saxon character, rather than rock-solid faith in the munificence of America's constitutional political system. In fact, Mendes projects a continuation of the bleak socioeconomic features of America's Gilded Age—political corruption, unjust wealth concentration, and violent worker radicalism—well into the twentieth century. America belongs

21. The image (if not cultural stereotype) of American Jews of Sephardic origins obsessively fussing about their illustrious lineages is popularized in Birmingham's portrayal of *The Grandees*, 1–17 and passim.

to the book's *dystopian* depictions, rather than to its messianic conclusion about world salvation. To some extent, this surprising absence of American patriotism reflects the author's own background and socialization. Having spent the first twenty-five years of his life in England, Mendes naturally envisioned that country and America as fraternal confederation allies in the coming century.

This aspect of *Looking Ahead* is relevant to the aforementioned challenge of categorization: the book belongs largely to a subgenre of fin-de-siècle books authored by theologians who envisioned the twentieth century in supernatural terms, beyond their own national frameworks. In view of the unrelenting anti-Russian polemic in *Looking Ahead*—these vituperative sections reflect the author's frustration about the tsarist empire's treatment of its Jews[22]—it might seem ironic to connect the book to the salvationist ecumenical utopia of a booklet published in 1900 by the Christian Russian theologian Vladimir Soloviev, *A Short Tale of the Anti-Christ*, but the comparison might nonetheless be warranted.[23]

In America's cultural landscape, the disarmingly explicit details in *Looking Ahead*'s restoration finale have an analogue in dispensationalist writings published by Christian evangelists. This dispensationalist genre was brought to the United States earlier in the nineteenth century by the Anglo-Irish preacher John Nelson Darby; in Mendes's time, it was popularized by W. E. Blackstone, a Christian Zionist, and by the end of the twentieth century, it reached millions of readers via the best-selling *Left Behind* series.[24] To be sure, these premillennial evangelists depict rapture events and other Christological elements that would never be found in a text such as *Looking Ahead.* Nonetheless, Mendes's Jewish restoration story shares a core with these evangelical utopias: the return of the Jews to their ancestral homeland after lavishly detailed apocalyptic occurrences is viewed as the start of humanity's salvation.

If *Looking Ahead*'s messianic restoration section connects contextually to evangelical Christians who, in many settings, including Zionism, operate as philosemites, its bleak portrait of twentieth-century chaos is linked contextually to a phenomenon of antisemitic dystopian writing. Much more than any

22. In the book's concluding disputation sequence, the only religious spokesman whose attestations of Holy Land devotion lack credibility is a member of the Greek Church. As he finishes his plea, "the eager look of the Russian plenipotentiaries" in the audience indicates that the speaker's performance masks profane bellicosity. Mendes, *Looking Ahead*, 303.

23. Vladimir Solviev, *Tri Razgovora* (Moscow: Sytin, 1991).

24. Yaakov Ariel, *An Unusual Relationship: Evangelical Christians and Jews* (New York: New York University Press, 2016), 38–39, 76–96, 46–56; Stephen Spector, *Evangelicals and Israel: The Story of American Christian Zionism* (Oxford: Oxford University Press, 2009), 13–15, 178–82.

resemblance to Bellamy's optimistic *Looking Backward*, Mendes's book draws heavily from descriptions in a morbid dystopia published by Ignatius Donnelly, a major figure in the Populist movement.[25] Published in 1890, *Caesar's Column: A Story of the Twentieth Century* ran through multiple editions, reaching a sales total of a quarter million.[26]

The most Donnelly-esque, Populist chapter in Mendes's book is called "The Social Aspect."[27] Unlike the book's other chapters, this one is introduced by an authorial footnote assuring the reader that all of its details are "fact." His long list of allegations about pernicious capitalism is lifted straight out Populist polemics of the era, which culminated with the divisive 1896 presidential election.[28] Also, several incidental details in *Looking Ahead* are suggestive of Mendes's responsiveness to *Caesar's Column.* These range from terrifying images of dirigible bombardment to demoralizing glimpses of co-opted religious ministers who pander to the elitist snobbery and greed of their rich congregations.[29]

Solicitous of Populism's reputation for left-wing idealism, the historian Norman Pollack once tried apologetically to soft-pedal the antisemitism in Donnelly's text, but his conclusions are untenable.[30] In fact, *Caesar's Column* should be regarded as one the most proactively impactful antisemitic texts ever to be published in the United States. Whereas later, more notorious texts mostly repeated antisemitic myths that were circulating in Europe, Donnelly's novel was relatively inventive in its Jew-hatred.[31] He framed his book around the

25. Lawrence Goodwyn, *The Populist Moment: A Short History of the Agrarian Revolt in America* (New York: Oxford University Press, 1978), 105–6.

26. Ignatius Donnelly, *Caesar's Column: A Story of the Twentieth Century* (Chicago: F. J. Shulte & Co., 1890).

27. Mendes, *Looking Ahead*, 76–91.

28. "Prominent among the disturbing forces were capitalists who skillfully wove their nets by combinations of interests, by trusts, by watered stocks or by wrecked roads, etc., or they built rival lines or bought them in, reorganized railway systems, put roads in receivers' hands, repudiated bonded interests, or by market manipulations they caused flurries, crashes, 'Black Fridays,' to the ruin of the many and the gain of the few." *Ibid.*, 78. For Populist politics, see Goodwyn, *Populist Moment*, 55–93.

29. However, unlike Donnelly, who doubted that clerics might save the world and whose colleagues were not themselves Jewish or Christian ministers, Mendes carefully pointed out that not all rabbis and priests preached in a smug vein that rationalized injustice and mass suffering.

30. Norman Pollack, "Handlin on Anti-Semitism: A Critique of 'American Views of the Jew,'" *Journal of American History* 51, no. 3 (1964): 391–403.

31. For instance, Henry Ford's *Dearborn Independent* essentially mimicked Europe's antisemitic screeds. See Neil Baldwin, *Henry Ford and the Jews: The Mass Production of Hate* (New York: Public Affairs, 2001).

fundamental idea of the *Protocols of the Elders of Zion* thirteen years *before* the *Protocols* forgery initially circulated in Russia. Donnelly's plot centers around two acidly defamatory claims about Jews: first, in willful conspiracy, or out of some unplanned yet natural ethnonational affinity, Jews operated simultaneously as left-wing socialists and as bankers and capitalists to subvert the world economic order; and second, they were deflowering America's pristine white Protestant core. In *Caesar's Column*, the leader of the capitalist cabal that cruelly rules the world and hatches genocidal schemes, a Jew named Jacob Isaacs (who masquerades as an Italian prince), has, with raping intent, purchased a young maiden named Estella, who descends from George Washington's family. While compiling information about Estella Washington, the book's Gentile narrator, who is cast by Donnelly as the rescuer of America's purity, learns that "the aristocracy of the world is now almost altogether of Hebrew origin."[32] In short, in Donnelly's dystopia, Jews are largely blamed for the afflictions of the tarnished Gilded Age: wealth concentration, currency manipulation, political venality, and other real or imagined ills that were of urgent concern to the Populist movement. Although Mendes accepts much in the diagnoses proffered by the Populists, his tale casts Jews not as America's nemesis, but rather as future saviors of modern society in general.

Looking Ahead is an unusual book, and its contextualization is complicated. In America, the fin-de-siècle publications that most closely resemble it, utopian books that also prophesied about "twentieth century happenings," were written either by Jew-haters whose scalding criticisms of Gilded Age corruption were, when shorn of their antisemitism, quite acceptable to Jewish idealists and activists, or by evangelical Jew-lovers whose restoration scenarios and philosemitic preaching made many Jews nervous. For the purposes of this article, the pertinent question is whether, despite its oddities, Mendes's *Looking Ahead* is representative of ways late nineteenth-century American Jews were thinking about the future.

Gilded Age Jewry as a Culture in Crisis

Mendes's fin-de-siècle pessimism is not wholly representative of the thoughts and sentiments of Jews in 1899, of course. The text that perhaps bears the closest resemblance to an "official" communal pronouncement that year is the inaugural edition of the *American Jewish Year Book*, published under the auspices of

32. Donnelly, *Caesar's Column*, 18.

the Jewish Publication Society of America.[33] In this influential publication's first annual summary statement about "The Jews of the United States," Abram S. Isaacs inserted some notes of caution, but was generally upbeat about the future. "While in many countries the medieval spirit still prevails, making the Jew a wanderer and an outcast, on American soil he seems to be preparing a distinctly new era," proclaimed Isaacs, editor of the *Jewish Messenger* and also a rabbi and university instructor. Synagogues and schools were sprouting up where a Jewish "wilderness" had existed just a decade before. Two or three notable Jewish books had been published in the preceding year, including Mendes's *Looking Ahead*, a "Zionistic fantasy," according to Isaacs. The growth of Zionism, spurred by the immigration of "our Russian brethren," was one of several indications of Jewish rejuvenation in America, he declared, and then added: "[E]ven opponents, who deplore the movement in the phase as outlined by Dr. Herzl, must acknowledge the warmth and devotion of the Zionists."[34]

New organizational developments were likely to ensure that Jews would hew more closely to their religion in the coming century, Isaacs predicted. For instance, within just a few years of its 1893 founding, the National Council of Jewish Women had six thousand contributing members, and the organization was enhancing "reverence" for Shabbat, helping to ensure that some radical Reform innovations, such as Sunday synagogue worship, would prove to be nothing more than passing "incidents." Just as Jews were fortifying their own religious identities, they were affirming their patriotic fitness as Americans for the coming century. Over the past year, American Jews had "furnished more than their quota of volunteers" for the Spanish-American War, Isaacs noted. Though he concluded that "American Israel meets with full confidence the currents of the time," Isaacs sounded unsure as to whether the country's Jewish communities were suitably organized for the challenges of the new century. The immigrant influx (more than 37,400 Jewish newcomers from June 1898 to June 1899) was compelling American Jews to establish "broader and more effective agencies"; but such organizational development was, in 1899, offering American Jews only a "certain degree" of "shape and direction" as they headed into the new century.[35]

The extent to which American Jews in the period 1865–1900 looked ahead to

33. For the *Year Book*'s founding and development, see Jonathan D. Sarna, *JPS: The Americanization of Jewish Culture, 1888–1988* (Philadelphia: Jewish Publication Society of America, 1989), 70–74.

34. Abram S. Isaacs, "The Jews of the United States," *American Jewish Year Book* 1 (1899–1900): 14–20.

35. *Ibid.*, 16, 15, 14.

the twentieth century with any specific attitude, pessimistic or otherwise, has received little scholarly research. Upholding what Jonathan Sarna identifies as the "immigrant interpretation," an early wave of post–World War II American Jewish historians maintained that the country's Jewish culture steadily eroded in the last decades of the nineteenth century and was revitalized only by the mass east European Jewish immigration.[36] Taking a harder line than did Isaacs in his 1899 summary, studies such as Henry Feingold's groundbreaking *Zion in America* (1974) doubted whether the country's established Jews created a "certain degree" of organizational cohesion in the 1880s and 1890s, and suggested that no real infrastructure for future American Jewish life would have arisen in the twentieth century had not the mass of newcomers forced the issue. Under this "immigrant interpretation," the communal spokesmen and activists of late Gilded Age Jewry could not have been bullish about the future.[37]

More recent one-volume histories of Jewish experience in America do not really dispute this conclusion.[38] These studies furnish little evidence of specific fin-de-siècle activity initiated by American Jews out of a particular outlook or agenda concerning the new century. Scholars such as Hasia Diner and Eli Lederhendler assertively revise the assumptions and contentions about immigrant arrival and adaptation that buttressed the earlier wave of scholarship; but their volumes are similarly immigrant-centered and do not focus on how native-born or relatively settled Jews in post–Civil War America might have been thinking and planning for their community's future outside of the complicated immigrant context.[39] Diner views American Jewish culture as arising "slowly" in a continuous process over a century of ongoing immigration and settlement, from 1820 to 1920.[40] Toward the end of this period, American Jewish religious and

36. Jonathan D. Sarna, *A Great Awakening: The Transformation That Shaped Twentieth Century American Judaism and Its Implications for Today* (New York: Council for Initiatives in Jewish Education, 1995), 2–5.

37. Henry Feingold, *Zion in America: The Jewish Experience from Colonial Times to the Present* (New York: Hippocrene Books, 1974), 112. Proponents of this interpretation were particularly critical of Reform Judaism; see Nathan Glazer, *American Judaism* (Chicago: University of Chicago Press, 1972), 60.

38. Eli Lederhendler, *American Jewry: A New History* (Cambridge: Cambridge University Press, 2017); Hasia R. Diner, *The Jews of the United States, 1654 to 2000* (Berkeley: University of California Press, 2004).

39. In this connection, see their earlier works: Eli Lederhendler, *Jewish Immigrants and American Capitalism, 1880–1920: From Caste to Class* (Cambridge: Cambridge University Press, 2009); Hasia R. Diner, *A Time for Gathering: The Second Migration, 1820–1880* (Baltimore: Johns Hopkins University Press, 1992).

40. Diner, *The Jews*, 76.

political culture had transformed significantly, she notes, but she does not focus on how these changes might have influenced Jews' thoughts about the coming century.[41] Lederhendler's study furnishes strong evidence about how, by the early years of the twentieth century, American Jewish business and professional notables, and precocious cultural figures, were constructing narratives about the past, noting rural-to-city transitions and highlighting "revered American traditions along with some less savory impressions about social discomfort and marginalization."[42] In some cases, as in the founding of the American Jewish Historical Society in the early 1890s, this turn to memory and nostalgia was intertwined with a future-oriented agenda by which Jews would claim "the American heritage [as] their own." Lederhendler refers in passing to "back to the soil" and other immigrant settlement ventures that implicitly or explicitly conveyed visions of the twentieth-century Jewish future in America, but he does not elaborate on them.[43]

Alongside these comprehensively framed studies of American Jewish history, some recent specialized studies of late nineteenth- and early twentieth-century Jewish immigrant culture in America convey important suggestions about future-related attitudes. Gil Ribak, for example, stresses how Jewish immigrant spokesmen articulated assumptions about the essential compatibility between Gentile, "Yankee," materialistic practicality, and their own Jewish culture, and thereby articulated a sense of optimism about the Jewish future in America.[44] Focusing on Orthodox newcomers in America and sermonic discourse expressive of their viewpoints, Kimmy Caplan notes a division between resisters and accommodators in the New World, and generally suggests a sense of Orthodox wariness about the twentieth-century future of Judaism, and of Jewish newcomers, in America.[45] Although these two specialized studies are not fully representative of the range of methods, concerns, and findings in ongoing research about American Jewish history, they are nonetheless indicators of a mixed and somewhat nonsystematic assessment of how American Jews were thinking about the future. Some scholars have observed that by

41. Her analysis of this century focuses on a transition from religious-based activism to ethnocentered politics: "By the end of the nineteenth century, the thrust of American Jewish politics shifted from the defense of Judaism to the defense of the Jews." *Ibid.*, 169.

42. Lederhendler, *American Jewry*, 95.

43. *Ibid.*, 127, 98.

44. Gil Ribak, *Gentile New York: The Images of Non-Jews among Jewish Immigrants* (New Brunswick: Rutgers University Press, 2012).

45. Kimmy Caplan, *Ortodoksyah ba-olam he-hadash: Rabanim ve-darshanut be-Amerikah, 1881–1924* (Jerusalem: Zalman Shazar Center, 2002).

the end of the nineteenth century, groups of American Jews were investing optimistically in a future of "abundance," as one study put it, whereas other scholars focus on subgroups or individuals who were pessimistic about American Jewish life in years to come, particularly about possible cultural/religious outcomes.[46]

Jonathan Sarna's research seems exceptional in its focus on the specific question of how late nineteenth-century Jews in America might have thought and organized for the future, operating on the basis of experiences that had accumulated over past decades, before the issue of mass immigration came to dominate Jewish consciousness and programming in the country. Sarna observes that following a spurt of post–Civil War growth through the 1870s, which culminated in a coast-to-coast landscape of three hundred synagogues and a Jewish population of a quarter million, the country's Jewish community became mired in a "cultural crisis of the highest order."[47] In 1881, on the cusp of the era conventionally identified with mass immigration, Reform rabbi Isaac Mayer Wise, heretofore a confident builder of a self-generating American Judaism, despaired about the future, remarking about how "sad experience upsets our beautiful theories and we stand confounded before the angry eruptions of the treacherous volcano called humanity."[48]

In Sarna's view, in the final two decades of the nineteenth century, small groups of young American Jews, most noticeably based in Philadelphia and led by figures of future prominence in the community such as Cyrus Adler and Cyrus Sulzberger, initiated an "organizing process" comparable to the Protestant Second Great Awakening. In a revival movement characteristic of the American religious scene as a whole, this youthful leadership reanimated American Jewish culture in a new mood of optimism about the future. This bullishness was buoyed by meaningful institutional growth in a fifteen-year period between the founding in 1886 of the Jewish Theological Seminary and the publication of the

46. Whereas the earlier wave of scholars, such as Feingold and Glazer, rested their case about late-century American Jewish cultural attenuation by focusing on Reform Judaism, newer, specialized studies convey arguments about the self-generating vitality of other American Jewish subcultures, thereby implicitly negating conclusions about how the community, as a whole, lacked infrastructure for optimism about the twentieth-century future. See, for instance, Jeffrey S. Gurock, *Orthodox Jews in America* (Bloomington: Indiana University Press, 2009), 109–46; Tony Michels, *A Fire in Their Hearts: Yiddish Socialists in New York* (Cambridge, Mass.: Harvard University Press, 2005), 1–25. The reference to a future of abundance is from Andrew Heinze, *Adapting to Abundance: Jewish Immigrants, Mass Consumption, and the Search for American Identity* (New York: Columbia University Press, 1990)

47. Sarna, *A Great Awakening*, 12.

48. Quoted in *ibid.*, 11.

Jewish Encyclopedia in the first years of the twentieth century.[49] Trends such as the rise of American Zionism and the dramatically increased presence of Jewish women in the community's organized sectors and religious culture propelled a "paradigm shift" that pivoted away from the earlier sharp drop of confidence about the Jewish future. Up to the 1920s, American Jewry revitalized around new principles: "a shift over time toward greater particularism as opposed to the earlier universalism"; "a heightened sense of Jewish peoplehood"; a newly positive orientation toward Zionism; and emphasis on "the spiritual and emotional aspects of Judaism."[50]

It is far from the case that American Jewry, in all its sectors, was sidelined by pessimistic inertia at the end of the nineteenth century, as Sarna's research resolutely shows. Yet there remains cause to wonder about the extent to which the programming impact and cultural shifts in the awakening he identifies could have been widely perceptible in the final years of the nineteenth century. Rabbi Mendes's status as JTS acting director in 1899 exemplifies how cultural institutions ushered in by this Jewish awakening were at the time in a state of flux and conveyed only a murky preview of their positive future impact. Revamped a few years later, the seminary became a powerful force in twentieth-century American Jewish culture, but its status at the time of *Looking Ahead*'s publication was uninspiring.[51]

Particularly in light of recent research about how the impact of Jewish immigrants from eastern Europe could have been manifest on the American scene before the 1880s, it remains difficult to separate the future thinking of American Jews from the anxieties, challenges, and opportunities posed by mass immigration.[52] Insofar as such winnowing can be done, there is no compelling

49. The emergence of the *American Jewish Year Book* in 1900 also figures as an endpoint in this period, and it was brought about by two key "awakening" figures mentioned in Sarna's pamphlet, *Cyrus Adler and Henrietta Szold.* See Sarna, *JPS*, 72.

50. Sarna, *A Great Awakening*, 30–31.

51. For the accepted view about the lack of viability of the original JTS by the end of the nineteenth century, see Jonathan D. Sarna, *American Judaism: A History* (New Haven: Yale University Press, 2004), 185–86. One revisionist scholar suggests that this portrait is overdrawn, and not surprisingly, this minority view was backed at the time by some early twentieth-century contemporaries who had vested interests in the original JTS. Mel Scult, "Schechter's Seminary," in *Tradition Renewed: A History of the Jewish Theological Seminary*, ed. Jack Wertheimer, 2 vols. (New York: Jewish Theological Society of America, 1997), 1:45–61; M. M. Silver, *Zionism and the Melting Pot: Preachers, Pioneers, and Modern Jewish Politics* (Tuscaloosa: University of Alabama Press, 2020), 175.

52. Gur Alroey, *Ha-mahpekha Ha-shketa: ha-hagira ha-yehudit meha-imperyah ha-rusit, 1875–1924* (Jerusalem: Zalman Shazar Center, 2008).

reason to overturn the judgment of the older historiographic school holding that many well-established or intellectually active Jews in late nineteenth-century America were gravely apprehensive about the future. Not unlike many American Jews exactly a century later, they wondered whether there would be one for their community.

There was not, in this fin-de-siècle period, a widespread renewal of confidence based on heightened pride in Jewish particularity—the perceived truths of universalism were viewed by many as a serious threat to Jewish continuity. The sudden surge of female expressiveness augured, in some measure, a new era of organizational efficiency and religious renewal, as exemplified by the establishment and quick impact of the National Council of Jewish Women.[53] In still greater measure, however, this gender trend reflected or instigated existential anxiety about the late nineteenth-century present and the twentieth-century future. Some scholars have argued in favor of vitality in organized Zionism in America in this early, Herzliyan period, before the flurry of activity led by Louis Brandeis in the World War I period.[54] But it is a stretch to imagine that First Aliyah settlement work in late nineteenth-century Ottoman Palestine inspired much confidence about the future among Jews in America.

The apocalyptic fervor of Mendes's text and its projection of Jewish national fulfillment into a post-historical, messianic future obviously exaggerated trends of pessimism among late nineteenth-century American Jews. Still, this 1899 publication can reasonably be viewed as an extension of an ongoing crisis of confidence about the coming century. Many late Gilded Age Jews were "looking ahead" to a tarnished future. The crisis of confidence persisted for a number of reasons; but I think that in emphasizing the impact of antisemitism generally and of specific, notorious incidents such as the exclusion of Joseph Seligman at the Grand Union Hotel, scholars have overlooked ongoing "internal," existential anxieties in late nineteenth-century American Jewish culture that were not directly occasioned by outside provocations.[55]

Unlike other American subgroups, Jews did not emerge from the Civil War with an emotionally satisfying, triumphalist narrative. Out of the bloody catastrophe, American culture reinvented myths of manhood, as evidenced by Rough Rider rhetoric in the period of Mendes's publication.[56] For Jews, however, acute

53. Faith Rogow, *Gone to Another Meeting: The National Council of Jewish Women, 1893–1993* (Tuscaloosa: University of Alabama Press, 1993).

54. Friesel, *Tenuah.*

55. Diner, *The Jews*, 169–73; Sarna, *A Great Awakening*, 7–9.

56. Gail Bederman, *Manliness & Civilization: A Cultural History of Gender and Race in the United*

manhood anxieties persisted. As new communication and transportation technologies shortened distances and post-Darwinian secularity challenged religious divisions, universalist discourses inspired soaring hope for the future in many sectors of American society, but the Jewish religious leadership was not really one of them.[57] Meaningful entry and rise in American society was becoming a realistic aspiration when American Jewish women thought about the twentieth-century future, but this prospect created anxiety about inclusion. In works by American Jewish women in this late nineteenth-century period, the problem of antisemitic exclusion has lesser salience than tension about intermarriage inclusion. In a kaleidoscopic way, we turn now to some examples of how such factors and trends sustained a sense of crisis among late nineteenth-century Jews, precluding optimism about the future.

The Civil War and Lingering Jewish Differences

For some Jews, the excruciating trauma of the Civil War reinforced faith in the moral tenacity and purpose of American democracy.[58] Especially among Jews who in Europe had experienced discrimination and the frustrating absence of liberal cornerstones such as church-state separation, postbellum patriotism became an elemental tenet of civil religion.[59] After Appomattox, they viewed the Jewish and global future through a hopeful prism of Americanism.

One such figure was Max Lilienthal, a Cincinnati-based Reform rabbi who, in an earlier phase of his career, had been devastated by the deceitful character of tsarist Russia's liberalization program for its Jews. Before the war, settled in the border state of Ohio, Lilienthal and his colleague Isaac Mayer Wise had been tongue-tied on political issues; then, during the war, Lilienthal was reviled by Southern firebrands.[60] "God bless America for this glorious redemption," Lilienthal sermonized gushingly at the end of the 1860s. Exile was over for

---

States, 1880–1917 (Chicago: University of Chicago Press, 1996), 1–44; David Pugh, *Sons of Liberty: The Masculine Mind in Nineteenth Century America* (Westport, Conn.: Greenwood Press, 1983).

57. The Gilded Age featured a mix of optimism about the prospect of social improvement wrought by popular protest and technical innovation, and caustically critical discourse about public corruption. See, generally, Richard White, *The Republic for Which It Stands: The United States During Reconstruction and the Gilded Age* (New York: Oxford University Press, 2017).

58. For this general topic, see Jonathan D. Sarna and Adam Mendelsohn, eds., *Jews and the Civil War: A Reader* (New York: New York University Press, 2010).

59. Matthew Silver, "Rabbi Max Lilienthal: From 'Compulsory Education' to the Separation of Religion and State" [Heb.], *Zion* 71, no. 3 (2006): 343–72.

60. Sefton D. Temkin, "Isaac Mayer Wise and the Civil War," in *Jews and the Civil War*, ed. Sarna and Mendelsohn, 161–80; Sarna, *American Judaism*, 114–15.

postbellum Jewry, he proclaimed: "Sunning ourselves in the golden rays of human and universal liberty we have ceased our wailings and cries of sorrow."[61] This surging patriotism expressed itself explicitly and implicitly on several levels, including adulatory attestations of devotion toward the martyred Abraham Lincoln and the confident willingness to invest newly marshaled resources in grand facilities, such as Reform synagogues, which symbolized expectations of a secure and prosperous Jewish future in America.[62]

The postbellum celebratory rhetoric trumpeted by religious leaders like Lilienthal may not have fully reflected the communal mood, however. One striking textual indication that it did not is an 1867 novel, *Differences*, written by Nathan Mayer, a Bavaria-born graduate of the Ohio Medical College who served as a surgeon in the 11th Connecticut Volunteers, distinguishing himself, in the words of one history, as "probably the most versatile Jewish soldier in the war between the States."[63] *Differences* includes engrossing Civil War scenes, with episodes that must have occurred in Mayer's proximity, including the real-life death of an 11th regiment captain, John Griswold, who courageously tried to ford Antietam Creek.[64] Graphic physical descriptions, such as trudging through Virginia's winter mud, lend credibility to the text. Mayer himself takes a few cameos in the novel, including one at the Battle of South Mountain, where a doctor peremptorily orders soldiers to obtain supplies; asked by them to furnish an officer's order for such foraging, the doctor authoritatively growls, "by order of *General* humanity."[65] Mayer's heroes operate in the aftermath of a real-life catastrophe, whereas Mendes's characters are cast on the rubble of an imagined apocalypse. In this thematic sense, they are bookends placed at the middle and end of the nineteenth century.

61. Quoted in Bruce L. Ruben, *Max Lilienthal: The Making of the American Rabbinate* (Detroit: Wayne State University Press, 2011), 193; Silver, "Rabbi Max Lilienthal," 371.

62. Jonathan D. Sarna and Benjamin Shapell, *Lincoln and the Jews: A History* (New York: St. Martin's Press, 2015); Gary Phillip Zola, ed., *We Called Him Rabbi Abraham: Lincoln and American Jewry, a Documentary History* (Carbondale: Southern Illinois University Press, 2014); Leon A. Jick, *The Americanization of the Synagogue, 1820–1870* (Hanover, N.H.: Brandeis University Press, 1976), 174–94.

63. Harry Simonhoff, *Jewish Participants in the Civil War* (New York: Arco, 1963), 105; cited in David G. Dalin and Jonathan Rosenbaum, *Making a Life, Building a Community: A History of the Jews of Hartford* (New York: Holmes & Meier, 1997), 31. The biographical information in this section relies on Dalin and Rosenbaum, 31–32, and also Janice Mathews, "Doctoring on the Field of Battle," *Connecticut Explored*, Spring 2007, https://www.ctexplored.org/doctoring-on-the-field-of-battle/.

64. Nathan Mayer, *Differences* (Cincinnati: Bloch and Co., 1867), 314.

65. *Ibid.*, 313.

Differences has, at first glance, a happy "Jewish" ending. Its protagonist, a Civil War hero and honorable, liberal-minded Jewish immigrant from Germany, marries a fetching, intelligent belle from an appealing Southern Jewish family. "United in love, notwithstanding former differences," exclaims Louis Welland, embracing his intended, Antonia Goldman, at the novel's conclusion. However, on this book's landscape, which is split physically between Claiborne County, Tennessee (itself a volatilely divided locale during the Civil War), and New York City, a large array of sectional, cultural, racial, religious, and gender "differences" either remain completely intact or are only superficially resolved.

One contrast developed by Mayer is between the Old World of his protagonist's birth (in the Rhenish Palatinate) and the United States. The novel's hero, Welland, is an idealist who is known to have fought with liberal German elements in the 1848 revolutions. Welland lost his family fortune and was forced from Europe due to a slanderous antisemitic accusation about money pilfering. His rigid yet admirable devotion to codes of gentlemanly European honor differentiates him in America's ruggedly capitalistic Yankee North. Welland never fully Americanizes, despite his heroic Civil War career; the novel's final conflict finds the protagonist equivocating between returning to an imperfect but improved Germany or remaining with his morally blemished but attractive and compatible fiancée in New York.

In addition to the contrast between German gentleman idealist and Yankee rugged materialist, the novel accentuates "differences" between Southern cavalier rowdiness and the temperate cohesiveness of Jewish family life. In Claiborne County, Antonia's Jewish family lives next to the estate of a restless slave owner, Frank Tourtelotte, who becomes a Confederate colonel and war hero. Though not a complete cur, Tourtelotte has a mean streak, and his affections for Antonia, with whom he becomes engaged during the war, combine love and financial motive. Suspense in the novel's latter parts revolves around the question of whether Antonia will consummate this unpromising mixed marriage.

The fundamental difference to be overcome in the novel is gender stereotype. Welland agrees to wed Antonia only after he is persuaded that her emotional inconstancy, the feminine equivalent of the Southern rowdiness of the male cavalier, can be remedied under the influence of his rigidly European sense of honor and devotion. Conversely, a Gentile New York woman, Emma Reichenau, originally rejects her Jewish suitor, Charles Goldman (Antonia's brother), because she finds him too effeminate. This Northern woman relents only after

Charles proves his manly mettle by becoming a hero for the Confederacy. By this formula, the Civil War made a "difference" for Jews, not as proof of their democratic patriotism, according to victorious Union standards, but rather as proof of their manhood.

None of these themes could have been terribly appealing to many contemporary readers, who by 1867 were quickly assimilating a victor's narrative, which fixated on the moral rectitude of the Northern cause. Jews in this novel seem to be following their own separate agendas, crossing religious lines while pretending that such lines are meaningless, and romantically overlooking the issue of who had fought for whom, which was becoming determinative for everyone else. While Welland fights nobly for the side of justice, he comes across in the novel's early parts as a weary, sometimes indifferent proponent of abolition. He accepts the inferiority of his aide-de-camp, a Tennessee slave named Ned, who follows him to the free North. Ned's subservience, in Welland's eyes, is not a racial-biological necessity, but rather an impairment inflicted by circumstances of education, cruelty, and deference that will not be remedied in the foreseeable future. More or less in the same spirit, Welland accepts that there are near impregnable differences between types of Jews. His sense of European idealism and the Goldman family's decency are contrasted with the crass materialism and sociopolitical opportunism of a stratum of New York Jews. Speaking for this class, one character, an unabashed war profiteer, exclaims: "What has a Jew to do with a country or rights? … Our country is our money, and the power and influence it gives us; these are our only acknowledged rights."[66]

Mayer's controlled prose conveys a sense of persistence about America as a reasonable choice for the Jewish future. Nonetheless, the novel has clear notes of equivocation. At the climax, Welland proposes to a Jewish woman who has previously betrayed her love vows to him, a woman who has also betrayed the democratic Union by rabble-rousing for the Confederacy with a stridency resembling that of a real-life counterpart, Octavia Harby Moses.[67] Welland resignedly weds himself to the future of a country whose past and present is imperfect; he is a symbol forecasting a late nineteenth-century sense of communal pessimism about the Jewish future.

66. *Ibid.*, 377.

67. For Octavia Harby Moses, see Diane Lichtenstein, *Writing their Nations: The Tradition of Nineteenth-Century American Jewish Women Writers* (Bloomington: Indiana University Press, 1992), 69–71.

Reform Jewish Worries: Would Progress Leave Room for Judaism?

Leaning heavily toward universalism, Reform Judaism's 1885 Pittsburgh Platform opened by proclaiming, "We recognize in every religion an attempt to grasp the infinite."[68] In a well-known debate, the platform's main patron, Rabbi Kaufmann Kohler, vociferously denigrated traditionalist Jewish observance, suggesting that such religious particularism was un-American. Essentially referring to Orthodoxy, Kohler exclaimed, "Orientalism on our free American soil will not stand the test of time."[69] Scholars have shown how Reform Judaism, in its late nineteenth-century "classical" period, systematically removed symbols of Jewish particularity from synagogue observance.[70] From the standpoint of Jewish continuity, this trend toward universalism posed clear challenges. Nathan Glazer provocatively made the point that, "Around the turn of the [twentieth] century, it would not have been far-fetched for a historian of ideas to predict a merger between Reform Judaism and liberal Christianity."[71] In their religious sphere, Reform rabbis ended the nineteenth century anxiously weighing the pros and cons of Jewish "differences" in a fashion qualitatively similar to the doubts about Jewish continuity in social and political spheres that were raised by Mayer in his post–Civil War novel.

One Reform rabbi who was tested, even tormented, by this question of "differences" was Emil G. Hirsch of Chicago's Sinai Congregation. For him, the question was palpable and poignant because his synagogue had divested itself of salient symbolic markings that separated Judaism from Christianity (worship was held on Sunday, for instance), and because his spirit of liberal activism politicized Judaism in a fashion that seemed to narrow the distance between it and then-prevailing Protestant models, such as the Social Gospel.[72] Hirsch's preaching seems saturated by spiritual crisis, by anguish over the possibility of Judaism's irrelevance in future epochs of universal faith. Time and again in his writings, Hirsch insists declaratively that Judaism has a future, but he then issues seemingly tepid justifications for its continued particularism. At a 1903

68. For the Pittsburgh Platform, see Walter Jacob, ed., *The Changing World of Reform Judaism: The Pittsburgh Platform in Retrospect* (Pittsburgh: Rodef Shalom Congregation, 1985).

69. Kaufmann Kohler, "Backward or Forward," in Kohler, *Studies, Addresses and Personal Papers* (New York: Alumni Association of Hebrew Union College, 1931), 205.

70. Michael Meyer, *Response to Modernity: A History of the Reform Movement in Judaism* (New York: Oxford University Press, 1988), 264–95.

71. Glazer, *American Judaism*, 53.

72. Tobias Brinkmann, *Sundays at Sinai: A Jewish Congregation in Chicago* (Chicago: University of Chicago Press, 2012).

Jewish Chautauqua assembly, for instance, Hirsch raised the vexing issue with concise pungency: "But what about the particularism of Judaism? Certainly the new religion will be all-inclusive. But is the famous particularism of the Jew in conflict with this demand?"[73] When compared with the urgency underlying the question's formulation, the answers furnished in this talk seem listless. Jewish particularism ought to have a future, Hirsch seems to conclude, because Jews are unusually philanthropic, progressive, and altruistic: "What then is the ruling thought of Jewish particularism? It resolves itself into the assumption of greater service without richer compensation."[74]

In the vein of fin-de-siècle anxiety, American Jewish religious leaders met a perceived crisis of Jewish particularism in different ways. Searching for an approach to make sense of his faith in the future of Jewish separatism, via the restoration of Jews as a spiritual nation in Palestine, Rabbi Mendes pessimistically found imaginative cause to obliterate politics and society in the twentieth century. Jews deserved their own future of separatism in Palestine because there would remain nothing else on earth to fight for. Searching for justification of his belief in interfaith activity for sociopolitical reform, Rabbi Hirsch split hairs when he advocated for a twentieth-century future of both universal religion and Jewish particularism. Jews would amalgamate with persons of other faiths in a crusade for social justice in America, but they deserved a somewhat special place in this endeavor because they were a little more charitable and altruistic than others.

American Jewish Women and the Future

By the late nineteenth century, a new American Jewish cultural subgenre emerged, one in which female authors and activists pondered an array of moral and spiritual problems and challenges, including intermarriage. This subgenre warrants comment here because, more than other American Jewish cultural niches, it was oriented toward the twentieth-century future. Given the limited socioeconomic opportunities for women in late nineteenth-century America, these Jewish authoresses were writing about characters who personified inequalities that were to be remedied in the future, but not always for their own personal benefit. These authors anticipated that their fictional characters' stifled ambitions would be realized by their Jewish and Gentile women successors in the twentieth century.

73. Emil Hirsch, "Judaism and Modern Religion," in Hirsch, *My Religion* (New York: Macmillan, 1925), 289.

74. *Ibid.*

These broad remarks are substantiated by two of the better-known novels authored by American Jewish women in the 1890s, Emma Wolf's *Other Things Being Equal*, which was published in 1892 and sold well, running through six editions,[75] and Annie Nathan Meyer's *Helen Brent, M.D.*, which was also published in 1892.[76] The protagonist of Wolf's novel, Ruth Levice, an energetic and sensitive personality, finds no clear outlets for her talents. At most, she gains temporary satisfaction in voluntary mentoring and social work tasks assigned to her by a Gentile physician, Dr. Herbert Kemp, her eventual fiancée. The Gentile protagonist of Meyer's book, Helen Brent, is a woman physician who struggles unsuccessfully to juggle her work as founder and director of a women's hospital and a romantic relationship. These are, in short, novels in which venues for romantic and career fulfillment for American Jewish women are restricted, if not shut off. If these women have a home, it is in the future.

Meyer treats topics—the challenges faced by women as they take up professional careers and the transformation of marriage roles in new eras of women's activism—that would become fundamental issues in twentieth-century culture. Up to the novel's bittersweet end, Dr. Brent's would-be partner, a prominent public figure named Harold Skidmore, voices traditional objections to marriage with a career woman. From our standpoint, Meyer's book is noteworthy both for its melancholy depiction of Dr. Brent's solitude, implying that work equality and a happy, equitable married life is not a reality for any woman in late nineteenth-century America, and for its lack of Jewish content, implying that Jewish women in the late nineteenth century are at least one step behind Gentile career women like Brent, who themselves are unhappy. Like other writings in this subgenre, Meyer's novel is not really committed to specific political agendas for the future. Much in Dr. Brent's ruminations and activities would appeal to subsequent generations of feminists, but the authorial voice also satirizes militant forms of late nineteenth-century women's activism. As director of her women's hospital, Dr. Brent is besieged by militant critics who demand that men not be allowed on its teaching staff. Meyer clearly recoils from such feminist stridency.

Her novel's moderate viewpoint about women's empowerment might be consistent with stances taken by Meyer herself on issues of urgency to women activists, particularly as an antisuffragist. But the determinants of Meyer's political

75. For background information about Wolf and this novel, see Barbara Cantalupo's introduction to the reprint of the book's 1916, revised edition: Emma Wolf, *Other Things Being Equal* (Detroit: Wayne State University Press, 2002), 9–58.

76. Annie Nathan Meyer, *Helen Brent, M.D.: A Social Study* (New York: Cassell Publishing Company, 1892).

outlook, particularly on the issue of voting rights, where family rivalry seems pertinent (Meyer's sister, Maud Nathan, was the most prominent American Jewish suffragette at the end of the nineteenth century), have never been resolutely analyzed.[77] In this subgenre, the personal and the political are interwoven in complicated ways.

Images of sickness in this subgenre acutely symbolize stresses and anxieties in late Gilded Age Jewish culture. Key characters in the novels by Meyer and Wolf, Helen Brent and Herbert Kemp, are physicians. Emma Wolf herself had a paralytic arm. In her novel, the origins and the consummation of the romance involve ailing Jewish parents. Ruth first becomes infatuated with Dr. Kemp when he prescribes a one-month rest cure for her mother, who suffers from attacks of emotional hysteria; and she marries the doctor after he diligently presides over her beloved father's final illness and death. (Since the mother's treatment is a hypnosis-induced state temporarily akin to death, the novel implicitly associates a future of Jewish intermarriage and assimilation in America with the death of Jewish parents.) Wolf's presentation of intermarriage as a future remedy is discernible yet tentative in *Other Things Being Equal.*

Finally, writing in this subgenre relates the American Jewish future to the issue of manliness, as did Mayer's Civil War–era novel. When American Jews thought about securing a creative, flourishing place in the country's future, they judged that much depended upon stifling what critical scholar Daniel Boyarin calls the "unheroic" image of effeminate Jewish males.[78] Wolf's novel is quite striking in this regard. Her antihero is Ruth's cousin, Louis Arnold, who is in his mid-thirties (and thus more than a decade older than the heroine). Originally from France, he has lived and prospered in business in America for twelve years. A companion and chaperone to Ruth, Arnold is viewed with affection by his San Francisco–based relatives. Wolf describes him as a wry, urbane figure, extenuates his cynicism, and casts him in a noble role in the novel's climax, when he steps aside and sets the stage for Dr. Kemp to wed Ruth. Yet there is something fundamentally repugnant about this male Jewish cousin. His wom-

77. For an overview of the opposing voting rights views taken by these two sisters, see Melissa Klapper, *Ballots, Babies, and Banners of Peace: American Jewish Women's Activism, 1890–1940* (New York: New York University Press, 2013), 18–32. Lynn Gordon entertains various interpretations of Meyer's antisuffragist stance, emphasizing the sibling rivalry factor; see Gordon, "Annie Nathan Meyer and Barnard College: Mission and Identity in Women's Higher Education, 1889–1950," *History of Education Quarterly* 26, no. 4 (1986): 503–22.

78. Daniel Boyarin, *Unheroic Conduct: The Rise of Heterosexuality and the Invention of the Jewish Man* (Berkeley: University of California Press, 1997).

anliness and superficial, westernized vanity are manifest in his first appearance. He is introduced as having the "fair complexion of a peachy-cheeked girl"; and, the narrator adds, "the delicate *pince-nez* he wore emphasized slightly [his] elusive air of supercilious courtliness."[79] In contrast, Ruth, embodies a cross between West Coast industriousness and the earthy wholeness of the biblical east (perhaps as an inverted representation of the Moabite Ruth, whose famed recognition in Jewish tradition was won by intermarriage with an Israelite). "There was something faintly oriental about Ruth," writes Wolf, "but the languorous air of Eastern skies was wholly wanting in the sweet sympathy of her glance."[80] Toward the end of the novel, Ruth's father, who professes to have strong attachment to his Jewish heritage but is more powerfully motivated by the concern that his daughter's intermarriage would leave her socially isolated, withholds his blessing and temporarily dissolves her engagement to the Gentile physician. Louis then proposes to Ruth. Wolf casts this futile exercise as a melodrama, but it reads more as a pathetic comedy in which the whiny, clingy male Louis injects fatuous legalism into an affair of the heart.[81] To the end, the novel's heroine dodges her cousin's advances, despite their acceptability in traditional Jewish terms. The only way Wolf can envision a salubrious heterosexual pairing for her heroine is to wed her outside of her faith, far from the unheroic, "peachy" sensuality of the Jewish male.

In keeping with these corporeal coordinates, for the Jewish woman, the prime attraction of intermarriage is Christian manliness. Whenever Dr. Kemp appears in the book, the metonyms evoke possessive power. Ruth is mesmerized by his "pleasantly authoritative gray eyes" and impressed by the commanding fashion in which he calms and hypnotizes her emotionally stressed mother: "'Be perfectly still,' he continued, holding her firmly. 'Obey this instant.' At the sound of his stern, brusque voice, the long, quivering shriek stopped halfway."[82] In a scene at a summer resort in the Russian River Valley, the Gentile physician sits in a rowboat, casting the magnetic pull of a medicinal sort upon Esther Levice and of a sexual type upon her daughter.

At the end of the Civil War, Jewish imaginative writing depicted the conflict as a battleground in which the Jewish male secured his place in the country's

79. Wolf, *Other Things Being Equal*, 72.

80. *Ibid.*

81. "You may think me a poor sort of a fellow even to wish you to marry me when you assure me that you love another. That means that you do not love me as a husband should be loved, but it does not prove that you never could love me so." *Ibid.*, 220.

82. *Ibid.*, 76, 80.

reunited future by proving his manly mettle. By end of the century, Jewish women writers were wondering whether the best way for them to seize opportunities in the next one was to marry manly Christians. This is not to say that a consistent theory about the place of the Jewish body in America could ever have been prescribed.[83] A few years into the twentieth century, when Israel Zangwill followed Wolf's train of thought and presented onstage a full-fledged ideology of melting pot intermarriage and assimilation, he scrambled the gender images and their carnal connotations. The talented Jewish musician (of Sephardic ancestry) who is the hero of his 1908 drama, *The Melting Pot*, has sexual pull precisely because he is a fragile, somewhat effeminate victim of the 1903 Kishinev pogrom. His fiancé, who personifies a heritage of Christian truculence, is the daughter of an antisemitic gang leader at Kishinev.[84]

Also, Lew Wallace's enormously influential 1880 novel, *Ben Hur: A Tale of the Christ*, conveys ambiguous messages about Jewish masculine valor or merciful effeminacy. The Jewish protagonist's manly courage and physical strength buttress *Ben-Hur*'s revenge and redemption themes, which are prominently and positively rendered by a non-Jewish author. On the other hand, at the end of the novel, drawn toward Jesus' daringly portrayed feminine-like qualities, Judah Ben-Hur abandons his faith in salvation as a this-worldly end to be attained by military victory and, according to the story's moral compass, correctly converts to the new faith in Christ, believing in its promises of deliverance in the next world. Arguably, the way Judah becomes a truer hero, by tapping the feminine side of his Jewish identity, is underscored. In various ways during the last decades of the nineteenth century, Wallace's novel figured as a symbol and catalyst of North-South reconciliation and postbellum American reconsolidation. In this capacity, it not only exploited images of Jewish conversion to Christianity, but also highlighted femininity in Jewish identity as a validator or generator of harmoniously forgiving national reconstruction.

Conclusion

In 1899, Dr. Henry Pereira Mendes had for more than twenty years presided over America's most venerable synagogue, an institution whose members took great pride in their families' heritages. However, his dystopian book, *Looking Ahead*, is unnervingly oblivious to the unparalleled rootedness, in American

83. For an interesting analysis of how this issue lingered and transformed in the first decades of the twentieth century, see Sarah Imhoff, *Masculinity and the Making of American Judaism* (Bloomington: Indiana University Press, 2017).

84. Israel Zangwill, *The Melting Pot: Drama in Four Acts* (New York: Macmillan Company, 1909).

Jewish terms, of his Congregation Shearith Israel setting. When he is finished drawing up his future of Jewish restoration in Eretz Israel, nothing remains from his Gilded Age American present, just as nothing lingers from the Spanish Golden Age heritage of his own past and that of his Sephardic synagogue congregants, at least apart from their obsessive evaluation of the messiah's lineage.

The detached, quietly dignified quality of Emma Wolf's prose is unlike the apocalyptic outbursts in Mendes's book. But this calmness only camouflages the fact that *Other Things Being Equal* sketches a blueprint for an entirely new epoch of Jewish experience in twentieth-century America. The novel's revolutionary imprint is on display in a pivotal scene where Ruth Levice and her Gentile suitor, Dr. Kemp, maneuver and plead to win her father's blessing for their mixed marriage. Yes, Ruth promises her father, she will continue to observe Jewish holidays and attend synagogue; but no, she will not allow her fiancé to celebrate Christmas alone. Why should she, since Jesus is in her eyes a morally inspiring figure, one whose birthday warrants celebration? No, she says, should she have children, they will not necessarily be Jewish. But they will not necessarily be Christian. They will have to choose for themselves. And so on and so forth.

In other words, as Emma Wolf saw it in 1892, the future in America would feature continuing negotiation between Jews and Christians, rather than a continuing state of equilibrium between two settled groups. The counterpart to her melting pot rhetoric of amalgamation and assimilation was Mendes's Zionist rhetoric of restoration and separation. He, too, believed that the terms of the future would have to be negotiated by Jews, this time in disputation with both Christians and Muslims; but he transported the discussion to Jerusalem's Temple Mount. On both visions—Zionist particularism and melting pot universalism—the terms of the Jewish future had barely started to be settled by 1899.

GILDED JEWS OF THE GILDED AGE

BENJAMIN STEINER

BOOSTED by structural economic and historical forces aligning in their favor, the prosperity of American Jews rose in the postbellum era. As the nation boomed, even Jewish immigrants who started out as peddlers could bound up the economic ladder in a single generation. Commercial fields such as storekeeping and garment production were the most typical catalysts for rapid individual advancement, but the "gilded Jews" of the Gilded Age were also well represented in the financial sector, and still others achieved prominence in fields ranging from newspaper publishing to mining. Chasing opportunity across the full expanse of the United States, these Jews were geographically distributed from New York to San Francisco. Many counted themselves members or leaders of Reform Judaism's classical Reform citadels, such as New York's Temple Emanu-El and Chicago's Sinai Congregation. Not a few dabbled in local, state, or national politics and befriended presidents, with a handful becoming ambassadors and congressmen. And fortune and philanthropy went hand in hand, so that America's wealthiest male Jews were frequently significant benefactors to Jewish and non-Jewish causes alike.

Jewish women found meager economic opportunities compared to the expansive possibilities open to Jewish men, but a similar innovative spirit and industriousness are visible in the variegated philanthropic and communal activities, activism, and social work initiated especially, though not exclusively, by the wealthiest among them. Freed from domestic labors, these individuals helped to further a significant expansion of women's societal roles outside the home, working within and outside the Jewish community to advance societal betterment. Whereas gilded Jewish men served as synagogue presidents and trustees, their wives often led sisterhoods and furthered the cause of Jewish education. They founded new national women's organizations to advocate Jewish causes within the United States and to promote public health in Palestine. They contributed substantially to myriad social reform efforts across America. And, in step with elite male Jews, they mobilized to support the growing number of impoverished Jewish immigrants who flooded into the United States from eastern Europe. The following short biographies are intended to provide a representative sampling of the activities of some of the most gilded Jews of the Gilded Age.

SHORT TITLES

Encyclopaedia Judaica: *Encyclopaedia Judaica*, ed. Michael Berenbaum and Fred Skolnik, 2d ed., 22 vols. (Detroit: Macmillan Reference USA, 2007).

Immigrant Entrepreneurship: German Historical Institute, *Immigrant Entrepreneurship: German-American Business Biographies, 1720 to the Present*, https://www.immigrantentrepreneurship.org/.

Shalvi/Hyman Encyclopedia: Jewish Women's Archive, *Shalvi/Hyman Encyclopedia of Jewish Women*, https://jwa.org/encyclopedia/.

Universal Jewish Encyclopedia: *The Universal Jewish Encyclopedia*, ed. Isaac Landman, 10 vols. (New York: The Universal Jewish Encyclopedia, Inc., 1939–1943).

1. Benjamin Altman (1840–1913)

Merchant, philanthropist, and art collector. Born in New York City to German immigrant parents, he received formative retail training at Hart & Dettlebach, an early department store in Newark, New Jersey, where he labored alongside future department store magnates Abraham Abraham (Abraham & Straus) and Lyman G. Bloomingdale (Bloomingdale's). At the age of twenty-five, Altman founded the forerunner of the luxury department store B. Altman & Co., and became a trendsetter in women's fashion. In 1906, he was the first department store owner to move his business to Fifth Avenue, helping to transform the thoroughfare into a retail mecca. Driven by the emerging trend of welfare capitalism, Altman created a foundation for the benefit of his employees, affording medical care and other assistance. His Fifth Avenue department store also provided subsidized meals to staff and contained employee restrooms. After Altman's death, B. Altman & Co. was run by a philanthropic trust benefiting many charities, among them Jewish organizations. Additionally, Altman was a devoted collector of Rembrandt paintings and Oriental porcelain, much of it acquired through the famous Jewish art dealer Henry Duveen. He bequeathed seventy-five old masters to the Metropolitan Museum of Art, to that date the most valuable donation in the museum's history.

SOURCES: Hanns G. Reissner, "Altman, Benjamin," *Encyclopaedia Judaica*, 2:21; Jeanne Abrams, "Benjamin Altman," *Immigrant Entrepreneurship*.

2. Sadie American (1862–1944)

Activist and social worker. Born in Chicago, she commenced her extensive involvement in Jewish and non-Jewish organizations in 1891. That year, American helped organize the Jewish Women's Congress held in tandem with the Chicago World's Fair of 1893. The Congress highlighted the activities of women in American Jewish religious life and spurred the creation of the National Council of Jewish Women (NCJW), for which American became the corresponding secretary. She remained active in the Council for twenty-three years, ensuring its success as an organization through her forceful speaking and by her zeal to organize local sections. American severed ties with the NCJW in 1916, as her brusque manner and position on the Sunday Sabbath created rifts with her colleagues. However, she remained committed to progressive social reforms in other volunteer capacities throughout her life. American worked to support eastern European Jewish immigrants at the Maxwell Street Settlement and taught Sunday school at her Chicago congregation, Sinai Temple. She was also active in the Women's Club of Chicago, vice president of the Illinois branch of the Consumers' League, and president of Chicago's League for Religious Fellowship.

SOURCE: Martha Katz-Hyman, "Sadie American," *Shalvi/Hyman Encyclopedia.*

3. Lizzie Spiegel Barbe (1856–1943)

Philanthropist and clubwoman. Born in East Liberty, Ohio, she moved to Chicago after her father, a Union army colonel, was killed in an ambush during the Civil War. There, Barbe became deeply involved in Jewish communal life like her cousin and lifelong friend, Hannah Greenebaum Solomon, founding president of the National Council of Jewish Women (NCJW). She was an officer for the Auxiliary of the Hebrew Union College and president of the Industrial School of Sinai Temple, which helped to educate immigrant children. Barbe also participated in the local chapter of the United Order of True Sisters, the oldest national Jewish women's organization. After the creation of the NCJW, of which she was a founding member, Barbe served as the third president of the Chicago section from 1902 to 1905. She also volunteered her energies to the NCJW's national executive board. Additionally, Barbe spearheaded the creation of Council Camp, a summer camp for Russian Jewish immigrants. In 1895, she was the inaugural president of the Conference Committee of the Jewish Women's Organizations. And Barbe took an active role in both the Chicago Sinai Temple Sisterhood and the national executive board of the National Federation of Temple Sisterhoods (today called Women of Reform Judaism). Through all of these activities, Barbe helped carve out leadership roles for women in the American Jewish community that had previously not existed.

SOURCE: Sandra K. Bornstein, "Lizzie Spiegel Barbe," *Shalvi/Hyman Encyclopedia.*

4. August Belmont (1813–1890)

Banker, diplomat, and politician. Born in Alzey, Germany, he started an apprenticeship with the Rothschilds' Frankfurt banking house at the age of fourteen. Recognizing his financial prowess, the firm transferred Belmont to Naples in 1833, where he was charged with the Rothschilds' financial negotiations. In 1837, Belmont was dispatched to Havana, Cuba, and to New York immediately thereafter. In New York, Belmont soon founded his own firm, August Belmont & Co., but he continued to represent the Rothschilds' interests. Between 1844 and 1850, he served as the consul general at New York for the Austrian government, but resigned over Austria's treatment of Hungarian rebels. In 1853, President Franklin Pierce appointed him the U.S. chargé d'affaires at The Hague. Subsequently, Belmont raised European money for the Union during the Civil War, and was Democratic National Committee chairman from 1860 to 1872. An avid horse racer and breeder of thoroughbreds, he helped fund the famous New York stakes race that bears his name.

SOURCES: Joachim O. Ronall, "Belmont, August," *Encyclopaedia Judaica*, 3:301; "August Belmont is Dead." *New York Times*, November 25, 1890, 1; Irving Katz, *August Belmont: A Political Biography* (New York: Columbia University Press, 1968); David Black, *The King of Fifth Avenue: The Fortunes of August Belmont* (New York: Dial Press, 1981).

5. Edward Albert Filene (1860–1937)

Businessman, philanthropist, and social reformer. Born in Salem, Massachusetss, to German immigrant parents, he learned the retail trade in high school and with his brother Lincoln took over his father's Boston dry goods business in 1891. Subsequently, Filene's would become among the most significant and profitable department stores in America, on a par with the likes of Macy's and Sears, Roebuck & Co. Edward's creative merchandising techniques and scientific approach to retail management, coupled with his renown as a progressive employer, helped to fuel the growth of the business. Among other innovations, Filene inaugurated a "bargain basement" plan, marking down the cost of merchandise unsold after thirty days. His firm also implemented a minimum wage, insurance and sick leave benefits, and weekly employee meetings, among other labor improvements, and pioneered welfare capitalism. Moreover, training programs were created to encourage employee advancement.

Filene's wealth and renown buoyed his efforts as a civic reformer. He served as a leading voice in the Boston Chamber of Commerce, United States Chamber of Commerce, and International Chamber of Commerce, all of which he helped organize, and was a key advocate of the minimum wage and workmen's compensation in Massachusetts. In the course of this advocacy he developed a longtime relationship with future Supreme Court justice Louis Brandeis. Most critically, Filene was a pivotal force behind the credit union movement in the United States, viewing it as a means by which any person could fairly obtain credit, and in 1909, the first credit union law in America was passed in Massachusetts. Filene joined with other prominent American Jewish entrepreneurs to promote the movement in the Greater Boston area, and his ceaseless advocacy helped credit unions to expand across the United States.

SOURCES: Robert Asher, "Filene," *Encyclopaedia Judaica*, 7:19–20; Saul Engelbourg, "Edward A. Filene: Merchant, Civic Leader, and Jew," *American Jewish Historical Quarterly* 66, no. 1 (1976): 106–22; Marcus Bacher, "Edward Albert Filene," *Immigrant Entrepreneurship*; Michael J. Lisicky, *Filene's: Boston's Great Specialty Store* (Mount Pleasant, S.C.: Arcadia Publishing, 2012).

6. Stella Heinsheimer Freiberg (1862–1962)

Advocate of Reform Judaism and arts patron. Born in Cincinnati, she married J. Walter Freiberg, who led the Reform Union of American Hebrew Congregations (UAHC) from 1911 until his death in 1921. While her husband served in that capacity, Freiberg helped to found the National Federation of Temple Sisterhoods (NFTS) as a subdivision of UAHC. She served as its inaugural vice president as well as on several national NFTS bodies, such as the Committee on Sabbath Schools and the National War Emergency Committee. Following her husband's death, Freiberg was president of the NFTS from 1923 to 1929, in which capacity she supported the decision to merge the UAHC and NFTS into the World Union for Progressive Judaism (WUPJ), and insisted that women have a voice in WUPJ proceedings. Freiberg was also involved in the leadership of the Cincinnati section of the National Council of Jewish Women and of the Jewish Social Agencies of Cincinnati, and she raised considerable funds for Hebrew Union College. Additionally, Freiberg was a founder of the Cincinnati

Symphony Orchestra, and she opened her home to prominent musicians of the day. In the 1940s, Freiberg created a professional catering business for musical gatherings.

SOURCE: Laura Lieber, "Stella Heinsheimer Freiberg," *Shalvi/Hyman Encyclopedia.*

7. Ida Weis Friend (1868–1963)

Philanthropist, suffragist, and advocate of progressive causes. Born in Natchez, Mississippi, she became active in Jewish philanthropy as a teenager, fundraising for Touro Infirmary in New Orleans. She founded the New Orleans chapter of Hadassah and became its inaugural president from 1917 to 1920. Subsequently, she served as national president of the National Council of Jewish Women. Weis also presided over chapters of several other organizations, including the New Orleans chapter of the Consumers' League, the Tulane Lyceum Association, the Voter's Registration League, the New Orleans Traveler's Aid, and the Urban League. Additionally, she was a member of the Commission on Interracial Cooperation. Aside from this organizational work, Friend became involved in political matters. She was a member of the Era Club, a New Orleans suffrage and service organization, and unsuccessfully campaigned for Louisiana's ratification of the 19th Amendment. And she advocated for a state increase in the minimum age for child labor, among other causes. In 1920, Friend served at the Democratic National Convention, the first Louisiana woman to do so, and a year later she was one of two female delegates to Louisiana's constitutional convention. Friend also patronized the arts, including as a founder of the New Orleans Symphony Orchestra society.

SOURCES: Karen Trahan Leathem, "Ida Weis Friend," *Shalvi/Hyman Encyclopedia*; Alan Smason, "Women of Valor: New Orleans Ladies," *Crescent City Jewish News*, https://www.crescentcityjewishnews.com/women-of-valor-new-orleans-ladies/.

8. Adam Gimbel (1817–1896)

Merchant. Born in Bavaria, Germany, he immigrated to America in 1835 and settled in New Orleans. After two years as a dockworker, Gimbel peddled along the Mississippi River before opening his own store in Vincennes, Indiana, in 1842. Five years later, he married Fridolyn Kahn-Weiler and ultimately raised eleven children to adulthood, including seven sons who helped to grow the family business. Over four decades in Vincennes, Gimbel acquired additional stores. He also served on the city council for four years. In 1887, the Gimbel family sold its stores in Vincennes and opened Gimbel Brothers, the largest dry goods store in Milwaukee, led by Adam's sons Jacob (1851–1922) and Isaac (1857–1931). A Gimbel Brothers location opened in Philadelphia that same year. After Adam Gimbel's death, the firm expanded to New York. Additionally, Gimbel Brothers purchased Saks & Co. in 1923 and acquired Kaufman & Baer of Pittsburgh in 1926.

SOURCES: Hanns G. Reissner and Ruth Beloff, "Gimbel," *Encyclopaedia Judaica*, 7:606; Paul H. Geenen, *Schuster's & Gimbels: Milwaukee's Beloved Department Stores* (Mount Pleasant, S.C.: Arcadia Publishing, 2012).

9. Henry Goldman (1857–1937)

Banker, philanthropist, and art collector. Born in Philadelphia, he was raised in New York in the rarified world of the German Jewish elite. His father, German-born banker Marcus Goldman, founded what became the financial firm Goldman Sachs. Following a brief stint at Harvard, the younger Goldman spent more than ten years as a traveling salesman for Dreyfuss, Willer & Co., before joining the family firm in 1884. Over time, he transformed the company, shifting its attention from international mercantile exchange to the domestic economy, and to higher-risk but more lucrative ventures. Together with Philip Lehman (son of Emanuel), a longtime business associate, Goldman engaged in the reconstruction of manufacturing industries. He helped list a myriad of mercantile companies, including Sears, Roebuck and F. W. Woolworth, recognizing these firms' potential for future revenue. And in 1911, Goldman Sachs together with Lehman Brothers refinanced and incorporated Studebaker Co. Despite these successes, Goldman's initial support for Germany in World War I proved his downfall in the world of finance, and he resigned from Goldman Sachs in 1917. An avid art collector, he amassed an immense collection of Renaissance and Baroque art. Toward the end of his life, Goldman aided Jewish intellectuals to escape Nazi Germany.

SOURCES: Eli Cook, "Henry Goldman: Immigrant Outsider as Empire Builder," *Immigrant Entrepreneurship*; June Breton Fisher, *When Money Was in Fashion: Henry Goldman, Goldman Sachs, and the Founding of Wall Street* (London: Palgrave Macmillan, 2010).

10. Selina Greenbaum (1866–1925)

Philanthropist. Born in New York City to German immigrant parents, she attended Normal College (now Hunter College) and married future New York State

Supreme Court justice Samuel Greenbaum in 1888. Subsequently, Greenbaum took advantage of expanding roles for women outside the home. She served on the board of directors of the nascent National Council of Jewish Women and became president of the downtown auxiliary of the recently organized Young Women's Hebrew Association. Additionally, Greenbaum supported the first recreation rooms on the Lower East Side. Most significantly, she played a pivotal role in the advent of the Jewish Working Girls' Vacation Society and became its long-serving inaugural president. With locations on Long Island and in the Adirondacks, the society afforded working women low-cost vacations. By 1917, the organization reached 800 girls each year and also afforded midweek vacations to young mothers.

SOURCE: Estelle C. Williams, "Selina Greenbaum," *Shalvi/Hyman Encyclopedia.*

11. Meyer Guggenheim (1828–1905; Fig. 91)

Merchant and industrialist. Born in Lengnau, Switzerland, he immigrated to America in 1848, settling in Philadelphia. Guggenheim established several successful importing businesses before purchasing a stake in Colorado's Leadville mines, where he made his early fortune. Guggenheim soon expanded to the refining business, constructing a major smelting operation at Pueblo, Colorado. In 1881, Guggenheim founded M. Guggenheim's Sons to focus exclusively on mining and refining, and many of his children took prominent roles in the business. The company soon opened profitable refineries in northern Mexico and across the United States.

In 1889, Meyer and his wife, Barbara (1834–1900), moved to New York City, America's economic and commercial epicenter, a symbol of their rising fortunes. By 1901, when M. Guggenheim's Sons merged with the American Smelting and Refining Company, the Guggenheims had become one of the wealthiest and most widely recognized Jewish families in the world. Meyer's son Simon (1867–1941) would go on to serve as a senator from Colorado, the sixth Jew elected to the upper house of Congress. And in 1925, Simon Guggenheim and his wife, Olga, endowed the prestigious Guggenheim Fellowships in honor of their son John, who died just before leaving for college.

SOURCES: Morton Rosenstock, "Guggenheim," *Encyclopaedia Judaica*, 8:124–25; Irwin Unger and Debi Unger, *The Guggenheims: A Family History* (New York: Harper Collins, 2005).

Fig. 91. Meyer Guggenheim, ca. 1910. (Library of Congress).

12. Lina Frank Hecht (1848–1921)

Philanthropist and social reformer. Born in Baltimore to German immigrant parents, she married the wealthy merchant Jacob Hecht in 1867 and subsequently moved to Boston. There, Hecht dedicated herself to philanthropic activities. With her husband, she worked to professionalize the United Hebrew Benevolent Association (UHBA), Boston's most significant Jewish charity. And as large numbers of east European Jewish immigrants began arriving in Boston, Hecht mobilized to support them. In 1878, she revived the Hebrew Ladies Sewing Circle and annexed it to the UHBA, which provided impoverished immigrants with free blankets and clothing. Hecht also spearheaded balls for the wealthy to fund the center's Hanukkah parties for the poor. Additionally, she created a Jewish Sunday school for immigrant children, and later the Hebrew Industrial School for Girls to acclimate students to American cultural mores. A school for boys soon followed with her support. Throughout her life, Hecht remained deeply connected with the UHBA as well its successor organization, the Federation of Jewish Charities, and she served as the Federation's first female vice president in 1908. Hecht was also a board member of both the Women's Educational and Industrial Union and the Boston Public Bath Department, vice president of both the Civil Service Reform Association and the National Council of Jewish Women, and honorary vice president of the Jewish Publication Society.

SOURCES: Ellen Smith, "Lina Frank Hecht," *Shalvi/Hyman Encyclopedia*; Julia Howe Ward, ed., *Sketches of Representative Women of New England* (Boston: New England Historical Pub. Co., 1904), 334–35.

13. Frances Wisebart Jacobs (1843–1892)

Philanthropist and social worker. Born in Harrodsburg, Kentucky, to German immigrant parents, she headed west to Colorado after marrying Abraham Jacobs in 1863. In 1870, the couple settled in Denver. Two years later, Jacobs organized and served as president of the Hebrew Ladies' Relief Society (now Jewish Family Service of Colorado), benefiting some 300 Jewish pioneers living in that city. Jacob's largesse soon expanded beyond Denver's Jewish community. Her leadership helped establish the Denver Ladies' Relief in 1874, and she served as the group's vice president and spokesperson. Six years later, Jacobs helped establish Denver's first free kindergarten for impoverished children. And in 1887, Jacobs joined with Protestant and Catholic leaders to form the Charity Organization Society, the forerunner of the national Community Chest. Additionally, Jacobs worked to create a sanatorium to benefit the large population in Colorado suffering from tuberculosis, and the Jewish Hospital Association of Colorado was incorporated in 1890. Though Jacobs did not live to see the sanatorium project completed, it was named the Frances Jacobs Hospital in her honor. By the time of her death, Jacobs had gained a national reputation and the title of Denver's "mother of charities."

SOURCE: Majorie Hornbein, "Frances Wisebart Jacobs," *Shalvi/Hyman Encyclopedia.*

14. Otto Hermann Kahn (1867–1934)

Banker, philanthropist, and arts patron. Born in Mannheim, Germany, he attended gymnasium and aspired to be a musician, becoming proficient at several instruments. He began work at the age of seventeen as a junior clerk at a bank in Karlsruhe. After serving in a cavalry unit in the German army, Kahn took a job at the London branch of Deutsche Bank, rising to assistant manager. In 1893, he accepted a position at the New York banking house of Speyer & Co., and in 1897 joined Kuhn, Loeb & Co. There, he gained fame at a young age for his financial prowess and peerless ability to reorganize railroads. He also reorganized the Metropolitan Opera in New York, serving variously as its chairman of the board and president, and was vice president of the New York Philharmonic. Philanthropically, Kahn supported universities, museums, art institutions, and artists of all kinds. He was a founder and great benefactor of the Federation of Jewish Philanthropies of New York.

SOURCES: Joachim O. Ronall, "Kahn, Otto Hermann," *Encyclopaedia Judaica*, 11:723; "Kahn, Otto Hermann," *Cyclopædia of American Biography*, ed. James E. Homans, vol. 8 (New York: Press Association Compilers, Inc., 1918), 50–52; Theresa M. Collins, *Otto Kahn: Art, Money, & Modern Time* (Chapel Hill: University of North Carolina Press, 2014).

15. Rebekah Bettelheim Kohut (1864–1951; Fig. 92)

Writer, educator, and community leader. Born in Kaschau, Hungary, she immigrated with her family to America in 1867, where her father, a rabbi, found work first in Philadelphia and then in Richmond. The family moved to San Francisco in 1875, and Kohut attended classes for two years at the University of California, though she did not graduate. In 1887, Kohut married traditionalist rabbi Alexander Kohut, recently elected to the pulpit of Congregation Ahawath Chesed (now Central Synagogue) in New York City. Using her stature

Fig. 92. Rebekah Bettelheim Kohut. From the cover of *American Jewess* 4, no. 2 (November 1896). (Princeton University Library. Gift of Leonard Milberg).

as a rabbi's wife to promote community improvement, she took part in the advocacy of the New York Women's Health Protective Association for improved public sanitation and organized a sisterhood at her husband's synagogue—only the second such organization in American Judaism. Kohut worked in the latter capacity to ameliorate the plight of new east European Jewish immigrants on the Lower East Side.

Following her husband's death in 1894, Kohut expanded her public activities. She became president of the recently created New York section of the National Council of Jewish Women (NCJW) and served as a spokesperson for the national organization. Additionally, Kohut was active in turn-of-the-century New York politics and became a trustee of the Young Women's Hebrew Association in 1914. During World War I, she raised money for war relief and served on New York's Women's Committee for National Defense. Kohut also chaired the NCJW's Reconstruction Committee, which assisted Jewish communities in Europe devastated by the war. Subsequently, she helped found and became the inaugural president of the World Congress of Jewish Women, established at a conference in Vienna in 1923. And in 1932, New York Governor Franklin D. Roosevelt appointed her the only female member of the Joint Legislative Committee on Unemployment. There, she advocated for the immediate creation of state unemployment insurance. Through her lifetime of service, Kohut was a model for women's deepening involvement in American Jewish communal life.

SOURCE: Karla Goldman, "Rebekah Bettelheim Kohut," *Shalvi/Hyman Encyclopedia.*

16. Simon Lazard (1828–1898)

Merchant and international banker. Born in Lorraine, France, he immigrated to America in 1844. Together with brothers Alexander and Lazare, Simon established Lazard Frères & Co. in New Orleans, which purveyed fine French clothing. After a fire destroyed their store, the brothers trekked to California, where gold had been recently discovered at Sutter's Mill. In 1849, Simon and Alexander reopened Lazard Frères in San Francisco, and it became the most significant dry goods business in the West. Lazard Frères also exported gold bullion to western Europe and gradually became involved in financial transactions. In 1876, Lazard Frères was remade into an international banking house with branches established in Paris (1854), London (1877), and New York (1880). In 1881, Simon Lazard became treasurer of the Sutro Tunnel Company. In 1888, the firm joined the New York Stock Exchange.

SOURCES: William D. Cohan, *The Last Tycoons: The Secret History of Lazard Freres & Co.* (New York: Broadway Books, 2007), 18–20; Hanns G. Reissner, "Lazard," *Encyclopaedia Judaica*, 12:558.

17. Simon Lazarus (1807–1877)

Clothing retailer and rabbi. Born in Württemberg, Germany, he immigrated to America in 1851, settling in Columbus, Ohio, where he opened a retail store. The business expanded after the Civil War, branching into the new market for ready-made menswear. Simon Lazarus was aided in this venture by his wife, Amelia, and their sons, Fred and Ralph. Simultaneously, he served as the first rabbi of Congregation Bene Jeshurun, the oldest synagogue in Columbus. In 1899, his sons changed the firm's name to F & R Lazarus & Co. Lazarus became a department store in 1926, and the company opened a branch in Cincinnati two years later. In 1929, the company was a founding member of the holding company Federated Department Stores alongside William Filene's Sons Co. and Abraham & Straus. Bloomingdale Brothers joined Federated a year later. Following a series of mergers and acquisitions, Federated was renamed Macy's, Inc. in 2007.

SOURCE: Hanns G. Reissner, "Lazarus," *Encyclopaedia Judaica*, 12:560.

18. Emanuel Lehman (1827–1907)

Banker. Born in Rimpar, Germany, he immigrated to America in 1847 and joined his older brother Henry's mercantile business in Montgomery, Alabama. Emanuel's younger brother Mayer also joined the firm, which became Lehman Brothers. After Henry's untimely death, Emanuel and Mayer turned their attention to cotton trading. Emanuel opened a branch of Lehman Brothers in New York in 1857, and Mayer joined him after the Civil War. Lehman Brothers helped form the New York Cotton Exchange in 1870. In the 1880s, the firm expanded into other commodities, including coffee, sugar, and petroleum. It also invested in cotton mills, iron and steel production, railway securities, real estate, and banks. Lehman Brothers joined the New York Stock Exchange in 1887. After the turn of the century, the firm moved away from commodities trading and became an investment bank under the guidance of a second generation of Lehmans.

SOURCES: Robert Archibald, "Mayer Lehmann," *Immigrant Entrepreneurship*; Peter Chapman, *The Last of the Imperious Rich: Lehman Brothers, 1844–2008* (New York: Portfolio/Penguin, 2010).

19. Adolph Lewisohn (1849–1938)

Businessman and philanthropist. Born in Hamburg, Germany, he began working at his father's mercantile business at the age of fifteen. Two years later, he followed his brothers to America, and by the late 1870s focused his attention on the copper trade, which proved an increasingly lucrative venture. Together with his brother Leonard (1847–1902), Adolph purchased his first copper mine in Montana in 1879 and formed the Montana Copper Company to quarry it. Later, the brothers constructed smelters to process the ore using the latest technology. They also formed Lewisohn Bros., a firm that sourced American copper globally. In 1887, the brothers partnered with other mine owners to form Boston & Montana Consolidated Copper and Silver Mining Company (B&M), one of the largest copper companies in the world. While consolidation in the industry after the turn of the century eroded the Lewisohns' dominant position in copper, they would go on to engage in a variety of other business ventures, including the production of fertilizer and sulfuric acid.

Philanthropically, Adolph Lewisohn supported many Jewish and non-Jewish causes in New York. He served as president of the Hebrew Sheltering Guardian Society and was a longtime trustee of Mount Sinai Hospital. He also held important leadership positions in the Hebrew Technical School for Girls and supported United Hebrew Charities and the Hebrew Free Loan Society. In 1913, he donated a German library to New York City's Hunter College. Additionally, Lewisohn's backed the construction of Lewisohn Stadium, a prominent amphitheater at the City College of New York. Among other social causes, Lewisohn worked for prison reform, chairing the National Committee on Prisons and Prison Labor and the Prison Survey Committee of New York. Finally, Lewisohn had a deep interest in literature and the fine arts, amassing extensive art (especially French Impressionism) and book collections. He gifted many of his best artworks to the Brooklyn Museum.

SOURCE: Henning Albrecht, "Adolph Lewisohn," *Immigrant Entrepreneurship.*

20. Minnie Low (1867–1922)

Social service leader. Born in New York, she moved with her family to Chicago at the age of ten and started her career in social work during the economic downturn of 1893. That year, Low co-founded the Maxwell Street Settlement House to aid east European Jewish immigrants in Chicago. Her longstanding friendship with Hull House leader Jane Addams started at this time, and Low would become known as the "Jane Addams of the Jews." Concurrent with her work for the Maxwell Street Settlement House, Low served as secretary to Hannah Greenebaum Solomon, founder of the National Council of Jewish Women (NCJW). In 1897, Low became the executive director of the Seventh Ward Bureau, founded by the Chicago NCJW, and in that capacity further assisted mostly impoverished Russian Jews with the goal of making them self-sufficient. To this end, Low also helped found the Woman's Loan Association. Moreover, Low was active with the Central Bureau of Jewish Charities, Desertion Bureau, Helen Day Nursery, Home for Jewish Friendless, and Jewish Home Finding Society, and she helped organized the Juvenile Court of Chicago. In 1914, Low was elected president of the National Conference of Jewish Charities, in which capacity she pushed for women's equality in the realm of Jewish social work. Unlike many of her female colleagues, Low was neither married nor wealthy.

SOURCE: Shelly Tenenbaum, "Minnie Low," *Shalvi/Hyman Encyclopedia.*

21. David Lubin (1849–1919)

Merchant and agriculturalist. Born in Klodowa, Poland, he immigrated to America with his family in 1855 following a two-year stay in England. At the age of twelve, Lubin got his first job working for a Massachusetts jeweler. He then drifted to California, working a variety of jobs there. By 1874, Lubin and his half-brother Harris Weinstock (1854–1922) had saved enough money to open their own store, D. Lubin One Price, in Sacramento, and the business grew dramatically. Within a decade, Lubin helmed the biggest department store and mail order business on the Pacific Coast. Meanwhile, his commercial interactions with farmers attuned him to the problems facing agriculturalists. Lubin's most lasting contribution in this sphere was his global campaign for an international agricultural congress to correct the problem of low prices for farm products. In 1904, he received the backing of King Victor Emmanuel III of Italy for this purpose, and the following year forty nations met in Rome to found the International Institute of Agriculture, a precursor of the United Nations Food and Agriculture Organization. Lubin also served for a time as the director of the International Society for the Colonization of Russian Jews.

SOURCES: Gabriel Davidson, "Lubin, David," *Universal Jewish Encyclopedia*, 7:223; Ava F. Kahn, ed., *Jewish Voices of the California Gold Rush: A Documentary History, 1849–1880* (Detroit: Wayne State University Press, 2002), 375.

22. Emma B. Mandl (1842–1928)

Social reformer, clubwoman, and communal worker. Born in Pilsen, Bohemia, she immigrated with her family to Chicago at the age of fifteen. Over four decades, Mandl established and presided over numerous charitable organizations in the city, many of them to benefit newly arriving east European Jewish immigrants. In 1889, she was a founder of the Baron Hirsch Woman's Club, an eminent Chicago philanthropic organization, and she later founded the associated Baron Hirsh Coworkers to further the club's work. In 1901, Mandl helped create the Chicago Home for Jewish Friendless and Working Girls and became its first president. Four years later, she spearheaded the creation of the Ruth Club, which afforded girls without proper homes a place to live. Additionally, in 1907, Mandl was a founder of the Jewish Home Finding Society, which helped poor mothers establish homes of their own. Later, when a tuberculosis epidemic swept Chicago, Mandl helped create the Chicago-Winfield Tuberculosis Sanitarium, serving as honorary president. She subsequently was a founder of the Home for Convalescent Men and Boys. Mandl was a director of the Bureau of Personal Service and became a probation officer of the Juvenile Court in conjunction with her efforts to aid impoverished children. Prominent activist and social worker Jane Addams as well as Julius Rosenwald were honorary pallbearers at her funeral.

SOURCES: Sandra K. Bornstein, "Emma B. Mandl," *Shalvi/Hyman Encyclopedia*; "Mandl, Emma B.," *Universal Jewish Encyclopedia*, 7:320–21; "Mrs. Emma B. Mandl, Charity Worker, Dead," *New York Times*, August 1, 1928, 21.

23. Marion Simon Misch (1869–1941)

Businesswoman, activist, and communal worker. Born either in Newark, New Jersey, or Allentown, Pennsylvania, she was raised in Pittsfield, Massachusetts, where she organized a Sabbath school at the age of fourteen. After graduating from college, Misch taught in Pittsfield public schools before marrying Caesar Misch, a New York merchant. Eventually, the couple settled in Providence, Rhode Island, where Misch became involved in communal affairs while her husband opened a department store. Over the next several decades, she held numerous positions in charitable, social, and educational organizations, both secular and Jewish. Misch long served on the Providence school board, led the Rhode Island Federation of Women's Clubs, founded the Providence Plantation Club, and directed the Providence Society for Organizing Charity and the Providence District Nursing Association. Misch also served as vice president of the Providence Civic and Park Association, president of the Rhode Island Federation of Music Clubs, and director of the Providence Association for the Blind. Within the Jewish community, she was honorary president of the Providence section of the National Council of Jewish Women, and led the national organization for five years. She also directed the National Federation of Temple Sisterhoods, served as president of the Montefiore Ladies Hebrew Benevolent Association, led the sisterhood of her synagogue, Temple Beth El, and served as vice president of the Jewish Orphanage. Misch traveled and lectured internationally, and, after the death of her husband in 1921, became the first woman in New England to run a department store.

SOURCES: Mary McCune, "Marion Simon Misch," *Shalvi/Hyman Encyclopedia*; Eleanor F. Horvitz, "Marion L. Misch—An Extraordinary Woman," *Rhode Island Jewish Historical Notes* 8, no. 2 (1980): 7–65.

24. Henry Morgenthau (1856–1946)

Lawyer, businessman, and diplomat. Born in Mannheim, Germany, he immigrated to America in 1865. He graduated from Columbia Law School in 1877, but subsequently made a fortune on real estate investments and gave up his practice. Morgenthau served as president of the Central Realty Bond and Trust Company and for a period as head of the Henry Morgenthau Company (1905–1913). He then transitioned from business to politics, fundraising for Woodrow Wilson, who appointed him ambassador to the Ottoman empire. Although not a Zionist, Morgenthau worked to improve the condition of Jews in Palestine during World War I, including by coordinating with relief organizations to ship emergency supplies. He also protested and raised American awareness of the Armenian genocide, the latter chiefly through his relationship with *New York Times* publisher Adolph Ochs. In 1917, he began an ultimately aborted mission to encourage Turkey to abandon the Central Powers. Additionally, Morgenthau was a leader of the American Red Cross, a patron of music organizations, and deeply involved in Jewish philanthropy. A committed Reform Jew, he served for a time as president of the Free Synagogue of New York, but resigned in protest of the Zionist leanings of its rabbi, Stephen S. Wise. Morgenthau's son Henry Morgenthau Jr. was the longtime U.S. Secretary of the Treasury in the administration of Franklin D. Roosevelt.

SOURCE: Morton Rosenstock and Isaiah Friedman, "Morgenthau," *Encyclopaedia Judaica*, 14:488–89.

25. Nelson Morris (1839–1907)

Meatpacker. Born Moritz Beisinger near the town of Hechingen in Baden-Württemberg, Germany, he immigrated to America at the age of twelve and settled with an uncle in New England. From there, Morris trekked to Pennsylvania, working as a coal miner and a charcoal burner. In 1853, he headed west to Chicago, finding employment as a stockyard watchman. Soon, Morris entered the cattle trade, and in 1861 won a significant contract to supply cattle for the Union army. By the war's end, he had acquired his own slaughterhouse and butcher shop, and his enterprise, Morris & Co., grew rapidly thereafter, opening processing plants across the Midwest fed by ranches throughout the western United States. By the 1890s, the Morris-owned Fairbank Canning Co. slaughtered upwards of 500,000 cattle a year. And by 1907, Morris's company had annual sales of around $100 million. Morris also held prominent social and economic positions, including as the first Jewish director of the First National Bank of Chicago. Despite conservative political leanings, in 1905 he helped found the Abraham Lincoln Centre, a Chicago settlement house.

SOURCE: Walter Roth, "Nelson Morris and 'The Yards,'" *Chicago Jewish History* 32, no. 2 (2008): 1, 4, 5.

26. Adolph Simon Ochs (1858–1935)

Newspaper publisher. Born in Cincinnati to German immigrant parents, he began working at the age of eleven as an office boy for the *Knoxville Chronicle.* At seventeen, he worked as a journeyman printer for the *Louisville Courier-Journal.* At nineteen, Ochs purchased a controlling half interest in the moribund *Chattanooga Times* for $250, which he then transformed into a leading Southern newspaper. In 1896, he purchased and subsequently rejuvenated the declining *New York Times,* which he ran for nearly four decades thereafter. During this time, Ochs increased circulation from 9,000 to more than 467,000 daily copies, and Sunday circulation eclipsed 780,000. He endeavored to make the *Times* fact-based and objective—in contrast with the sensationalist "yellow" journalism in vogue at the time—and comprehensive, adopting as the *Times*'s masthead motto "All the News That's Fit to Print." Ochs was an executive committee member of the Anti-Defamation League and used his position in journalism to discourage prejudicial references to Jews in the media. He further served as a trustee of New York's Temple Emanu-El. In 1883, Ochs married Effie Miriam Wise, the daughter of Reform institutional patriarch Isaac Mayer Wise.

SOURCES: "Adolph S. Ochs," *New York Times*, April 9, 1935, 20–21; Louis Rich, "Adolph S. Ochs," *American Jewish Year Book* 37 (1935–1936): 27–53; Susan S. Lukesh, "Adolph Ochs," *Immigrant Entrepreneurship*.

27. Joseph Pulitzer (1847–1911)

Newspaper editor and publisher. Born in Mako, Hungary, he immigrated to America at the age of seventeen and fought for the Union during the Civil War. In 1868, he became a reporter for the *Westliche Post*, a German-language newspaper in St. Louis. He rose to managing editor and purchased an interest in the publication, later selling it for a handsome profit. In 1878, Pulitzer bought the St. Louis *Dispatch* and combined it with the St. Louis *Post* to create the *Post-Dispatch*, which soon netted him large earnings. The paper was a leader in sensational journalism, championing the underdog and populism, and boasted eye-catching illustrations and typography. In 1883, Pulitzer purchased the *New York World* from financier Jay Gould and revitalized that publication, creating the *Evening World* as a late edition of the paper four years later. These publications, too, were organized along sensationalist lines. The hard-working Pulitzer also had a career in politics. At the age of only twenty-two he won a seat in the lower house of the Missouri legislature, and in 1885 he briefly served in the U.S. House of Representatives from New York. In 1912, Pulitzer founded the Journalism School at Columbia University. Additionally, he endowed the famous prizes for journalism that bear his name.

SOURCES: Irving Rosenthal, "Pulitzer, Joseph," *Encyclopaedia Judaica*, 16:731–32; James McGrath Morris, *Pulitzer: A Life in Politics, Print, and Power* (New York: Harper Collins, 2010).

28. Julia Richman (1855–1912)

Educator and social reformer. Born in New York City, she attended Normal College, graduated at the age of seventeen, and began teaching grammar at New York City Public School 59. A few years later she was promoted to principal of Public School 77, the first Jewish woman to hold such a position. Simultaneously, Richman became involved in charity work. She was a founder of the Young Women's Hebrew Association and a trustee of the Hebrew Free School Association. Richman also worked as a director for the Educational Alliance, a vehicle by which established German Jews sought to Americanize newly arriving east European immigrants. This program aligned with Richman's broader pedagogical belief that public education must transform immigrants into culturally assimilated Americans. In 1903, Richman became superintendent of Lower East Side schools, in which capacity she introduced Americanization classes. Her criticism of immigrant mores, however, elicited controversy and an ultimately failed petition for her removal. Richman became deeply involved with reforming religious education as well. She served as chairman of the Sabbath School Committee of the National Council of Jewish Women and helped establish the Jewish Religious Union of New York to provide courses of study for religious schoolteachers.

SOURCES: Selma Berrol, "When Uptown Met Downtown: Julia Richman's Work in the Jewish Community of New York, 1880–1912," *American Jewish History* 70, no. 1 (1980): 35–51; Selma Berrol, *Julia Richman: A Notable Woman* (Philadelphia: Balch Institute Press, 1993).

29. Julius Rosenwald (1862–1932; Fig. 93)

Merchant and philanthropist. Born in Springfield, Illinois, to German immigrant parents, he moved to New York in 1879 to apprentice at his uncle's wholesale clothing business. He then began to manufacture men's summer garments with his brother and moved the business to Chicago, where, along with a cousin, they founded Rosenwald & Weil Clothiers. In 1895, Rosenwald purchased a one-quarter interest in the new mail order business Sears, Roebuck & Co. from his brother-in-law for $37,500 and became company vice president a year later. He became company president in 1908. Meanwhile, laws passed by Congress eased the delivery of parcels to rural areas, which proved a boon for his firm's business. For his part, Rosenwald worked to streamline the process of filling orders, implemented a satisfaction guarantee, and created a system for testing merchandise for quality. He also expanded distribution of the firm's mail order catalog. Between 1895 and 1909, annual sales ballooned from $750,000 to $50 million. In 1924, Rosenwald resigned the presidency to focus more attention on philanthropy.

Rosenwald's most significant charitable giving promoted black education and health. From 1917 to 1932, he helped erect 5,357 public schools for African Americans in the South, and his challenge grants facilitated the construction of YMCA buildings for blacks in twenty-five cities. He also provided for the construction of model housing for African Americans in Chicago and was a longtime trustee of the Tuskegee Institute. In addition, Rosenwald gave to Jewish causes, including the Associated Jewish Charities of Chicago, a resettlement plan for Russian Jewish refugees in Crimea and Ukraine, and more modestly to causes in

Fig. 93. Julius Rosenwald, ca. 1929. (Library of Congress).

Palestine. And the University of Chicago and the Chicago Museum of Science and Industry benefited greatly from his largesse. The Julius Rosenwald Fund, established in 1917 to further his philanthropic interests, distributed more than $70 million before depleting its funds in 1948.

SOURCES: Morton Rosenstock, "Rosenwald," *Encyclopaedia Judaica*, 17:457–58; Pauline K. Angell, "Julius Rosenwald," *American Jewish Year Book* 34 (1932–1933): 141–76; Lawrence P. Bachmann, "Julius Rosenwald," *American Jewish Historical Quarterly* 66, no. 1 (1976): 89–105; Stephanie Deutsch, "Julius Rosenwald," *Immigrant Entrepreneurship*; Peter M. Ascoli, *Julius Rosenwald: The Man Who Built Sears, Roebuck and Advanced the Cause of Black Education in the American South* (Bloomington: Indiana University Press, 2006); Hasia R. Diner, *Julius Rosenwald: Repairing the World* (New Haven: Yale University Press, 2017).

30. Joseph Schaffner (1848–1918)

Businessman and philanthropist. Born in Reedsburg, Ohio, to German immigrant parents, he moved with his family to Chicago in 1871. For seventeen years he served as a bookkeeper in a textile company before joining as a full partner in Hart, Abt & Marx, a firm that specialized in high-quality men's suits. An innovative campaign of illustrated advertising under Schaffner's direction grew the firm, now renamed Hart Schaffner & Marx (HSM), into a national brand of ready-to-wear clothing. By 1910, HSM's Chicago sweatshops employed more than 8,000 workers. Following a massive garment workers' strike that originated at Schaffner's firm that year, HSM became the first major clothing producer in Chicago to recognize organized labor—a pivotal moment in the history of labor relations in the city. After 1910, Schaffner devoted more attention to charitable giving. He helped found the School of Commerce at Northwestern University in 1908, today one of America's premier business schools, and served as a Northwestern trustee from 1910 until his death.

SOURCE: Tobias Brinkmann, "Joseph Schaffner," *Immigrant Entrepreneurship.*

31. Jacob Henry Schiff (1847–1920; see Fig. 15)

Financier, philanthropist, and foremost Jewish leader. Born in Frankfurt, Germany, to a family of distinguished rabbinic lineage, he followed his father into banking. He immigrated to America at eighteen and became a partner in Budge, Schiff & Co. In 1875, Schiff married Therese Loeb, the eldest daughter of Solomon Loeb of Kuhn, Loeb & Co., and joined the firm. A decade later, he became its leader. Schiff's firm facilitated rapid American industrialization in the late nineteenth and early twentieth centuries through shrewd investments in companies such as Westinghouse Electric, U.S. Rubber, Armour, and American Telephone and Telegraph. Schiff proved particularly influential in the growth and consolidation of railroads that powered the nation's economic growth, including the Union Pacific Railroad and the Great Northern Railway. Kuhn, Loeb & Co. also floated loans to sovereign nations, most famously a $200 million bond issue for Japan during the Russo-Japanese War in 1904–1905. At the same time, Schiff used his influence to prevent Russia from raising capital as a protest against the antisemitic policies of the tsarist regime.

While personally affiliated with the Reform movement, Schiff had multifaceted philanthropic interests that spanned the Jewish religious spectrum, and he marshaled his enormous wealth and influence in defense of his coreligionists everywhere. He was especially involved in the formation of the Jewish Theological Seminary, which he lauded for its "reasonable Orthodoxy," but the Reform citadel, Hebrew Union College, and the Orthodox Rabbi Isaac Elchanan Yeshivath (today Yeshiva University) were also considerably boosted by his largesse. Schiff supported the Bureau of Jewish Education of the New York Kehillah and institutions of Jewish learning of all types. He backed the Jewish Publication Society and funded the acquisition of prominent Jewish libraries. Schiff was a major contributor to the Montefiore Hospital in New York and many other organizations, to which he dedicated considerable personal attention. He raised money for victims of Russian pogroms (1903–1905) and for Jewish relief efforts during and after World War I. He helped found the American Jewish Committee (1906) to advocate for Jewish interests globally. And while Schiff eschewed Zionism, he supported agricultural and technical initiatives in Palestine. His munificence also reached countless non-Jewish organizations, from Barnard College to the Tuskegee Institute to the American Red Cross, but he remained ever devoted to his Jewish roots. Speaking at the dedication of the Semitic Museum at Harvard College in 1903 (which he had funded), Schiff quoted the German writer Johann Wolfgang von Goethe: "Happy he who in gladness remembers those he sprang from."

SOURCES: Morton Rosenstock, "Schiff, Jacob Henry," *Encyclopaedia Judaica*, 18:130–31; Cyrus Adler, "Jacob Henry Schiff: A Biographical Sketch," *American Jewish Year Book* 23 (1921–1922): 21–64; Bernice Heilbrun, "Jacob H. Schiff," *Immigrant Entrepreneurship*.

32. Therese Loeb Schiff (1854–1933)

Social welfare activist and philanthropist. Born in Cincinnati, she was the eldest daughter of Solomon Loeb, a German immigrant who arrived in America after the failed revolutions of 1848. She married financier Jacob Schiff in 1875. Jacob's considerable largesse enabled Therese's diverse volunteer and philanthropic initiatives, as was not uncommon among upper-crust German Jewish women of her day. Unencumbered by domestic labors, these women threw their energies into charitable organizations. While Jacob Schiff directed the family's charitable giving during his lifetime, Therese Schiff shaped her own philanthropic legacy after his death. She supported Lilian Wald's Henry Street Settlement as a memorial to her husband and served as an honorary vice president and advisory board member of Temple Emanu-El's Sisterhood of Personal Service. Later, she donated substantial sums to the United Jewish Campaign, Montefiore Hospital for Chronic Diseases, the Loeb Convalescent Home, and the YMHA, among other organizations. And in 1931, Therese Schiff supported the development of a national training center for the Boy Scouts of America in memory of her only son, Mortimer.

SOURCE: Idana Goldberg, "Therese Loeb Schiff," *Shalvi/Hyman Encyclopedia.*

33. Isaac Newton Seligman (1855–1917; Fig. 94)

Banker and communal worker. Born on Staten Island, New York, this son of banker Joseph Seligman began his career at the New Orleans branch of his father's firm. He later transferred to New York and rose to lead J. & W. Seligman & Co. in 1895 after the death of his brother Jesse. Under his direction, the firm helped to finance the construction of the Panama Canal in the early 1900s, refinance the debts of Venezuela, and extend loans to several states in Central and South America and elsewhere. Seligman was also intensely involved in municipal political reform movements, including as treasurer of the Citizens Union and vice president of the New York Chamber of Commerce, where he spearheaded efforts to reform public finance. He was further invested in the elimination of social ills of all kinds, including as a founder of the Child Labor Association. His philanthropic largesse extended to such organizations as United Hebrew Charities and the St. John's Guild (which rendered medical services to the poor), and he was a patron of the arts and a trustee of Temple Emanu-El.

SOURCE: "Isaac N. Seligman," *Publications of the American Jewish Historical Society* 28 (1922): 306–8.

Fig. 94. Isaac Newton Seligman, ca. 1911. (Library of Congress).

34. Joseph Seligman (1819–1880)

Banker and businessman. Born in Baiersdorf, Germany, the eldest of eleven children, he immigrated to America at the age of seventeen and soon began to work as a clerk for a wealthy cousin in Pennsylvania. Then he peddled, and saved sufficiently to bring three of his brothers from Germany. The quartet opened stores in Alabama, but, discomfited by the institution of slavery, made New York their wholesale clothing headquarters, which Joseph managed. At this point, all of his siblings had settled in the United States, and offshoots of the business were established in San Francisco, St. Louis, and Watertown, New York. (In Watertown, the Seligmans became friendly with then Lieutenant General Ulysses S. Grant, a relationship that paid dividends when Grant became president.) During the Civil War, Joseph Seligman disposed of bonds in Europe in support of the Union, though the quantity is disputed. In 1864, the investment bank J. & W. Seligman & Co. was formed in New York, with branches ultimately opened in London, Paris, Frankfurt, New Orleans, and San Francisco. The company was a preeminent financial force in the postbellum era, playing a prominent role in railroad financing and refunding the U.S. national debt.

Joseph Seligman loomed large in Jewish communal and religious affairs. He was a founder of the Hebrew Orphan Asylum and a leader in supporting the oppressed Jews in Romania. Though a prominent member of New York's Temple Emanu-El, he also later backed Felix Adler, serving as the inaugural president of Adler's humanistic Society for Ethical Culture. Additionally, Seligman would be the victim of an infamous incident of American antisemitism. In 1877, Judge Henry Hilton, the owner of the Grand Union Hotel in Saratoga Springs, New York, denied Seligman accommodations. The event garnered national publicity and was a harbinger of developments to come. Within just a few years, social discrimination against Jews spread widely.

SOURCES: Joachim O. Ronall, "Seligman," *Encyclopaedia Judaica*, 18:266; George S. Hellman, "Joseph Seligman, American Jew," *Publications of the American Jewish Historical Society* 41, no. 1 (1951): 27–40; Elliott Ashkenazi, "Joseph Seligman," *Immigrant Entrepreneurship.*

35. Hannah Greenebaum Solomon (1858–1942; Fig. 95)

Clubwoman and social activist. Born in Chicago, she was raised in a prosperous Jewish family and became involved in prominent social clubs and organizations in the city. In the Jewish sphere, Solomon helped to orchestrate the Jewish Women's Congress at the Chicago World's Fair in 1893, where the National

Fig. 95. Hannah Solomon and her daughter Helen S. Levy and granddaughter Frances Levy Angel. Colorado Springs, Colorado, 1918. (Photographic post-card. Hannah G. Solomon Papers, Manuscript Division, Library of Congress).

Council of Jewish Women was founded, with Solomon serving as its inaugural president. Additionally, she founded the Bureau of Personal Service to aid Jewish immigrants in Chicago and served on the executive board of Associated Hebrew Charities. Solomon also promoted an array of non-Jewish causes. She worked with Jane Addams at Hull House and became president of the Illinois Industrial School for Girls. She took leadership roles in the Chicago Civic Federation and the Illinois Federation of Women's Clubs. She established penny lunch stations in public schools across America and a nationwide program placing probation officers in municipal courts for delinquent children. And Solomon was an advocate for women's suffrage, serving as a delegate to the 1904 International Council of Women convention in Berlin alongside her friend Susan B. Anthony. During World War I, she helped to coordinate efforts in Chicago in support of troops. Through all of these societal contributions, Solomon modeled expanded roles for women outside the confines of the home.

SOURCE: Beth Wenger, "Hannah Greenebaum Solomon," *Shalvi/Hyman Encyclopedia.*

36. Nathan Straus (1848–1931)

Merchant and philanthropist. Born in Otterberg, Germany, he immigrated to America at the age of six. His family moved from Georgia to New York after the Civil War, where his father founded the pottery and glassware firm Lazarus Straus & Son, for which Nathan served for a time as salesman. The firm grew into the crockery department of R. H. Macy & Co. (today's Macy's), where Straus and his brother Isidor became partners. The two would ultimately co-own R. H. Macy & Co. and Abraham & Straus, two of New York's largest department stores. Straus also served in city government in a variety of capacities and considered a deeper involvement in its politics. From 1889 to 1893, he was park commissioner of New York City. A year later, he declined the Democratic Party's nomination for mayor of the city. Straus was president of the Board of Health and commissioner of the Department of Health in 1898.

Straus retired from business in 1914 to focus on his charitable giving, which had already elevated the cause of public health in New York City and beyond. He achieved this goal most prominently through efforts to distribute pasteurized milk to nursing mothers, and he became a major advocate in a successful campaign for compulsory pasteurization of all milk. By 1906, seventeen milk stations distributed millions of bottles and glasses of pasteurized milk at his expense, significantly reducing infant mortality and tuberculosis. Straus also funded, in 1909, the Tuberculosis Preventorium for Children at Lakewood Township, New Jersey, which became a global model. Fittingly, President William H. Taft appointed him as the only U.S. delegate to the International Congress for Protection of Infants in Berlin in 1911, and the next year as a delegate to the Tuberculosis Congress in Rome. Straus also gave widely to Jewish causes. In 1916, he sold his yacht and donated the proceeds to war orphans in Palestine. A proud Zionist, he contributed more than $2 million, some two-thirds of his fortune, to support infrastructure in Palestine. There, too, his largesse was especially impactful in the realm of public health. The Israeli city of Natanya is named in his honor.

SOURCES: Naomi W. Cohen et al., "Straus," *Encyclopaedia Judaica,* 19:248–50; David de Sola Pool, "Nathan Straus," *American Jewish Year Book* 33 (1931–1932): 135–54.

37. Levi Strauss (1829–1902)

Businessman and philanthropist. Born in Bavaria, Germany, Strauss immigrated to America at the age of eighteen. He first peddled goods from his brothers' wholesale business in New York and then, in 1853, opened a West Coast branch in San Francisco under the name Levi Strauss & Co. In 1873, Strauss and Nevada tailor Jacob Davis patented work pants made out of blue denim with copper rivets, which proved popular with gold miners. These "blue jeans" brought Strauss millions of dollars, with which he supported a variety of charitable initiatives, including the University of California, the Pacific Hebrew Orphan Asylum and Home, the Eureka Benevolent Society, and the Hebrew Board of Relief, as well as Protestant and Catholic orphanages. Strauss also joined the San Francisco Board of Trade and served as director of a variety of significant enterprises, including wool mills, a bank, and an insurance company.

SOURCES: Hanns G. Reissner and Ruth Beloff, "Strauss, Levi," *Encyclopaedia Judaica,* 19:253; Lynn Downey, "Levi Strauss," *Immigrant Entrepreneurship*; Lynn Downey, *Levi Strauss: The Man Who Gave Blue Jeans to the World* (Amherst: University of Massachusetts Press, 2016).

38. Adolph Heinrich Joseph Sutro (1830–1898; Fig. 96)

Entrepreneur, engineer, and civic leader. Born in Aachen, Germany, he began work at his family's woolen cloth factory at the age of sixteen and immigrated to New York in 1850. Reaching California soon thereafter, Sutro sold a variety of merchandise in Stockton and San Francisco, including especially lucrative tobacco products. He invested heavily in Nevada after silver was struck at

Fig. 96. Adolph Heinrich Joseph Sutro, ca. 1880. (The National Portrait Gallery, Smithsonian Institution. Gift of Robert L. Drapkin).

the Comstock Lode, and devised a tunnel through the area to facilitate safer and more efficient mining. By the time his Sutro Tunnel Company completed the project in 1878, the height of the silver rush had passed, but Sutro made an immense profit by selling his tunnel stock at the right time. He returned to California in 1880 and invested heavily in real estate and companies. Running as the Populist Party candidate, Sutro was elected the twenty-fourth mayor of San Francisco and served from 1895 to 1897, but was widely criticized for his inability to work with others.

Sutro's largesse benefited the people of San Francisco. He built the Sutro Baths, a massive saltwater pool complex intended to serve recreational and health needs. He provided the land for the medical center at the University of California Medical School at San Francisco. He supported the Home for Aged Israelites. And he built a home at Sutro Heights, the expansive landscaped grounds of which he opened to the public. An avid book collector, Sutro amassed a library of some 125,000 volumes, including more than 10 percent of the world's early printed books, many of which were destroyed in the 1906 San Francisco fire. Fortunately, a considerable amount Hebraica from the collection survives, including Bible fragments and scrolls, Bible commentaries, lexicons, prayer books, philosophic and Kabbalistic works, and poetry.

SOURCES: Robert E. Levinson, "Sutro, Adolph Heinrich Joseph," *Encyclopaedia Judaica*, 19:329–30; Hermann-Victor Johnen and Jack Chai, "Adolph Sutro," *Immigrant Entrepreneurship*; William R. Huber, *Adolph Sutro: King of the Comstock Lode and Mayor of San Francisco* (Jefferson, N.C.: Macfarland & Company, 2020).

39. Henrietta Szold (1860–1945; see Fig. 56)

Educator, Zionist organizer, and communal worker. Born in Baltimore, she received a rich education from her father, the Hungarian-born rabbi Benjamin Szold, and began her working career as a teacher of English, German, French, Latin, mathematics, history, botany, and physiology. Simultaneously, she contributed to the *Jewish Messenger* under the pseudonym "Sulamith" and taught religious school and adult education classes at Oheb Shalom, her father's Baltimore pulpit. In 1889, Szold began teaching night school for east European immigrants in conjunction with the Isaac Baer Levinsohn Literary Society. Four years later, she joined the Zionist Association of Baltimore, and in 1898 became a founding member of the executive committee of the Federation of American Zionists. Szold also served as secretary of the Jewish Publication Society from 1893 to 1916, in which capacity she oversaw the translation, indexing, and publication of eighty-seven volumes. Separately, she helped to compile the *Jewish Encyclopedia.* And in 1902 she enrolled in the Jewish Theological Seminary to study Hebrew and Talmud, on the condition that she would not pursue the rabbinate.

In 1912, Szold was instrumental in the formation of the Hadassah Chapter of Daughters of Zion and was elected its president. The organization focused on improving public health and opened its first office in Jerusalem in 1913. Over the ensuing years, Hadassah transformed medical care in Palestine, and in 1920 Szold moved to Palestine to oversee these efforts herself, and remained there for most of the last twenty-five years of her life. In 1932, Szold became the director of Youth Aliyah, which ultimately brought 11,000 Jewish youth to Palestine from Germany and other countries that fell under Nazi control.

SOURCES: Michael Brown, "Henrietta Szold," *Shalvi/Hyman Encyclopedia*; Jewish Women's Archive, Women of Valor, "Henrietta Szold," https://jwa.org/womenofvalor/szoldlower; Lotta Levensohn, "Henrietta Szold: December 21, 1860–February 13, 1945," *American Jewish Year Book* 47 (1945–1946): 51–70; Shulamit Reinharz, "Szold, Henrietta," *Encyclopaedia Judaica*, 19:409–11; Joan Dash, *Summoned to Jerusalem: The Life of Henrietta Szold* (New York: Harper and Row, 1979).

40. Lillian D. Wald (1867–1940; Fig. 97)

Nurse, social worker, and activist. Born in Cincinnati, Ohio, to German immigrant parents, she graduated from the New York Hospital Training School in 1891 and subsequently worked as a nurse at the New York Juvenile Asylum orphanage. Additionally, Wald took medical school classes and taught home nursing to immigrants on New York City's impoverished Lower East Side. Soon, she began tending to Lower East Side residents as a visiting nurse. Observing firsthand the hardships they faced, Wald left medical school to devote her undivided energies to the tenement community. In 1895, backed by philanthropist Jacob Schiff, she founded the Nurses' Settlement (later renamed the Henry Street Settlement) to provide social services, including equitable healthcare. Around the same time, Wald coined the term "public health nurse" to describe individuals whose "organic relationship with the neighborhood should constitute the starting point for a universal service to the region."

Wald was deeply involved in an array of additional activities. In 1902, she spearheaded the first American public school nursing program in New York City. In 1903, she helped found the National Women's Trade Union League. In 1904, she was an early leader of the National Child Labor Committee. In 1909,

Fig. 97. Lillian D. Wald, ca. 1937. (Library of Congress).

she was a founding member of the National Association for the Advancement of Colored People. Three years later, Wald became the inaugural president of the National Organization for Public Health Nursing. Additionally, Wald served as president of the American Union Against Militarism. And she advocated for other political causes, including women's right to birth control and women's suffrage. During World War I, Wald was chairman of the Committee on Community Nursing of the American Red Cross, though she opposed American intervention in the war. Later, she led the Red Cross's efforts to stop the Spanish flu epidemic of 1918 through the organization's Nurses' Emergency Council. In 1922, the *New York Times* named Wald one of the twelve greatest living American women. Wald wrote about her lifetime of community health work in *The House on Henry Street* (1911) and *Windows on Henry Street* (1934).

SOURCES: Irwin Yellowitz, "Wald, Lillian," *Encyclopaedia Judaica*, 20:600–601; Marjorie N. Feld, "Lillian D. Wald," *Shalvi/Hyman Encyclopedia*; Marjorie N. Feld, *Lillian Wald: A Biography* (Chapel Hill: University of North Carolina Press, 2008).

INDEX

INDEX

Italic numbers indicate illustrations

C

H

I

Q

R

T

U

Y

PRINTED BY

PURITAN CAPITAL

HOLLIS, NEW HAMPSHIRE

BOUND BY

SUPERIOR BOOKBINDING

BRAINTREE, MASSACHUSETTS

DESIGNED BY

MARK ARGETSINGER

HOLYOKE, MASSACHUSETTS